ISBN 978-1-330-87508-7
PIBN 10088393

1 MONTH OF
FREE
READING

at

www.ForgottenBooks.com

By purchasing this book you are eligible for one month membership to ForgottenBooks.com, giving you unlimited access to our entire collection of over 700,000 titles via our web site and mobile apps.

To claim your free month visit:
www.forgottenbooks.com/free88393

English
Français
Deutsche
Italiano
Español
Português

www.forgottenbooks.com

Mythology Photography **Fiction**
Fishing Christianity **Art** Cooking
Essays Buddhism Freemasonry
Medicine **Biology** Music **Ancient
Egypt** Evolution Carpentry Physics
Dance Geology **Mathematics** Fitness
Shakespeare **Folklore** Yoga Marketing
Confidence Immortality Biographies
Poetry **Psychology** Witchcraft
Electronics Chemistry History **Law**
Accounting **Philosophy** Anthropology
Alchemy Drama Quantum Mechanics
Atheism Sexual Health **Ancient History**
Entrepreneurship Languages Sport
Paleontology Needlework Islam
Metaphysics Investment Archaeology
Parenting Statistics Criminology
Motivational

HISTORY

OF THE

COUNTIES

OF

BERKS AND LEBANON:

CONTAINING A BRIEF ACCOUNT OF THE INDIANS

Who inhabited this region of country, and the numerous Murders by
them, notices of the first Swedish, Welsh, French, German, Irish,
and English settlers, giving the names of nearly five thousand
of them, Biographical Sketches, topographical descriptions
of every Township, and of the Principal Towns
and Villages; the Religious History, with
much useful Statistical information,
notices of the Press & Education

EMBELLISHED BY SEVERAL APPROPRIATE ENGRAVINGS.

COMPILED FROM AUTHENTIC SOURCES
BY I. DANIEL RUPP,
AUTHOR OF HE PASA EKKLESIA, ETC., ETC

PUBLISHED AND SOLD
BY G. HILLS, PROPRIETOR;
LANCASTER, PA.

1844.

JOHN H. PEARSOL, PRINTER, LANCASTER, PA.

PREFACE.

The writer made no attempt in this compilation, as can be done in regular history, in which causes and effects are minutely given, to preserve a consecutive chronological arrangement of facts; it was not his design to do so; he simply aimed at embodying in a convenient form, notices of the leading incidents that occurred in Berks and Lebanon, from their earliest settlements; and with that view, preserved, as far as practicable, original documents, letters, extracts, etc., knowing that these are always read with much interest by the great majority.

The design of this work is to preserve the most interesting local facts relating to the Indians who inhabited this region of country, the numerous sanguinary massacres committed by them; to give brief historical sketches of the first Swedish, Welsh, French, German, Irish, and English settlers, and as far as practicable, to preserve the names of those who resided a century ago, within the limits of these counties, and to occasionally intersperse biographical sketches of some of the pioneers or their immediate descendants, of ministers of the gospel, so far as they had been connected with the church in these counties, &c. How far this has been done, is left to the candid reader to say. Nothing has been left undone on the part of the compiler, to collect facts from authentic sources and arrange them according to the best of his judgment.

To compile a work like this, is attended with difficulties that none know of, except those whom experience has taught. A remark corroborative of this may be found in the preface to "The Description of the Borough of Reading," by Major William Stahle. The author says:—"That the execution of his design was not free from difficulty, may be inferred from the fact that it was undertaken many months ago, and has been prosecuted with unremitted diligence to the present moment. The difficulties attending a work of this description far exceed those of ordinary authorship. It is easy to write an essay, or a plausible argument, on almost any subject, but difficult to ascertain facts. It is pleasant to sit at one's ease and write out a tale of fictitious love or woe; not so, to scour the streets, noting the material, and measuring the height of houses, and inquiring into the business of their inmates. It was the gathering of the *materiel* for the book that gave me the most trouble, and it is in the fidelity with which this task has been performed, that its principal merit consists."

In a compilation of this kind, made up of letters, &c., with original remarks occasionally, a diversity of style cannot be avoided; especially where the very words of authors quoted, and contributors, are preserved. Where the sentiment, or a mere fact of an author is embodied in these pages, the usual marks of credit are given.

The acknowledgments of the compiler are due the following gentlemen, for facts furnished by them:

Messrs. H. K. Strong, State Librarian; Charles M'Clure, Secretary of the Commonwealth; Charles Kessler, John S. Richards, T. P. Jones, Joel Ritter, John K. Longnecker, William Rank, Jacob Weidle, Jacob Beam, Charles Troxel, Abraham De Tirk, Thomas E. Lee, Joseph Light, Adam Ulrich, Doctors Leineweaver, Isaac Hiester, C. H. Hunter, the Hons. John Ritter, H. A. Muhlenberg, the Revd's Miller, Bucher, Pauli, Herman, Ulrich, Leinbach, Ernst, Wagner, Rothrauff. To those gentlemen who received the writer, while collecting materials, so hospitably, he would thus publicly return his thanks for their kindness.

Lancaster, Pa., July 12, 1844.

CONTENTS

OF THE HISTORY OF BERKS COUNTY.

~~~~~~~~~~~~~~

CONTENTS

OF THE HISTORY OF LEBANON COUNTY.

ERRATA.

~~~~~~~~~~~~

Numerous typographical errors occur, some of which it is important that they should be noted to prevent mistakes in dates, facts and names. The first numerals, in these corrections, indicate the page; those at the close of the correction, the line; always counting from the top of the page, unless otherwise stated.

Page 17, *Alligewi,* read Alliwegi, line 25; 71, *Mechir,* Melchior, 9; 71, 1754, 1757, 3; 77, *spring,* sprang, 13; *Yon,* Ton, 7; 1910, 1710, 26; 93, *Redemptions,* Redemptioner, 16; 94, *makeweights,* makeweights, 5; 105, *after,* often, 20; 125, *cannot be enabled,* on not being able, 12; 125, *Allummapees,* Allummapees, 11; 131, *life,* lives, 8; 145, *manufactures,* manufactory, 17; 174, 1828, 1758, 6; 181, 1735, 1758; 183, *filed,* field, 12; 184, 1841, 1741, 30; 185, *school,* church, 38; 186, 1852, 1752; 1836, 1756, 8; 196, 34, 14, 9; 197, *purlien,* purlieu, 29; 199, *wherefrom,* wherefor, 8; 190, 1818, 1718, 10; 199, *Reads,* Revds., 25; 199, *deputies was,* deputies' case was, 29, 200, *south-east,* southwest, 30; 201, *five,* four children, 3; 201, *Anna, Madlina,* Anna Madlina, 4; in the foot note, page 201, first line read, page 181. in a note we stated on the authority of family tradition. 204, *Wilson,* Weiser, 13; 204, *mild,* wild, 33; 205, *Pyrlacus,* Pyrlaeus, 17; 205, *Shamokin,* Shekome-ko, 32; 205, *Shemokin,* Shekomeko, 36; 210, *Teedpiscung,* Teedyscung, 11; 222, *Loner,* Lower, 35; 223, 1744, 1844, 3; 245, *respectively,* repeatedly, 29; 247, *better,* bitter, 24; 259, *turnpikes,* townships, 26, 427, *Krichel,* Kriebel, 12.

Errors—Union township in Lebanon county, was taken entirely from East Hanover, and no part of it from Swatara township.

Lebanon contains one or two taverns less than stated on page 312.

Omissions.—We omitted to state in its proper place, that there were se-veral Banks in the Borough of Reading, viz:—The Farmers' Bank of Reading, incorporated in 1814, and the Berks County Bank, incorporated in 1826. The latter is in bad repute; its paper is quoted at 63 per cent. discount!

INTRODUCTION.

CHAPTER I.

Two hundred and ten years ago, no white man held possession among the red men of the woods within the extended limits of an uncultivated territory of Pennsylvania, three hundred and ten miles in length, and one hundred and sixty in breadth, containing rising thirty million acres of land; and, at present, inhabited by a white population numbering nearly two millions—a region of country, which, in its mountains and hills, its vallies and glens, rivers, creeks and cascades, presents all the varieties of the grand, "rugged, sheltered and romantic scenery;" and, in the bosom of whose variegated surface, useful minerals, ores, and indispensable fossils are embedded. A little more than two centuries ago, the lords of the soil were Indians, and whose prerogative it was, that alone "their fear and their dread were upon every beast of *Pennsylvania*, and upon every foul of the air, and all that moved upon the earth in *that domain*, and upon all the fishes of the *streams*," but who have since been *obliged* to leave their hunting grounds and wigwams, and of whom some account will be given in the sequel. The Swedes were the first who settled among the Indians within the limits of Pennsylvania; as early as 1638, they made purchases from them, though at a cheap rate. The Indians sold them the use of lands in and about Tinicum isle, at one yard of baize, or a bottle of brandy, for four hundred acres.

At Tinicum isle, the seat of government of the **New** Sweden colony, John Printz, erected in 1642, a spacious mansion, well known in history as Printz's Hall. The Swedes, however, were not left long in quiet possession of their new home; the Dutch, in 1655, subdued and brought them under the jurisdiction of Peter Stuyvesant, governor of New Netherlands, who, himself and country, were shortly afterwards conquered **by Charles II.,**

1

of England, and New Netherlands was afterwards called New York; and, as a consequence, the settlements on the Delaware, first made by the Swedes, then held by the Dutch, fell into the possession of the English, in 1664.

In Europe, a spirit of religious persecution, caused many an aching heart to yearn after a place of peace and repose; where, in obedience to the dictates of conscience, the Almighty might be worshipped without an impious interposition by man between the homage of man and his Creator. At this time the founder of Pennsylvania, on account of his religious sentiments, suffered much in this way; and in order to escape persecution, and to establish a colony for the oppressed of all denominations, turned his eye upon the western world.

William Penn, born in London, October 16, 1664, grandson of Giles Penn, and son of Sir William Penn, Admiral of the English Navy, availed himself of the claims he had upon the British Government, on account of the eminent services his father had rendered that country, petitioned King Charles II., that, in lieu of a large sum of money, sixteen thousand pounds, due the Admiral, at his death, to grant him letters patent for a tract of land in America, "lying north of Maryland; on the east, bounded by Delaware river; on the west, limited as Maryland; and northward, to extend as far as plantable."

Penn obtained a charter from Charles II., dated at Westminster, March 4, 1681. Having now been sole proprietary of Pennsylvania, he made sales of lands to adventurers, called first settlers, who embarked, some at London, others at Bristol, in 1681, for America, and arrived at Upland, now Chester, on the 11th December. Penn, with many of his friends, chiefly from Sussex, England, sailed for America, and landed at New Castle on the 27th October, 1682, where he was received with demonstrations of joy. Penn went to Upland, where he convened an assembly, December 4th; and in a brief session of three days enacted several important laws, one of which was an act to naturalize the Dutch, Swedes, and other foreigners.

The same year that Penn arrived, there was quite an accession. The two next succeeding years, settlers from London, Bristol, Wales, Holland, Germany, &c., arrived to the number of fifty sail; among these were German Quakers from Cresheim, near Worms in the Palatinate. The banks of the Delaware was one bustling scene—some lodged in the woods in hollow trees, some in caves, which were easily dug on the high banks of the Wissahickon and the Delaware, and others in haste erected huts.*

To do justice, secure the smiles of the Indians, and to meet the approbation of Heaven, Penn held treaties of peace and friendship with the tawny sons of the forest, and contracted with them for *their* lands—this done, he proceeded to lay out a city, by the assistance of his surveyor, Gen. Thomas Holme. Eighty houses were erected, the first year, in Philadelphia.. Next was a survey of lands for the *first settlers*—this having been completed, the Proprietary, in 1682, divided the country into six counties—three in the territory of Delaware; namely, New Castle, Kent, and Sussex; three in the province of Pennsylvania; namely, Philadelphia, Buck, and Chester; the first and last, embracing *all*, and much more, of the land within the present limits of Berks and Lebanon.

Penn remained but a short time on his first arrival; he sailed for Europe, August 16, 1684, leaving the province under the government of five commissioners, chosen from the Provincial council; however, previous to his departure, he made a league of amity with nineteen Indian nations, between them and all the English America.† In 1699, Penn again visited the colony, and remained only till November 1st, 1701, when he returned to England, where he died July 30th, 1718, at Rushcomb, near Twyford, in Buckinghamshire, aged about seventy-four years. In 1712, he had been seized with some fits of the appoplectic kind, which for the last six years of his life, had rendered him incapable of doing public business.

* Proud II, 220.   † Oldmixon.

CHAPTER II.

THE INDIANS.

When the Europeans first discovered the American continent, they erroneously applied the name, Indians, to the indigenes that inhabited the "New World." This name was given to the aborigines of America, under a mistaken notion of having arrived, as Columbus supposed, at the eastern shore of the continent of India. The erroneous application of this name was not discovered till it had so obtained, that a change could not have been conveniently made. However, in a historical point, it is to be regretted that the name of the indigenes, as well as the name of the continent which they inhabited, should have been misapplied. The name of the continent should have been derived from *Columbus*, the discoverer of the New World, instead of *Americus*.

The writer of this sketch of the Indians that inhabited the portion of Pennsylvania, comprising all within the present limits of the counties of Berks and Lebanon, does not deem it compatible with the plan of this work, to give "probable theories" concerning the origin of the aborigines of the western continent. *By what means the Indians got from the old world to the new*, has never been satisfactorily answered, by all the numerous, long, and laborious disquisitions that have appeared from able pens, since the discovery of America in 1492, to the present time. Among the modern theorists who have written upon the peopling of America, the following are the leading ones, and to whose works the reader who wishes to inform himself on this subject, is referred: St. Gregory, Herrera, T. Morton, Williamson, Wood, Tosselyn, Thorowgood, Adair, R. Williamson, C. Mather, Hubbard, Robertson, Smith, Voltaire, Mitchill, McCulloh, Lord Kaim, Swinton, Cabrera, Jefferson, Heckewelder, Drake, Flint, and others.

When the Swedes arrived in this country and settled on the shores of the Delaware, and also when the English landed in 1681, they found a numerous race of Indians, who met the *strangers* in a friendly manner; and when, the following year, William Penn, with his train of pacific followers arrived, he also, with his friends, was affectionately hailed. He was treated as their *Miquon, or elder brother*."

At the time of Penn's arrival there were not less than ten native tribes in Pennsylvania, comprising about six thousand in number; these, however, formed only a portion of the Indians inhabiting the country between Virginia and Canada; those who were principally seated on the Delaware, were the Lenni Lenape, and were considered the grandfathers of near forty tribes. The others were the Mengwe, or usually called Iroquois, who inhabited the more northern portion of the United States. The Iroquois were also divided into numerous tribes.

According to popular tradition, the numerous tribes of the Delawares and Iriquois, trace their origin to two sources. The traditions, as handed down by their ancestors run thus:—The Lenni Lenape, or for brevity's sake, "*Lenape*," meaning, *The original people*, were an unmixed and unchanged race, residing, many centuries ago, towards the setting of the sun—somewhere in the *west* of this continent. For some reasons, not explained, they determined to migrate towards the rising of the sun. After their journeying they arrived at the *Fish River*, the *Namasi Sipu;* (Mississippi,) here they fell in with a nation, also in quest of a new home eastward—these were the Mengwe, or Iroquois, as they have since been called. They here united their forces, anticipating opposition from a people of gigantic form, and a populous race, the Alligewi, on the east of the Mississippi. Not many days, after their union, before they advanced, many and mighty battles were fought—the Alliwegi to escape total extermination, abandoned the country to the people of "*The New Union*," fled far southward, and never returned. The victors now divided the spoil—the country was shared out between themselves—the Iroquois made choice of the north—lands in the vicinity of the great lakes, and on their tributary streams; the *Lenape* took possession of more southern parts, where they lived in peace for many years till the Europeans came.

The Lenape; or, as they were called by the Europeans, *Delawares*, were divided into three tribes—the *Unamis*, or Turtle; the *Wunalachtikos*, or Turkey; and the *Minsi*, or Wolf. "The *Minsi* or Monceys, the most warlike of the three tribes, inhabited a country that extends from the Minisink on the Delaware, to the Hudson on the east, to the Susquehannah on the southwest, to the head waters of the Delaware and Susquehan-

1*

nah rivers on the north, and to that range of hills now known in New Jersey by the name of Muskenecum, and by those of Lehigh and Coghnewago in Pennsylvania."

The Monceys embraced a number of subordinate tribes, who were known by names derived from their residence, or some accidental circumstance. Such were the Susquehannas, Neshamines, Conestogas, and other tribes in the province of Pennsylvania, on Penn's arrival. The limits of this chapter will not admit of a further detail of the several smaller tribes. This part of the narrative will therefore be closed by an extract from one who was a man of more than ordinary observation, and whose opportunity to make them correctly, was not surpassed by any of those who have written on the Indians at the time of the first settlements made in the province of Pennsylvania. An occasional remark will be introduced.

Extract of a letter from William Penn, Proprietor and Governor of Pennsylvania, to the committee of traders of that the Province, residing in London, dated, Philadelphia, the 16th of the sixth month, called August, 1683.

"The natives I shall consider, in their *persons, language, manners, religion,* and *government,* with my sense of their *original.*

"For their *persons,* they are generally tall, straight, well-built, and of singular proportion; they tread strong and clever, and mostly walk with a lofty chin. Of complexion, black, but by design, as the *Gypsies,* in England, they grease themselves with bear's fat, clarified; and using no defence against the sun, or weather, their skin must needs be swarthy. Their eye is little and black, not unlike a straight-looked Jew. The thick lip, and flat nose, so frequent with the East *Indians* and blacks, are not common to them; for I have seen as comely European-like faces among them, of both, as on your side the sea; and truly, an Italian complexion hath not much more of the white; and the noses of several of them have as much of the *Roman.*

"Their *language* is lofty, yet narrow; but, like the *Hebrew,* in signification, full; like short-hand, in writing, one word serveth in place of three, and the rest are supplied by the understanding of the hearer: imperfect in their tenses, wanting in their moods, participles, adverbs, conjunctions, and interjections. I made it my business to understand it, that I might not want an Interpreter on any occasion; and I must say, that

I know not a language spoken in Europe, that hath words of more sweetness, or greatness, in accent and emphasis, than theirs; for instance, *Octocockon, Rancocas, Oricton, Shak, Marian, Poquesion,* which are all the names of places; and have grandeur in them. Of words of sweetness, *Anna,* is mother; *Issimus,* a brother; *Netcap,* friend; *Usquerot,* very good; *Pane,* bread; *Metsa,* eat; *Matta,* no; *Hatta,* to have; *Payo,* to come; *Spassen, Passijon,* the names of places; *Tamane, Secane, Menanse, Secatereus,* are the names of persons; if one asks them for any thing they have not, they will answer, *Matta ne hatta,* which, to translate, is, *not I have,* instead of, I have not."

According to Heckewelder and others, there appear to have been four principal Indian languages, which branched out in various dialects. These were the *Karalit* spoken by the Greenlanders and Esquimaux—the *Iroquois,* spoken by the *Six Nations,* from which many and various dialects prevail—the *Floridian,* spoken by all the southern Indians, and the *Lenape* or *Delaware,* the most widely extended of all of those languages which were spoken on this side of the Mississippi. The *Iroquois* was the next.

Those skilled in the *Delaware,* tell us the pronunciation is quite easy. An extract from a translation of John's espistles, by C. F. DENCKE, as a specimen of the Delaware is presented.

Pennamook! elgiqui penundelukquonk Wetochwink, wdaoaltowoagon, wentschi hewilchqussiank Gettanittowit wdamemensemall. Guntschi matta woachgussiwuneen untschi pemhakamixitink, eli pemhakamixit taku wohaq Patamawossall.

Behold, what manner of love the Father hath bestowed upon us, that we should be called the sons of God; therefore, the world knoweth us not, because it knew him not.

The letters *f, v, ph,* and *r,* are wanting in their alphabet. The Iroquois or Six Nations have the letter *r.* The following is the Lord's prayer in that language.

Soungwauncha, caurounkyauga, tehseetaroan, saulwoneyousta, es a, sawaneyou, okettauhsela, ehneawoung, na, caurounkyauga, nugh, wonshauga, neattewehnesalauga, taugwaunautoronoantoughsick, toantangweleewheyoustaung, cheneeyent, chaquatautaleywheyoustaunna, toughsan, langwassareneh, tawantottenaugaloughtoungga, nasawne, sacheautaugwass, contehsalohaunzaikaw, esa, sawauneyou, esa, sashantzta, esa, soungwasoung, chenneauhaungwa, anwen.

Their language is highly figurative. They are fond, says Heckewelder, of metaphors. They are to their discourse what feathers and beads are to their persons, a gawdy but tasteless ornament. The following specimens will afford an idea of their metaphors. *The sky is overcast with dark blustering clouds;* meaning, We shall have trouble some times; we shall have war. *A black cloud has arisen yonder*—War is threatened from that quarter, or from that nation. *Two black clouds are drawing towards each other*—Two powerful enemies are drawing towards each other. *The path is already shut up*—Hostilities have commenced, the war is begun. *The rivers run with blood*—War rages in the country. *To bury the hatchet*—To make or conclude a peace. *To lay down the hatchet, or to slip the hatchet under the bedstead*—To cease fighting for a while, during a truce. *You did not make me strong*—You gave me nothing. *The stronger you make me, the more you will see me*—The more you give me, the more I will do for you. *You now speak from the heart*—Now you mean what you say. *You keep me in the dark*—You deceive me. *You stopped my ears*—You did not wish me to know it. *Now I believe you*—Done! agreed! It shall be so! *Your words have penetrated into my heart!*—I consent! am pleased with what you say. *You have spoken good words*—I am pleased with what you say. *Singing birds*—Tale-bearers, liars. *Don't listen to the singing of birds which fly by*—Don't believe what stragglers tell you. *To kindle a council fire at such a place*—To appoint a place where to transact national business. *Don't look the other way*—Don't join with those. *Look this way*—Join our party. *I have not room to spread my blanket*—I am too much crowded on. *I will place you under my wings*—I will protect you at all hazards! *Suffer no grass to grow on this war path*—Carry on the war with vigor. *The path to that nation is again open*—We are again on friendly terms. *I am much too heavy to rise at this present time*—I have too much property! (corn, vegetables, &c.) *I will pass one night yet at this place*—I will stay one year yet at this place. *To bury the hatchet beneath the root of a tree*—To put it quite out of sight. *To bury injuries done, deep in the earth*—To consign injuries done, to oblivion. *One night's encamptment*—A halt of one year at a place.

"Of their *customs and manners* there is much said. I will begin with children: So soon as they are born they wish them in water; and while very young, and in cold weather, they

plunge them in the rivers to harden and embolden them.
Having wrapped them in a clout, they lay them on a strait,
thin board, a little more than the length and breadth of the
child, and swaddle it fast, upon the board, to make it straight;
wherefore all the Indians have flat heads; and thus they carry
them at their backs. The children will go, very young, at nine
months commonly; they wear only a small clout round their
waste, till they are big; if boys, they go a fishing, till they are
ripe for the woods, which is about fifteen; then they hunt:
and after having given some proofs of their manhood, by a good
return of skins, they may marry; else it is a shame to think of
a wife. The girls stay with their mothers and help to hoe the
ground, plant corn, and carry burdens; and they do well to
use them to that, young, which they must do when they are
old; for the wives are the true servants of the husbands, otherwise the men are very affectionate to them.

"When the young women are fit for marriage they wear something upon their heads for an advertisement; but so as their
faces are hardly seen, but when they please. The age they
marry at, if women, is about thirteen and fourteen; if men,
seventeen and eighteen; they are rarely older.

"Their houses are mats, or barks of trees set on poles, in the
fashion of an English barn; but out of the power of the winds;
for they are hardly higher than a man; they lie on reeds, or
grass. In travel, they lodge in the woods, about a great fire,
with the mantle of duffils, they wear by day, wrapped about
them, and a few boughs stuck around them.

"Their diet is maize or Indian corn, divers ways prepared;
sometimes roasted in the ashes, sometimes beaten and boiled
with water, which they call homine; they also make cakes, not
unpleasant to eat. They have likewise several sort of beans
and peas that are good nourishment; and the woods and rivers
are their border.

"If an European come to see them, or calls for lodging at their
house or wigwam, they give him the best place and first cut.
If they come to visit us, they salute us with an *Itab;* which is
as much as to say, *Good be to you,* and set them down; which is
mostly on the ground, close to their heels, their legs upright;
it may be, they speak not a word, but they observe all passages. If you give them any thing to eat or drink, well; for
they will not ask; and be it little, or be it much, if it be with
kindness, they are well pleased; else they go away sullen, but
say nothing.

"They are great concealers of their own resentment; brought to it, I believe, by the revenge that hath been practised among them. In either of these they are not exceeded by the Italians. A tragical instance fell out since I came into the country: A king's daughter thinking herself slighted by her husband, in suffering another woman to lie down between them, rose up, went out, plucked a root out of the ground and ate it; upon which she immediately died; and for which, last week, he made an offering to her kindred for atonement and liberty of marriage; as two others did to the kindred of their wives, who died a natural death. For, till widowers have done so, they must not marry again. Some of the young women are said to take undue liberty before marriage, for a portion; but when married, chaste. When with child they know their husbands no more till delivered; and during their month they touch no meat; they eat but with a stick, lest they should defile it; nor do their husbands frequent them till that term be expired.

"But, in liberality they excel; nothing is too good for their friend. Give them a fine gun, coat, or any thing, it may pass twenty hands before it sticks; light of heart, strong affection, but soon spent. The most merry creature that lives, feast and dance perpetually; they never have much, nor want much; wealth circulates like the blood; all parts partake; and though none shall want what another hath, yet exact observers of property. Some kings have sold, others presented me with several parcels of land; the pay or presents I made them were not hoarded by the particular owners; but the neighboring kings and their clans being present when the goods were brought out, the parties chiefly concerned, consulted what, and to whom they should give them. To every king then, by the hands of a person for that purpose appointed, is a proportion sent, so sorted and folded, and with that gravity that is admirable. Then that king subdivides it, in like manner, among his dependants; they hardly leaving themselves an equal share of their subjects; and be it on such occasion as festivals, or at their common meals, the kings distribute, and to themselves last. They care for little, because they want but little; and the reason is, a little contents them. In this they are sufficiently revenged on us; if they are ignorant of our pleasures, they are also free from our pains. They are not disquieted with bills of lading and exchange, nor perplexed with chancery suits, and exchequer reckonings. We sweat and toil to live; their pleasure feeds them; I mean their hunting, fishing, and fowling;

and their table is spread every where. They eat twice a day, morning and evening; their seats and table are the ground. Since the European came into these parts, they are great lovers of strong liquor, rum especially; and for it they exchange the richest of their skins and furs. If they are heated with liquor, they are restless till they have enough to sleep; that is their cry, some more, and I will go to sleep; but when drunk, one of the most wretched creatures in the world!

"In sickness impatient to be cured, and for it give every thing, especially for their children, to whom they are extremely natural. They drink at those times, a *teran*, or decoction of some roots in spring water; and if they eat any flesh, it must be of the female of any creature. If they die they bury them with their apparel, be they man or woman; and the nearest of kin fling in something precious with them, as a token of their love; their mourning is blacking of their faces, which they continue for a year. They are choice of the graves of their dead; for, lest they should be lost by time, and fall to common use they pick off the grass that grows upon them, and heap up the fallen earth, with great care and exactness.

" *These poor people are under a dark night in things relating to religion,* to be sure the tradition of it; yet they believe a God and immortality, without the help of metaphysics; for, they say, there is a Great King that made them, who dwells in a glorious country to the southward of them; and that the souls of the good shall go thither, where they shall live again. Their worship consists of two parts, sacrifice and cantico. Their sacrifice is their first fruits; the first and fattest bucks they kill goeth to the fire, where he is all burnt, with a mournful ditty of him that performeth the economy; but with such marvellous fervency and labor of body, that he will even sweat to a foam. The other part is their cantico, performed by round dance, sometimes words, sometimes songs, then shouts; two being in the middle that begin; and, by singing and drumming on a board, direct the chorus. Their postures in the dance are very antick and differing, but they all keep measure. This is with equal earnestness and labor, but great appearance of joy. In the fall when the corn comes in, they begin to feast one another. There have been two great festivals already, to which all come that will. I was at one myself: their entertainment was a great feast by a spring, under some shady trees, and twenty bucks with hot cakes of new corn, both wheat and beans; which they make up in a square form, in the leaves of

the steam and bake them in the ashes; and after that they fall
to dance.   But they that go must carry a small present, in their
money; it may be sixpence; which is made of the bone of a
fish, the black is with them, as gold; the white, silver; they
call it *wampum*."

Conrad Weiser's letter to a Friend respecting the Indians views
on the subject of religion; showing that they have a strong
confidence in the overruling Providence of God.

Heidelburg, Berks co., 1746.

ESTEEMED FRIEND:—I write this in compliance with thy
request, to give thee an account of what I have observed among
the Indians, in relation to their belief and confidence in a Divine
Being, according to the observations I have made, from 1714,
in the time of my youth, to this day.

If, by the word *religion*, people mean an assent to certain
creeds, or the observance of a set of religious duties; as appointed prayers, singing, baptism, or even *Heathenish worship*,
then it may be said, the Five Nations and their neighbors, have
no religion.   But, if by religion, we mean an *attraction* of the
soul to God, whence proceeds a confidence in, a hunger after,
the knowledge of Him, then this people must be allowed to have
some *religion* among them, notwithstanding their sometimes
savage deportment.   For we find among them some traces of
a confidence in God alone; and, even, sometimes, though but
seldom, a vocal calling upon Him: I shall give one or two
instances of this, that fell under my own observation.

In the year 1737, I was sent, the first time, to *Onondago*, at
the desire of the Governor of Virginia; I departed in the latter
end of February, very unexpectedly, for a journey of five hundred English miles, through a wilderness, where there was
neither road nor path, and at such a time of the year, when
animals could not be met with for food.   There were with me,
a Dutchman and three Indians.   After we had gone one hundred and fifty miles on our journey, we came to a narrow valley, about half a mile broad and thirty long, both sides of which
were encompassed with high mountains; on which the snow
laid about three feet deep: in it ran a stream of water, also
about three feet deep, which was so crooked that it kept a continued winding from one side of the valley to another.   In order
to avoid wading so often through the water, we endeavored to
pass along the slope of the mountain; the snow being three

·feet deep, and so hard frozen on the top that we walked upon it: but we were obliged to make holes in the snow with our hatchets, that our feet might not slip down the mountain; and thus we crept on. It happened that the old Indian's foot slipped, and the root of a tree by which he held breaking, he slid down the mountain, as from the roof of a house; but happily he was stopped in his fall, by the string which fastened his pack, hitching on the stump of a small tree. The two Indians could not go to his aid, but our Dutch fellow-traveller did; yet not without visible danger of his own life. I also could not put a foot forward, till I was helped; after this we took the first opportunity to descend into the valley, which was not till after we had labored hard for half an hour with hands and feet. Having observed a tree lying directly off from where the Indian fell, when we were got into the valley again, we went back about one hundred paces, where we saw, that if the Indian had slipped four or five paces further, he would have fallen over a rock one hundred feet perpendicular, upon craggy pieces of rocks below. The Indian was astonished, and turned quite pale; then, with outstretched arms, and great earnestness, he spoke these words: "*I thank the great Lord and Governor of this world, in that he has had mercy upon me, and has been willing that I should live longer.*" Which words I, at that time, put down in my journal: this happened on the 25th of March, 1737.

On the 9th of April following, while we were yet on our journey, I found myself extremely weak, through the fatigue of so long a journey, with the cold and hunger, which I had suffered; there having fallen a fresh snow about twenty inches deep, and we being yet three days journey from Onondago, in a frightful wilderness, my spirit failed, my body trembled and shook; I thought I should fall down and die; I stepped aside, and sat down under a tree, expecting there to die. My companions soon missed me; the Indians came back and found me sitting there. They remained awhile silent; at last, the old Indian said: "My dear companion, thou hast hitherto encouraged us, wilt thou now quite give up? remember that evil days are better than good days; for when we suffer much we do not sin; sin will be driven out us by suffering, and God cannot extend his mercy to them; but contrary wise, when it goeth evil with us, God hath compassion on us." These words made me ashamed; I rose up, and travelled as well as I could.

The next year, (1738,) I went another journey to Onon-

3

dago, in company with Joseph Spangenberger, and two others.
It happened that an Indian came to us in the evening, who had
neither shoes, stockings, shirt, gun, knife, nor hatchet; in a
word, he had nothing but an old torn blanket, and some rags.
Upon enquiring whither he was going, he answered to Onondago.   I knew him, and asked him how he could undertake a
journey of three hundred miles so naked and impoverished,
having no provisions, nor arms, to kill animals for his suste-
nance?   He answered, he had been among enemies, and had
been obliged to save himself by flight; and so had lost all; for
he had disposed of some of his things among the Irish, for
strong liquors.   Upon further talk, he told me very cheerfully,
"That God formed every thing, which had life, even the rattlesnake itself, though it was a bad creature; and that God would
also provide, in such a manner, that he should go thither; that
it was visible God was with the Indians in the wilderness, because they always cast their care upon him; but that, contrary
to this, the Europeans always carried their bread with them."
He was an *Onondago Indian;* his name was *Onontagketa* —the
next day we travelled in company; and the day following I
provided him with a knife, hatchet, flint, tinder, also shoes and
stockings, and sent him before me, to give notice to the council at Onondago, that I was coming; which he truly performed,
being got thither three days before us.

Two years ago, I was sent by the Governor to Shamokin,
on account of the unhappy death of John Armstrong, the Indian trader, (1744.)   After I had performed my errand, there
was a feast prepared, to which the Governor's messengers
were invited; there were about one hundred persons present;
to whom, after we had in great silence, devoured a fat bear, the
eldest of the chiefs made a speech, in which he said: "That, by
a great misfortune, three of the brethren, the *white men,* had
been killed by an Indian; that nevertheless the sun was not
set, (meaning there was no war,) it had only been somewhat
darkened by a small cloud, which was now done away; he that
had done evil was like to be punished, and the land to remain
in peace: therefore, he exhorted his people to thankfulness to
God; and therefore he began to sing with an awful solemnity,
but without expressing any words; the others accompanied
him with their voices: after they had done, the same Indian
with great earnestness of fervour, spoke these words: "*Thanks,
thanks, be to thee, thou great Lord of the world, in that thou*

*hast again caused the sun to shine, and hast dispersed the dark
cloud—the Indians are thine.*"

"Their government is by Kings, which they call *Sachama;*
and those by succession, but always of the mother's side. For
instance, the children of him, who is now king, will not succeed, but his brother, by the mother, or the children of his sister, whose sons, and after them the children of her daughters
will reign, for no woman inherits. The reason, they render for
this way of descent is, that their issue may not be spurious.

"Every King hath his council; and that consists of all the
old and wise men of his nation; which, perhaps, is two hundred people. Nothing of moment is undertaken, be it war,
peace, selling of land, or traffick, without advising with them;
and, which is more, with the young men too. It is admirable
to consider how powerful the kings are, and yet how they
move by the breath of their people. I have had occasion to
be in council with them, upon treaties for land, and to adjust
the terms of trade. Their order is this: The king sits in the
middle of an half moon, and hath his council, the old and wise,
on each hand; behind him, or at a little distance, sit the young,
or fry, in the same figure. Having consulted and resolved their
business, the king ordered one of them to speak to me; he stood
up, came to me, and, in the name and authority of his King,
saluted me, then took me by the hand, and told me, he was
ordered by his king to speak to me, and that now it was not
he, but the king that spoke, because what he should say was
the king's mind. He first prayed me, "To excuse them, that
they had not complied with me, the last time; he feared there
might be some fault in the Interpreter, being neither Indian nor
English: beside it was the Indian custom to deliberate and take
up much time in council, before they resolved; and that if the
young people and owners of the land had been as ready as he,
I had not met with so much delay." Having thus introduced
his matter, he fell to the bounds of the land they had agreed
to be disposed of, and the price, which now is little and dear;
that which would have bought twenty miles, not buying now
two. During the time that this person spoke, not a man of
them was observed to whisper or smile; the old, grave; the
young, reverent in their deportment. They spoke little, but
fervently, and with elegance. I have never seen more natural
sagacity, considering them without the help, (I was going to

say) the spoil of tradition; and he will deserve the name of
wise that outwit them, in any treaty, about a thing they understand.   When the purchase was agreed, great promises passed
between us, of kindness and good neighborhood, and that the
Indians and English must live in love as long as the sun gave
light.   Which done, another made a speech to the Indians, in
the name of all the Sachamakers or kings; first to tell them
what was done, next to charge and command them, "To love
the Christian, and particularly live in peace with me and the
people under my government; that many Governors had been
in the river, but that no Governor had come himself to live and
stay here before; and having now such an one that had treated
them well they should never do him, or his, any wrong."   At
every sentence of which they shouted, and said, Amen, in their
way.

   "The justice they have, is pecuniary.   If they commit any
wrong or evil, be it murder itself, they atone by feasts, and presents of their wampum; which is proportioned to the quality of
the offence, or persons injured, or of the sex they are of.   For,
in case they killed a woman, they pay double; and the reason
they render is, that she breedeth children, which men cannot
do.   It is rare that they fall out, if sober; and, if drunk, they
forgive it, saying, "It was the drink and not the man that
abused them."

   "We have agreed that in all differences between us, six of
each side shall end the matter.   Do not abuse them, but let
them have justice, and you do win them.   The worst is, that
they are the worse for the Christians, who have propagated
their vices, and yielded them tradition for ill, and not for good
things.   But as low an ebb as these people are at, and as in-
glorious as their own condition looks, the Christians have not
outlived their sight, with all their pretensions to an higher
manifestation.   What, good then, might not a good people graft,
where there is so distinct a knowledge left between good and
evil?   I beseech God to incline the hearts of all that come into
these parts, to outlive the nations, by a fast obedience to their
greater knowledge of the will of God; for it were miserable
indeed for us to fall under the just censure of the poor Indian's
conscience, while we make profession of things so far transcend-
ing.

   "For their original, I am ready to believe them of the Jewish
race; I mean, of the stock of the ten tribes; and that, for the

following reasons: First, they were to go to a "land not planted, nor known;" which, to be sure, Asia and Africa were, if not Europe; and He that intended that extraordinary judgment upon them, might make the passage not uneasy to them, as it is not impossible in itself, from the easternmost parts of Asia to the westernmost of America.

"In the next place, I find them of the like countenance, and children of so lively resemblance, that a man would think himself in Duke place, or Berry street, London, when he seeth them. But this is not all; they agree in rite; they reckon by moons; they offer their first fruits; they have a kind of feast of tabernacles; they are said to lay their altar on twelve stones; their mourning a year; customs of women, with many other things, that do not now occur."

Peter Kalm, the Swedish natural philosopher, a great traveller and a clear observer, visited this country, in 1748, wrote a work, in which he gives a minute account of them. An extract, it is thought, will not be out of place here. Speaking of their *food and mode of living*, he says:

Maize, (Indian corn,) some kinds of beans, and melons, made up the sum of the Indian's gardening. Their chief support arose from hunting and fishing. Besides these, the oldest Swedes, related that the Indians were accustomed to get nourishment from the following plants, to wit:

Hopniss, so called by the Indians, and also by the Swedes, (the Glycine Apios of Linnæus,) they found in the meadows. The roots resembled potatoes, and were eaten boiled, instead of bread.

Katniss, so called by the Indians and Swedes, (a kind of Sagittaria sagittifolia,) was found in low wet ground; had oblong roots nearly as large as the fist; this they boiled or roasted in the ashes. Several Swedes said they like to eat of it in their youth. The hogs liked them much, and made them very scarce. Mr. Kalm, who ate of them, thought they tasted like potatoes. When the Indians first saw turnips, they called them katniss, too.

Taw-ho, so called by the Indians and Swedes, (the Arum Virginicum, or Wakerobin, and poisonous!) grew in moist ground, and swamps; they ate the root of it. The roots grew to the thickness of a man's thigh; and the hogs rooted them up and devoured them eagerly. The Indians destroyed their poisonous quality by baking them. They made a long trench in the ground, put in the roots and covered them with earth, and over them they made a great fire. They tasted somewhat like potatoes.

Taw-kee, so called by the Indians and Swedes, (the Orontium Aquaticum,) grew plentifully in moist low grounds. Of these they used the seed, when dried. These they boiled repeatedly to soften them, and then they ate somewhat like peas. When they got butter and milk from the Swedes, they boiled them together.

Bilberries, or whortleberries, (a species of Vaccinium,) was a common diet among the Indians. They dried them in the sun, and kept them parched as close as currants.

Of their implements for domestic or field use. The old boilers or kettles of the Indians were either made of clay, or of different kinds of pot-stone, (Lapis Ollaris.) The former consisted of a dark clay, mixed with grains of white sand or quartz, and probably burnt in the fire. Many of these kettles had two holes in the upper margin; on each side one, through which they passed a stick, and held therewith the kettle over the fire. It is remarkable that none of these pots have been found glazed either inside or outside. A few of the old Swedes could remember to have seen the Indians use such pots to boil their meat in. They were made sometimes of a grayish pot stone; and some were made of another species of a pyrous stone. They were very thin. Mr. Bartram, the botanist, showed him an earthen pot, which had been dug up at a place where the Indians had lived. On the outside it was much ornamented. Mr. Bartram has also several broken pieces. They were all made of mere clay, in which were mixed, according to the convenience of the makers, pounded shells of snails and muscles, or of the crystals found in the mountains; it was plain, they did not burn them much, because they could be cut up with a knife. Since the Europeans have come among them, they disuse them, and have even lost the art of making them.

The hatchets of the Indians were made of stone, somewhat of the shape of a wedge. This was notched round the biggest end, and to this they affixed a split stick for a handle, bound round with a cord. These hatchets could not serve, however, to cut any thing like a tree; their means, therefore, of getting trees for canoes, &c., was to put a great fire round the roots of a big tree to burn it off, and with a wet swab of rags on a pole to keep the tree constantly wet above until the fire below burnt it off. When the tree was down, they laid dry branches on the trunk and set fire to it, and kept swabbing that part of the tree which they did not want to burn; thus the tree burnt a hollow in one place only; when burnt enough, they chipped or scraped it smooth inside with their hatchets, or sharp flints, or sharp shells.

Instead of knives, they used little sharp pieces of flints or quartz, or a piece of sharpened bone.

At the end of the arrows they fastened narrow angulated pieces of stone; these were commonly flints or quartz. Some made use of the claws of birds and beasts.

They had stone pestles of about a foot long and five inches in thickness; in these they pounded their maize. Many had only wooden pestles. The Indians were astonished beyond measure, when they saw the first windmills to grind corn. They were, at first, of opinion that not the wind, but spirits within them gave them their momentum. They would come from a great distance, and set down for days near them, to wonder and admire at them!

The old tobacco pipes were made of clay or pot stone, or sepertine stone, and were seen chiefly with the Sachems. Some of the old Dutchmen, at New York, preserved the tradition that the first Indians seen by Europeans made use of copper for their tobacco pipes, got from the second river, near Elizabeth river. In confirmation of this, it was observed that the people met with holes worked into the mountains, out of which some copper had been taken; and they even found some tubes which the Indians probably used for the occasion. They used bird's claws instead of fishing-hooks; the Swedes saw them succeed in this way.

"The Indians made their ropes, bridles, and twine for nets, out of a wild weed, growing abundantly in old corn fields, commonly called Indian hemp, (i. e., Linum Virginianum.) The Swedes used to buy fourteen yards of the rope for a loaf of bread, and deemed them more lasting in the water than that made of true hemp. Mr. Kalm himself saw Indian women rolling the filaments of this plant upon their bare thighs, to make of them thread and strings, which they dyed red, yellow, black, &c.

"The Indians at first were much more industrious and laborious, and before the free use of ardent spirits, attained to a great age. In early time they were every where spread about among the Swedes. They had no domestic animals among them before the arrival of the Europeans, save a species of little dogs. They readily sold their lands to the Swedes for a small price. Such tracts as would have brought $400 currency in Kalm's time, had been bought for a piece of baize or a pot of brandy!

The Indians told Kalm, as their tradition, that when they saw the first European ship on their coast, they were perfectly persuaded that *Manitto*, or God himself, was in the ship; but when they first saw the negroes, they thought they were a true breed of devils.

"The last of the Lenape, (Delaware,) nearest resident to Philadelphia, died in Chester county, in the person of "Old Indian Hannah," in 1803. She had her wigwam many years upon the Brandywine, and used to travel much about, selling her baskets, &c. On such occasions she was often followed by her dog and pigs—all stopping where she did. She lived to be nearly a hundred years of age—had a proud and lofty spirit to the last—hated the blacks, and scarcely brooked the lower order of whites; her family before her; had dwelt with other Indians in Kennet township. She often spoke emphatically of the wrongs and misfortunes of her race, upon whom her affections still dwelt. As she grew old, she quitted her solitude, and dwelt in friendly families.

"As late as 1705, the Shawnese had their wigwams at the Beaver pond, near Carlisle, Cumberland county; and as late as 1760, Doctor John, living in Carlisle, with his wife and two children, were cruelly murdered, by persons unknown. He was a chief. The governor offered $100 reward."

"*Present state and refuge of the Indians.*—The Indian nation of the *Delawares*—our proper Indians—was once one of the most numerous and powerful tribes, but are now reduced to about four or five hundred souls, and scattered among other tribes. The chief place, according to Watson, where they now hold any separate character and community, is at the river Thames, (1830,) in Upper Canada, about seventy miles from Detroit, where they settled about the year 1793.—*Watson's Annals.*

CHAPTER III.

In the year 1744, open hostilities were declared between Great Brittain and France, which involved not only the mother country, but also the colonies; and, of course, Pennsylvania, that had up to this time enjoyed tranquillity, now began to feel the effects of the war between France and England. Shortly after the declaration of hostility between those great rival nations, the French hovered along the great lakes, and succeeded in their machinations to a great extent in seducing the Indians from their allegiance to the English. Many of the Indians, being dissatisfied with the English on account of their lands, went over to the French, and the affairs of the colonies changed aspects on Braddock's defeat, in 1755. From that period, till 1764, Berks and Lebanon counties were scenes of murder and burning of houses, &c. The apprehensions of those who feared the consequences of Braddock's defeat, were shortly realized. Governor ROBERT MORRIS, in his message of July 24, 1755, to the Assembly, has the following language in relation to the defeat: "This unfortunate and unexpected change in our affairs deeply effect every one of his majesty's colonies, but none of them in so sensible a manner as this province, while having no militia, is thereby left exposed to the cruel incursions of the French and barbarous Indians, who delight in shedding human blood, and who make no distinction as to age or sex—as to those that are armed against them, or such as they can surprise in their peaceful habitations—all are alike the objects of their cruelty—slaughtering the tender infant, and frightened mother, with equal joy and fierceness. To such enemies, spurred by the native cruelty of their tempers, encouraged by their late success, and having now no army to fear, are the inhabitants of this province exposed; and by such must we now expect to be overrun, if we do not immediately prepare for our own defence; nor ought we to content ourselves with this, but resolve to drive to and confine the French to their own just limits."*

The following extracts from the official documents at Har-

* Votes Ass. 4, 416.

risburg, and the Gazettes of that day, as well as copies from original manuscript letters, written at the time, will afford some idea of the extent of depredations and murders committed upon the frontier inhabitants, coming legitimately within the bounds of that portion of territory, of which a history is attempted.

A brief narrative of the incursions and ravages of the French and Indians, in the Province of Pennsylvania, made by the Secretary of the Province, at Philadelphia, 27th December, 1755. *Provincial Records*, N. p. 340–2.

October 15, 1755, a party of Indians fell upon the inhabitants on *Mahahany* (or Penn's) creek, that runs into the river Susquehannah, about five miles lower than the Great Fork made by the juncture of the two main branches of the Susquehannah, killed and carried off about twenty-five persons, and burnt and destroyed their buildings and improvements, and the whole settlement was deserted."—*Provincial Records*, N. 340.

A petition to Governor Morris, from inhabitants on the west side of the Susquehannah, is presented here, to show the alarming condition of the settlers in that part of the province, at, the time alluded to in the Secretary's narrative.

"We, the subscribers, near the mouth of Penn's creek, on the west side of the Susquehanna, humbly show, that on or about the 16th inst., (October, 1755,) the enemy came down upon said creek and killed, scalped, and carried away all the men, women, and children, amounting to twenty-five in number, and wounded one man, who fortunately made his escape, and brought us the news, whereupon the subscribers went out and buried the dead, whom we found most barbarously murdered and scalped.

"We found but thirteen, who were men and elderly women; and children we suppose to be carried away prisoners. The house where we suppose they finished their murder, we found burnt up; and the man of it, named Jacob King, a Swisser, lying just by it. He lay on his back, barbarously burnt, and two tomahawks sticking in his forehead; one of those marked newly with W. D.—we have sent them to your honor. The terror of which, has driven away almost all the back inhabitants, except the subscribers, with a few more who are willing to stay and endeavor to defend the land; but as we are not all able of ourselves to defend it for the want of guns and ammunition, and but few in number, so that without assistance, we must flee and leave the country to the mercy of the enemy. ·

"We, therefore, humbly desire it, that your honor would take the same into consideration, and order some speedy relief for the safety of these back settlements, and be pleased to give us speedy orders what to do.

"George Gliwell, Gates Auchmudy, John McCahon, Abraham Soverkill, Edmund Matthews, Mark Curry, William Doran, Dennis Mucklehenny, John Young, John Simmons, George Snabble, George Aberheart, Daniel Braugh, George Lynn, and Gotfried Fryer."*

In continuation of the Secretary's narrative, he adds: "October 23, 1755, forty-six of the inhabitants on Susquehannah, went to Shamokin to enquire of the Indians there, who they were who had so cruelly fallen upon and ruined the settlements on Mahahony creek; on their return from Shamokin, they were fired upon by some Indians who lay in ambush, and four were killed, four drowned, and the rest put to flight, on which all the settlements, between Shamokin and Hunter's Mill, for the space of fifty miles along the river Susquehannah, were deserted."
—*Prov. Rec.* N. 340.

The following letters from John Harris, of Harris's Ferry, (Harrisburg,) and other gentlemen, to Governor Morris, will cast some additional light upon this point.

Paxton, October 20, 1755.

May it please your Honor—

I was informed last night, by a person that came down our river, that there was a Dutch (German) woman, who made her escape to George Gabriel's, and informs us that last Friday evening, on her way home from this settlement on Mahahony, or Penn's creek, where her family lived, she called at a neighbor's house, and saw two persons lying by the door of said house, murdered and scalped; and these were some Dutch (German) families that lived near their places, immediately left, not thinking it safe to stay any longer. It is the opinion of the people up the river, that the families on Penn's creek being scattered, that but few in number are killed or carried off, except the above said woman, the certainty of which will 'soon be known, as there are some men gone out to bury the dead.

By report this evening, I was likewise informed by the belt of wampum and these Indians here, there were seen, near Sha-

* Provincial Records, N. p. 242-3. Votes of Assembly 4, 495.

mokin, about six days ago, two French Indians of the Cana-
wago tribe.   I a little doubted the truth·of the report at first;
but the Indians have seemed so afraid, that they despatched
messengers immediately to the mountains above my house, to
bring in some of their women that were gathering chestnuts, for
fear of their being killed.

By a person just arrived down onr river, bring information
of two men being murdered within five miles of George Gabriel's, four women carried off, and there is one man wounded
in three places who escaped to Gabriel's, and it is imagined that
all the inhabitants on Penn's creek and Little Mahahony, are
killed or carried off, as most of them live much higher up, where
the first murder was discovered.   The Indian warriors here
send you these two strings of white wampum, and the women the black one, both requesting that you would lay by
all your council pipes, immediately, and open all your eyes
and ears and view your slain people in this land, and to put a
stop to it immediately, and come to this place to our assistance
without any delay; and the belt of wampum particularly mentions that the proprietors and your honor would immediately
act in defence of their country, as the old chain of friendship
now is broken by several nations of Indians, and it seems to be
such as they never expected to see or hear of.   Any delay on
our acting vigorously now at this time, would be the loss of
all Indian interest, and perhaps our ruin in these parts.

I am your honor's
Most obedient servant,
JOHN HARRIS.

P. S.   I shall endeavor to get a number of my neighbors to
go out as far as the murder has been committed; and, perhaps,
to Shamokin, to know the minds of the Indians, and their opinions of these times, and to get what intelligence I can from
them, and to encourage some of their young men to scout about,
back of the frontiers, to give us notice of the enemy's approach,
if possible, at any time hereafter.   I heartily wish your honor
and the assembly, would please to agree on some method at
this time towards protecting this province, as this part of it
seems actually in danger now; for should but a company of Indians come and murder, but a few families hereabouts, which
is daily expected, the situation we are in would oblige numbers to abandon their plantations, and our cattle and provisions,
which we have plenty of, must then fall a prey to the enemy.

Our Indians here seem much discouraged at the large number of families passing here, every day, on account of the late murders done on the Potomack, and will be much more so, if it should happen to be our case. There were two Indian women set out from here two days ago, for the Ohio, to bring some of their relations (as they say) down here; and should the French, or their Indians hear by them, as they will be enquiring for news, the effect that their late murders has had among our inhabitants, it will be a matter of encouragement to them.[*]

I conclude, your honor's

Most obedient and must humble servant,

JOHN HARRIS.

———

Paxton, October 28, 1755.

To GOVERNOR MORRIS.

May it please your Honor—

This is to acquaint you, that on the 24th of October, I arrived at Shamokin, in order to protect our frontiers up that way, till they might make their escape from their cruel enemies, and to learn the best intelligences I could. The Indians on the west branch of Susquehannah, certainly killed our inhabitants on Mr. Penn's creek, and there are a hatchet and two English scalps sent by them up the north branch to desire them to strike with them, if they are men.

The Indians are all assembling themselves at Shamokin, to council; a large body of them was there four days ago. I cannot learn their intentions; but it seems Andrew Montour and Monacatootha are to bring down the news from them. There is not a sufficient number of them to oppose the enemy; and, perhaps, they will join the enemy against us. There is no dependance on Indians, and we are in imminent danger.

I got certain information from Andrew Montour, and others, that there is a body of French with fifteen hundred Indians coming upon us. Picks, Ottaways, Orandox, Delawares, Shawanese, and a number of the Six Nations; and are now, not many day's march from this Province and Virginia, which are appointed to be attacked; at the same, some of the Shamokin Indians seemed friendly, and others appeared like enemies.

———

' [*]Provincial Records, N. p. 241-2. Votes of Assembly 4, 495

4

Montour knew many days of the enemy being on their march, against us, before he informed me; for which I said as much to him, as I thought prudent, considering the place I was in.

On the 25th of this instant, on my return with about forty men, at Mr. Penn's creek, we were attacked by about twenty' or thirty Indians—received their fire, and about fifteen of our men and myself took to the trees and attacked the villains, killed four of them on the spot, and lost but three men; retreating about half a mile through woods, and crossing Susquehannah, one of whom was shot off an horse riding behind myself, through the river. My horse before me was wounded, and failing in the river, I was obliged to quit him, and swim part of the way.

Four or five of our men were drowned crossing the river. I hope, our journey, though with fatigue, and loss of our substance, and some of our lives, will be of service to our country, by discovering our enemy, who will be our ruin, if not timely prevented.

I just now received information that there was a French officer, supposed a captain, with a party of Shawanese, Delawares, &c., within six miles of Shamokin, two days ago; and no doubt, intends to take possession of it, which will be a dreadful consequence to us, if suffered. Therefore, I thought proper to despatch this messenger to imform your Honor. The Indians here, I hope, your Honor, will be pleased to cause them to be removed to some place, as I do not like their company; and as the men of those here were not against us, yet did them no harm; or else I would have them all cut off the old belt of wampum promised at Shamokin; to send out spies to view the enemy, and upon his hearing of our skirmishes, was in a rage; gathered up thirty Indians immediately and went in pursuit of the enemy, I am this day informed.

I expect Montour and Monacathootha down here this week, with the determination of their Shamokin council. The inhabitants are abandoning their plantations, and we are in a dreadful situation.*

I am your Honor's
Most obedient and humble servant,
JOHN HARRIS.

P. S. The night ensuing our attack, the Indians burnt all George Gabriel's houses—danced around them.

*Provincial Records, N. p. 247-8.

Extract from the Provincial Records, N. p. 243: I, Thomas Foster, Esq., Mr. Harris, and Mr. McKee, with upwards of forty men, went up the 23d inst., (October, 1755,) to Captain McKee, at New Providence, in order to bury the dead, lately murdered on Mahahany creek; but understanding the corpse were buried, we then determined to return immediately home. But being urged by John Sekalamy, and the Old Belt, to go up to see the Indians at Shamokin, and know their minds, we went on the 24th, and staid there all night—and in the night, I heard some Delawares talking—about twelve in number—to this purpose: "What are the English come here for?" Says another: "To kill us, I suppose; can we then send off some of our nimble young men to give our friends notice that can soon be here?" They soon after sang the war song, and four Indians went off, in two canoes, well armed—the one canoe went down the river, and the other across.

On the morning of the 25th, we took our leave of the Indians and set off homewards, and were advised to go down the east side of the river, but fearing that a snare might be laid on that side, we marched off peaceably, on the west side, having behaved in the most civil and friendly manner towards them while with them; and when we came to the mouth of Mahahany creek, we were fired on by a good number of Indians that lay among the bushes; on which we were obliged to retreat, with the loss of several men; the particular number I cannot exactly mention; but I am positive that I saw four fall, and one man struck with a tomahawk, on the head, in his flight across the river. As I understood the Delaware tongue, I heard several of the Indians that were engaged against us, speak a good many words, in that tongue, during the action.

ADAM TERRANCE.

The above declaration was attested by the author's voluntary qualification, no magistrate being present; at Paxton, this 26th October, 1755, before us.

John Elder, Thomas McArthur, Michael Graham, Alex. McClure, Michael Teass, William Harris, Thomas Black, Samuel Lenes, Samuel Pearson, William McClure.

N. B. Of all our people that were in the action, there are but nine that are yet returned.

A Letter to Governor Morris from Conrad Weiser.

Reading, October 22, 1755.

HONORED SIR:

I take this opportunity to inform you, that I received news from Shamokin, and that six families have been murdered on John Penn's creek, on the west side of the Susquehannah; about four miles from the river, several people have been found scalped, and twenty-eight or more missing. The people are in great consternation, and are coming down, leaving their plantations and corn behind them. Two of my sons are gone up to help down one of their cousins with his family.

I hear of more that will defend themselves; but George Gabriel——the people down here seem to be for ourselves, and say: The Indians will never come this side the Susquehannah river; but I fear they will, since they meet with no opposition any where. I do not doubt, your Honor has heard of this melancholy affair before now, by the way of Lancaster, perhaps more particularly; yet, I thought it my duty to inform you of it; and when my sons come back, I will write again, if they bring any thing particular.

I have heard nothing of the Indians that have gone up to fight against the French on the Ohio; their going, I fear, has been occasion of this murder. I have nothing more to add, but am, Honored Sir,

Your very humble servant,

CONRAD WEISER.

———

Letter to Governor Morris from Conrad Weiser.

HEIDELBERG, IN THE COUNTY OF BERKS, }
October 26, 1755, at 5 o'clock, Sunday evening. }

SIR:

Just now, two of my sons, Frederick and Peter, arrived from Shamokin, where they have been to help down their cousin with his family. I gave them orders before they went, to bring me down a trusty Indian or two, to inform myself of the present circumstances of the Indian affairs; but they brought none down; they saw Jonathan, but he could not leave his family, in these dangerous times.

While they were at George Gabriel's, a messenger came from Shamokin, sent by James Logan, one of Shickelamy's sons, and Capachpitan, a noted Delaware, always true to the English, to let George Gabriel know that they had certain intelligence, that a great body of French and Indians had been seen on their march towards Pennsylvania, at a place where the Zinaghton river comes out of the Allegheny hills, and that if the white people will come up to Shamokin and assist, they will stand the French and fight them.

They say, that now they want to see their brethrens faces, and well armed with smooth guns—no rifled guns, which require too much cleansing. They, in particular, desired the company of men gathered at George Gabriel's—Capt. McKee's and John Harris's men—they being informed that people had gathered there—and that they are extremely concerned on account of white people running away, and said, they alone could not stand the French.

The message was delivered to George Gabriel, and to about ten whites more, among whom were my two sons, by a Delaware Indian, named Enoch, and a white man called Lawrence Book, who came with the Indians as a companion. The Indian messenger that brought the news, from the Indians living up the river Zinaghton, (the north-west branch of the Susquehannah,) arrived at Shamokin, at midnight, upon the 23d of this inst. The Indians are extremely concerned, as my sons tell me, that the people are coming away in a great hurry—the rest that stay are plundering the houses and making the best of peoples' misfortunes.

The French want to see Jonathan taken prisoner, &c. All this is in great hurry. I pray, good sir, don't slight it. The lives of many thousands are in the utmost danger. It is no false alarm.

I am, dear sir, your humble and
obedient servant,
CONRAD WEISER.

P. S. If a body of men would go up, they could gather plenty of Indian corn, beef, and other provisions. Now every thing is in the utmost confusion. I suppose in a few days hence, not a family will be seen on the other side of Kittatiny hills.

4*

A Letter to James Read, Esq., at Reading, from Conrad Weiser.

Heidelberg, October 26, at 11 o'clock, }
Sunday night, 1755. }

MR. JAMES READ,

Loving Friend :

About one hour ago, I received the news of the enemy having crossed the Susquehannah, and killed a great many people, from Thomas McKee's down to Hunter's mills.

Mr. Elder, the minister at Paxton, wrote to another Presbyterian minister, in the neighborhood of Adam Reed, Esq. The people were then in a meeting, and immediately designed to get themselves in readiness, to oppose the enemy, and lend assistance to their neighbors.

Mr. Reed sent down to Tulpehocken—and two men, one that came from Mr. Reed's, are just now gone, who brought in the melancholy news. I have sent out to alarm the townships in this neighborhood, and to meet me early in the morning, at Peter Spicker's, to consult together what to do, and to make preparations, to stand the enemy, with the assistance of the Most High.

I wrote you this, that you may have time to consult with Mr. Seely and other well-wishers of the people, in order to defend your lives and others. For God's sake let us stand together, and do what we can, and trust to the hand of Providence—perhaps, we must, in this neighborhood, come to Reading; but I will send armed men to Susquehannah, or as far as they can go for intelligence.

Pray let Sammy have a copy of this, or this draft for his Honor, the Governor. I have sent him, about three hours ago, express to Philadelphia, and he lodges at my son Peter's. Despatch him as early as you can. I pray, beware of confusion, be calm, you and Mr. Seely, and act the part of fathers of the people. I know you are both able; but excuse me for giving this caution—time requires it.*

I am dear sir,

Your very good friend and

Humble servant,

CONRAD WEISER.

* Provincial Records, N. p. 244-5.

From the following letter, it will be seen that Weiser's letter was immediately despatched as requested.

Reading, October 27th, 1755,
6 o'clock, A. M.

GOVERNOR MORRIS,

Sir,

I must not detain the bearer a moment. I have sent the original letter from Mr. Weiser, that no mistake may arise by any doubts of the justness of a copy.

I shall raise our town in an hour, and use all prudent measures for our defence. I could wish your Honor could order us two or three swivel guns and blunderbusses, with a few muskets, some powder, and swan shot. Nothing shall be wanting in me, who have the misfortune of being major of two associated companies; but know not how my people will behave, as they are under an infatuation of an extraordinary sort.[*]

I am, may it please your Honor's
Most humble servant,
JAMES READ.

P. S. Many wagons that are got thus far, are bound back again, immediately upon hearing this news.

Letter to Gov. Morris, from Conrad Weiser, Esq.

Reading, October 27th, 1755.

May it please your Honor—

Since the date of my last letter, which I sent by express, by Sammy Weiser, dated last Sunday evening, 5 o'clock, and about 11 o'clock, the same night, I sent a letter to Mr. Read, in this town, who forwarded it to your Honor, by the same opportunity.

The following account of what has happened since, I thought it was proper to lay before your Honor, to wit:—After I had received the news that Paxton people above Hunter's mills, had been murdered, I immediately sent my servants to alarm the neighborhood. The people came to my house by the break of day. I informed them of the melancholy news, and how I

----

[*] Provincial Records, N. p. 244-5.

came by it, &c. They unanimously agreed to stand by one
another, and march to meet the enemy, if I would go with
them. I told them that I would not only myself accompany
them, but my sons, and servants should also go— they put
themselves under my direction. I gave them orders to go
home and fetch their arms, whether guns, swords, pitch-forks,
axes, or whatever might be of use against the enemy, and to
bring with them three days provision in their knapsacks, and
to meet at Benjamin Spicker's, at three of the clock that afternoon, about six miles above my house, in Tulpehocken township, where I had sent word for Tulpehocken people also to
meet.

I immediately mounted my horse, and went up to Benjamin
Spicker's, where I found about one hundred persons who had
met before I came there; and after I had informed them of the
intelligence, that I had promised to go with them as a common
soldier, and be commanded by such officers, and leading men,
whatever they might call them, as they should choose. They
unanimously agreed to join the Heidelberg people, and accordingly they went home, to fetch their arms, and provisions for
three days, and came again at 3 o'clock. All this was punctually performed; and about two hundred were at Benjamin
Spicker's, by two o'clock.

I made the necessary disposition, and the people were divided
into companies of thirty men in each company, and they chose
their own officers; that is, a captain over each company, and
three inferior officers under each, to take care of ten men, and
lead them on, or fire, as the captain should direct.

I sent privately for Mr. Kurtz,* the Lutheran minister, who
lived about one mile off, who came and gave an exhortation to
the men, and made a prayer suitable to the time. Then we
marched towards Susquehannah, having first sent about fifty
men to Tolheo, in order to possess themselves of the gaps or
narrows of *Swahatawro*,† where he expected the enemy would
come through; with those fifty, I sent a letter to Mr. Parsons,
who happened to be at his plantation.

We marched about ten miles that evening. My company
had now increased to upwards of three hundred men, mostly
well-armed, though about twenty men had nothing but axes,
and pitch-forks—all unanimously agreed to die together and

* Kurtz lived where Rev. Daniel Ulrich resides at present, 1844.
† Swatara.

engage the enemy, wherever they should meet them; never to enquire the number, but fight them, and so obstruct their way of marching further into the inhabited parts, till others of our brethren come up and do the same, and so save the lives of our wives and our children.

The night we made the first halt, the powder and lead was brought up from Reading, (I had sent for it early in the morning,) and I ordered it to the care of the officers, and to divide it among those that wanted it the most.

On the 28th, by daybreak, we marched; our company increasing all along. We arrived at Adam Reed's, Esq., in Hanover township, Lancaster (now Lebanon) county, at about ten o'clock—there we stopped and rested till the rest came up. Mr. Read had just received intelligence from Susquehannah, by express, which was as follows, to wit: That Justice Forster, Capt. McKee, John Harris, and others, to the number of forty-nine, went up to Shamokin to bury the dead bodies of those that had been killed by the enemy on John Penn's creek, and coming up to George Gabriel's, about five miles this side Shamokin, and on the west of Susquehannah, they heard that the dead bodies had been buried already, and so they went along to Shamokin, where they arrived last Friday evening, and were seemingly well received, but found a great number of strange Indians, the Delawares, all painted black, which gave suspicion; and Thomas McKee told his companions that he did not like them, and the next morning—that is, last Saturday—they got up early, in order to go back; but they did not see any of the strangers. They were gone before them. Andrew Montour was there, painted as the rest; he advised our people not to go the same road they came, but to keep on this side the Susquehannah, and go the old road; but when they came to the parting of the roads, a majority was for going the nighest and best road, and so crossed Susquehannah, contrary to Andrew Montour's counsel, in order to go down on the west side of the river, as far as to Mahahany; when they came to John Penn's creek, in going down the bank, they were fired upon from this side by the Indians that had waylaid them; some dropped down dead; the rest fled and made towards Susquehannah, and came to this side, and so home, as well as they could. Twenty-six of them were missing and not heard of as yet, last Monday.

Upon this we had a consultation, and as we did not come up

to serve as guards to the Paxton people, but to fight the enemy, if they were come so far, as we first heard, we thought best to return and take care of our own townships.

After I had given the necessary caution to the people to hold themselves in readiness, as the enemy was certainly in the country, to keep their arms in good order, and so on, and then discharged them—and we marched back, with the approbation of Mr. Reed. By the way, we were alarmed, by a report, that five hundred Indians had come over the mountain at Tolheo, to this side, and had already killed a number of people. We stopped and sent a few men to discover the enemy, but, on their return, proved to be a false alarm, occasioned by that company that I had sent that way the day before, whose guns getting wet, they fired them off, which was the cause of alarm—this not only had alarmed the company, but whole townships through which they marched. In going back, I met messengers from other townships about Conestoga, who came for intelligence, and to ask me where their assistance was necessary, promising that they would come to the place where I should direct.

I met also at Tulpehocken, above one hundred men well-armed, as to fire arms, ready to follow me; so that there were in the whole, about five hundred men in arms that day, all marching up towards Susquehannah. I, and Mr. Adam Reed, counted those that were with me—we found them three hundred and twenty.

I cannot send any further account, being uncommonly fatigued. I should not forget, however, to inform your Honor, that Mr. Reed has engaged to keep proper persons riding between his house and Susquehannah, and if any thing material shall occur, he will send me tidings to Heidelbreg or to Reading, which I shall take care to despatch to you. I find that great care has been taken at Reading, to get the people together, and near two hundred were here yesterday morning; but upon hearing that the people attending me, were discharged, the people from the country went off without consulting what should be done for the future, through the indiscretion of a person who was with them, and wanted to go home; and near the town they met a large company coming up, and gave such accounts as occasioned their turning back. I think most of the inhabitants would do their duty; but without some military regulations, we shall never be able to defend the province.

I am sure we are in great danger, and by an enemy that can travel as Indians, we may be surprised when it would be impossible to collect any number of men together to defend themselves, and then the country would be laid waste. I am quite tired, and must say no more than that*

I am your Honor's
Most obedient servant,
CONRAD WEISER.

Under date of October 31, 1755, the Secretary, states: "An Indian trader and two other men, in Tuscarora valley, were killed by Indians, and their houses, &c., burned; on which most of the settlers fled and abandoned their plantations. Nov. 2, 1755, the settlements in the Great Cove were attacked, their houses burned, six persons murdered, and seventeen carried off, and the whole settlement broken up and destroyed."

From the following extract, taken from the *Pennsylvania Gazette*, of Nov. 13, 1755, the names of the murdered and missing at Great Cove, may be seen—Elizabeth Gallway, Henry Gilson, Robert Peer, William Berryhill, and David McClelland were murdered. The missing are John Martin's wife and five children; William Gallway's wife and two children, and a young woman; Charles Stewart's wife and two children; David McClelland's wife and two children. William Fleming and wife were taken prisoners. Fleming's son, and one Hicks, were killed and scalped."

The inhabitants of Berks county were kept in a state of consternation from the time they had received intelligence of the massacre of the people on Penn's creek; and every day's news added to their alarm, as may be seen from the following communication sent to Governor Morris.

Reading, October 31, 1755, }
At 8 o'clock at night. }

May it please your Honor—

We have scarce strength left to write. We are forever employed, and without clerks. We have within one hour received letters from Justice Forster, from Mr. James Galbreath, and John Harris, by several messengers, with the accounts that the people at Auckwick and Juniata are cut off, and among others

* Provincial Records, N. p. 249-251.

George Croghan.   The date of Mr. Foster's letter is the 29th
inst., Mr. Galbreath's the 30th; but Harris's is, through confusion, not dated.

We cannot find clerks; we cannot write ourselves any thing
of considerable length.   We must, therefore, depend upon it,
that we shall be credited without sending copies; and originals
we must keep to convince the unhappily scrupulous of the truth
of our accounts.

We are all in an uproar—all in disorder—all willing to do,
and have little in our power.   We have no authority—no commission—no officers practiced in war, and without the comise-
ration of our *Friends* in Philadelphia, who think themselves
vastly safer than they are.   If we are not immediately supported, we must not be sacrificed; and therefore, are determined
to go down with all that will follow us to Philadelphia, and
quarter ourselves on its inhabitants, and wait our fate with
them.*

We are your Honor's most
Obedient, humble servants,
JOHN POTTS,
CONRAD WEISER,
WILLIAM MAUGRIDGE,
JONAS SEELY,
JAMES REED.

P. S.   Mr. Bird was obliged to go home, or would certainly
have signed this.

Towards the close of October, the enemy neared the borders
of Berks county.   A letter from William Parsons to the Rev.
John Nicholas Kurtz, at Tulpehocken, shows this.

October 31st, 1755.

To the Rev. Kurtz and all other Friends:

This morning, very early, between four and five o'clock,
Adam Rees, an inhabitant over the first mountain, about six
miles from Lawrance Hout's, who lives on this side of the
mountain, came to my house, and declared, that yesterday, between 11 and 12 o'clock, he heard three guns fired towards the
plantation of his neighbor, Henry Hartman, which made him
suspect that something more than ordinary had happened there.
Whereupon he took his gun and went over to Hartman's house,

*Provincial Records, N. p. 257.

being about a quarter of a mile off, and found him lying dead upon his face; his head was scalped; but saw no body else. He thereupon made the best of his way through the woods to the inhabitants on this side of the mountain, to inform them of what had happened.

He further informs me, that he had been to Adam Reed's, Esq., and related the whole of the affair to him, and that Reed is raising men to go over the mountain in quest of the murderers.*

I am your very
Humble servant and most
Hearty Friend,
WM. PARSONS.

—————

Another Letter from William Parsons to Adam Reed, Esq.

Stoney Kiln, November 1, 1755.

SIR—

I wrote you yesterday, that I intended to be with you at the unhappy place, where Henry Hartman was murdered; but when I got to the top of the mountain, I met some men, who said they had seen two men lying dead and scalped, in the Shamokin road, about two or three miles from the place where we were; wherefore, we altered our course, being twenty-six in number, and went to the place, and found the two men lying dead, about three hundred yards from each other, and all the skin scalped off their heads.

We got a grubbing hoe and a spade, and dug a grave as well as we could, the ground being very stony, and buried them both in one grave, without taking off their clothes or examining at all their wounds; only we saw that a bullet had gone through the leg of one of them. I thought it best to bury them, to prevent their bodies from being torn to pieces by wild beasts. One of the men had a daughter with him that is yet missing; and the other man had a wife, and three or four children, that are also missing.

I shall be obliged to return home in a day or two, but hope to see you sometime about Christmas, and to find my unhappy countrymen somewhat relieved from this distressed condition.

*Provincial Records, N. p. 258.

5

I can't help thinking that it would be well for a good number of the inhabitants to go next Monday, and help to bring the poor peoples grain and corn to this side the mountain—it will help to maintain them, which we must do, if they can't maintain themselves; and tis very likely those barbarous Indians will set fire to, and burn all, if it be not soon secured.*

I am, Sir, your very humble servant,
WM. PARSONS.

In another part of the Secretary's narrative, he states that, "November 16th, 1755, a party of Indians crossed the Susquehannah, and fell upon the county of Berks, murdered thirteen persons, and burnt a great number of houses, destroyed vast quantities of cattle, grain and fodder, and laid waste a large extent of country."—*Provincial Records.*

The following letters will afford the reader some idea of the state of things in Berks at the time. The first is from Mr. E. Biddle, to his father, then in Philadelphia.

Reading, November 16, 1755.

MY DEAREST FATHER:

I'm in so much horror and confusion, I scarce know what I'm writing. The drum is beating to arms—bells ringing—and all the people under arms. Within these two hours, we have had different, though *too certain* accounts, all corroborating each other!—and this moment is an express arrived and despatches news from Michael Reis's, at Tulpehocken, eighteen miles above this town, who left about thirty of their people engaged, with about an equal number of Indians, at said Reis's. This night we expect an attack. Truly alarming is our situation. The people exclaim against the Quakers, and some are scarce restrained from burning the houses of those few who are in this town. Oh, my country! my bleeding country!!

I recommend myself wholly to the divine God of armies. Give my dutiful love to my dearest mother, and my best love to brother Jemmy. I am, honored sir,

Your affectionate and obedient son,
EDWARD BIDDLE.

P. S. *Sunday,* 10 *o'clock.*—I have rather lessened than exaggerated our melancholy account.

*Provincial Records, N. p. 258.

The following is from Peter Spycker, near the present Stouchtown, to Conrad Weiser, then in Philadelphia, on public business.

Tulpehocken, the 16 *November,* 1755.

CONRAD WEISER, ESQ.

John Anspack and Frederick Reed came to me and told me the miserable circumstances of the people murdered this side the mountain. Yesterday the Indians attacked the Watch, killed and wounded him, at Derrick Sixth, (Dietrich Six,) and in that neighborhood, a great many in that night.

This morning the people went out to see, and about 10 o'clock came to Thomas Bower's house, finding a man dead—killed with a gun shot. They soon heard a noise of firing guns; running to that place, saw four Indians setting on children scalping them—three of the children are dead, two are still living, though scalped. Afterwards our people went to the Watch-house of Derrick Sixth, where the Indians made the first attack. They found six dead bodies; four of them scalped; about a mile on this side of the Watch-house, as they came back, the Indians had set fire to a stable and barn; burnt the corn, cows and other creatures—here they found five Indians in a house eating their dinner and drinking rum which had been in the house; two of them were on the outside the house. They fired upon them, but without doing execution. The Indians have burnt the improvements on four other plantations.

I have this account from those above named, and from Peter Anspack, Jacob Caderman, Christopher Noacre, Leonard Walborn, George Dollinger, and Adam Dieffenbach.

We are, at present, in imminent danger to lose our lives, or estates; pray, therefore, for help, or else whole Tulpehocken will be laid waste by the Indians, in a very short time—all the buildings will be burned, the people scalped. Do, therefore, lose no time to get us assistance. The Assembly may learn from *this work,* what kind, and fine *friends* the Indians are!! We hope members of the Assembly will get their eyes opened, and manifest tender hearts towards us; and the Governor the same. They are, it is hoped, true subjects to our king George

II., of Great Britain, or are they willing to deliver us into the hands of these cruel and merciless creatures?*

I am your friend,

PETER SPYCKER..

N. B.   The people are fled to us from the Hills; Peter Kyger and John Wise are the last.

Since our last, says the Editor of the Pennsylvania Gazette, Nov. 20, 1755, we have had several letters from Berks county, advising us of a great deal of mischief done in Tulpehocken by the Indians; yesterday a gentleman arrived express from that county, who brought with him two scalps, one of a white person, the other of an Indian—and the following deposition.

Berks county, Pennsylvania, ss.

Jacob, Morgan, a captain in Col. Weiser's regiment, being sworn on the Holy Evangelists of Almighty God, doth depose and say, That on Sunday, the 16th November inst., (1755,) at about five o'clock, P. M., he, the deponent, Mr. Philip Weiser and Mr. Peter Weiser, set out from Heidelberg towards Dietrich Six's, to get intelligence of the mischief done at Tolheo, or thereabouts, and to get a number of men to join them to go and seek for the persons who were scalped by the Indians; and to help in the best manner they could, the poor distressed inhabitants.   That about nine miles from Mr. Weiser's, they found a girl about six years old, scalped, but yet alive, and a vast number of people there; but he knows not at whose house it was, nor the name of the child.   That at the request of the people there, Mr. Weiser's son and deponent, went back to Mr. Weiser's for powder and lead.   That at or about 2 o'clock, yesterday morning, they were alarmed at Mr. Weiser's with an account that the Indians had beset George Dollinger's house, and his family were fled; whereupon Philip Weiser, and the deponent, and a person whose name deponent does not know, set off immediately, and at Christopher Weiser's, overtook a large company, consisting of about one hundred men, and with them proceeeed to George Dollinger's and surrounded his house, where they found a deal of damage done, and in the garden, a child about eight years old, daughter of one Cola, lying dead and scalped, which they buried.

* Provincial Records, N. p. 287.

That the whole company went on to a plantation of Abraham Sneider, and found in a corn-field the wife of Cola, and a child about eight or nine years old, both dead and scalped, and in the house they found another child of the said Cola's, about ten years old, dead and scalped; but the deponent knows not of what sex, either of these two children was. That while they were preparing the grave, they were alarmed by the firing of a gun, and flying to their arms, they went (a few staying to take care of the dead) to the place from whence the sound came, and about half a mile from the place they came from, they met the company, one of whom had indiscreetly discharged his musket, and then went back to bury the dead; in their return they found the scalp of a white person. That having buried the woman and children, they went to Thomas Bower's in whose house they found a dead man scalped, whose name, the deponent thinks was Philip, by trade a shoemaker, but knows no more of him.

That the company increased fast, and were now about one hundred and thirty men, who marched on the Shamokin road to near Dietrich Six's; about half a mile from whose house, they found Casper Spring dead and scalped, and having buried him, they marched about one hundred rods and found one Beslinger dead and scalped—they buried him. That at the same distance from Beslinger's they found an Indian man dead and scalped, which Indian, it was generally believed, was a Delaware. Mr. Frederick Weiser scalped him the day before.

That twenty of their body, who had gone a little out of the road, about two miles from Dietrich Six's, found (as the deponent and the rest of the company were informed, and as he believes without any doubt) a child of Jacob Wolf—he cannot say whether a boy or a girl—which was scalped? Its age the deponent does not know, but the father carried it in his arms to be buried, as they were informed. That the deponent was informed, by Mr. Frederick Weiser, that a company, with whom he had been the day before, had buried John Leinberger and Rudolph Candel, whom they found scalped.

That the deponent and company finding no more scalped or wounded, they returned, being then by the continual arrival of fresh persons, about three hundred men, to George Dollinger's. That Casper Spring's brains were beat out; had two cuts in his breast; was shot in the back, and otherwise cruelly used, which regard to decency forbids mentioning; and that Beslinger's brains were beat out, his mouth much mangled, one of his eyes cut out, and one of his ears gashed, and had two knives lying on his breast. That the whole country thereabouts desert their habitations, and send away all their household goods. The horses and cattle are in the corn-fields, and every thing in the utmost disorder, and the people quite despair. And further, that he heard of much mischief done by burning houses and barns; but not having been where it was reported to have been done, he chooses not have any particulars thereof inserted in this deposition.

JAMES MORGAN.

Sworn at Reading, the 18th of November, 1755, before us.

JONAS SEELY,
HENRY HARRY,
JAMES READ.

Besides the persons mentioned in the above deposition, one Sebastian Brosius was murdered and scalped, whose scalp was brought to Philadelphia at the beginning of this week, having been taken from an Indian.

To Governor Morris, from Conrad Weiser.

HEIDELBERG, BERKS COUNTY, }
November 19, 1755. }

HONORED SIR:

On my return from Philadelphia, I met, in the township of Amiety, in Berks county, the first news of our cruel enemy having invaded the county, this side of the Blue mountain, to wit: Bethel and Tulpehocken.

I left the papers as they were, in the messenger's hands, and hastened to Reading, where the alarm and confusion were very great. I was obliged to stay that night and part of the next day, to wit: the 17th inst., and sat out for Heidelberg, where I arrived that evening. Soon after, my sons Philip and Frederick arrived from the pursuit of the Indians, and gave the following relation, to wit: that on Saturday last, about 4 o'clock in the afternoon, as some men from Tulpehocken were going to Dietrich Six's places, at the foot of the hill, on the Shamokin road, to be on the watch appointed there, they were fired upon by the Indians; but none were hurt nor killed. Our people were but six in number—the rest being behind—upon which our people ran towards the Watch-house, which was about one half mile off; the Indians pursued them, killed and scalped several of them. A bold, stout Indian came up to one Christopher Ury, who turned about and shot the Indian right through his breast. The Indian dropped down dead, but was dragged out of the way by his companions—he was found next day, and scalped by our people.

The Indians divided themselves into two parties. Some came this way, to meet the rest going to the Watch, and killed some of them; so that six of our men were killed that day, and a few were wounded. The night following, the enemy attacked the house of Thomas Bower, on Swatara creek. They came, in the dark night, to the house, and one of them put his fire-arm through the window, and shot a shoemaker, who was at work, dead on the spot. The people being extremely surprised at this sudden attack, defended themselves by firing out of the windows, at the Indians. The fire alarmed a neighbor, who came with two or three men—they fired by the way and made a great noise, and scared the Indians away from Bower's house, after they had set fire to it; by Thomas Bower's diligent exertions the fire was timely extinguished. Thomas Bower, with his family, left the house that night, and went to his neighbor's, David Sneider, who had come to assist him.

By eight of the clock, parties came up from Tulpehocken and Heidelberg. The first party saw four Indians running off. They had some prisoners, whom they scalped immediately. Three children lay scalped, yet alive; one died since; the other two are likely to do well.

Another party found a woman just expired, with a male child lying at her side—both killed and scalped. The woman lay upon her face; my son Frederick turned her about to see who she might have been—to his, and his companions surprise, they found a babe of about fourteen days old, under her, wrapt in a small cushion; his nose was quite flat, which was set right by Frederick, and life was yet in it, and recovered again!

Our people came up with two parties of Indians that day, but they hardly got sight of them. The Indians ran off immediately. Either our people did not care to fight them if they could avoid it, or, which is more likely, the Indians were alarmed first by the loud noise of our peoples coming, because no order was observed.

Upon the whole there are about fifteen of our people, including men, women, and children killed; and the enemy is not

beaten, but scared off. Several houses and barns were burned.
I have no true account how many.

We are in a dismal situation—some of the murders were
committed in Tulpehocken township. The people abandon
their plantations to within six or seven miles from my house.
I am now busy to put things in order, to defend my house
against another attack.

Guns and ammunition are much wanted here: my sons have
been obliged to part with most of that which was sent up for
the use of the Indians. I pray your Honor, will be pleased, if
it is in your power to send us up a quantity, upon any conditions. I must stand my ground, or my neighbors will all go
away, and leave their habitations to be destroyed by the enemy,
or our own people. This is enough of such melancholy accounts for this time. I beg leave to conclude,

That I am, Sir, your
Very obedient,
CONRAD WEISER.

P. S. I am creditably informed just now, that one Wolf, a
single man, killed an Indian, at the same time when Ury killed
the other; but the body has not been found as yet. The poor
young man since died of his wound in the abdomen.*

The savages now fully bent upon fell destruction, continued
their excursions, and wherever they went, the whites fell victims to their relentless cruelty.

"We hear from Reading, in Berks county, that on Sunday
last, about nine o'clock at night, the guard belonging to that
county, about seventeen miles from that town, were attacked by
some Indians, with whom they exchanged several fires, and put
them to flight; that none of the guard were wounded; though
one of them had the skirt of his jacket shot away, and that
they supposed some of the Indians were badly burnt, as they
heard a crying among them as they ran off; but that the
guard having spent their ammunition, could not pursue them."†

The Indians extended their excursions into Northampton,
when, on the 25th November, 1755, they destroyed a fine
settlement of Moravians, called Gnaden-huetten, on the west
branch of the river Delaware, killed six of the inmates, burnt
down their dwellings, meeting houses, and all their out-houses,

* Provincial Records, N. p. 342.
† Pennsylvania Gazette, Dec. 18, 1755.

their grain, hay, horses, and upwards of fifty head of cattle that were under cover.*

The Secretary in his narrative, continues—"During December, 1755, the Indians having been destroying all before them in the county of Northampton, and have already burnt fifty houses here, murdered above one hundred persons, and are still continuing their ravages, murders, and devastations, and have actually overrun and laid waste a great part of that county, even as far as within twenty-five miles of Easton, is chief town. And a large body of Indians under the direction of French officers, have fixed their head quarters within the borders of that county, for the better security of their prisoners and plunders."

"This," continues he, "is a brief account of the progress of these savages, since the 18th of October, on which day was committed the first inroad, ever made, by Indians, upon this Province, since its first settlement; and in consequence of all our frontier country which extends from the river Potomack to the river Delaware, not less than one hundred and fifty miles in length, and between twenty and thirty in breadth, but not fully settled, has been deserted, the houses and improvements reduced to ashes, the cattle, horses, grain, goods and effects of the inhabitants, either destroyed, burnt or carried off by the Indians—whilst the poor planters, (farmers) with their wives, children, and servants, who could get away, being without arms, or any kind of defence, have been obliged, in this season of the year, to abandon their habitations, naked and without support, and thrown themselves upon the charity of the other inhabitants within the interior parts of the province, upon whom they are a very heavy burthen.

"Such shocking descriptions are given, by those who have escaped, of the horrid cruelties, and indecencies committed by the merciless savages, on the bodies of those unhappy wretches, who fell into their hands, especially the women, without regard to sex or age as far exceeds those related of the most abandoned pirates! Which has occasioned a general consternation, and has struck so great a panic and damp upon the spirits of the people, that hitherto, they have not been able to make any considerable resistance, or stand against the Indians."†

*Pennsylvania Gazette, Dec. 18, 1755.
†Provincial Records, N. p. 342.

A Letter from Valentine Probst to Jacob Levan, Esq., of Maxatany.

February 15, 1756.

MR. LEVAN:

I cannot omit writing about the dreadful circumstances of our township, Albany. The Indians came yesterday morning, about eight o'clock, to Frederick Reichelderfer's house, as he was feeding his horses, and two of the Indians ran upon him, and followed him into a field ten or twelve perches off; but he escaped and ran towards Jacob Gerhart's house, with a design to fetch some arms. When he came near Gerhart's, he heard a lamentable cry, *Lord Jesus! Lord Jesus!*—which made him run back toward his own house; but before he got quite home, he saw his house and stables in flames; and heard the cattle bellowing, and thereupon ran away again.

Two of his children were shot; one of them was found dead in his field, the other was found alive, and brought to Hakenbrook's house, but died three hours after. All his grain and cattle are burnt up. At Jacob Gerhart's they have killed one man, two women, and six children. Two children slipped under the bed; one of which was burned; the other escaped, and ran a mile to get to the people. We desire help, or we must leave our homes.

Yours,

VALENTINE PROBST. —

Mr. Levan immediately repaired to Albany township, but before he reached the scene of horror, additional intelligence was received by him, of other murders. In a letter from him to James Read and Jonas Seely, of Reading, he says: "When I had got ready to go with my neighbors from Maxatany, to see what damage was done in Albany, three men, that had seen the shocking affair, came and told me, that eleven were killed, eight of them burnt, and the other three found dead out of the fire. An old man was scalped, the two others, little girls, were not scalped."

From the above, as well as from the following, it will be seen that the Indians were marauding in various parts of Berks, and the upper part of Lancaster, now Lebanon county, in the spring and summer of 1756.

In March, 1756, the Indians laid the house and barn of Barnabas Seitle in ashes, and the mill of Peter Conrad, and killed Mrs. Neytong, the wife of Baltser Neytong, and took his son, a lad of eight years old, captive. Next morning Seitle's servant informed Capt. Morgan of the injury done by the Indians, whereupon the Captain and seven men went in pursuit of the enemy, but did not find any. On his return, he met a person named David Howell, who told him that when on his way to the watch-house, these Indians shot five times at him—the last shot he received a bullet through his arm.

And on the 24th of March, the house of Peter Kluck, about fourteen miles from Reading, was set on fire by the savages, and the whole family killed—while the flames was still ascending, the Indians assaulted the house of one Linderman, in which there were two men and a woman, all of whom ran up stairs, where the woman was shot dead through the roof. The men then ran out of the house to engage the Indians, when Linderman was shot in the neck, and the other through the jacket. Upon this Linderman ran towards the Indians, two of whom only were seen, and shot one of them in the back, when he fled and he and his companion scalped him and brought away his gun and knife.*

About two weeks before the assault upon the house of Kluck, the Indians had committed depredations in another part of the country. In a copy of a letter, dated March 8, 1756, from Hanover township, Lancaster county, now within the limits of Lebanon county, it is said, that the morning, before (March 8,) Andrew Lycan, who lived over the mountain, was attacked by the Indians. He had with him a son, John Lycan, a negro man, and a boy and two of his neighbors, John Revolt and Ludwig Shut. That Andrew Lycan and John Revolt went out early that morning to fodder their creatures, when two guns were fired at them, but did not hurt them: upon which they ran into the house and prepared themselves for an engagement. That then the Indians got under cover of a hoghouse near the dwelling house, John Lycan, Revolt, and Shut, crept out of the house, in order to get a shot at them; but were fired at by the Indians, and all wounded, and Shut in the abdomen. That Andrew Lycan saw one of the Indians over the hoghouse, and got a little distance from it; and also saw *two white men* run out of the hoghouse and get a little distance

* C. Sauer's German Paper, March, 1756.

from it. That upon this, our people endeavored to escape; but were pursued by the Indians to the number of sixteen or upwards, and John Lycan and Revolt being badly wounded, were able to do nothing, and so went off with the negro, and left Andrew Lycan, Shut and the boy, engaged with the Indians. That the enemy pursued so closely, that one of them came up to the boy and was going to strike his tomahawk into him, when Shut turned and shot him dead, and Lycan shot another, and he is positive that he killed him—saw a third fall, and thinks they wounded some more of them. That they being now both ill wounded, and almost spent, they sat down on a log to rest themselves, and the Indians stood a little way off looking at them.

That one of the said Indians killed was Bill Davis, and two others they knew to be Tom Hickman and Tom Hayes, all Delawares, and well known in these parts. That all our men got into Hanover township, and under the care of a doctor, and are likely to do well; but have lost all they are worth. And that the people of that township were raising a number of men to go after the enemy. The above people lived twenty-five miles below Shamokin, at or near Wiskinisco creek.*

In another from Hereford township, Berks county, dated March 28, 1756, it is dated, That on the 22d of that month, one John Kraushar, and his wife, and William Yeth, and his boy, about twelve years old, went to their places to find their cattle, and on their return, were fired upon by five Indians, who had hid themselves about ten perches from the road, when Yeth was mortally wounded in the back; Kraushar's wife was found dead and scalped, and had three cuts in her right arm with a tomahawk. Kraushar made his escape, and the boy was carried off by the enemy. That on the 24th March, ten wagons went up to *Allemaengel*† to bring down a family with their effects; and as they were returning, about three miles below George Zeisloff's, were fired upon by a number of Indians from both sides of the road; upon which the wagoners left their wagons and ran into the woods, and the horses frightened at the firing and terrible yelling of the Indians, ran down a hill and broke one of the wagons to pieces. That the enemy killed George Zeisloff and his wife, a lad of twenty, a boy of twelve, also a girl of fourteen years old, four of whom they

*Pennsylvania Gazette, March 18, 1756.
†Albany township.

scalped. That another girl was shot in the neck, and through the mouth, and scalped, notwithstanding all which she got off, and was alive, when the letter was written.

That a boy was stabbed in three places, but the wounds were not thought to be mortal. That they killed two of the horses, and five are missing, with which it is thought the Indians carried off the most valuable of the goods that were in the wagon.[*]

At the same time, the Indians carried off a young lad, named John Schoep, about nine years old, whom they took by night, seven miles beyond the blue mountain; where, according to the statement of the lad, the Indians kindled a fire, tied him to a tree, and took off his shoes and put moccasins on his feet—that they prepared themselves some mush, but gave him none. After supper they marched on further. The same Indians took him and another lad between them, and went beyond the second mountain; having gone six times through streams of water, and always carried him across. The second evening they again struck up fire; took off his moccasins, and gave him a blanket to cover himself; but at midnight when all the Indians were fast asleep, he made his escape, and by daybreak had travelled about six miles. He passed on that day, sometimes wading streams neck-deep, in the direction of the blue mountain—that night he stayed in the woods. The next day, exhausted and hungry, he arrived, by noon, at Uly Meyer's plantation, where Charles Folk's company lay, where they wished him to remain till he had regained strength, when they would have conducted him to his father. He was accordingly sent home.[†]

In June, 1756, the Indians once more commit deliberate murder, in Bethel township, Lancaster county, (now Lebanon.) A letter dated Bethel township, June 9, makes mention that, yesterday, the 8th inst., in the afternoon, between three and four o'clock, four or five Indians made an incursion, at a place called "THE HOLE," where the Great Swatara creek runs through the blue mountain—they crept up unobserved behind the fence of Felix Wuensch, shot him, as he was ploughing, through the breast. He cried lamentably, and run, but the Indians soon came up with him. He defended himself some-

* Pennsylvania Gazette, April 1, 1756.
† C. Sauer's German Paper, March, 1756.

time with his whip; they cut his hand and breast in a cruel manner with their tomahawks, and scalped him.   His wife hearing his cries, and the report of two guns, ran out of the house, but was soon taken by the enemy, who carried her with one of her own and two of her sister's children, away with them, after setting the house on fire.   A servant boy who was at some distance, seeing this, ran to their neighbor, George Mies, and told him what had happened.   Upon which Mies, though he had a bad leg, with his son, ran directly after the Indians, and raised a great noise, which so frightened the Indians, that they immediately took to their heels, and in their flight left a tub of butter, and a side of bacon behind them.   Mies then went to the house, which was in flames, and threw down the fences, in order to save the barn.   They drank all the brandy in the spring house, and took several gammons, a quantity of meal, some loaves of bread, and a great many other things, with them.   Had Mr. Mies not been so courageous, they probably would have attacked another house.   They shot one of the horses in the plough, and dropped a large French knife.*

From additional intelligence it appears, that immediately on the above murder being perpetrated, twenty families went into Smith's Fort—"which was but *one mile and a quarter* from where Wuensch lived," and that still more were expected to go into the fort—and immediately a party was sent out after the enemy, but to no purpose.†

The Editor of the Gazette, of June 24, says: We have advice from Fort Henry, in Berks county, (Bethel township,) that two children of one Lawrence Dieppel, who lives about two miles from said fort, are missing, and thought to be carried off by the Indians, as one of their hats has been found, and several Indian tracks seen.   In relation to this statement, the Editor says, in the first of July No.—We learn that one of Lawrence Dieppel's children, mentioned in our last to be carried off, has been found cruelly murdered and scalped, a boy about four years old, and that the other, also a boy, eight years old, was still missing.

Another onslaught upon the inhabitants of Swatara township was made by the Indians, in the latter part of June, 1756.

July 1, 1756.‡   We have advice that on Saturday last, nine

* Pennsylvania Gazette, June, 1755.
† Ibid., June 17, 1776.   ‡ Ibid.

Indians came to "*The Hole*," in Swatara, and killed and scalped four persons and shot two horses, and that a party of men went in pursuit of them, but to no purpose.

In the early part of October, incursions were again made into Hanover township, about three miles west of *The Hole*. The following letter from Adam Reed, Esq. to Edward Shippen, Esq. and others, dated Hanover township, Oct. 14, 1756, details the shocking circumstances:

"*Friends and Fellow Subjects:*

I send you in a few lines, the melancholy condition of the frontiers of this county. Last Tuesday, the 12th inst., ten Indians came on Noah Frederick, while ploughing, killed and scalped him, and carried away three of his children that were with him—the eldest but nine years old—and plundered his house and carried away every thing that suited their purpose; such as clothes, bread, butter, a saddle, and a good rifle gun, &c.—it being but two short miles from Captain Smith's fort, at Swatara gap, and a little better than two miles from my house.

Last Saturday evening, an Indian came to the house of Philip Robeson, carrying a green bush before him—said Robeson's son being on the corner of his Fort, watching others that were dressing, flash by him—the Indian perceiving that he was observed, fled; the watchman fired, but missed him. This being about three-fourths of a mile from Manady Fort; and yesterday morning, two miles from Smith's Fort, at Swatara, in Bethel township, as Jacob Farnwal was going from the house of Jacob Meylen to his own, was fired upon by two Indians, and wounded, but escaped with his life; and a little after, in said township, as Frederick Henly and Peter Sample were carrying away their goods in wagons, were met by a parcel of Indians, and all killed, lying dead in one place, and one man at a little distance. But what more has been done, has not come to my ears—only that the Indians were continuing their murders!j

The frontiers are employed in nothing but carrying off their effects; so that some miles are now waste! We are willing, but not able, without help—you are able, if you be willing, (that is including the lower parts of the county) to give such assistance as will enable us to recover our waste land. You may depend upon it, that without assistance, we, in a few days, will be on the *wrong side* of you; for I am now on the frontier, and I fear that by to-morrow night, I will be left some miles.

Gentlemen, *consider what you will do, and don't be long about it;* and let not the world say, that we died as fools died! Our hands are not tied, but let us exert ourselves, and do something for the honor of our country, and the preservation of our fellow subjects. I hope you will communicate our grievances to the lower parts of our country; for surely they will send us help, if they understood our grievances.

I would have gone down myself, but dare not, my family is in such danger. I expect an answer by the bearer, if possible.*

I am, gentlemen,
Your very humble servant,
ADAM REED.

P. S. Before sending this away, I would mention, I have just received information, that there are seven killed and five children scalped alive, but have not the account of their names.

In the month of January, 1844, the writer called on Mr. Martin Meylin, grandson of Jacob Meylin, mentioned in Mr. Reed's letter, who stated, he heard it from his father and others, that one Mr. Spitler, son-in-law to Jacob Meylin, was shot dead on the spot while fixing up a pair of bars, and that Mrs. Spitler escaped by taking refuge in the watch-house at her father's, about two miles from Stumptown. And that at the same time several men, were riding towards Williamsburg, (Jonestown,) were fired upon by the Indians, and two of them were killed.

The reader will pardon a digression, to give place to the following communication, from JACOB WEIDLE, Esq., with whom the writer spent a night at his residence, January 27, 1844, in Union township, Lebanon county.

Union Forge, February 13, 1844.

DEAR SIR—The following facts I obtained from Mr. Daniel Musser, who is nearly seventy. He suggests that there may probably be an error to locate *Fort Smith*, where Union Forge is. Mr. Musser's maternal grandfather, Peter Heydrich, who

<hr>

*Provincial Records, P., p. 69.

emigrated from Germany and located, previous to 1738, about three-fourths of a mile due north from this place, it appears, owned the place on which Fort Smith was erected. My informant says, he knows that a fort had been erected on his grandfather's farm, to which, in great emergencies, the neighbors fled for safety.

The persons whom Mr. Musser remembers of having heard of, that resided in this township, as old settlers, were Mr. Noacre or Noecker, who was shot dead in his field while ploughing, on the farm now owned by John Zehring. He says that one Philip Maurer was shot dead while cradling oats on the farm now occupied by John Gross. Martin Hess, who escaped unhurt, his house also had been a place of refuge—often half a dozen of families would resort to Hess's house, which was about one mile south-west from Peter Heydrich's, and a half a mile west from this place. Mathias Boeshore (your mother's relative) was also an old settler, who, on one occasion retreated from the enemy, the Indians, towards Hess's. Just as he had got inside the house, seized his gun, and turned upon his pursuers, levelling his deadly weapon at them, and while in the act of drawing the trigger, he received a shot from an Indian, which wounded him but slightly. The bullet of one savage's gun struck that part of Boeshore's rifle, to which the flint is attached; the ball glancing a little to one side, wounded him in the left side. Boeshore lived to be a very old man.

The land on which this fort was erected, is now owned by widow Elizabeth Shucy. The old people are unanimous in locating the fort on Mrs. Shucy's farm, at that time the property of Peter Heydrich. None of them seems to know that the house on Mr. Weidman's place here was ever used as a fort. May it not, like the house of Mr. Hess, have been only a kind of blockhouse; as the house of Hess, as well as the one here, has also some apertures, or port holes, which were evidently used to fire out upon the enemy?

Of Peter Heydrick, it is related, that on certain occasions, the Indians appeared in great numbers—and nearly all the neighbors being in their own houses—Heydrich gave immediate notice to the people to resort to the fort, and in the mean time, (having both fife and drum in the fort, and could beat and fife

6*

well) took the drum and fife, marched *himself* into the woods
or thickets, now beating the drum, then blowing the fife;
then and again gave the word of command, *loud and distinct*, as if it had been given to a large force—though he was
the only one to obey orders—by this *Guerre de ruse, slight of
war*, he managed to keep the savages away, and collect his
neighbors securely. *Noth bricht Eisen.*

Yours,
JACOB WEIDLE.

Some time in the latter part of October, the Indians again
returned into Hanover township, where they murdered, under
circumstances of much cruelty, several families, among whom
was one Andrew Berryhill. On the 22d October, they killed
John Craig and his wife, scalped them both, burnt several
houses, and carried off a lad, about thirteen years old. The
next day they scalped a German, whose name has not been
given.[*]
Many of the settlers had fled, and not a few were killed.
The writer has examined the tax collector's duplicate of several townships, for 1756, and found, from entries made in these,
by the collectors, that in East Hanover, Lancaster county, now
principally, if not wholly, within the limits of Lebanon county,
the following had fled.
Andrew Karsnits, John Gilliland, John McColloch, Walter
McFarland, Robert Kirkwood, William Robison, Valentine
Stoffelbeim, Andrew Cleaman, Rudolph Fry, Peter Walmer,
John McCulloch, James Rafter, Moses Vance, John Brower,
Frederick Noah, Jacob Moser, Philip Mauerer, Barnhart Be-
shore, Jacob Beshore, Matthias Beshore, William McCullough,
Philip Calp, Casper Yost, Conrad Cleck, Christian Albert,
Daniel Moser, John McClure, John Anderson, Thomas Shirley,
James Graham, Barnett McNett, Andrew Brown, Wm. Brown,
Andrew McMahon, Thomas Hume, Thomas Strean, John
Hume, Peter Wolf, Henry Kuntz, William Watson, John Stu-
art, John Porterfield, David Strean, John Strean, Andrew
McCrath, James McCurry, Conrad Rice, Alexander Swan,
John Grean.
Andrew Berrihill, (killed,) Samuel Ainsworth's son, (was.

<hr>

[*] Pennsylvania Gazette, November 4, 1756.

taken,) John Kreag, (killed and boy taken captive.*) The whole tax list contains some names less than one hundred.

The enemy, in the month of November, made great havoc, in various parts of Berks. We have, says the Editor of the Pennsylvania Gazette, advices from Fort Lebanon, in Berks county, that on the 3d inst., (November, 1756,) a fire was seen about seven miles from said fort, supposed to be at the house of John Flnsher; upon which a party was despatched, who on coming to the place, found Finsher's house, barn, out-houses, and a considerable quantity of corn, on fire; but saw no Indians, nor any body that belonged to the house.

They discovered a great many tracks, which they followed till they came to the house of Philip Culmone, whose wife, daughter, and one Martin Fell, his son-in-law, were all killed and scalped; and Fell's wife, with a child, about a year old, and a boy about seven years old, were missing. That they then sent notice to the fort of what had happened; when the captain with some men went out, but could not find the enemy; however, they carried all their neighbors, women, and children, into the fort, to the number of about sixty.

We hear also from the fort, near North Kill, (creek,) in the same county, that a child was carried off by a number of Indians the same day. That Lieut. Humphreys, with a party, went out in pursuit of them, and next morning came up with them, at Nicholas Long's, whose house they had set on fire, had killed two old men,† one of whom was scalped; and they would have destroyed ten women and children, that had got into the cellar. That they then engaged the Indians—twenty in number—put them to flight; two of whom it was thought were badly wounded.

They extinguished the fire at Long's, and got the women and children, and carried them to the fort. Lieut. Humphreys had one man wounded, and his own coat was shot through in four places. They brought off a gun and a blanket. The Indians had all red hats and red blankets.‡

On the sixth of the same month, the wife and three children of John Adam Burns, of Allemaengel (Albany) township, were

---

* See tax daplicate for 1756, Isaac Sharp, collector, in the commis-, sioner's office, Lancaster.—*Compiler.*

† Old Mr. Zeuchmacher & Bernhart Motz.—*Sauer's Journal.*

‡ Pennsylvania Gazette, November 12, 1756.

carried off by the Indians. The youngest child was only four weeks old.*

Letter from Col. Conrad Weiser, to Gov. Denny.

HEIDELBERG, IN THE COUNTY OF BERKS, }
November 19, 1756. }

HONORED SIR—

Last night about ten o'clock, I received the melancholy news, that the enemy Indians had again made an incursion in Berks county, killed and scalped two married women, and a lad fourteen years of age, wounded two children of about four years of age,. and carried off two more—one of the wounded is scalped and is likely to die, and the other has two cuts on her forehead, given by an Indian, who attempted to scalp her, but did' not succeed. There were eight men, of Fort Henry, posted in different neighbor's houses, about one mile and a half off, when they heard the noise of the guns firing, made immediately towards it, but came too late.

The people are moving away, leaving their barns full of grain behind them, and there is a lamentable cry among them. It is, with submission, a very hard case, that so many men are taken away to protect Shamokin, (all wilderness,) and the inhabited parts to be without protection. I have ordered eighteen men out of the town of Reading, to re-inforce Fort Henry immediately, of which I hope your honor will approve.

Captain Busse will have reached Fort Augusta last Sunday evening, according to what he wrote me, in his last letter, from Fort Hunter, dated 15th inst. He complains bitterly of the poor condition the detachment is in, for want of clothes. I entreat your honor, that as soon as the companies of the First Battalion receive their pay, (so that they can furnish themselves with necessaries against the winter,) Captain Busse, and the detachment under him, may be relieved before the winter sets in.

I am very sorry that I cannot attend in Philadelphia, at this time. I have now an intermittent fever upon me; thought it, therefore, necessary, to send my son Samuel, in order to serve

---

* C. Sauer's German Paper, November, 1756.

your honor, as an interpreter, at New Castle, or any other of the Six Nations.*

I am, honored sir,
Your very obedient,
CONRAD WEISER.

We have heard that a woman has been missed from Heidelberg township, Berks county, for three weeks past, supposed to be carried off by the enemy.†

Extract of a letter, dated

Reading, December 23, 1756.

We have an account from Fort Babel, that on Friday last, a boy was killed and scalped; and another who had the small pox, was dangerously wounded by the Indians, within a mile and a half of said fort. Lieut. Humphreys went out, but could find nothing of the enemy. The wounded lad says, he saw but two Indians, one was painted black, the other red; they cut him badly, but would not scalp him for fear of the infection, as is supposed.‡

From Reading, Berks county, there is advice that a man was lately killed by the Indians. A letter from Fort Lebanon states, that sixteen Indians were seen near that place.§

In a letter from Hanover, Lancaster county, dated May 2d, 1757, it is said that on the night of the 29th ult., the house of Isaac Snevely was set on fire, and entirely consumed, with eighteen horses and cows.||

Since our last, we hear from Lancaster, that on the 17th May, five men, and a woman, *enciente*, were killed and scalped by the Indians, about thirty miles from Lancaster, and that the bodies of the men and the women, had been brought down there by some in the neighborhood where the murders were committed. We are likewise informed that an express arrived in Lancaster, on Saturday last, with an account of seven people being killed in one house, the night before. And there are letters in town, which advice of more murders being committed; the number uncertain, but is thought there are above twenty

---

* Provincial Records, P., p. 69.
† Pennsylvania Gazette, Dec. 9, 1756.   ‡ Ibid, January, 1757.
§ Ibid, May 5, 1757, || Ibid, May 19, 1757.

destroyed, besides what may be carried off; and that the frontier inhabitants are in great distress, and moving from their plantations as fast as they can. The number of the Indians that have done, and are doing the mischief, not known. These late murders have been done in Bethel, Hanover, and Paxton townships.*

Extract of a letter, dated

Reading, June 25, 1757.

Last night, Jacob Levan, Esq., of Maxatany, came to see me, and showed me a letter of the 22d inst., from Lieutenant Engle, dated in Allemangel, by which he advised Mr. Levan of the murder of one Adam Trump, in Allemangel, by Indians, that evening, and that they had taken Trump's wife and his son, a lad nineteen years old, prisoners; but the woman escaped, though upon her flying, she was so closely pursued by one of the Indians, (of which there were seven,) that he threw his tomahawk at her, and cut her badly in the neck, but 'tis hoped not dangerously. This murder happened in as great a thunderstorm as has happened for twenty years past; which extended itself over a great part of this and Northampton counties—for I found much mischief done, as I came from Easton, Northampton county, to this town, the length of fifty-two miles—the day before yesterday, and which I hear has broken down the dams of seven forges, and six grist mills, on Maxatany creek, chiefly in this county; the rest in Philadelphia county.

Mr. Levan told me that at the same time that the Indians did the mischief in Allemangel, another party killed and scalped a man near Fort Henry, in this county, and the next day carried off a young woman from the same neighborhood. I am told too—though I cannot tell what credit is to be given to it—that two persons were killed and scalped near the fort at Northkill, in this county, Wednesday evening last, at the time of the thunderstorm.

I had almost forgot to mention (but I am so hurried just now, 'tis no wonder,) that the Indians, after scalping Adam Trump, left a knife, and a halbert, or a spear, fixed to a pole of four feet, in his body.   JAMES READ.

* Pennsylvania Gazette, May 26, 1757.
† John S. Richards, Esq., of Reading, politely furnished a transcript of this from among original letters in his possession.—*Compiler.*

We hear from Berks county, from a letter, dated at Tulpehocken, July 4, 1754, that the Indians are murdering, about six miles from my house,* says the writer—three women and four children were murdered, and if we do not get assistance from the country, all the inhabitants of Tulpehocken will move away.†

The Rev. John Nicholas Kurtz, pastor of the Lutheran congregation, at Tulpehocken, Lebanon county, in writing to Rev. Henry Mechir Muhlenberg, pastor of the Lutheran church, at New Providence, Montgomery county, under date of July 5, 1757, says:

"Diesen Morgen, wurden sieben ermordete und gescalpte, nemlich drey Maenner und vier Kinder, zur Beerdigung auf unsern Kirchhof gebracht, so gestern bey Somnen Untergang, fuenf Meilen von hier von den Indianern umgebracht worden, und alle in einem House!‡

Extract of a letter, dated

Heidelberg, July 9, 1757.

Yesterday, about three of the clock, in the afternoon, between Valentine Herchelroad's, and Tobias Bickell's, four Indians killed two children; one about four years, the other five; they at the same time scalped a young woman of about sixteen; but, with proper care, she is likely to live and do well.

A woman was terribly cut with the tomahawk, but not scalped—her life is despaired of. Three children were carried off prisoners. One Christian Schrenk's wife, being among the rest, bravely defended herself and children, for a while; wresting the gun out of the Indian's hands, who assaulted her, also his tomahawk, and threw them away; and afterwards was obliged to save her own life—two of her children were taken captives in the mean time. In this house were also twenty women and children, who had fled from their own habitations, to take shelter; the men belonging to them were about one half mile off, picking cherries—they came as quick as possible and went in pursuit of the Indians, but to no purpose, the Indians had concealed themselves.||

* Pennsylvania Gazette, May 26, 1757.
† Reverend Kurtz.
‡ Pennsylvania Gazette, July 4, 1757.
§ Hallische Nachricten, fuer 1757.
|| Pennsylvania Gazette, July, 1757.

We hear that in Bethel township, Lancaster county, (now Lebanon,) one man was murdered last Saturday, a second one wounded so badly that he died, and a third shot in the hand.*

We hear, says C. Sauers, from Linn township, (now Greenwich,) Berks county, that, as Adam Klaus and his neighbors were reaping rye, July 9th, they were surprised by a party of Indians; two men, two women, and a young girl escaped. Martin Yaeger, (Hunter,) and his wife, were killed and scalped. John Kraushaar's wife and child, Abraham Seckler's wife and one of Adam Clauss's children were scalped, and are still living, though badly wounded; one of the women is wounded in the side and the other in the hip. Two of Kraushaar's children were killed; one of Seckler's and one of Philip Eschton's, but were not scalped. The alarm being raised, a party went in pursuit of them, and overtook nine, and fired upon them. But they soon eluded the pursuit of the whites.†

Extract of a letter, dated

Hanover, Lancaster (now Lebanon) county, ⎱
August 11, 1757.   ⎰

Last Thursday, John Andrew's wife, going to a neighbor's house, was surprised by six Indians, had her horse shot under her, and she and her child were carried off. On Saturday, in Bethel township, as John Winkleblech's two sons, and Joseph Fischbach, (a soldier in the pay of the Province,) went out about sunrise, to bring in the cows, they were fired upon by about fifteen Indians; the two lads were killed; one of them was scalped; the other got into the house before he died, and the soldier was wounded in the hand.

The same morning, about seven o'clock, two miles below Manaday gap, as Thomas McQuire's son was bringing in some cows out of a field, a little way from the house, he was pursued by two Indians, and narrowly escaped. The same day, in the middle of this township, four miles from the mountain, as Leonard Long's son was ploughing, was killed and scalped; on the other side of the fence, Leonard Miller's son was ploughing; he was made prisoner.

John Graham, who lives near the gap of the Indian town creek, had a steer killed, about sunrise, or before, and John

---

* Pennsylvania Gazette, August 11, 1757.
† C. Sauer's Journal, July, 1757.

Brown had two cows killed; all except the first mischief done in' one day; so that last Saturday there must have been, at least, four parties of Indians in this township.

Having notice of this on Sunday morning, I set out with four men, and we ranged till after midnight. Monday morning I set out again, with forty men, intending to go over the mountain. We ranged the first day in the forest, and had intended to lie out on the mountain all night, but a heavy rain falling, we took to a house. On Tuesday morning we set out over the mountain to find tracks, if possible; but we found not the least appearance of any, or Indians, over the mountain, or in any of the waste houses; so we returned on Tuesday night.

Monday, 8th. Many tracks were seen among the inhabitants, and in the waste houses, where the Indians lodged. In one of the houses they left a scalping knife, and had killed and scalped a man. Wednesday, we intended to rest, but at about 12 o'clock had another alarm.

Near Benjamin Clarke's house, four miles from the mill, two Indians surprised Isaac Williams' wife, and the widow Williams, alias Smelley, killed and scalped the former, in sight of the house, she having run a little way, after three balls had been shot through her body; the latter they carried away captive.

About the same time, as George Maurer was cutting oats in George Scheffer's field, he was killed and scalped, two miles from the hill, so that it was not all done by one party.

There is now such a severe sickness in these parts—the like has not been known—that many families can neither fight nor run away, which occasions great distress on the frontiers. Had it not been for forty men, which the province has in pay, in this township, little of the harvest could have been saved, and as the time for which they have been engaged is nearly elapsed, the inhabitants hope the government will continue them in the service, else the consequences must be dreadful.*

We hear from a gentleman that six persons were taken away by the Indians from Lancaster county, 17th August.†

Since our last, we learn from Lancaster, that there was nothing but murdering and capturing among them by the Indians. That on the 17th August, one Beatly was killed in Paxton— that the next day, James Mackey was murdered in Hanover,

* Pennsylvania Gazette, August, 1757.　　　† Ibid. Aug. 11.

7

and William and Joseph Barnet wounded. That on the same day were taken prisoners, a son of James Mackey, a son of Joseph Barnet, Elizabeth Dickey and her child, and the wife of Samuel Young and her child; and that ninety-four men, women and children, were seen flying from their places, in one body, and a great many more in smaller parties, so that it was feared the settlements would be entirely forsaken.

We hear from Berks county, that several Indians have lately been seen near Fort Lebanon; and that on Sunday, the 21st August, the house and barn of Peter Semelcke were burnt, and three of his children carried off; himself, wife and one child, being from home at the time. This was done within two miles of the fort.*

Our accounts, in general, from the frontiers, are most dismal; all agreeing that some of the inhabitants are killed or carried off; houses burnt and cattle destroyed daily—and that at the same time they are afflicted with severe sickness and die fast, so, that in many places, they are neither able to defend themselves, when attacked, nor to run away.†

We hear from Lebanon township, Lancaster (now Lebanon) county, that on last Friday, four children were carried off by the Indians. From Reading, Berks county, that on Thursday and Friday last, some people were murdered in Bern township, by the Indians, and others carried off.

A letter from Hanover township, Lancaster county, dated October 1st, 1757, says that the children mentioned of having been carried off from Lebanon township, belonging to Peter Wampler, that they were going to the meadow for a load of hay; and that the Indians took from the house what they thought most valuable, and destroyed what they could not take away, to a considerable value.

In the same letter it is said, that the frontiers are almost without inhabitants, and on that day, and on the day before, several creatures were killed by the enemy in Hanover township, and that on Thursday before, four persons were killed in Berks county, and four made prisoners, near the Northkill, by a party of Indians, supposed to be about fifty.‡

On the 25th of November, Thomas Robinson, and a son of Thomas Bell, were killed and scalped by the Indians, in Hano-

---

* Pennsylvania Gazette, September 1, 1757.   † Ibid, September 8.
‡ Ibid, October 6 and 13.

ver township; but that the Indians immediately went off after committing the murder.*

The condition of the frontier settlers or inhabitants was truly deplorable; not only were they surprised by the ferocious, blood-thirsty savages, but sickness rendered their unenviable condition still more dismal. They had not the means to engage forces or scouters to apprize them of the Indians' invasions, or prevent their incursions. In these deplorable circumstances they had to appeal to a deaf government, and to the sympathies of their fellow citizens, for means.

The following is given to show the nature of their appeal to their fellow brethren. It has been copied from a file of papers in the possession of the Hon. JOHN RITTER, of Reading. It is from C. Sauer's German paper, printed at Germantown, in July, 1757.

Die hintern Einwohner zu Dolpehocken bitten um eine Beysteurer, dass sie mehr Wacten bezahlen koennen zu ihre Sicherheit, weil die Festengen so weit aus einander liegen, und die Voelcker drinnen wenig Dienste thun. Wer willen ist etwas zu steuern, der kan es ablegen in Lancaster by Herrn Oterbein, und Herrn Gerock, Lut. Pred.; in New Hanover und Providentz by Hr. Muehlenberg und Leydig; in Madetsche by Dr. Abraham Wagner; in Goschenhoppen by Mr. Michel Reyer; in Germantown by Christoph Sauer, sr.; und in Philadelphia bey Hr. Handschuh, und dabey schreiben, wie viel gegeben worden; und diese koennen es uebersenden an Col. Conrad Weiser, oder Peter Spycker, oder an Hr. Kurtz, wie es einem jeden beliebt.

Diejenigen, welchi in Ruhe und Sicherheit ihre Erndte haben koennen schneiden und heinbringen, haben Ursache Gott davor zudanken.

Extract of a letter, dated

Tulpehocken, April 8, 1758.

I and Mr. Kern have just arrived at Mr. Jacob Sherman's, where we have been informed that a woman was killed and scalped by the Indians last night, about three miles from here. We are now ready to pursue them. The persons killed, besides one taken captive, are two young men at Swatara—

* Pennsylvania Gazette, Sept. 8, 1757.

brothers, by the name of Shetterly—one Michael Sauter, and William Hart, and a widow woman taken captive.

At Tulpehocken, a man by the name of Lebenguth and his wife were killed and scalped. At Northkill, Nicholas Geiger's wife and two of his children were killed; and also Michael Ditzelar's wife was killed—these were all scalped. The Indians have divided themselves into small parties, and surprise the settlers unawares.[*]

On Monday, the 22d of May, 1758, Barnabas Tolon was killed and scalped in Hanover township, Lancaster county. And we are well informed that one hundred and twenty-three persons have been murdered or carried off from that county, by the Indians, since the war commenced; and that three have been scalped and yet alive.[†]

A letter from Fort Henry, in Berks county, dated June 17, 1758, mentions the wife of John Frantz, and three children, being carried off by the Indians; and that the woman was murdered a little way from Frantz's house, she being weakly and not able to travel. Also, that the son of Jacob Snavely, a shoemaker, was killed and scalped about the same time. From the tracks of the enemy, their number is supposed to be about twenty.[‡]

We have advice from Swatara township, Lancaster (now Lebanon) county, that on Tuesday, the 20th inst., a Dutchman (German) was shot and scalped by the Indians; and the next day one Samuel Robinson was shot, but got into a house—he soon after died.

Extract of a letter, dated
Fort Henry, Berks county, October 4, 1758.
The first of October, the Indians burnt a house on Swatara, killed one man, and three are missing. Two boys were found tied to a tree and were released. We are alarmed in the fort almost every night by a terrible barking of dogs; there are certainly some Indians about us.[§]

* C. Sauer's German Paper, April, 1758.
† Pennsylvania Gazette, Jan. 1, 1756.
‡ Ibid, Jan. 29.   § Ibid, Oct. 19, 1758.

Reading, Nov. 15, 1758.

We learn that on the 13th inst., Jacob Mosser and Hans Adam Mosser, were killed by the Indians, in Bethel township, Lancaster county. There were some others in the company who made their escape, and being pursued by the enemy, got into the house, the door of which the Indians endeavored to force open, when one of them was shot down, by a white boy, upon which the others wrapped him in a blanket and went off.

1763, *September* 9.—"A few of the Rangers who had encamped in Berks county, were apprized of the approach of Indians by their outscouts; the Indians advanced cautiously to take them by surprise; when near, with savage yells, they rushed forward, but the Rangers, springing on their feet, shot the three in front; the rest fled into a thicket and escaped. The Indians were armed with guns, and provided with ammunition. These Indians, it is supposed by some, had been on their way from the Moravian Indians, in Northampton county, to the big island. Runners were sent to the different parties of Rangers, with information, and others set out in pursuit of those who fled.*

Letter from Jonas Seely, Esq., dated

Reading, Sept. 11, 1763.

We are all in a state of alarm. Indians have destroyed dwellings, and murdered with savage barbarity their helpless inmates; even in the neighborhood of Reading. Where these Indians came from, and where going, we know not. These are dangerous times. Send us an armed force to aid our Rangers of Berks and Lancaster.†

JONAS. SEELY.

————

Another letter, dated

Reading, September 17, 1763.

It is a matter of wonder, that Indians living among us, for numbers of years, should suddenly become grum friends, or

———
* Pennsylvania Gazette, Oct. 19, 1758.
† Laid before the Assembly, Sept. 16, 1763. Votes of Assembly.

most deadly enemies! Yet there is too much reason for sus-.
picion. The Rangers sent in word, that these savages must
consist of fifty, who travel in companies from five to twenty,,
visiting Wyalusing, Wichetunk, Nain, Big Island and Conestogue, under the mark of friendly Indians. Our people have
become almost infuriated to madness. These Indians were not
even suspected of treachery, such had been the general confidence in their fidelity. The murders recently committed are
of the most aggravating description. Would it not be proper
to institute an inquiry into the cause of our present distress?
We are in want of force, and money; we require aid.

The Senecas, there is much reason to believe, have been
tampering with our Indians.

JONAS SEELY.

To the Hon. Gov. James Hamilton.

In the early part of September, in the afternoon, eight well-
armed Indians came to the house of John Fincher, a Quaker,,
residing north of the Blue mountain, in Berks county, about
twenty-four miles from Reading, and within three-quarters of a
mile of a party of six men of Captain Kern's company of Ran-.
gers, commanded by ensign Scheffer. At the approach of the
Indians, John Fincher, his wife, two sons and daughter, immediately went to the door and asked them to enter in and eat;
expressed their hopes that they came as friends, and entreated
them to spare their lives. The Indians were deaf to the en-
treaties of Fincher. Both parents and two sons were deliberately murdered; their bodies were found on the spot. The
daughter was missing after the departure of the Indians, and it
was supposed from the cries, that were heard by the neighbors,
that she also was slain.

A young lad, who lived with Fincher, made his escape, and
notified ensign Scheffer, who instantly went in pursuit of these
heartless, cold-blooded assassins. He pursued them to the
house of one Millar, where he found four children murdered;
the Indians having carried two others with them. Millar and
his wife being at work in the field, saved their lives by flight.
Mr. Millar himself, was pursued near one mile by an Indian,,
who fired at him twice while in hot pursuit. Scheffer and his
party continued their pursuit and overtook the savages, firing
upon them. The Indians returned the fire, and a sharp, but.

short conflict ensued,—the enemy fled, leaving behind them. Millar's two children, and part of the plunder they had taken..

These barbarous Indians had scalped all the persons whom they had murdered, except an infant, about two weeks old, whose head they had dashed against the wall, where the brains with clotted blood on the wall was a witness of their cruelty. The consequence of this massacre was the desertion of all the settlements beyond the Blue mountain.

A few days after these atrocious murders, the house of Frantz Hubler, in Bern township, eighteen miles from Reading, was attacked by surprise—Hubler was wounded; his wife and three of his children were carried off, and three other of his children scalped alive; two of these shortly afterwards died.

"Murder and cruelty marked the path of these Indians. From the many acts of savage ferocity committed in Berks county, may be noticed that on the 10th of September, 1763, when five of these Indians entered the house of Philip Martloff, at the base of the Blue mountain, murdered and scalped his wife, two sons and two daughters, burnt the house and barn, the stacks of hay and grain, and destroyed every thing of any value. Martloff was absent from home, and one daughter escaped at the time of the murder, by runniug and secreting herself in a thicket. The father and daughter were left in abject misery."*

* See Votes of Assembly, vol. v. p 285. Oct. 21, 1765.

CHAPTER IV.

THE SWEDES.

Some descendants of this hardy race, of whom it is said, that when Penn arrived, "they had made great improvements—had houses full of fine children; are still found in the lower parts of Berks county, and others in Alsace. Among their descendants are those of the name of Jones, Kirlin, Umsted and others, whose names are mentioned in speaking of Douglass, Amity and Alsace townships.

One hundred and fifty years ago, the Swedes were a very plain, remarkably strong, and exceedingly industrious people. As it may prove interesting to the reader, a brief sketch from the pen of an able writer is given, with some additional remarks, concerning this interesting people.

"Numbers of Swedes lived at Kensington and on Sunner's creek, before the arrival of Penn. They had grants of land from Alexander Henoyon, the governor of New York, as early as 1664—that is the date of the deed to old Peter Cock, for Shackamaxon. On that creek, three-fourths of a mile from its mouth, now so diminished, they once built large sloops, and afterwards a brig, at its mouth.

The Swedes dwelt in numbers on Tinicum, calling the place New Gottenburg. At their church there, the first corpse ever buried was Catharine, daughter of Andrew Hanson, October 24, 1646.

To the church upon Tinicum Island, all the Swedes, settled along the Delaware, used to go in their canoes from long distances. They did the same in visiting the primitive log church at Wiccoco,—almost all their conveyances were preferred by water. There was a stone upon Darby, to which they always went by water, even when the land route was often nearest.

The old Swedish inhabitants were said to be very successful in raising chick turkies; as soon as hatched, they plunged them into cold water, and forced them to swallow a whole pepper corn,—they then returned it to the mother, and it became as hardy as a hen's chick. When they found them drooping, their practice was to examine the rump feathers, and such two or three as were found filled with blood, were to be drawn out, and the chick would revive and thrive.

"Kalm, the Swedish traveller, who was here among his countrymen, in 1748, has left notices as follows, concerning them:—The ancient Swedes used the sassafras for tea, and for a dye. From the persimmon tree they made beer and brandy. They called the mullen plant the Indian tobacco; they tied it round their arms and feet, as a cure, when they had the ague. They made their candles generally from the bayberry bushes; the root they used to cure tooth ache; from the bush they also made an agreeable smelling soap. The magnolia tree they made use of for various medicinal purposes.

"The houses of the first Swedish settlers were very indifferent; consisting of but one room; the door was so low as to require you to stoop. Instead of window panes of glass they had little holes, before which a sliding board was put, or, on other occasions, they had isinglass; the cracks between logs were filled with clay; the chimnies in a corner, were generally of gray sandstone; or for want of it, sometimes mere clay; the ovens were in the same room. They had separate stables for the cattle; but after the English came and set the example, they left their cattle to suffer in the open winter air. The Swedes wore vests and breeches of skin; hats were not used, but little caps with flaps before them. They made their own leather and shoes, with soles like moccasins, of the same materiel as the tops. The women, too, wore jackets and petticoats of skins; their beds, excepting the sheets, were of skins of bears, wolves, &c. Hemp, they had none; but they used flax, for ropes and fishing tackle. This rude state of living was, however, in the country places principally, and before the English came.

"The Swedes seemed to have retained for a long time a hereditary attachment to the skin garments; for within the memory of some of their oldest, still living, some are remembered who were seen wearing calf-skin vests and jackets, and buckskin breeches.

"Many Swedes settled along the western side of the Schuylkill. Matthias Holstein, a primitive settler in Upper Merion, took up one thousand acres there. Mauntz Rambo, an aged Swede, alive about sixty-five years ago, born near Swedes

Ford, was a celebrated hunter in his day; he killed numerous deer in his neighborhood in his time—once he shot a panther which he found attempting to attack his dog. He remembered many still among them, in his younger days.

"My friend," says Watson, "Major M. Holstein, fond of his Swedish descent, tells me, that when he first went to the Swedes' church, in Merion, as a boy, all the men and women came there on horseback, and all the women wore 'safe-guard petticoats,' which they took off and hung along the fence.

"His grandmother, born at Malothan, four miles from Potts-grove, remembered the Indians once about them, and that she, herself, when young, had been carried some distance on a squaw's back. They then did all their travelling by canoes, on the Schuylkill. When married, she and her wedding friends came down to Swedes Ford, in their canoes. In the same manner they always made their visits to Philadelphia."

A settlement was commenced by the Swedes, at Moletton, prior to 1700. At Douglasville, there is still standing a sub-stantially built house, erected nearly one hundred and thirty years ago, by a Mr. Johns or Jones. The orthography of Swedish names, has been so much changed since their first im-migration, that descendants from the same family can scarcely be recognized. Jonasson, has been changed into Johnson; Johns, now Jones; Halling, into Hulings or Hewlings; Von Culen, into Culen; Mats, into Matthias; Bengt, into Bene-dict; Olave, into William; Kohnig, into King; Longaker, into Longenecker; Jocom, into Yocum; Omstadt, into Ulmstead or Umsted; Gostasson, into Justis.

The Swedish language is very little spoken among their de-scendants. A specimen of it is given below, being the Lord's Prayer in that language.

Fader waer som aest i Himmelen. Helgat warde titt Nampn. Tillkomme titt Ricke. Skee tin Wilie sae pae Jordenne som i Himmelen Waert, dagliga Broed giff ofs i dagh. Och foerlaet oss waera skulder sae som ock wi foerloeten them oss skyldige aero. Och in leed oss icke i frestelse. Ut an frals oss i frae ondo, Tu Ruket aer titt, och Machten och Haerligheten i Ewigheet. Amen.*

* Copied from the Stockholm Edition of 1674.

CHAPTER V.

FRENCH PROTESTANT, OR HUGUENOTS.

A small body of these persecuted persons, settled at a comparatively early period, in Oley, Alsace, and other townships of Berks county. It is supposed by some that they were termed Huguenots, by way of reproach. Before giving an account of those who settled in Berks county, a few remarks will be submitted as to the name by which the French Protestants are now generally known.

Many and various are the sources to which the *learned* have traced the etymology of "*Huguenot.*"

Some have asserted that the term was originally applied to the members of the Reformed, by the dignitaries of the Catholic Church, as one of reproach. To sustain this position, it is argued that when the new doctrine was first preached in France, a number of the inhabitants of the city of Tours—which afterwards, and next to the city of Rochelle, ranked as the strongest hold of the Reformed party—embraced the same. Unlike the Catholics, their worship was conducted in the evening as well as in the day. Cultivating a spirit of genuine piety, they met after night in each others houses, for social prayer. In this, they imitated the example of primitive Christians, and like them, they became the subjects of a persecution almost as relentless. Going from house to house as the place of meeting might chance to be, after the labors of the day were over, to attend to this pious duty, and returning therefrom at a later hour, their enemies, the papists, endeavored to prevent the extension of their doctrines, by reporting at first that they were engaged in some foul conspiracy against the government, and afterwards against the people. Failing in their attempts to affect them in this way, and finding that the fallow ground was being broken up daily, with the promise of a rich return, and that the seed of the true faith which was sown in confidence, was germinating and yielding an abundant harvest, despite their efforts, to the contrary, they next changed their mode of warfare, and endeavored to effect their object by bringing them into ridicule and contempt. For this purpose, they seized upon the fact of their meeting after night, and connected with it a story, then current, concerning the city of Tours. One of the gates of the city, it seems, was called *Hugo,* and according to a popular tradition from Hugo, comte Tours, who it seems, according to the same tradition, was eminent in life only for his crimes, oppression and cruelty. After his death—so runs the the story—his spirit, incapable of repose, haunted immediately after nightfall, the scene, which was the neighborhood of the gate in question, of its cruelty and crimes, when embodied in the flesh. Many and strange pranks were played, and many a hapless wight was bruised and beaten by this pugnacious spirit, all of which added to horrible sounds and unearthly noises in the immediate vicinity of its walks, so alarmed the inhabitants, as to induce them to keep closely housed, whenever the hour for its appearance drew near. Hence, Hugo and ghost came to be synonymous; and as has been already shown, the social worship of night meetings of the Reformers being so widely different from the imposing ceremony of the Catholic church, and requiring them consequently to be out more after night than the latter, each individual of the former was called a *Hugo;* the whole, *Huguenots.* Thus much for this derivation, and the tale that thereby hangs.

The next supposed derivation, is that it was a term voluntarily assumed by themselves, as a party name, when their religion was attacked, and they were forced to take arms against the government in self-defence. As they were rigid Calvinists, of great sanctity of character and purity of morals, Caseneuve has pretended to have discovered the original in the Flemish word Heghenon or Huguenon, which means Cathari or Puritan; but this is not very probable, inasmuch as it is not likely, that having a word in their own vocabulary, so expressive as "Puritan," they would be disposed to borrow from a language no more known than the Flemish.

Another author has attempted to trace its origin to *Huguenote,* a name given to an iron or earthen pot for cooking, by connecting it with the persecutions to which the Reformed were subjected in France; and basing it upon the hypothesis, that some of their number may have been roasted or tortured and exposed to the flames like a vessel used for culinary purposes.

These are all, however, but mere surmises, unsupported and

unsustained by any thing at all calculated to give them a proper title to serious consideration. The only etymology then, which in our humble opinion remains, is undoubtedly the true one—this we shall briefly attempt to prove by the history of the times and the people.

Eidgenoss is a German compound word, in the Saxon and Dutch dialects, *Eedgenotten;* of which the singular is *Eidgenoss*, or *Eedgenot.** It is formed from *Eid,* an oath, and *Genoss*, a confederate or partaker of the oath; and was the original designation of the three Swiss patriots, William Tell, Walter Fuerst, and Arnold of Melcthal,† on the night of the 7th November, 1307, met at Ruetli, on the lake of Luzerne, and there bound themselves by a solemn oath, to shake off the yoke of their Austrian oppressors, and to establish the liberties of their country. The conspiracy thus formed was embraced with delight by all to whom it was communicated, each member of which was called an *Eidgenoss*, and afterwards, January, A. D. 1308, when the people of the Waldstetter, composed of the Cantons, Appenzell, Glaris and Uri, met in solemn council, and took the oath of perpetual alliance, they were designated as the *Eidgennossenschaft*, i. e. Confederation.— Through successive generations they were thus known, and when in aftertimes, the people of Geneva, which had now been included in the Swiss confederation, embraced the doctrines of John Calvin; they threw off the allegiance of the Duke of Savoy; and in order to maintain their independence, formed a confederacy after the example of the Waldstetter, with the Cantons of Bern and Freibourg, which was also confirmed by an oath of all the contracting parties. Like the original patriots, they in turn were called *Eidgenossen*. This movement being half temporal, and half ecclesiastical or spiritual, related to their freedom of government as *men,* and the rights of conscience as *Christians*. Hence in its popular usage, this term conveyed the primary idea of *freemen,* in contradistinction to *mamelukes, serfs, or slaves*, by which name the party of the Duke was better known; and also the secondary idea of a religious reformation in the mind of the adherents to the Catholic faith. For the city of Geneva, having embraced the Reformed doctrines, and immediately thereafter, thrown off the allegiance, under the circumstances already given, the term *Eigenossen*

* Lewis Mayer, D. D.   † Davenport, article Fuerst.

8

became identified among the papists, with the notion of *rebels*
or *apostates* from the church, and was therefore consequently
used as a term of reproach.

From Geneva, where he had taught with so much success,
that instead of Zurich, it became the metropolis of the Reformed
Churches, Calvin, ardent in the discharge of what he conceived
his duty, pushed his doctrines with eminent success into his native kingdom of France. They were readily embraced by the
learned and the pious, without regard to caste or standing in
society. The Admiral Caspar de Coligni, D'Andelot, Mornay,
Duplesis, La Renandie, the Prince de Gonde Ann Dubourg,
Theodore Beza, and a host of others equally worthy and eminent for their virtues, were among the firmest supporters of the
Reformation, and the teacher of its doctrines. Sustained by
such men against the power of the court; in the midst of persecutions and civil wars—the professors of the Reformed religion were spoken of with respect; and although the term
Eidgenoss, or *Eedgenot,* was known in France at that time,
still no effort was made to bring them into disrepute by the
application of this, or any other term of ridicule, except when
they were occasionally called "*the pretended reformed,*" or,
"*seditionists,*" in the state papers. Thus they remained, until
on the accession of Frances II. to the throne, and his early marriage with Mary, Queen of Scotland. Being very young in
years, and devotedly attached to his young Queen, he readily
transferred the care of his kingdom to his wife's uncles, the
Dukes of Guise and Loraine. This begat discontent among
the protestants, who only wanted a leader to organize them
into a formidable body. Calvin, like Thomas Cranmer, the
celebrated reformer, had taught that the king was supreme, and
acting upon this principle, the French Calvinists maintained that
the king being yet in his minority, was to be protested by his
subjects from the tyranny of his uncles; to this end a plan was
concerted, known as the conspiracy of Amboise, for their overthrow, of which the Prince de Conde, was unanimously chosen
leader; but without his knowledge, nor was he considered as
a participator, until the time of action arrived. John de Bari,
and the Sieur La Renandi, in the meantime were to direct all
their movements. In conformity with this plan they convened
a meeting of the protestant leaders at Nantes, in the darkness
of the night, in a ruined building on the outskirts of the town.

Before they proceeded to develope their schemes, La Renandi administered solemn oaths, that "nothing be done or attempted against the King and Queen-mother, or princes, his brothers." To this agreement they all swore; and after praying for success, they parted with fraternal embraces, and in tears. The time and place of carrying their plot into execution, was to be at Blois, on the 15th of March, 1550. By some means the plot was discovered to the Count, and therefore, the Duke of Guise was appointed Lieutenant General of the Kingdom, with supreme power in all cases, civil and military. Armed with this authority he adopted the most energetic measures to suppress the protestants, and although he succeeded in defeating and killing La Renandi and a few of his companions, yet the effect was not produced which the Count anticipated; but on the contrary, the Reformed party increased in numbers, and displayed additional zeal and activity in all their movements, much to the annoyance of the Guises and their adherents."

It is only at this period of history in France then, that we find the professors of the Reformed religion first designated by the term Huguenots. They were identified in faith with the Reformed of Geneva, and like them, upon the discovery of the conspiracy referred to, were called *Eidgenossen;* that is, in the Papist sense, rebels and apostates. From this, owing to their ignorance of the orthography of the German word, and their inability to pronounce it correctly; but yet well knowing its import, it is easy to conceive that Frenchmen would readily corrupt it into *Huguenot.* The analogy is striking, the facts undoubted, and the reasons given, to our mind, at least, satis-factory.

With this brief enquiry into the origin of the term *Eidgenossen,* i. e. *Huguenot,* we might rest, but as there are many descendants of this brave, moral, religious and much persecuted people, residing in Berks county, and in some instances still living upon the farms originally patented by their refugee ancestors, we feel bound to say a word concerning them. After the Huguenot colonies at New Rochelle, West Chester county, Esopus, Ulster county, New York, had been formed; some of their number at an early day, emigrated to this county and commenced settlements. Of this number were the De Tircks or De Turcks, and others, who had emigrated from Esopus, in New York, to Oley township, prior to 1712.

Abraham De Turck, of Oley township, in a note, dated March, 1844, says: Meine Voraeltern, Namens Isaac De Turck wohnten in Frankreich, waren von den sogenannten Huguenoten, fluechteten wegen Religion nach der Pfalz in die Stadt Franckenthal; von dorten, wandente sie aus nach America, liessen sich nieder im Staat New York, in der Gegend Esopus in der Zeit der Koenigen Anna; zogen von da nach Oley zwischen 1704 und 1712. Das Patent von meinem land ist 1712.

This soon opened the way for a direct emigration of their persecuted brethren still remaining in France, and of others who had sought protection of the protestant powers of Switzerland, Germany, Holland, and England. Among the most prominent of these early Huguenot settlers in this county, we give the names of several head of families, as follows: besides the De Turcks, Bertolets, are Levans, Loras, Beseaurs, Sharodin, Berdos, De La Plains, Delangs and others. (See Oley township.)

These pious and persecuted men, with their fellow refugees and families, passed "through much tribulation," until at length they secured for themselves and posterity an asylum where they could "worship God according to the dictates of their own consciences." Although they succeeded far beyond their most sanguine expectations, still they looked back with regret, and in many instances with home-sick hearts, upon the vine-clad hills and sunny fields of their own much loved France. They were exiles from the land of their nativity; the broad billows of the Atlantic rolled between them and the graves of their fathers. Separated from friends and kindred, who in their turn were driven to seek the protection of foreign potentates, or restrained by the policy of the government, after the revocation of the edict of Nantes, from emigrating, and forced into an abjuration, of their faith—how harassing must have been their feelings and how sore their trials! But, "He who tempers the wind to the shorn lamb," was still gracious unto them; he who had protected and defended them from dangers, imminent and terrible, was still "their strength and abiding place." Time blunted the keenness of their sorrows, and as the forest began to bloom beneath their labors, they sat down in contentment, and in daily prayer returned thanksgiving unto Him, who is the Author of every good and perfect gift.

Some of the Huguenots brought with them French Bibles. Daniel Bartolet, a descendant of Jean Bartolet, who, with his wife and five children, emigrated into Oley in 1726, has the very Bible brought with the family. It is esteemed a precious relic.

The following, being the Lord's Prayer, has been copied from one of these French Bibles. It is from the Maresior edition of 1669.

Nostre pere, qui es es cieux. Yon Nom soit sanctifie. Ton regne vienne. Ta volonte soit faite ainsi en la terre comme au ciel. Donne nous aujourd hui nostre pain quotidien. Et nous quitte nos debtes, comme aussi nous quitons a nos detteurs les heurs. Et ne nos indui point en tentation, mais delivre nos du malin. Car a toi est le regne et la puissance et la gloire a jamais. Amen.

8*

CHAPTER VI.

THE GERMANS.

The Germans, who first emigrated into the Province of Pennsylvania, came chiefly for conscience's sake; those who arrived at a later period, came to improve their temporal, as well as their spiritual condition. Not many names of the first German emigrants, except a few of the German Quakers who came in with Penn, are preserved.

Among the very first, whose name has been handed down, is that of Henry Fry, who arrived two years before William Penn. His widow was still living in 1754.* One Plattenbach came a few years later.† In 1682, a considerable number came from Cresheim—these were principally Quakers. They settled at Germantown. About the year 1684 or '85, a company was formed in Germany, called the "Frankfort Land Company," consisting at first of ten gentlemen, living in Frankfort, on the Mayne; their articles were executed in that city on the 24th of November, 1686. They seem to have been men of note by the use of each of his separate seal. Their names were G. Van Mastrick, Thomas V. Wylick, John Le Bran, F. Dan. Pastorious, John J. Schuetz, Daniel Behagel, Jacobus Van Dewaller, John W. Peterson, Johannes Kimber, Balthasur Jowest. They bought 25,000 acres of land from Penn. The Germantown patent for 5350, and the Manatauney patent for 22,377 acres. T. D. Pastorious was appointed the attorney for the company, and after his resignation, Dan. Faulkner was in 1708 made attorney.

In 1708, 1709, 1710 to 1720, thousands of them emigrated who were known as Palatines, because they had come from the Palatinate, whither some had been forced to flee from their homes in other parts of Europe. Many of these had gone first to England on the invitation of Queen Anne, at whose bounty, not a few were transported to America. Hundreds of them were gratuitously furnished with religious and useful books, before their departure by the Read Anton Wilhelm Boehm, Courtchaplain, of St. James. The principal book was Arndt's.

* Hal. Nach.   † Ibid.

Wahres Christenthum. Among these German emigrants were Mennonites, Dunkards, German Reformed, and Lutherans. Their number was so great, as to draw the remarks from James Logan, secretary of the Province of Pennsylvania, in 1717—"We have," said he, "of late, great number of Pala-tines poured in upon us without any recommendation or notice, which gives the country some uneasiness, for foreigners do not so well among us as our own English people!"

In 1719, Jonathan Dickinson remarks, "We are daily expecting ships from London which bring over Palatines, in number about six or seven thousand. We had a parcel who came out about five years ago, who purchased land about sixty miles west of Philadelphia, and prove quiet and industrious. Some few came from Ireland lately, and more are expected thence.* This is besides our common supply from Wales and England. Our friends do increase mightily, and a great people there is in the wilderness, which is fast becoming a fruitful field."

From 1720 to 1725, the number of Germans from the Palatinate, Wurtenberg, Darmstadt, &c., increased; these settled principally in what is Montgomery, Berks, and Lancaster county. Those who came in between 1720 and 1725, were accompanied by ministers of the gospel, and some schoolmasters—among the German Reformed was Rev. Bochm, who had come in prior to 1720, and Rev. George Michael Weiss, who came subsequent to 1720. Among the Lutheran ministers were the Rev. Falckner, Hinckel, and Stoever. Their schoolmasters, for the want of a supply of ministers, read sermons and prayers. Among the Dunkards were the Rev. Peter Becker, and Alexander Mack, as ministers.

In the period between 1720 and 1725, a number of Germans emigrated from the State of New York, and settled at Tulpehocken. Of these, a detailed account will be given when speaking of Tulpehocken township.

From 1725 to 1740, there was another great influx of Germans of various religious opinions, German Reformed, Lutherans, Catholics, Moravians, and Swenckfelders, arrived; of the latter, a particular account will be given when speaking of Herford township. It appears from a letter written by James Logan, in 1725, that many of the Germans were not over scrupulous in their compliance with the regulations of the Land

* These were the Mennonites in Pequea valley.

Office. He says, and perhaps with much truth, "they come in, in crowds, and as bold, indigent strangers from Germany, where many of them have been soldiers. All these go in the best vacant tracts, and seize upon them as places of common spoil. He says they rarely approach him on their arrival to propose to purchase; and when they are sought out and challenged for their rights of occupancy, they allege it was published in Europe that we wanted and solicited for colonists, and had a superabundance of land, and, therefore, they had come without the means to pay. The Germans in after time embroiled with the Indians at Tulpehocken, threatening a serious affair. In general, those who sat down without titles acquired enough in a few years, to buy them, and so generally they were left unmolested.

The character then known to him, he states, are many of them a surly people—divers of them Papists—the men well armed, and, as a body, a warlike, morose race. In 1727, he states that 6000 Germans more are expected, (and also many from Ireland,) and these emigrations, he hopes, may be prevented in future by act of parliament, else he fears those colonies will, in time, be lost to the crown!—a future act.

"In 1729, he speaks of being glad to observe the influx of strangers, as likely to attract the interference of parliament; for truly, says he, they have danger to apprehend for a country where not even a militia exists for government support. To arrest in some degree their arrival, the Assembly assessed a tax of twenty shillings a head on new arrived servants.

"In another letter, he says, the numbers from Germany at this rate will soon produce a German colony here, and perhaps such an one as Britain once received from Saxony in the fifth century. He even states as among the apprehended schemes of Sir William Keith, the former governor, that he, Harland and Gould, have had sinister projects of forming an independent province in the west, to the westward of the Germans, towards the Ohio—probably west of the mountains, and to be supplied by his friends among the Palatines and Irish, among whom was his chief popularity at that time.

From 1740 to 1752, emigrants came in by hundreds. In the autumn of 1749, not less than twenty vessels, with German passengers, to the number of twelve thousand, arrived at Philadelphia. In 1750, 1751, and 1752, the number was not much less. Among those who emigrated in the years from 1740 to 1752, there were many who bitterly lamented that they had forsaken their houses, for the Province of Pennsylvania. At that time there was a class of Germans who had resided some time in Pennsylvania, well known by the name of *Neulaender,* who made it their business to go to Germany and prevail on their countrymen to sacrifice their property, and embark for America. In many instances persons in easy circumstances at home, with a view to better their condition, come to America, but to their sorrow found that their condition was rendered none the better, but in numerous instances worse, if not wretched. Others again, who had not the means of paying their passage across the Atlantic, were, on their arrival at Philadelphia, exposed at public auction to serve for a series of years to pay their passage. Those, thus disposed of, were termed *Redemptioners.* The Palatine Redemptions were usually sold at ten pounds, for from three to five years servitude. Many of them, after serving out their time faithfully, became, by frugality and industry, some of the most wealthy and influential citizens of the State. The years that were peculiarly remarkable for the importation of Palatine Redemptions were 1728, '29, '37, '41, '50, and '51.

In 1751, the writer's paternal grandfather, (a native of Zinsheim,) Jonas Rupp, arrived in the ship Phœnix, commanded by Captian Spurrier, September 25th. Out of four hundred and twelve who embarked in the same vessel, only one hundred and eighty survived to land at Philadelphia, and of these, many died soon after their arrival.* Rupp and others were exposed at auction, as Redemptioners. Leonard Umberger, near Lebanon, bought him, with whom he served two years and six months, on a farm, now owned by Mr. Lichty, near Lebanon. At the expiration of his term he married the step-daughter of Mr. Umberger,—a Miss Elizabeth Burst, whose father had died in 1741, and her mother, Barbara Burst, the widow of Michael Burst, deceased, had intermarried with Leonard Umberger.

A few years after his marriage, he settled several miles south of Millerstown. In 1771 he sold his tract of land to one Sieg, and moved to Cumberland, and settled among the Irish, who

* Provincial Records, for 1751.

have since been nearly wholly supplanted by the Germans.. He died at an advanced age in 1801.

"In later times, say about the year 1753 to 1756, the Germans having become numerous, and therefore powerful as *makewights* in the political balance, were much noticed in the publications of the day. They were at that period of time, in general, very hearty co-operators with the Quakers or Friends, then in considerable rule in the Assembly. A MSS. pamphlet in the Franklin Library at Philadelphia, supposed to have been written by Samuel Wharton, in 1755, shows his ideas of the passing events, saying, that the party on the side of the Friends derived much of their influence over the Germans, through the aid of C. Sauers, who published a German paper in Germantown, from the time of 1729, and which, being much read by that people, influenced them to the side of the Friends, and hostile to the governor and council. Through this means, says be, they have persuaded them that there was a design to enslave them; to enforce their young men, by a contemplated militia law, to become soldiers, and to load them down with taxes, &c., from such causes, he adds, have they come down in shoals to vote, (of course, many from Berks,) and carrying all before them. To this I may, says Watson, add, that I have heard from the Norris family, that their ancestors in the Assembly were warmly patronized by the Germans in union with Friends. His alarms at this German influence at the polls, and his proposed remedies for the then dreaded evils, as they show the prevalent feelings of his associates in politics, may serve to amuse the present generation. He says the best effects of these successes of the Germans will probably be felt through many generations! Instead of a peaceable, industrious people as before, they are grown now insolent, sullen, and turbulent,—in some counties threatening even the lives of all those who oppose their views, because they are taught to regard government and slavery as one and the same thing. All who are not of their party, they call "*Governor's men*," and themselves, they deem strong enough to make the country their own! Indeed, they come in, in such force, say upwards of 5000 in the last year, I see not but they may soon be able to give us law and language too, or else, by joining the French, eject all the English. That this may be the case, is too much to be feared, for almost to a man they refused to bear arms in the time of the late war, and they say, it is all one to them which king gets the country, as their estates will be equally secure. Indeed it is clear that the French have turned their hopes upon this great body of Germans. They hope to allure them by grants of Ohio lands. To this end, they send their Jesuitical emissaries among them to persuade them over to the Popish religion. In concert with this, the French for so many years have encroached on our province, and now are so near their scheme as to be within two days march of some of our back settlements"—alluding, of course, to the state of the western wilds, overrun by French and Indians just before the arrival of Braddock's forces in Virginia, in 1755.

"The writer (Wharton) imputes their wrong bias in general to their "stubborn genius and ignorance," which he proposes to soften by education—a scheme still suggested as necessary to give the general mass of the inland country Germans right views of public individual interests. To this end, he proposes that faithful Protestant ministers and schoolmasters should be supported among them. That their children should be taught the English tongue; the government in the meantime should suspend their right of voting for members of Assembly; and to incline them the sooner to become English in education and feeling, we should compel them to make all bonds and other legal writings in English, and no newspaper or almanac be circulated among them unless also accompanied by the English thereof."

"Finally," the writer concludes, that "without some such measure I see nothing to prevent this province from falling into the hands of the French."

A scheme to educate the Germans, as the one alluded to, was put on foot about the year 1755, and carried on for several years. The details of this scheme are given at the close of this chapter.

Nine-tenths of the first settlers of Berks county were Germans. They made settlements early, on the east side of the Schuylkill on Mahanatawny creek, and in Oley township. Those who had located themselves in the lower parts of the county, were attacked by some Indians in 1728. In the Colonial Records it is said that at Mahanatawny Ironworks, a skirmish occurred between the inhabitants of that region of country, and

a party of foreign Indians. Intelligence thereof reaching Gov.
Gordon, he, and divers gentlemen, left there on Friday, the
10th of May, 1728, for Mahanatawny. On his return to Philadelphia, he met the council, May 15th, "and acquainted the
board that he had just retured from Mahanatawny, where he
found the people in very great disorder, by the noise of the
skirmish that happened between some of our people and a small
party of Indians; that many of the back inhabitants had quitted
their houses, and seemed under great apprehensions of numbers
of Indians coming to attack them; that several *Palatine families*,* numbering some hundreds of persons, were gathered together at a mill near New Hanover township, in order to defend
themselves, and that there he saw the man who was said to
have been killed by the Indians, but he appeared to be only
slightly wounded in the belly." The report had been, that the
Indians had fired upon some of our people, had wounded several slightly, and one man mortally.† That having examined
several persons there and at Colebrookdale, touching the said
Indians, he understood that they were eleven in number
"painted for war, armed with pistols, guns, &c.,"‡ and had
been in that neighborhood for some days; that they were all
armed, and had a Spanish Indian for their captain, and that
having been rude in several houses, where they forced the people to supply them with victuals and drink; some of our inhabitants, to the number of twenty, were armed with guns and
swords, went in search of the Indians, and coming up with them
they sent two of their number to treat with the captain, who,
instead of receiving them civilly, brandished his sword and
commanded his men to fire, which they did, and wounded two
of ours, who, thereupon, returned their fire; upon which they
saw the captain fall, but he afterwards got up and ran into the
woods after his party, having left his gun and watch coat behind, and that since that time they had been seen no more."§
    From subsequent communications from some of the chiefs, the
skirmish above alluded to, was between some Shawanese Indians on the one part, and the whites on the other."‖ You
have heard, said Gordon, to Sassoonan and others, at a council held at Philadelphia, January 4, 1728, my brethren, that
some Shawanese, about twenty days ago, came from about Pe-

* Col. Rec. vol. 3, p. 330.   † Ibid, 320.   ‡ Ibid, 330
§ Ibid, 321.   ‖ Ibid, 333.

choquealin, armed with guns, pistols and swords, and painted
for war; they fell in amongst some of our inhabitants, and behaved foolishly; our people thought they were strange Indians,
and believed there were much greater numbers behind in the
woods; they met together with arms to defend themselves,
&c."*

From a verbal message to the Governor from Kakow-watchy,
chief of the Shawanese, sent by Nicholas and Schonhoven, two
Indian traders from Pechoqueahin, near Durham Ironworks,
Berks county, it appears, that the Shawanese had heard that
the Flathead Indians, were come into the Province with a design to make war upon the Indians here—Kakow-watchy had
sent eleven of his armed men to enquire into the truth of the
report, with orders to assist our Indians in case that the same
should be true—that their provisions failed them, and that they
were obliged to get provisions from the white inhabitants to
subsist upon; but that the Indians offered no rudeness till the
whites used them ill, and fired upon them.

Kakow-watchy expressed great sorrow for what had happened, and sent assurances, that he has a great love for all his
white brethren, but that one of their number is wounded, and
lost his gun, which he desired might be returned.

The above message was submitted by the Governor to the
Board, who returned Kakow-watchy a message, informing
him, that they considered the conduct of the *eleven* Indians
very imprudent; that they regretted the consequences which
resulted from this imprudence; warning them to be more cautious hereafter in their future behaviour, and that the gun
spoken of should be enquired for.†

As early as 1723, a considerable settlement was made in
Tulpehocken, by Germans, who had emigrated from New
York, on an invitation by Sir William Keith, when he was at
Albany. For a particular account of their emigration, the
reader is referred to the chapter, "*Tulpehocken.*"

Many of the names of the first settlers at Tulpehocken, are
preserved in the Provincial Records. An extract from the
Records, being a petition from those Germans, contains some
of the names.

* Col Rec., vol. 3, p. 336.   † Ibid, 327.

"*To his Excellency, William Keith, Baronet Governor of Pennsylvania, &c., &c., the Honorable Council.*

"The petition of us, the subscribers, being thirty-three families in number, at present inhabiting Tulpehocken creek,

"HUMBLY SHEWETH,

"That your petitioners being natives of Germany, about fifteen years ago, were by the great goodness and royal bounty of her late Majesty, Queen Anne, relieved from the hardships which they then suffered in Europe, and were transported into the colony of New York, where they settled.* But their families increasing, being in that Government confined to the scanty allowance of ten acres of land to each family, whereon they could not well subsist. Your petitioners being informed of the kind reception which their countrymen usually meet with in the Province of Pennsylvania, and hoping they might, with what substance they had, acquire larger settlements in that Province, did last year, (in the spring of 1723,) leave their settlements in New York Government, and came with their families into this province, where, upon their arrival, they applied themselves to His Excellency, the Governor, who, of his great goodness, permitted them to inhabit upon Tulpehaca creek, (being the farthest inhabited part of the province northwest of Philadelphia,) on condition that they should make full satisfaction to the proprietor or his agents, for such lands as should be allotted them, when they were ready to receive the same. And now, your petitioners, understanding that some gentlemen, agents of the proprietor, have ample power to dispose of lands in this province. And we, your petitioners, being willing and ready to purchase, do humbly beseech your Excellency and Council to recommend us to the favorable usage of the proprietor's agents, that upon paying the usual prices for lands at such distance from Philadelphia, we may have sufficient rights and titles made to us for such lands as we shall have occasion to buy, that our children may have some settlement to depend on hereafter, and that by your authority we may be freed from the demands of the Indians of that part of the country, who

---

* Ten vessels or ships with about four thousand Palatines arrived at New York, June 13, 1710.—*Conrad Weiser's private German MSS. Journal.*

pretend a right thereto. And we humbly beg leave to inform
your Excellency and Council, that there are fifty families more
who, if they may be admitted upon the same conditions, are desirous to come and settle with us. We hope for your favorable answer to this our humble request, and as in duty bound
shall ever pray, &c.

Johannes Yans,	Johannes Claes Shaver,
Peter Ritt,	Jo. Hameler Ritt,
Conrad Schitz,	Antonis Shart,
Paltus Unsf,	Johan Peter Pacht,
Toritine Serbo,	Jacham Michael Cricht,
Josap Sab,	Sebastian Pisas,
Jorge Ritt,	Andrew Falborn,

Godfreyt Filler.

☞ The names to the petition being mostly in a deep German hand, could not be read, but by one skilled in German
writing; they are given as above.*

The following is the scheme alluded to in a preceding page
for instructing the Germans:

"A brief history of the rise and progress of the charitable
society, carrying on by a society of noblemen and gentlemen
in London, for the relief and instruction of poor Germans and
their descendants, settled in Pennsylvania, &c., published for
the information of those whom it may concern, by James Hamilton, William Allen, Richard Peters, Benjamin Franklin, and
Conrad Weiser, Esquires, and the Rev. William Smith, Trustees General, appointed for the management of the said charitable scheme.

For several years past, the small number of Reformed Protestant ministers, settled among the German emigrants in Pennsylvania, and finding the harvest great, but the laborers few,
have been deeply affected with a true Christian concern, for
the welfare of their distressed countrymen, and the salvation of
their precious souls. In consequence of this, they have from
time to time, in the most solemn and moving manner, entreated
the churches of Holland, to commisserate their unhappy fellow
Christians, who mourn under the deepest affliction, being settled in a remote corner of the world, where the light of the gos-

* Col. Rec., vol. 3, p. 341.

pel has but lately reached, and where they are very much destitute of the means of knowledge and salvation.

The churches of Holland, being accordingly moved with
friendly compassion, did, from time to time, contribute to the
support of religion in these remote parts. But in the year
1751, a very moving representation of their state having been
made by a person, whose unwearied labors for the benefit of
his dear countrymen have been for some years conspicuous, the
states of Holland aud West Frisland, granted 2000 gilders *per
annum*, for five years, from that time, to be applied towards the
instruction of the said Germans and their children, in Pennsylvania. A considerable sum was also collected in the city of
Amsterdam, and elsewhere, and upon a motion made by the
same zealous person, the Rev. Mr. Thomson* was commis-
sioned by the Synod of Holland, and Classis of Amsterdam, to
solicit the friendly assistance of the churches of England and
Scotland.

When Mr. Thomson arrived in Great Britain, he found the
readiest encouragement among persons of the first rank, both in
church and State. In this peculiar glory of the British government, equally to consult the happiness of all who live under
it, however remote, wherever born, or of whatsoever denomination. Wicked and inhuman tyrants, whose ambition is to rule
over slaves, find it their interest to keep the people ignorant.
But, in a virtuous and free government, like that of Great Britain, the case is far otherwise. By its very nature and spirit,
it desires every member of the community enlightened with
useful knowledge, and especially the knowledge of the blessed
gospel, which contains the best and most powerful motives for
making good subjects, as well as good men. Considered in
this light, Mr. Thomson's design could not fail to be encouraged in our mother country, since it was evidently calculated
to save a multitude of most industrious people from the gloom
of ignorance, and qualify them for the enjoyment of all those
privileges, to which it is now their good fortnne to be admitted, in common with the happy subjects of a free Protestant
government.

Mr. Thomson having thus made his business known in England, and prepared the way for encouragement there, he, in the

* Mr. T. is a minister of one of the English churches in Amsterdam, and
a member of said Synod and Classis.

meantime, went down to Scotland; and, himself being known in that country, he represented the case to the General Assembly of the church, then sitting at Edinburgh, upon which a national collection was made, amounting to upwards of £1200 sterling. Such an instance of generosity is one out of many, to show how ready that church has always been to contribute towards the advancement of *Truth, Virtue, and Freedom*.

Mr. Thomson, upon his return from Scotland, found that his pastoral duty called him back to Holland. He saw likewise that it would be absolutely necessary to have some person in London, not only to manage the monies already collected, but also to solicit and receive the contributions of the rich and the benevolent in England, where nothing had yet been collected, and where much might be hoped for. With this view, he begged a certain number of noblemen* and gentlemen, of the first rank, to take the management of the design upon themselves.

This proposal was readily agreed to by those noble and worthy persons. They were truly concerned to find that there were any of their fellow subjects, in any part of the British dominions, not fully provided with the means of knowledge and salvation. They considered it a matter of the greatest importance to the cause of Christianity in general, and the protestant interest in particular, not to neglect such a vast body of useful people, situated in a dark and barren region, with almost none to instruct them, or their helpless children, who are coming forward in the world in multitudes, and exposed an easy prey to the total ignorance of their savage neighbors on the one hand, and the corruption of our Jesuitical enemies, on whom they border, on the other hand; and of whom there are always, perhaps, too many mixed among them. Moved by these interesting considerations, the said noblemen and gentlemen, with a consideration peculiar to great and generous souls, did accord-

---

* The first members of this society were as follows, though we believe several are added this winter, (1775,) whose names have not yet been transmitted to us.

The Right Hon. Earl of Shaftesbury, Earl of Morton, Earl of Finlater, and Lord Willoughby, of Parham. Sir Luke Schaub, and Sir Joshua Van Neck, Paronets. Mr Commission Vernon, Mr. Chitly, and Mr. Fluddyer, Aldermen of London John Fance, Robert Furguson, and Nathaniel Paice, Esqrs., of London. Rev Benjamin Avory, L. L. D, Rev. Thomas Birth, D. D., Rev. Mr. Casper Wetstein, Rev. Mr. David Thomson, and Rev. Samuel Chandler, Secretary.

ingly take the good design into their immediate protection, and formed themselves into a society for the effectual management of it.

The first thing said society did, was to agree to a liberal subscription among themselves; and, upon laying the case before the king, His Majesty, like a true father of his people, granted £1000 towards it. Her Royal Highness, the Princess Dowager of Wales, granted £100; and the honorable proprietors of this province, willing to concur in every design for the ease and welfare of their people, generously engaged to give a considerable sum yearly for promoting the most essential part of the undertaking. From such a fair beginning, and from some hopes they reasonably entertain of a more public nature, the honorable doubt not of their being able to complete such a fund as may effectually answer their pious design, in time coming. In the meantime they have come to the following general resolutions, with regard to the management of the whole.

I. To assist the people in the encouragement of pious and industrious protestant ministers that are, or shall be regularly ordained and settled among the said Germans, or their descendants, in America; beginning first in Pennsylvania, where the want of ministers is greatest, and proceeding to the neighboring British colonies, as they shall be enabled by an increase of their funds.

II. To establish some charitable schools for the pious education of German youths of all denominations, as well as those English youths who may reside among them. Now, as a religious education of youth, while the tender mind is yet open to every impression, is the most effectual means of making a people *wise, virtuous, and happy,* the honorable society have declared that they have this part of their design, in a particular manner, at heart; it being chiefly from the care that shall be taken of the rising generation, that they expect the success of their whole undertaking.

III. The said honorable society, considering that they reside at too great a distance, either to know what ministers deserve their encouragement, or what places are most convenient to fix the schools in,—and as they would neither bestow their bounty on any who do not deserve it; therefore they have devolved the general execution of the whole upon us, under the name of *Trustees General,* for the management of their charity among the German emigrants in America.   And as our residence is in this province, where the chief body is settled, and where we may acquaint them with the circumstances of the people, the generous society hope that we cannot be imposed upon, or deceived, in the direction or application of their excellent charity.

IV. And lastly, considering that our engagements in other matters, would not permit us personally to consult with the people in the country, nor to visit the schools as often as it might be necessary for their success, the honorable society have, out of their true fatherly care, appointed the Rev. Mr. Schlatter, to act under our direction, as *Visitor* or *Supervisor* of the schools, knowing that he has already taken incredible pains in this whole affair, and being acquainted with the people in all parts of the country, can converse with them on the spot, and bring us the best advices from time to time, concerning the measures fit to be taken.

This is a brief history of the rise and progress of this noble charity, till it was committed to our management, under which we hope it shall be so conducted, as fully to answer the expectation of the worthy society, and give all reasonable satisfaction to the parties for whose benefit it is intended.   We shall spare no pains to inform ourselves of the wants and circumstances of the people; as will appear by the following plan which we have concerted for the general examination of our trust, leaving room to alter or amend it, as circumstances shall require, and time discover defects in it.

With regard to that part of the society's design which proposes the encouragement of pious protestant ministers, we shall impartially proportion the monies set apart for this purpose according to the instruction of the said society; as soon as such ministers shall put it in our power so to do, by making their labors and circumstances known to us, either by their own personal application, or by means of Mr. Schlatter, or any other creditable person.

As to the important article of establishing schools, the following general plan is proposed, which may be from time to time, improved or perfected.

1st. It is intended that every school to be opened upon this charity, shall be equally to the benefit of protestant youth of all denominations; and therefore the education will be in such things as are generally useful to advance industry and true godliness. The youth will be instructed in both the English and German languages; likewise in writing, keeping of common accounts, singing of Psalms, and the true principles of the holy protestant religion, in the same manner as the fathers of those Germans were instructed, at the schools in those countries from which they came.·

2dly. As it may be of great service to religion and industry, to have some schools for girls, also, we shall use our endeavors with the honorable society, to have some few school mistresses encouraged, to teach reading, and the use of the needle. And though this was no part of the original design, yet as the society have nothing but the general good of all at heart, we doubt not they will extend their benefaction for this charitable purpose also.

3dly. That all may be induced, in their early youth, to seek the knowledge and love of God, in that manner which is most agreeable to their own consciences, the children of all protestant denominations, English and Dutch, (German) shall be instructed in catechism of sound doctrine, which is approved of and used by their own parents and ministers. All unreasonable sort of compulsion and partiality is directly opposite to the design and spirit of this *charity*, which is generously undertaken to promote useful knowledge, true religion, public peace, and Christian love, among all ranks and denominations.

4thly. For the use of the schools, the several catechisms that are now taught among the Calvinists, Lutherans, and other protestant denominations, will be printed in English and Dutch, (German) and distributed among the poor, together with some other good books, at the expense of the society.

5thly. In order that all parents may be certain of having justice done to their children, the immediate care and inspection of every school will be committed to a certain number of sober and respectable persons, living near the place where every such school shall be fixed. These persons will be denominated *Assistant or Deputy Trustees;* and it will be their business, monthly or quarterly, to visit that particular school for which they are appointed, and see that both master and scholars do their duty. It will also be their business to send an account of the state and progress of the schools, at every such visitation, to us as Trustees General. These accounts we shall transmit from Philadelphia to the society in London; and the society will from time to time, be enabled, by these means, to lay the state of the whole schools before the public; and thus charitable and well disposed people, both in Great Britain and Holland, seeing the good use that has been made of their former contributions, will be inclined to give still more and more for so glorious and benevolent an undertaking.

This method cannot fail to be of great advantage to the schools, since the Deputy Trustees, being part of the very people for whom the work is undertaken, and having their own children at the same schools, they must have an interest in the reputation of them, and do all in their power to advance good education in them. Besides this, being always near at hand, they can advise and encourage the master, and help him over any difficulties he may meet with.

But, 6thly. As the keeping up a spirit of emulation among the youth is the life of all schools, therefore, that we may leave as little room as possible for that remissness, which sometimes hurts charities of this nature, we shall, as far as our situation will permit, have a personal regard to the execution of the whole. As the Assistant Trustees may after want our advice in removing difficulties and making new regulations, we shall so contrive it, that Mr. Schlatter shall be present with them at their quarterly meetings, to consult with them, and concert the proper measures to be taken. Besides this, we shall have one general visitation of the whole schools every year, at which one or more of us shall endeavor to be present. On these occasions, such regulations shall be made, as may be wanted; and careful inquiry will be made whether any parents think themselves injured, by any unjust exclusion of their children from an equal benefit of the common charity, or by the partiality of the masters or otherwise. At such visitations, books will be given as rewards and encouragement, to the diligent and deserving scholars. The masters will likewise have proper marks of esteem shown them in proportion to their fidelity and industry in the discharge of their office.

7thly. With regard to the number of schools to be opened, that will depend partly on the encouragement given by the people themselves, and partly on the increase of the society's funds. A considerable number of places are proposed to fix schools in; but none are yet absolutely determined upon, but New Hanover, New Providence, and Reading.* These places were first fixed upon because the people of all persuasions, Lutherans, Calvinists, and other Protestants, moved with a pious and fatherly concern for the illiterate state of their helpless children, did, with true Christian harmony, present their petitions, praying that their numerous children of all denominations in these parts, might be made the common object of the intended charity. And for this benevolent purpose, they did further agree to offer school houses in which their children might be instructed together, as dear fellow Christians, redeemed by the same common Lord and Saviour, and travelling to the same heavenly country, through this valley of tears, notwithstanding they may sometimes take roads a little different in points of smaller moment.

This striking example of 'unanimity and good agreement among all denominations, we hope, will be imitated by those who shall afterwards apply to us for fixing schools among them; since it is only upon the aforesaid generous plan for the common benefit of all, that we find ourselves empowered to institute such schools. But while the petitions are agreeable to this, our plan, as now explained, they will not be overlooked, as long as the funds continue. And if the petitioners shall recommend school masters, as was the case at New Hanover, New Providence, and Reading, such school masters will have the preference, provided they are men of sufficient probity and knowledge, agreeable to all parties, and acquainted with both the English and Dutch (German) languages, or willing to learn either of these languages which they may not then be perfectly acquainted with. .

These are essential qualifications; and unless the generous society had made provision for teaching English as well as Dutch, (German) it would not have answered their benevolent design, which is to qualify the Germans for all the advantages of native English subjects. But this could not have been done,

---

* Since the original publication, petitions have been sent to the Trustees General, from Upper Solfort, from Vincent township, in Chester county, from the borough of Lancaster, from Tulpehocken, and several other places, all which will be considered as soon as possible. Feb. 25, 1755.—*Penna. Gazette.*

NOTE.—Schools were also established in 1756, besides the places mentioned, at Lancaster, York, and several other places.

without giving them an opportunity of learning English, by speaking of which they may expect to rise to places of profit and honor in the country. They will likewise be thereby enabled to buy or sell to the greater advantage in our markets, to understand their own causes in courts of justice, where pleadings are in English, to know what is doing in the country around them, and, in a word, to judge and act entirely for themselves without being obliged to take things upon the word of others, whose interest it may be to deceivepand mislead them.

We have only further to add, that having thus published, in our names, a true and faithful account of the rise and progress of this excellent charity, down to the present time, we hope it will candidly be received as such, and prevent many wrong conjectures and insinuations, that might otherwise have been made, if we had not given this genuine and necessary information concerning it. From the foregoing plan it plainly appears, that as the chief management is in the people themselves, it must be entirely their own faults, if these schools do not become the greatest blessing to many generations, that ever was proposed in this country. Such, and so benevolent are the designs of this new society!

And surely, now, we may be permitted in their name, to address you, countrymen and fellow Christians, for whose benefit the great work is undertaken! We cannot but entreat you to consider, of what importance such a scheme must be to you, and your children after you. We are unwilling to believe that there are any persons, who do not heartily wish success to a design so pious and benevolent. But, if, unhappily for themselves, there should be any such among us, we are bound in charity to suppose they have never yet reflected that, whilst they indulge such wishes, they are in fact acting a part, plainly repugnant to the interests of liberty, true religion, and even of human nature.

Mankind in general are, perhaps, scarcely raised more, by their nature, above the brutes, than a man *well instructed* above the man of no knowledge or education; and whoever strives to keep a people in ignorance, must certainly harbor notions or designs that are unfavorable, either to their civil or religious liberty. For whilst a people are incapable of knowing their own interests, or judging for themselves, they cannot be governed by free principles, or by their own choice; and though they should not be immediate slaves of the government under which they live, yet they must be slaves or dupes to those whose councils they are obliged to have recourse to, and follow blindly on all occasions, which is the most dishonorable species of slavery.

But on the other hand, a design for instructing a people, and adorning the minds of their children with useful knowledge, can carry nothing in it but what is friendly to liberty, and auspicious to all the most sacred interests of mankind.

Were it otherwise, why are so many of the greatest and best men, both of the British and the German nations, engaged in the undertaking? Why have they, as it were, stooped from their high spheres, and even condescended to beg from house to house, in order to promote it! Is not all this done with the glorious intention of relieving from distressful ignorance that was like to fall upon you? Is it not done with a view to call you up to all the advantages of free and enlightened subjects, capable of thinking and acting for yourselves? And shall they call you in vain? God forbid! If by any infatuation, you should neglect the means of knowledge and eternal happiness, now offered you, think seriously what must be the consequence. You will be accountable in the sight of Almighty God, not only for your own sad negligence, but for all that misery and slavery, which you may thereby entail upon your hapless offspring to the latest generations. Your very names will be held in abhorrence by your own children, if, for the want of instruction, their privileges should either be abridged here, or they should fall a prey to the error and slavery of our restless enemies.

But on the contrary, if proper instruction are begun now, and constantly carried on among you, no design can ever be hatched against your religion or liberties, but what you shall quickly be able to discover and defeat. All the arts of your enemies will be of no avail to sever you from your true interests, as men and as protestants. You shall know how to make the true use of all your noble privileges, and instead of moving in a dry and barren land, where no water is, you and your posterity shall flourish from age to age, in all that is valuable in human life. A barren region shall be turned into a fruitful country, and a thirsty land into pools of water. The wilderness and solitary place shall be glad through you, and the desert shall rejoice and blossom as the rose. Isa. 35.

'That you may soon be placed in these happy circumstances, shall be our continual endeavor, as it is our sincere prayer. But if ever you hope to be so, or to transmit the glorious privileges of Protestants and Freemen to your posterity, we must observe, that in this time of danger, (when a popish enemy has advanced far into our country, even to your very doors,) it becomes you to be extremely jealous for your safety. It becomes you to exert yourselves for the calm enjoyment of that religion, for the sake of which you crossed the stormy occean, and encountered the horrors of the desert. It becomes you to secure your children the full and free possession of these fair seats, which your own hands have formed out of the vast wilderness. Whatever unfavorable notions you may apprehend the government at home may have fallen into concerning your conduct, on account of the great distance you may now be sure, that while you do your duty as good subjects, we shall at all times present you in the most impartial light to the honorable society of London; and as this Society consists of some of the best and greatest men of the English nation, who have generously taken you and all your concerns under their protection, they will always be glad to receive you in kind and acceptable terms, to the continuance of our most gracious Sovereign.

By order, and in behalf the Trustees General.

WILLIAM SMITH, Secretary.

Philadelphia, Feb. 25, 1755.

10

CHAPTER VII.

THE WELSH.

In the very incipient stage of the first settlements made in the Province, many Welshmen arrived in Pennsylvania. They were of sterling worth and of a most excellent character. They were, says a certain writer, of the last century, "A hardy, active, hospitable and kind-hearted people—only a little hasty and quarrelsome."

Among the most influential, at early day, was THOMAS LLOYD, one of Penn's Deputy Governors. He died in 1694, aged fifty-four years. His father, says Proud, was a person of fortune, rank and esteem; of an ancient family and estate, called Dolobran, in the North of Wales. THOMAS LLOYD, the late Deputy Governor, was educated in the best schools; from which he was removed to the University at Oxford; where, it is said he attained considerable proficiency; and being endowed with good natural parts, and an amiable disposition of mind, he attracted the regard and esteem of persons of rank and figure, and was afterwards in the way of considerable preferment in the world; but being of a sober and religious way of thinking, he joined with the Quakers, and renounced all worldly considerations, for that peace of mind, and real mortal felicity, which he believed to be the effect of true religion; and become a highly esteemed preacher in that Society. In consequence of which, having suffered much unmerited reproach, persecution and loss of property, in his native country, he afterwards removed to Pennsylvania, among the first or early settlers, and was one of William Penn's most intimate friends. He was mostly one of the principal persons in the government, from his first arrival, and of very great service in the public affairs."*

The Welsh had early purchased of William Penn, in England, forty thousand acres of land, and settled on the west side of the Schuylkill river. Only a few years elapsed when their number was considerably increased—it was sufficiently augmented, that they had settled, before the year 1692, not less than six townships in Chester county.

The custom of the Welsh, and that of the Swiss and Palatins, in settling parts of Pennsylvania, was similar. They would either purchase extensive tracts in England, to settle many of their friends in one body, as did the Menonites in Pequea valley in 1709 and 1710; or like the Frankfort company in 1686, or as they did, as just alluded to above; or they did in some instances, send persons across the Atlantic, to take up land for them, and make some preparation for the reception of their friends and families.

Among the Welsh, who thus acted as pioneers, was the well known Rowland Ellis, who sent over Thomas Owen and family to commence a settlement. No sooner had Owen made improvement, in which he spent a few years, when Ellis and one hundred other Welsh passengers left Wales, and embarked for America in 1686.

In 1698 many other Welsh families arrived, among whom were William Jones, Thomas Evans, Robert Evans, Owen Evans, Cadwallader, Evans, Hugh Griffith, Edward Foulke, John Humphrey, Robert Jones, and others, who purchased ten thousand acres of land from Robert Turner, in Guinedd township, Chester county.

Not many years afterward, the Welsh extended their settlements into the present borders of Berks county; principally in the townships of Cærnarvon, Brecknock, and Cumru. For the names of the first settlers, the reader is referred to the description of the three named townships.

They had settled in the midst of the Indians. It appears from the Colonial Records, and the public records at West Chester, that in 1728, two brothers, Welshmen, cruelly murdered some Indians on the frontiers. It is said, the brothers appear to have been maddened with sheer fright, and killed the first unoffending Indians they met.* The affray took place on or near the Cacoosing, or Cucussea creek; as appears from the following extract:

In 1728, two individuals, named John and Walter Winters, without any provocation given, cruelly murdered an Indian man and two women, who were of the friendly natives. They were, says Governor Gordon, most inhumanly knocked on the

* Watson.

head, by three or four of our people, and this without any pro--
vocation from the sufferers, that I could possibly learn.   The
Governor being at this time at Maxatany, immediately on hearing the melancholy news, by an express from Samuel Nutt,.
Esq., repaired to Cucussea, and on his arrival, caused a "Hue
and Cry" to be issued, for the apprehension of the perpetra-
tors; three of whom were taken, and committed to Chester jail,
and put in irons.   The Governor likewise caused search to be
be made for the dead bodies; the two murdered women were
found while he was there, who, by his order, were laid in a
grave, covered with shirts and strowds, and buried.   On further
search the body of the Indian man was found and buried.[*]

Before the Governor left, he called in other friendly Indians,
who were not far from the neighborhood, to acquaint them of
the unhappy accident—using his utmost endeavor to prevent
the worst impressions, or if such had already been made, to
remove them— inviting them to attend a treaty, then contemplated, to be held at Conestogue in the course of a few weeks.

The descendants of the first Welsh settlers in the county,
are numerous and respectable.   Little or no Welsh is spoken
by them at present.   A few printed specimens of the Welsh
language are presented; the first, the Lord's prayer, the second the one hundred and thirty-fourth Psalm.   Copied from
a London edition of 1718, in the possession of GEORGE FORD,
Esq., Lancaster, Pa.

Ein Tad yr hwn yn y nefoedd, Sancteiddier dy Enw. Deled
dy deyrnas.   Gwncler dy ewyllys, megis yn y nef, *felly* ar y
ddaear hefyd.   Dyro i ni heddyw ein bara beunyddiol.   A
madden i ni ein dyledion, fel y maddeuwn ninnau i'n dyledwyr.
Ac nacarwain ni i brofedigaeth, eithr gwared ni rhagdrwg.
Canys eiddot ti yw 'r deyrnas, a'r nearth, a'r gogoniant, yn
oes oesoedd.   Amen.

PSALM CXXXIV.

Wele holl weision Arglwydd nef,
   bendi thiwch ef, lle 'r ydych
Yn feyfyll yn nhy Dduw y nos,
   ai gyntedd diddos trefn-wych.

[*] Col. Rec., III, 320.

Dyrchhefwch chwi eich dwylo glan
  yn ei gysserg-lan annedd:
A bendithiwch a chalon rwydd,
  yr Arglwydd yn gyfanneddi.

Yr Arglwydd, a'i ddeheulaw gref
  hwn a wnaeth Nef a daear,
A roddo ei fendito a'i ras,
  i Seion ddinas howddgar.

10*

CHAPTER VIII.

THE IRISH.

The Irish emigrants, says Watson, did not begin to come to Pennsylvania till about the year 1719. Those which did come were generally from the north of Ireland. Such as come out first, generally settled at, and near the disputed Maryland line. James Logan, writing of them to the Proprietaries, in 1724, says, they have generally taken up the southern lands, (meaning in Lancaster, towards the Maryland line,) and as they rarely approached him to propose to purchase, he calls them bold and indigent strangers, saying as their excuse, when challenged for titles, that we had solicited for colonists, and they had come accordingly. They were, however, understood to be a tolerated class, exempt from rents by an ordinance of 1720, in consideration of their being a frontier people, forming a kind of cordon of defence, if needful. They were soon called bad neighbors to the Indians, treating them disdainfully, and finally were the same race who committed the outrages called Paxtang Massacre. The general ideas are found in the Logan MSS. collection. Some of the data are as follows:

"In 1725, James Logan states, there that are so many as one hundred thousand acres of land, possessed by persons, (including Germans,) who resolutely set down and improved it without any right to it, and he is much at a loss to determine how to dispossess them.

"In 1729, he expresses himself glad to find that the Parliament is about to take measures to prevent the too free emigration to this country. In the meantime the Assembly had laid a restraining tax of twenty shillings a head for every servant arriving; but even this was evaded in the case of the arrival of a ship from Dublin, with one hundred papists and convicts, by landing them at Burlington. It looks, says he, as if Ireland is to send all her inhabitants hither, for last week, not less than six ships arrived, and every day two or three arrive also. The common fear is, that if they continue to come, they will make themselves proprietors of the province. It is strange, says he, that they thus crowd where they are not wanted. But besides convicts are imported thither.* The Indians themselves are alarmed at the swarms of strangers, and we are afraid of a breach between them—for the Irish are very rough to them.

"In 1730, he writes and complains of the Scotch Irish, in an audacious and disorderly manner, possessing themselves of the whole of Conestoga manor, of fifteen thousand acres, being the best land in the country. In doing this by force, they alleged that it was against the laws of God and nature, that so much land should be idle, while so many Christians wanted it to labor on, and to raise their bread, &c. The Paxtang boys were great sticklers for religion and scripture quotations against "the heathen." They were, however, dispossessed by the Sheriff and his *posse,* and their cabins, to the number of thirty, were burnt. This necessary violence was, perhaps, remembered with indignation; for only twenty-five years afterwards, the Paxtang massacre began by killing the Christian unoffending Indians found in Conestoga. The Irish were generally settled at Donegal."

But few Scotch Irish settled within the present limits of Berks county. A respectable number settled in East Hanover township, Lancaster county, which is now partly included within the bounds of Lebanon county. For the names of the first Irish settlers, the reader is referred to the history of the towhship in the western part of Lebanon county. The Irish who settled here were Presbyterians.

There are still some of the descendants of this "generous, quick-witted, hospitable, and cheerful people," occupying the farms first owned by their ancestors. The Irish language which many of the first settlers spoke, is no longer spoken. To give the reader a specimen of the printed language of the sons of Erin, the writer has copied the Lord's prayer from Gr. Daniel's edition of an Irish Bible, printed in 1602.

Air nathir ataigh air nin. Nahz fat hanimti. Tigiuh

---

* Augustus Gun, of Cork, advertised in the Philadelphia papers, that he had powers from the Mayor of Cork, for many years, to procure servants. for America

da riathiate.   Deantur da hoilamhuoil Air nimh agis air
thalambi.   Air naran laidthuil tabhair dhuin a niomb.   Agis
math duin dairf, biacha ammnil Agis mathum vid dar feu-
thunuim.   Agis na trilaic astoch sin anau sen.   Ac sar sino
ole.   Amen.

CHAPTER IX.

ERECTION OF BERKS COUNTY.

The lands on the Tulpehocken were still owned by the Indians till 1732–'33, when Thomas Penn purchased them, which more effectually opened the door to emigrants into that part of the province within the limits of Berks and Lebanon. Germans and others, especially the former, who were already seated, sent for their relatives and kindred; and they in turn, on their arrival here, enticed others—till several thousand had settled in various parts on the Schuylkill, Tulpehocken, and other places—till every glen, vale, hill, and mountain, was more or less settled—and under such circumstances the inhabitants felt the want of a new county, and were led to petition the Assembly for privileges which Penn and successors had awarded. For, William Penn, shortly after his arrival, in 1682, established several counties, namely, Philadelphia, Bucks, and Chester. Philadelphia county then extended indefinitely towards the northwest, bounded on the east by Bucks, and on the west by the Schuylkill, which separated it from Chester county, which included, at that time, Delaware county, and all the territory, except a small portion now within the limits of Philadelphia county, south-west of the Schuylkill, and extended to the extreme limits of the province, north, west, and south. In 1729, Chester was reduced, by erecting Lancaster county out of it. In 1749, York county was erected, and in 1750, Cumberland was established. Berks was erected, March 11th, 1752.

At the time of erecting Berks county, its population was from six to eight thousand. As it may be interesting to the reader, a copy of the petition to the Assembly, and sundry papers, have been copied, and are inserted.

A petition from a considerable number of the inhabitants of READINGTOWN, upon Schuylkill, was presented to the house, February 4th, 1752, and read, setting forth, that they had settled in the said town, expecting that it would be a great place of trade and business, and had put themselves to vast expense in building and removing thither with their families,

several of whom left tolerable good plantations; that though
the said town had not above one house in it about two years
ago, (1750,) yet it now consists of one hundred and thirty
dwelling houses, besides forty-one stables, and other out-houses,
and that there are one hundred and sixty families, consisting
of three hundred and seventy-eight persons settled therein; that
they have good reason to believe that in another summer they
will be much increased, as the chief part of the province that
can be settled is already taken up, and the settling of the
town will be of great benefit to tradesmen and others, who are
not able to purchase tracts of land to live on; that they humbly conceived it to be their interest, to the honorable proprietaries, as well as themselves, and that unless this house will be
pleased to erect part of the counties of Philadelphia, Chester,
and Lancaster, into a separate county, they shall be entirely
disappointed of their expectations, notwithstanding all the cost
and trouble they have been at; that, therefore, they pray this
house would take their case into consideration, and grant them
relief, by erecting such parts of said counties, as they shall
think most proper, into a new county, with the same privileges
that the other counties of this province enjoy; and that the
seat of judicature be fixed within the said town of Reading.*

Another petition was presented, February 5, 1752, from
which the following extract is presented: "They find the
causes of their complaint still growing, they humbly beg leave
further to represent, that they are settled at a very great distance from the place of judicature, many of them not less than
one hundred miles, which is a real hardship upon those who are
so unhappy as to be sued for debts, their charges in long jour-
neys, and sometimes in severe weather, with the officer's fees,
amounting to near as much, if not more, than the debts; that
the hardships on jurymen, constables, and in being obliged to
attend when required, is also very great; that now there is a
new town laid out by the proprietaries' order, within fifteen
perches of the division line between Philadelphia and Lancaster counties, and above one hundred and thirty houses, and near
as many families living therein, it is very easy for rogues and
others to escape justice by crossing Schuylkill, which has already been their practice for some years; that though their

* Votes of Assembly, vol. iv., p. 204.

grievances were laid before the Assembly some years past,* were not redressed, because of other weighty affairs being at that time under consideration; yet the prayer of their petition was thought reasonable, and the number of petitioners being since doubled by the increase of the back inhabitants, they therefore pray, that this house would grant relief in the premises by erecting them into a separate county, bounded, as to the wisdom of this house shall seem best.†

The prayer of the petitioners was granted by the.passing of act, March 11th, 1752,‡ directing the erection of a county out of parts of Philadelphia,§ Chester,|| and Lancaster counties.¶

"Whereas a great number of the back inhabitants of the county of Philadelphia, and the adjacent parts of Chester and Lancaster, by their petition, have humbly represented to the Governor and Assembly of this province, their remote situation from their respective county towns, where the courts of justice are held, and public offices kept, whereby they are frequently put to extraordinary expense of money, and loss of time, in their long journies thither, as parties in cases, witnesses, jurymen, &c. For remedying which inconveniences, and relief of the inhabitants in those remote parts in the premises, be it enacted by the Hon. James Hamilton, Esq., Lieutenant Governor, under the Hon. Thomas Penn and Richard Penn, true and absolute proprietaries of the province of Pennsylvania, and of the counties of New Castle, Kent and Sussex, upon Delaware, by and with the advice and consent of the representatives of the freemen of the said province, in general assembly met, and by the authority of the same—That all and singular the lands lying within the province of Pennsylvania aforesaid, within the limtis and bounds as hereinafter described, be erected into a county, and the same are hereby erected into a county, named, and henceforth to be called BERKS ; bounded as follows : by a line, at the distance of ten superficial miles south-west from

* 1739–'40. Feb. 4, a petition signed by Conrad Weiser, John Davis, James Lewis, and others, was presented.
† Votes of Assembly, vol 4, p. 205.
‡ A, vol. iii , p. 227 of the Rolls at Harrisburg.
§ Alsace, Exeter, Amity, Allimengle or Albany, Oley, Colebrookdale, and Hereford townships, then organized, were parts of Philadelphia county
|| Coventry and part of Nantmill, now Union, part of Chester county.
¶ Cærnarvon, Robeson, Heidelberg, Bethel, Tulpehocken, Cumru, and Bern, then organized part of Lancaster county.

the western bank of the river Schuylkill, opposite to the mouth of a creek called *Monocasy,** to the run north north-west to the extremity of the province, and south-east, until it shall intersect the line of Chester county, then on one straight line of McCall's manor, then along the said line to the extremity thereof, and continuing the same course, to the line dividing Philadelphia and Bucks counties, then along the said line northwest, to the extent of the county aforesaid.

That it shall and may be lawful to and for Anthony Lee, Francis Parvin, William Mangridge, William Bird and Joseph Millard, or any three of them to purchase and take assurance to them and their heirs, of a piece of land, situate in some convenient place in the town of *Reading*, in trust, and for the use of the inhabitants of said county, and thereon to erect and build a court house and prison, sufficient to accommodate the public service of the said county, and for the ease and conveniency of the inhabitants." For which purpose three hundreds pounds were authorized to be assessed and levied, for purchasing land, and finishing the court house and prison.

By the same act, Edward Scull of Philadelphia county, Benjamin Lightfoot of Chester county, and Thomas Cookson of Lancaster county, were appointed to run, mark out and distinguish the boundary line between the said counties of Philadelphia, Chester, Lancaster, and of Berks.

An act was passed, February 18, 1769, appointing William McClay, William Scull, and John Biddle, jr., to settle and fix the boundary line dividing the counties of Lancaster, Berks, and Cumberland. The former commissioners, Edward Scull, Benjamin Lightfoot, and Thomas Cookson, not having continued said line further than the settlement at that time (1752) made. And, whereas, many were then (1769) settled, and new settlements then making beyond the said lines of 1752, and disputes having then already risen, and others were likely to arise, concerning the limits and bounds of the said counties of Lancaster, Cumberland, Berks, and Northampton; by reason of the boundary lines of 1752, not being completed, the act of February 18, 1769, authorized and required Messrs. McClay, Scull, and Biddle, and enjoined it that they should, within the space of nine months from the passage of the act, "to assemble themselves together, and to extend, run, and mark out, by

* Feb. 18, 1769, an act was passed to settle this line.

actual survey, the boundary lines between the said counties of Lancaster, Cumberland, and Berks, and between the county of Berks and that of Northampton, by continuing the said due north-west course, from the south-east ends of the lines already run between the said counties respectively, as far as the lands lately purchased by the honorable, the proprietaries of this province from the Indians, do extend; and that the costs, charges, and expenses of running, surveying, and marking out the said line, so far as the same shall run between the said counties of Berks and Lancaster—and that the costs, charges, and expenses of running the said line, so far as the same shall extend between the said counties of Cumberland and Berks, shall be paid equally between the said counties of Berks and Cumberland."

Berks, since its organization or erection in 1752, has been reduced by annexation of a part to the county of Northumberland, March 21, 1772, which was erected out of parts of Lancaster, Cumberland, Berks, Bedford, and Northampton; and by the erection of Schuylkill, March 1, 1811—the townships of Brunswick, Schuylkill, Manheim, Norwegian, Upper and Lower Mahantango, and Pine Grove, were a part of Berks county. The average length of Berks county, at present, is about thirty-two miles, and in breadth not exceeding twenty-eight; containing an area of nine hundred and twenty-seven square miles. The present population may exceed seventy thousand.

As above stated, Berks county was formed out of Philadelphia, Chester, and Lancaster counties. All on the east side of the Schuylkill was, at the erection of Berks, part of Philadelphia, and was divided into the following townships: Alsace, Exeter, Amity, Allimengle or Albany, Oley, and Colebrookdale. The southern portion of Berks was part of Chester, and divided into two townships, Coventry and Nantmill; parts of each of these townships are now included in Union township, organized since the erection of the county. The west and north-west portion was part of Lancaster, and divided into the following townships, namely: Cærnarvon, Robeson, Tulpehocken, Heidelberg, Bethel, Tulpehocken, Cumru, and Bern.

11

CHAPTER X.

In giving the history, extent, &c., of the townships as now
organized, each will be given as bounded at present; but in
giving the names of the first settlers, these will be introduced,
speaking of the townships as they were bounded at, or soon
after the organization of the county.

ALBANY TOWNSHIP.

Albany township, lying a little east of due north from Reading, is one of the most northern townships in the county, and
on account of its partial barrenness, was known for many years
by the name of "*Allemeangel*"—*All-wants.* It was, however,
settled at a comparatively early period. In 1741, as it was
then bounded, it contained thirty-seven taxables, and in 1758,
it contained eighty-five taxables. The first settlers were Germans, as will appear from the following list of names, including
those who resided therein prior to 1756.
Valentine Brobst, Martin Brobst, Henry Ritter, Michael
Brobst, Christian Hechter, Philip Stambach, Arnold Bittich,
John Kunstler, George Klingerman, William Stampf, Cornelius
Dries, Tobias Stabelton, Frantz Bety, Andreas Hagenbuch,
John Miller, Martin Kemp, Peter Knoper, Jacob Wirth, Jacob
Gerhardt, Heinrich Reichelsderfer, George Trump, Johannes
Hein, John Wilt, Jacob Pohr, Jacob Kuntz, Simon Uries, Val-
entine Petri, George Lili, John Steygerwald, John Uries, Philip
Kugler, John Kluck, Michael Maurer, Christian Heinrich, An-
tony Adam, Nicholas Wenner, Nicholas Muldenberger, Chris-
tian Linseberger, Jacob Bachert, Nicholas Bachert, Henry
Zimmerman, George Stimperd, George Kunckell, Jacob Stamm,
John Bricker, Jacob Lantz, Frederich Hauer, Johan Nicholas
Strasser, Martin Kasser, Christian Kielbach, Michael Hollen-
bach, Wilhelm Smedder, Michael Herpster, Johan Nicholas
Emerich, Jacob Gordner, Johannes Smedder, Peter Seebold,
George Rau, Nicholas Smith, Henry Ruppert, Frederick Hesse,

Christian Scherff, Samuel Leydy, Christian Brancher, George Kautzman, Jacob Biely, Daniel Paulscher, Jacob Donath, Dewald Beilman, Solomon Bacher, Philip Shelhame, Christian Schwenck, John Lieps, Frederick Reichelsderfer, Daniel Smith, Henry Kœnig, Henry Fallweiler, Elias Rothschoen, Philip Bauer, Jacob Driess, Jacob Hagenbach.

In the early part of February, 1756, the Indians committed several cruel and barbarous murders in this township. On the 14th of February, 1756, the Indians came to the house of Frederick Reichelsderfer, shot two of his children, set his house and barn on fire, and burnt up all his grain and cattle. Thence they proceeded to the house of Jacob Gerhart, where they killed one man, two women, and six children. "Two children slipped under the bed, one of which was burned; the other escaped, and ran a mile to get to the people.

When the intelligence of this murder had reached Maxatany, many of the inhabitants of that township repaired to Albany, to see what damage had been done; while on their way, they received accounts of other murders: "When," says Jacob Levan, in a letter to Mr. Seely, February 15, 1756, "I had got ready to go with my neighbors from Maxatany, to see what damage was done in Albany; three men that had seen the shocking affair came and told me, that eleven were killed, eight of them burnt, and the other three found dead out of the fire. An old man was scalped, the two others, little girls, were not scalped."*

On the 24th of March following, says the Pennsylvania Gazette, April 1, 1756, ten wagons went up to Allemaengle (Albany) to bring down a family with their effects; and as they were returning, about three miles below George Zeisloff's, were fired upon by a number of Indians from both sides of the road; upon which the wagoners left their wagons and ran into the woods, and the horses frightened at the firing and terrible yelling of the Indians, ran down a hill and broke one of the wagons to pieces. That the enemy killed George Zeisloff and his wife, a lad of twenty, a boy, of twelve, also a girl of fourteen years old, four of whom they scalped. That another girl was shot in the neck, and through the mouth, and scalped, notwithstanding all which she got off. That a boy was stabbed in three places, but the wounds were not thought to be mor-

* See page 58

tal. That they killed two of the horses, and five are missing, with which it is thought the Indians carried off the most valuable goods that were in the wagon."

Sometime in November, 1756, the Indians appeared again in this township and carried off the wife of, and three children of Adam Burns—the youngest child was only four weeks old. In the month of June, 1757, the Indians murdered one Adam Trump—they took Trump's wife and his son, a lad nineteen years old, prisoners; but the woman escaped, though upon her flying, she was so closely pursued by one of the Indians, (of which there were seven,) that he threw his tomahawk at her, and cut her badly in the neck. The instances of murder were both numerous and barbarous in this township.

Its present boundary is as follows: On the north and west by the Blue mountain, owing to the singular configuration of the mountain; on the east by Lehigh county, and on the south by Greenwich township. It contains about twenty-one thousand acres of land. The soil in the north-western part is slats or shale, and in the south-eastern part somewhat sandy; but upon the whole, the soil is of inferior quality throughout the township, and the surface broken and hilly. It is drained by Maiden creek, which flows through the south-eastern part, intersecting the township unequally, and its tributaries, which are Mill creek and Stony run on the east, and Pine creek and one or two smaller streams on the west. Besides the mountain on the north, noted for its prominent termination, there is *Round Top* or "*Peaked Mountain*," rising in the form of a sugar loaf, to the height of a thousand feet or more. There are three churches in this township, two forges, seven grist mills, five saw mills, six public houses, two stores, eight schools, two justices of the peace, John Miller and George Reagan, Esqs. There are two post offices in the township, viz. at Featherolfsville, and at Union Iron Works. Population in 1810, was 996; in 1820, 1182; 1830, 1129; 1840, 1057, according to the census: 181 horses, 643 horned cattle, 604 sheep, 585 swine; raise 1158 bushels of wheat, 9982 rye, 6852 corn, 4590 oats, 2932 buckwheat, 6302 potatoes, 590 tons of hay, 822 pounds of wool. Tax valuation for 1844, for county purposes, $281,088; for State purposes, $271,613; county tax $562,17. Gross amount of State tax, $312,45.

AMITY TOWNSHIP.

Amity township, in the southern part of the county, was among the first settled townships in the county, originally settled by Swedes* and Germans. There is, at present, a durably built house standing on the east bank of the Schuylkill, erected in 1716, as appears from a stone in the front wall of the house, with the initials, probably of the builder's name, "I. M. I. 1716." The house stands near Douglasville, near which is the old Swedish church, known as the Molatton church, a place of considerable note in the early history of the province.

It was at Molatton that the Indian chiefs, Allummapces, Opekasset, and Manawkyhickon, cannot be enabled to attend a treaty at Conestoga, proposed to meet the Honorable Patrick Gordon, lieutenant governor of Pennsylvania, in relation to the unfortunate affray between the Palatines and Indians, at the iron works at Mahanatawny.

"June 3d, 1728, the governor informed the Board of the Council, convened at Philadelphia, that while he was at Conestoga, he received an answer to the messages sent by order of the Board, the 15th May, to Allummapecs, Opekasset, and Manawkyhickon, which were in substance, that Allummapecs and Opekasset had received the governor's letter and present, that they had nothing in their hearts but love and good will towards the governor and all his people, 'that they would have apprehended some danger if the governor had not sent to them, but that now their doubts are over and offer to meet the governor at Molatton, because they cannot reach Conestoga by the time appointed."

"The governor then said, that understanding Allummapecs and Opekasset, were come to Molatton, he despatched messengers to them, with an invitation to come down to Philadelphia; and that accordingly they were now come, and had brought with them some of the relations of those Indians lately killed by the Winters, and therefore he was now to advise with the Board upon what might be proper to be paid to them, and the presents, necessary on the occasion.

As early as 1741, there were rising of seventy taxables in

* See chapter iv., page 80.

11*

the township. In 1752, the following persons were returned as taxables to the county commissioners, namely:

Cornelius Gehard, Ellis Griffith, George Lutz, Joseph Brown, William Winter, Philip Snear, Joseph Boon, Mathias Hipser, John Adam Bickly, John Waren, Edward Drury, Enos Ellis, Gilbert Dehard, Baltzer Schultz, Thomas Brownfield, John Wolf, John Lowry, Jacob Weaver, Daniel Andraes, Michael Trump, Nicholas Boyer, Martin Becker, John Webb, Lawrence Cropper, Maurice Ellis, Jacob Rhoads, Peter Weaver, Jacob Crust, Cornelius Dehart, Daniel Fraily, Samuel Emwigh, Rinichots Oningthun, Philip Boyer, Michael Messinger, Jacob Early, John Sands, John Fitergrinder, Daniel Ludwick, John Campbell, John Huling, William Davis, Hugh Mitchell, Shedrick Lord, Hernis Shegal, Henry Gibson, Francis Gibson, John Childs, John Samuel Hatt, Thomas Bansfield, John Hoose, Philip Balser Crissman, John Marlain Fritz, Roland Harris, John Rafesnider, Hugh McCaffry, John Taylor, John Sue, Nicholas Jones, John Adam Ludwick, Lenard Roadermell, Jonas Jones, James Waren, Jacob Waren, Peter Kerlin, Ludowick Gouogar, Henry Vanreed, Daniel Woombledorf, William Champbell, Conrad Barlett, Abijah Sands, Mathias Maiday, Marcus Huling, John Ewalt, John Kerlin, John Yocomb, Andrew Ringberry, Peter Yocomb, Peter Livergood, George Shitler, Conrad Lutz, Garrad Deways, George Fritz, Charles Smith, George Adam Fisher, Adam Livergood, George Hanselmah, David Buchard, Jacob Neagly, Edward Harding, Felty Cackly, Michael Cougler, Christopher Wickle, Derrick Cleaver, Adam Hatfield, Samuel Bosarder, Andreas Bosarder, George Adam Weidner, Isaac Wiseman, Thomas Mains, Mathew Culford, Frederick Haws, Charles Herman, Frederick Hoppman, William Williams, Solomon Broonfield, Abraham Andrews, John Peter Wyler, Valentine Ems, James Burn, Rudulph Mictz, Joseph Thomas, Jacob Barnet, William Walker. Many of these were Swedes, or their descendants.

It is bounded on the north-east by Oley and Earl townships; on the south-east by Douglass; south-west by the Schuylkill, separating it from Union; and north-west by Exeter; being nearly a square of four miles, containing about ten thousand five hundred acres of land, principally red shale and gravel; the surface undulating, except the central part, which bears a mountain aspect on account of Monakesy Hill, which strongly marks the prominent features of that part of the township. Though the soil is red gravel and shale, it has been in many places rendered highly productive; and land is rated from twelve to sixty dollars per acre.

This township is intersected by two considerable streams, by Monokesy creek in the north-west, and the Mahanatawny creek, in the north-east; on both of which are several mills; there are six grist mills, five saw mills, and one fulling mill in the township; besides these two streams there are several smaller ones, all winding their course to the Schuylkill. There are several small villages in the township; Douglassville, near the line between Douglass and Amity township, Warrensburg, and Weavertown—there is a church held in common by the Lutherans and German Reformed. There is also one English Presbyterian church at Warrensburg—one near Manokesy hill. The Perkiomen turnpike road, and the Reading railroad pass through the township; the latter along the Schuylkill, and the former within a few miles of it. The population in 1810, 1090; 1820, 1279; 1830, 1378; 1840, 1664,—278 horses, 903 horned cattle, 535 sheep, 840 swine; raise 9912 bushels of wheat, 13,775 rye, 18,543 corn, 22,745 oats, 589 buckwheat, 4038 potatoes, 1703 tons of hay, 1220 pounds of wool, 920 flax. Valuation of articles for county tax for 1844, $543,321; amount of tax, $1090 64. Gross amount of State tax, $791 44.

BERN TOWNSHIP.

Bern township, contiguous to, and north-west of the borough of Reading, was settled by those whose ancestors had emigrated from a canton in Switzerland, one of the largest, and second in rank in the Swiss confederation, called Bern; and in memory of the canton of their forefathers, named their new and future home, *Bern*.

Many of the first settlers were men of wealth, influence, and possessed weight of character, and some of whose descendants are conspicuous in the annals of our country, both as soldiers, statesmen and divines—of these were the Hiesters and others. The primitive settlements in this township were made between the years 1728 and 1740, and principally by Germans, as will appear on examining the following list of taxables for the year 1752 :

Abraham Hause, Joseph Richards, Albright Straus, Philip Straus, Joseph Shoemaker, Jacob Good, Christian Stutsman, Jacob Hanslerf, Anenias Sickle, Walter Rumford, George Sheel, Hans Filbert, Jacob Weisner, Jacob Beiler, George Wagoner, Jacob Kaufman, Fredrick Moir, Ludowick Nicholas, Samuel Minks, Felty Long, Ludowick Meily, Joseph Solendbrien, John Sever, Albright Fright, Rynard Chartle, Jacob Stutsman, Henry Steely, Jacob Westlar, Jacob Beiler, John Sreber, Valentine Helmberger, Nicholas Miller, Henry Busand, Nicholas Runch, Michael Burner, John Passman, Matthew Turnbeh, Philip Jacobs, Christian King, George Crusel, Cortes Crusel, Ludowick Semarr, William Tumbleson, John Smith, Christopher Four, Benjamin Kepler, Samuel King, Christian Pike, Pence Leman, John Holy, Pence Benedict, Henry Adam, John Hertzberger, Christopher Yader, Jacob Bader, Martin Geek, John Fisher, John Kaufman, Everhard Caspin, Gerry Wagoner, jr., Jacob Pertgoble, John Young, John Zimmerman, Bastian Rood, Christian Yader, Philip Faust, Hermann Weaver, Daniel Hiester, George Gardner, John Faust, Christian Albright, Michael Stout, Jacob Bois, Peter Harpin, Matthew Weaver, Jacob Rezer, jr., Martin Cheaner, Joseph Heck, John Runch, John Bucks, John Meater, John Snider, senr., Jacob Rude, William Leymeister, George Bellman, Casper Philip, David Grim, Jacob Grim, Nicholas Klee, Philip Bower, Michael Hansel, John Snider, jr., John Althaus, John Richards, Titus Denning, John Elfman, Nicholas Souder, James Williamson, Adam Rickebach, John Stout, Christian Kaufman, Jacob Albright, Andreas Weiler, Jacob Runcle, Christian Berer, George Kirsner, Christian Zuch, Samuel Wallison. John Apler, Adam Bohn, Frederick Trum, John Mackimore, Woolrick Rathmacker, Jacob Fuchs, Philip Mackimore, Peter Brown, Valentine Epler, John Heister, John Rebert, Jost Hiester, Adam Stump, William Hettrich, Nicholas Haller, Jacob Summer, Jacob Rezer, Joseph Obelt, Heronimus Henig, Hans Michael Leep, Jacob Miller, Wondle Brecht, David Brecht, Jacob Allwene, Henry Kettner, George Gernant, Peter Zuber, Samuel Wallison. Not a few of these were descendants of the Huguenots, of whom something has been said in chapter v., pages 83, 88.

The inhabitants of this township, in common with all the frontier townships, suffered much from the cruel enemy, marauding the county. The last murders, of which we have any notice, committed on this side the Blue Mountain, in Berks, were committed in Bern township. The following letter from Jonas Seely to Governor Penn, (son of Richard Penn,) contains this account:

Reading, September 11, 1763.

HONORED SIR—

This moment at Reading, as I was sending off the express, certain intelligence came that the house of Frantz Hubler, in Berne township, about eighteen miles from here, was attacked on Friday evening last, by the Indians—himself is wounded, his wife and three children carried off—and three other of the children scalped alive—two of whom are since dead.

I am, Honored Sir,
Your humble and
Obedient servant,
JONAS SEELY.

In another letter, the same writer says: "We are all in a state of alarm; Indians have destroyed dwellings, and murdered with savage barbarity, their helpless inmates; even in the neighborhood of Reading. Where these Indians came from, and where going, we know not. These are dangerous times. Send us armed force to aid our rangers of Berks."

This township is bounded on the north by Centre township, which has been organized out of parts of Bern and Upper Bern, since 1830; on the east by the Schuylkill river, separating it from Maiden Creek, and Alsace township; south-west by the Tulpehocken creek, separating it from Cumru and lower Heidelberg townships; north-west by Penn township, which was formed out of Bern and Upper Bern; extreme about seven miles and a half, and greatest breadth seven miles; average length and breadth about five miles; area of about 20,000 acres, and the surface considerably undulative; the soil principally gravel, but considerably improved by a proper course of tillage. Bern presents a kind of Delta, lying in the fork of the Tulpehocken creek and the Schuylkill river, which, together with Plum creek, afford abundance of water power for

mills and other purposes.   In 1840, there were one flouring
mill, six grist mills, seven saw mills, one powder mill, and three
tanneries in the towdship.   There are two churches in the
township, Epler's, six miles from Reading, and Bern church.
The first church here was singularly decorated by a grotesque
painting.   Bernville, fourteen miles from Reading, is a post
village.

The following, which is " clipt" from the " Schuylkill Journal" of May, 1839, shows that some native genius is to be
found in Bern.   To stimulate some dormant genius, whose eye
may be caught by this, space is given to a tribute of praise.—
The Editor of the Journal says :   " A short time since I called
to see *Jacob Miesse, Esq.*, of Bern township, Berks county,
Pa., who showed me a number of engravings executed by his
son Gabriel Miesse.   The young gentleman has an undoubted
claim to talents.   The first piece of work of the kind he performed, is surprisingly well done, when it is recollected he had
never seen a copper-plate—in fact, not even a graver, for this instrument was constructed by a neighboring blacksmith, according to a pattern furnished by the young man himself.   In consequence of the development of such promising talents, he was
prevailed upon by the liberality of his father, to resort to
Philadelphia, and put himself under the care of an experienced artist.   But from great constitutional delicacy of
frame, he did not remain there more than ten days or two
weeks, before he was attacked by a severe illness, which obliged
him to return to the country, and abandon those opportunities
so congenial to his taste.   He continued, however, to amuse
himself by engraving a great variety of pieces, among which
are plants, flowers, animals, the human figure, &c., executed
with a spirit of fidelity, truly astonishing, and turned off by an
apparatus wholly constructed by himself, from the stile to the
press."

Population in 1810, 1,240 ; 1820, 1,791 ; 1830, 2,154 ;
1840, 3,149.   Horses 907 ; horned cattle 1,774 ; sheep
1,135 ; Swine 2,105 ; bushels of wheat 29,960 ; rye 39,267 ;
corn 37,885 ; oats 48,227 ; buckwheat 1,354 ; potatoes 16,-
219 ; tons of hay 4,307 ; pounds of wool 2,122 ; flax 3,261.
Valuation of articles for county tax $602,884 ; county tax
$1,205 ; State tax $672,35.

BETHEL TOWNSHIP.

Bethel township was, no doubt, so called after a colony of *United Brethren* or Moravians, who had a small establishment on the Swatara, in this township, called *Bethel* ; the literal meaning of which is, " *The House of God.*"

Bethel township is the most north-western township of Berks county ; primitively settled by Germans, whose descendants are still the owners of their ancestors farms and homestead. In no township of the county were more life sacrificed to glut the destructive propensities of the barbarous Indians, during the French and Indian war, than in this township. It was in this township Captain Busse, under the direction of the province and inspection of Conrad Weiser, Fort William and Henry was erected, and well garrisoned by one company and a half—part of a regiment consisting of nine companies, under the command of Colonel Conrad Weiser ; and notwithstanding the fort being within this township, the Indians killed many of the inhabitants.

Under date of November 19, 1755, Conrad Weiser, in a letter to Governor Morris, says : " On my return from Philadelphia, the first news of our cruel enemy having invaded the county, this side of the Blue Mountain, to wit : *Bethel* and Tulpehocken."

In a deposition, signed by James Morgan, it is stated that on Sunday, the 16th November, 1755, a company of one hundred and thirty inhabitants of Berks, principally from Heidelberg and Tulpehocken, went to Bethel township ; and that near Dieterich Six's, about half a mile from his house, they found Casper Spring dead, and scalped, whose brains had been knocked out, and having buried him, they marched about one hundead rods and found one Beslinger dead, and scalped ; his brains were also knocked out, his mouth much mangled, one of his eyes cut out, and two knives lying in his breast—they buried him. That twenty of their body, who had gone a little out of the road, about two miles from Six's, found a child of Jacob Wolf—and that the day before, some of the same company had found John Leinberger and Rudolp Candel, dead and scalped.

It is further stated, " the whole country thereabouts deserted their habitations, and sent away all their household goods—

that much mischief had been done by the Indians, by burning houses and barns.

Loskiel, in speaking of the Moravian settlements, in 1756, thus alludes to the colony in Bethel :—" The savages continued to commit murders in Allemaengel ; and a lance lost by them on the road, proved them to be some of the very people who had attended the Congress (Indian treaty) at Easton. Roving parties infested the borders of the country, the public roads, and all those places in which they feared no resistance ; so that the small colonies of Brethren settled in Allemaengel and *Bethel, on Swatara,* who had held out with uncommon patience, were at last obliged to take refuge, the former in Bethlehem, and the latter in Lebanon."*

Some time in the month of June, 1758, the Indians carried off the wife of John Frantz, and three of his children. Mrs. Frantz being rather infirm and sickly, not able to travel, was most cruelly murdered by the savages ; the children they took with them.†

At the time this murder was committed, Mr. Frantz was out at work ; his neighbors having heard the firing of guns by the Indians, immediately repaired to the house of Frantz ; on their way there apprised him of the report—when they arrived at the house they found Mrs. Frantz dead, and all the children gone ; they then pursued the Indians some distance, but all in vain. The children were taken and kept captives for several years.

A few years after this horrible affair, all of them, except one, the youngest, were exchanged. The oldest of them, a lad of twelve or thirteen years of age, at the time when captured, related the tragical scene of his mother being tomahawked and shamefully treated. Him they compelled to carry the youngest.

The anxious father, having received two of his children as from the dead, still sighed for the one that was not. Whenever he heard of children being exchanged, he mounted his horse to see whether among the captured, was not his dear little one. On one occasion he paid a man forty pounds, who had reported he knew where the child was, if he restored it. To another he paid a hundred dollars, and himself went to Canada

* Loskiel's His. Mis U. F La Trobe's Translation, Part ii., p. 180.
† Pennsylvania Gazette, June 1758.

in search of the lost one—but, to his sorrow, never could trace his child. A parent can realize his feelings—they cannot be described.

The following persons were returned to the county commissioners, as taxables of this township, in 1754:

Martin Kepler, Charles Smith, Michael Grossman, Casper Snevely, George Reninger, Loretz Stautz, Wendel Reeger, John Schuie, Peter Bixler, Martin Eichgelberger, Martin Eisenhauer, John Eichgelberger, Michael Groff, George Groff, Frederick Sixth, George Bceshor, John Kunkle, Martin Speck, Jacob Dehn, Adam Kussel, George Emrich, Michael Wieland, Nicholas Marke, David Marke, Nicholas Gebhart, Andreas Smith, Jacob Sierer, John Apple, Daniel Sneider, Henry Kobel, Conrad Fuerther, Ulrich Spies, Henry Shuie, Christopher Herold, Frantz Legenberger, Adam Daniel, Nicolaus Pontius, George Berger, Henry Berger, Andrew Kremer, John Emrich, Jacob Smith, Jacob Emrich, Jacob Zerbe, Baltzer Emrich, Leonard Emrich, Jacob Leyninger, Ulrich Seltzer, Baltzer Smith, Frederick Tresler, Martin Tresler, Bastian Stein, Thomas Bauer, Rudy Mayer, John Frantz, Peter Mayer, John Adam Walborn, John Adam Bartorf, William Parsons, Esq., Christel Neucommer, Wendel Seibert, Christopher Knebel, Peter Dietrich, Christopher Reier, Dietrich Markle, Nicholas Wolf.

The quantity of land owned by the above, was 2,230 acres, whereof were cleared and sowed in grain, 168 acres; horses 68; mares 25; cows 103; sheep 41; servants 4; one hired man, Dietrich Markle.

Bethel, as it is at present, is bounded on the north by the Blue Mountain, for the distance of fifteen miles, which separates it from Schuylkill county; east and south by the Little Swatara creek, which divides it from Upper and Lower Tulpehocken townships; south and west by Lebanon county; its mean length is about eight miles, and mean breadth about five miles, having an area of about 27,000 acres of land. The surface is diversified; in the north, somewhat mountainous; soil nearly all gravel, some yellow shale, and upon the whole, not productive. Parts of it, however, have been rendered productive by the shield and care of the provident husbandman.

The main road from Jonestown, in Lebanon county, to Rehrersburg, passes through the south part of it—the road to Pine

Grove crosses it on the east; that to Sunbury, centrally, and the State road to the west. The Little Swatara and Grosskill, are the principal streams, affording good water power. There are four grist mills, six saw mills, one fulling mill, and one woollen factory in the township; two tanneries and several distilleries—but at present, not in operation. Millersburg is the only village in the township, containing between thirty and forty dwellings, several taverns, and stores; one church, held in common by the Lutherans and German Reformed. The German Baptists, or Dunkers, have one or two meeting places.

The population in 1810, 924; 1820, 1,294; 1830, 1,482; 1840, 1,458; horses 463; horned cattle 1,480; sheep 836; swine 966; bushels of wheat 11,852; rye 16,491; corn 18,822; oats 26,880; buckwheat 587; potatoes 5,662; tons of hay 1,886; pounds of wool 1,427; flax 836. Valuation for county tax for 1844, $524,501; county tax $1,049 00; State tax $608,45.

BRECKNOCK TOWNSHIP.

Brecknock township, in the southern part of the county, was called so, after Brecon or Brecknock, an inland county of South Wales, whence some of the first settlers in this part of Berks county have emigrated. The primitive settlers of this township were the following, among whom were a few Germans:

George Douglass, Charles Hornberry, George Hesong, Jacob Fry, Adam Beamer, Daniel Commer, Henry Miller, John Black, Casper Koch, John Long, David Commer, M. Geyman, Abraham Stein, Leobald Yost, John Aldibery, Jacob West, James Ratliff, Bernhard Pealer, Adam Philabaum, Hans Ruble, Jeremiah Seemor, Michael Finfrock, Christian Acre, Michael Frankhauser, Adam Neide, Hans Hamigh, Hans Moser, Michael Slaugh, Henry Brindle, Henry Ourwasher, Daniel Cooper, Joseph Wenger, Nicholas Shans, Peter Baltsly, Christian Geyman, John Comier.

It is bounded on the north by Cumru township; on the east by Robeson township, and south-east by Cærnarvon; southwest by Lancaster county, and on the northwest by Cumru; greatest length seven miles; mean breadth about two and a half; contains rising of ten thousand acres of land. The surface is generally hilly, and the soil gravel; but pretty well improved, though there is still much room for greater improvement.

The township is well supplied with water. Allegheny creek rises near the centre of this township, and in a north-eastern direction meanders through the glens, and seeks its way towards the Schuylkill, affording water power to several mills within the limits of the township. Big and Little Muddy creeks have their sources in this township; the former rises in the eastern, the latter in the western part of the township, and unite in Lancaster county, and empty into the Conestoga. There is a German Reformed church in this township. Population in 1810, 495; 1820, 536; 1830, 866; 1840, 935. Horses 335; horned cattle 956; sheep 749; swine 671; bushels of wheat 2,491; rye 7,056; corn 8,072; oats 5,991; buckwheat 792; potatoes 6,523; tons of hay 909; pounds of wool 1,357; flax 1,397. Valuation of articles for tax for 1844, $148,131; county tax $296,26; State tax $179,14.

CÆRNARVON TOWNSHIP.

Cærnarvon township, is the extreme southern township of the county; was originally settled by Welsh, who named it after a maritime county of North Wales, whence they had emigrated. The following list embraces all the primitive settlers who lived at the time of the organization of Berks county.

Nicholas Hadson, John Wilson, George Martin, Richard Smith, Moses Martin, Jacob Cymerlin, Archibald Mahon, William Robeson, Daniel Jones, Aaron Rattue, John Davis, John Light, John Hamilton, Nicholas Hudson, John Bracken, Aaron Ash, Alexander Adams, Mathias Broadsword, Valentine Carberry, Joseph Davis, Robert Ellis, John Evans, Daniel Fox, John Fern, Daniel Gillis, Thomas Harper, Jacob Hofman, David Jones, Francis Morgan, Daniel Owen, Mark Pealor, Richard Philips, Charles Richardson, Moses Robinson, William Robinson, Cornelius Shea, John Stephens, Benjamin Talbert, John Morgan, Daniel Davis, John Talbert.

The township is bounded on the north by Robeson township; south-east by Chester county, and north-west by Lancaster. Its mean length five miles; mean breadth two miles and a half; contains upwards of ten thousand acres of land; the surface is diversified—the soil is gravel and limestone, the greater part of which is well cultivated.

The township lies principally in the great valley. In no part of Berks county, do farms surpass those in this township. They are well cultivated, and very productive. "Few travellers," says a certain writer, speaking of this part of the county, "who pass through it, can well avoid the breach of the tenth commandment, or refrain from envying the inhabitants their tranquil life and abundant comforts—their spacious and neat dwellings of stone, and their capacious and overflowing garners, their fields studded with cattle and whitened with sheep, are substantial witnesses of their happiness."

It is pretty well watered; the Conestoga creek affords water power, on which, within the borders of Cærnarvon, are several mills. There is some iron ore in this township, but mixed with some copper. This is stated upon the authority of the Assistant State Geologist. He says, speaking of Berks county: "Copper ore occurs at several places within the county, but generally in such small quantities, and so mixed with iron, as to render the expediency of working it very doubtful. Near Morgantown is a mine of this character, which is not at present in a productive state." It contains three stores, one flouring mill, three grist mills, and three saw mills. Morgantown, a post village, is a small town, though pleasantly situated on the Conestoga turnpike road, thirteen miles from Reading; it contains between forty and fifty dwellings, the usual handicrafts, several stores and taverns; population rising of three hundred; contains a German Reformed Church.

The population of this township was in 1830, 1440; 1840, 1830. Horses 208; horned cattle 705; sheep 544; bushels of wheat 13,570; rye 4,205; corn 9,764; oats 12,859; buckwheat 491; potatoes 3,597; tons of hay 713; pounds of wool 804; flax 1,121. Valuation of articles for county tax for 1844, $244,617; county tax $480,23; State tax $324,75.

COLEBROOKDALE TOWNSHIP.

Colebrookdale township, was among the first organized townships, and settled at a comparatively early period. Among the first settlers were a number of Palatine families, of whom mention is made in the Coloniel Records, in the year 1728. In 1741, this county contained eighty-five taxables; and in 1752, the year Berks county was organized, the following were the names of the taxables of this township:

Conrad Rode, Thomas Potts, Conrad Read, Mathias Datterow, John Potts, Peter Gars, Casper Richard, Leopold Long, Paul Picteo, Thomas Weasor, Casper Bowman, John Shouts, Conrad Mone, Manues Sossiminius, (Sassamanhous,) Godfried. Kesabaer, Barnebas Rhodes, Thomas Schohn, Adam Gerber, David Potts, John Wartler, Adam Ritznover, John Michael Dotterer, Fredrick Erne, Nicholas Eiss, Conrad Boehm, Andrew Eschenbach, John Moir, Conrad Seihiber, John Buckwalter, Peter Lower, Bernhard Wanemacher, Philip Filtz, Daniel Stover, Paul Finsman, John Baily, Paul Mosner, Michael Hartlein, Michael Klein, Jacob Ganz, Stephen Hautz, Jacob Mathias, Ruben Tuders, Jacob Miller, Adam Lintz, Jacob Bush, John Beicker, Jacob Hauk, Frederick Potts, Jacob Tangler, Henry Schweitzer, Leonard Thomas, Jacob Machlin, Francis Carle, John Pile, George Kirch, Thomas Walker, George Hartley, Daniel Stover, Jacob Klotz.

This township is at present bounded, as follows: North-east by Washington township, formed out of part of Colebrookdale and Hereford; south-east by Montgomery county, south-west by Douglass, and north-west by Earl and Pike; it is near a square of three miles, and contains rising of six thousand acres of land; surface rather hilly; soil principally gravel, and some loam; generally, however, of a good quality, and rendered, by a proper system of culture, productive. The Stone and Swamp creek have their sources in this township. There are several grist mills, saw mills, fulling mills, in this township. Black lead has been discovered, and iron ore of the magnetic variety, connected with the primary rocks, abounds—one of these is near Boyerstown. These mines were formerly worked for the supply of furnaces, in the vicinity of the mines.

Boyerstown, a post village, is situated in the south-eastern

12*

part of the township, where there is a church, common to the Lutherans and German Reformed.

Population in 1810, 792; 1820, 1,046; 1830, 1,219; 1840, 1,124. Horses 193; horned cattle 678; sheep 292; swine 393; bushels of wheat 3,303; rye 4,174; corn 7,010; oats 6,985; buckwheat 545; potatoes 3,422; tons of hay 812; pounds of wool 692; flax 1,392. Amount of valuation for tax for 1844, $333,872; county tax $667,74; State tax $432,47.

CUMRU TOWNSHIP.

Cumru township was, like the last named townships, primitively settled by the Welsh emigrants. It was within the limits of this township, that two Welshmen, brothers, by the name of Winters, murdered three friendly Indians. The circumstances connected with this affair are given in the Colonial Records, as detailed by Governor Gordon, who was, after the murder had been committed, in the neighborhood, in 1728. In laying an account thereof before the Council, "The Governor proceeded and said, that after having used several methods to quiet the country, (alluding here to the disturbance at Mahanatawny,) and to induce the people to return to their habitations, and having ordered some powder and lead to be distributed in case of any attack. He was preparing to return home, when he received the melancholy news by an express from Samuel Nutt, Esq., that one Indian man and two women were cruelly murdered, at Cucussea, by John and Walter Winters, without any provocation given, and two Indian girls much wounded, upon which a hue and cry was immediately issued against the murderers, and he returned back next day to Mahanatawny to make enquiry into this matter, where he learned that the said Winters and one Morgan Herbert, an accomplice in said murders, were apprehended, who being brought thither and examined, the said Winters confessed the murder, as did likewise Herbert, his being present when they perpetrated the same, as appears from the several examinations now laid before the Board, and that they had nothing else to say in their justification, than that, from the reports in the country of the Indians having killed some white men, they thought they might lawfully kill any Indian whom they found."

The following list of taxables for 1756, contains the names of many of the first settlers in the township:

Adam Ziegler, Abraham Eckert, Andrew Woolf, Adam Householder, Amos Jenkins, Andrew Bossard, Bastian Morgan, Benjamin Horning, Casper Steff, Christian Bowman, Christian Stehute, Christian Brinckle, Conrad Ohard, David Edward, Daniel Shea, David Evans, Dietrich Fernsler, Dennis Brady, Francis Yarnal, Francis Kreck, Francis Steele, George Jacob, George Bollman, George Burkhard, George Eckert, George Bauer, George Krimlauf, George Englehardt, George Bower, George Riehm, George Geminder, George Lewis, Hans Ruthey, Henry Alsbach, Henry Frelick, Harman Rule, Hans Zovalle, John Emy, Jacob Bauman, Jacob Eshellman, Isaac Willets, Jacob Stehly, John Selegan, John Davis, John Smith, John Morris, John Hengle, Jacob Ruth, James David, Jacob Freimeyer, Jona Stephen, Jacob Beyerly, Joseph Missler, John Richard, James Lewis, John Eaton, Jacob Syder, James Perst, John Englebrown, Joseph Wollinson, John Reed, Joseph Althouse, Jacob Clower, John Davis, John Bryninger, John Klinegenny, John Binckley, Jacob Worst, John Moon, John Creek, John Henton, Jonas Seely, John Bollman, John Pugh, Ludwick Herman, Ludwick Moon, Michael Lamb, Martin Kollmer, Michael Meyer, Michael Shoemaker, Michael Grauel, Michael Ruth, Martin Beyer, Melchoir Steel, Martin Bryminger, Martin Kromer, Nicholas Creager, Nathan Evans, Nicholas Killian, Peter Hoeckert, Peter Road, Peter Flick, Peter Shearman, Nicholas Cowyer, Peter Neagley, Peter Eshelman, Rudolph Hueberling, Reinhard Rorebach, Richard Lewis, Reinhard Waltz, Samuel Embree, Stephen Lash, Samuel Phipps, Vernor Moone, Walter Burk, Vernor Weystel, William Jones, William Thomas, William Lerch, Nicholas Lerch, William Davis, Thomas Jones, Thomas Pest, Isaac Willets, Peter Road, Henry Beyerley, Edward Harry, William Lewis, Nathan Lewis, James Jones, Evan Harry, Nathaniel Morgan, John Peter, Solomon Davis, James Davis, John Davis, Daniel Bossert, Jacob Creek, John Bopkin, Reuben Davis.

The following letter written, in this township, may be interesting to some of the readers here—though not exactly *in place,* it is given.

Sinking Spring, Sept. 10, 1763.

JOHN PENN, ESQ.
    Honored Sir—
    I am sorry I have to acquaint your honor of the following melancholy accounts, which I received by express from Capt. Kern, last night.   On the 8th inst., a party of Indians came to the house of one John Fincher, about three-quarters of a mile distant from a party of Captain Kern's men, commanded by Ensign Sheffer.   They killed Fincher, his wife, and two of his sons;·his daughter is missing; one little boy made his escape from the savages, and came to the Ensign, who went immediately to the place with his party.   But the Indians were gone, and finding by their tracks which way they went, pursued them to the house of one Nicholas Miller, where he found four children murdered.   Our paity still pursued, and soon came up with the enemy, and fired on them.   They returned the fire; but the soldiers rushed on them so furiously, that they soon ran off and left behind them two prisoners, two tomahawks, one hanger and a saddle—the Indians were eight in number, and our party, seven.   Three of the enemy ₋were much wounded. The two prisoners which our party wounded, were two of said Miller's children, whom they had tied together, and so drove them along.   Miller's wife is missing—in all, there are eight killed, and two missing in that neighborhood.
                    I am, honored sir,
                        Your most obedient
                            Humble servant,
                                JONAS SEELY.

    This township is bounded on the north-east by the Schuylkill river, separating it from Bern and Alsace township; on the south by Robeson township and Brecknock; south-west by Lancaster county; and on the north-west by Lower Heidelberg township.   The mean length and mean breadth, a little more than seven miles; and contains rising of thirty-one thousand acres of land; the surface variegated; partly level and partly hilly; the soil diversified, gravel and limestone of excellent quality, and highly productive.
    The Welsh mountain and Flying hill, in the southern part of the township, are distinguished prominences, and give boldness

to the southern borders of Cumru. This township is well watered. Besides the Schuylkill and Tulpehocken, other streams,
such as the Cacoosing creek, Wymising, Angelica, and Flying
Hill run, afford water power to propel the "gearings" of one
furnace, two forges, one fulling mill, twelve flouring mills, five
grist mills, and five saw mills.

There is also the Sinking Spring, near the Harrisburg turnpike, about five miles from Reading, which is quite a natural
curiosity to those who may not be familiar with the circumstances frequently attending large springs in a limestone region.
"The water here rises and sinks again in the same basin, which
is very deep; thence finding its way again under ground, through
fissures and hidden caverns in the limestone rock, probably once
more to seek the light of day in some other place."

Near this spring is a village, deriving its name from the spring.
It contains fifteen or eighteen dwelling houses, one or two
taverns, and several stores, and a church held in common by
the German Reformed and Lutherans.

The county poor house—a "lordly palace"—is in this township, about three miles from Reading, upon Angelica Farm,
formerly the property of Governor Thomas Mifflin.

The population in 1810, 2,017; 1820, 2,462; 1830, 2,705;
1840, 2,930. Horses 725; horned cattle 1,880; sheep 1,921;
swine 2,178; bushels of wheat 33,535; rye 26,766; corn
34,997; oats 44,337; buckwheat 1,311; potatoes 11,451;
tons of hay 2,541; pounds of wool 1,993; flax 3,750. Whole
amount of valuation on all articles made taxable by law for
county purposes, for 1844, $1,138,900; whole amount of
county tax $2,277 80; State tax $1,316 66.

DISTRICT TOWNSHIP.

District township, is one of the north-western townships in
the county, and was settled primitively and principally by Germans, whose choice was among the hills, preferring this land
on account of the springs. In 1756, the following persons
were all taxables, and nearly all of whom were land holders:

George Hartlein, Conrad Arnold, Thomas Banfield, Jacob
Bush, Jeremiah Bacon, Israel Burget, John Barns, Frederick

Potts, George Brown, Henry Dener, George Trust, Joshua De La Plain, (Delaplain) George Dotterer, Nicholo Eis, Jacob Bernhard, George Oyster, Jacob Frey, Jacob Fridge, John Fare, Jacob Grues, Bernhard Gembling, Jacob Hill, George Hartline, Michael Hoffman, Michael Hartman, Andreas Hacker, Peter Hardman, Lorentz Hauck, George Haltzlhech, Stephen Hanch, Jacob Hard, Paul Hartman, Jacob Herb, Michael Klein, John Kabron, George Koutz, Conrad Keim, Nicholas Koutz, Adam Kildan, Geroge Klauser, George Lantz, George Lintz, Tobias Manek, Jacob Mathias, Dietrich Mathias, Wm. Mackey, S. Mayberry, John Moatzer, Peter Miller, John Miller, Wm. Miller, Henry Machanet, Frederick Mayer, Frederick Martin, Andeas Norgang, Frantz Moser, John Reidenauer, Michael Radicher, George Schall, William Stork, Jacob Steinbrenner, Lawrence Sheeler, sen. and jr., George Stevenson, Nicholas Schlister, Henry Schoerham, Valentine Schaeffer, Adam Urich, Jacob Walter, Peter Weller, Philip Weismiller, Casper Weisner, Jacob Schweitzer, George Adam Weidner, Jacob Roth, Charles Weis, Christopher Schock, Michael Schuhmacher, Christian Brensinger, Samuel Oyster, Daniel Eyst, John Cobron.

This township is bounded on the north by Long Swamp township; east by Hereford and Washington; south by Pike, and west by Rockland. Greatest length four miles and a half, and breadth about three and a half; containing rising of seven thousand acres of land? the surface in many places very hilly; soil, gravel, and of rather, naturally, an inferior quality; average value, when improved, not exceeding twenty-five dollars per acre. The land is susceptible of greater improvement than has been made. Pine creek and branch of Mahanatawny, rises in this township, on which there is a furnace—there is one forge, a grist mill, and a saw mill, in the township.

Population in 1830, 562; 1840, 583. Horses 187; horned cattle 418; sheep 331; swine 300; bushels of wheat 1,572; rye 3,371; corn 3,845; oats 3,416; buckwheat 1,458; potatoes 2,946; tons of hay 392; pounds of wool 742; flax 379.— whole amount of valuation on all articles made taxable by law, for county purposes $139,029; county tax $278,06; State tax $160,63.

DOUGLASS TOWNSHIP.

Douglass township had been organized prior to 1740; that year it contained as many as fifty-eight taxables, and like Cole-brook, was principally settled by Palatines.* Its early settlers were alarmed by Indian skirmishes, mentioned in a preceding page. In 1755, the following persons resided in this township: Jacob Nagle, Daniel Wills, sen., Adam Miller, Henry Shomberger, Valentine Foght, Jacob David Hiser, Samuel Buzard, Christian Kasebeer, sen., John Slice, Christian Wigle, Michael Coglar, Michael Kaspotz, Yoakam Negice, Valentine Keely, George Hanselman, Philip Walter, sen., George Shadler Peter Levengood, Peter Yoakam, Andrew Ringberry, Frederick Wambach, Martin Nahr, Michael Hoffman, Crhistian Sheeler, George Fritz, Andrew Huling, Derick Clever, Wm. Keepers, Heronimus Spies, Leonard Hersger, John Keffer, Nicholas Reem, Christian Conrad, Christian Bender, Geo. Geringer, John Clows, Andrew Miller, James Bevin, Peter Sheener, Philip Barthner, Simon Ringberry, Philip Hapelbaker, John Potts, jr.

This township is bounded north by Colebrookdale; east by Montgomery county; south by the Schuylkill river; on the west by Amity and Earl township; the greatest length, five miles and a quarter, breadth two miles; contains seven thousand acres of land—surface undulating—soil good—not very productive. The Mahanatawny creek passes through the south ern part of it, on which there is a Pine forge. Iron Stone creek divides the northern portion longitudinally, and nearly equally, till it reaches the Mahanatawny. The Philadelphia & Reading turnpike, and the Railroad to Philadelphia, pass through the southern part of it. There is a furnace, a forge, a fulling mill, four grist mills, three saw mills and an oil mill, in this township.

Population in 1810, 660; 1820, 1,046; 1830, 1,210; 1840, 1,113. Horses 475—horned cattle 754—sheep 306—swine 504—bushels of wheat 3,115—rye 8,768—corn 10,445—oats 7,330—buckwheat 1,268—potatoes 2,131—tons of hay 794—pounds of flax 295—wool 880. Whole amount of valuation on all articles made taxable by law, for county purposes, for 1844, $282,212—county tax $564 42—State tax $342 31.

* Col Rec. iii. 321.

ELSACE, OR ALSACE TOWNSHIP.

Alsace township was named after the province from which the first settlers had chiefly emigrated. They had come from a French province, called Alsace, forming the departments of the upper and lower Rhine. Among the first settlers were some descendants of French Reformed or Huguenots, and Swedes; the latter were Lutherans. The greater part were Germans. The following were returned as taxables by the assessor in 1756. Some of them were Swedish Lutherans, others descendants of Huguenots.*

Jacob Debery, Jacob Sheffer, John Umstat, Michael Fischer, John Ebling, Rudolph. Gehrhart, Henry Ganet, Peter Smith, John Haberacker, Samuel High, Nicholas Yost, Harry Schneider, Baltzer Moone, John' Schmeck, Harry Becker, Herman De Haven, Christopher Spengler, Adam Garret, Adam Reifle, Dewalt Baum, Nicholas Highshoo, Frederick Goodhart, George Heyer, Peter Rothenberger, Philip Resser, John Lehmer, Rudolph Schleer, Michael Glasser, Michael Seiler, Jacob Lanciscus, Christian Kinsey, Adam Wagner, Baltzer Schwenck, William Noll, Casper Millhause, Adam Schwartzbach, Harry Shillt, Jacob Becker, Adam Bauman, Ernst Seitel, Conrad Bobb, Conrad Keller, Isaac Levan, jr., Lorentz Wentzel, Geo. Nees, Mathias Trenckel, Nicholas Kreisher, Jacob Heitschuh, Dietrich Bettleman, Adam Wordenberger, Victor Spies, Henry Bingeman, John Close, Richard Hockley, Jacob Boyler, Henry Koch, Baltzer Marthew, Adam Eple, Mathias Knob, Christopher Rodecker, George Wolf, Michael Spohn, George Sietz, Michael Reitmayer, David Kinsey, Daniel Hargang, Michael Shegtel, John Bingeman, Peter Fisher, Jonas Bauman, John Schmeck, Henry Bauman, Adam Scheurer, Nicholas Fisher, George Rothenberger, Mathias Sauermilch, George May.

The present boundaries of this township, including the Borough of Reading, are as follows: On the north-west side by Maiden creek township; on the north-east by Ruscommanor; east by Oley and Exeter; and on the west by the river Schuylkill. It contains about twenty-one thousand five hundred acres of land. The surface of the eastern part of the township

---

* See chapter iv.; p. 80; and chapter v., p. 83.

hilly and mountainous, embracing a great proportion of Penn's mountain and Never Sink. The western part is somewhat undulating—parts of it are level. A considerable proportion of the township is limestone, and highly productive. The hilly parts have, within the last fifteen years, been much improved, and the cultivator is abundantly repaid for labor bestowed upon the soil.

In the south-eastern part of the township, and within two miles of Reading, is a chaybelate spring, well known as *Kessler's Spring.* It is one of the most pleasant places of resort during the heat of the summer, in the county. The lover of the " rugged beauties" of nature, may regale himself in this pleasant place of retreat, being in a secluded and highly romantic gorge of Mount Penn. Many to while away ennui, resort thither,—" and to sip the fluid of a rivulet which there precipitates itself, sparkling and leaping down the ravine."

Under an excitement so prevalent in the late war—at every rivulet to erect without adequate protection—a manufacturer, Mr. Kessler, the venerated father of *Charles Kessler, Esq.,* of Reading, established a woollen factory; but it has since been abandoned; and the building is now used for other purposes— a hotel, which is "so completely hedged by mountains, and well shaded with original forest trees, as to be almost entirely screened from the influence of the sun, and is ten or fifteen degrees cooler in summer than the open country around. A house, and various works designed for the comfort and entertainment of visiters, are kept in excellent repair—and present no ordinary attractions."

During the Revolution of '76, a number of British prisoners had taken *lodgings* near *Kessler's Spring.* " A body of Hessian prisoners, captured at Trenton in 1776, together with many British, and the principal Scotch Royalists, subdued and taken in North Carolina, were brought to Reading, and stationed in a grove on the bank of the river Schuylkill, in the south part of the borough. In the fall of the same year, they were removed to the hill, *east of the town,* which is called the *Hessian Camp* to this day. There they remained some time, and built themselves *huts* in regular camp order, the greater part of which may be seen at the present day."*

Among the prisoners of war at Reading, July 16, 1777,

* Stahle's Description of Reading, p. 64

13

were the following : Major Allen M'Donald, taken at Moore's creek, North Carolina, March 2d, 1776 ; Lieutenant Alexander M'Donald and Major James Hepburn, all taken at the same time and place.

Captain Duncan Nicol, of Royal Highlanders, or Regiment of emigrants, Lieutenant Hugh Frasier, Captain John Battut, of the fourteenth British Regiment, and Lieutenant Christopher Foster of the fifty-fifth Regiment, and Lieutenant James Willson, of the same Regiment, Lieutenant John Cameron, of the seventy-first Regiment, Lieutenant Simon Wilmot, of Light Dragoons, James Forster, master of a transport ship, and John Wilkinson, mate of the same, Samuel Elphinston and James Horns, mates of a British ship of war, Allan McDonald, Rannold McDonald, and Archibald McDonald, taken in New York, Thomas Leonard, of Monmouth county, New Jersey, and John Duyckunck, of Brunswick.

Some of the British prisoners had servants who were not prisoners. Among these was one, a negro who called himself Richard Barley, who attended on Lieutenant Wilmot—it was thought the negro was a runaway.

The following is a copy from an original MSS. letter, before me, addressed to the committee for the care of prisoners of war at Reading.

March 16, 1777.

Gentlemen—

By direction of the late Council of Safety, now the Board of War, I enclose you a copy of Lieutenant Simon Wilmot's parole; he is to set out to-morrow, under the conduct of Lieutenant Boehm, of the City Guards.

I am, gentlemen, your very obedient servant,
Lewis Nicola, *Town Major.*

Besides Kessler's spring, other streams have their sources from Penn's mountain, such as Roush's creek, upon which are several mills. The small tributaries of Dry run, and other smaller streams, one of which supplies the Reading reservoir, near the head of Penn street.

Iron ore is abundant—Mount Penn alone contains an inexhaustible quantity.

This township is intersected by the turnpike from Philadelphia to Pottsville, which passes through the western part, and by that which passes from Reading to Harrisburg. The Schuylkill canal, and the railroad from Philadelphia to Pottsville, both pass through Alsace.

There are, besides the churches in the borough of Reading, two churches in this township; Alsace church, about two miles from Reading, and Spies' church in the north-east angle of the township—both common to the German Reformed and Lutherans. It contains two fulling mills, four grist mills, and three saw mills. The population of Alsace township, exclusive of Reading, was in 1810, 1,275; 1820, 1,640; 1830, 1,943; 1840, 2,501. Of these there were 1,245 males, 1,256 females. Horses 214; horned cattle 624; sheep 409; swine 658; bushels of wheat 8,113; rye 6,196; corn 6,220; oats 8,094; buckwheat 307; potatoes 3,742; tons of hay 820; pounds of wool 230; flax 725. Whole amount of valuation on all articles made taxable, for county purposes, for 1844, $686,220; county tax $1,372 46; State tax $889,56.

READING is on the east bank of the Schuylkill,* and about fifty-two miles from both metropolis and capital of the State. The following sketch of the primitive settlement, and early history of Reading, is from the pen of DANIEL B. KEIM, Esq., and was originally published in the *Ladies' Garland*, for February, 1839.

"As early as 1733, warrants were taken out by John and Samuel Finney, and four hundred and fifty acres of land surveyed under their sanction, which are now entirely embraced within the limits of Reading. Whether the inducements to this selection were other than its general beauty and fertility, it is now difficult to say, though it is asserted that when the Proprietaries, John and Richard Penn, became aware of its advantages, and proposed to re-purchase for the location of a town, the Messrs. Finney long and firmly resisted all the efforts of negotiation. This produced a momentary change in the design of the Proprietaries, as they employed Richard Hockley to survey and lay out the plan of a town on the margin of the Schuylkill, opposite its confluence with the Tulpehocken. This

---

* Schuylkill, Schuil-kill, or Skoal-kill, i. e. hidden-creek, or channel— the native Indians called this stream *Manijunk*, according to a Swedish MSS.—*Proud* ii., p. 251.

survey is still to be found on record, though divested of any
date or name by which the precise period in which it was made
can be ascertained. It is now only known as an appended
portion to Reading, under the designation of the 'Hockley Out-
Lots.'

"The importance as well as the reality of the design, now
appears to have subdued the objections of the Finneys to the
sale of their claim, as they immediately relaxed in their demands, and finally yielded them to the proprietaries, who at
once caused the 'Hockley plot' to be abandoned, and in the fall
of the year 1748, that of Reading to be laid out.

"The difficulty in obtaining water, even at great depths,
through the limestone, was the specious reason generally assigned for the sudden vacation of the former site, as the new
one was remarkable for the numerous large and copious springs
existing within its limits.

"Thus, Thomas and Richard Penn, proprietaries and governors in chief of the province of Pennsylvania, became private
owners of the ground plot of Reading, the lots of which they
carefully subjected in their titles to an annual quit or ground
rent. Singular as it may seem, this claim became almost forgotten through neglect, and the circumstances that resulted
from the change in the *old order* of things produced by the revolution; indeed, when recurred to at all, it was generally believed to have become a forfeit to the State, by the nature of
that event. But a few years ago it was revived by the heirs,
and its collection attempted under the authority of the law;
but so excited were the populace, and adverse to the payment
of its accumulated amount, that it was generally, and in some
cases, violently resisted, till the deliberations of a town meeting had suggested measures, leaning to a more direct, amicable
and permanent compromise.

"Like most of the primitive towns of the State, Reading is
indebted for its name, as also for the county in which it is situated, to the native soil of the Penn's.

"Its area comprises about 2,194 acres of a rich calcareous
soil, sloping gently from Penn's Mount, an elevation on its
eastern side, to the river Schuylkill; thus presenting natural
facilities for its drainage, and the prevention of accumulated
filth, and adding a decided feature to its well-established character for health.

" The streets intersect each other at right angles, and form in their direction almost correct indices to the cardinal points of the compass. Their original names were retained to a very recent date, (Aug. 6, 1833,) and were characteristic of the loyalty of the proprietary feeling, as well as family attachment and regard.

" King, Queen, Prince, Duke, Earl, and Lord streets, sufficiently evidence the strength of the former, whilst the main or central streets, Penn and Callowhill, are as distinctly indicative of filial regard.

" Hannah Callowhill, their mother, was the second wife of William Penn, and had issue beside *Thomas* and *Richard*, of John, Margaret and Dennis, whence also had originated the names of Thomas, Margaret, and Richard streets. Hamilton street, from James Hamilton, Esq., who was Deputy Governor of the Province at that period.

" The names now substituted ' as more compatible with the republican simplicity of our present form of government,' are similar to those of Philadelphia, as the streets running north and south commence at Water street, on the Schuylkill, and extend to Twelfth street, while those running east and west are called Penn, Franklin, Washington, Chestnut and Walnut streets.

" In 1751, Reading contained 130 dwelling houses, besides stables and other buildings—106 families, and 378 inhabitants, though about two years before it had not above one house in it.

The original population was principally Germans, who emigrated from Wurtemberg, and the Palatinate, though the administration of public affairs was chiefly in the hands of the Friends.

" The former by their preponderance of number, gave the decided character in habits and language to the place, as the German was almost exclusively used in the ordinary transactions of life and business, and is yet retained to a very great extent."

As late as 1754, bears were still plenty in the vicinity of Reading. From an extract of a letter dated at Reading, Sept. 22, 1754, to a gentleman in Philadelphia, it would appear so. " The bears were never half so numerous as now; you can

13*

scarce go à mile without seeing one. Several of them have been killed near this town lately."—*Phil. Gazette*, 1754.

The following were returned by the assessor in 1757, as taxables of the town of Reading:

Adam Geier, Andreas Fighthorn, Adam Eppler, Adam Ege, Abraham Smith, Andreas Engle, Alexar.dei Klinger, Abraham Kerber, Anthony Fricker, Adam Widman, Adam Fas, Adam Schlegle, Adam Wirenberger, Adam Brosius, Bastian Krauser, Bernhard Rhorbauch, Benjamin Pearson, Baltzer Sneyder, Baltzer Henning, Baltzer Meuerlin, Conrad Weiser, Esq., Conrad Bower, Christopher Lehman, Conrad Braun, Conrad Dress, Christian Samet, Christopher Smid, Conrad Reichstein, Christian Banse, Christian Merchel, Conrad Stichler, Conrad Neihard, David Henderson, David Meuerlen, David Schreck, Henry Aaun, Dorst Phister, Erst Maurer, Edward Drury, Erhard Rose, Eberhard Martin, Amos Evans, Evan Price, Francis Wenrich, Frederick Miller, Frederick Perlet, Francis Gibson, Frederick Zinn, George Diehl, George Bernhard, George Yoe, George Deible, George Springer, George Jock, George Handschuh, Gottlieb Strohecker, George Heist, Gabriel Schop, George Geisler, George Schultz, George Sourbry, George Wunder, George Stump, Henry Dosselbauer, Henry Gulhard, Henry Ruhl, Henry Wolf, Henry Gossler, Henry Degenhard, Henry Rightmeyer, Henry Singer, Henry Hahn, Isaac Wickersham, John Schorb, John Sweitzer, Jacob Lutz, Joseph Henck, John Smith, Jacob Kern, Jacob Fisher, Joseph Shamon, John Richner, James Keemer, Jacob Rabold, John Schneider, Jacob Hettler, Jacob Dehn, Israel Jacobs, Jacob Yaeger, Jacob Bucher, John Dengler, John Gross, John Weaber, John Henrich, John Jacobs, John Lebo, John Schried, Jacob Leybrock, James Read, Esq., Jacob Balde, Isaiah Ris, John Wideman, Joseph Brintlinger, John Bertolet, John Koch, John Eisenbeis, John Bernheisel, Jacob Nagle, John Morge, Isaac Young, John Hardman, Joseph Ritner, Joseph Perret, Julius Kerber, Jacob Dick, John Philippi, John Kurtz, Henry Kraft, Ludwig Weidman, Ludwig Ember, Leonard Spang, Lorentz Fix, Michael Reitmoyer, Michael Brecht, Martin Kast, Michael Seister, Michael Hag, Michael Fedder, Mathias Feigle, Mathias Mayer, Michael Rosch, jr., Michael Rosch, senr., Martin Ege, Michael Spaz, Mathias Bonhman, Mathias Hein-lein, Michael Fichthorn, Nicholas Seysinger, Nicholas Godschalk, Nicholas Morris, Nicholas Schabert, Nicholas Neidle, Nicholas Keim, Philip Weis, Philip Smith, Peter Loch, Philip Nagle, Philip Sehler, Peter Feder, Peter Dehm, Peter Weiser, Peter Kleim, Peter Haas, Peter Klinger, Philip Mayor, Peter Baum, Philip Marselaaf, Paul Perlet, Philip Phising, Samuel Hush, Stophel Widman, Samson Mitelberger, Samuel Shultz, Stophel Neidley, Simon Nagle, Stophel Mileisen, Thomas Dehm, Thomas Lincoln, Valentine Kerper, Valentine Urledig, William Reiser, William Clues, William Iddings, William Max, William Orman, William Ermel, William Miller, Huttenstein, William Frick, William Koch, William Gress, William Miller, Wolfgang Haga, Jacob Bulkert, Martin Young, Martin Kraft, Andrew Smith, Samuel Weiser, David Rine, Henry Witman, John Sourmilk, James Whitehead, Benjamin Lightfoot, Nathan Lyon, James Starr, Robert Popkin, Isaac Lebo, Samuel Jackson, Thomas Barcher, Elijah Pearson, Michael Scherchtoly.

During the French and Indian war, the inhabitants were occasionally alarmed on account of the Indians. [See chap. iii., pp. 47, 50, 54.] Their hopes and fears, owing to the alliance between the Indians and French, and conduct of some inhabitants among them, were often excited, as will appear from the following public documents:

To THE HON. GOV. MORRIS,[*]

SIR:—As all our *Protestant inhabitants* are very uneasy at the behavior of the *Roman Catholics*, who are very numerous in this county, some of whom show great joy at the very bad news lately from the army,[†] we thought it our duty to inform your honor of our dangerous situation, and to beg your honor to enable us by some legal authority to *disarm* or otherwise to *disable the papists* from doing injury to other people, who are not of their vile principles. We know that the people of the Roman Catholic church are bound by their principles to be the worst subjects and worst of neighbors; and we have reason to fear, at this time, that the Roman Catholics in Cussahoppen, where they have a very magnificent chapel, and lately have had large processions, have bad designs; for in the neighborhood of that chapel, it is reported, and generally believed, that

---

[*] Provincial Records, N. p. 125.
[†] Alluding to Braddock's defeat.

thirty Indians are now lurking, well armed with guns and swords, or cutlasses. The priest at Reading, as well as Cussahoppen, last Sunday gave notice to their people, that they could not come to them again in less than nine weeks, whereas they constantly preach once in four weeks to their congregations; whereupon some imagine, they are gone to consult with our enemies at Du Quesne. It is a great unhappiness, at this time, to the other people of this province, that the papists should keep fire arms in their houses, against which the protestants are not prepared, who, therefore, are subject to a massacre whenever the papists are ready. We pray that your Honor would direct us in this important business, by the bearer, whom we have sent express to your honor.

We are, may it please your honor,

Your honor's most obedient servants,

HENRY HARVEY,

JAMES READ,

WILLIAM BIRD,

JONAS SEELY,

CONRAD WEISER,

Justices of Berks County.

Heidelberg, July 23, 1755.

This excitement was not only among the inhabitants of Berks—but the people of Northampton had strong objections to the Catholics about the same time.

"To the Worshipful, the Justices of the Court of General Quarter Sessions of the Peace, held at Easton, for the county of Northampton, the 18th June, 1755.

"The petition of divers inhabitants of said town and others, humbly showeth:—That your petitioners are very apprehensive your worships have been greatly imposed upon, in granting recommendations to his honor, the governor, for sundry Roman Catholics, out of legiance of his present majesty, our most gracious sovereign, for keeping public house, in this town, when an open rupture is now daily expected between a Roman Catholic powerful and perfidious prince, and the crown of Great Britain; as the Romans have thereby a better opportunity of becoming acquainted with our designs against them, and thereby better enabled to discover those designs and render them abortive.

" Your petitioners therefore pray, that your honors will make proper inquiry into this matter, and grant such redress as the circumstances of things may require; and your petitioners will ever pray, &c.

"John Fricker, a Catholic applicant, was then refused a recommendation, because he was a Roman Catholic."

Time has tested the grounds of the suspicions of those opposed to Catholics. Facts settle doubts, and remove or confirm prejudices. The current is still strong against them. They induce it by their importunities for office, and their consequent success, naturally engenders these feelings against them; especially among the Germans against the Irish portion of them. The blustering and swaggering of some at the polls, are offensive, not only to Germans, but to all true Americans; and the day is not distant, when an end must be put to these encroachments for the safety and permanency of our free institutions. A general diffusion of knowledge is the only remedy.

During the revolution of '76, Reading was resorted to by Philadelphians, and a place equally safe from the dangers to which the metropolis was more exposed, as a place of retirement from the political commotions of the city. Alexander Graydon, born at Bristol, April 10, 1752, and who had been taken prisoner at New York, but while on parole visited his mother, who had removed her residence to Reading, gives some interesting incidents by way of reminiscences of his stay here, in 1777.

In his *Memoirs*, page 263, he says, " My mother, as already mentioned, having removed her residence to Reading, thither, in company with the lady so often adverted to, whose family was also established there, we proceeded in high spirits.

"Many other Philadelphians had recourse to this town, as a place of safety from a sudden incursion of the enemy; and, among a score or more of fugitive families, were those of Gen. Mifflin and my uncle, as I have called Mr. Biddle, though only standing in that relation by marriage.

"It was also the station assigned to a number of prisoners, both British and German, as well as of the principal Scotch royalists, that had been subdued and taken in North Carolina. I soon discovered that a material change had taken place

during my absence from Pennsylvania; and that the pulses of
many, that at the time of my leaving it, had beaten high in the
cause of whigism and liberty, were considerably lowered.
Power, to use a language which had already ceased to be or-
thodox, and could therefore only be whispered, had fallen into
low hands: The better sort were disgusted and weary of the
war.   Congress, indeed, had given out that they had counted
the cost of the contest; but it was but too apparent, that very
many of their adherents, had made false calculations on the
subject, having neither allowed enough for disasters in the field,
nor domestic chagrins, the inevitable consequence of a dissolu-
tion of old power and the assumption of new.   It was, in fact,
just beginning to be perceived, that the ardor of the inflamed
multitude is not to be tempered; and that the instigators of
revolutions are rarely those who are destined to conclude them,
or profit by them.

The great cause of schism among the whigs, had been the
declaration of independence.   Its adoption had, of course, rendered numbers malcontent; and thence, by a very natural transition, consigned them to the tory ranks.   Unfortunately for
me, this was the predicament in which I found my nearest and
best friend, whose example had no doubt contributed to the
formation of my political opinions, and whose advice, concur-
ring with my own sense of duty, had placed me in the army.
I now discovered, that we no longer thought or felt alike; and
though no rupture took place, some coldness ensued, and I have
to regret a few words of asperity which passed between us, on
occasion of the French alliance.   But this was but a momentary blast; as neither of us was affected with that hateful bi-
gotry, which too generally actuated whigs and tories, and led
to mutual persecution, as one or other had the ascendancy.

As to the whigs, the very cause for which they contended, was
essentially that of freedom, and yet all the freedom it granted
was, at the peril of tar and feathers, to think and act like themselves, the extent indeed of all toleration proceeding from the
multitude, whether advocating the divine right of a king, the
divine sovereignty of the people, or of the idol it may be pleased
to constitute its unerring plenipotentiary.   Toleration is only
to be looked for upon points in which men are indifferent, or
where they are duly checked and restrained, by a salutary authority.

Mr. Edward Biddle, then in a declining state of health, and no longer in Congress, apparently entertained sentiments not accordant with the measures pursuing; and in the fervid style of elocution, for which he was distinguished, he often exclaimed, that he really knew not what to wish for. " The subjugation of my country," he would say, "I deprecate as a most grievous calamity, and yet sicken at the idea of thirteen, unconnected, petty democracies; if we are to be independent, let us, in the name of God, at once have an empire, and place Washington at the head of it."*

Fortunately for our existence as a nation, a great proportion of those, whose early exertions tended to that issue, were not aware of the price by which it was to be acquired; otherwise, my knowledge of the general feeling at this time, so far as my means of information extended, obliges me to say, that it would not have been achieved. Not that disgust and despondence were universal among the leading and best informed whigs, but an equal proportion of disaffection to independence, in the early part of the year 1776, must have defeated the enterprize. Still, it may be observed, that as whigism declined among the higher classes, it increased in the inferior; because they who composed them, thereby obtained power and consequence. Uniforms and epaulets, with militia titles and paper money, making numbers of persons gentlemen who had never been so before, kept up every where throughout the country, the spirit of opposition; and if these were not real patriotism, they were very good substitutes for it. Could there, in fact, be any comparison between the condition of a daily drudge in agricultural or mechanic labor, and that of a spruce, militia-man, living without work, and, at the same time, having plenty of continental dollars in his pocket! How could he be otherwise than well effected to such a cause!

The success of General Howe; the loss of Philadelphia; as well as the ground given in the northern quarter by the retreat of General St. Clair, were amply counterbalanced by the utter extinction of Burgoyne's army, on the 15th of October. As

* I have presumed to put in the wrong, those who were adverse to the declaration of independence; and the high ground on which we have since stood, fully justified me: but present appearances seem again to unsettle the question, in the minds of those at least who are heterodox enough to doubt the eligibility of a dependence on France.

Reading lay in the route from Saratoga to Yorktown, where Congress was now assembled, we received, before that body, the particulars of this glorious event, from Major Wilkinson, who was charged with the despatches of General Gates. But without loading my memoirs with obvious and trite reflections on this memorable occurrence, I turn a moment to myself, to observe: That were I prey to the vulture of ill-star'd ambition, the mention of a gentleman, with whom I commenced in the same rank, my military career, and who is now in the chief commands of the American force, might suggest, somewhat unpleasantly, the immeasurable distance he has left me behind; but the recollections his name awakens with infinitely more interest, are of a nature wholly different. They relate to pursuits and occupations of a character more congenial to that season of life, when, as a student of physic, he attended medical lectures in Philadelphia, before either of us wore a uniform, and before a foundation was laid for the many strifes which have since ensued. Thus much, without connecting him with any of them, I freely pay to the remembrance of an early friendship, ever renewed when casualities have brought us together, maugre the enstranging influence of different party associations.

The ensuing winter, at Reading, was gay and agreeable, notwithstanding that the enemy was in possession of the metropolis. The society was sufficiently large and select; and a sense of common suffering in being driven from their homes, had the effect of more closely uniting its members. Disasters of this kind, if duly weighed, are not grievously to be deplored. The variety and bustle they bring along with them, give a spring to the mind; and when illumined by hope, as was now the case, they are, when present, not painful, and when past, they are among the incidents most pleasing in retrospection. Besides the families established in this place, it was seldom without a number of visiters, gentlemen of the army, and others. Hence the dissipation of cards, sleighing parties, balls, &c., was freely indulged. General Mifflin, at this era, was at home, a chief out of war, complaining, though not ill, considerably malcontent, and apparently, not in high favor at head-quarters. According to him, the ear of the commander-in-chief was exclusively possessed by Greene, who was represented to be neither the most wise, the most brave, nor most patriotic of counsellors. In short, the campaign in this quarter, was stigmatised as a series of blunders; and the incapacity of those who had conducted it, unsparingly reprobated.

The better fortune of the northern army, was ascribed to the superior talents of its leader; and it began to be whispered, that Gates was the man who should, of right, have the station so incompetently sustained by Washington. There was, to all appearance, a cabal forming for his deposition, in which, it is not improbable, that Gates, Mifflin and Conway, were already engaged; and, in which, the congenial spirit of Lee, on his exchange, immediately took a share. The well known apostrophe of Conway to America, importing "that Heaven had passed a decree in her favor, or her ruin must long before have ensued, from the imbecility of her military counsels," was, at this time, familiar at Reading; and I heard him myself, when he was afterwards on a visit to that place, express himself to that effect: "That no man was more a gentleman than General Washington, or appeared to more advantage at his table, or in the usual intercourse of life; but as to his talents for the command of an army, (with a French shrug,) they were miserable indeed." Observations of this kind, continually repeated, could not fail to make an impression within the sphere of their circulation; and it may be said, that the popularity of the commander in chief, was a good deal impaired at Reading. As to myself, however, I can confidently aver, that I never was proselyted; or gave into the opinion for a moment, that any man in America, was worthy to supplant the exalted character, that presided in her army.

I might have been disposed, perhaps, to believe that such talents as were possessed by Lee, could they be brought to act subordinately, might often be useful to him; but I ever thought it would be a fatal error, to put any other in his place. Nor was I the only one, who forbore to become a partizan of Gates. Several others thought they saw symptoms of selfishness in the business; nor could the great *eclat* of the northern campaign, convince them, that its hero was superior to Washington. The duel which afterwards took place between Generals Conway and Cadwalader, though immediately proceeding from an unfavorable opinion expressed by the latter, of the conduct of the former at Germantown, had perhaps a deeper origin, and some reference to this intrigue; as I had the means

14

of knowing, that General Cadwalader, suspecting Mifflin had instigated Conway to fight him, was extremely earnest to obtain data from a gentleman who lived in Reading, whereon to ground a serious explanation with Mifflin. [Not that General Cadwalader was induced from the intrigue to speak unfavorably of General Conway's behavior at Germantown. That of itself, was a sufficient ground of censure. Conway, it seems, during the action, was found in a farm-house by Generals Reed and Cadwalader. Upon their enquiring the cause, he replied, in great agitation, that his horse was wounded in the neck.— Being urged to get another horse, and at any rate to join his brigade which was engaged, he declined it, repeating that his horse was wounded in the neck. Upon Conway's applying to Congress, some time after, to be made a major general, and earnestly urging his suit, Cadwalader made known this conduct of his at Germantown; and it was for so doing, that Conway gave the challenge, the issue of which, was, his being dangerously wounded in the face from the pistol of General Cadwalader. He recovered, however, and some time after went to France.] So much for the manœuvring, which my location at one of its principal seats, brought me acquainted with; and which, its authors were soon after desirous of burying in oblivion.

Among the persons, who, this winter, spent much time in Reading, was one Luttiloe, foreigner, who was afterwards arrested in London on suspicion of hostile designs; also, Mr. William Duer, who either was, or lately had been, a member of Congress. His character is well known. He was of the dashing cast, a man of the world, confident and animated, with a promptitude in displaying the wit and talents he possessed, with very little regard to the decorum, which either time or place imposed. Of this, he gave an instance one day, at Mr. Edward Biddle's, which, had it been on a theatre, where the royal cause was predominant, I should have relished it: as it was, it was unpleasant to me.

Captain Speke, of the British army, a prisoner, was present, with his eye on a newspaper, several of which had lately come out of Philadelphia, when Duer, taking up another, began to read aloud, commenting with much sarcasm on the paragraphs as he went along. Speke bore it a good while, but at length Duer's remarks became so pinching, that he was roused to a reply. To this he received a ready rejoinder, and a warm altercation was on the point of taking place, when captain Speke prudently took the resolution of relinquishing the field; and taking up his hat, abruptly retired. As Speke, although a thorough Englishman, was a well bred man, with whom I had become acquainted, and had exchanged some civilities, I was not a little hurt at this circumstance, as the company in general seemed to be.

Duer, for his part, triumphed in his success, displaying a heart, which, however bold on the safe side of the lines, might nevertheless have been sufficiently meek on the other; at least, such a conduct would but conform to the result of my observations on persons who play the bashaw in prosperity; and I believe it is pretty generally agreed, to be no mark of game to crow upon a dunghill. While upon the subject of Captain Speke, I will finish the little I have to say of him. He belonged, if my recollection does not fail me, to the same regiment with Mr. Becket; at least, he was acquainted with him, and told me had heard him speak of me. He was young and lively, with an addiction to that sly significance of remark, characteristic both of his profession and his nation; and which may be pardoned, when accompanied with good humor. Taking up my hat one day, when at his quarters to take coffee with him and one or two others of his fellow prisoners, he observed, that it was a very decent one, which is more, said he, than I can say of those generally worn by the officers of your army; they have precisely, what we call in England, the *damn my eyes cock*. At another time, having called upon me at my mother's, I was led by some circumstance, to advert to the awkward form and low ceiling of the room; but "faith," said he, looking round, "you have made the most of it with furniture;" which was true enough, as it was unmercifully overloaded with chairs, tables and family pictures.

Such freedoms may fully justify me in scanning Mr. Speke, who, to say the truth, was, in point of information, far above the level which is allowed to the gentlemen of the British army, by Swift and other writers of their nation. As to "your *Noveds*, and *Blutarks*, and *Omars* and stuff," I know not, if he was of the noble captain's opinion, in Hannah's animated plea for turning Hamilton's bawn into a barrack; but he had read some of the English poets; and speaking of Prior and Pope, I remember his saying, that the former was much preferred to the latter, by people of taste in England. But grant what we may to the sprightliness and easy gaiety of Prior, this can hardly be the award of sound criticism. Being heartily tired of the condition, Mr. Speke was extremely anxious to get rid of it, and to this effect suggested, that by mutual exertion, we might be exchanged for each other. He said that if I could obtain permission for him to go to Philadelphia on parole, he had no doubt of having sufficient interest to effect it. I accordingly took the liberty to write to General Washington on the subject, but was a long time in suspense as to the success of my application. An additional inducement to the step, was, that both Colonel Miles, and Major West, had by requisition of General Howe, repaired to Philadelphia; and I every day expected a similar summons.

It had been given out that these gentlemen had not observed all the passiveness which had been enjoined upon them by their parole; and I well knew that I was charged with a like transgression. I spoke freely, it is true, of the treatment of prisoners; and this was considered by the tories and some of the British officers in our hands, as very unpardonable in one who had been favored as I had been; and I was aware that I was threatened with a retraction of the indulgence. I remained, however, unmolested. The situation of Miles and West in the neighborhood of the army at White Marsh, was, perhaps, the circumstance which gave color to the accusation against them; but they were not long detained.

Besides, that it would have ill comported with the indulgence I enjoyed, it was abhorrent to my feelings, to behave haughtily to a prisoner. There were two puppies, however, in that predicament, in whom I immediately recognised the insolent manner of a genuine *scoundrel in red;* and these, I cautiously avoided. They were subalterns; one of whom, of the name of Wilson, was base enough, under the false pretence of being related to Captain Wilson, who he had some how learned, had treated me with civility, to borrow a few guineas of my mother, which it unluckily slipped his memory to repay. Had I been aware of the application, the loan would have been prevented; but I never knew of the circumstance, until after his exchange.

With the exception of these fellows, who, I had the mortification to hear, had found their way to Gen. Washington's table, at the time of their being taken, all the prisoners in Reading behaved with much decency. Among them, were a number of German officers, who had really the appearance of being, what we call, downright men. There was a Major Stine, a Captain Sobbe, and a Captain Wetherholt, of the Hessians, whom I sometimes fell in with.

There were several others, with whom I was not acquainted, and whose names I do not remember. One old gentleman, a Colonel, was a great professional reader, whom, on his applica- cation, I accommodated with such books of the kind, as I had. Another of them, a very portly personage, apparently replete with national phlegm, was, nevertheless, enthusiastically de- voted to music, in which he was so absorbed, as seldom to go abroad. I did not know this musical gentleman, except by sight; but I have understood from those who did, that call upon him at what time they would, and, like another Achilles in re- tirement,

> Amus'd at ease, the godlike man they found,
> Pleas'd with the solemn harp's harmonious sound ·

For this was the obsolete instrument, from which he extracted the sounds that so much delighted him. But of all the pri- soners, one Graff, a Brunswick officer taken by General Gates's army, was admitted to the greatest privileges. Under the pa- tronage of Dr. Potts, who had been principal surgeon in the northern department, he had been introduced to our dancing parties; and being always afterwards invited, he never failed to attend. He was a young man of mild and pleasing manners, with urbanity enough to witness the little triumphs of party, without being incited to ill humor by them. Over hearing a dance called for, one evening, which we named *Burgoyne's surrender*, he observed to his partner, that it was a very pretty dance, notwithstanding the name; and that General Burgoyne himself would be happy to dance it in such good company. There was also a Mr. Stutzoe, of the Brunswick dragoons, than whose, I have seldom seen a figure more martial, or a manner more indicative of that manly openness, which is sup- posed to belong to the character of a soldier. I had a slight acquaintance with him; and recollect with satisfaction, his call- ing on me at the time of his exchange, to make me his acknowledgments, as he was pleased to say, for my civilities to the prisoners.

Perhaps I may be excused for these trifling details, when it it is considered, that they serve to mark the temper of the times, and to shew, that they were not all fire and fury, as certain modern pretenders to the spirit of *seventy-six,* have almost persuaded us they were. It ought to be granted, indeed, that an equal degree of toleration, was not every where to be met with. It would scarcely have been found in that description of persons, which soon arrogated, and have since voted themselves the exclusive possession of all the patriotism in the nation. Even that small portion of the monopolists which resided at Reading, revolted at a moderation they did not understand; and all who were less violent and bigoted than themselves, were branded as tories. All the families which had removed from Philadelphia were involved in this reproach; and, in their avoidance of the enemy to the manifest injury, of their affairs, they were supposed to exhibit proofs of disaffection. Nor was I much better off: my having risked myself in the field was nothing: I should have staid at home, talked big, been a militia-man, and hunted tories.

In confirmation of my remark, that toleration was not among the virtues affected by those who were emphatically styled *the people,* I will instance the case of a young Scotch officer of the name of Dunlap, who was one day beset in the street, by certain persons overflowing with whigism; and, for presuming to resent the insults he received from them, was not only cudgelled, but afterwards put to jail. This treatment might have fairly squared with that of our officers from the royal side, in relation to the fish sellers; though I will undertake to aver, that, generally speaking, the prisoners in our hands were treated both with lenity and generosity. Some time after this affray, happening, at a table, in Philadelphia, to be placed by the side of Doctor Witherspoon, then a member of Congress, I took occasion to mention it to him, and to intercede for his good offices in regard to the liberation of Dunlap, who was still in jail.

I counted something upon the national spirit, supposed to be so prevalent among North Britons; and yet more, upon the circumstance of knowing from Dunlap and two other young Scotchmen, his fellow prisoners, that Doctor Witherspoon had been well acquainted with their families. I did not find, however, that the doctor was much melted to compassion for the mishap of his countryman, as he contented himself with coldly observing, that if I could suggest any substantial ground for him to proceed upon, he would do what he could for the young man.

It appeared to me that enough had been suggested, by my simple relation of the facts; and I had nothing more to offer. But whether or not my application was of any benefit to its object, my presentation of the *laddies* to the recollection of the doctor, seemed to have something of national interest in it; and had the effect, to incite him to a shrewd remark, according to his manner. He told me he had seen the young men soon after they had been taken, and was surprised to find one of them, whose name I forgot, so much of a cub. His father, said he, was a very sprightly fellow, when I knew him. This lad is the fruit of a second marriage; and I immediately concluded, when I saw him, said the doctor, that Jemmey, or Sawney something, mentioning the father's name, had taken some *clumsy girl* to wife, for the sake of a fortune.

On looking back here, and adverting to the free observations I have from time to time made, both on revolutionary men and measures, I am aware that I have no forgiveness from many, for attempting to rub off the fine varnish which adheres to them. But I set out with the avowed design of declaring the truth; and to this, I have most sacredly and conscientiously conformed, according to my persuasions, even as to the coloring of each particular I have touched upon.

The same veracity shall direct my future delineations, well knowing, that, independently of my obligations to do justice, this alone must circumscribe the merit of my memoirs. That we were not, and still are not without patriotism, in an equal degree, perhaps, with other nations, I have no inclination to question; but that a noble disinterestedness and willingness to sacrifice private interest to public good, should be the general disposition any where, my acquaintance with human nature, neither warrants me in asserting, or believing. The prevalence of generous sentiment, of which, no doubt, there is a portion in all communities, depends very much upon those, who have the direction of their affairs. Under the guidance of Washington, both during the revolution and his administration of the general government, the honorable feelings being cher-

ished and brought into action, they had a temporary predomi-
nance over those, which were selfish and base. But these, in
their turn, having acquired the ascendancy, we may sadly re-
cognize with the poet, that

> An empty form
> Is the weak virtue that amid the shade
> Lamenting lies, with future schemes amus'd,
> While wickedness and folly, kindred powers,
> Confound the world

Reminiscences of Reading in 1798-'99.—Shortly after the
election of John Adams, several acts were passed by Congress,
which were obnoxious to a portion of the people of East Pennsylvania, in consequence of which, Berks, Bucks, and Northampton, presented scenes of excitement. In Northampton, a
party headed by one Fries, resisted attempts by the federal
government to collect a *direct tax*—well known by the name
of *"the house tax."* John Fries, a desperado, and his associates, not only resisted the assessors, but in hot pursuit chased
them from township to township. It is said there were parties
of them—fifty and sixty in number—most of them well armed.
Fries himself was armed with a large horse pistol, and accompanied by one Kuyder, who assisted him in command. They
seized several assessors.

In some parts of the counties named, in demonstration of
their opposition to government, they erected *liberty poles.* To
quell the insurrection, troops, in obedience to Adams' instructions, were raised in Lancaster county—several companies
marched from Lancaster, April 1, 1799; wending their *front*
toward the arena of dispute, by way of *Reading,* when Captain Montgomery's troop of light horse arrived on the evening
of the 1st of April. Their first act, to display their prowess
and gallantry, was to go clandestinely to the house of Jacob
Gosin, who in the spirit of the times had erected a liberty pole
on his own premises, which they cut, without meeting any resistance.

To give undoubted proof of their daring bravery, they brandished their damascene weapons—drew pistols, to show that
they were armed, in the house of the inoffensive father, whose
minor children were scared "half to death," at the martial ma-
nœuvers of the Lancaster troops.

To let no time slip, and while they were undaunted, they proceeded from Gosin's to the house of John Strohecker, whither their eagle eyes were drawn by a recently erected pole, tipped with a rag, "flapping in the breeze." This pole, to show the independence of some sturdy urchins, had been erected by some children, in which Strohecker's were ringleaders. To deter these young heroes, the soldiers took down the pole, stripped it of its insignia—entered the house where they found the little wights—and as they did at Gosin's, so did they here—brandished weapons of war—presented pistols and swords to the youthful company, to no small alarm of both parents and children!!

To consummate their martial plans and designs, they molested the house of Jacob Epler—maltreated him unprovokedly.— Like bravos ever merit—these merited the contempt of all refleeting persons—rendering themselves obnoxious to the orderly and well disposed among all classes.

Satisfied of having rendered their country some service, the troop next morning started for Northampton, to fully execute the specific purpose of their mission. This done, they again returned by way of Reading, where they entered the office of the "*Adler,,*" a paper edited and printed by Jacob Schneider, whom they rudely denuded, by violently taring his clothes from his body, in a somewhat inclement season, and by force of arms, dragged him before the commanding captain, who peremptorily ordered the editor, for writing and printing some offensive articles, to be whipped; "twenty-five lashes," said he, shall be well laid on his denuded back, in the market house"— which order was, however, not executed, because of the timely and manly interposition of some *gentlemen* of Captain Leiper's company, of Philadelphia. A few lashes, however, had been inflicted before these men had time to fully interpose—these were laid on by one accustomed to beat, when little resistance is to be dreaded—he was a drummer !!

Colonel Epler, who it appears, had by this time erected, by the assistance of his neighbors, a *liberty pole* in place of the pole erected by his children—thither the soldiery resorted, where they attempted to compel a common laborer to cut down the "offensive wood," notwithstanding that he protested against doing so, at the same time, on most solemn asseverations,

declaring he also was a federalist—Ich bin auch ein Federal-
ihr liebe Leut; das bin.—Ja ich auch ein Federal!!

They succeeded in divesting the pole, and with it appended
as a trophy, they rode, vociferating as they went, through the
streets of Reading, to their place of quarters. In a few days
they left; but on the 24th of April, an army under the command of Brigadier General W. McPherson, arrived at Reading,
apprehending some of the insurrectionists, who were afterwards
tried before Judge Peters,—some found guilty—some were
fined and imprisoned—some were condemned to be capitally
punished— but none atoned with their lives—they were pardoned through executive clemency! Their names are here with-
held.

"The borough is divided into four nearly equal parts, by the
intersection of its principal streets—Penn and Fifth. This division is recognized in various borough arrangements, and is of
much practical convenience. The houses are numbered from
these streets. The boundaries of the wards are also marked
by them. There are four wards, N. E. ward, the S. E. ward,
the S. W. ward, and the N. W. ward."

Reading is a flourishing town, containing rising of ten thousand inhabitants. It is beautifully situated on a "gentle de-
clivity" or "sloping plain, between Penn's mountain and the
eastern bank of the Schuylkill. The streets, most used, are
regularly graded, and are covered with a hard white gravel,
derived from the sand-stone of the mountain, east of the town,
which forms a very compact, smooth, and durable roads, superior to most paved or McAdamized roads."

It is, comparatively speaking, a great place for trade. It possesses superior advantages for manufacturing purposes; and will
no doubt, ere long, be a great manufacturing place. "It may,"
says Major William Stahle, to whose labors we owe much of
this article, "be safely predicted that within twenty-five years
from this time, (1841,) that those fertile fields between the railroad and the river, will all be converted into town, compactly
built."

This town was erected into a *borough* by an act of assembly
in 1783; altered and repealed by an act of 1813, under which
it elects a legislative town council and burgesses, whose duty
it is to carry the ordinancy into effect.

Formerly, and till within a few years, the *Jahr Markts,* or

The Court House at Reading

yearly markets, held on the 4th of June and 22d of October, as privileges granted by the proprietors in 1776, were always *"thickly"* attended—crowded by the boys and girls, fathers and mothers, from the country, for the purpose of hilarity, and " to the reverse of morals."

Reading contains the usual number of public buildings, court house, jail, state house, &c. The new court house, finished in 1840, is superior to most others in the State. It stands on an elevated ground plot, and measures 120 feet in front, and is 230 feet deep, inclosed with iron railing. The cost of it is $58,846 42. The jail was erected in 1770; it is a large stone building. The *State House*, as it is usually called, was erected in 1793. The market house is in the centre of Market square, in which provisions are sold on Wednesday and Saturday mornings.

There are several churches in the borough of Reading. The first erected in Reading, it is supposed, was the Friends meeting house, erected in 1766. It is a one story log-house. The German Reformed erected a building in 1753. In 1761, the first building, which was of logs, was taken down and a stone one built; this also was taken down, and the present one erected in 1832; which is 75 feet in length, 55 in breadth, and has a steeple 151 feet high, and a chime of bells. *Rev. John Casper Bucher* is the present pastor. In 1751, the Lutherans erected a building, which was torn down, and the present one erected in 1791. It is a very spacious building. It has a steeple 201 feet and 7 inches high. The *Rev. Jacob Miller* is the pastor. The Catholic church was erected in 1791.— The Presbyterian was erected in 1824. The present pastor, *Rev. William Sterling*. The Episcopal church was erected in 1826, pastor, *Rev. R. V. Morgan*. The Methodist church was erected in 1839. The Baptist church in 1837, and the Universalist in 1830. Besides these churches, there are three others belonging to the colored people—the Union African, the Presbyterian African and Methodist African.

The Reading Academy is a two story brick building, 50 by 60 feet, in which male and female schools are taught; besides the academy, there is an adequate number of public school houses. There are a number of charitable, literary and other associations in Reading. *See chap. on Education and the Press.*

There is also a Water Company, styled "The Reading Water Company," established prior to 1722; in that year the
company first brought water into the borough.   Since that
time, their works have been greatly improved.   The town
is supplied with excellent spring water, led into a reservoir,
near the head of Penn street, from whence it is carried through
the various streets, by means of iron pipes."*

That Reading is destined to become a great manufacturing
place, cannot be questioned, if a retrospect of the past be an
index of the future.

Some idea of the ordinary business of Reading, may be gathered from the account of trades and pursuits, given in a preceding chapter.   But this Borough is, of late, assuming an importance from its manufactures and public improvements, which
demands for these a separate notice.

No manufncturing was done in Reading previous to the year
1836, except in the articles of boots and shoes, hats and stone
ware.   Since that period the Iron and Nail Works of Messrs.
Keim, Whitaker & Co., the Iron & Brass Foundry of Messrs.
Darling, Taylor & Co., the Locomotive Engine Manufactory
and Machine shop of D. H. Dotterer & Co., the Stationary
Steam Engine and Rifle Barrel Manufactory of William G.
Taylor, the Foundry of Adam Johnson, the Auger Manufactory of Messrs. Rankin & Philips, the Steam Saw Mill and
Chopping Mill of Messrs. Ferry & Frill, and three shops for
manufacturing Horse Power Threshing Machines, Corn Shellers, Patent Ploughs, Revolving Hay Rakes, Cultivators, &c.,
have been established.

There are also three Flour Mills in the borough, including
the steam mill lately put into operation by Davis & Co.   The
extensive flouring Mill occupied by Mr. George Smith, is a
large brick building, four stories high.   It has four pair of
stones, and manufactures 8,000 barrels of flour a year.

The following description of some of the principal Iron
Works, have been obligingly furnished me.

"*The Reading Iron and Nail Works* were erected and went
into operation, June, 1838.   They were built by Messrs. Benneville Keim, George M. Keim, Simon Seiffert, and James
Whitaker, and are advantageously situated within a short distance of the Philadelphia and Reading Railroad, and the

* Stahle's Dis. Reading, p. 50.

Schuylkill Navigation. A track or *turn-out,* made for us by the Railroad Company, connecting with one of the store houses, and a basin situated on the canal within twenty yards of the door of another store house, afford every desirable facility for a safe and rapid transition of our iron and nails to the market. The Reading Iron and Nail Works are now owned by Messrs. Benneville Keim, James Whitaker, Simon Seiffert, and John McMann. The articles manufactured at these works are, as the name imports, iron, and nails. That is, the pig iron is here converted into malleable iron and rolled into various sizes and shapes to suit the market. The crude metal or pig iron, for that purpose, is purchased exclusively in Pennsylvania, a large quantity of which Berks county supplies. We use at the rate of four thousand tons per annum of this pig iron: this immense quantity of raw metal is, in that division of the work, called the Puddling Mill, converted into puddled iron, or No. 1 iron, by the process of puddling and rolling.

For this purpose we have six large puddling furnaces, conveniently placed near the rolls. This mill has a squeezer attached, for forming the ball or loops of iron coming from the furnaces, into a convenient shape for entering the large rolls. We puddle at the rate of twelve tons pig iron per day. This division of the mill is also fitted up for rolling sheet and boiler iron. The second division is that for rolling nail plates, band, and gas pipe iron, and the larger sizes of merchant bar iron. Here we have the reverberatory heating furnace; the flues of which are so constructed, that the superfluous heat is applied to the boilers of the steam engine. Some of the flues of the puddling furnaces are constructed in the same manner, thus economising on the consumption of coal. We roll in this mill at the rate of nine tons per day. The third division is the mill for making all kinds of small iron—round, square and flat, from a quarter of an inch to one inch, with their intermediate sizes. Another reverberating furnace is attached to this mill, and is used for beating the billets of iron, preparatory to rolling. Here we make ready for the market, at the rate of 650 tons finished iron, per year. The rolling mill is a heavy frame building, 130 by 166 feet. Immediately adjoining the rolling mill, and connected therewith, is the nail factory—a substantial and massive brick building, 75 by 50 feet, two stories high, having on its principal floor 33 machines, calculated

15

for making all descriptions and sizes of nails, brads and spikes. The lower story contains the drums and belts that drive the machinery above, and also the grind stones. It is also a store house and will contain several thousand kegs of nails. The whole machinery of these works is driven by a steam engine of 180 horse power, (this is not, however, its maximum power,) it is high pressure, and was built in 1835, by McClurg, Wade & Co., of Pittsburg.

This establishment employs at the rate of 130 men and boys, per day, and consumes fuel at the rate of 7000 tons of Anthracite coal per year. This kind of coal is now used here exclusively. Our blasts for the various furnace is created by fans.

Besides the principal buildings already mentioned, there are several others in the immediate vicinity, and belonging to the same concern, viz: a blacksmith shop with two fires; a cooper shop where from 8 to 10 coopers are constantly employed in making nail kegs; also a counting house, store houses for iron and nails, tool house, &c. &c. The cost of these works for building, was over one hundred thousand dollars. Referring again to the nail factory, we forgot to say that we make at the rate of eighteen hundred tons of nails per year.

" *The Locomotive and Steam Engine Manufactory*, of D. H. Dotterer & Co., is situated immediately on the Canal, and a short distance above the Lancaster Bridge. The machine shop is a brick building, 145 by 32 feet, one-half of which is 3 stories high. The smith shop and engine house is 95 by 24 feet, and one and a half stories high. The stationary engine of this establishment is of 15 horse power, and used for propelling the machinery, and blowing cylinders for the foundry of Messrs. Darling, Taylor & Co. D. H. Dotterer & Co., have built, in the last year, 6 first class locomotive engines, and rebuilt 3. In the same time they have built 3 stationary engines, besides doing the work of a general machine shop. The buildings and machinery are sufficient to turn out 12 first class locomotives a year, along with the other work. This establishment has been in successful operation about three years; and the average number of hands employed, is 30 journeymen and 16 apprentices.

" Adjoining the above establishment is the *Iron and Brass Foundry* of Darling, Taylor & Co. The iron foundry is a brick building, 90 by 45 feet, and one story high, with a steeple and bell. Bellows and cupola house, 70 by 30 feet, part of which is two stories high. Connected with the foundry is an air furnace of the largest class ; building, 20 by 30 feet, and a cupola of the largest class, the air for which is supplied by a pair of iron blowing cylinders, constructed upon the most improved plan. The above establishment is calculated to make castings of all dimensions—also, forge hammers, anvils, &c. The number of hands employed is 16. The brass foundry and smith shop, is 100 by 25 feet, one and a half stories high, of brick. The brass department is calculated to cast brasses of every description, and bells of all sizes, equal in point of tone, to any cast in the U. States. The other part of the building is occupied by two forge fires for the use of foundry and threshing machine shop, 50 by 30 feet, and 2 stories high; in which are built horse power and threshing machines of the most improved construction, and all kinds of agricultural implements. Number of hands employed—5 journeymen; and have manufactured for sale, from 75 to 100 machines the past season.

The above foundry has been in operation since 1835."

The Reading Stationary Steam Engine Manufactory of W. G. Taylor, is situated on Water, near Penn street.

These works employ a large number of hands, and do a large and extensive business. They have constructed a great num ber of engines of various power, which have uniformly proved of excellent quality. Boilers for locomotive and other engines are made here ; and also mill gearing, lathes, drills, and a variety of other machinery. Connected with this establishment is a rifle barrel manufactory, which turns out over 3000 barrels annually.

The new foundry of Mr. Adam Johnston, was put in operation during the last year, and is situated at the corner of Chestnut and Eighth streets. The building is of brick, 25 by 59 feet, and at present employs eight hands. The machine shop is 26 by 36 feet. From the experience of Mr. Johnston, in the business, and his well known skill as a practical moulder, there is little doubt that this new establishment will thrive and prosper in business, and prove a valuable acquisition to the borough.

The extent to which manufactories have grown up in Reading within the last four or five years, and their success thus

far, add confidence to the opinion, now pretty generally entertained, that this town possesses no ordinary advantages for
manufacturing operations.   As yet they are confined principally
to some branch of the iron business; but woollen and other
factories will probably soon be established.   The borough already feels the benefits of this new interest, in the increase of
population and business, which it has brought to the place.—
Stahle's Des. of Reading.

Population in 1810, 3,462; 1820, 4,278; 1830, 5,631; 1840,
8,392—at present (1844) rising of 10,000.   In 1840 there
were in Reading, horses 566; horned cattle 378; sheep 5;
swine 1,115; bushels of wheat 3,872; rye 3,290; corn 3,472;
oats 2,486; buckwheat 271; potatoes 1,043; tons of hay 465.

Whole amount of valuation on all articles made taxable by
law for county purposes for 1844, $1,712,321; whole amount
of county tax on the same, at two mills on the dollar, $3,424 64
cts.   State tax, $3,091 57 cts.

MISCELLANEOUS MATTERS.—*Stahle's Des. of Reading.*

" Old Berks was erected into a county, and Reading established as the county seat, in the year of grace, one thousand
seven hundred and fifty-two.   The first *Deed* was recorded in
the office, November the seventeenth, and the first *Will* November the twenty-ninth of that year; and to complete the
honors of the new county, a *law suit* was instituted about the
same time.

" Here follow some records of the doings of His Majesty,
George the Third's Justices of the Peace.

" BERKS COUNTY.

To one of ye Constables of Reading.

Henry Christ Subpœna Philip Adam Klauser and Joseph
          Seal   Sollenberger of ye township of Bern, so that
they be and appear before me and Wm. Reeser, on ye first day
of September next at one of the clock in ye afternoon, then and
there to give evidence in a certain dispute now depending before us and undetermined, between ye Lutheran and Reformed
Congregations about Sanct. Michael's Church.—Hereof you
are not to fail at your peril.   Given under my hand and seal at
Reading ye 27th day of August 1770.

HENRY CHRIST.

"Berks ss.

L. S. Apprehend George Geisler, and bring him immediately before me, or the next Justice to ansr unto such matters and things, as on his Majesty's behalf shall be objected against him by Catharine Reese; hereof fail not.—Given under my hand and seal, **Decr ye 26th 1770.**

JAMES DIEMER.

To Samuel Jackson, Constable.

That is the true magisterial style, and I have no doubt that between the Justice and.Catharine Reese, poor George Geisler had a hard time of it.

The following documents are interestsng as illustrative of the times.

"Ann appraisement of the goods late the property of Wm. Kees taken in execution—by SAMUEL JACKSON, *Constable.*

One gunn,	15s	£0	15s	0d.
One pair of Leather Breeches 15s.		0	16	0
		£1	10	0"

But see how they stript Samuel Dehart of the comforts of life.

"A list of the goods taken in execution from Samuel Dehart by the Constable, and appraised by us the subscribers as follows. Amity August 24th 1770, to wit—

One coat	30s.	£1	10	0d
One Jacket and trowsers,	12s	0	12	0
One rugg	5s	0	5	0
One pillow 2s		0	2	0
		£2	9	0

I am not quite sure that Mr. Dehart would congratulate himself that his *body* vras left."

" The oldest houses standing in the borough are, the house of Widow Graeff, No. 134 East Penn Street, formerly kept as a tavern; the house of Daniel Graeff, No. 133 East Penn Street; No. 158 in 8th st., between Penn and Washington, and the Spring Garden house."

There are several newspapers printed in Reading; when speaking of education and means of diffusing knowledge, they will be fully noticed.

" The corner house, occupied by Keim & Stichler, was built

15*

in the year of 1755, by *Conrad Weiser*, the Indian interpreter and agent for Government, and was for many years occupied as a Wigwam, where many tribes met for treaty."

Christian Frederick Post, on a message frcm the Governor of Pennsylvania to the Indians in Ohio, in the month of October, 1828, called at the house of Conrad Weiser, in Reading, the 27th of that month, as will appear from extracts of Post's Journal.

"October 27, 1758, about seven o'clock in the morning, I came to Reading, and there found captain Bull, Mr. Hays, and the Indians just mounted, and ready to set out on their journey; they were heartily glad to see me; *Pisquetcmen* stretched out his arms, and said,—"Now, brother, I am glad I have got you in my arms, I will not let you go, I will not let you go again from me, you must go with me:" and I likewise said the same to him, and told him, "I will accompany you, if you will go the same way as I must go." And then I called them together, in Mr. Weiser's house, and read a letter to them, which I had received from the Governor, which is as follows, viz:

"To Pisquetomen and Thomas Hickman, to Totiniontonna and Shickalany, and to Isaac Still.

BRETHREN, Mr. Frederick Post is ccme express from the General, who sends his compliments to you, and desires you would come by the way of his camp, and give him an opportunity of talking with you.

By this string of Wampun I request you to alter your intended rout by way of Shamokin, and to go to the General, who will give you a kind reception. It is a nigher way, in which you will be better supplied with provisions, and travel with less fatigue and more safety.

WILLIAM DENNY,

Easton Oct. 23, 1758."

To which I added : "Brethren, I take you by this string, by the hand, and lift you from this place, and lead you along to the General."

"After which they consulted among themselves, and soon resolved to go with me. We shook hands with each other, and Mr. Hays immediately set out with them; after which, having with some difficulty procured a fresh horse, in the King's service, I set off about noon, with Captain Bull, and when we came to Conrad Weiser's plantation, we found Pisquetoman lying on the ground very drunk, which obliged us to stay all night, the other Indians were gone eight miles farther on their journey.''

———

The following Biographical Memoir, copied from the United States Gazette, will, it is believed, be read with interest:

BIOGRAPHY OF GOV. HIESTER.

Circumstances put me in possession of many facts in relation to the life of the late GENERAL JOSEPH HIESTER, which induce a belief that their publication, more especially those which relate to his conduct in the war of independence, would be acceptable to a people who have in truth delighted to do him honor, while he remained amongst them. I think the facts cannot fail to imbue our population with the same sound principles and zealous feelings of patriotism, which at an early period, and throughout a long rnd unostentatious but useful and honorable life, animated the deceased. No man knows how soon the day may come, when his services may be required by his country, and he may be called upon to make sacrifices of feeling and interest to contribute his mite towards her freedom and happiness. Our political horizon is not cloudless.— There are floating dark spots in the south, which, though now no larger than a man's shield, may, by the breath of faction, be blown together, and form a dark mass, which shall overshadow the Union. In such times it behooves every citizen to examine the great questions which agitate the Union, and make up his mind to adopt that course of conduct which patriotism and honor shall make out. The early, manly, and disinterested course of devotion to their country's welfare, which distinguished the lives of many of our citizens, will now well bear to be reviewed, not only to do honor to them and their memories, but to invite us to emulate their virtues.

It was in the twenty-third or twenty-fourth year of his age, that General Joseph Hiester, first rallied under the standard of his country, and took up arms in defence of her independence. It was a gloomy period, at which many hearts, that had beat-

en high, were sickened and sad in the bosoms of those who
now had melancholy forebodings of the issue of the contest in
which they had cheerfully embarked; at a time when the great,.
the good, the peerless Washington, had much cause to complain
of the want of men and means to meet the enemies of his
country.

It was late in the year 1775, or early in 1776, that Joseph
Hiester, then a vigorous, powerful, and influential young man,
called together, by beat of drum, his fellow townsmen of Reading, Pennsylvania, to take into consideration the alarming state
and gloomy prospects of their country Reading was then an
inconsiderable town, with a small population. Having convened about twenty-five or thirty, he explained to them the
necessity there was that they also should be up and doing in
the cause of their common country. He stated that their beloved General was then believed to be in a most perilous situation in New Jersey; that his friends and fellows oldiers were
but few, while his foes and the foes of America were thicken-
ing and multiplying on every side. Having so far as in his
power, embarked the sympathies and roused the patriotism of
his hearers, he expressed his anxious desire to raise a company of volunteers, and march to the assistance of Washington.
He was heard with attention and respect, and .his proposition
was kindly received. He then laid $40 on the drum head and
said, "I will give this sum, as a bounty, and the appointment
of a sergeant, to the first man who will subscribe the articles
of association to form a volunteer company, to march forthwith,
and join the Commander-in-chief, and I also pledge myself, said
he, to furnish the company with blankets and necessary funds
for their equipment, and on the march." This promise he honorably and faithfully fulfilled. After our young Captain had
thus addressed his neighbors, they consulted together, and Mathias Babb stepped forward, from amongst them, signed the articles, and took the money from the drum head. This example, and further advancements of smaller sums of money, induced twenty men, on that evening, to subscribe to the articles of association. Notices and invitations were sent through
the neighborhood; other meetings were held, and in ten days
from the first meeting, Captain Hiester had eighty men enrolled. They were promptly organized and ready to march to
join the Commander-in-chief.

This company and other troops were, at that time, enlisted and organized under the legislature or the executive council of Pennsylvania, I do not recollect which, for the purpose of forming a disposable force called the Flying Camp. The success which was consequent upon Capt. Hiester's efforts to raise a volunteer company, led to the determination to raise a battalion, or regiment. It was early ascertained, that the liberality and popularity of Captain Hiester, would secure him the highest office in the troops, about to be raised. This state of public opinion could not be mistaken or misunderstood, and Captain Hiester was generally regarded as the future commander of the troops about to be raised. At this point of time, Mr. Haller, also a citizen of Reading, called upon Mr. Hiester, and expressed strong desire to join the army, but on condition that he, Mr. Hiester, would relinquish in his, Mr. Haller's favor, all claims to the command.

Mr. Haller frankly admitted that he was not disposed to go, unless elected Colonel, and that he well knew he could not attain that rank in any other way, than through the resignation and good offices of Capt. Hiester. Mr. Hiester heard with patient attention, all that was argued and suggested by Mr. Haller, and in answer said: The office you seek must be the gift of our fellow soldiers, but I do assure you I am not anxious for command or distinction, further than they may enable me the more effectually to serve our country. I will willingly yield all claim, rather than that our country shall not have your services. The declaration thus made, was followed up by Capt. Hiester, who freely conversing with the troops, and declining to be a candidate for the office claimed, used his influence in favor of Mr. Haller. The facility with which Capt. Hiester consented to the wishes of Mr. Haller, and a reliance upon the pure motives which had induced him thus to yield rank and precedence to another, was the cause of a new application of a similar nature. Mr. Edward Burd was desirous to obtain the rank of Major, yet was satisfied how hopeless would be any opposition he could make to the election of Capt. Hiester, whose promotion to that rank was the more anxiously desired by the men, from the public spirited and handsome manner in which he had declined the Colonelcy, and succeeded in. persuading the men to elect another. The feelings thus every where manifested, did not, however, deter Mr. Burd from at-

tempting to attain the station which he ardently desired. He·
waited on Capt. Hiester, laid before him his wishes, stated his.
knowledge of public opinion, his belief that he could be of advantage to the public service, and his anxiety that Capt. Hiester would forego his own promotion, and assist him, Burd, to
the rank he sought. Capt. Hiester unhesitatingly assented to,
the request of Mr. Burd ; he addressed his fellow soldiers, assured them how satisfied he was to continue to serve as Captain, and even declared a willingness to serve in the rank, if
by such service he could better serve their common country.—
This address had the desired effect, the officers were elected as
he wished, and Capt. Hiester and his company, marched from
Reading for New Jersey.

On their arrival at Elizabethtown, they learned that General Washington had moved with his forces to Long Island.—
Lord Sterling had been sent into Jersey to expedite the march
of the American troops. On communicating this information
to the companies commanded by Captain Hiester and Captain
Graul, Capt. Graul's men, and some of Capt. Hiester's, declared
their determination to march no further. They declared that
they could not have been compelled to leave their native state,
and that it was unreasonable to expect that they should
advance further. This was a critical and painful state of affairs. What was to be done; what could be done, to induce
the men to go forward? They were drawn up in a compact
body, and Capt. Hiester addressed them in such honest, suitable and impassioned language, that they warmed as he warmed, and they soon felt as he felt, and their hearts beat in unison
with his. One who was present on that trying occasion, said
to me, I wish to God, I could tell you what the captain said,
and how the men looked and felt; you have marched thus far
said he, resolved to fight your country's foes, and defend your
homes and families, and will you now prove cowards, and desert your country when your country most wants your help?
I would be ashamed to return home with you ! I will go forward ; yes, if I go by myself. I will go and join Gen. Washington as a volunteer, as a private; and if you will not go, I
will go alone; but surely, said he, you will not turn your backs
upon the enemy, and leave your country at their mercy. I
will try you once again—Fall in !—Fall in to your ranks, men,
and those who are ready to fight for freedom and America,,

will, when the drum beats, and the word is given, march to
join George Washington.   The men fell in; they shouldered
their muskets; the drums were beat, and on the word "march,"
the whole line, except three men, moved forward. Those three
soon sprang into the ranks, three cheers were given, and they
were forthwith on their march to Long Island.   On their arrival at Long Island, they came frequently in hostile contact
with the enemy; some were killed and some were wounded; at
length the British army having concentrated, the American
troops generally, were captured; how very ill they were used,
and how severely they were treated, is of historical record, to
the dishonor of the British name.   Capt. Hiester, with many
of the American officers, was confined for a long time on board
the prison ship Jersey.   The cruelties inflicted, and the sufferings and the privations of the prisoners, will long be remembered and felt.   From the prison ship, Capt. Hiester was taken
and cast into prison in New York, where the scarcity of food
and the general ill treatment of the Americans, was scarcely a
remove better than they had experienced on board the Jersey.
Capt. Hiester was attacked with a slow fever, and became so
feeble and emaciated, that he was reduced to the painful necessity of passing up and down stairs on his hands and feet. After some months confinement, his exchange was effected, and
he was liberated after having been plundered of his stores,
money, and clothing.   After his liberation he returned to Reading, where having recovered his strength, and made all necessary arrangements, he again joined the army near Germantown.
In a skirmish, with an advanced company of the enemy's horse,
his head was slightly grazed by a bullet.   He continued in the
army till the close of the war, after which he returned to the
bosom of his family.   The popularity, deservedly acquired by
Gen. Hiester, by his public spirit and devotion to his country
during the revolutionary war, he never lost; in all the revolutions of party, his neighbors and those all around him, who had
the best opportunities of knowing his private worth, and good
qualities, continued firmly attached to him.

He was, soon after the war, elected to the Legislature of
Pennsylvania, where he, for many years, honorably and faithfully represented and served his constituents.   He was elected
with a host of good men, and of sound understandings to the
convention, which, after the formation of the Federal Constitu-

tion, were assembled to frame a Constitution for Pennsylvania, and they did frame the very excellent form of government under which we have so long prospered as a State, and lived happily as citizens of the Union. Under that constitution to which he was so zealously attached, he served many years in the General Assembly of Pennsylvania. He has frequently been chosen a member of the College of Electors of President and Vice President of the United States. He was an Elector, at the time John Adams was chosen President, and Thos. Jefferson Vice President. He had the further honor of serving his country in the great Council of the Nation, for fourteen years, and after having declared a re-election to Congress, he acceded to the solicitation of his friends, became a candidate for the office of Governor, and was elected. It is a fact well known to the political and personal friends of Gen. Hiester, that he was reluctantly induced to become a candidate for the office of Governor, and that he yielded his consent upon the express and well understood condition, that he would serve but one period. It is equally well known, that at the end of that period of service, he resolutely refused again to permit the use of his name, although urged by partisans and by many friends, solicited to be a candidate, at the expiration of the three years he had consented to serve as Governor. He returned to the bosom of his family, still residing in the borough of Reading, where, surrounded by friends and neighbors, by whom he was greatly esteemed and respected, he lived happily, and descended to his grave full of years and honor. He died on the 10th of June, 1832, in the 80th year of his age. He was buried in the burial ground of the German Reformed Church of Reading, on the 13th of June; his remains were followed to the grave by a numerous concourse of mourning relations and fellow citizens. The profound attendance of the military, and other demonstrations of respect and attachment, all of which were promptly tendered, were respectfully declined, and his well attended but unostentatious funeral, was in perfect keeping with the truly republican simplicity which had marked the whole course of his long and useful life.

CAPTAIN JACOB YODER, was born in Reading, 1758—a highly respectable and wealthy Farmer, of Spencer county, Kentucky. To him belongs the honor of having descended the Mississippi, in the first Flat Boat—and if no other powers than those of time, and wind, and storm, shall assail the *tablet,* of which an account is given below, which will preserve the fact recorded in deep indentations upon it, through a series of ages to come.

The iron tablet was cast by Hanks & Niles, of Cincinnati, in 1834, and now marks the spot where remains the bones of Captain Yoder. It is one of the first of the kind ever execu- ted west of the Alleghenies. It has this inscription:

JACOB YODER
Was born in Reading, Pennsylvania,
August 11th, 1785;
And was a Soldier in the Revolutionary Army
In 1777 and 1778;
He emigrated to the West in 1780, and in May
1782, from Fort Redstone, on the
Monongahela River,
in the
FIRST FLAT BOAT
That ever descended the Mississippi,
He landed at New Orleans, with a cargo of
Produce.
He died April 7, 1832, at his farm in Spencer
County, Kentucky, and lies here
Interred beneath this tablet.

No one who has any pretensions to the possession of a soul, can contemplate this tablet without a variety of emotions. A brilliant series of associations enchain the mind of the gazer, as with a spell, to it—that the man who navigated the first flat boat that ever descended the Mississippi, should have lived to see a magnificent steamboat ploughing the same watery track—is a truth which affords a subject of admiration. When he launched his little bark on the Monongahela, what were his anticipations? Such as time has proved! No, he then thought of the wily savage, whose covert was a wide and untrodden wilderness. He proceeded on his precarious voyage. Instead

16

of cheering aspects of busy cities, flourishing villages, and cul‑
tivated farms, which now claim the voyager's attention, he saw
a range of hills, unshorn of their primeval widerness; whence
the lugubrious howl of the wolf proceeded, the vast wilderness
which the foot of the civilized man had not trodden, *instinct*,
'tis true, *with life;* but it was the life of the forest derizen,
the trembling fawn, and the myriad songsters of the wild. He
reached his destination, but his safety was a marvel to himself,
and his dangers, in after recital, awakened up a fear stricken
excitement in the minds of those who listened to his tale of
perils "by field and flood." He lived to see the country
change masters, the wilderness blossom as a rose, and human
energy achieve a conquest over a thousand obstacles.

This is the greatest triumph that man has yet achieved.—
History records no parallel. To the future generations of
America, it will be what the fabulous age of the Titans was to
the ancient Greeks.

———

COLONEL THOMAS HARTLEY—the subject of this notice—
was born in the vicinity of Reading, September 7th, 1748.—
His parents sent him to the common, as well as to the schools
of more advanced standing, in which he made more than ordi‑
nary proficiency—he left not a moment to pass without some
improvements. At the age of eighteen he went to York, Penn‑
sylvania, where he entered upon a regular course of Purdy's
jurisprudence, under the direction of Samuel Johnson, Esq.—
So great was his proficiency, that before he had attained the
age of twenty-one, he was admitted to practice at the bar.

Never has any one risen higher, in the same time, in his pro‑
fessional business, than Thomas Hartley; this was mainly
owing to his thorough knowledge of law, and in his intimate
acquaintance of the English and German languages—both es‑
sential, in that day, to succeed as a lawyer at that bar. Per‑
haps the great extent of his practice was also owing in part to
the paucity, as to the number of lawyers—for young Hartley
and the Honorable James Smith, were for some time, the only
practicing attorneys—Mr. Johnson, his preceptor, was the
prothonotary of the county, from 1764 to 1777.

Hartley, unlike many of that day, though much engrossed

with professional business, was the warm friend of his country —much of his time was devoted, both in the field and cabinet, to his country's cause. As early as 1774, the citizens of York county elected him as a member of the provincial meeting of deputies, held at Philadelphia, July 15, 1774. In 1775, he again attended a provincial convention, held at Philadelphia, 23d of January.

The crisis was now arriving that was to try men's souls— the time was approaching when stern requisition demanded decision of character. The committee of safety for Pennsylvania, who never recommended any that would falter in duty, recommended among others, Mr. Hartley to Congress, for filed officers to the sixth battalion, ordered to be raised in Pennsylvania. The merits of the respective gentlemen, recommended, were inquired into by Congress; whereupon, January 10, 1776, the following persons were elected:—William Irwin, Esq., as Colonel; Thomas Hartley, as Lieutenant Colonel; and James Dunlap, Esq., as Major. But not many months passed before Lieut. Col. Hartley was promoted to the rank of Colonel. He was distinguished as a soldier—devoted three years to the service of his country, in that capacity. After thus faithfully serving, at the expiration of three years, on the 13th of July, 1779, he respectfully addressed Congress, asking permission to resign his commission. The reasons set forth to Congress, were deemed sufficient to grant him his reasonable request—his resignation was accepted, and at the same time, it was resolved by that honorable body, that "they had a high sense of Colonel Hartley's merit and services."

His fellow citizens were determined to have his services, if not in the field, at all events in the legislative hall; they accordingly elected him in October, 1778, to represent the county of York in the General Assembly.

In 1783, he was was elected a member of the council of censors, under the constitution of '76—the first day of their meeting was the 10th of November, 1783. At the close of the year 1787, he was a member of the State convention which adopted the constitution of the United States.

Having so faithfully represented the interests of his constituents, and honorably discharged the duties of the several stations he held, his fellow citizens were determined on his further services, and they accordingly elected him as a member of Congress. As a new order of things had now commenced, the public mind was engrossed alike with hope and fear. The citizens of York county had taken a great interest in the establishment of the new constitution, and as Colonel Hartley was the first person who was to go forth from among them, as a member of Congress, under that constitution, they determined in the warmth of their feelings, to show him every honor.— When he set out from York, on the 23d of February, 1789, on his way to the city of New York, where Congress was to set, he was accompanied to the Susquehanna by a great number of the inhabitants of the borough and its neighborhood, and was there received by a company from that part of the county, and from Lancaster. The citizens then partook of a dinner, and the whole was one splendid celebration. When on the way of his return, he arrived at Wright's Ferry on the 6th of October, he was met at that place by a number of gentlemen from the borough of York, and was from there conducted to his house, in town, amidst the acclamations of his friends and fellow citizens."

He was for many years a member of Congress. He was the first gentleman from the State of Pennsylvania, that was admitted a counsellor in the Supreme Court of the United States. He closed his eventful life on the morning of the 21st of December, 1800, aged 52 years, 3 months, and 14 days. His remains rest in the burial ground of the Church of St. John's, York, Pennsylvania.

EXETER TOWNSHIP.

Exeter township was settled prior to 1720, and numbered, fifteen or twenty years afterwards, rising of three hundred of a population. In 1841, the number of taxables was seventy-six; and a few years after the organization of Berks county, the following were taxables in Exeter township, as then bounded:

Adam Wink, Michael Zeister, Paul Durst, Isaac Levan, Leonard Lebo, Jacob Scherer, Adam Garrett, Henry Lees, Frederick Kunkle, Conrad Kehler, Henry Boyer, Henry Alder, Moses Ellis, Abraham Levan, Jacob Lanciscus, Frederick Christian, George Engle, Nicholas Herner, John Aurand, Francis Rutter, Martin Allstat, Christian Weeks, George Hinton, Samuel Hughes, Edward Hughes, Jonathan Price, Robert

Dickey, William Boone, Henry Hernor, Morris Ellis, John Webb, William Russel, James Boone, Peter Schneider, Rudolph Hegler, George Messersmith, Adam Young, Martin Waltz, George Gerich, Valentine Messersmith, Jacob Weiler, Christian Boyer, Jacob Boechtel, Peter Boechtel, James Thompson, Peter Rein, Jacob Rawn, Wm. Maugridge, Philip Near, John Boyer, Henry Thompson, Jacob Boyer, Daniel Conrad, Robert Patterson, William Kirby, Peter Kirby, Geo. Hart, Peter Smith, Mordecai Lincoln, Jacob Huget, Benjamin Parks, Ulrich Mahn, Peter Huet, Francis Wallich, Mathias Detert, Frederick Kehler, Michael Lodwick, Benjamin Boone, Leonard High, Joseph Boone, John Hugh, John Wainwright, Jacob Yoder, John Zug, Yost Sees, Henry Shleigh, Christian Boyer, Peter Noll, Stephen Kreitscher, Mathias Feeder, John Boone, James Thompson, Philip Saddler, Peter Alstat, Hezekiah Boone, John Conrad, Jacob Dibler, Frederick Herner. Wm Patterson, Frederick Wallick, Peter Fisher, John Boechtel, Abraham Lincoln, George Ritter John Frellweiler.

Exeter township is bounded north-east by Oley township; on the east by Amity; on the south by the Schuylkill river, which divides it from Robeson and Cumru; and on the northwest by Alsace. Greatest length, four miles and a half, and breadth the same; the surface generally undulative, except in the north-western part, which is hilly; soil a reddish shale and gravel; naturally not productive, but in many places it has been rendered, by the husbandman's care, very productive. The western boundary is strongly marked by Mount Never Sink and other prominent hills.

Roush creek, which enters this township on the north-west, passing through it in a southern course, wending its way to the Schuylkill and the Manokesy, which crosses the north-east corner of the township, affords water power to several grist mills, saw mills, an oil mill, a fulling mill, and a forge.

The Perkiomin and Reading turnpike pass through it for a distance of five or six miles. Exeter, a small village, is on the turnpike, eight miles from Reading. It contains not more than eight or ten houses, a tavern and a store.

There is a school held in common by the German Reformed and Lutherans, near the centre of the township.

Population in 1810, 1,194; 1820, 1,416; 1830, 1,455; 1840, 1,911. Horses 321; horned a   770; sheep 691; swine
16*ttle

1,118; bushels of wheat 11,670; rye 12,367; corn 18,564; oats 23,802; buckwheat 304; potatoes 5,089; tons of hay 1,686; pounds of wool 1,274; flax 1,284.

Whole amount of valuation on all articles made taxable by law, for county purposes, $614,092; county tax $1,228 18; State tax $06,10.

GREENWICH TOWNSHIP.

Greenwich township was formed about 1852, out of part of Allemangel, which had been settled prior to 1836. .It was originally nearly wholly settled by Germans, . among whom were a few of the descendants of French Huguenots. During the French and Indian war, from 1754 to 1760, the inhabitants, in common with all the frontier settlers of Berks, were occasionally alarmed by their cruel enemies.

In March, 1755, the Indians burned the house of Barnabas Seitel, who lived on the borders of the township, and the mill of Peter Conrad; killed the wife of Balsar Neytong, and made captive his son, a lad of eight years of age. They fired five times upon David Howell, and the last time shot him through the arm.

The settlers were also alarmed by the news of murders committed in the township, immediately north; namely, in Albany township, when they heard of the horrid massacre of Jacob Gerhart's family, and others. These were trying times.

In 1756, the following taxables resided within this township, as it was then limited: .

George Herring, Adam Smith, Adam Baner, Andrew Onengst, Adam Boose, Adam Zolman, Charles Balmer, Christopher Rein, Christian Ungerer, Frederick Kremer, Frederick Hene, Frederick Shallenberger, Dietrich Mayer, Dietrich Leiby, Godfried Stern, Gabriel Eisenberger, George Kosser, Gottfried Kremer, George Ley, George Miller, George Breiner, George Wilhelm Riegel, Gerhart Schallenberger, George Slaus, Geo. Kremer, George Kemp, George Herring, George Bauman, George Ussinger, Henry Ballender, Henry Mayer, Henry Berke, Henry Krall, Henry Eschbach, Hantorns Kiel, Jacobus Diehl, Jacob Liebe, John Schwedner, John Sassamanhaus, John Raush, John Dunkle, John Wary, Jacob Hetrick, John Collon, Jacob Zettelmayer, Jacob Gronable, Jacob Leydick, Lorentz

Biever, Leonard Bauman, Mathias Reamer, Melchior Biel, Michael Crans, Michael Mauser, Michael Lesher, Matthias Keffer, Mathias Ley, Martin Hetinger, Michael Leiby, Michael Gottschall, Nicholas Stein, Philip Lenhart, Peter Lenhard, Peter Herdinger, Philip Kallbach, Peter Dell, Philip Mayer, Peter Buns, Peter Steuerwald, Peter Hauck, Rudolph Bussart, Rudolph Zimmer, Simon Dierick, Simon Essenberg, Urbanus Frieferly, Ludwig Beckel, Nicholas Essenberg, Geo. Spang, Abraham Kles, Jacob Hoffman, Hans Christian Baum, Nicholas De Hoop, John Riebsaamen, Martin Onangst, Jacob Mack, George Krubach, Daniel Manensmith, Michael Smith, John Manser, Andrew Seitle, Henry Smith, Adam Faust, Henry Faust, Jacob Lantzard, Henry Shullenberger, Peter Dempkle, Christian Manensmith.

Greenwich is bound north by Albany township, north-east by Lehigh county, south-east by Maxtawny township, south by Richmond, and west by Windsor; mean length six miles and a half, and mean breadth four and a half; contains nearly fourteen thousand acres of land, generally hilly ; and the soil, gravel, of an ordinary quality. Round-top hill, or Peaked mountain, on the northern boundary of the township, presents a prominent feature, and gives a similar character to the aspect of the surface in its vicinity.

The Maiden creek, which passes through the north-western part of the township, affords water power, as do several other streams in the township; among these is Lacony creek, a branch of Maiden creek, which flows in a serpentine course of five miles along the southern boundary, receiving, as it progresses, Mill creek, and several smaller rivulets. There are six grist mills, five saw mills, four tanneries, one forge, an oil mill and a pottery, in the township.

There are two small towns, Klinesville, seven miles from Hamburg, on the State road, leading from Hamburg to Allentown; Grimsville, on the same road, ten miles from Hamburg —three stores, and seven taverns. In 1840, the following Revolutionary pensioners lived in this township:—Andreas Camp, George Hincley, and Peter Steger.

Population in 1830, 1,407; 1840, 1,629. Horses 200; horned cattle 572; sheep 459; swine 644; bushels of wheat 2,275; rye 6,030; corn 5,621; oats 6,465, buckwheat 2,575; potatoes 5,621; tons of hay 601; pounds of wool 597; flax 350.

Whole amount of valuation on all articles made taxable by law for county purposes $467,975; county tax $935 95; State tax $581 59.

HEIDELBERG TOWNSHIP.

Heidelberg township was so called by the first settlers, after the capitol of the country whence many of them had emigrated to America. It was named after Hiedelberg, a city of south Germany, in the duchy of Baden, and the seat of a town and district bailiwick, at the foot of the Kaiserstuhl, on the Neckar, about twelve miles above its confluence with the Rhine, at Manheim.

When settlements were commenced by the Germans, (of whose coming and settling a detailed account will be given below,) they scattered themselves in the midst of the Indians, who complained much to government, of the "foreigners," that their corn had been destroyed by those *people's* creatures.— Sassoonan or Allummapees, at a council held at Philadelphia, in the Great meeting house, June 5, 1728, complained bitterly of the intrusions by the Germans at Tulpahoca, (Hiedelberg.) In addressing secretary Logan, he said: " He was grown old, and was troubled to see the christians settle on lands that the Indians had never been paid for—they had settled on *his* lands, for which he had never received any thing. That he is now an old man, and must soon die, that his children may wonder to see all their father's lands gone from them, without his receiving any thing for them, that the christians now make their settlements very near them, and they shall have no place of their own left to live on.—*Col. Rec.* iii. *p.* 338.

A few years after this complaint by Sassoonan, Thomas Penn purchased the Tulpehocken lands, now forming Berks and Lebanon counties. At the time of Penn's purchase, 1732, and ten or fifteen years later, the tawny sons of Tulpahoca had a cluster of Indian villages, north of the present site of Wommelsdorf, under the Kittatiny or Blue Mountain.

In a preceding chapter,[*] it has been stated, that some Germans had settled in Tulpehocken, the greater part of which lay within the bounds of Heidelberg township, when Berks county was organized. As it may be interesting to the general

* Chapter vi , p. 98, 99.

reader, and especially to the numerous descendants of the first settlers of this portion of the county, a brief account will be given of their emigration to Pennsylvania.

About the years 1707, '8, '9, thousands of Germans were oppressed by Romish intolerance, many of whom, to the number of three thousand or more, on a proclamation of Queen Ann, of England, 1708, went from the Palatinate to Holland, and were thence transported to England. They encamped near London. About this time, the colonists of New York, looked to the mother country for aid to repel the incursions of the French. In 1710, Cols. Nicholas and Schuyler, accompanied by five Sachems, or Indian chiefs, had returned from America to England, to solicit additional forces against Canada.* While at London, the chiefs in their walks in the outskirts of London, saw the unenviable condition of the houseless and homeless Germans; though Indians, they were moved by human woe and suffering, commisserated their destitute condition, and no doubt, being informed of the yearnings of the Germans' aching hearts for a country free from persecution, one of them, unsolicited and voluntarily, presented the Queen a tract of *his* land, in Schoharie, New York, for the use and benefit of the distressed Germans.†

About this time, Colonel Robert Hunter, having received the appointment of Governor, for New York, and sailing for America, brought with him not less than three thousand of these Germans, or Palatines, to the town of New York, where they encamped several months; and in the autumn of 1710, many of whom were removed at the expense of Queen Ann, to Livingston district; others settled in the city of New York, some in Germantown, others elsewhere.

Those who were removed to Livingston's District, or Manor, were required, in order to repay freightage from Holland to England, thence to New York, to raise hemp, and manufacture tar.‡ In this business they did not succeed; however, they were released in 1713, from all claims upon them for freightage across the Atlantic.

One hundred and fifty of the families, willing to avail themselves of their *present* from the Indians, made to Queen Ann,

* His. N. Y., p. 39.—Holmes Annals i. 501.
† Hallische Nachrichten, 973—981.
‡ Hal. Nach. 974.

for their use, moved in the spring of 1714, through a dense forest to Schoharie, west of Albany, and seated themselves among their Magua or Mohawk neighbors and friends, the Indians. On their arrival, they were wholly destitute, both of food, and the implements of husbandry. Their sufferings, for some time, were very great. Their neighbors, the Indians, had not laid up any provisions for themselves; and of course had none to spare, to supply the wants of their white brethren —depending entirely upon Nature's store-house—believing that their hands were not made to perform manual labor, other than hunting and fishing.

The Palatines, in this new home, made many a meal upon ground-nuts and wild potatoes. The former, the Indians called *otachraquara*, and the latter *ochnanada*. The nearest place where flour or meal could be procured, was at a distance of fifty miles from the new settlement; and these they had to purchase on credit, which was not readily obtained—unenviable condition.

In Schoharie, having only permission from the Indians, the Germans commenced, under all these discouraging circumstances, improving lands, and building houses. In a few years, and after persevering efforts, they succeeded in improving several settlements; for they had settled in hamlets, (Doerfer,) or lodges, of these there were seven, namely : Kneskern's Gerlack'sdorff, Fuchsendorff, Hans George Schmit'sdorff, Weiser's or Brunnendorff, Hartman'sdorff, and Ober-Weiser'sdorff.— They seemed now to prosper ; having in a great degree overcome nearly all obstacles, which so readily presented, and still present themselves, in commencing settlements in a remote forest country. Having, however, neglected to comply with the formalities of the law of New York, and improving lands without the full consent of Government, the titles to their lands were defective, and as a consequence, they were involved in new difficulties. After much vexation, and many fruitless efforts to secure to themselves, what was intended for them by the Indian present to Queen Ann; some having heard of unoccupied lands in Swatara and Tulpehocken, in Pennsylvania, united, and left Schoharie, wended their faces in a south-western direction, and travelled through the forest, till they reached the Susquehanna river, where they made canoes, freighted them, with their families, and some household goods, floated down the river to the mouth of the Swatara creek, thence they worked their way up, till they reached a fertile spot on Tulpehocken creek, where they settled amidst the Indians, in the spring of 1723. Their cattle they drove by land.* Here they commenced the world anew, with some disorder. Weiser, who joined them afterwards, and knew them well, says:—"Es war niemand unter dem Volk der es regieren konnte; ein jeder that was or wollte; and ihr starker Eigensinn hat ihnen bis auf diese Stunde (1745) in Wege gestanden." There was none among the people who could govern them; every one did as he pleased; their obstinacy, to this day, (1745,) has been much against them. There were thirty-three families of them at Tulpehocken in 1728. The names of some of them are still preserved in the Provincial Records. There are given below as then spelled: Johannes Yans, Peter Ritt, Conrad Schitz, Paltus Unfs, Toritine Serbo, Josep Sab, Jorge Ritt, Gotfrey Filler, Joannes Claes Shaver, Jo Hameler Ritt, Johan Peter Pacht, Jocham Michael Cricht, Sebastian Pisas, Andrew Falborn.†

These expected in 1728, fifty families more, " who, if they might be admitted on certain conditions," would come and settle among them at Tulpehocken. In 1729, there was an important accession. Among these were the Hoehns, Fischers, Lauers, Anspachs, Badtorfs Spickers, Crists, Cadermans, Noacres, Lebenguths, Conrad Weiser and his sons—the latter settled near Wommelsdorf, of whom more will be said in the sequel.‡

In 1756, the following were assessed and returned as taxables of Heidelberg township, many of whose descendants are still the owners of the lands first possessed by the first settlers. Heidelberg then embraced upper and lower Heidelberg, having since 1830, been divided.

Philip Weiser, Frederick Weiser, Andrew Boyer, John Oorth, John Boyer, jr., John Eckert, Michael Schauer, Henry Fitler, George Deer, Leonard Groh, Nicholas Ried, Jacob Klein, John Zerbe, Peter Hoffman, George Lauch, Henry Shuger, Henry Gruber, Adam Schauer, Casper Hoehn, Joseph Felsmayer, Ga-

---

* Conrad Weiser's German MSS. Journal.
† Col Rec. iii. p. 342, and preceeding pages 97-99.
‡ Heidelberg twp. is noted for having been the place of the Heidelberg meeting in 1829, in opposition to Sunday Schools, &c. See Appendix, A.

briel Radgee, Antonie Faust, Adam Spohn, Thomas Jones, Lodowick Deer, Eliezar Evans, Michael Malle, Peter Betz, Wilhelm Fuser, Peter Eberle, Dieterich Marschall, Frederick Koble, John Koble, Peter Bricker, Christian Daube, Sebastian Obald, Jacob Boyer, Conrad Scharff, Peter Knop, Ullerich Michel, Valentine Frei, Henry Staer, Michael Lauer, Tobias Bickel, Conrad Erns., Martin Barteberger, Michael Kaiser, Joseph Hetterich, Peter Riedi, Conrad Finck, Lorentz Storck, (Strong,) Michael Miller, Melchior Knauer, Dietrich Scholl, Jacob Kreiter, Henry Deckert, John Doutrick, Simon Bimoch, Adam Hoehn, Frederick Gerhart, John Kohler, John Disler, Henry Boyer, Nicholas Bechtel, Paul Engle, Lazarus Wengert, Peter Fege, Christian Hoehn, George Hoehn, Frederick Hoehn, Peter Newman, Adam Brown, W. Mauntz, Jacob Sensebach, Samuel Nickel, Jacob Cull, Andrew Gross, Francis Bosman, Henry Spohn, Michael Busch, John Klinger, Nicholas Schaeffer, Christian Miller, Peter Warner, Conrad Smith, Christian Freimeier, Christian Frantz, Christian Paffenberger, Frederick Stump, John Bayer, jr., Mathias Jacobi, Ulrich Brunner, Adam Boniwitz, Baltzer Wenrich, John Planck, Jacob Orths, William Jones, John Riegel, Henry Martin, George Boeshor, John Strohschneider, Charles Bomberger, George Newman, John Mayer, Jacob Spatz, Martin Linck, Ludwig Held, John Dieter, John Rose, Nicholas Glatt, John Fischer, Casper Scheffer, Abraham Kessler, Mathias Schallhorn, Michael Overhouse, Michael Kessler, Henry Prince, Joseph Fuchs, Ulrich Rickert, George Hetterick, Michael Kurtz, Christian Michel, Leonard Schnell, Christopher Mohr, Dieterich Steinbrecher, Peter Haas, Christopher Witmer, Henry Hetterick, Michael Borger, George Michael Hehl, John Shuger, Henry Seitel, Martin Long, George Brindel, Jacob Slauch, Jacob Fischer, Christian Everhart, Michael Scheffer, Peter Bolender, John Heckert, Nicholas Schweigart, George Aumiller, Abraham Stover, Antonie Crandeberger, Jacob Schwob, Peter Riegel, Henry Dock, Peter Schoenfelter, John Walter, Philip Zerbe, Joiacham Schmit, Rudolph Schmaltz, Peter Foltz, Da-Miller, Henry Gerverd, George Rabb, Frederick Schwartz, Jacob Minig, Henry Christ, Baltzer Koenig, John Hartman, Peter Fischer, William Allen, Peter Werle, Michael Schneider, Adam Potteiger, Martin Armheld, John Servey, Andrew Ruhl, Christian Plank, Charles Plank, Samuel Boyer, Adam

Gruber, John Lesch, Henry Sohl, Thomas Jones, Christopher Lerch, Mathias Miller, Jacob Erntt, Casper Conrade, John Zerbe, Henry Minig, Peter Smith, George Manntz, Nicholas Yung, Philip Baner, Henry Weaver, Henry Seidel, Henry Deckert.

From the following communication, addressed by George Washington to Gen. Wayne, it appears he had been in this township in the fall of 1777 :

Sept. 17, 1777.
Reading Furnace, 6 o'clock P. M.

DEAR SIR:—I have this instant received yours of half past 3 o'clock, A. M. Having written to you already to *move forward* upon the enemy, I have but little to add. Generals Maxwell and Porter, are ordered to do the same, being at Pott's Forge. I could wish you and those Generals to act in conjunction, to make your advance more formidable, but I would not have too much time delayed on *this* account. I shall follow as speedily as possible with jaded men—some may probably go off immediately, if I find they are in a condition for it. The horses are almost all out upon patrol. Cartridges have been ordered for you. Give me the earliest information of every thing interesting, and of your moves, that I may govern mine by them. The *cutting off* the enemy's baggage would be a great matter.

Yours, sincerely,
GEO. WASHINGTON.

Gen. A. Wayne.

Heidelberg township is bounded on the north by upper Tulpehocken township; north-east by Penn, a recently organized township; south-east by lower Heidelberg; south-west by Lancaster county, and west by Marion township—about being formed out of part of Heidelberg and lower Tulpehocken; contains between eighteen and nineteen thousand acres of good land, much of it level; more than one half of it limestone soil, the other gravel, and when tilled, highly productive.

It is well watered by the Tulpehocken, and its tributary streams has ample water power. There are in it one furnace, two fulling mills, two woollen factories, four grist mills, three saw mills, one paper mill, and four or five churches.

17

The Reading and Harrisburg turnpike passes through it.—
The Wommelsdorf is on this pike, fourteen miles from Reading.
This town, originally called Middletown, was laid out by John
Wommelsdorff, in 1762. The first house erected here was the
one now occupied by Michael Seltzer, whose grandfather, Jacob Seltzer, erected it in 1761, '62 The town contains 125
houses; population 900; 3 stores and 3 taverns; a Lutheran
and German Reformed church, a New Presbyterian, and also
one owned by the Evangelical Association; three or four
schools, and an Academy, built in 1834. Rev. Morse is principal.

General Washington staid all night at Wommelsdorf, the
13th November, 1793, as appears from the following:
Wommelsdorf, den 14 ten Nov. 1793.
Gestern Abends hatten die Einwohner dieser Stadt das Vergnuegen den Presidenten, George Washington, der Vereinigten
Staaten von America zu bewirthen, und ihm bey dieser, Gelegenheit folgende Addresse zu ueberreichen:
Ihro Excellentz!
Moechten sie unsere aus Dankbarkeit und Gehorsam entste-
hende Freudensbezeugungen, in diesem gluecklichen Augen-
blick da wir die persoenliche Gegenwart von Ihro Excellentz
geniessen, in Dero angebornen und gewohnlichen Guete an-
zunehmen belieben.
Die kluge und mit gluecklichem Erfolg gekroente Thaten,
die Sie unter dem Schutz des Allerhoechsten Wesens in dem
letzten glorreichen Krieg ausgefuehret haben, dan Glueck und
Zufriedenheit das wir unter Dero Regierung seithin in Fried-
enszeit geniessen, und des letzhin sowohl ueberlegte zum rech-
ten Zeitpunct anempfohlne Neutralitaete-System, ermuntert
alle Menschen aufs Neue zur Hochachtung und Liebe gegen
sie.
Die Einwohner dieser Gegend werden niemals unterlassen,
langes Leben und Gesundheit von Gott fuer sie zu erbeten.

To which Washington sent the following very appropriate
reply:

Die Aufmerksamkeit die sie mir erzeigen, und der Beifall
von meinen Bemuehungen, giebt mir das groeste Vergnuegen.

A company of volunteers assembled, and amidst repeated firing of guns, near the door of the house in which be lodged, exclaimed:—Lang lebe George Washington! Lang lebe George Washington!!

Newmanstown, on the road from Wommelsdorf, on the boundary line between Lebanon and Berks county, was laid out by Walter Newman, 1762. The proprietors was known for many years as *"Der Irische."* The names of the original lot holders are still preserved; they are as follows:—Fage, Lasch, Kapp, Gartner, Keenzer, Zeller, Nall, Strickler, Eisenmenger, Manerer, Reed, Brown, Schenkel, Jacobs, Knauer, Moor, Stoop, Shup, Minig, Schall, Ensminger, Spatz, Hildebeitel, Brenner.

It contains 54 houses; two stores and two taverns; a church, common to Lutherans and German Reformed. Population 455. The present proprietors are Peter and Jacob Schoch, to whom eight shillings, per annum, are paid per lot, by the holders.

Population of the township before it was divided: in 1830, 4,101; 1840, 2,827.* Horses 1,107; horned cattle 3,312; sheep 1,713; swine 3,448; bushels of wheat 56,189; potatoes 15,825; tons of hay 4,120; pounds of wool 3,057. Whole amount of valuation, made taxable for county purposes, in 1844, $761,308; county tax $1,522 60; State tax $921 66.

CONRAD WEISER.†

Conrad Weiser, whose name is intimately associated with the early history of his adopted country, both as a private individual, and as a useful citizen in a public capacity, was born at Herrenberg, in Wittemberg, Germany, November 2d, 1696. His father's name was John Conrad Weiser.

Conrad was kept at school till he had mastered the rudiments of the German language, and had been instructed in the elements of the christian religion, according to Martin Luther's catechism. At the age of twelve, he was, by death, deprived of a pious and affectionate mother of sixteen children. She

* Since 1840, Heidelberg has been divided into upper and lower.
† Conrad Weiser was the grand-father, on the maternal side, of DOCTOR MUHLENBERG, of Lancaster, and of the Rev. and Hon. HENRY A. MUHLEN-BERG, lately Minister to Austria, and now residing at Reading, Pa.

died May 1st, 1709.   Conrad, in his private journal, speaking
of his mother, says:—"Sie war eine Gottesfuerchtige, und bey
ihren Nachbarn sehr geliebte Frau.   Ihr Wahlspruch war:
Jesus, dir lebe ich, dir sterbe ich; dein bin ich todt und leben-
dig."

Shortly after the death of Mrs. Weiser, the father, with
eight of his children, in company with several others of his
countrymen, left Germany for England, where they arrived at
London, June 34, 1709; and there they were maintained at the
expense of Queen Ann, npon whose invitation they had gone
thither, till towards the close of December, when about four
thousand of them embarked for America, where they arrived,
at the town of New York, the 13th of June 1710.

Conrad, the subject of this notice, and seven brothers and
three sisters, accompanied their father.   Conrad's oldest sister,
Catharine, having married Conrad Boos, remained at the old
homestead.   " Mein Vatter," says Conrad, " lies ihnen sein
Haus Aecker, Wiessen, Wein-Garten, u. s. u. fuer 675 Gulden."

In the autumn of 1710, John Conrad Weiser, with several
of his children, among whom was Conrad, and several hundred
German families, were transferred, at Queen Ann's expense, to
Livingston district, where many of them remained till 1713.—
Two younger brothers of Conrad Weiser, namely, George
Frederick and Christopher Frederick, were shortly, on their
arrival at New York, by the consent of their sick father, bound
out, or apprenticed by the Governor of New York, to a gentleman on Long Island.

In Livingston district, under the direction of commissioners
Johan Cast, Henry Mayer, and Richard Seakott, appointed by
Governor Hunter, it was allotted to these Germans to manufacture tar, and raise hemp, to repay freightage from Holland
to England, and thence to New York.   This business proved
unsuccessful; they were, however, released in 1713, of all
freightage upon them.   Shortly afterwards, the Germans were
dispersed through the province of New York—many remained
in this district, and about one hundred and fifty families resolved
to move to Schoharie, forty miles west of Albany.   Previous
to their removing, they sent deputies thither to consult with
the Indians, touching their locating at that place; for one of
the Chiefs, when in England a few years previous, at the time

these Germans were there, made Queen Ann a present of some land, for the behoof of the Palatines. John Conrad Weiser, Conrad's father, was one of their deputies.

Having, in a preceding part of this book, mentioned the leading circumstances, of this *present.* It is hoped, the reader will nevertheless excuse the apparent episode, if the substance of the former be repeated in this connection.

In 1708, the French in America, continued their aggressions eastward. Having penetrated to Haverhill, on the Merrimack, and reduced the town to ashes, it was then proposed by Colonel Vetch, to subdue Acadia, Canada, and Newfoundland; an attack was made upon Quebec, by a squadron with five regiments from England, and 1200 provincials from Massachusetts and Rhode Island, whilst 1500 men, under Colonels Vetch and Nicholson, from the central colonies, attempted Montreal, by way of Lake Champlain. The inhabitants of New York entered into this scheme with great alacrity—raised funds for that purpose, and made other necessary preparations. The *Five Nations,* by the influence of Col. Peter Schuyler, had been induced to take up the hatchet, and to send 600 warriors to the field, leaving theirs to be maintained by the provincial treasury.

At this critical juncture, Colonel Nicholson returned to England to solicit further assistance; he was accompanied by Col. Peter Schuyler, with four *Sachems* of the confederate Indians. While in London, these chiefs saw the miserable condition in which the Germans were; for they had just arrived from Germany, and encamped in the purliens of London. The Indian chiefs commisserated their case, and one of them voluntarily presented Queen Ann a tract of his land in Schoharie, New York, for the benefit of the distressed Germans, whose hearts ached for a place of rest from oppression.

John Conrad Weiser was one of the deputies to Schoharie. After they returned from the Mohawk or Maqua country, in which Schoharie lay, many of the families moved from Livingston district in the autumn of 1713; some to Albany, others to Schenectady, with a view of moving, the following spring, to Schoharie. Conrad's father also moved that fall, to Schenectady, and remained with his family, during the winter, with one Johannes Meynderten,. Here he was repeatedly visited by an Indian chief, called Quagnant, of the Maqua or Mohawk

nation. Quagnant proposed to take Conrad with him to his
own country, and teach him the language spoken by his nation.
The father acceded, and Conrad, the son, accompanied his future instructor, and took lodings among the Indians.

While here, and acquiring a knowledge of the Mohawk language, his sufferings, according to Weiser's own journal, were
almost intolerable.   He had scarce clothes enough to cover his
nudity, much less to protect him securely against the inclemency
and piercing cold of a severe winter; and he was afterwards
pressed by hunger, in addition to the pinchings of frost—and
still to heighten the keen sufferings of the stranger and scholar,
he was repeatedly menaced with death by the inebriate Indians,
to escape which, he had frequently to flee and conceal himself,
till reason was restored, and "a sober second thought" had restrained the execution of their threats.   While the young suf-
ferer was among the savages, his father moved in the spring of
1714, from Schenectady to Schoharie, being accompanied by
one hundred and fifty German families.

In the month of July, 1714, having spent the winter with
Quagnant, Conrad returned to his father's house.   Having,
however, acquired considerable knowledge of the Mohawk language.   At home, he perfected his knowledge of that language,
by being repeatedly called on to act as interpreter between the
German settlers and the Maqua or Mohawk Indians.   Several
families of the Maqua nation, lived within a mile of his father's
house.   He complains, however, in his journal, that he had to
interpret gratuitously.   " So lagen auch allezeit Maquaische
hie und wieder auf der Jagd, da es oefters was fehlte dass ich
viel zu dalmetschen hatte, *aber ohne Lohn.*"   Poor recom-
pense.

The Germans, amid hardships, sufferings, and trials, with
which original settlers, in new countries, ever meet, made considerable improvements.   Their flattering prospects, however,
were blasted in their incipient efforts, and all their labor lost.
Owing to a defect in their titles to the land, which they had
with so much care and solicitude improved, in not conforming
to the requisitions of the laws of New York, before they located, to secure to themselves their improved lands.   The Governor of New York sold these lands in Schoharie, to seven
wealthy merchants, four of whom resided in Albany, and three
in the town of New York; those of the former place, were

Méyndert Shyller, John Shyller, Robert Livingston,* and Peter Non Brughen; those of New York, were George Clark, the Secretary of the Province, Doctor Stads, and Rip Von Dam.— This caused a great excitement at the time, both at Schoharie and at Albany. There were many at Albany, anxious to see it, that the poor Germans might retain the land. The Germans, at Schoharie, were divived in opinion—two parties arose— the stronger refused to submit, wherefrom they sent three deputies, or commissioners, to England, to appeal to King George the first. The deputies sailed from Philadelphia, in 1818; but they had scarcely left Delaware Bay, when the vessel in which they sailed, was surprised and captured by pirates. John Conrad Weiser—Conrad's father—one of the deputies, was tied three times by the pirates, and bastinaded, with a view to compel him to give up what money he might have; he would not yield. William Schaff, another of the deputies, addressed the pirates; stating, that the purse they had taken from him, was theirs in common—that the bounden man had no more to give; whereupon they left the vessel.

They were now compelled—having been robbed of all their provisions—to sail into Boston harbor, to procure a fresh supply. They then sailed for England—but to their sorrow, regret, and great disappointment, times had changed since the demise of Queen Ann. They found but few friends; among these were the Reads, Boehm and Roberts, Chaplains at St. James. These did all that lay in their power, to bring their case before the Lords, Commissioners of Trade and Plantations.

The consideration of the deputies was deferred, from time to time, till they were involved in debt, and in great difficulties.

Mr. Walrath, the other deputy, resolved to return to America. He embarked for New York, but died before he arrived. Weiser and Schaff were imprisoned for debt. They wrote to their friends, at Schoharie, for money, but owing to the treachery of some, the forwarding of money was deferred: in the

---

* Robert Livingston was also the proprietor of Livingston Manor, or District, mentioned above, and originally contained that tract of land in Columbia county, New York, what now composes the township of Livingston, Taghkanie, Copake, Ancram, Gallatin, Clermont, and Germantown — The royal grants to R. Livingston, are dated respectively 1684, and 1686, and were confirmed in 1714.

In June, 1710, seventy of the Palatines sent out by Queen Ann, settled in German township, then part of Livingston Manor—among these was Weiser.

meantime, the Governor of New York appeared before the Lords of Trade and Plantations, while the deputies were still in prison; of course nothing to relieve them was effected. Ultimately, the money they had written for, was received; and the two deputies paid their debt, and were released. They now supplicated—*de novo*—finally, they received an order on the new Governor, William Burnet, (of New York,) who was requested to grant the Germans such lands as were not disposed of, which had been presented to Queen Ann by the Indian Sachem, for the benefit of the Germans. Towards the close of 1720, said William Burnet arrived at New York.

Conrad Weiser, in his private journal, says, "I was sent, in the early part of 1721, to New York, to said Governor Burnet, to hand him a petition. He received me kindly, and informed me that he had received instructions from the Lords of Trade, which he had resolved to follow implicitly."

The two surviving deputies were still in England, and were quite dissatisfied with what had been done, but could effect nothing more. In 1721, Schaff being displeased with John Conrad Weiser, returned. "Siehatten," says Conrad, "beide harte Koepfe." Both were obstinate. Finally, Mr. Weiser returned in November, 1723. Schaff died six months after his arrival.

Governor Burnet granted patents to the few who agreed to settle in the Mohawk country, in Stoney Arabia,* or near the Falls;† but as only a few were disposed to settle at the Falls, some moved to the Mohawk country, others remained at Schobarie—some having heard favorable reports of lands in Pennsylvania, turned their faces thitherward. They united; wending their course in a southeastern direction, till they struck the Susquehanna river, where they made canoes; these they freighted with their children and effects—floated down on the broad bosom of the river, to the mouth of the Swatara creek; thence they worked their way up, till they reached a fertile spot in Tulpehocken—settled in the spring of 1723, in the midst of the Indians. Here they also commenced improvements, without permission from the Land Commissioners."

Conrad Weiser having married his beloved Anna Eva, (the daughter of respectable Christian parents,) the 22d Nov. 1720,

* Now in Montgomery county, N. Y
† Falls in the Mohawk river.

while his father was in England; and having settled in life, and being employed as interpreter, he remained at Schoharie till 1729, when he, with his wife and five children, his sons Philip and Frederick, and daughters Anna, Madlina and Maria, followed his relations and friends at Tulpehocken, and chose this valley as his future residence; he located himself half a mile east of the present site of Wommelsdorf.*

Conrad Weiser, as occasion demanded it, acted in various, both private and public capacities. Few men were more useful in his day and generation, than he. Though he had determined to spend his remaining days in private, his talents soon attracted the attention of his own countrymen, as well as those of his adopted country.

In August, 1730, John Peter Miller, a native of Oberant Lautern, of the Electoral Palatinate, and a graduate of the University of Heidelberg, arrived in Philadelphia, and there made application to the Scotch Synod, for clerical ordination. Before receiving ordination, a question for discussion was proposed, and in answering it, showed he was a man of rare endowments. "We gave him, says Rev. Andrews, in a letter to a friend, "a question to discuss about *justification*, and he answered it, in a whole sheet, in a very notable manner. He speaks Latin as readily as we do our vernacular tongue."

Shortly after his ordination, Mr. Miller visited Mr. Weiser, at Heidelberg. Here Mr. Miller labored as a minister of the gospel, among the Germans, for several years.

Weiser's skill, as an interpreter of the Indian language, was

* When writing the History of Lancaster county, page 184 in a note, authority of "Family tradition," that Conrad Weiser's father come to Pennsylvania in 1723. This is an error. The Hallische Nachrichter enables us to correct this. Dr Henry Melchior Muhlenberg says, "In the year 1746, came my wife's grandfather to my house, he had resided in New York since 1710, and lately on the borders of New England He left that country on account of the dangers which he apprehended from the French and Indians, who had already murdered several German families. Moreover, he was also anxious to see his children and grand-children, to converse with them on the subject of religion, and to spend his last days, unmolestedly, among his kindred in Pennsylvania. He was very infirm and frail when he came, and was confined in bed for some time after his arrival; after he had been somewhat convalescent, his son Conrad, my father-in-law, who resided at Heidelberg, fifty miles off, sent a wagon with suitable bedding for them — He reached Heidelberg with much difficulty—lived but a short time afterwards with his son—and fell asleep in death, in the presence of his weeping children and grand-children." He had lived to the age of between 80 and 90 years.—Hal. Nach., p. 161-163.

soon known and appreciated. His services were required, in that capacity, by the Hon. P. Gordon, Lieutenant Governor of the province of Pennsylvania, as early as 1731. For that purpose, Weiser accompanied Shekelemy and Cehachquey—Indians—from his residence, to Philadelphia.* He was repeatedly called on, to act as interpreter, while pursuing the improvement of his farm. Weiser and Shekelemy were, by the treaty of 1732, appointed as fit and proper persons to go between the Six Nations and the Government, and to be employed in all actions with one another, whose bodies, the Indians said, were to be equally divided between them and us; we to have one-half—that they (Indians) had found Conrad Weiser faithful and honest—that he is a true, good man, and had spoken *their* words, and *our* words, and not his own.†

Weiser was a man of integrity, and of unbounded benevolence. He was disposed "to hope all things." He was easy of access, and readily yielded to religious influences. He was neither a rigid sectarian, nor a sanctimonious bigot; though educated a Lutheran, and thoroughly indoctrinated in the principles of that church, he gave countenance to the sincere and good of other denominations.

Several years after the arrival of the Rev. Miller, among the Germans, at Heidelberg and Tulpehocken, a religious excitement prevailed through that region; scores imbibed the sentiments promulgated by Conrad Beisel, the founder of the "German Seventh Day Baptist Association," at Ephrata."

Among the number of converts to that doctrine, were Miller and Weiser, both of whom were initiated into that church, by the ordinance of baptism, in May, 1735. Weiser soon forsook the society, but Miller resorted to Ephrata, where he remained till the day of his death, September 25, 1796.

George Thomas, Governor of the province of Pennsylvania, tendered Weiser the appointment of Justice of Peace, which he accepted, and soon after, he was appointed Indian agent and interpreter, for which he was exceedingly well qualified. In this, the threefold capacity, he rendered his country essential service for many years. From this time forth, till the day of his death, he commenced, and continued in a most active career.

* Col. Rec., iii, 453.
† Prov. Rec. Book P., p. 96.

In September, 1736, the chiefs of the Six Nations were expected in Philadelphia, to confirm a treaty that had been previously made in 1732. Weiser was active here, as we learn from the Public Records. "Conrad Weiser, our interpreter, about the beginning of September, 1736, advised from Tulpehocken, that he had certain intelligence from some Indians, sent before him, that there was a large number of those people, with many of the chiefs, arrived at Shamokin, on the Susquehanna, upon which he was directed to repair thither to attend them, and supply them with necessaries on their journey here, (Philadelphia.)

On the 27th September, the chiefs came with Conrad Weiser to the President's house, at Stenton, being near the road, when a suitable entertainment was provided for them; and the next day, the honorable proprietor, Thomas Penn, and some of the council, with other gentlemen, coming thither from Philadelphia; after dinner, a council was held at Stenton, September 28. The council continued till the 29th; then adjourned, to meet Oct. 2d, in the Great Meeting House, in Philadelphia."*

Weiser attended the adjourned council.

A resolution was offered Oct. 4, 1736, "That Conrad Weiser, the interpreter, who is extremely useful on all such occasions—and on the present one has been very serviceable—there be given him twenty pounds."†

In the year 1737, he was sent to Onondago, N. Y., at the desire of the Governor of Virginia. He departed quite unexpectedly, towards the close of February, on a journey of five hundred miles, through a wilderness, when there was neither road nor path, and at a time of the year when arrivals could not be met with for food. The sufferings and privations he endured, were indescribably great. He gives a very interesting account of this journey, in a letter, which is inserted in a previous page, (see p. 24, &c.)

The following year, in May, he again went to Onondago, in company with Bishop Spangenberger, David Zeisberger, and Shebosch, Moravian Missionaries to the Indians. They suffered many hardships, but experienced also, says Loskiel,‡ some re-

* Prov. Rec , Book P., p 90.
† Prov. Rec., Book I , p. 94.
‡ Loskiel's His. of Miss., P. II., p. 79

markable proofs of the kind Providence of God.   Having been
without provisions for several days, they found a quarter of
bear, hung up for the use of travellers·by an Indian hunter, who
could not carry it off, according to a prevalent custom among
the Indians—"When, says Loskiel, huntsmen kill a deer, they
take the skin and as much of the flesh as they can carry; the
rest they hang upon a tree for the use of such as pass that way."

Such timely relief they received more than once, and were
therefore encouraged to assist other hungry travellers whom
they met on the road.   One day they found two Iroquis warriors, who had lost all their provisions, were almost naked, and
had travelled nearly four hundred miles.   One of them was also
on the road to Onondago.   Conrad Wilson asked him how he
intended to reach that place in such a situation?   His answer
was: "God, who dwells in heaven, has created the earth and
all creatures therein, and he feeds numbers of men and beasts
in the wilderness."   He can and will feed me also.   While
they were in company with Weiser and his companions, they
received their full share out of the common kettle, and thus he
was fed according to his faith.   Weiser cites this (see p. 25, 26,)
as an illustration of the Indian's belief in the Providence of God.

Though an active and efficient public officer, still his mind was
not so wholly engrossed as to give no heed, or devote some
time to religious matters.   He not only accompanied the Moravian missionaries to Onandago; but in August, 1742, we
find him again at Bethlehem, where he set out in company with
Count Zinzendorf, who had just lately arrived in America, for
Tulpehocken, to render the Count all necessary aid, affording
him an opportunity of preaching to the Indians.   On the 14th
of August, they met a numerous embassy of Sachems, or heads
of the Six Nations, returning from Philadelphia.   Though they
were extremely mild, and had on the same day, shot one of
their own people, Zinzendorf would not omit so good an opportunity of preaching the gospel, but desired Conrad Weiser
to tell them, that he had a word from God to them, and their
nations, which he and his brethren, would proclaim to them;
further, that his intention was neither to buy land, nor to trade,
but to point out to them the way to everlasting life.   Conrad
Weiser added: "This is the man whom God hath sent, both to
the Indians and the white people, to make known his will to

them," confirming his words, after the Indian custom, by a present of a piece of red cloth.*

Shortly after this, Weiser accompanied the Count to Shamokin, where they were kindly received by Shikelimus. After spending some time here, Weiser returned again to Tulpehocken settlement.

In January, 1743, at the request of Governor Thomas Weiser, again set out for Shamokin. In his journal, he says:—"On the 30th of January, 1743, in the evening, I received the Governor's order, together with the deposition of Thomas McKee, and set out next morning with Mr. McKee for Shamokin, where we arrived on the first of February. I left Shamokin the 6th, and arrived at home in the night, the 9th of February.†

So deeply was Weiser interested in the success of the missionary efforts of the Moravians, in converting them to christianity, that aside from accompanying the heralds of the cross, he devoted much time to teaching them the Indian language.— Pyrlacus, who arrived with Buettner and Zander, from Europe, in October, 1741, as missionaries, to convert the Mahikander and Delaware nations, resolved to preach the gospel to the Iroquois nation; however, as a thorough knowledge of the Maqua or Mohawk language was required, to be able to preach the gospel to them, Pyrlacus went to Tulpehocken settlement, to the house of Conrad, in 1743, where he remained three months to study this language with him. Weiser's superior skill as a qualfied instructor, soon enabled his pupil to master the language, so as to address the tawny sons of that nation; and with that view, he afterwards moved with his wife into the interior part of the Iroquois country, and took up his abode with the English missionaries, in Juntarogu. Conrad Weiser had, says Loskiel, an inclination to follow Pyrlacus, and on his way, called at Shamokin. His astonishment, at what he saw and heard at this place, is evident, from the following letter to another of the missionaries, namely Buettner, who was stationed at Shamokin:

" I was very sorry not to have seen you at Shemoken, owing to your indisposition. But the pleasure I felt, during my abode there, has left a deep impression upon me. The faith of the

* Loskiel, P. ii., chap. 2, p. 27.
† Prov. Rec., Book K, p. 276.

18

Indians in our Lord Jesus Christ—their simplicity and unaf-
fected deportment—their experience of the grace procured for
us by the sufferings of Jesus, preached to them by the brethren,
has impressed my mind with a firm belief, that God is with
you.   I thought myself seated in a company of primitive christians.

" The old men sat partly upon benches, and partly upon the
ground, for want of room, with great gravity and devotion;
their eyes steadfastly fixed upon their teacher, as if they would
eat his words.   John was the interpreter, and acquitted himself in the best manner.   I esteem him as a man annointed with
grace and spirit.   Though I am not well acquainted with the
Mahikander language, yet their peculiar manner of delivery
renders their ideas intelligible to me, as to any European in this
country.   In short, I deem it one of the greatest favors bestowed upon me in this life, that I have been at Shamokin.

" That text of scripture, "Jesus Christ, the same yesterday
and to day, and for ever," appeared to me as an eternal truth,
when I beheld the venerable patriarchs of the American Indian
church sitting around me, as living witnesses of the power of
our Lord Jesus Christ, and of his atoning sacrifice.   Their
prayers are had in remembrance in the sight of God—and may
God fight against their enemies.   May the Almighty give to
you and your assistants an open door to the hearts of all the
heathens.   This is the most earnest wish of your sincere friend,

CONRAD WEISER."

In April, 1743, he went again, in a public capacity, to Shamokin, on affairs of Virginia and Maryland.   He says:—
"April 9th, I arrived at Shamokin, by order of the Governor of
Pennsylvania, to acquaint the neighboring Indians, and those
on Wyoming, that the Governor of Virginia was well pleased
with the mediation, and was willing to come to agreement with
the Six Nations about the land his people were settled upon, if
it was *that* they contended for, and to make up the matter of
the late unhappy skirmish, in an amicable way."

In June, he went to Onondago, in obedience to the orders
of the Governor and Council of Pennsylvania.   Of this journey
there is a full report, and of the proceedings, in the Provincial
Records, Book K., p. 280, 283, 287.

As stated above, the governor of Virginia proposed to adjust all amicably, and the Indians acceded to attend a treaty to be held the spring following, at Lancaster; in the interval an occurreuce took place, and Weiser was again obliged to go to Shamokin. April, 1744, Governor Thomas received a letter dated, April 22, Lancaster, signed by Cookson, stating that John Armstrong, an Indian trader, with his two servants, Woodward Arnold, and James Smith, had been murdered at Juniata, by three Delaware Indians; he was despatched to the chiefs of the Delaware Indians, at Shamokin, to make strict enquiry, which resulted in the apprehension of the murderer, who was imprisoned at Lancaster, and from that removed to Philadelphia, to await his trial.*

When the time arrived for the conference, or treaty, to be held at Lancaster, which took place, it was attended by the Governor himself, in person, and agents of Virginia and Maryland; Conrad Weiser attended as interpreter. Here all matters of dispute between the parties were satisfactorily settled. Weiser was paid £15 3s. 6d., to defray the expenses of the treaty.†

From, and after 1743, Conrad Weiser did not, so efficiently as formerly, co-operate with the Moravians. Whatever may have led him to measureably, if not wholly, decline acting in concert with them, it was probably owing to the fact, that public business demanded more of his attention, and that he devoted himself more to sustaining the church of his fathers; for an effort was made, at that time, by the Rev. Muhlenberg, who had arrived from Europe in 1742, as the Apostle of Lutheranism in America, to build up their churches; and in conse-

---

* In a letter to a friend, Weiser says, alluding to this occurrence—the death of John Armstrong, &c.—"After I had performed my errand, there was a feast prepared, to which the Governor's messengers were invited; there were about one hundred persons present; to whom, after we had, in great silence, devoured a fat bear, the oldest of the chiefs made a speech, in which he said·'That by a great misfortune, three of the brethren—the *white men*—had been killed by an Indian; that nevertheless, the sun was not set; (meaning there was no war,) it had only been somewhat darkened by a small cloud, which was now done away; he that done evil was likely to be punished, and the land to remain in peace; therefore, he exhorted his people to thankfulness to God; and he began to sing with an awful solemnity, but without expressing any words; the others accompanied him with their voices; after they had done, the same Indian, with great earnestness and fervor, spoke these words: Thanks, thanks be to thee, thou great Lord of the World, in that thou hast again caused the sun to shine, and hast dispersed the dark cloud—the Indians are thine.'"

† Votes of Assembly, III, p. 546—Gordon's Pa., 247.

quence, from his success, is justly entitled to the appellation of "Patriarch of the American Lutheran Church." He visited the Tulpehocken settlement in 1743, where he formed the acquaintance of Conrad Weiser, and a connection that would naturally enlist his feelings, and secure his efforts, in building up and sustaining the Lutheran church, in preference to any other.

Muhlenberg, Weiser's son-in-law, alluding to this circumstance, says: "Im Jahr, 1743, ward unser Freund, Conrad Weiser, bekannt mit dem ersten hereingesandten Deutschen Evangelischen Prediger, gewan ihn und seine Lehre lieb und gab ihm 1745, seine aelteste Tochter zur, Ehegenossin. Diese Freundschafts-Verbindung verursachte dann und wann einen Besuch und eine anhaltende Correspondence; beide wurden, so viel Gott Gnaden verliehen, auf die seelen-Erbau ung gerichtet vobei er verschiedene Jahre ziemlich munter und lebhaft im Glauben schien. Die heilige Bibel war ihm durch und durch bekant. u. s. f.*

"In 1745, May 19, I set out," says Weiser, "for Onondago, incompany with Shikelamy, one of the Indian chiefs, his son, and Andrew Montour, and we arrived safe at Onondago on the 6th of June following. The 7th, early in the morning, Canassatego, Cahesh, Carrawano, the Black Briar, and Casehayion, came to receive me and my company. The best part of the day was spent with discourses concerning news, &c., &c."

It was probably while at Onondago this time, the current anecdote, related by Dr. Franklin, touching Weiser and Canassatego, which is found in Drake's Indian Biography, Book V., p. 12, 13. As the editors of the valuable Encyclopedia Perthensis have thought this anecdote worthy a place in that work, it has gained one here:

"Dr. Franklin tells us a very interesting story of Canassatego, and at the same time makes the old chief tell another.—In speaking of the manners and customs of the Indians, the doctor says, "The same hospitality, esteemed among them as a principal virtue, is practised by private persons; of which Conrad Weiser, our interpreter, gave me the following instances: He had been naturalized among the Six Nations, and spoke well the Mohawk language. In going through the Indian country, to carry a message from our governor to the

* Hal. Nach., p. 976.

council at Onondago, he called at the habitation of Canassatego, an old acquaintance, who embraced him, spread furs for him to sit on, placed before him some boiled beans, and venison, and mixed some rum and water for his drink. When he was well refreshed, and had lit his pipe, Canassatego, began to converse with him; asked how he had fared the many years since they had seen each other; whence he then came; what occasioned the journey, &c. Conrad answered all his questions; and when the discourse began ·to flag, the Indian to continue it, said, ‘Conrad, you have lived long among the white people, and know something of their customs: I have been sometimes at Albany, and have observed, that once in seven days they shut up their shops, and assemble in the great house; tell me what that is for; what do they do there?’ ‘They meet there,’ says Conrad, ‘to hear and learn good things.’ ‘I do not doubt,’ says the Indian, ‘that they tell you so; they have told me the same; but I doubt the truth of what they say, and I will tell you my reasons. I went lately to Albany, to sell my skins, and buy blankets, knives, powder, rum, &c. You know I used generally to deal with Hans Hanson; but I was a little inclined this time to try some other merchants. However, I called first upon Hans, and asked him what he would give for beaver.— He said he could not give more than four shillings a pound; but says he, I cannot talk on business now; this is the day when we meet together to learn good things, and I am going to the meeting. So I thought to myself, since I cannot do any business to-day, I may as well go to the meeting too, and I went with him. There stood up a man in black, and began to talk to the people very angrily; I did not understand what he said, but perceiving that he looked much at me, and at Hanson, I imagined that he was angry at seeing me there; so I went out, sat down near the house, struck fire, and lit my pipe, waiting till the meeting should break up. I thought too that the man had mentioned something of beaver, and suspected it might be the subject of their meeting. So when they came out, I accosted my merchant. ‘Well, Hans,’ says I, ‘I hope you have agreed to give more than 4s. a pound.’ ‘No,’ says he, ‘I cannot give so much, I cannot give more than three shillings and sixpence. I then spoke to several other dealers, but they all sung the same song,—three and sixpence, three and sixpence. This made it clear to me that my suspicion was right;

18*

and that whatever they pretended of meeting to learn good
things, the purpose was to consult how to cheat Indians in the
price of beaver.   Consider but a little, Conrad, and you must
be of my opinion.   If they met so often to learn good things,
they would certainly have learned some before this time.   But
they are still ignorant.   You know our practice.   If a white
man, in travelling through our country, enters one of our cabins,
we all treat him as I do you; we dry him if he is wet; we
warm him if he is cold, and give him meat and drink, that he
may allay his thirst and hunger; and we spread soft furs for him
to rest and sleep on: we demand nothing in return.   But if I
go into a white man's house at Albany, and ask for victuals
and drink, they say, get out you Indian dog.   You see they
have not yet learned those little good things, that we need no
meetings to be insiructed in, because our mothers taught them
to us when we were children; and therefore it is impossible their
meetings should be, as they say, for any such purpose, or have
any such effect: they are only to contrive the cheating of Indians in the price of beaver.' "

In June, 1747, he again started for Shamokin, charged with
a message to the Indians there to notify them of the death of
the late Proprietary, John Penn.   In his report of this mission,
to the Secretary; Weiser says, that in his journey to Shamokin,
in obedience to the command of the President and Council, he
fortunately met, at Chamber's mill, in Pextang, with Shikelamy and several Indians, among whom was Scaienties, a man of
note, of the Cayuga nation, which accidental meeting rendered it unnecessary for him to go farther, he here communicated them the message, &c.*

The reader, it is believed, will excuse the apparent episode,
in giving a place to an extract from the *Hallische Nachrichten*, containing Weiser's views, as to instructing the Indians in
the doctrines of Christianity; and to show that he was fearless
in the discharge of public duty, as a Justice of Peace.

"July 5, 1747, I (Muhlenberg) preached at Northkill, in
Bethel township, Lancaster county, (now Berks,) on the gospel, of the lost and found sheep, Luke xv.—baptized several
children—confirmed some of the young people—there was
much and deep religious feeling—dispersed the Lord's Supper.
In the afternoon hastened to another appointment, eight miles

* Prov. Rec , Book L., p. 7.

off, to Tulpehocken, to preach at 3 o'clock in the afternoon.— Having preached and taken my leave from the congregation, and in going with my father-in-law, Conrad Weiser, to his house, we overtook an Indian chief, who was accompanied by his son and son-in-law, on his way to Mr. Weiser's, to confer with him concerning some lands."

"If we consider," says M., " the blindness and darkness in spiritual matter, of those Indians, we feel disposed to deplore their condition; because we have the light of the gospel, but we generally love darkness rather than light." The French Papists, many years ago, made an effort to convert the Canadian Indians to christianity, but succeeded illy, because several of their missionaries violated the seventh commandment.

According to Mr. Weiser's statement, our Indains are very astute and witty in *natural things*—of quick perception; and although they cannot write, they retain much of the past history; because they handed it down by oral tradition, from one generation to another. They generally entertain deep-rooted prejudices against the whites, and mistrust them greatly, saying the whites had crept out of the earth on the other side of the great deep, and they on this side. The whites should have reemained on their own ground, whence they came, and there maintain themselves as they do on theirs. That the whites came for no other purpose to this country, than to take away their lands—and have spoiled their hunting ground, and thus made life a burden, by rendering the procuring of game and fish more arduous, in order to supply their natural wants.— They also complain that decease is more common among them since the introduction of intoxicating liquors.

If an attempt is made to instruct them in the truths contained in the revealed word of God, it is impracticable to do it with any degree of success, for the want of suitable terms or words to convey to their mind spiritual perception. Natural theology, and the historical portions of scripture might be taught them to a considerable extent in their own language, scanty as it is.

Mr. Weiser made repeated efforts, yet in a great degree, without much success, to communicate to them, historical facts from the writings of Moses. They invariably replied:—"This may all be true, and it is likely the Great Spirit may have revealed this to you on the other side of the great water; but it

does not concern us. Our God has revealed to us, on this side
of the great water, something else; do you adhere to what has
been revealed to you, and we will hold to that which has been
revealed to us."

Mr. Weiser is of the opinion, that to convert them to christianity, it would be essential, among other methods, to adopt
something like the following:

1. Several missionaries should take up their abode in the
midst of the Indians, and strive to make themselves thoroughly masters of their language—conform as far as possible
to their costumes, manners and customs, yet reprove their natural vices by a holy, meek, and virtuous deportment.

2. Translate revealed truth into their own language, and
present the whole as intelligibly as possible.

3. The missionaries should study the Indian's tunes and melodies, and convey to them the law and gospel, in such tunes
and melodies, in order to make an abiding impression—and
thereby, under the blessings and increase of God, patiently wait
for the fruits of their labors.

Weiser, as a justice of the peace, was fearless in the discharge
of his duty. He incurred the displeasure of the lawless. Muhlenberg says, in the Hallische Nachrichten, p. 209—an attempt
was made to fire his house in 1747.

"There was a certain family living in the neighborhood of
my father-in-law, Conrad Weiser, against whom he pronounced
the sentence of the law for a certain flagrant violation thereof.
Shortly afterwards, the doors and the windows of his house
were fastened, by some ill-disposed persons, in the night, and a
large heap of straw, with other combustibles, was placed under
the roof of the portico, and fire set to it. The smoke, and the
noise of the burning roof, wakened one of the children, who
aroused the other inmates instantly. But as the doors had
been fastened, they were obliged to force their way through
the window, to extinguish the fire. Thus they narrowly escaped—his whole family were in danger of being consumed,
except two children, who had gone to a neighbor's house before
night, and remained there.

In November of the same year, he was sent upon another
mission to Shamokin; the object of the mission was to administer relief to some of the suffering Indians there. "On the
6th of Oct., 1747," says Weiser, "I set out for Shamokin, by

way of Pextang— the weather was bad. I arrived at Shamokin on the 9th, about noon; I was surprised to see Shikalimy in such a condition as my eyes beheld. He was hardly able to stretch forth his hand, to bid me welcome. In the same condition was his wife—his three sons not quite so bad, but very poorly; also one of his daughters, and two or three of his grandchildren. All had the fever. There were three buried out of the family, a few days before, namely: Cajadis, Shikalimy's son-in-law, who had been married to his daughter above fifteen years, and was reckoned the best hunter among all the Indians, and two others. I administered medicine to them, under the directions of Dr. Graeme."* Shikalimy soon recovered from his sickness. Weiser returned, and arrived at home the 15th of October; but we soon find him again at Paxton, or Harris' Ferry.

Paxton, Nov. 28, 1747.

RICHARD PETERS, ESQ.

SIR:—Last night I arrived here with the Indians, all in good health but Canachquasy, the speaker.

Scaiohady told Shikalimy at my house, very privately, that Peter Chartier and his company, had accepted of the French hatchet: but kept it in their bosom till they would see what interest they could make in favor of the French.

Yours, &c.,
CONRAD WEISER.

This was a manifesto of what was brooding among the Indians, and the dangers apprehended from Indian hostilities, induced the Assembly to use every exertion to secure the aid of those not yet disaffected, and if possible, to gain over the disaffected. The government had a subtle enemy to fear, " for the Indians were well disposed to make the most of their fears of their good friends, the whites; and by continual suggestions of their inability long to resist the French, who endeavored to intimidate them by threats, and to seduce them by promises, they gave occasions for new conferences, which were always accompanied by presents. Distant and vagrant tribes, also, sent their ambassadors, proffering friendship, and soliciting the bounty of the Province."

* Prov. Rec., Book L., p. 7.
t Prov. Rec., Book L., p. 145.

"Some Indians, on the banks of the Ohio, connected with the Six Nations, visited Philadelphia, to tender their homage, and to invite the Province to send commissioners to a council fire, at which the neighboring nations were to be present. Impressed with the importance of such a conference, the council invited the governments of Maryland and Virginia to send their agents, and to unite in preparing a suitable present. On the part of Pennsylvania, goods were provided to the amount of ten thousand pounds, and Conrad Weiser was selected as envoy. He was charged to obtain a perfect knowledge of the numbers, situation, disposition and strength of the Indians of the vicinity; whether friends, neutrals or enemies; what reliance might be placed upon them to protect the Province against the French." Previous to his entrance upon his journey westward, Weiser consulted the friendly Indians, as is evident from the following communication:

TULPEHOCKEN, March 28, 1748.

Richard Peters, Esq., Secretary of Pa.*

Sir—

I let you know by these lines, that Shikalimy, with his eldest son, came down from Shamokin, at my request. They arrived this afternoon. I wanted to consult with him about the journey to Ohio, and to hear what passes among the Indians on Susquehanna river, and elsewhere.

Yours, &c.,
CONRAD WEISER.

On the receipt of this communication, Mr. Peters wrote to Weiser, requesting him to come forthwith to Philadelphia—he accordingly went, and spent a few days. In the meantime, he took preliminary measures to bring things to a happy issue. Under date of 13th June, 1748, Weiser again addresses the Secretary:

"Last night arrived at my house, Fanataraykon, Sogogockiathen, Achnoara, Kattake, and Sanagaranet, sent by Shikalimy, to inform me that a message from the Six Nations was sent, &c."†

On the 23d of the month, Weiser attended the council at

* Prov. Rec. Book, L., p. 211.
† Ibid, 320.

Philadelphia. "He and Andrew Montour were without, but were called in; and Mr. Weiser presented Mr. Montour to the Board, as a proper person who might be of service to the Province, as an Indian interpreter and messenger; informing them that he had employed him in sundry affairs of consequence, and found him faithful, knowing and prudent—that he had engaged him for his own private information, as Andrew lives among the Six Nations, between the branches of the Ohio and Lake Erie, &c."

At this time, Weiser received special instruction. The instructions were handed him in writing, and are as follows:

"Sir—This Government having promised the Indians, who came from Ohio in November last, to send *you* to them, early in the Spring, and having provided a present of considerable value, you are to proceed thither, with all convenient despatch. Mr. George Croghan, the Indian trader, who is well acquainted with the Indian country, and the best roads to Ohio, has undertaken the convoy of you and the goods, with his own man and horses, at the public expense, &c.

These instructions had been drawn up in March previous, when Mr. Weiser was on the point of going to Ohio, and laid before the Assembly in May; but his journey being postponed, for reasons set forth, were not sooner delivered to him.[*]

August 11th, 1748, Weiser set out from his house for Ohio; travelled that day about thirty miles; staid all night at the house of James Galbraith, in Cumberland county, east Pennsboro township. His journal of this mission, is replete with thrilling incidents. The want of space allows no extracts here. Weiser returned from Ohio, and arrived at home September 29, 1748.[†]

Notwithstanding the efforts made on the part of the government to quiet the Indians, they committed depredations. In order to adopt decisive measures, the Secretary of the Province, Mr. Richard Peters, and Conrad Weiser, were directed to proceed to cumberland county in 1749, to expel some white intruders, who caused the Indians great uneasiness, and induced them to commit depredations. Peters and Weiser were joined by the magistrates of the county, the delegates from the Six

[*] Prov. Rec. Book, 334.

[†] The writer has transcripts of several of Weiser's journal, amounting to several hundred ordinary sized pages.

Nations, a chief of the Mohawks, and Andrew Montour, the interpreter from the Ohio.*

About this time, Weiser was nearly constantly abroad in the discharge of the public duty as Indian agent. In the month of August, 1750, he undertook a journey to Onondago, with a message from the Honorable Thomas Lee, Esq., President of Virginia, to the Indians there.

Place is given to a brief abstract from his journal:—August 15, 1750, I set out in the afternoon, from my house at Heidelberg, came to Reading on Schuylkill, 14 miles. The 17th, to Nazanth, 27 miles. The 18th, to Nicholas Depue, in Smithfield, on the Delaware, 30 miles. The 19th, to Henry Cortrecht, at the Minisinks, 20 miles. The 20th, to Emanuel Pascal, 35 miles. The 21st, to Kingston, 44 miles. The 22d, rain all day. The 23d, crossed Hudson's river, came to Reinbeck, 10 miles. The 24th, came to the Manor of Livingston, 18 miles. The 25th, came to Albany, 24 miles. Sunday 26, met Henry Peters and Nickas, two chiefs of the Mohawks, &c."

In this journey, he had an interview with Livingston, and Col. Johnson. On page 89, he recommends to John Pickert, his sisters son, to learn the Mohawk tongue perfect among the Indians, to serve as an interpreter for Pennsylvania. Pickert's father resided one mile from Canawadagy.

Sept. 21, Weiser went towards Schoharie or Huntersfield— he spent some time here. Arrived at home, Oct. 1, 1750.†

In June, 1751, he again went to Albany, to meet the Indians there on public business.‡ July, 1753, he went once more to the Mohawk country. "July 24, 1753, I set out from my house in Heidelberg, in Berks county; arrived at Philadelphia the 26. August 1, I arrived at New York—being taken ill, I sent my son Sammy with one Henry Van den Ham, to Flushing, on Long Island, to wait on Governor Clinton, to deliver Hamilton's letters. August 7, took passage board a sloop to Albany." After transacting his business, he returned to Philadelphia, where he arrived August 30th.§

About this time, a society of noblemen and gentlemen of

* Gordon's Pa , 260.
† Prov. Rec., book M., p. 84.
‡ Ibid, 133.
§ Ibid, 341.

London, England, formed a scheme for the relief and instruction of poor Germans, and their descendants, settled in Pennsylvania, and considering that they resided too great a distance to know where schools were most needed, they appointed a Board of *Trustees General*, for the management of their scheme; Conrad Weiser was appointed as one of them—his colleagues were Gov. James Hamilton, Chief Justice Allan, Richard Peters, Secretary of the Land Office,. Benjamin Franklin, Esq., and the Rev. William Smith, D. D. This board appointed the Rev. Michael Schlatler, Visitor General.*

In 1755, during the alarms on the frontiers, Weiser was appointed Colonel of a regiment of volunteers from Berks county. He exerted himself by day and night in the protection of his suffering fellow citizens, and repelling the savage Indians in their incursions. He was vigilant, brave and active. See his numerous letters on this subject, in preceding pages 33 to 79, inclusive. A number of forts and block houses were put up under his directions, on the frontiers of Lancaster and Berks.

During the Indian and French war, he had command of the second battalion of the Pennsylvania regiment, consisting of nine companies. These he distributed very judiciously—he stationed one company at Fort Augusta, one at Hunter's mills, seven miles above Harrisburg, on the Susquehanna, one half company on the Swatara, at the foot of the North Mountain, one company and a half at Fort Henry, close to the gap of the mountain, called the *Tolhea Gap*, one company at Fort William, near the forks of the Schuylkill river, six miles beyond the mountain, one company at Fort Allen, erected by Benj. Franklin, at Gnadenhurlen, on the Lehigh, the other three companies were scattered between the rivers Lehigh and Delaware, at the dispositions of the captains, some at farm houses, others at mills, from three to twenty in a place.†

During the period of the French and Indian war, he attended many treaties and conferences. In November 1755, he attended the meetings of the Council at Philadelphia.‡   In January, 1756, he attended an Indian conference at John Harris' Ferry. "January 29, 1756, I set out from my house with a

* The reader is referred to preceding pages, 99, 109, for a particular account of this scheme
† Gordons Pa. p. 341.
‡ See preceeding page, 51.

hired man; arrived at Harris' Ferry the 30th, being rainy weather. I met the Indians that evening, acquainted them that I was sent, &c. Early in the morning, on the 31st, I met them in the Belt's cabin, &c. In July, 1756, he was interpreter at a council held at Easton.* Next year, 1757, he attended the Indian treaty held at Lancaster, May 29, and another at Easton, held in August; on all these occasions he was interpreter.

At this time he had taken his residence† in the town of Reading, where he still acted as Indian agent, and in the capacity of commissary; having plenary powers granted for that purpose, as appears from the following document:

$\left\{ \text{SEAL} \right\}$ WILLIAM DENNY.

By the Honorable William Denny, Esq., Governor and Commander-in-Chief of the Province of Pennsylvania, and counties of New Castle, Kent, and Sussex on Delaware.

WHEREAS, Brigadier General Stanwix hath represented to me, that his Majesty's service is in immediate want of a number of wagons and horses, for the transportation of provisions, and other necessaries for the army under his command, and that he hath contracted with Conrad Weiser, Esq., of the county of Berks, to supply the quota assigned to be raised, within the said county of Berks, to grant unto the said Conrad Weiser, impress warrants, in case he shall at any time find himself obliged to apply to the said justices for the same. These are, therefore, in his Majesty's name, and in pursuance of the Act of Assembly, to require you to issue your warrants to the constables within your respective districts, for the impressing of as many wagons as shall at any time be demanded by the said Conrad Weiser, or his deputies, in order to enable him and them to carry on the King's service according to his contract. Hereof fail not, as you will answer to the contrary at your peril.

* Prov. Rec., Book O, p. 23.

† "On the corner of Penn and Callowhill streets, stood Weiser's house.— In old times it was the principal hotel in the place. Here the war-song of the savage was sung—the war-dance wound down, and the calumet of peace finally smoked."—*Reading Times.*

Given under my hand and seal at arms, at Philadelphia, the ninth day of June, Anno. Dom., 1759, in the sixty-second year of his Majesty's reign.

To the Justices of Peace for the county of Berks.

WILLIAM DENNY.

His opinion touching public as well as private affairs, was always regarded, and in emergencies, he was freely consulted. The following is a case in point. We quote an extract of the proceedings of the Provincial Council held in Philadelphia.

"Sept. 19, 1759, Mr. Weiser was sent for, and desired to give his sentiments about the request of Teedpuscung, an Indian chief, for fixing a certain price for scalps, and that the Governor would send him a black belt to give to the Delawares, and the Ten Confederate Nations, to go to war against the French; and *secondly*, on building an Indian Fort and houses for the Delawares, and appointing a proper person to direct and superintend the works."

On this occasion he wished it, as a favor, to be permitted to give his views in writing, which he did as follows:

September, 19, 1759.

May it please your Honor:—

I have weighed the discourse about Indian affairs, at this time passed in your Honor's presence; it is my humble opinion, that no encouragement should be given to the Indians for scalps, for fear we must then pay for our own scalps, and those of our fellow subjects, as will certainly be the case; allow as much for prisoners as you please, rather more than was intended.

Great caution should be used in requiring the Indians to be settled on Wyomink, to take up the hatchet against the French and their Indian allies, for fear they will have it to say, that we made peace with them in order to make them fight our battles, and to make them a barrier and throw away their lives, by setting them against the French, and their numerous allies. The Ohio Indians will say, we will rather stay where we are, we are on the strongest side now, and will not hazard our lives and families in breaking with the French, in favor of the English, who have been beaten several times, and are not likely to do any thing for themselves.

I am in a very low state of health, and cannot without great hazard undertake any journey; besides, if the Six Nations should not be pleased with the building of a Fort at Wyomink, they would blame me more than any body else, because they would have it to say, that I knew their rights, &c.   Though I believe if the building of a Fort at Wyomink is cautiously carried on, merely for the use of the Indians, and left to them when finished, all will be well.

A trading house at Fort Augusta, should immediately be erected, else our Indian interest, what little we may yet have, will be entirely lost.   If the Government cannot agree about the condition, some well disposed men should be appointed to keep stores at Fort Augusta, and furnish the Indians with what they want, clothing especially, as they must be for the most part naked at this time.   This article requires all possible care and speed.

Rum should not be allowed to be sold or given by any licensed trader.   A little, or just a dram, might be given by the commanding officer of Fort Augusta, and he to deny obstinately, and absolutely a second; and the Indians will like it the better, when they judge of the thing coolly, and by themselves.

Sir William Johnson, or rather the Six Nations, by means of Sir William, should be made acquainted with this, and be told, it was done at the request of our Brethren, the Delaware Indians; and that we claim no right, by means of that Fort, to the lands of Wyomink, but leave the fort to be possessed and defended by the Indians.

CONRAD WEISER.

From the preceding communication we learn, that Weiser's health began to fail him.   "*I am,*" says he, "*in a very low state of health, &c.*   Even at the time he accepted the appointment of Colonel, he was infirm, yet, remarkable as it may appear, discharged efficiently and ably, all the ardent and responsible duties devolving upon him, as a soldier, Justice of the peace, and interpreter, to the satisfaction of the Government.   Before his appointment as Colonel, he had resolved to live retired.   His patriotism would not, though he made great sacrifices of comfort and gain, suffer him to enjoy the ease and quiet of life, so desirable when on the verge of three score years.

"Als aber," says Muhlenberg in his Biographical notice,

"der gefaehrliche Krieg in diesem Theil der Weltzwischen den Franzosen und England ausbrach, und unsere benachbarte Wilde Nationen meist bundbrichen worden, den Feinden zufielen, und unsere Grenzen verwuesteten, gerieth Conrad Weiser in neue Versuchungen. Die Landes Obrigkeit verordnete ihn zum Obrist-Leutnant. Die Aemter sind hier bisweilen nur fuer die Personen, und die Personen nicht fuer die Aemter geschaffen.

Und weil man seiner nun besonders in diesen Umstaenden benoethigt war, und ihm noch viel mehr muehe und Last auf legen wollte, so sollte das Salariam einst Obrist-Leutnants alles ersetzen u. s. f. Diese Bedienung, charge, oder Last, wie man es nennen, mag, that ihm und seinen Kindern mehr Schaden an Seel und Lieb, als einiges zuvor. Er war schon alt an Jahren, Schwach an Leibeskraeften, der haeuslichen Pflege gewohnt, muste viel abwesend von Hause seyn und auch oft mit den Vornehmen in der Stadt und Europaeischen Kriegshelden wegen der Indianer Sachen conferriren.

Der Allergnaedigste und Erbarmungsvolle Mittler und Menschen--Freund, der nicht Lust hat an des Menschen-Verderben, erhielte sein natuerliches Leben bis fast zum Ende des wunderlichen Kriegs, und verlich ihm noch eine besondere Gnadenfrist, so dass er Zeit hatte sich zu recalligiren; im Blute des Lammes die Befleckung des Geistes abzuthun, seine Kleider helle zumachen, seine Seeligkeit mit Furcht und Zittern zu schaffen, und ein gnaediges Ende zu erwarten. Es kostet gewiss Viel ein Christ zu sein, und zu bleiben.—*Hal, Nach., p.* 974.

He closed his eventful life July 13, 1760. On Saturday, the 12th, he went from his residence in Reading, in the enjoyment of his wonted health, to his country seat, near the present site of Wommelsdorf. He was suddenly seized by a violent *colica pituitosa*, which terminated his life on Sunday about noon. His remains were interred in the family burying ground, on the 15th, on which occasion the Rev. Kurtz preached a very impressive. discourse from these words: "And thou shalt go to thy fathers in peace; thou shalt be buried in a good old age. Sen. 15: 15." Compared with Ps. 84: 11, 12; for the Lord God is the sun and shield: the Lord will give grace and glory: no good thing will he withhold from them that walk uprightly. O Lord of hosts, blessed is the man that trusteth in thee.

20*

He left seven children (having been the father of fifteen children, eight of whom had died,) and a widow, to lament his departure. The spot, exposed as it is, where he lies, is about half a mile east of Wommelsdorf, south of the turnpike. A rough hewn sand-stone, singly and alone, stands there with the following (almost obliterated) inscription:

Dieses ist die
Ruhe Staette des
weyl ehren geachteten M. Conrad Weiser
derselbige ist gebohren 1696 den 2 November
in Astaet im Amt Herrenberg im
Wittenberger Lande, und gestorben
1760 den 13 Julius, ist
alt worden 63 jahr
8 Monat und 13 Tage.

Tradition has it, that from a high regard for his character, the Indians, for many years after his death, were in the habit of making visits of affectionate remembrance to his grave. Respect paid, which puts to shame the respect of some kindred.

The writer visited the grave of Weiser, February 21, 1844; and was pained to see no inclosure or fence around the grave of so great and good a man. Will not his wealthy descendants think of this? Remember the respect paid him by the Indians. *Verbum sat.*

HEREFORD TOWNSHIP.

Hereford township was settled at a comparatively early period. It, like many other parts of Pennsylvania, was sought as a place of refuge for the oppressed. Many of the present inhabitants are descendants of those who came hither to seek a home free from oppression.

In this and adjacent townships of Berks and Bucks, the Schwenkfelders settled at a comparatively early period. As a Christian, they are named after Casper Schwenkfeld von Ossing, Selisian knight, and counsellor to the duke of Lignitz. He was born (seven years after Luther) in Loneer Selisia, in 1490, in the principality of Lignitz. As a reformer, he, like others, had his adherents. For a particular account of Schwenkfeld, a work lately prepared for press by the writer, and published by James Y. Humphreys, Philadelphia, 1744. The work is entitled *He Pa s a Ekklesia*, &c.

The Schwenkfelders were sorely persecuted in Europe, from time to time. In 1719, the Jesuits thought the conversion of them an object worthy of attention; accordingly they sent missionaries to Silesia, who preached to them the faith of the emperor. The missionaries produced imperial edicts, that all parents should attend their public worship, and bring their children to be instructed in the Catholic faith, under severe penalties.

The Schwenkfelders sent deputies to Vienna, to solicit for toleration and indulgence; and though the emperor apparently received them with kindness and condescension, yet the Jesuits had the dexterous address to procure another imperial edict, ordering that such parents as would not bring every one of their children to the missionaaries for instruction, should at last be chained to the wheel-barrow, and put to hard labor on the public works, and their children should, by force, be brought to the missionaries.

Upon this, families fled in the night, into Lusatia, and other parts of Saxony, in 1725; sought shelter under the protection of the Senate Gorlitz, and also of Count Zinzendorf—leaving behind them their effects, real and personal, (the road being beset, in day time, to stop all emigrants.) They dwelt unmolested, in their late sought shelter, about eight years; when this protection being withdrawn, they resolved to seek a permanent establishment in Pennsylvania. A number of them in 1734, emigrated to Altona, a considerable city of Denmark and Holland, thence to Pennsylvania.

In April, 1734, they left for Altona, where they arrived May 17; thence sailed for America, and after a tedious voyage, arrived at Philadelphia on the 22d September, 1734; and on the 5th October, of the same year, others of them arrived. They settled principally in Montgomery, Bucks, Lehigh and Berks, where their grand-children reside at present. Of those of them who first settled in Hereford township, were the Rev. Christopher Schultz, sen., George Schultz, Melchior Schultz, Melchior Wiegner, David Mester, Gregorius Mester, Baltzer Yeagle.

The township was pretty well settled, as early as 1745.

The following were the taxables in 1758:

Melchir Wagoner, George Acker, Andrew Altendorff, Deobald Beck, Abraham Bechtel, Abraham Bauer, Michael Bauer, Gerhardt Bechtel, John Bechtel, Peter Bishop, Conrad Been, Martin Kreter, Martin Klever, George Dee, John Erly, Joseph Ehrenman, John Ebener, Nicholas Funck, Jacob Fisher, Peter Fetterhof, Ludwig Gauer, Heronimus Greber, Christian Gehman, Leonard Gressemer, Jacob Gressemer, George Herbst, Daniel Haw, John Gregory, Richard Gregory, Francis Lussehar, John Kunius, Benedict Leeser, Frantz Lussehar, Philip Lohr, George Lohr, Casper Leydecker, Moritz Lorentz, Jacob Lebenguth, Casper Meyer, Christian Meister, David Meister, Henry Miller, Andrew Mauer, George Mastdel, Jacob Miller, Frederick Nestor, William Richard, Nicholas Nickour, George Rohrbach, Martin Rehr, John Schaurner, Nicholas Seitle, Frederick Seiler, Michael Schalle, A. Steinmann, Melchior Schultz, Martin Stertzman, Benedict Strohm, Christopher Schultz, Wolf Wolfgang, Jacob Stauffer, John Stapp, Andrew Schwartz, Peter Schner, Jacob Fress, Jacob Fren, Jacob Frollinger, William Taunss, Melchior Weigner, Jost Wyant, Jacob Wetzel, Valentine Weybel, William Mayberry, Roland Young, Bernhard Young, Baltzer Zimmermann, George Beyer, Henry Gable, Abraham Stauffer, Peter Wolf, Abraham Gehman, Henry Bortz, Philip Leydecker, Philip Neiss, Christian Kretter, Geo. Weigner, Philip Raush, Theodorus Schneider, John Schleiger.

Hereford township has been reduced to its present limits and boundaries, by erecting Washington township, in 1839—*Ser Washington township*—it is bounded on the north-east by Lehigh county, and the south-east by Montgomery county; on the south-west by Washington and District; on the north-west by District and 'Long-swamp; length about four miles, mean breadth, not exceeding three miles; contains about twelve thousand acres of land; generally hilly; soil, gravel, naturally not fertile; but in some places rendered very productive. Shoub's mountain, near Lehigh county, is a striking feature of landscape.

This township, by the principal and west branches of Perkiomin creek, which afford water power sufficient. There were in 1840, three forges, one fulling mill, one woollen factory, five grist mills, six saw mills, two oil mills, and several tanneries in this township.

There are several churches in this township; one Roman Catholic, one belonging to the Schwenkfelders, and two common to the German Reformed and Lutherans.

Population in 1830, 1,716; 1840, 1,244; horses 316; horned cattle 883; sheep 506; swine 839; bushels of wheat raised 8,533; rye 11,835; corn 1,268; oats 11,338; buckwheat 2,992; potatoes 6,402; tons of hay 1,130; pounds of wool 1,027; flax 1,021. Whole amount of valuation on all articles made taxable for county purposes for 1844, $341,301; amount of county tax $682 60; state tax $365 44.

LONG-SWAMP TOWNSHIP.

Long-swamp township, was like all the townships contiguous to it—settled primitively by Germans. During the years, from 1754 to 1763, it was the occasional scene of Indian barbarities. The following named persons resided here in 1756, and many of them nearly thirty years earlier:

Bernhard Klein, Jacob Long, Valentine Dillinger, Jacob Harne, John Hess, Paul Hamrig, Michael Coller, Philip Finck, Adam Dietrich, Simon Moser, Adam Len, Rinehard Abendseheim, Peter Bechtel, Jacob Stall, Bartel Kieffer, Peter Bucher, Baltas Klever, Martin Kerger, Philip Fenstermacher, Andrew Scherle, Mathias Fenstermacher, Adam Gery, Jacob Danner, Nicholas Schwartz, Daniel Schwartz, Christian Steinberger, Deobald Grub, Nicholas Mertz, Nicholas Schreter, Peter Mertz, Ludwig Haspelhorn, Henry Bollinger, Jacob Weimer, Adolph Mayer, Simon Loydecker, Augustin Speckler, Nicholas Gress, Christian Abendscheim, Bernhard Schweizig, Deobald Carl, John Diehl, Michael Smith, Baltas Trit, Adolph Arnold, Barnhard Fegely, Christian Trevelstet, Michael Nothstein, Jacob Schenck, Andrew Same, Mathias Eigner, Peter Redler, Friedrich Popenmayer, Joseph Bery, Valentine Fleck, Enos Nael, John Flammer, Henry Shefer, Michael Biever, Samuel Burger, Jacob Long, Philip Burger, Philip Dall, John Hilpert, Jacob Fenstermacher, Peter Klein, Michael Nietrauer, Frederick Helwig, Christian Hofman, Nicholas Helm, Lewis Nits, Peter Aller, Joseph Richard, Christian Reisinger, Martin Boger,

George Kumph, John Kaufman, Philip Hene, Deobald Klein,. Adam Helwig, Mathias Eigner.

Long-swamp is bounded on the north-east by Lehigh county south-east by Hereford township, south by District and Rockland, north-west by Maxatawny; mean length about five miles, and breadth four and a half; containing nearly fourteen thousand acres of land, somewhat hilly, especially the north-eastern part, south of Little Lehigh river; the soil is partly limestone, and considerable gravel; but portions of it well cultivated.

The township is principally watered by the tributaries or sources of the Little Lehigh river; and by a creek which rises near the line of Rockland township, and running about four miles and a half, it disappears near the Lehigh county line, and is lost in a limestone fissure.

Mertztown, near the north-eastern corner of the township, is a small village, containing between twelve and fifteen dwellings, a tavern and store, a German Reformed and Lutheran church. Trexler's furnace is near the District township line.—There are several fine mills—six or seven in this township.

Population in 1810, 998: 1820, 1,371; 1830, 1,702; 1840, 2,112. Horses 499; horned cattle 805; sheep 652; swine 1,050; bushels of wheat raised 8,506; rye 13,284; corn 10,050; oats 11,130; buckwheat 2,318; potatoes 4,965; tons of hay 671; pounds of wool 871; flax 876. Whole amount of valuation on all articles made taxable for county purposes in 1844, $485,671; amount of county tax $661,73; gross amount of State tax, $661 73.

MAIDEN CREEK TOWNSHIP.

Maiden creek township has its name from a considerable stream of that name, which crosses the township diagonally from its extreme northern point to its remotest southern bounds. The Indian name of the stream was *Onteelaunee.* Whence the name Maiden creek? In answer to the question, the following is plausible: "It is told, as a tradition, that the river called *Schuylkill,* by the Dutch, bore the Indian name *Manajung,* meaning *the Mother,* and the *Onteelaunee,* the *Little Daughter of the Great Mother; that is Maiden creek.*"

The primitive settlers were Friends or Quakers; upwards of seventy families resided in this township in 1738. Owing to a large emigration westward, their number has been decreased. The taxables in 1741, were seventy-five; at that period the township embraced a portion of what was afterward included in Ruscommanor. In 1757 the following taxables were returned by the assessor to the county commissioners:

Francis Parvin, Esq., Francis Parvin, jr., Myrick Starr, Joseph Burger, John Koch, Adam Mingle, Edward Mourn, Thomas Pearson, Mordecai Lee, James Jordan, Moses Starr, Thomas Lewis, Barnhard Unhorn, William Penrose, Joseph Penrose, Richard Penrose, Mary Wily, George Fegler, Felty Keime, John Goonbord, Michael Arnold, John Reeser, John Fraufelter, Frederich Blat, John Hutton, James Hutton, Stephen Barnhard, Ulrich Hoy, Michael Doonkel, Lewhard Mayer, Christian Zugg, Jacob Lightfoot, Thomas Kerby, Peter Rodarmel, Rudolph High, Paul Rodarmel, Elias Reed, Moses Starr, jr., James Kees, Thomas Parvin, Frederick Hess, Philip Wax, Urban Shuttle, John High, John Finsher, Rudolph High, Benjamin Parvin, Owen Hughes, Jonathan Hughes, John Starr, Peter Nanhorn, Thomas Reed, Casper Strahl, John Barto, Stanly Kirby, Joseph Lightfoot, George Plot, Jeremal Starr, John Nanhorn.

This township is bounded on the north by Windsor township; on the north-east by Richmond; on the south by Ruscommanor and Alsaci; on the west by the Schuylkill river, dividing from Berne and Centre; mean length four miles and three-fourths; breadth four miles; containing thirteen thousand acres of first-rate level, limestone, and gravel land; many portions of which is highly productive. This township has a good supply of water power from the Schuylkill, and its great tributary, Maiden creek, on which are five or six mills.

There is a Friends meeting house, near the centre, on the east side of Maiden creek, and a German Reformed and Lutheran church, called Garndnt's church, near the northern boundary, about nine miles from Reading. The turnpike road to Sunbury passes, for the distance of four or five miles, parallel with the Schuylkill, through the township, and passes Maiden creek, over a wooden-covered bridge, of one arch.

Leesport, laid out by Drs. Darry and Young, in 1840, nine miles from Reading, is on the turnpike. It contains some twenty

or twenty-five dwellings, a steam mill, and the usual handicraft
of country villages.   Efforts were making in 1844, to erect an
Academy.

Population in 1810, 918; 1820, 1,192; 1830, 1,350; 1840
the number of inhabitants were 875 white males, 850 females,
14 male colored persons, 8 females; in all 1,747.   Horses 131;
cows 425; sheep 804; swine 679; bushels of wheat raised
14,743; rye 8,527; corn 10,200; oats 11,184; buckwheat
170; potatoes 11,130; tons of hay 492; pounds of wool 947.
Whole amount of valuation on all articles taxable for county
purposes $765,343; whole amount of county tax $1,530 68;
gross amount of State tax $945 12.

MAXATAWNY TOWNSHIP.

Maxatawny township—no doubt the inviting aspect of the
country, and other considerations, induced many of the Germans,
to settle here shortly after Penn's new purchase from the Indians, in 1732.   A few years after the erection of Berks, the
number of taxables was rising of one hundred, among whom
were the following in 1757, principally Germans:

Abraham Barling, Andrew Sassamanhausen, Adam Roads,
Abraham Zimmerman, Anthony Fisher, Andrew Heck, Chris-
tian Ruth, Charles Kern, Casper Smeck, Conrad Mane-
smith, Conrad Boader Christian Wenner Durst Kershner,
Daniel Levan, Deobald Wink, Deobald Kemp, David Hutten-
stein, Frederick De La Plank, (Delaplank,) Jacob Meyer,
Daniel Ott, George Scheffer, George Sassamanhausen, George
Roads, Geo. Baeder, Henry Wetstone, Henry Christ, Henry
Luckenbill, Henry Hock, Joseph Liegfried, John Hergarather,
John Hartman, John Beaver, John Bost, Jacob Levan, Julius
Kerber, John Hill, Jacob Shoradin, John De Long, Jacob
Roads, Michael Att, Michael Christman, Nicholas Harmany,
Nubiles Roads, Nicholas Musfel, Nicholas Queery, Peter
Brann, Peter Sherer, Philip Granel, Peter De Long, Paul Sho-
radin, Sebastian Levan, Sebastian Zimmerman, Thomas Roads,
Dietrich Biever, William Groose, Anthony Bensinger, Andrew
Balich, Anthony Altman, Abraham Ely, Casper Killion, Chris-
tian Shlinker, Christian Baum, Daniel Dosser, David Musgen-

Bast

ing, Daniel Young, Frantz Jacob Keill, George Esser, George Stibe, George Markle, Geo. Wild, Henry Lutz, Jacob Shaffer, Jacob Baner, Jacob Fisler, John Miller, Jacob Miller, Jacob Wildbrant, John Smaus, John Pott, Gustavus Urban, John Baner, John Hood, Leonard Saul, Michael Baner, Martin Sea, Martin Wanner, Michael Henninger, Michael Knebel, Michael Andreas, Nicholas Schumacher, Philip Hahn, (Haun,) Peter Gross, Peter Sturtz, William Gross, Wm. Trautman, Jacob Kumerer, George Breinnig, Conrad Henninger, Valentine Sterner, Philip Ruth, William Edleman, Adam Schebele, Wm. Wann, Frederick Hausman, Benedict Neidlinger, Peter Minich, Michael Hide, Conrad Mesker, Jacob Stimmel, George Steinbach, George Selb, George Hamberd, Jacob Grauel, George Etzler, Jacob De Long, Nicholas Boader, Joseph Gross, Andrew Heck, Abraham Dunkelberger.

Maxatawny township is bounded on the north-east by Lehigh county, south-east by Long-swamp township and Rockland, south and south-west by Rockland and Richmond; and north-west by Greenwich township.

Greatest length, five miles and a half; breadth, four miles and a half; forming an oblong, and containing nearly fifteen thousand acres of land, generally level, limestone and gravel soil, and very productive too; a great portion of it being in what is called Maxatawny valley, which is pronounced by competent judges, "a fertile vale of deep-soiled red shale and limestone." Brown argillaceous iron ore occurs near Kutztown.

This township is remarkable for being intersected by a score of roads in various directions. It is not so well supplied with water power as some townships in the county are. The principal stream, affording water power, is Sacony creek, a branch of Maiden creek, passing through the south-western part of the township, turning several mills as it seeks a northern direction towards Maiden creek; and Mill creek, a branch of Sacony, runs south-west for the distance of three miles in the township; there are several mills on this stream. There are several churches in this township, one in the southern part, and another at Kutztown, both common to the German Reformed and Lutherans.

Kutztown, on the west side of Sacony creek, in this township, is a considerable post village—a borough—having been incorporated by an act of Assembly, March 1st, 1815—situated
20

in Maxatawny valley, on the Allentown and Readine road, being midway between both, and 17 miles from either. It contains about one hundred and twenty-five dwellings, with a population rising of seven hundred; several stores, taverns, an academy of advanced standing, and a church, as mentioned above.

A certain gentleman, who spent a few days at this place, two years ago, in writing to a friend, speaking of Kutztown and vicinity, says:—"The peasantry are honest, hard-working Germans. Here they lock no doors. The congregations of different sectarian faiths, worship in the same chuich on alternate Sundays. The church is filled with attentive people, and a very great proportion are communicants. They have an excellent organ, made in this county. Preaching in German. It pains me to observe in every country church yard, the naked marble slabs, unsheltered by a single tree, and unadorned by a single shrub or flower."

The following Revolutionary pensioners lived in this township in 1840: Henry Grim, aged 75; Frederick Bower, 83; Jacob Wink, 82; Philip Noyes, 84; Christian Smick, 76.

Population in 1810, 1,530; 1850, 1,845; 1830, 2,108; 1840, 2,564; of these there were 1,330 males, and 1,264 females.— Horses 528; horned cattle 1,379; sheep 1,302; swine 1,872; bushels of wheat raised 28,556; rye 29,235; corn 17,946; oats 18,810; buckwheat 13,582; potatoes 12,190; tons of hay 1,732; pounds of wool 1,434; flax 2,439. Whole amount of valuation on all articles made taxable for county purposes in 1844, $844,700; whole amount of county tax, $1'686 40; gross amount of county tax, $1,084 48.

OLEY TOWNSHIP.

Oley township was settled at an early period. On examining the Land Office, we find deeds for land in Oley, dated 1682, some time before William Penn, the Proprietary, left England for the Province. The farm now owned by Gideon Hoch, in the north-eastern part of this township, is part of a tract sold by William Penn to John Snashold, then both of England. The deed calls for five hundred acres—dated May 6, 1682.

The farm owned by Daniel Bartolet, was conveyed by William Penn to Thomas Bond, the 17th and 18th of June, 1682. De Tirck, the maternal great grand-father of Bartolet, purchased it in 1721.

The first settlers, it would appear, were French Huguenots, and some of their descendants, who located in Oley, between 1704 and 1710. [See Chapter V.] The De Turks, who settled here in 1710 or '11, were from Esopus, New York, where a number of Huguenots had settled, between 1650 and 1660. They had remained but a short time at Esopus. They came to America in the early part of the reign of Queen Ann, who ascended the throne in 1703; settled at Esopus, thence came to Oley, 1710 or '11.

Several families of Friends, or Quakers, settled in this township as early as 1713 or 1715. George Boone, a native of England took out a warrant, in 1718, for four hundred acres of land in Oley, then in Philadelphia county. And it is believed, that Arthur Lee, also a native of England, had previously settled to Boone's arrival. Lee's nearest neighbors were Indians—who delighted to have him in their country, knowing the peaceable principles of the Friends; they never, molested him. Nay, rather ever manifested a strong disposition to defend him. Of this we have a striking instance, in an occurrence, which has been handed down by tradition in the Lee family. The neighboring Indians having received intelligence that a hostile tribe was about making incursions into the settlements of the whites, came, by night, painted and equipped, to do the stern duty of war, to Arthur Lee's dwelling, and surrounded it. This formidable attitude of the Indians, alarmed some of the inmates, especially the younger of them, who, to escape for life, made efforts to get out the house, but were prevented by the Indians, assuring them that their object in coming was to protect them against the assaults of hostile Indians, and not to injure them. The Indians then inquired into the truth of report touching the hostile Indians; and being assured by Mr. Lee, that it was unfounded, they then, to manifest their joy at such news, fired their guns in the air, with a shoult of exultation—returned to their homes, instead of proceeding against their red brethren, as had been their intention.

After the Friends, and some Huguenots had settled here, the way was open for others of their persecuted brethren in France,

In 1726 Jean Bartolet, a native of Chasteadeux, and family, embarked for America, and on his arrival, settled in Oley.

Before leaving the country, whither he had fled from France, like an honest and religious man, he procured, as a good citizen, a certificate, showing that he did not leave his country without the consent of the proper authorities, as appears from the following *original* paper:

Wir zu Endte Unterschriebenen Oberamtman der Hochfuerstlichen Pfaltzgraefflichen Gemeinschaft Guttenberg, attestieren hiermit und in Kraft dieses Brieffs dass Vorweiser dieses der wohlehrbare und bescheydene Jean Bertolet gebuertig von Chasteaudeux in der Schweitz Berner Gebiets, nebst seiner Hausfrau, sich seit vierzehn Jahren als bestandere des alhier gelegenen und hochloeblicher, Stiffts-Seltz gehoerigen Hoffs, fromm, ehrbar, aufrichtig, und redlich verhalten, und dergestalten, wie es einem ehrlichen Manne geziemen will loeblicht auffgefuehret, dass wir demselben, so wohl als dessen Hausfrau, andersters nichts dann alles Liebes und Gutes nachzusagen wissen; weylen nun diese beide Eheleute, nebst bey sich habenden fuenf Kindern um ihres verhoffenden bessern Nutzen und Gelegenheit willen sich in das Neue Land oder *Pennsylvanien* zu begeben und sich alda selbsten Haeuslich nieder zu lassen, gaentzlich entschlossen und gesinnt seynd. Als wir Maenniglicher Standes gebuehr respective gehorsam auch dienste und freundlichen ersuchet und gebetten bemelte Jean Bartolet nebst dessen-Hausfrau Susanna und fuenf Kindern nicht allein aller Orthen frey, sicher und ohngehindert passieren auch beyneben wegen ihres ruehmlichen Wohlverhalten allen Gerichten willen und Assistentz wiederfahren zu lassen, Ein solches seynd wir dergleichen Occasionem freundlichst zu senproeiren so erbiethig als bereit: Diessen zu wahren Urkundt haben wir nebst eigenhaendigen subscription unser gewoehnliches Paetschafft hieran gehenckt. So gegeben im zwanzigsten Monaths Tag Apriles als man zaehlt ein Tausand sieben hundert zwanzig und sechs.

J. G. WIMPHFEN,
NICHOLATS SCHOENLEUCH,

Anwald
Hans Ehrhart, Sect des Gerichts.

Oley township is remarkable in the annals of Pennsylvania,

as place for religious excitement, at an early period. A singular sect was started in Oley, headed by one Mathias Bowman. Before his arrival in this country, there were some who
professed to be impeccable; or having attained to a state of
sinlessness; they were, in their own estimation, *perfect.* They
styled themselves "*New Born.*"

Mathias Bowman, who assumed the right as leader, was a
native of Lamshelm, Palatinate; born in 1701; and no doubt,
having heard of the shepherdless few, embarked for America
in 1719. It is reported, he was an honest and sincere man—
not very solicitous to accumulate wealth; but, this was not said
of Peter Kilwain,* or Kuehlenwein, Yotter, and others of his
followers—some of these loved the good things of the world
inordinately.†

Bowman's followers, as said, professed sinless perfection—
boasted that they were sent of God to conform others. Their
disputations were frequently heard in the market places of
Philadelphia. On one occasion, Bowman, as empirics are wont
to do, to show that *his* doctrine from God, proposed to walk
across the Delaware river.

Many of them were, as it ever was, and is to this day—Mil-
lerites not excluded—enthusiasts, brainless fanatics, contentions,
perfect babblers, wandering through the country, displaying a
blind zeal for *their* doctrines—the whims and caprices of men,—
by angrily controverting with all who differed from them in
matters of faith. None, no matter how retired seemed to escape the *New-Born leader;* even Conrad Beissel, the founder
of the *Sieben Taeger,* was occassionally annoyed in his recluse
situation, by Bowman and his disciples.

From the following letter, written before Bowman's arrival
in Oley, by one of his subsequent adherents, a female, in answer
to a letter from a friend in Germany, will afford the reader
some idea of the sentiments held by the New-Born.. The
original, of which a copy is given, is still preserved. It is
dated:

OLEY TOWNTHIP.
May 14, 1718.

"Ich gruesse euch alle hertzlich, Brueder, Schwestern,
Schwaeger und Geschwistern, als, Freunde und Bekannte. Wir

---

* Col. Rec. iii. 349.
† Chron. Ephra.

20*

haben euren Brief bekommen und daraus ersehen wir was ihr wissen wolt; aber das ist mir nun zu schlecht zu beantworten.

"Ich will euch mein Weg kund thun wie es mit mir steht.— Ich bin nun in einem bessern Stand also ich, da ich draussen war; hier hat mich der liebe Gott Suenden frei gemacht, dass ich nicht mehr suendigen kann, und davor lobe ich ihn jetzt und in Ewigkeit. Ich habe mich zu Gott gehalten, so ist er zu mir kommen und hat Wohnung bei mir gemacht.

"So ihr Lust habt mit mir die Neuegeburt zu geniessen, der muss seinen Sinn und Gedanken von allen Dingen, von der Welt abziehen, und nichts mehr suchen als Gott allein, und anhalten mit Beten und Seufzen, Tag und Nacht, dass ihn Gott moege neugebaehren, und so er es getreu meinet so wird der Mensch Wunder erfahren.

"Menschen ruehmen sich Christen, und wissen nicht wass die Neugeburt ist. Die Neugeburt ist der neue Stein dass Niemand weiss war er ist, als der ihn bekomt.

"In Pennsylvanien zu reisen ist nicht der werth so wir in Suenden seyn. Wer weis es ob man habin koemmt! Die meisten Menschen muessen Krankheiten ausstehen, und viele gar den Tod, und hier in Pennsylvanien ist sowohl Unruh als draussen; ist es nicht vom Krieg, so ist etwas anders das uns nicht gefaellet.

"Die Menschen werden in der Welt keine Ruhe finden, sie moegen hingehen wo sie wollen. Bey Gott ist Ruhe und sonst an keinem andern Ort. Gedenket ihr nach einem andern so seyd ihr unruhig, und also auch hier in America; wann einer aber Suendenfrey ist so mag einer reisen oder dorten bleiben, dan hat er den besten Schatz bey sich, und ist zufrieden wo er ist und had Vergnuegen an seinem Schatz in der ganzen Welt.

"Lehrer und Zuhoerer sind alle keine Christen den sie sind Suender, und Christus ist kommen die Suenden wegzunehmen Wer dan nicht Suendenfrey ist dem ist Christus noch nicht in die Welt gekommen. Alle Lehrer in der ganzen Welt die nicht Suendenfrey sind gemacht, und nicht mehr suendigen koennen, das sind falsche Lehrer, sie moegen sein fromm oder boes. Es gilt nichts im Reiche Christi, als Christus selber. Wer den nicht hat der ist nicht seyn, und wo er ist, da ist man Suendenfrey.

"Ich gruesse euch noch einmal alle herzlich. Gedenket was

ich euch habe kund werden lassen, und nehmet es zu herzen, es soll euch besser seyn als alle Dinge in der Welt.

MARIA DE TÜRK,
Gebohrne De Heroken.

In connection with the above letter, and from an extract of the *Hallische Nachrichten*, the views of the *New-Born* may be learnt. The Rev. Muhlenberg says, in p. 227, Hal. Nach. "Junii 10, 1747, reisete ich von Neuhanover ab; kehrte 8 meile von dem Ort bey einem alten so genannten Neugebornen ein, welcher vor zwanzig und etlichen Jahren eine Witwe geheurathet, und mit derselben 5 Kinder gezeuget, welche mir die Mutter in den ersten Jahren, erwachsen, zum Unterricht und heiliger Taufe, wieder des Vaters Willen, uebergab, und deswegen von ihrem Manne vieles leiden musste.

Der alte mann giebt vor dass er in der Pfalz neugeboren sey. Die Kennzeichen solcher Geburt erstrecken sich aber nicht weiter nach seiner oft wiederholten Aussage, als dass er sich von der Reformirten Kirche und den Sacramenten separirt, und dem damals zur Regierung gekommenen Churfuersten nicht den Eid der Treue ablegen wollte, worueber er nebst andern vor das Consistorium gefordert, auch mit Gefaergniss belegt, und seiner Meinung nach, um Christi und der Wahrheit willen verfolget worden. Er nimt weder vernuenftigen Beweis, noch die hoehere Offenbarung nach allen Theilen und ihren ganzen Inhalt an; laesset sich auch nicht belehren, wel er vom Schwachem Verstand, halstarrigem Eigenwillen und stuermenden Affecten ist, und die Pennsylvanische Freiheit zum Schaden missbraucht.

Nachdem er hier ins Land gekommen, hat er sich mit einigen vereiniget, welche Secte den Namen der *Neugebornen* tragen. Dieselbe giebt eine Neugeburt vor, welche sie durch unmittelbare Einsprache, Erscheinungen vom Himmel, Traeume und dergleichen, ploetzlich erlangen. Wenn sie die Neugeburt auf solche Weise bekommen; so sind sie ihrer Einbildung nach, Gott und Christus selber, koennen nicht mehr suendigen noch irren. Daher gebrauchen sie von dem heiligen Wort Gottes nicht mehr, als eben dasjenige, was ihren falschen Seckten zu favorisiren scheint. Die heiligen Sacramenten sind ihnen laecherlich, und ihre Ausdruecke von denselben hoechst aegerlich.

Oley township is also further remarkable for several Mora-

vian Synods held in it, shortly after the arrival of Count Zinzendorf.

Towards the close of the year 1741, Count Zinzendorf came
to Pennsylvania; shortly after his arrival he sent Gotlieb Buettner to visit a Moravian minister, the Rev. Rauch, at Shekomeko,* to invite him to attend a synod about to be held under
the auspices of the Count, whose object in coming to America
was to enquire into the general condition of the Christians, impart instruction, and give directions to his brethren. Buettner, on his arrival at Shekomeko, found some fruits of Rauch's
labors, which was cause of considerable joy to him; here he
tarried some eight or ten days among the sons of the forest, and
preached to them, January 14, 1742; he preached to thirty-
two Indians, from these words: "He hath delivered us from
the power of darkness, and hath translated us into the kingdom
of his dear son."

The time having arrived to repair to the Synodical meeting,
they made ready to depart; the Indians hearing that their
spiritual instructors were about leaving, three of them, Shabash,
Seim. and Kiop, obtained permission to accompany them.—
They left Shekomeko, January 22d, on foot, but being in company with Indians, were refused admittance at some inns, on
their way to Philadelphia, via which they went to Oley, where
they arrived the 9th of February, and met Count Zinzendorf,
"and many laborers and ministers of various denominations assembled together." The appearance of the three Indian visiters,
whose hearts were filled with the grace of Jesus Christ and the
love of God, made a deep impression upon all present. Soon
after their arrival, a party of Delaware Indians came to see
them, to whom they immediately spoke of Jesus Christ, their
God and Saviour. They likewise declared to their brethren
how much they wished for baptism. Having received the gospel with a believing heart, been faithfully instructed in the doctrine of salvation, and earnestly desiring to obtain mercy and
pardon in the blood of Jesus; the synod first declared them
candidates for baptism, and then resolved, without delay, to administer holy baptism to them in the presence of this whole
assembly."

The 11th of February was the day appointed for this so-
lem act—it was a day, says Loskiel, never to be forgotten in

* On the borders of Connecticut.

the annals of missions. The awful presence of Him, who has promised to meet with his own, was powerfully felt—the greatest solemnity prevailed, and the spirit of God was sensibly felt, during the morning exercises, which consisted of prayer, and praising the Father of all in spiritual song. Here, as in the days of yore, when the sons of God met, Satan was also present, especially in his devoted servants; for while the humble believers were engaged in preparatory exercises to baptize the contrite Indians, "some ill-disposed people coming from the neighborhood, raised such distui bance, that the whole company was upon the point of dispersing, and postponing this transaction for the present. However, peace and quietness being happily restored, there was a solemn meeting in the afternoon, in which Rauch and Buettner were ordained deacons by the two bishops, David Nitchman and Count Zinzendoif. After this act, preparations were made in a barn belonging to *De Tirk*—(or Van Dirk, as it is written in German.) There was no church in Oley at this time. In this barn the above named Indians were baptised by Christian Henry Rauch, the missionary from Shekomeko. "The whole assembly being met, the three catechumens were placed in the midst, and with fervent prayer and supplication, devoted to the Lord Jesus Chiist, as his eternal property; upon which Rauch, with great emotion of heart, baptised these three firstlings of the North American Indians into the death of Jesus, in the name of the Father, and of the Son, and of the Holy Ghost, calling Shabash, *Abraham;* Seim, *Isaac;* Kiop, *Jacob.*"[*]

The same writer continues, and says, "The powerful sensation of the grace of God, which prevailed during this sacred transaction, filled all preseut with awe and joy, and the effect produced in the baptised Indians, astonished every one. Their hearts were filled with such rapture, that they could not keep silence, but made known to all the white people who came into their hut, what great favor had been bestowed upon them.— They preached a whole night to a party of Delaware Indians, who were in the neighborhood, and by the providence of God were just at that time led to return back to Oley. When one ceased the other began, and their animated testimony of Jesus filled their hearers with admiration. Soon after this, they set out with Rauch, went first to Bethlehem, and having spent

[*] Loskiel's His. Miss., Part 2, p. 21.

some days with *their* brethren to mutual edification, they proceeded on their journey, full of spiritual life, in the company of
their beloved teacher.   When they came home, they testified
to all their relations and friends, of the grace bestowed upon
them by God, and their words made an abiding impression in
the minds of the heathen."

In 1757, the following were taxables in this township:
Conrad Rife, Samuel High, John Lisher, John De Turk,
Samuel Guldin, Anthony Hunter, John Lee, Jonathan Harpine,
W. Kelbach, John High, Abraham Levan, Lazarus Weidner,
Dietrich Weidner, Nicholas Lisher, Jacob Keim, William Pott,
Peter Lobach, Jacob Yoder, John Yoder, sen., Gabriel Boyer,
Jacob Kaufman, John Yoder Yost, Casper Grismer, Nicholas
Hunter, George Dollinger, Jacques De La Plank, (James Dela-
plank, Valentine Hufnagle, Benjamin Hufnagle, Elias Hufnagle, Peter Breil, Peter Herple, Thomas Lee, Samuel Lee,
Abraham Bartolet, Jacob Stover, Isaac Bardo, Abraham Peter,
John Hill, John Frederick, David Weiser, John Pott, Frederick
Bartolet, John Hunter, Benjamin Longaworthy, W. Richards,
Martin Slaugenhans, Valentine Young, George Schits, Michael
Knob, Jacob Schneider, Henry Sheffer, Peter Harpine, W.
Yonkman, Frederick Leinbach, John Leinbach, Conrad Fisher,
George Windbigler, John Great, Adam Boligh, John Marke,
Melchior Moyer, John Holly, Simon Kepler, Nicholas Shoemaker, William Collins, Frederick Collins, Henry Herson, Michael Regleitor, Peter Catzenmoyer, Frederick Hill, Jacob
Stots, George Kalteisen, Adam Michel, Philip Hartzman,
Christian Sammet, Christopher Kentner, Christopher Gerhart,
Valentine Huff, Jacob Byder, William Byder, Francis Kirling,
Jonas Weaver, George Wicker, Christopher Fur, John Zook,
Jeremiah Channel, George Brown, Jacob Karner, Jacob Ominsettle, Michael Brush, Philip Hartman, John Dewalt, (Dewald)
Jacob Seary, Anthony Kempfer, Henry Neukirch, sen., Jacob
West, Stephan Repperts, Mordecai Ellis, Martin Schenckel,
Mordecai Ellis, Samuel Gulden, Daniel Gulden, George Michel, George Yaeger, Jacob Yoder, George Kerstner, John
Herger, Peter Knobb, John Knobb, Jacob Weisner, George
Sinsinger, Joseph Lauch, Jacob Hassinger, Matthias Mosser,.

Peter Read, John High, Ludwick Marburger, George Kleim, Henry Fonal.

This township is bounded north by Rockland and Pike; east by Earl; south by Amity and Exeter; and on the west by Alsaoe and Ruscommanor; mean length five miles; breadth four and a half; contains thirteen thousand six hundred acres of land, generally very level, and principally first rate limestone,— some in a very high state of cultivation. The average value of land, from thirty to sixty-five dollars per acre; watered by the sources of Manokisy and Manatawny creeks. It contains a score of mills, one furnace, two forges. and three churches— both splendid edifices—near Manatawny creek. The one belongs to the German Reformed, (some of whom are the descendants of Huguenots) and the other belongs to the Lutherans; and one in which the Evangelical Association holds meetings.

Friedensburg, in this township, is a small village of some ten or fifteen houses; some of them built of stone. It contains a store and tavern.

Population in 1810, 1,274; 1820, 1,410; 1830, 1,469; 1840, 1,875; horses 458; horned cattle 1,479; sheep 865; swine 1,102; bushels of wheat raised 19,747; rye 13,648; corn 27,800; oats 34,252; buckwheat 1,366; potatoes 7,092; tons of hay 1,783; pounds of wool 1,533; flax 1,675. Whole amount of valuation on all articles taxable for county purposes for 1844, $875,815; whole amount of county tax, $1,751 63; gross amount of State tax, $1,283 59.

RICHMOND TOWNSHIP.

Richmond township was organized shortly after the erection of the county, lying partly within the same vale of Maxatawny, was also settled at an early period, and by the same class of persons, honest and industrious Germans.

In 1768, the following taxables resided in this township: Stophel Teischer, Abraham Keiser, Adolph Peter, Andrew Millegle, Balthaser Rehm, Christian Denoher, Christian Schlegel, Christian Rodarmel, Christian Schick, Conrad Miller, Cas-

per Merkle, Chas. Hellen, David Oehly, Daniel Hoch, David
Kemp, Frederick Hill, George Sheffer, George Michael Wine-
man, George Merkle, George Ohl, George Folk, George Nutz,
Henry Kelchour, Henry Keismer, Henry Orthly, Henry Dil-
boren, Henry Borghardt, John Rodarmel, Jacob Treibelbiss,
John George Merkle, Joakin Sleisly, Jacob Shoemaker, John
Glass, Jonas Resler, Joseph Luler, Michael Reeber, Michael
Wilhelm, Michael Keneher, Melchior Fritz, Michael Kepler,
Melchior Braun, Nicholas Keiser, Peter Bull, Peter Spohn,
Peter Dellborn, Peter Merkle, Peter Greenwalt, Philip Sohns,
Philip Hedrick, Theobald Biber, Valentine Hussman, Vincent
Lescher, Geo. Michael Derr, Henry Conrad, Nicholas Raush,
Frederick Brown, Christian Hoffman, John Andreas Reh, Geo.
Zerr, John Mering, John Adam Schelkop, Nicholas Mauckly,
Michael Dieber, George Merkle, Jacob Wanner, Peter Krob,
Michael Grist, Philip Groh, Nicholas Barou, Christian Rink,
Michael Gellinger.

Richmond is bounded on the north by Greenwich; on the east
by Maxatawny; south by Rockland and Ruscommanor; south-
west by Maiden creek, and west by Windsor township. Mean
length five miles, and breadth four, containing twelve thousand,
four hundred and eighty acres of land, generally pretty level;
gravel and limestone soil of a superior quality, and well cultivated. Brown argilaceous iron ore occurs at Moselem; it is
extensively mined, and affords ore for Hunter's Furnace on
Moselem creek. Sacony, Maiden creek, and Moselem creek,
all afford water power. There are four or five mills in this
township; three churches; the Moselem church was erected in
1761.

There are several villages in this township; Coxtown, in the
extreme south part of the township, was laid out about fifty
years ago by one Cox, whose name it bears; there are two stores
and two taverns in it, and the usual handicraft. Walnut town,
a few miles west of Cox town, has some eight or ten houses.
Virginsville consists of half a dozen houses, two taverns and
a store.

There is a remarkable natural curiosity in this township. It
is called the *Dragon's cave*. It has been described by a gentleman of Berks county. "The entrance to the cave," he
says, "is on the brow of a hill, in the edge of a cultivated field.

Passing into it, the adventurer descends about fifty yards by a rough narrow passage, and then turns to the left at an acute angle with the passage hitherto pursued.   After proceeding about thirty yards farther, he enters the great chamber, about fifty feet long, twenty wide, and fifteen to twenty feet high, in a rock of limestone.   Near the end of this chamber, opposite to the entrance, is the *altar*, a large mass of Stalactile, which rings under the hammer, and is translucent.   Formations of Stalactile are found in other parts of the cave, though none so large as the mass just mentioned."

Population in 1810, 971; 1829, 1,135; 1830, 1,550; 1840, 2,006.   Horses 383; horned cattle 911; sheep 800; swine 1,440; bushels of wheat raised 19,715; rye 16,177; corn 17,-980; oats 25,125; buckwheat 2,050; potatoes 6,498; tons of hay 1,469; pounds of wool 1,579; flax 2,448.   Whole amount of valuation on all articles made taxable for county purposes in 1844, $519,272; whole amount of county tax $1,158 54; gross amount of State tax $734 75.

———

ROBESON TOWNSHIP.

Robeson township was settled at an early period.   Among its first and principal settlers, were the Friends or Quakers.— These were Gaius Dickinson, John Scarlet, and Peter Thomas— all Friends, and who settled when the country was a wilderness.

Little has been preserved of the first settlers, of interest.— Our friend, T. E. Lee, of Exeter, has furnished the following: "Thomas," says Lee, "was in the habit of turning out his cattle to browse upon the bushes, and sending a boy and girl in the evening to collect them; one evening, the dark shades began to spread gloom over the forest, but they did not return. The old man, like the father of Saul, left caring for the cattle, and cared only for the children.   He set off in search of them, and proceeding along a path through the thick woods for a distance, he met the children returning, while the wolves and bears were howling around them."

Among the early, or first settlers of this township, may be named, Thomas Ellis, of Wales, William Morris, Mordecai
21

and Thomas Ellis; John, George, and Thomas Booné, of Eng-
land; John, William, and Edward Hugh, of Wales; John,
James, Joseph, Benjamin, and Samuel Webb, of England. ⌐
  In 1756, the following persons were assessed as taxables:

  Michael Kern, John Scarlet, James Bird, Arnold Sheafer,
Jacob Redcay, Peter Licken, John Griffith, George Sower,
Gerhart Dewees, John Howman, David Jarred, Thos. Thomas,
Ephraim Jackson, Owen Humphrey, Owen Long, David Thom-
as, Edward Goff, George Dykes, Enos Ellis, George Donhower,
Adam Bedenhower, John Williams, William Northen, Gaius
Dickenson, Philip Hoyle, Melchior Swisher, Christian Treat,
Henry Reicher, Stephen Doughty, Elias Redcay, John Sheaver,
John Evans, George Wendle, Baltzer Schneider, Nicholas Mil-
ler, Jones Liken, Conrad Moore, James Thomas, Jenkin Mor-
ris, James Cadwallad, Sebastian Harleman, John Philips, Wil-
liam Harvot, John Hollem, Felty Ems, Henry Pennybecker,
Felty Haun, Josiah Boone, Michael Miller, Michael Snousser,
Christian Ehrgott, Anthony Bernhard, Daniel Bane, Christian
Keiger, Jacob Bechtel, Philip Hart, Michael Kern, Israel
Robinson, Benjamin Williams, Samuel Overholtzer, Adam
Staut, Jacob Koch, Richard George, Robert Morris, Ellis
George, David James, Edward George.

  Robeson township is bounded on the north-east by the
Schuylkill river, separating it from Exeter township; on the
east by Union township and Chester county; on the south by
Cærnarvon; on the south-west by Brecknock, and north-west
by Cumru. Mean length, six miles and a quarter; breadth,
five; containing twenty-one thousand acres of land, of a very
ordinary quality, naturally hilly. It is watered by the Allegheny creek, and Hay creek, on both of which, are forges, and
several mills. There are two churches in this township, and
a Friends meeting house.
  Population in 1810, 1,807; 1820, 2,2065; 1830, 1,970;
1840, 1,965; of these there were white males, 971; females
963; colored males 17; females 14. Horses 422; horned cattle 1,304; sheep 830; swine 810; bushels of wheat raised
7,229; rye 14,120; corn 20,691; oats 1,505; buckwheat 1,360;
potatoes 9,997; tons of hay 1,270; pounds of wool 1,106; flax
1,621. Whole amount of valuation on all articles made taxa-

ble for county purposes in 1844, $424,444; whole amount of county tax $648 88; gross amount of state tax $470 22.

ROCKLAND TOWNSHIP.

Rockland township was settled at the time those were by which it is bounded, and by a similar class of persons, nine-tenths of whom were Germans.   In 1757, the following were its taxables:

John Albrecht, George Angstadt, John Angstadt, Charles Bernhard, Nicholas Blatner, Jacob Boger, Philip Berminger, Nicholas Benninger, John Bot, William Bot, Conrad Bair, Jacob Boral, Casper Bicking, Mathias Beck, Peter Breifogel, Ludwig Brem, Nicholas Clementz, Michael Dressler, Melchior Donner, Henry De Long, William Dabitsch, Jacob Drog, Nicholas Dehb, Deobald Drumheller, John Eck, Peter Ernst, Jacob Ellinger, George Fleck, William Folck, Peter Folck, George Hefner, Christian Henry, Frederick Hersch, Jacob Hoffman, George Hoffman, Peter Luder, Nicholas Jacobi, Michael Kerber, Michael Klein, Peter Klassmoyer, Andreas Krett, Simon Kerber, Jacob Krebs, Jacob Keim, Michael Keim, Peter Lobach, Henry Long, Nicholas Long, Ludwig Long, Michael Long, John Moll, Henry Mertz, Nicholas Moyer, Geo. Oberdorff, Peter Ruff, sen., Peter Ruff, jr., Lorentz Berig, Casper Rap, Peter Remer, Frederick Reish, Conrad Roth, Casper Rubbert, Ludwig Rouzanner, Henry Showash, Christian Shumachir, George Schumachir, Frederick Schackler, John Scheuerer, George Scheffer, George Seibert, (Seuwert) Frederick Ubrick, Adam Wagner, Adam Wecht, Jacob Ziegemfuss, Henry Mertz, Herman Emrich, George Reif, Jacob Hefner, Peter Kieffer, Michael Jacobi, Peter Anstat, Michael Scheffer, Christian Kolb, Ludwig Bitting.

Rochland is bounded as follows, at present. Some slight alterations in the boundary having been made within a few years. It is bounded on the north by Maxatawny township; on the north-east by Long-swamp; on the east by District; south-east by Pike; on the south by Oley; on the west by Ruscommanor; and north-west by Richmond; mean length five miles; breadth four; containing twelve thousand acres of land;

rather hilly, gravel soil, and indifferently cultivated. With a little care, as to rotation of crops, and the application of vegetable and mineral manures, it might be rendered productive. It is not well watered; still there are several mills, one furnace, and two forges, in this township.

There is some iron ore in this township, from which the furnace is supplied. There is one church in this township, common to the Lutherans and German Reformed.

Population in 1810, 1,026; 1820, 1,131; 1830, 1,342; 822 white males, 825 females, 3 colored males and 5 females. Total, 1,655; horses 252; horned cattle 581; sheep 591; swine 871; bushels of wheat raised 4,380; rye 9,511; corn 8,382; oats 6,387; buckwheat 1,923; potatoes 5,986; tons of hay 653; pounds of wool 1,027; flax 1,710. Whole amount of valuation on all articles made taxable by law for county purposes, for 1844, $289,907; amount of county tax $579 81. Whole amount of valuation for state purposes, on all articles made taxable for county purposes, excepting trades, occupations and professions, above $200, for state purposes, $265 17; gross amount of state tax, $312 80.

RUSCOMMANOR TOWNSHIP.

Ruscommanor township, like all the adjacent townships, was beginning to be settled between the years 1732 and 1745. As early as 1749, the following were landholders within this township:

David Foll, Andrew Brenst, John Miller, John Wilkhammer, Adam Shumble, John Williams, Conrad Bruse, Jacob Perteller, Yost Waggoner, Martin Spiegelmeuer, Martin Nerr, Frederick Sprung, Embrich Billiar, Mathias Beck, Peter Rise, Philip Miller, John Fogell, Derick Swath, Derick Long, Mathias Rhole, George Angstad, Peter Crell, John Shous, George Hefner, Casper Burk, John Shamber, Jacob Mickle, Peter Hidleman, Felty Becker, Jacob Libhart, Jacob Simer, Ulrich Becker, Philip Smith, Christian Shoemaker, Jacob Ely, Bastian Garnard, Ber. Fogle, Peter Rise.

It is almost a matter of astonishment that this portion of Berks should have been thus early and densely settled, when it is considered that the soil is of the most ordinary kind, and the surface hilly. About the year 1760, the number of taxables had almost doubled itself from 1740, to that period.

Ruscommanor is bounded on the north by Richmond, north-east by Rockland, on the east by Oley, south-west by Alsace, and north-west by Maiden creek; contains about ten thousand acres of ordinary, and hilly land; soil gravelly, and very indifferently cultivated—much room for improvement.

There are one or two villages in this township. Pricetown, laid out by Conrad Price nearly seventy years ago; contains twenty-five houses—one store and two taverns. Population 165.

Speachtown, a village with seven houses and twenty-five inhabitants—this place was laid out between thirty and forty years ago, by a certain Boarsmith. There are three or four grist mills in this township.

Population in 1801, 932; 1820, 1,056; 1830, 1,243; 1840, 1,189: horses 88; horned cattle 222; sheep 247; swine 288; bushels of wheat raised 1,502; rye 2,943; corn 2,465; oats 2,958; buckwheat 337; potatoes 2,970; tons of hay 253; pounds of wool 477; flax 458. Whole amount of valuation on all articles made taxable for county purposes in 1844, $227,528; county tax $455 05; gross amount of State tax $258 90.

––––––

TULPEHOCKEN TOWNSHIP.

Tulpehocken township was so named after a tribe of Indians called *Turpyhockin*, who inhabited this region of country, whose chief was named Manangy, called the Indian chief on Schuylkill. This region of country is respectively mentioned in the Provincial Record of Pennsylvania. It appears to have been a place of thorough pass, from an Indian village, called Peixtan, on the Susquehanna, to Philadelphia.

We find that in 1707, that one Nicole, French and Indian trader, was apprehended by persons, sent by government at Peixtan, and carried to Philadelphia, via Turpyhocken.—
" Martin went again to Peixtan, and brought Nicole where we we lay in concealed, and asking him to drink a dram, he seized

21*

him; but Nicole started from him, and run for it, when immediately we started out and took him, and presently carried him to the village (Peixtan) through which we were obliged to pass; and there we found some Indians, with guns in their hands, who looked much displeased at what we had done; but being in readiness against any surprise, they thought it not fit to attempt any thing.   Here we staid about half an hour, and then parted for Turpyhocken—having mounted Nicoli on a horse, and tied his legs under the belly, we got within a mile of Turpyhocken at about two of the clock.   On Friday morning, about seven, the governor went to the town, from thence we went to Manatawny that night, and the next day to Philadelphia."*

The first white settlers were Palatines, who had emigrated from New York, of whom a general notice has been given, when speaking of the first settlers in Heidelberg township, to which the reader is referred.

John Adam Diffebach, Christian Lower, John Spycker, Jacob Lederman, Jacob Fisher, John Soller, Jacob Sorbert, Francis Wenrich, Ulrich Schwartz, Stephen Conrad, Conrad Sherf, John Livergood, Peter Sanns, Adam Stein, John Edwards, George Null, Jacob Livergood, Francis Parvin, Henry Seller, Ludowick Ansbach, George King, Peter Krieger, John Weiser, Peter Lebo, Christopher Weiser, George Beistein, Jacob Ketterman, Peter Ansbach, Michael Ried, Herman Walborn, Frederick Reed, George Landauer, Henry Boyer, Martin Stip, Abraham Lauch, Peter Serby, Casper Reed, (Ritt) Peter Reed, Lenard Rees, Adam Lesh, Philip Brown, Peter Shever, Felty (Onroo) Unruth, John Fohrer, Christopher Keiser, John Trautman, Michael Detweiler, Nicholas Kinser, John Moir, Henry Stein, Christian Moir, George Sherman, Peter Keephart, William Keyser, George Jacob Sherman, Gottfried Rohrer, Jacob Hoffman, Mathias Doebler, George Wolf, Bartel Dissinger, George Tollinger, Jacob Reed, Frederick Kaufman, Christian Frank, Rudolph Moir, Michael Kofner, George Brosius, Jacob Bortner, Jacob Casert, Casper Reed, Christopher Ulrich, Johann Jacob Snebly, Mathias Bricker, John Pontius, Peter Criser, Daniel Lucas, William Keyser, Philip Gebhart, George Ulrich Fisher, William Dieler, Jacob Miller, Jacob Hubelor,

* Col. Rec., ii., p. 405.

Jacob Wilhelm, Jacob Bartner, Nicholas Olly, John Hovershen, Simon Scherman, John Riegel, Jacob Schwaner, Henry Millberger, Wolf Miller, George Paffinberger, Geo. Kantrico, Daniel Moir, Martin Schell, Adam Jordan, Jacob Tantor, Jacob Fullman, Mathias Noffziger, John George Meirslem, Jacob Miller, Simon Bogenreif, Andrew Wollinbeck, George Gotyman, Henry Reidenbach, John Baltzer Shever, Valentine Brindseil, Martin Warner, William Brath, Gottfried Fitler, Peter Mink, Casper Stump, Mathias Wagner, Nicholas Hamber, Nicholas Miller, George Weaver, Philip Meade, John Philip Bunger, George Christ, Conrad Wirth, Conrad Reber, Valentine Bungardner, Nicholas Lang, Frederick Stap, Valentine Neu, Christian Kurtz, John Ebberts, Michael Albert, Thomas Kern, Mathias Shefer, John Ridnore, Jacob Stough, John George Mats, William Sassaman, Adam Rehm, Johan Adam Weaver, Peter Laux, Jacob Houksvert.

This, like many other townships, was the scene of Indian massacres, as may be seen on examining the third chapter of this book. Here I will insert one of many soul-stirring stories of Indian massacres, which we find in the Hallische Nachrichten. This is from the pen of the Rev. Muhlenberg, the great apostle of American Lutheranism. "It may teach us, says a certain writer,* alike to appreciate the security of our worship, and the better cost at which our fathers provided for it, may teach us that we are reaping the fruits of their sweat and blood." The case was that of a man whose two grown daughters had attended a course of instruction by Mr. Muhlenberg, and been solemnly admitted by confirmation to the communion of the church.

"This man afterwards went with his family some distance into the interior, to a tract of land which he had purchased.— When the war with the Indians broke out, he removed his family to his former residence, and occasionally returned to his farm, to attend to his grain and cattle. On one occasion he went, accompanied by his two daughters, to spend a few days there, and bring away some wheat. On Friday evening, after the wagon had been loaded, and every thing was ready for their return on the morrow, his daughters complained that they

* Dr. S S. Schmucker, see *He Pasa Ekklesia*, pp. 385, 386, by *I. D. Rupp*, published by James Y. Humphreys, Phila., 1844.

felt anxious and dejected, and were impressed with the idea that they were soon to die. They requested their father to unite with them in singiug the familiar German funeral hymn, Wer Weiss wie nahe mein Ende? "Who knows how near my end may be?"—after which they commended themselves to God in prayer, and retired to rest.

"The light of the succeeding morn beamed upon them, and all was yet well. Whilst the daughters were attending to the dairy, cheered with the joyful hope of soon greeting their friends, and being out of danger, the father went to the field for the horses, to prepare for their departure home. As he was passing through the field, he suddenly saw two Indians, armed with rifles, tomahawks, and scalping knives, making towards him at full speed. The sight so terrified him, that he lost all self command, and stood motionless and silent. When they were about twenty yards from him, he suddenly, and with all his stregth exclaimed, "Lord Jesus, living and dying, i . m thine." Scarcely had the Indians heard the words "Lord Jesus," (which they probably knew as the white man's name of the Great Spirit,) when they stopped short, and uttered a hideous yell.

"The man ran with almost supernatural strength into the dense forest, and by taking a serpentine course, the Indians lost sight of him, and relinquished the pursuit. He hastened to an adjoining farm, where two German families resided, for assistance. But on approaching near it, he heard the dying groans of the families, who were falling beneath the murderous tomahawk of some other Indians.

"Having providentially not been observed by them, he hastened back to learn the fate of his daughters. But, alas! on arriving within sight, he found his home and barn enveloped with flames! Finding that the Indians had possession here, too, he hastened to another adjoining farm for help. Returning, armed with several men, he found the house reduced to ashes, and the Indians gone. His eldest daughter had been almost entirely burnt up, a few remains only of her body, being found! And awful to relate, the younger daughter, though the scalp had been cut from her head, and her body horribly mangled from head to foot with the tomahawk, was yet living! "The poor worm," says Muhlenberg, "was yet able to state all the circumstances of the dreadful scene." After having done so, she requested her father to stoop down to her, that she might give him a parting kiss, and then go to her dear Saviour; and after she had impressed her dying lips upon his cheek, she yielded her spirit into the hands of that Redeemer, who, though his judgments are often unsearchable, and his ways past finding out, has nevertheless said, ' I am the resurrection and the life, if any man believe in me, though he die, yet shall he live.' ''—This is only one of many similar cases that has occurred in Berks and Lebanon counties.

Tulpehocken (Lower) was separated from Upper Tulpehocken. It is bounded north by Little Swatara creek, which separates it from Bethel township—on the east by Upper Tulpehocken, and south by Marion—a township about being organized out of part of Heidelberg and Lower Tulpehocken; and on the west by Lebanon county; contains about 20,000 acres of land—limestone and gravel—very productive; mean length eight miles; breadth six miles. Besides the Swatara on the north, (and its tributaries,) it is also watered by Mill creek, which also rises in this township. There are two churches, one near Mill creek, and one at Rohrersburg, common to the Lutherans and German Reformed. There are several villages or towns in this township. There are several mills in the township.

Rohrersburg is on the road from Reading to Sunbury, about twenty-two miles from Reading, counting rising of fifty houses, several stores and taverns. Population about 300.

Wohleberstown is a small village, not numbering more than fifteen or eighteen houses, a tavern and store, and several mechanic's shops. It is on the road to Myerstown, in Lebanon county, and on the Jonestown road.

Population in 1830, 3,200: 1840, 2,941; horses 713; horned cattle 1,923; sheep 765; swine 2,581; bushels of wheat raised 29,397; rye 10,756; corn 30,300; oats 47,212; buckwheat 837; potatoes 5,986; tons of hay 651; pounds of wool 1,027; flax 1,710. Whole amount of valuation on all articles taxable for county purposes in 1844, $1,027,212: county tax $2,054 42: gross amount of State tax $1,291 10.

UNION TOWNSHIP.

Union township was settled originally by Swedes, Welsh and English. Among them we still find the Olmsteds or Umsteads, Kerlins, and others.

Among the principal settlers, as early as 1740 to 1745, were the following:

John Godfrey, Thomas Pratt, Jacob Stover, Benjamin Millard, Timothy Millard, Thomas Millard, Joseph Millard, Abraham Wanger, David Yoder, John Kensey, Charles Mc-Grew, Isaac Adams, Jonathan Millard, Samuel Harris, John Godfrey, Christian Stanly, Richard Otty, Edward Hugh, Cadwalader Hughes, Peter Henry, James Kelly, Solomon Davis, Andrew Smith.

In 1758 the following, including some of the above named persons, were returned as taxables of this township:

Casper Singhouse, William Bird, John Harrison, Henry Winterberg, John Lincoln, Joseph Hunt, John Stone, George Kerst, Thomas Pratt, Joseph Burgoyne, Timothy Millard, Thomas Millard, Joseph Millard, Abraham Wenger, Daniel Yoder, Jacob Swisser, John Madery, Charles McGrew, Woolrich Reinhard, Jacob Basence, Thomas Baufield, John Godfrey, Mordecai Harris, Jonathan Millard, Peter Flickinger, Andrew Gibson, John Haas, Stephen Lewis, Andrew Hoofman, Mounce Jones, Evan Evans, Penal Evans, Frederick Hoofle, Morgan Lewis, Peter Funk, Conrad Walter, Richard Otta, James Robert, Edward Hughes, William How, Aron Hartman, Lochlan Doyle, Jacob Mizel, Robert Galoway, George Trouck, Mordecai Millard, Peter Roofner, Frederick Haas, James McGrew, Adam Helmstater, William Adams, Owen Hugh.

Union township is bounded north-east by the Schuylkill, which separates it from Amity; south by Chester county, west and north-west by Robeson. Its mean length five miles—breadth four miles: containing about twenty-one thousand acres of land, of the most ordinary quality—the greater part is poor and hilly, and upon the whole not well improved. It contains but one small village—Unionville. It is watered by the Schuylkill, Hay creek and Sixpence run—upon which is a forge—mill creek and two branches of French creek, on one of which is Hopewell furnace. There are six mills in this township.

Population in 1810, 706: 1820, 921: 1830, 1,046: 1840, 1,298: horses 303: horned cattle 976: sheep 569: swine 688: bushels of wheat raised 6,386: rye 11,013: corn 14,839: oats 18,062: buckwheat 598: potatoes 8,375: tons of hay 1,719: pounds of wool in 1844, 234,710: county tax $469 43: state tax $263 26.

WINDSOR TOWNSHIP.

Windsor township was began to be pretty generally settled between 1740 and 1752, the time when Berks was organized. The natural advantages it would secure, at presens, were not great to induce the first settlers to locate here: notwithstanding, we find a large number of taxable inhabitants—four or five years after the erection of the county—there were nearly one hundred then.

Michael Kreisher, Adam Kuhn, Adam Kleim, Andrew Seitle, Adam Lukenbill Conrad Kerschner, Conrad Hausman, Christian Hausenknecht, Clementz Dunkelberger, Conrad Heiser, Broch, Christopher Brenninger, Daniel Kemp, Deobald Werner, Daniel Hill, Elias Stein, Edward Shopple, Gerhard Will, Geo. Anstat, George Haner, George Adam Wagner, George Bauman, George Gatschall, George Ressler, George Stenger, Geo. Folb, George Charles, George Schneider, George Paust, Geo. Gartner, George Crane, George Miller, Henry Keim, Henry Gross, Henry Scheuerer, Henry Popst, Henry Kalbach, John Kerber, Jacob Wingerd, Jonathan Worrell, John Hover, John Herd, Jeremiah Schoble, Jacob Petery, Jacob Hauer, Jacob Hill, Jacob Hummel, Jacob Kraeff, Jacob Roush, John Hauser, John Hess, John Mayer, Yost Kreischer, Melchior Keiber, Killian Dunkel, Leonard Reber, Lawrence Kuntz, Leonard Keplinger, Michael Rentzler, Michael Deobald, Mathias Braun, Michael Schlaire, Mathias Alsbock, Martin Werner, Mathias Frieher, Martin Roush, Michael Eisenman, Nicholas Wingerd, Nicholas Frieh, Dietrich Leonard, Peter Bordelein, Philip

Hensel, Peter Weber, Philip Hill, Peter Dunkelberger, Philip Hinckel, Reinhard Alsbach, Sebastian Kreischer, Wendel Kieffer, William Bussler, Wendel Hauer, Wendel Ernst, Jacob Miller, Jacob Martin, John Miller, Casper Schmidt, Charles Havelle, Philip Schweitzer, Philip Wentzel, George Mauty, Anthony Adam, David Alsbach, Casper Breninger, John Conradi, Jacob Linch, Nicholas Hallabach.

This township, as well as all the other townships along the Blue Mountain, was the repeated scenes of Indian massacres. For a particular account of persons who fell victims to the cruelties of the Indians, the reader is referred to the third chapter of this book.

Windsor township is bounded on the north-west by Schuylkill county; north-east by Albany and Greenwich; and on the east by Maiden creek, which separates it from Richmond township, and from Greenwich for several miles; on the south by Maiden creek township; on the west by the Schuylkill river, separating it from Centre and Upper Bern; mean length, eight miles; breadth four miles and a half; containing nearly twenty-nine thousand acres of gravel land, somewhat hilly. " The Schuylkill river and canal run along the western boundary: and Maiden creek forms the eastern boundary.— The Blue Mountain fills the north-western corner. The village of Hamburg (see below) lies on the turnpike road to Northumberland, near the river below the Water Gap. A church, used by the Lutherans and German Reformed, is centrally situated in the township, and another near Hamburg.— There is a furnace at the foot of the Blue Mountain, at the head of a tributary of Maiden creek." There are several mills in this township, one of them near Hamburg.

Hamburg is a considerable village on the east bank of the Schuylkill river. It contains between ninety and one-hundred dwellings: several stores, taverns, and one church: population nearly six hundred. There is a bridge over the Schuylkill here. Considerable improvement has lately been made on the country around this town. Some of the land has been rendered highly productive. This shows what can be done by proper culture.

Population of the township in 1730, 2,298; 1840, 2,839. Hores 340: horned cattle 845: sheep 584: swine 1,029: bush-

els of wheat raised 3,998; rye 16,945; corn 13,562; oats 21,-
884; buckwheat 2,531; potatoes 9,439; tons of hay 1,095;
pounds of flax 602.   Whole amount of valuation on all articles
made taxable for county purposes in 1844, $626,959; county
tax $1,252 31; state tax $690 15.

UPPER TULPEHOCKEN.

Upper Tulpehocken, and Upper Bern, lie at the base of the
Blue mountain.   For the names of the first settlers, the reader
is referred to the townships of Bern and Lower Tulpehocken.

The following list embraces all who had settled on and along
the mountain between the Schuylkill and Swatara, and as far
as the first ridge of mountains between these two streams, at
the time Berks county was organized:
Jacob Shaver, George Mock, George Webb, Burgoin Bird,
Thomas Willots, Francis Yarnal, Rudolph Henry, William
Hughs, Richard Stephen, John Fincher, Thomas Ellis, John
Green, John Willots, Paul Himes, Rudolf Kendle, Joseph Jor-
don, John Jones, Jacob Fudge, Jacob Grosshaup, Mathias
Swisie, Philip Hope, Michael Homel, George Seiffer, William
Anderson.

This township is bounded on the north by Schuylkill county,
on the east by Northkill river, which divides it from Upper Bern
and Penn township; on the south by Tulpehocken creek, separating it from Heidelberg; on the west by Lower Tulpehocken
and by Bethel township; mean length seven miles; breadth,
four; containing about twenty-eight thousand acres of land of
a good quality; soil, limestone and gravel; surface somewhat
diversified.   Much of this township is in a good state of cultivation.   It is well supplied with water by the Northkill,
Tulpehocken, Little Northkill and Swatara creeks. The Union
Canal follows the Tulpehocken along the southern boundary of
the township.
There is a brick church, common to the Lutherans and German Reformed, near Little Northkill, and the road from Hamburg and Rohrersburg.   There are six mills in this township.
22

Population in 1830, 1,456; 1840, 1,537; horses 538; horned cattle 1,484; sheep 781; swine 1,207; bushels of wheat raised 9,341; rye 22,752; corn 14,201; oats 21,318; buckwheat 2,266; potatoes 9,531; tons of hay 1,457; pounds of wool 1,358; flax 1,787; whole amount of valuation on all articles made taxable for county purposes in 1844, $448,531; county tax $897 06; state tax $489 37.

UPPER BERN.

Upper Bern—this township was originally included, as also Centre and Penn, at the time when Berks county was erected, under the name of Bern. The names of the first settlers of this portion, are given when speaking of Bern. Upper Bern has, since its organization, been considerably reduced, by taking portions from it, in erecting Centre and Penn townships. Its present boundary is as follows: on the north it is bounded by Schuylkill county; on the east by the Schuylkill river, which divides it from Windsor township; on the south by Centre and Penn; on the west by Northkill, which separates it from Upper Tulpehocken. The surface on the north part is hilly—somewhat level in the southern part—soil of an ordinary quality, nearly all gravel.

The township is watered by the Schuylkill, Northkill, and some smaller streams. There are several mills in it. There is one church, four taverns, and two stores in it.

Population in 1810, 1,342; 1820, 2,017; 1830, 2,117; 1840, 2,750: horses 906, horned cattle 1,912, sheep 1,126, swine 1,846, bushels of wheat raised 12,667, rye 28,113, corn 30,905, oats 24,747, buckwheat 3,596, potatoes 16,318, tons of hay 1,844, pounds of wool 1,677, flax 352: whole amount of valuation on all articles made taxable for county purposes in 1844, $357,248; county tax $741 49; state tax 603 45.

WASHINGTON TOWNSHIP.

Washington township was divided off from the south-western part of Hereford, and the north-eastern part of Colebrookdale. For the names of the first settlers of this part of Berks county, the reader is referred to Hereford and Colebrookdale townships, in this book.

This township is bounded on the north-east by Hereford; south-east by Montgomery county; south-west by Colebrookdale; north-west by Earl, Pike and District. It is watered by the west branch of Perkiomen creek and Swamp creek, in the southern part of the township.

This township has two small villages—Schultzville, near the centre of the township, laid out by C. K. Schultz. It is on the cross roads leading from Kutztown to Philadelphia, and from Allentown to Boyerstown. It has four houses, one tavern and a post office.

Bechtelsville laid out by *J. S. Bechtel*, is on the Allentown and West Chester state road. The cluster of houses embraces four dwellings, one grist mill, one saw mill, one oil mill, one black-lead mill, and several mechanics shops.

The township has three stores, three taverns, four grist mills, four saw mills, one wool carding machine, one shoe peg manufactory, two forges, one iron foundry, two oil mills. A Roman Catholic chapel, and two meeting houses—the Schwenkfelder and Mennonite meeting houses.

———

CENTRE TOWNSHIP.

Centre township was formed out of the southern part of Upper Bern, and northern part of Bern, and is bounded as follows: on the north by Upper Bern, on the east by the Schuylkill river, dividing it from Windsor and Maiden creek, on the south by Bern and Penn, and on the west by Penn; mean length and breadth six miles, containing twenty thousand acres of land of ordinary quality—gravel soil—somewhat undulating. It is watered by the Schuylkill river, Irish creek and Plum creek. There are three or four mills in this township. Bellman's church, common to the Lutherans and German Reformed, is the only church in the township.

Population in 1840, 1,216: horses 226, horned cattle 560, sheep 481, swine 473, bushels of wheat raised 4,949, rye 5,612, corn 6,618, oats 6,708, buckwheat 972, potatoes 4,050, tons of hay 793, pounds of wool 429, flax 1,425: whole amount of valuation on all articles made taxable for county purposes in 1844, $365,273; county tax $730 54; state tax $342 31.

PENN TOWNSHIP.

Penn township—like Centre—was formed since 1840, out of a portion of Upper Bern and Bern townships. It is bounded on the north by Upper Bern, on the east by Centre and Bern, on the south by Bern, south-west and west by Tulpehocken creek and Northkill, separating it from Heidelberg and Upper Tulpehocken townships. It embraces some good land, though principally gravel soil. Scull Hill, nearly central, gives it a variegated aspect. This township is well watered. Besides the Tulpehocken and Northkill, several smaller streams rise in this township—such as Irish creek, Plum creek and Licking creek. There are several mills in it, and Northkill church, not far from Bernville, a small village fourteen miles from Reading. This town contains some fifty houses, and several stores and taverns. It has a population of about three hundred. The country around this village has been much improved within the last ten years.

Whole amount of valuation on all articles made taxable for county purposes in 1844, $399,317; county tax $798 63; state tax $363 68.

LOWER HEIDELBERG TOWNSHIP.

Lower Heidelberg was originally a part of Heidelberg. For the names of the first settlers, see Heidelberg—it is bounded on the north-east by the Tulpehocken creek, separating it from Bern, south-east by Cacoosing creek, dividing it from Cumru, south-west by Lancaster county, and north-west by Heidelberg: average length eight miles, breadth four and a half—containing rising of fourteen thousand acres of land—some of it very good —limestone soil, others ordinary—soil, gravel—surface level and hilly. It is watered by the Tulpehocken, Cacoosing and

Spring creeks: a branch of the Cocalico rises in the south-. eastern corner of this township. There are several mills in it, one church, called Hain's church. Present population probably between 1200 and 1300. Whole amount of valuation on all articles made taxable for county purposes in 1844, $680,094; county tax $1,360 05; state tax $706 84.

MARION TOWNSHIP.*

Marion township is about being organized out of part of Heidelberg and Lower Tulpehocken. This township embraces a portion of country settled primitively by emigrants from New York.

It was within the limits, near the present site of Stouchstown, that Benjamin Spicker, the contemporary and intimate fiiend of Conrad Weiser, resided. His house was a very public and conspicuous place during the French and Indian war. Some thrilling incidents occurred here. One of which is circumstantially detailed in a letter from Conrad Weiser to Gov. Morris, dated October 27, 1755, an extract of which is presented.

"After I had received the news that the Paxton people above Hunter's mills, had been murdered, I immediately sent my servants to alarm the neighborhood. I informed them of the melancholy news, and how I came by it, &c. They unanimously agreed to stand by one another, and march to meet the enemy, if I would go with them. I told them that I would not only myself accompany them, but my sons and servants should also go—they put themselves under my direction. I gave them orders to go home and fetch their arms, whether guns, swords, pitch-forks, axes, or whatever might be of use against the enemy, and to bring with them three days provision in their knapsacks, and to meet at Benjamin Spicker's, at three of the clock that afternoon, about six miles above my house, in Tulpehocken township, where I had sent word for Tulpehocken people also to meet.

"I immediately mounted my horse, and went up to Benja-

* In January 1844, it was still undecided whether this township, with its boundaries as given, would be confirmed by the proper authority.

min Spicker's, where I found about one hundred persons who had met before I came there; and after I had informed them of the intelligence, that I had promised to go with them as a common soldier, and be commanded by such officers, and leading men, whatever they might call them, as they should choose.— They unanimously agreed to join the Heidelberg people, and accordingly they went home, to fetch their arms, and provision for three days, and came again at 3 o'clock. All this was punctually performed; and about two hundred were at Benjamin Spicker's, by two o'clock.

I made the necessary disposition, and the people were divided into companies of thirty men in each company, and they chose their own officers; that is, a captain over each company, and three inferior officers under each, to take care of ten men, and lead them on, or fire, as the captain should direct.

I sent privately for Mr. Kurtz, the Lutheran minister, who lived about one mile off, who came and gave an exhortation to the men, and made a prayer suitable to the time. Then we marched towards Susquehanna, having first sent about fifty men to Tolheo, in order to possess themselves of the gaps or narrows of *Swahatawro*, where we expected the enemy would come through; with those fifty, I sent a letter to Mr. Parsons, who happened to be at his plantation.

We marched about ten miles that evening. My company had now increased to upwards of three hundred men, mostly well-armed, though about twenty men had nothing but axes, and pitchforks—all unanimously agreed to die together and engage the enemy, wherever they should meet them; never to inquire the number, but fight them, and so obstruct their way of marching further into the inhabited parts till others of our brethren came up and do the same, and so save the lives of our wives and children."

For further particulars the reader is referred to pages, 43, 44, 45, and 46.

Marion is bounded on the north by Tulpehocken; on the south-east by Heidelberg, and on the south-west by Lebanon county.

It is watered by Tulpehocken creek, which divides it into two unequal portions, and Millbach. It lies in the form of an isoceles triangle. It embraces some of the best land in Berks county. The turnpike road from Reading to Harrisburg passes through for the distance of four miles. There are two churches in this township, two mills, and one small town.

Stouchstown contains between twenty and thirty houses, one store and tavern. It is situated on the turnpike.

_____

EARL TOWNSHIP.

Earl Township was originally part of Oley, and of course was settled shortly after settlements had been commenced in Oley. For the name of original or primitive settlers, the reader is referred to the list in Oley township.

Earl is bounded on the north by Pike, on the east by Colebrookdale and Douglass, on the south by Amity, and on the west by Oley: mean length four miles and a half; breadth three miles and a quarter—containing nine thousand, five hundred and twenty acres of land—soil, gravel—surface very hilly—the South mountain passes through its south-west corner, on which is Spring Forge. Iron creek has its sources in this township. Population in 1810, 653; 1820, 924; 1830, 979; 1840, 1,160: horses 165, horned cattle 526, sheep 236, swine 434, bushels of wheat raised 2,291, rye 4,872, corn 6,282, oats 5,402, buckwheat 659, potatoes 2,502, tons of hay 504, pounds of wool 454, flax 360: whole amount on all articles made taxable for county purposes in 1844, $219,000; county tax $438,000; state tax $242 19.

_____

PIKE TOWNSHIP.

Pike township was formed out of parts of the several contiguous turnpikes. For the names of the first inhabitants of this and Earl township, the reader is referred to Oley and Colebrookdale townships.

Nothing of any remarkableness, not common to the adjacent townships, occurred in this township. Passing, it might be remarked that a certain Maria Yung, or, as she was wont to be called "*Die Berg Maria*," lived as a *solitaire* for many years in this township, near Motz's mill. It is said she led the life of a hermitess for thirty years—that she had been visited by persons from various parts of the country—some from the distance of four hundred miles. She died at an advanced age, in 1819.

A gentleman of Oley, to whom we are indebted for these facts, says he frequently, in company with others, visited Maria. On her death he wrote the following epitaph:

Hier unter diesem Steine,
Sanft ruhen die Gebeine,
Der frommen Maria.
Ihr Herz und ganzes Leben,
War ihrem Gott ergeben,
Dass man's an ihrem Wandel sah

Sie hat ganz unverdrossen,
Bis dreisig Jahr verflossen,
In Einsamkeit gewohnt :
Ihr Angesichtes-Zuegen,
Verriethen Gottes Lieb,
Damit der Herr sie hat belohnt

Nachdem sie schon verschieden,
Sah man den Suesen Frieden
In ihrem Angesicht;
Es war voll Lieb und Wonn
Als zur Gnaden-sonn,
Noch immer hingericht.

Nun ist sie wegenommen;
Gott hies sie zu sich kommen,
Aus diesem Jammerthal :
Wo auf den Himmels-Auen,
Sie Jesum wird anschauen,
Mit seiner auserwaehlten Zahl

This township is bounded on the north-east by District, south-east by Washington and Colebrookdale, on the south by Earl and Oley, on the west by Rockland—mean length four miles and a half; breadth two miles and a half—containing six thousand, five hundred acres of land—surface, large hills—soil, gravel—poor and very ordinarily cultivated. It is watered by Pine creek and other sources of Manatawny creek. Swamp creek rises in this township. There are nine or ten mills in this township, and a forge: one church, near the south-east corner, owned by the Lutherans and German Reformed.

Population in 1810, 552; 1820, 645; 1830, 752; 1840, 784; horses 157, horned cattle 590, sheep 413, swine 483, bushels of wheat raised 4,244, rye 5,356, corn 6,441, oats 4,628, buckwheat 1,467, potatoes 3,301, tons of hay 694, pounds of wool 606, flax 716: whole amount of valuation on all articles made taxable by law for county purposes $151,911; county tax $303 82; state tax $197 33.

CHAPTER XI.

Statistics of Agriculture of Berks county, for 1838. Only twenty-five, of thirty-five districts, had reported. By adding about one-third to what is given below, we may approximate to the true, or full amount.

The number of acres of limestone land cleared, is thirty thousand four hundred; of uncleared limestone land, thirteen thousand eight hundred acres; cleared slate land, eleven thousand six hundred acres; uncleared slate land, four thousand eight hundred and fifty; gravel land cleared, eighty thousand two hundred and sixty acres; uncleared gravel land, thirty-six thousand six hundred acres; sandy land, twenty-six thousand seven hundred acres—mountain or rock land, thirty-six thousand seven hundred and eighty—seven acres containing iron ore. The whole quantity of cleared land, as *reported*, of all kinds, is one hundred ninety thousand, and six hundred acres. This falls far short of the actual quantity of cleared land, in 1844, which cannot be less than two hundred and fifty thousand acres. The whole quantity of uncleared land, but fit for cultivation, as reported in 1838, is thirty-six thousand three hundred acres. This, it is believed, is also much below its actual amount. The probable number acres of uncleared land, but fit for cultivation, is about one hundred thousand acres. The whole quantity of uncleared land, unfit for cultivation, is sixty-four thousand two hundred acres, according to the report of 1838. This is also too low; there are rising of one hundred thousand acres that come under this denomination. Berks county contains rising of five hundred thousand acres in all, [516,320.]

The average value per acre of cleared land, is thirty dollars; and that of woodland fit for cultivation, twenty-seven dollars per acre: woodland unfit for cultivation, twenty dollars per acre; the whole value of cleared land, as reported in 1838, is four millions, eight hundred ninety-nine thousand and five hundred dollars. The valuation in reality approximates eight millions. The whole valuation of uncleared land in 1838, was one million eight hundred, twenty-five thousand, three hundred and fifty dollars. The true valuation approximates three millions. For, in 1844, the whole amount of valuation on all articles made taxable by law for county purposes, approximated nineteen millions of dollars, [18,617,569.]

According to the report of 1838, there were two thousand and twenty-one farms, averaging seventy-five acres each. The whole number of stone farm houses, was one thousand two hundred and fifty-four; brick houses, two hundred and seventy-nine; wood farm houses, one thousand nine hundred and fifty-five; tenant houses on farms, (not farm houses) one thousand two hundred and five. There were one thousand one hundred and eighty-eight stone barns; of brick thirty-nine: one thousand five hundred and seventy-five barns built of wood.

The whole number acres of wheat in 1838, was seventeen thousand four hundred acres; of rye, nineteen thousand four hundred and ten; of oats, fifteen thousand seven hundred; of barley nine hundred and eighty: of Indian corn seventeen thousand two hundred: in clover eleven thousand seven hundred: in timothy six thousand six hundred: of natural meadow ten thousand two hundred acres: in potatoes four thousand acres: turnips one thousand five hundred and ten: buckwheat one thousand nine hundred and ninety: in flax seven hundred.

The average yield of wheat per acre in bushels, fifteen; of rye thirteen, oats twenty, barley twenty-five, corn thirty, cloverseed two bushels, timothy seed two, natural meadow seed two, potatoes eighty, turnips seventy-five, buckwheat twelve bushels. Dressed flax per acre, seventy-five pounds. The whole quantity of wheat produced in 1838 for market, two hundred eight thousand and four hundred bushels; valued at three hundred twelve thousand and six hundred dollars; rye two hundred one thousand and eight hundred bushels; valued at one hundred and sixty-six thousand and six hundred dollars; oats two hundred forty-six thousand bushels, valued at eighty thousand one hundred dollars; barley one thousand and forty bushels, valued at eight hundred and eighty dollars; Indian corn one hundred forty-seven thousand and two hundred dollars, valued at one hundred eleven thousand and one hundred dollars.

Clover produced in tons, seven thousand three hundred dollars, valued at seventy-three thousand dollars; timothy hay, four thousand five hundred and fifty tons, valued at forty-eight thousand one hundred dollars; meadow hay, four thousand tons, valued forty-four thousand one hundred dollars; potatoes, fifteen thousand two hundred bushels produced for market, valued at seven thousand one hundred dollars; turnips produced and sold at market, five hundred and ten bushels, valued at three hundred and seventy dollars; buckwheat, nine thousand seven hundred bushels, valued at seven thousand seven hundred and eighty dollars; flax produced and dressed, fourteen thousand eight hundred pounds, valued at two thousand nine hundred dollars.

Lime, used as a manure, four hundred and forty-three thousand bushels; cost per bushel, delivered in the field, twelve and one half cent; the average quantity per acre, applied in one season is seventy-five bushels—the whole quantity supposed to form a complete dressing; whole quantity of plaster or gypsum used, one thousand four hundred and thirty-tons—three-fourths of a bushel applied to an acre; the cost per ton, ground, ten dollars. The number of hands steadily employed in farming during the year, six thousand six hundred and fifty; the average compensation per month of a hand, nine dollars. Work horses employed in farming, six thousand nine hundred and five during the year the aggregate value of which is three hundred and sixty-five thousand five hundred dollars; forty-six work oxen were employed, aggregate value, one thousand six hundred and fifty-five dollars; the whole number of horses of all kinds, nine thousand one hundred, the aggregate value, five hundred fifteen thousand seven hundred; the whole number of oxen of all kinds, three thousand seven hundred and eighty; the aggregate value was seventy-five thousand four hundred dollars; the whole number of all kinds, thirteen thousand six hundred and forty: aggregate value, two hundred and forty-two thousand eight hundred dollars; sheep of all kinds, twelve thousand four hundred and sixty: aggregate value, twenty-six thousand dollars; Merino sheep, only twenty: Saxony, thirty-five. The whole number of swine of all kinds, twenty-one thousand nine hundred and thirty: aggregate value, seventy-nine thousand one hundred dollars. The whole number of pounds of beef sold and killed, three hundred and thirty-two thousand seven hundred pounds, at seven cents per pound; pork salted and sold, one hundred and one thousand four hundred pounds, at eleven cents per pound; pounds of mutton sold, thirty-one thousand four hundred and fifty, at seven cents per pound.

The number of pounds of fine wool sold, two hundred pounds, at fifty cents; coarse wool, five thousand one hundred pounds, at forty cents. Butter sold, two hundred and forty-four thousand seven hundred pounds, at eighteen cents; one hundred and twenty pounds of cheese, at ten cents.

————

MANUFACTURING STATISTICS.

The number of threshing machines in use, one hundred; corn shellers one hundred and fifty-two; revolving horse rakes fifty-three; cultivators and shovel harrows one thousand and thirty. Valuation of oak firewood two dollars; hickory three per cord; stone coal five dollars per ton, delivered.

Number of grain mills one hundred and seven—twenty-three thousand one hundred barrels of flour made—average price per barrel, eight dollars. Whole number bushels of wheat ground, two hundred and forty-five thousand five hundred bushels—gross value three hundred seventy-two thousand, nine hundred and seventy bushels. Whole number bushels of corn ground, ninety-eight thousand four hundred—gross value seventy thousand one hundred dollars. Barley ground, two hundred bushels—gross value one hundred and fifty dollars. Whole number bushels of rye ground, three hundred and twenty-seven thousand one hundred bushels—gross value two hundred and two thousand, six hundred dollars. Whole number of hands employed in grain mills, one hundred and fifty. Amount of capital invested in mills, ninety-nine thousand two hundred. Forty-eight distilleries were reported, which consumed fifteen thousand seven hundred bushels of grain—produced forty-three thousand eight hundred gallons: gross value of spirits distilled, eighteen thousand eight hundred dollars: these distilleries consumed, as fuel, one hundred and twenty tons of mineral coal, and six hundred and ten cords of wood—employed fifty hands: capital invested, twenty-eight thousand two hundred dollars. There were three breweries, consuming four thousand one hundred and fifty bushels of grain, and brewed sixty-eight thousand

23

three hundred gallons of malt liquor, and consumed eighty tons of mineral coal, and one hundred and fifty cords of wood—giving employment to seven hands, having invested three thousand five hundred dollars—seven hundred gallons of grape wine made: gross value seven hundred dollars: seven hundred and twenty barrels of cider made: gross value one thousand four hundred and seventy dollars. Eight furnaces for manufacturing pig iron—three hot blast furnaces—three thousand seven hundred and ninety tons of pig iron made—gross value one hundred and eighteen thousand six hundred dollars: consumed three hundred and fifty-four thousand, three hundred bushels of charcoal—employed two hundred and ninety hands in manufacturing pig iron: amount of capital invested in manufacturing iron, one hundred and fifty-one thousand six hundred dollars. Five air and cupola furnaces, made two hundred tons of casting—gross value twenty-four thousand nine hundred dollars—consumed five hundred tons of mineral coal, employed thirty hands, and invested a capital of fifteen thousand dollars. Twenty-two forges manufactured six hundred and ten tons of bar iron—gross value forty thousand eight hundred dollars—number tons of blooms, two thousand three hundred and fifty: gross value one hundred and forty thousand eight hundred dollars—consumed one hundred and ninety-nine thousand five hundred bushels of charcoal—employed two hundred and seventy hands: amount of capital invested, two hundred and ten thousand dollars. Number of rolling mills two—manufactured two hundred tons of rolled iron: gross value two hundred thousand dollars: consumed five hundred tons of mineral coal—employed one hundred and twenty hands: amount of capital invested, one hundred and twenty-five thousand dollars. One nail factory manufactured one thousand tons of nails—gross value one hundred and twenty thousand dollars—consumed five tons of mineral coal—employed twenty hands—capital invested, twenty-five thousand dollars. Two steam engine factories, two locomotive factories, and seven stationary, of all kinds—the whole number of horse power of all the engines made, is one hundred and ninety horse power: gross value of engines manufactured, thirty-five thousand dollars—twelve hundred tons of mineral coal consumed—two thousand bushels of charcoal—employed thirteen hands: amount of capital invested, sixteen thousand dollars. Two scythe or sickle manufactories, manufactured two thousand scythes: gross value of scythes and sickles manufactured, one thousand seven hundred and seventy dollars—consumed one ton of mineral coal, and two thousand three hundred bushels of charcoal—employed three hands—capital invested, seven hundred and eighty dollars. Seven axe and other edge tool manufactories, manufactured three hundred and twenty axes: gross value seven hundred dollars: consumed thirty tons of mineral coal, and four thousand three hundred bushels of charcoal—employed twelve hands—amount of capital invested, nine hundred dollars. Seven gun factories manufactured three hundred and seventy guns: gross value, one thousand nine hundred and thirty dollars—consumed one thousand three hundred and fifty bushels of charcoal—employed ten hands—amount of capital invested, one thousand one hundred and thirty dollars. Twelve copper and sheet iron ware manufactories—gross value of tin ware manufactured, eight thousand nine hundred and fifty dollars—value of copper ware manufactured, one thousand dollars—value of sheet iron manufactured, two thousand and fifty dollars—consumed six tons of mineral coal, and one thousand seven hundred and fifty-one bushels of charcoal—employed thirty hands—amount of capital invested, seven thousand five hundred dollars. Saw mills one hundred and three—saws in use one hundred and three—quantity of stuffs sawed in superficial feet of one inch thick, four millions, five hundred and one thousand feet—employed one hundred and eleven hands—amount of capital invested, seven thousand dollars. Carriage, car and wagon manufactories, twenty-four—carriages manufactured, one hundred and four, railroad cars nineteen, wagons one hundred and fifty-three—gross value of vehicles of all kinds, fifteen thousand five hundred—employed fifty-eight hands—amount of capital invested, twelve thousand six hundred dollars. Thirty-three manufactories of chair and cabinet ware—gross value manufactured, twelve thousand two hundred and ten dollars—employed fifty hands—amount of capital invested, four thousand seven hundred and forty dollars. Ploughs manufactured, two hundred and twenty-four—gross value, two thousand three hundred and thirty dollars—employed fifteen hands. Value of wooden ware, of all kinds manufactured, including cedar and cooper's ware, two thousand two hundred dollars—employed twenty hands. Woollen mills seven—setts of woollen machinery seventeen—quantity of wool consumed, seven thousand two hundred and fifty pounds—manufactured, six thousand eight hundred yards of cloth—gross value of woollen goods manufactured, five thousand and seventy dollars —consumed three tons of mineral coal—number of hands employed, eighteen males and two females—amount of capital invested, three thousand three hundred dollars. Seventeen fulling mills—twenty-one thousand eight hundred yards of cloth fulled—employed twenty hands—amount of capital invested, two thousand one hundred dollars. Stocking factories, three— manufactured five thousand five hundred pairs of stockings— gross value manufactured, one thousand seven hundred dollars —employed seven hands. Tanneries, fifty-one—thirty-seven thousand eight hundred and thirty hides of all kinds tanned— gross value of leather tanned and curried, ninety-six thousand six hundred dollars—used two thousand one hundred and seventy cords of bark—employed seventy-eight hands, amount of capital invested, ninety-one thousand two hundred and twenty dollars. Saddle and harness manufactories, seventeen—gross value of saddles and harness made, thirteen thousand seven hundred and ninety dollars—employed thirty-five hands— amount of capital invested, eight thousand and forty dollars. Boot and shoe manufactories, fifty-four—manufactured four thousand two hundred pairs of boots, twenty-two thousand seven hundred pairs of shoes—gross value, fifty-seven thousand dollars—hands employed, one hundred sixty males, and twenty-two females—capital invested, thirteen thousand nine hundred dollars. Hat manufactories, eight—manufactured seven thousand hats—gross value, fourteen thousand four hundred and fifty dollars—consumed sixty-two tons of mineral coal— employed twenty-six males, and thirteen females—amount of capital invested, ten thousand three hundred and fifty dollars. Five paper mills manufactured fifty-five ton weight of stock— gross value of paper manufactured, fourteen thousand eight hundred dollars—consumed twelve tons of mineral coal—employed ten hands—amount of capital invested, seven hundred and fifty dollars. Oil mills, eight—manufactured fourteen thousand and twenty gallons of oil—used seven thousand one hundred bushels of flaxseed—gross value of oil made, ten thousand one hundred and ten dollars—consumed ten tons of mineral coal—employed ten hands—amount of capital invested, seven thousand four hundred and forty dollars. Ten potteries—gross value of ware made, four thousand two hundred dollars—employed twenty hands. Brick-yards, sixteen—number of bricks made, three millions eight hundred and eighty-four thousand—gross value, nine thousand five hundred dollars—number of hands employed, ninety. Number of mulberry trees raised, forty-eight thousand eight hundred and sixty—eighteen pounds cocoons produced—five males and three females employed—amount of capital invested, one thousand dollars. One comb manufactory—value of combs manufactured, one thousand dollars—employed three hands—consumed three tons of mineral coal. Three soap and candle factories, made one hundred and thirty thousand pounds of candles—whole value of candles made, fifteen thousand six hundred dollars—consumed twelve tons of mineral coal—employed four hands—amount of capital invested, seven hundred dollars. Ten tobacco and snuff factories, twisted forty thousand pounds of tobacco, and made nineteen millions eight hundred and ninety thousand segars—gross value of tobacco manufactured, eighteen thousand three hundred and thirty dollars—forty-seven hands employed—capital invested, nine thousand one hundred dollars. Ropewalks, one—made ten tons of rope—gross value, four hundred dollars—employed three hands. Whole number of shoemakers, not general manufacturers, two hundred and seventy-two; tailors, one hundred and eighty-five; weavers, seventy-four; hatters, ninety-five; butchers, forty-two; watchmakers, eighteen; blacksmiths, one hundred and ninety-four; whitesmiths, seven; carpenters, two hundred and sixty; wheelwrights, seventy-seven; printers, ten; book-binders, one.

STATISTICS OF COMMERCE.

Number of importers of tobacco, one—gross value of tobacco imported, thirty-seven thousand dollars—amount of capital invested, two thousand dollars. Number of retailers of foreign goods, ninety-three—gross amount of sales, two hundred and ninety-nine thousand two hundred dollars—employed one hundred and forty-six hands—amount of capital invested, two hundred and ten thousand four hundred dollars. Number of retailers of domestic dry goods, fifty-eight—gross amount of *sales, one hundred and seventy thousand six hundred dollars—number of hands employed, one hundred and twelve—amount of capital invested, eighty-three thousand nine hundred dollars. Retail groceries, fifty-eight—gross amount of sales, one hundred thousand three hundred dollars—employed ninety-five hands—amount of capital invested, fifty-seven thousand nine hundred dollars. Retailers of hardware, thirty-four—gross amount of sales, one hundred and nineteen thousand two hundred dollars—employed fifty-five hands—amount of capital invested, seventy-four thousand four hundred and fifty dollars. Retailers of foreign liquors, (not tavern-keepers,) thirty-nine—gross amount of sales, sixty-one thousand one hundred dollars—employed seventy-three hands—amount of capital invested, twenty-four thousand nine hundred and seventy dollars. Retailers of domestic spirits, thirty-three—gross amount of sales, nineteen thousand one hundred dollars—hands employed, sixty-three—amount of capital invested, seventeen thousand four hundred and fifty dollars. Retail Drug & Chemical stores, twelve—gross value of sales, eight thousand dollars—sixteen hands employed—amount of capital invested; seven thousand four hundred dollars. Taverns, one hundred and thirty-five—gross amount of sales of liquors, forty-eight thousand five hundred and fifty dollars—number of hands employed, one hundred and fifty-four. Flour and feed stores, eighteen—gross amount of sales, ten thousand eight hundred dollars—number of hands employed twenty—amount of capital, $6,970 00—five lumber yards—gross amount of sales, three hundred and twenty-five thousand dollars—employed eight hands—amount of capital invested, twelve thousand one hundred dollars. Six coal yards—gross amount of sales of anthracite coal, eight thousand five hundred dollars—amount of capital invested, seven thousand one hundred dollars.*

STATISTICS OF MINING.

Seven iron ore banks in operation, mined twelve thousand tons of ore—whole value of all the ore mined, nineteen thousand seven hundred dollars—smelted ten thousand eight hundred tons of ore in the county—sent out of the county one thousand seven hundred tons—employed seventy-three hands in mining—employed fifteen hands in transporting—amount of capital invested, two hundred thousand dollars. Ninety limestone quarries in operation, quarried twenty-two thousand nine hundred perches of limestone—valued at fifteen thousand six hundred dollars—employed one hundred and seventy hands. Lime-kilns in operation, three hundred—burned six hundred and sixty-five thousand bushels of lime, valued at eleven cents per bushel—whole value, seventy-three thousand one hundred and fifty dollars—employed seventy hands at kilns, and thirty in transportation.

APPENDIX.

A. On page 191, in a foot note, the reader is referred to *Appendix A.*, touching a meeting held in 1829, in opposition to Sunday Schools, &c. The proceedings of the meeting are given, with *remarks* by A CHRISTIAN FREEMAN.

APPENDIX.

A.

Meeting of Freemen in Heidelberg township, Berks county.

At a numerous and respectable meeting of citizens assembled at the house of George Gernand, on Thursday the 21st of May, 1829, pursuant to public notice, given by the committee of correspondence, appointed by the Committee in Cocalico township, Lancaster county, on the 19th of March last, to deliberate and consult upon the causes and tendency of the religious excitement at present prevailing in the county; Joseph Hain, Esq., was appointed President; Henry Bennetsch and John Sohl, jr., and Daniel Wenrich, Secretaries; John Shitz, Jacob Seitzinger, Henry Shoner, Martin Texter and John Hain (of Adam) being appointed a committee to report proceedings for the consideration of the meeting; after retiring for a short time, reported the following address and resolutions, which were unanimously adopted:

The committee appointed to report proceedings for the consideration of this meeting, respectfully submit the following:

That a religious excitement exists in many sections of the country, not calculated, as they apprehend, to promote the interests of genuine rational Piety, and tending eventually, if not arrested in its progress, to abridge the civil and religious liberties of the people. The cause of this excitement may be found in the extraordinary conduct of certain ecclesiastical Professors, who appear to have undertaken a crusade, for the spreading of particular religious opinions, and the advancement of church

establishments. Pervading the country in every direction, they
alarm the weak minded and youthful part of the community
with unusual and vehement denunciations of divine wrath, and
thus obtain an influence over minds which is not the result of
rational conviction, and which is destined to be directed to the
elevation of the clerical profession to a degree of authority in-
consistent with the people's welfare, and the spirit of the free
constitutions under which we live.

It appears to your committee that the Clergy of the United
States in general, have exhibited many manifestations of a
spirit of worldly ambition. That measures have been projected
by that class of men, calculated and designed to promote their
own interests at the expense of those of the people; to enable
them to dictate to the consciences of their fellow-men; and to
assume a right of interference in the direction of state affairs.
They have observed with dissatisfaction and alarm, the establishment of opulent and influential societies, the management of
which is committed to ecclesiastical hands or subjected to ecclesiastical control. Amongst these they number Bible and
Missionary Societies, Theological Seminaries and Sunday
School Unions. They regard these institutions as unnecessary
burdens upon the church going part of the community, appro-
priating vast sums of money to purposes for the most part un-
called for, and tending directly to increase the influence of the
clergy. They have witnessed the attempts recently made to
induce the Congress of the U. States, to prohibit the transportation of the mail on Sunday, and regard them as ebullitions
of the fanatical spirit, so widely disseminated by the Clergy.—
They consider all endeavors to procure legislative interference
in matters of religion, as attempts to infringe upon the rights
of conscience, and all measures adopted to compel particular
observance of the Sabbath as incipient approaches to the establishment of spiritual tyranny. Your committee would shrink
from proposing a single objection to the extension of the Christian Religion. They believe the revealed Religion of the old
and new Testaments to be the most inestimable gift of a beneficent
Creator to the human family. They regard it as a written law for
the guidance of human conduct, exhibiting a sublime and perfect
system of morals, and holding incentives to the pursuit of virtue in those immortal rewards which Divinity alone could offer.
But in revolving the histories of bye-gone ages they are ad-

monished by the wails of nations, and the groans of oppressed people, to beware of a body of men assuming to be the interpreters of the Divine word, and the Directors of men's consciences. They contemplate with horror, the intolerance and bloody persecutions of the church of Rome, and the debased condition of the people in every nation where ecclesiastical rulers have the sway. They look upon England, the most free of European governments, and behold a Union of Church and State, which has burdened the people for ages with an oppressive hierarchy that maintains a luxurious Clergy with the hardworn earnings of the Agriculturalist and Mechanic. They look forward with prophetic apprehensions to the termination of the race, which fanaticism is running in our own country, and behold in anticipation, misery and slavery, and ecclesiastical tyranny beyond the goal.

Your committee with a view to counteract the efforts which are making to promote ecclesiastical supremacy, respectfully submit the following resolutions for the consideration of the meeting:

Resolved, That in the opinion of this meeting, the institution of Bible and Missionary Societies, Theological Seminaries and Sunday School Unions, are works of supererogation, considered in reference to the wants and welfare of the people; that they are designed to elevate and sustain the authority of the Priesthood, and so considered, are dangerous to the liberties of the people, and that we will not assist in maintaining Clergymen who advocate them or are concerned in their support.

Resolved, That we consider the extraordinary zeal for religion, which manifests itself in the condemnation of innocent amusements and the requisition of an ascetic severity of life, as originating in the false pretences of designing men, or the erroneous opinions of over-heated enthusiasm, believing as we do, that hilarity in enjoying the bounties of Providence, is not unacceptable in the sight of the Almighty dispenser of all things.

Resolved, That our religious and moral duties are plainly set forth in the language of the holy Scriptures; that they consist in visiting the sick, feeding the hungry, clothing the naked, rendering due honor to parents and the exercises of charity towards all men, and that no amount of mortification or prayer can justify the omission of any of them.

24

Resolved, That we duly appreciate the advantages of the Sabbath, considered as a day of worship and temporal repose; but that we cannot regard innocent recreations on that day, not prohibited by the laws of the land, as infractions of its duties or those of rational piety.

Resolved, That hereafter we will receive no preacher into our congregation who is an adherent or supporter of any Theological Seminary, of the Sunday School Union, or the Bible, Missionary, Tract or any other similar societies, or who is engaged in distributing any so called religious papers or Magazines, because we sincerely believe those institutions have been introduced for no other purpose than to collect large sums of money, which is to be applied towards erecting an influence and power of the Clergy over the people, and consequently may eventually lead to the destruction of our civil and religious liberties.

Resolved, That it is our sincere opinion that all those persons who so conspicuously disseminate principles so dangerous in their consequences, are either hypocrites seeking their own aggrandizement, or deluded fanatics, whose blindness seeks to involve twelve millions of free and happy people between the fangs of an overreaching and ambitious priesthood. That our Saviour came into the world to make men free and happy is an undeniable truth; but that priestcraft, under the garb of religion, endeavors to enslave the world is also a fact seriously to be deplored.

Resolved, That we view those arrogant and haughty beggars, who, in imported broad cloths, strut about our country, distributing tracts and asking money for Missionary purposes, as a set of imposters, too lazy to earn, by the sweat of their brow, the food that sustains them.

Resolved, That we are, as we have been ever, ready to reward upright and unassuming ministers for their services, and to render their stay among us as agreeable as circumstances will allow; with this proviso, however, that they remain free and independent from all connexion with those societies, whose ostensible object may seem laudable, but whose intentions are the promotion of themselves and the slavery of the people.— Should, however, no such preacher be found, we will nevertheless frequent the house of God and appoint one of the number present to read an appropriate sermon, a chapter from Holy writ, and conclude by prayer and hymns of thankfulness to the supreme creator of all his mercies.

Resolved, That we approve of the proceedings of the meeting held on the 19th of March last, in Cocalico township, Lancaster county, and that we will endeavor our utmost to aid in fulfilling them.

Resolved, That the proceedings of this meeting be signed by the officers of the day, and published in all the papers friendly to the cause of the people.

JOSEPH HAIN, President.

HENRY BENNETSCH, } Vice Presidents,
JOHN GERHART,

JOHN SOHL, Jr. } Secretaries.
DANIEL WENRICH,

REMARKS BY A CHRISTIAN FREEMAN.

Believing that the cause of the Redeeemer is best promoted, when its friends are apprised of the evil as well as of the good, which attends it, and have it in their power to know the strength of its enemy, the weapons he employs, and the nature of the conflict which it is their duty to maintain, I request the insertion in the Magazine of the accompanying report and resolutions adopted by a meeting held in Berks county, in this State.   This production can afford neither pleasure nor edification to your readers; but they can learn from it how much of heathenism is yet to be purged away in our own country and our own church; and how much they ought to do.

The persons who composed this meeting are, at least principally, Germans, and a portion of them are members of the Reformed Church.   I mention these facts with deeper shame and regret:—they are a blot upon our character and will fill a dark page in our history.   I would say, "Tell it not in Gath; publish it not in the streets of Ashkelon," but the authors have already proclaimed their own reproach by publishing it in all the papers which would insert their strange production.

These men profess to regard the Christian religion as "the most inestimable gift of a beneficent Creator to the human family," and "to shrink from proposing a single objection to the extension of it." They may possibly be sincere: but it is too manifest that they neither possess the spirit of Christianity, nor know what it is, and that their resolutions strike with the most reckless violence at all the means of promoting or extending it. The religious institutions which are the glory of the present age, and whose effects in promoting the knowledge and the influence of Christianity, have been already so important, are pursued with a rancorous and deadly hostility, as dangerous to the liberties of the people; their friends and supporters are characterized as "hypocrites who seek their own aggrandizement, or deluded fanatics;" and the clergy who promote them, are denounced as an "over-reaching and ambitious priesthood."

In this virulent opposition, these people have been preceded by the Pope of Rome, and the Patriarch of the Popish Maronite Christians in Asia, who have fulminated their anathemas against Bible Societies and Bible-men, denouncing them as pests and instruments of the devil, calculated to undermine their "holy faith." The Turkish Sultan, if I remember right, has also issued his *firman* prohibiting the distribution of the Bible, and of other Christian books in his dominions, by Protestant Missionaries. And there can be no doubt that Satan regards them with no kinder thoughts, and is doing what he can to drive them out of his kingdom.

It is easy to perceive why the Pope and his adherents should be opposed to the religious institutions of Protestants, and particularly to Bible Societies; since it is manifest, that if the Bible, without note or comment, be every where circulated and read, nothing can be more dangerous to the superstitions and the priestly tyranny of that church: and accordingly it has been the constant policy of the Popish Hierarchy to shut up the Bible from the people.

Nor is it difficult to comprehend why the Turkish Sultan should be opposed to the distribution of the Bible and of religious tracts. He and his people are Mahomedans: their sacred book is the Koran: and he knows that, if the Bible and Christian tracts be circulated and read in his dominions, his religion must fall before them; or, at best, it cannot be benefitted by them.

It is equally as easy to discover why the Prince of Darkness should hate Bible Societies, whose object is to distribute the Word of Eternal Life; and Tract societies, which endeavor to spread Christian knowledge and piety by distributing those tracts which are so well adapted to inform the understanding and to improve the heart; and Sunday schools, whose aim is to store the mind at an early period of life, with the principles of Christianity; and the Missionary Societies, whose design is to propagate the religion of Christ among all nations, and to gather souls from the four winds into his kingdom; and Theological Seminaries, in which ministers of the Gospel are suitably prepared for their holy office; and Evangelical Religious Periodicals, by which knowledge is increased, zeal awakened, and piety promoted. He well knows that all these are destructive to his power, and that if they are permitted to exert their energies in peace, his kingdom cannot prosper.

But it is impossible to explain why Christians, who declare that they "would shrink from proposing a single objection to the extension of the Christian religion," why Protestant Christians, why members of the Reformed and the Lutheran churches, should join in the same hostility and unite in the same warfare, against these things. What has the Protestant Christian to fear from them, that he should join with such associates in such a crusade?

A reason for this conduct is assigned in the first resolve, viz: that these institutions "are designed to elevate and sustain the authority of the Priesthood, and so considered, are dangerous to the liberties of the people."

Is it not difficult to comprehend what these Christians and Patriots mean by the sneering term priesthood: they apply it to those ministers-of religion, in the Protestant Christian Church, who foster the benevolent institutions which they abhor. It is well known that the ministers of the Protestant Churches are no Priesthood in the literal sense of the term; as they do not pretend, in that sense, to offer up sacrifices of any sort. The ministry of the Church of Rome assert that, the mass is literally a sacrifice which they offer to God; and they claim for that reason to be a Priesthood. Protestant ministers maintain that Jesus Christ is the only priest, and his death upon the cross the only sacrifice of his church. They, therefore, disclaim the office of priests, and profess to be only pastors and teachers. This fact, I presume the Committee who reported these resolutions, knew; but the term Priesthood presented so inviting an opportunity to confound Protestant ministers with

24*

Popish priests, and to involve them all in a common odim, that they could not forbear to use it. There is some malignity in this conduct, and a pleasure is evidently felt in the indulgence of it.

It is not so easy to understand what they mean by the *authority* of the Priesthood, which our benevolent institutions "are designed to elevate and sustain." In the United States, ministers of all denominations possess no other than purely spiritual authority: they are officers of a kingdom which is not of this world: as such, they are authorized to teach and propagate the religion of Christ, to administer his sacraments, and to exercise the discipline which is necessary for the purity and the edification of his church. This authority they have from God who gave some Apostles and some Prophets, and some Evangelists, and some Pastors and Teachers, for the perfecting of the saints, for the work of the ministry, for the edifying of the body of Christ; and commanded them to teach all nations, to preach his gospel to every creature, to seek first his kingdom and its righteousness, and to labor as well as to pray that his name may be hallowed, that his kingdom may come, and that his will may be done on earth as it is in heaven,* (i. e., in all places, by all, and with delight.) This authority can neither be "elevated" nor depressed, neither "sustained" nor overthrown, by any thing which men can do. But the benevolent institutions, which the zealous disciples and friends of Jesus establish, bring together a great store of means, and a powerful co-operation of fellow christians, to enable ministers of the gospel more effectually to execute their Lord's commands. If this be what is meant by "elevating and sustaining the authority of the Priesthood," I should like to be informed what harm it can possibly do to the liberties or the happiness of man; or how Jesus Christ himself can escape the reproaches of those who can see nothing but danger, harm and wickedness in it.

If Christian ministers were aiming at temporal power, I cannot conceive how the institutions which they cherish could possibly subserve their design. The learned and candid authors of the report refer us to the "history of by-gone ages" for proof of the danger to be apprehended from "a body of men, assuming to be the intepreters of the divine word, and the directors

* Ephes. 4, 11, 12. Math. 28, 19, 20. Mark 16, 15. Math. 5, 33.— Math. 6, 9, 10.

of men's consciences;" but they have not informed us by what means those wicked men established their tyranny and introduced so much corruption and misery into Christendom. Was it by supplying every destitute family with a copy of the Bible in the vulgar tongue? by distributing tracts in which the doctrines of the Bible were stated and explained? by establishing Sunday Schools in which children, and especially the poor, were taught to read, and were instructed in the Holy Scriptures? by publishing periodicals in which Christian doctrines and duties were freely discussed and illustrated? or by preaching repentance, faith in Christ, and holiness of life, and denouncing the wrath of God against impenitent and wicked men? By such means, the "Priesthood" might indeed have enlightened and improved their flocks, and made them happy, both in this world and in the next; but they could not possibly have established a priestly tyranny in the church. The people would have known what Christianity is: they would have understood both their rights and their duties; they would have discerned the nature and design of the Christian ministry, and would have been in a condition to judge the claims and the conduct of their spiritual guides by the unerring rule of the Holy Scriptures. An iniquitous spiritual domination can subsist only where the people are very ignorant and superstitious. This the "ambitious Priesthood" of " by-gone ages" were sagacious enough to perceive, and they accordingly took the measures to introduce a sottish ignorance and superstition into the church. The Bible was taken away and shut up as a dangerous book; permission to read it could be obtained only as a special favor by a very few in whom the Priesthood confided; and the people were told that they must learn the will of God from the lips of the priest only, and receive his statements as the oracles of truth. The sermons which the people heard and the books which they were permitted to read, if they could read at all, were filled with the senseless legends of pretended saints, and extravagant commendations of the pope, the saints, images, relics, pilgrimages, prayers and masses for the dead, &c., &c. It was denounced as an insolent impiety, if proof was demanded for the truth of any of these things. A contented ignorance and implicit faith in the infallibility of the church was, with them, the very summit of Christian excellency. It was not even necessary that a Christian should know

what the church believed. It was sufficient if he admitted
that, whatever it be, it must be true. An "overreaching and
ambitious priesthood" claimed to be the interpreters of the
word of God, and the directors of men's consciences. Putting
themselves in the place of the Bible, they shut out the light
from every other source of information, and demanded that
their decisions should be received as the rule of men's faith and
practice: and having thus got men's consciences into their power, they filled their minds with superstitious trumperies, instead
of healthful truth. It was in this manner that their wicked
dominion was established. How long would their tyranny
have lasted, if the priesthood of that age had changed their
system, and adopted the measures which the enlightened meeting in Heidelberg so much reprobate in the Protestant clergy
of the present age? It would have disappeared in a very little
time. The Reformers attacked, and in part demolished it, by
preaching the same doctrine which is now preached; by trans-
lating the bible into the vulgar tongue, and circulating it as
much as possible; by publishing great numbers of religious
books and tracts; by establishing primary schools for the instruction of youth, and seminaries of learning which were especially designed to prepare young men for the ministry of the
Gospel; by catechising the children on Sundays, and compiling
catechisms and other suitable books for their use; and, in short,
by a system of measures the same in its nature and tendency,
though somewhat different in its form, from that which is now
pursued. If this system had been permitted to operate universally. not a vestige of the priestly tyranny of Rome would have
remained. The Hierarchy could maintain their ground, as far
as they kept it, only by setting bounds to these operations, and
extinguishing, as far as possible, the light which the Reformers
had kindled; and they effected this by fire and sword, by dun-
geons and racks, by the terrors of the Inquisition, and by calumnies which were designed, like those of the good men of Heidelberg, to ruin the fair fame and destroy the influence of the
men whom they opposed. Wherever this system can now
operate in popish countries, it either destroys popery, or re-
forms it and bring it near in its spirit to protestantism. The
pious and liberal portion of the Romish priesthood are its
warm friends and supporters. There are in that communion
such men as Leander Van Ess. But the other part, who are

intent only on the maintenance of their own power and emolu-
ment, treat it, as it was treated in the days of the Reformation,
with anathemas, calumnies, and persecutions; and join very cordially in the sentiments and language of the meeting in Heidelberg.

If by the "elevating and sustaining of the authority of the
Priesthood," these men, who have so much respect for the
Christian religion, and for the office of the Christian ministry
as an appointment of Jesus Christ, mean that the various institutions and religious operations, which they oppose, will increase the influence of clergymen, I freely admit the fact to a
certain extent. They will enlighten the public mind on the
subject of religion, spread the influence of pure Christianity,
improve public and private virtue, withdraw the affections
from earth to heaven, light up the hope of immortality, and
open the fountains of divine consolation. In accomplishing
this, they will place in a stronger light the excellency of true
religion and the value of an intelligent and devoted ministry,
and will consequently procure for those clergymen, who are
men of the right character, a larger measure of confidence, respect, and love, and a more extensive influence than they would
otherwise have enjoyed; but they will not increase the influence
of a man in whom an enlightened and virtuous community can
discern no just claims to their esteem. *He* will succeed only
among the ignorant and ungodly, who are like himself as he is
like them. *He* might be popular with the corrupt party in the
church of Rome; or figure at a meeting where Bible Societies,
Sunday Schools, &c., are reprobated and denounced. *He* may
raise himself to consequence and power where the people love
darkness rather than light, and are not likely to discover his
unfitness for the sacred office. But *he* must be a man of real
merit, who can sustain himself in a community where there is
much intelligence, much piety, and much devotedness to the
Redeemer's cause; and *his* influence in it will be only in the
proportion in which he deserves to be esteemed. It is the interest of preachers of low grovelling minds and little worth, to
discourage every thing, by which the community may be enlightened and improved, and a higher standard of fitness for the
gospel ministry is raised; or which may oblige them to more
activity and self denial. Such men will not be the originators
of Bible Societies, Sunday Schools, Theological Seminaries,

&c.; nor will they ever give them a cordial support, when others have originated them. If the meeting at Heidelberg choose to select their preachers from this class, I beg leave to refer them to Paul's affecting charge to Timothy.— 2 Tim., 4, 1—4.

I am unable to comprehend how the influence which the Clergy may gain by the measures they have adopted and the objects they are pursuing, can possibly be dangerous to the liberties of the people. If their influence be in proportion to the confidence reposed in them by an enlightened and virtuous community; if it be acquired by spreading christian knowledge and virtue, and by making themselves more useful and worthy of esteem; it can be dangerous to nothing but vulgarity, ignorance and vice. If by liberty the Heidelberg patriots mean licentiousness, the whole matter is very clear: that sort of liberty is in much danger from such an influence; but if they mean by it the unrestrained enjoyment of the rights which God has given us, it is a thing which can only be safe where men are intelligent and truly virtuous. Nothing can be more congenial to it than the influence of a body of clergy whom such a people honor with their confidence. Nothing, on the contrary, can be more pernicious to it than the principles of those who are at open war with Bible Societies, Missionary Societies, Sunday Schools, Theological Seminaries, &c.

The Heidelberg meeting ought to have known that the clergy are not exclusively the authors and promoters of these institutions. They have been originated, supported, and promoted by associations of the zealous friends of the christian religion, consisting of persons of both sexes and of every condition in life, of whom the clergy form but a very small part. They are not confined to any one denomination of Christians, nor to any one country, but are found in all christendom, where any religious liberty exists. Among their supporters are a very large portion of the most intelligent, virtuous and patriotic citizens of every country; whose opinions upon political questions and upon other points of religion are, in many instances, as opposite as the Poles, and who would be induced to unite in no other common object than that of propagating the religion of Jesus Christ, and thereby promoting the happiness of mankind. Many of these refuse to unite with general associations, preferring societies composed exclusively of members of their own religious denominations, and designed to propagate their own peculiar mode of faith and worship; because that alone appears to them entirely scriptural; but the main design is still the same, namely to spread the religion of Christ.

Can it be imagined, without absurdity, that all these individuals have conspired to raise "a corrupt Priesthood" over their own heads and to make themselves and their fellow christians slaves? Do they contribute their money, their talents and their time to destroy the precious boon of religious liberty, for which so many myriads of Protestants, whose memory they cherish with the warmest affection, suffered the loss of all things, and so much christian blood was shed; or are they ignorant of the design and tendency of their religious operations, the dupes of a crafty and wicked priesthood, and do they need to have their eyes opened by the more enlightened meeting at Heidelberg? So this singular publication would have us to believe!

But, it is urged, that these religious institutions are "committed to ecclesiastical hands, or subjected to ecclesiastical control" The ignorant reader would infer from these words that the entire management of them is exclusively in the hands of clergymen. But this surely is not the truth. The business of every religious association is transacted by a Board of Managers, elected by the associaton, of whom a part only are clergymen. The reason why clergymen are appointed is a very plain one. The confidence they usually enjoy, the nature of their office as ministers of religion, and their disengagedness from the distractions of worldly business, are supposed to fit them best for management of a religious or charitable institution; but it is the moral and religious transactions only that receive their attention: as Treasurers whose duty it is to manage the pecuniary concerns of the institution, laymen are almost universally appointed. A report of their proceedings, together with a statement of the receipts and expenditures, is laid before the Society at its anniversary meeting, and is afterwards published for the information of the public. If the members of the Heidelberg meeting had *read* the religious periodical, instead of *proscribing* them, they would have obtained some knowledge of the subject which they have undertaken to expose; and they would then have seen that the dangers, which have so much alarmed them, are like those that frighten children, and that they might very safely dismiss their fears and remain at home in peace.

The officers of religious Societies receive no compensation for their services, except in those few instances where the duties of the office require so much attention, that they require the whole or a very large portion of the officer's time, and make it necessary that a suitable provision be made for his support. This is the case of the treasurers, secretaries, and general agents of some societies, whose business is very extensive. All others contribute their services gratuitously, and in addition to these contribute their money also.

It is therefore no temporal advantage to clergymen, if they are appointed to the management of religious and charitable institutions. On the contrary, it is very often a disadvantage; and sometimes a pretty serious one too. Because religion and charity are considered more properly their concern, more is expected from them than from other officers, and they are obliged, for that reason, more frequently to attend meetings and to take an active part in transacting their business. A single clergyman in one of our cities spends more time, labour and money, in the cause of humanity, without receiving any earthly compensation for it, than, perhaps, the whole meeting at Heidelberg, officers and all, have ever devoted to that object. On this account selfish, covetous and narrow-minded clergymen, usually avoid all connexion with these institutions, and still more with the management of them; or, if they cannot for shame avoid it, are very heartless and negligent in it.

This report produces not a single argument or fact to show that these institutions have been abused, or that their tendency is dangerous, or that their authors and promoters are corrupt and plotting men. All this is insinuated again and again, with sufficient boldness; and it is abundantly evident that, if proof were at hand, it would be triumphantly exhibited; but these righteous judges content themselves with merely resting such heavy charges upon *opinions* for entertaining which they assign no reason: "We regard," "We consider," "It is our sincere opinion," &c., &c. This it seems must suffice. The public must believe them, because *they think so:* and upon this ground all the friends of religious and charitable institutions, who endeavor by such means to diffuse the religion of the Bible, are denounced as " hypocrites seeking their own aggrandizement, or deluded fanatics, whose blindness seeks to involve twelve millions of free and happy people between the fangs of an over-reaching and ambitious priesthood," and ministers of Christ, who cannot conscientiously abandon these institutions, are to be driven from their pulpits and churches, and turned out upon the world together with their families, without bread or shelter!!! Here are patriotism and christianity with a vengeance. If this be not the spirit of popery in its worst form, I have yet to learn what that spirit is. O shame upon such professors of religion—such members of a Protestant church!

There is a good reason to believe that the master spirits, both at this meeting, and at the former one in Lancaster county, were some intriguing infidels; some wolves in sheep's clothing. Of these our country has enough; and that section of it is not without them. By these an ill informed and credulous body of men are wrought into a phrenzy of passions by representations that their liberties are in danger. I have been informed, by good authority, that the author of the report and resolutions adopted by the meeting in Lancaster county, is the editor of an irreligious publication called the German Reformer. This second production, contains abundant internal evidence of a similar authorship. How much of it the meeting at Heidelbern understood, I know not. I believe that what they have done was done in their ignorance, and I am disposed to pray in their behalf, "Father, forgive them for they know not what they do." I have the satisfaction to know that no clergymen in connexion with our Synod had any connexion with this unworthy transaction.—*Mag. Ger. Reformed Church.*

25

ADDENDA.

Every effort made to ameliorate the condition of man or to alleviate his pains and sufferings, should claim the attention of the philanthropist. To bring to notice, and preserve to future days, an effort of the kind, the following has been introduced:

MEDICAL FACULTY OF BERKS COUNTY.

The practising physicians of this county, having associated and become a body politic in law, under the above style and title, met agreeably to public notice, on Saturday evening, the 7th of August, 1824, at the public building of this borough, and duly organized their institution.

Doct. *Isaac Hiester* was called to the Chair, and Doct. *Charles Baum* appointed Secretary.

The charter and by-laws having been read, the following gentlemen were elected officers for the ensuing year:

Isaac Hiester, M. D., *President.*
C. L. Schlemm, M. D. } *Vice Presidents.*
John B, Otto, M. D. }
Charles Baum, M. D., *Recording Secretary.*
Wm. J. C. Baum, M. D. } *Coresp'ng. Sec'rys.*
Edward Haydock, M. D. }
George Eckert, M. D., *Treasurer.*
Dr. Bernard M'Neil, } *Curators.*
Dr. Gerh. G. Bishop, }

The President delivered a short address to the association, and then proceeded agreeably to the by-laws to appoint a standing committee of three members for the examination of candidates for the grade of junior membership.   The following gentlemen compose the committe, C. L. Schlemm, M. D., John B. Otto, M. D., and Charles Baum, M. D.

The following resolutions were then offered, discussed and adopted.

Resolved, That the members of the Medical Faculty be requested to furnish monthly to the corresponding secretaries, a list of the diseases and deaths that may occur in their respective neighborhoods, and an account of the general health of the county, together with such remarks as they may deem proper for publication.

Resolved, That it is expedient to apprize the public of the existence of small pox in this borough, and that inasmuch as this body retains undiminished confidence in vaccination, this mild and safe preventative be strongly recommended in all cases deemed liable to the infection of that loathsome and too often fatal disease.

Resolved, That the students in medicine of Berks county have permission to attend the meetings and deliberations of this body.

Resolved, That one hundred copies of the constitution and by-laws of the medical faculty of Berks county, be printed in pamphlet form, under the superintendence of a committee consisting of Drs. Otto, Baum and Bishop, and that the proceedings of this evening, together with the inaugural address of the president, be published in the several papers of this borough, signed by the President and attested by the Secretary.

On motion, Resolved, That the President deliver an oration in public as soon as may be convenient, in the name and on behalf of this faculty.

The faculty adjourned to the next stated meeting on the first Saturday in October next, at 7 o'clock, P. M.

CHARLES BAUM, Recording Secretary.

ADDRESS.

Gentlemen of the Medical Faculty:—My warmest acknowledgments are due to you for honoring me, by an unanimous vote, with the first office of your society; and the best pledge I can offer of my future zeal for its prosperity, is the interest I have already taken in its establishment.

Now that our institution, (which is the first of the kind in Pennsylvania, except the college of physicians and medical society of Philadelphia,) is organized, permit me to remark that, we commence our operations under auspices solemn and impressive. We have not, like those of most other associations, chosen to form ourselves into a self constituted body, liable to be dissolved by every adverse breeze; but have boldly demanded the sanction of the proper authorities, and we found our existence on the permanent basis of an act of incorporation.

The invitation we have thus virtually given to the profession elsewhere, and to the public generally, to mark our origin and observe our progress, imposes upon us new and weighty obligations, in addition to those ordinarily incumbent on the practising physician. Carefully to observe diseases, diligently to watch their immense variety of symptoms, and faithfully to charge the memory with the effects of remedies, as guides in future practice, are duties indispensable to every practitioner who aims at individual excellence: But associated as we now are, for the avowed as well as substantial purpose of improving medical knowledge in this part of the country, and thereby enlarging our usefulness to the community, more will justly be expected from us in our collective capacity. "I hold," says Lord Bacon, "every man a debtor to his profession; from which as men of course do seek countenance and profit, so ought they of duty to endeavor themselves, by way of amends, to be a help and an ornament thereunto." The imperfect state of the medical profession in common with all others, its dependence mainly, for improvement on an accumulation of practical facts, and above all its immense importance to mankind, renders it peculiarly incumbent on its members, wherever they may be located, to contribute their aid to its advancement. Dispersed, however, as we are, in different parts of the country, and confined to our respective circles of practice by a pursuit at once arduous and painful, we have little leisure, and perhaps less inclination to commit to paper, for the inspection of others, the results of our individual experience and observation. Insulated with regard to our professional brethren, the only competent judges of our merit, and accustomed to the indiscriminate praises of our patients, we are in continual danger of mistaking the reputation we enjoy for actual superiority of skill; while we daily drop in the rear of our contemporaries by neglecting to cultivate those vast accessions of knowledge to our science that so pre-eminently distinguish the age in which we live.— Without the advantage of a frequent exchange, and comparison of knowledge with our brethren in practice, we are inclined to listen to the suggestions of vanity, and imagine ourselves standards of perfection, while we glide into a dull routine of practice *exclusively* founded on our own limited experience.   The solemn obligation of every practitioner, to bring to the bedside of his patient the most enlightened views of disease, and the best curative means, afforded by the present state of the healing art, is forgotten, and there is a disposition in cases of failure, to seek refuge from the reproaches of an offended consciences in the miserable reflection that "we have done our duty to the best of our knowledge."   An unlimited sanction is thus given to indolence or ignorance, as the case may be; while the high responsibilities, and real dignity of the profession in relieving the sufferings of our fellow creatures, and preserving human life, are lost in their subserviency to a sordid subsistence, and prostituted to purposes purely mercenary.   Deprived of professional intercourse, and little inclined to invigorate the judgment by study and reflection, our intellects tend to assimilate with those of our associates as certainly as heat tends to an equilibrium; and such, moreover, is the disposition of the human mind to collapse, that without the application of powerful incentives, the mere practising physician is especially liable to deteriorate rather than improve.   Other professions would seem to have the advantage of being better comprehended by the mass of mankind, than that of medicine.   Law and theology, although abstract sciences in their extended ramifications, are nevertheless founded in the constitution of human nature.— As every one has a sense of Deity, which is the origin of the one, so every individual has a sense of right and wrong, which is the *sub*-structure of the other science; but where is the man who without much study, and a knowledge especially of anatomy, and the laws of the animal economy, can clearly comprehend a single disease?   While the lawyer therefore, or the divine, may be said to meet with a professional companion in some measure, in every one with whom he is disposed to con-

25*

verse, the physician alone feels himself a stranger in thought, in language, and in action. Whatever may be his stock of knowledge when he begins his career in practice, he soon discovers, if he was not before aware, that he has been taught a science and a language not intelligible to any one out of his profession. To avoid the imputation of pedantry, he retreats within himself, and is in danger of losing not only the principles but even the very nomenclature of his science. To counteract such tendency by creating a spirit of generous emulation, to elevate the profession by exciting a thirst for general knowledge, and to cultivate a taste for observation and inquiry by combining the efforts and skill of physicians in various parts of the country, are surely objects worthy of our institution.

ISAAC HIESTER, M. D., *President.*

Attest: CHARLES BAUM, *Secretary.*

BRIEF SKETCH OF THE HIESTER FAMILY.

The name of Hiester is so extensively connected with the general and State governments, that a brief sketch of the family may not be uninteresting. Their remote ancestors were of Silesian origin. From that country they were distributed throughout Austria, Bavaria, Saxony, Switzerland, and the countries bordering on the river Rhine. The immediate anoestors of the present race of that name in this country, emigrated from Witzenstein, in Westphalia, and arrived in America in the early part of the 18th century. They consisted of three brothers, Daniel, John, and Joseph, who all took up their residence in the first place at Goshen-hoppen, then in Philadelphia, now in Montgomery county. Here Daniel at once purchased a farm which was somewhat improved. After exploring and becoming better acquainted with the country, they united in purchasing from the Proprietary government, between two and three thousand acres of land in Bern township, now Berks county. Here John and Joseph settled, while Daniel remained at the old homestead. Having thus, with the characteristic prudence of those primitive days, first secured the means of supporting families, they next, in due time, formed matrimonial alliances with American women, and "set themselves down, each under his own vine and fig tree," to enjoy, in the pursuit of Agriculture, the fruits of their virtuous enterprize.

As they had been induced to leave their own native country by the vassalage of an oppressive government, which exacted, not only onerous taxes, but also a portion of the time and labor of its subjects, they naturally cherished in the minds of their descendants, a lofty spirit of freedom. Accordingly, when the revolutionary war broke out, they were among the first to enroll themselves in the list of "Associaters." The efficient services of this class of citizen soldiers, which were organized by electing two Brigadier Generals at Lancaster on the 4th of July, 1776, afterwards rendered in the campaigns of N. Jersey, N. York, Delaware, and the lower parts of Pennsylvania, is a well known matter of history. Daniel, of Montgomery, John, of Chester, and Gabriel, of Berks, the three eldest sons of Daniel, entered the service as field officers, the two former with the rank of Colonel, and the latter with that of Major. William, the fourth and youngest son of Daniel, although also enrolled, did not, on account of his extreme youth and the infirmity of his aged parents, serve more than one campaign. Joseph Hiester, afterwards Governor of Pennsylvania, the only son of John, entered the service as a captain in the " Flying Camp," and having been made a prisoner at the battle of Long Island, and confined on board the notorious Jersey Prison Ship, New Jersey, he was, after his exchange, promoted to the rank of Colonel. After the war, he and his two cousins, Daniel and John, were elected to the rank of Majors General of the militia in their respective districts. The popularity these men gained by their devotion to country, and the public spirit during the eventful struggles of the revolutionary war, never forsook them. After the conclusion of peace, they all enjoyed, by the suffrages of the people, a large share in the councils of the State, and general Government. General Daniel Hiester was the first representative in Congress, under the present constitution, from Berks county, of which he had in the meantime become a citizen. In 1796 he removed to Maryland, where he was again repeatedly elected to the same office, from the districts composed of Washington, Frederick and Allegheny counties, until the time of his decease, which occurred at Washington city, in the Session of 1801—2. Joseph Hiester was elected a member of the convention which met in Philadelphia, in November, 1787, to consider and ratify, or reject the present constitution of the United States; and in 1789, he was a member of the convention which formed the second constitution of this State. Under that constitution, he and Gabriel Hiester, who had also been a member of the convention which formed the first State constitution, were repeatedly elected to the legislature, the latter continuing either in the Senate or House of Representatives, uninterruptedly, for nearly thirty years.   General Joseph Hiester, after the removal of Daniel to Maryland, represented his district, composed in part of Berks county, in Congress, and about the same time General John Hiester, was also chosen a member of the same body from Chester county.   Both were re-elected for a series of years—the former, until he resigned in 1820, when he was elected Governor of Pennsylvania, and the latter until he declined a re-election, and retired to private life.*

* See pages 175 to 180, antea.

HISTORY

OF

LEBANON COUNTY.

CHAPTER I.

LEBANON COUNTY ERECTED.

It has been shown, in a preceding page, (117,) that Philadelphia, Bucks and Chester counties were established in 1682; Lancaster in 1729; York in 1749; Cumberland in 1750; Berks in 1752; which, prior to that time, was a part of Lancaster county, as well as Lebanon; and afterwards, till 1785, when Dauphin county was separated from Lancaster, embracing the whole of Dauphin and Lebanon counties, till then.

Lebanon county was formed from parts of the counties of Dauphin and Lancaster, by an act of Assembly, passed February 16, 1813. Its present limits are as follows:

It is bounded on the north-east by Berks and Schuylkill counties, on the south-east by Lancaster, on the south-west and north-west by Dauphin; length and breadth, seventeen miles—containing two hundred and eighty-eight square miles—being a little more than one-fourth the superficial area of Berks county.

Though Lebanon is small, yet it is one of the finest counties in the State of Pennsylvania. It forms a part of the great transition formation, lying chiefly between the south mountain and the Kittatiny range. "It is distinguished for the fertility of its soil, and the value of its agricultural productions. The

26

limestone land is generally considered the best; but in the cal-
careus portions of the slate formation, there are many excellent and highly productive farms:"*

The greater proportion of the original settlers of this part of
Pennsylvania, was German, except the western and north-western part of Lebanon county, Londonderry township, which
was originally settled by Scotch and Irish, whose descendants;
however, have nearly all disappeared, and given place to the
present industrious, frugal and thrifty German population.

The history of the early settlements and Indian massacres;
is so completely merged with the history of Berks, that little
of interest, separately considered, remains to be noticed. Besides, but little has been preserved, by record or tradition, of
the early history of the portion embraced within the present
limits of Lebanon county. What has been preserved, and what
has been gleaned, is, however, of an authentic character. The
best sources have been resorted to.

In the history, as well as the topographical description of the
townships of this country, Lebanon township being among the
first settled and organized, claims precedence.

LEBANON TOWNSHIP.

Lebanon township was, till 1739, a large township, when in
May of that year, the Court of Lancaster, ordered that _Bethel_
township be erected, which was then bounded as follows:—
"That the division line begin at Swatara creek, at a stony
ridge, about half a mile below John Tittle's, and continuing
along the said ridge easterly to Tolpehocken township, to the
northward of Tobias Pickels, so as to leave John Benaugle,
Adam Steel, Thomas Ewersly and Mathias Tise, to the south-
ard of the said line; that the northernmost division be named,
and called Bethel—the southern division continue the name
Lebanon. When Berks county was erected the greater part
of Bethel was included by and separated with that county.

Lebanon township was first settled by Germans; many of
whose descendants are still the owners of their ancestors'

* C. B. Trego's Geog. of Pa., p. 274.

first warranted lands. The first settlers of the county were some families of the Tulpehocken settlements, in the western part of it—now within the eastern limits of Lebanon. These have been noticed before.

The rude huts, erected and occupied by these and others of the first settlers, have long since peiished, and in their stead, others were erected, and these in their turn are superseded by others of more durable materials, and more commodious. Where the scrub oaks stood thick, there are now highly improved farms, fertile fields, and smiling gardens. The persevering efforts of the husbandman are richly crowned.

The first settlers, for the want of better ones, had to help themselves, as well as they could, with simple and rude utensils, furniture and fixtures, both culinary and agricultural; their accommodations and comforts were agrestical. Wide contrast —instead of puncheon floors, carpets deck smooth plained ones.

One instance—hundreds might be given—of the first settlers in this township will be noticed. The writer's father's maternal grandfather, *Michael Burst*, a Palatine, on arriving in Philadelphia, in August 1729, wended his course by Manatawny and Tulpehocken, westward some seventy-five miles into the wilderness, from the town of Philadelphia, squatted among the Indians, on a tract of land two miles north-west from the present site of the town of Lebanon. The farm is now owned by *Joseph Light*, near Lebanon.

Burst's nearest white neighbors were the Noacres and Spykers, and others, who had settled in 1723 to 1729, at the west end of the Tulpehocken settlement. To answer his wants, he erected a cabin or hut—not unlike the shantees put up by the Irish a few years ago, near the same place, when excavating the canal.

When Michael Burst ,or Boarst, left Germany for America, he was accompanied by rising of seventy Palatine families, making in all about one hundred and eighty persons. They were imported in the ship Mortonhouse, James Coultas, master, from Rotterdam, but last from Deal, as by clearance thence dated, 21st of June, 1729. They arrived in August, and signed the following declaration the 19th of August.

We, subscribers, natives and late inhabitants of the Palatinate

upon the Rhine, and places adjacent, having transported ourselves and families into this Province of Pennsylvania, a colony
subject to the crown of Great Britain, in hopes and expectation
of finding a retreat and peaceable settlement therein, do solemnly promise and engage, that we will be faithful, and bear true
allegiance to his present Majesty, King George the Second,
and his successor, King of Great Britain, and will be faithful
to the Proprietor of this Province; and that we will demean
ourselves peaceably to all his said Majesty's subjects, and
strictly observe and conform to the laws of England, and of
this Province, to the utmost of our power, and best of our understanding.

Among others who sailed in the same ship, were the following:—John Philip Rank, John Miller, Michael Urelick, Jacob
Bowman, Dirick Adam Weidle, John Rice, Christopher Bum-
garner, Johannes Orde, Jacob Fetter, Jacob Eshelman, Christopher Fry, Jacob Over, David Mantandon, Martin Alstadtant,
Adam Schambach, Valentine Fikus, Conrad Killinor, Johannes
Brinkler, Casper Dorest.*

The region of country in which he located, was previously known
among the Indians as "*Quitopaheela,*" i. e., *Snake Harbor;* for
Burst's first work, in the morning, was, to kill snakes, in and
outside of the hut. For the want of earthen ware, they used
gourds or calabashes, as drinking cups, and for "milk pans."

Burst's location formed a kind of nucleus for a more dense
and extended settlement. George Steitz soon followed Burst,
and located south-east from him, on the Quitopahila creek.
The greater proportion of land between Steitz's and Burst's,
was located by Casper Wiester, the brass button-maker, (and
son-in-law of Mr. Zimmerman, of Lancaster county,) who sold
several hundred acres, in 1738, to John Licht, grandfather of
Joseph Licht; or, as now spelt—Light. The Deed describes
the southern boundary of this farm, "South by George Steitz's
settlement," &c.

Among others who settled in and about Burst's and Steitz's,
besides Licht, at this period, were Peter Kuecher, Martin
Meylin, Henrich Klein, John Adam Kettring, John George
Hederick, Jacob Rieger, Anastatius Uhler. Though many of
them commenced with small means, they acquired so much of

* Col. Rec. iii 390.

this world's goods, as to render them not only comfortable, but many grew rich. From the subjoined inventory of goods and chattels, the property of Michael Burst, deceased,* it will be seen that he was well calculated to settle in a new country. It is evident he had all the necessaries to get along, and help his neighbors too.

An account of the effects that belonged to the dec'd, Michael Burst.

Five head of horses and mares, £14, 10, 0. Eight head of cows, £13, 10, 0,	£28
Six sheep, £1, 10. The dec'd, Michael Burst's clothes, £1, 3,	3 10 0
A gun, 6s. Two spinning wheels, 8s. Woollen and linen yarn, £1, 3,	1 17 0
A piece of linen cloth, £2. Two stone bottles 4s,	2 4 0
Four books, £1. Two chests, 7s. A tailor's shears and goose, 3s,	1 10 0
A hammer and anvil, 4s. Two augurs and a drawing knife, 5s,	0 9 0
A log chain, 13s. A plantation wagon, plough and gears, £2, 10,	3 3 0
A cutting knife and steel, 9s. Old iron tools, £1,	1 9 0
Earthen ware, 4s. Wooden vessels, 13s. Eight bags, 15s,	1 12 0
A saddle and bridle, 10s. A sow and pigs, 12s. The plantation, £40,	41 2 0
Debts owing to Michael Burst from Adam Clately, £8, 10, and Henry Peters, £4,10,	13 0 0
	£99 15 0

This part of the county being the garden spot, soon a large number of families, Mennonites and others, settled thick around here. The massive three story house, with a "hipped roof," erected by John Licht in 1742, was a regular monthly meeting place, where the Mennonites met for worship. The Moravians also had a house of worship erected prior to 1743, hard by the

* Michael Burst died in 1741 The widow, Barbara Burst, administered, entered into bond, to faithfully execute her trust. Her sureties were George. Steitz and Anastatius Uhler Bond, entered at Lancaster, Nov. 3, 1741.

Quitopahilla, a mile east of the present site of Lebanon, and a few hundred yards north from the stone *Oratorium*, which was built in 1750.

The Moravian communion was considerable. In 1748, they held a synod for the transaction of ecclesiastical business in the wooden building, on the banks of Quitopahila. Loskiel says:

"Soon after Bishop Cammerhof's return from Shamokin, a synod was held in Quitopahila; in which the mission among the Indians was considered with much attention, and the following principles reviewed and approved:

1. The Brethren do not think, that they are called to baptize whole nations; for it is more to the purpose, to gain one converted soul, than to persuade many to take merely the name and outward form of christianity.

2. We are not discouraged by the dangers and hardships attending the labor among the heathens, but always bear in remembrance, that our Lord endured distress and death itself, to gain salvation for us, and rested not till the great work was finished. If, after the most strenuous exertions of soul and body, one soul is gained for Christ, we have an ample reward.

3. We will continue to preach nothing to the heathen but Jesus, and him crucified, repeating the same testimony of his gospel, till the hearts of the heathen are awakened to believe; being fully convinced, that the power of the eross is the word of God, which is alone able to bring souls from darkness into light.

4. The missionaries should never reject any heathen, not even the most abandoned and profligate, but consider them as persons, to whom the grace of Jesus Christ ought to be offered."—Loskiel, P. ii. p. 108, 109.

The names of the principal families connected with the Hebron station, or Quitopahila church, were Kuecher, Meylin, Klein, Kettring, Hederick, Rieger, Huber, Rathforn, Wagner, Waschebach, Olinger, Schmal, George, Teis, Trachsler, Rewald, Mies, Urich, Danneberger, Heckedorn, Christman, Struebig, Stoehr, Etler, German, Orth.

Lebanon township contained in 1750, nearly one hundred and thirty taxables, as appears from the Tax Duplicate. Adam

Ulrich, was collector for that year. Their names have been preserved, and are as follows:

Jacob Steiner, Ulrich Burkholder, Robert Boyd, John Espy, Jacob Helenger, George Berger, John Schnog, Michael Boarst, Benjamin Brechtbill, Jacob Maron, Joseph Gingerich, Christian Neave, Michael Gingerich, George Miller, Ulrich Zollinger, Nicholas Huber, Peter Smith, Wollerich Steiner, Baltsar Road, Peter Witmer, Martin Miley, Felix Landis, Henry Bowman, John Gerber, Jacob Stouffer, Peter Gingerich, John Heisey, George Hetterick, Michael Holt, John Adam Schneider, Oswald Neis, George Strohm, Jacob Woolf, Andrew Wild, William Burgholder, Abraham Witman, George Peters, Leonard Young, John Helams, Christian Better, Harman Egel, Daniel Seiler, Abraham Corman, Michael Wambler, Jacob Diets, Jacob Meyers, Nicholas Neig, Jacob Hubman, Michael Schuneher, Adam Wenrich, Mathew Strawer, Henry Sanders, John Schalley, Philip Park, Jonathan Heid, Ralph Whiteside, John Troxel, Casper Lieper, John Licht, sen., George Elliger, Thomas Hammersly, John Hallenbach, Leonard Umberger, Thomas Clarke, John Clarke, Michael Polter, John M'Clintick, Richard Robertson, Peter Gingerich, Jacob Geremor, Philip Byers, John Brechtbill, Christopher Simonus, John Bernwalt, Henry Smith, Jacob Bian, Adam Bog, John Kreider, Henry Little, Jacob Graf, Christian Kreider, Christopher Myers, Jacob Hersberger, John Dewalt, Martin Hooi, Peter Woolf, Philip Ologer, Robert Warner, Conrad Braun, Adam Wolert, John Schwob, George Schitz, Martin Hostetter, Geo. Huber, John Whitmore, Peter Hailman, Peter Yoder, Christian Long, Peter Yerte, Nicholas Erb, Nicholas Ellenberger, John Myers, Benjamin Noll, Jacob Freely, Adam Brand, Michael Teis, Philip Schaeffer, Henry Waschenbach, John Stohler, Thielman Waschenbach, Warner Fuller, John Licht, Michael Wagoner, Francis Reynolds, John Egesohn, Charles Schally, Christopher Meyer, Andrew Miller, Peter Ebersohl, Michael Bachman.

That the increase of population was constant, will appear on comparing the names of the taxables of the above list with the names that follows, for 1755:

Philip Sheffer, Jacob Sheffer, Michael Tyce, Adam Brand, Adam Brand, jr., John Brand, Abraham Smutz, Baniel Higendorn, Peter Kucher, George Hettrick, Jno. Light, jr., Jacob

Light, John Light, sen., George Steitz, John Miller, Peter
Slosser, Herman Orendorff, John Seiler, Martin Hoff, Adam
Weibel, Jacob Zolicker, John Schultz, Michael Singer, Henry
Ushenbach, Jacob Gemberling, Christopher Miller, John Adam
Reifwein, Conrad Ziegler, Jacob Schwobe, John Adam Miller,
Conrad Wise, Hermau Eckel, John Atkinson, Jacob Creesman,
Jacob Blaser, Michael Stegbed, John Kemmerling, Bartholo-
maus Kuntzelman, Lenhart Umberger, Anastasius Uhler, Michael
Wagner, Philip Meeshy, William Blegher, Peter Wolf, Nich-
olas Ackerman, Jacob Heger, Dietrich Weitzel, Christ. Bren-
zer, Heury Ehler, Menhard Sebold, Geo. Elinger, Jacob Graff,
Adam Bough, Christian Kreiter, Martin Kreiter, John Kreiter,
Henry Little, Christopher Mier, Felix Landis, Henry Bowman,
Henry Smith, Jacob Giles, John Gerber, Philip Star, Conrad
Brown, Jacob Stouffer, Peter Gingerich, Michael Gingerich,
Jost Gingerich, John Hiesey, Michael Horst, Jacob Meyer,
Adam Nicodemus, Geo. Diehl, Oswal Neave, Dorst Thomas,
Christian Strohm, Jacob Schock, John Becher, Geo. Gloss-
brenner, Geo. Huber, Philip Clinger, John Haushalter, John
Dinius, Adam Steger, Martin Illy, Jacob Graff, jr., John Gam-
ber, Ralph Whiteside, Joseph Espy, Charles Shally, Michael
Bachman, Christian Burkholder, John Ebersohl, Michael Boor,
Abraham Heit, Michael Boltz, Philip Rudesill, Jacob Froliek,
Ludwick Shally, Geo. Berger, John Snook, Gerhard Etter,
Michael Zimmerman, Christian Blouch, Benj. Knall, Geo. Die-
trich, John Brechbill, Dewalt Lichty, Daniel Resor, Philip
Byer, Michael Fernsler, Hans Ulrich Huber, Frederick Kauf-
man, Nicholas Ellingberger, John Wilhelm, Peter Frank, John
Ellenberger, Nicholas Erb, Goo. Hopengortner, Peter Eschel-
man, Christian Long, John Doner, Henry Xander, Peter Wit-
mer, Casper Weaver, John Bachman, Ulrich Burkholder, Con-
rad Mintziger, Jacob Benedict, Mathias Boger, Henry Frick,
Michael Wampler, Jacob Brenizer, Christian Miller, Jacob
Horschberger, Delman Klein, Jacob Wolf, Jacob Killinger,
Jacob Beam, Peter Reise, Michael Henry, Michael Kinnert,
Casper Seller, Peter Schweigert, Mathias Strayer, Christian
Neave, John Huber, Richard Crain, Geo. Mintzer, Michael
Ulerich, Ulrich Stephan, Martin Kerstetor, Adam Ulrich, Hen-
ry Humberger, Thomas Clark, John Clark, Adam Steer, Henry
Peter, Peter Yorty, Martin Mily, Adam Hailman, Abraham
Kornman, Peter Hailman, Rudolph Miller, Peter Smith, Chris-

tian Herschberger, Nicholas Neu, Richard Robison, John Spiger, Andrew Weltz, Peter Kremer, John Siegrist, Michael Boltz, Daniel Seiber, Abraham Weidman, John M'Clintock, John Casper Stover, Conrad Templeman, Abraham Sheafer, Ulrich Wampler, George Crusman, Henry Smith, Henry Bowman.

Lebanon, the county seat, is in this township; little, however, of its early history has been preserved. There is a diversity of opinion, even as to the time when it was laid out.— According to *Robert Proud*, who wrote a *History of the Province* between 1760 and 1773, "Lebanon was laid out about the year 1759; and in 1772, it is said to contain above two hundred good dwelling houses, many of them large and well built of stone, dug out of the ground where the houses stand, and principally inhabited by Germans."*

Another writer, Rev. George Lochman, D. D., whose opportunities for research were favorable, and whose statement is worthy of credit, says, " Diese Stadt, *Libanon*, ist im Jahr, 1756 von George Steitz ausgelegt worden, und liegt an dem Fluss *Quitopahilla* (ein Indianischer Name, der auf Deutch, *Schlangenloch* heist.)†

An eastern gentleman, S. Day, says, "Lebanon—or Steitzetown, as it was for a long time called, and still by many of the old Germans—was probably laid out about the year 1750, by one Steitze."‡

Touching Day's statement, it might, *passing*, be remarked, that there is nothing *problematical* as to the town *being laid out*. No German seems to doubt this. All agree it *was laid out*. As to the time *when*, there is some difference of opinion. As to this, there is some "guessing."

The late Col. Adam Ritscher's father, was, says Day, one of the first settlers, and paid ground rent, as appears by receipts still extant, as early as 1751, (1761?) He cleared the lot west of the one upon which his son Adam *lived*, from the forest then standing.§

During the French and Indian war, this place being then

* R. Proud's His. Pa. ii. 284.
† Evang. Mag. for 1812, vol. i, p. 20
‡ S. Day's His. Col. 420.
§ S. Day's His. Col. 420.

already densely settled, was resorted to, as a place of safety,
by hundreds of families, who fled from the frontier settlements,
to escape being murdered by the barbarous savages, whose cruelty knew no bounds—they were insatiable. Sixty families
had, at one time, taken shelter in the house of John Light,
which is still standing, and known among the people there, as
the "Old Fort." The house of Mr. George Gloninger was
also a place of usual resort. Besides these, and some other
private houses, the Moravian church, erected in 1750, a mile
and a half east of Gloninger's, was occupied by refugees, the
principal part of whom had fled from the Moravian settlements
in Bethel township.* Loskiel, alluding to this fact, says, "the
savages continued to commit murders in Allemaengel—and a
lance lost by them on the road, proved them to be some of the
very people who attended the Congress (treaty) at Easton.
Roving parties infested the borders of the country, the public
roads, and all other places in which they found no resistance, so that the small colonies of brethren settled in Allemaengel and Bethel, on Swatara, who had held out with uncommon patience, were at last obliged to take refuge, the former in Bethlehem, and the latter in Lebanon†—this was in
1756. Some of them soon returned again to their farms, and
not a few of them were surprised by the Indians and cruelly
murdered. One John Spitler, son-in-law to Jacob Meylin,
who was the grandfather of Martin Meylin, of Jonestown, was
shot dead while fixing up a pair of bars—his body cruelly mangled. Mrs. Miley escaped by taking refuge in the watch-house,
at her father's, a few miles from Stumptown. This happened
in May, 1757. Spittler's mangled corpse was interred in the
grave-yard at Hebron, near Lebanon.

The following, touching the murder of Spittler, is found in
the Records of the Hebron Church. "1751, May den 16,
wurde Johannes Spitler, jr., ohnweit von seinem Hause an der
Schwatara von moerderischen Indianern ueberfallen und ermor-
dert. Er war im acht und dreisigsten Jahr seines Alters, und
verwichenes Jahr im April, an der Schwatara auf genommen.
Seine uebelzugerichttete Leiche wurde den 17ten May bieher

* Loskiel, P. ii., p. 180.
† There is still an old meeting house remaining at Swatara, in which the
Rev. Simon reaches occasionally.

gebracht, und bei einer grossen Menge Leute begleitet auf unsern hiesigen Gottes-acker beerdigt.

During the Revolutionary war of '76, many of the residents
of this place, a few of whom are still living, took up arms in
common with many of their fellow patriots, in defence of American liberty, and were engaged in the battle of Trenton, N. Jersey, December 25, 1776, when the Hessians were routed with
great slaughter, and one thousand of them taken prisoners, and
not a few of them taken to Reading, and to Lebanon, where
they were confined in the old Lutheran Church in town, and
the Moravian Church below town. Some of the citizens of
Lebanon also took a part in the battle at Germantown, October 4th, 1777. They constituted a portion of the Pennsylvania
militia, three thousand strong, under the command of General
Armstrong, whose march on this occasion, it is said, is enwrapt
in mystery. "Some reports say, that he actually engaged the
Hessian division of the enemy, others state that the alarm of
the Americans retreating from Mr. Chew's stone house reached
his ear, as the vanguard of his command entered Germantown,
near the market house, and commenced firing upon the chas-
scurs who flanked the left wing of the British army." But to
return to the county town. In 1840, the following pensioners
were still living in the borough; George Hess, aged 79 years;
Andrew Hoover, 75; Dilman Daup, 81; M. Weaver, 75 years
old.

Lebanon, so called after the county, which was so named, as
some suppose, in allusion to the Lebanon of the Scripture, a
famous range of mountains in the north of Canaan, is pleasantly
situated on a branch of Quitopaheela creek, twenty miles from
the Capitol, and seventy-five miles from the metropolis of the
State, on the turnpike; and contiguous to the Union Canal. It
is well laid out, and regularly built—the buildings are principally of stone, or brick, and generally commodious, though there
are but few large buildings in it, except the court house, which
is a spacious and splendid edifice of brick, surmounted by a cupola. The county officers are in this building. In the area,
in the centre of the borough, is a market house. There is, as
a necessary indispensable, a jail; but, of late, it has had only
a few inmates. There are, in the borough proper, which was
incorporated Feb. 20, 1821, about three hundred dwellings—

some ten or more taverns, and a like number of stores, one grist mill, one clover mill, a foundry, and many mechanics shops.

There are in this place a number of churches—the Lutheran which was erected in 1798, and dedicated the 3d of June—it is built of stone, with a large steeple. In 1808 it was supplied with an organ. The Lutherans had, previously, a log church, erected in 1766. Prior to that time, a congregation had been organized—they had held their meetings in a private house, rented for that purpose.

The German Reformed church, was erected of stone about the year 1787, and is at present undergoing some alterations. A Catholic chapel of brick; a Methodist meeting house of brick; one owned by the Evangelical Association; a United Brethren Church; a Mennonite meeting house are here. At present here is another Lutheran Church building under the pastoral care of Rev. J. Rothrauf.

The respective pastors of these churches are the Rev. Ernst, of the Lutheran congregation, who officiates in German; Rev. Rothrauf, in English. The Lutherans number rising of four hundred members. The Rev. Henry Wagner is the pastor of the German Reformed church—this congregation numbers between two hundred and fifty, and three hundred members.— The Evangelical Association has upwards of one hundred members—their pastors are, the Rev'ds Danner and Sailor. The Methodist Episcopal has about one hundred members; the Rev. Greenbank has the pastoral charge of this congregation. Rev. Steinbach officiates in the Catholic chapel; number of members about eighty. The United Brethern number probably twenty members.

There are five Sabbath Schools here, and all well attended; numbering between 500 and 600 children. The Borough contains 404 families, and an adult population of 1092. The entire population, by the census of 1840, was, of the borough proper, 1,860.

The Union canal passes contiguous to the borough, affording great facilities to business, where the bustling, neat village of North Lebanon is growing up beautifully and rapidly. It will outgrow Lebanon proper.

The means of education are favorable. There is a fine academy here, and ably conducted by Mr. Kluge, whose efficient system of instruction cannot be too highly appreciated.—

has been said that he is not sufficiently encouraged, because the importance of a proper education of youth, and its influence upon the habits and character, in after life, do not seem to be well considered. This is to be much regretted. The academy contains between thirty and forty scholars. It was incorporated in 1816, to which the State made a donation of $2000. There is also a female seminary here, and it is said to be well conducted. All the young ladies in town and country should attend it. Where the acquisition of wealth is appreciated and trade understood, a bank would be deemed necessary—such an institution is here—it is judiciously managed. The inhabitants are nearly all German, who usually, in addressing a stranger, speak in their vernacular tongue, though nearly all can speak some English. They are hospitable, frugal and industrious; many of them own out lots, and may be seen at work, in summer, barefooted.

There are several newspapers published here—of these some account is given when speaking of the " Press." Near the town is a stationary steam engine, by which water is raised from the Quitopahila and conducted to the canal!!

The original boundaries of Lebanon township have, by reducing and dividing it, since its erection, June 9th, 1729, been materially changed. In 1729, its boundaries were thus defined : " Lebanon township beginning under the aforesaid hill, (i. e., the *Kehtotoning** hill*, above Peter Allen's,) at the north-east corner of *Peshtank*,† thence by the said hill, easterly, to the Tolpehocken manor, thence southerly by the said line, to the hills bounding Warwick township, thence by the said hills and township, westerly, to the corner of Derry, on Conewago, thence northerly by Derry and Peshtank, to the place of beginning."

In 1739 it was reduced, by erecting Bethel township. In 1830, it was bounded as follows :—but since, divided into North and South Lebanon—on the north, by Swatara and Bethel townships; east by Jackson and Heidelberg townships; south by Lancaster county, and west by Londonderry and Annville townships. Greatest length, eleven miles; greatest breadth, seven miles—containing 44,700 acres of first rate land—surface very level, and principally limestone soil. The improvements

---

* Kittatinny, or Blue mountain.
† Paxton.

27

are of the first rate order. There are many fine buildings in this township:

North and South Lebanon are well watered: The Quitopahila creek, a beautiful, fine stream, flows through the borough of Lebanon, and in its course propels several mills. The Union Canal, and Reading and Harrisburg turnpike, pass through North Lebanon township. Iron ore is found in abundance—in South Lebanon, in the Conewago hills, and in the south part of this township. Cornwall Furnace, erected at the head of Furnace creek, is supplied with ore from these mines. The furnace is owned by B. D. Coleman. The streams are the head of Tulpehocken, Hammer creek, Kuder creek, Meadow run, and head of Conewago creek.

North and South Lebanon, in 1840, contained seventeen stores, three lumber yards, eight grist mills, five tanneries, three distilleries, two breweries, three potteries, four printing offices, three weekly papers and one periodical, one academy—fifty students, eleven schools—four hundred and twenty scholars: Population in 1830, 3,556; in 1840, 6,197. Tax valuation for North Lebanon in 1844, $569,465; county tax, $854 20: South Lebanon, $1,238,750; county tax, $1,858 13.

BETHEL TOWNSHIP.

Bethel township was part of Lebanon township, till May, 1739, when it was separated, by an order of Court, at Lancaster. It was divided, and bounded as follows, viz:

" That the division line begin at Swatara creek, at a stony ridge, about half a mile below John Tittle's, and continuing along the said ridge, easterly, to Tolpehocken township, to the northward of Tobias Pickel's, so as, in the course, to leave John Benaugle, Adam Steel, Thomas Ewersly and Mathias Tise, to the southward of the line—that the northermost division be named and called Bethel—the southern division continue the name Lebanon." Bethel then embraced, also, what is now Swatara township and part of Union.

When Berks county was erected, in 1752, part of this township was separated and included within the limits of that county. It was, no doubt, so called after a colony of Moravians,

who had a small establishment on the Swatara, in this township, called Bethel—the literal import of the term, is "the
house of God." The Moravian colony, formed here, was one
among their first in Pennsylvania. In 1737, Mr. Spangenberger, a Moravian missionary, having fulfilled his appointment in
establishing the mission in Georgia, came to Pennsylvania,
where he remained for some time, and thence to St. Thomas,
one of the West India islands, to hold a visitation in that mission. He then returned, and remained in Pennsylvania till
1739. Through him, it is said, the United Brethren were made
attentive to other Indian nations, especially the Iroquois, or Six
Nations. Mr. Spangenberger received the first notice of them
from Conrad Weiser, justice of the peace, and interpreter to the
government in Pennsylvania.*

They erected a church here about 1740. The Rev. Johannes Brand Mueller officiated here, about the year 1744. The
names of their members are still preserved—a few of them we
were permitted, by the politeness of the Rev. Henry Francis
Simon, their present pastor at Hebron, near Lebanon, to copy
from the " Schwatarer Kirchen Buch, containing ein Verzeich-
niss der Brueder der Gemeine und deren Kindern welche von
den Bruedern sind getauft worden von April Anno 1743.

Among their first members here, were Rudolph Hauck, Ja-
cob Dueps, Wilhelm Fischer, Ludwig Born, Johan Frederich
Weiser, Christian Bimmer, George Miesse, Jacob Gausser
Thomas Williams, Franz Albert, Jacob Haentchy, Daniel
Born, Michael Kohr, Johannes Spitler, Bernhard Faber, Casper
Korr.

This township was originally, nearly wholly settled by Germans and some French Huguenots: of the latter, was Franz
Albert, a native of *Deux-ponts*, born in 1719, July 20, and who
came to this country when a young man, and was afterwards
cruelly murdered by the Indians, June 26, 1756. As early as
1751, the following taxables resided in this township:

*John Ebrecht, James Macnees, David Fischer, Jacob Mire,
Mathias Grey, Mr. Folk, Edmund Schnebly, John Schnebly,
John Reynolds, John King, Abraham Stettler, Jacob Miley,
Urbin Long, Peter Groff, Han Nickle Garst, Dewalt Garst,
Philip Wolf, Rudy Huntsecker, Widow Gray, Widow Brecht-*

* Loskiel His Mis. P. ii., p. 4.

bill, Casper Sherrick, Jacob Oberholtzer, Henry Wagoner, Henry Dubs, Henry Souter, Peter Kenny, Christian Leaman, Peter Clop, Adam Berger, Abraham Hubbler, Wendel Heyl, Barned Boughs, Jacob Weaver, Killian Long, Christian Long, Jacob Schnebly, Jno. Kneagy, Dewald Nabinger, Abraham Grove, Jacob Wagoner, Adam Snider, Jacob Miller, Jacob Carner, Nicholas Benner, Casper Hisler, Frederick Tibbin, Jno. Bickle, Henry Bohn, Henry Mark, Isaac Schnelby, Henry Kelker, John Martin, Henry Sietz, Crom Jacob Mire, George Miess, Nicholas Wirrigh, Martin Kemmerling, Ludwig Waiten, Andrew Hollo, Christian Lantz, Adam Kline, Christian Leaman, John Mish, Frederick Rudy, Peter Forster, Jacob Goldman, Joseph Stout, Wm. Jones, Samuel Stout, Andrew Kaufman, Conrad Gerhart, Valentine Gerhart, John Wingerd, Henry Schnebly, Henry Stiegle, Ulrich Yeakle, Valentine Keifer, Peter Gray, John Bop, Philip Creesman, Thos. Mottern, George Fredrick, Anthony Nagle, Casper Stover, jr., Isaiah Casaway, Peter Smith, Thomas Mayberre, Jacob Albert, Daniel Schuhy, Ludwick Schuhy, Michael Frantz, Mathias Loser, Conrad Lor, Gotlieb Torrom, Nicholas Schonty.

During the French and Indian war, notwithstanding there was a line of provincial forts extending along the frontiers of Dauphin, Lebanon and Berks counties, intended as defences against the incursions of the savages, and as places of security, many of the inhabitants of this part of the county were most cruelly murdered, their houses burnt, their children taken captive. In November, 1755, twenty persons were killed, and some children carried off by the Indians. "Shocking," says the Secretary of the Province, in his statement to the Assembly, "are the descriptions given, by those who escaped, of the horrid cruelties and indecencies, committed by the merciless savages, on the bodies of those unhappy wretches, who fell into the hands, especially the women, without regard to age or sex, these far exceeds those related of the most abandoned pirates."[*]

In June, 1756, the Indians again appeared in this township, and committed, in cold blood, cruel and deliberate murder.

On the 8th of June, in the afternoon, between three and four o'clock, four or five Indians made an incursion, at a place called " The Hole," where the Great Swatara runs through the

Prov. Rec. N., p. 342.

Blue mountain—they crept up, unobserved, behind the fence of Felix Wuench, shot him, as he was ploughing, through the breast—he cried lamentably, and run, but the Indians soon came up with him: he defended himself some time with his whip—they cut his head and breast with their tomahawks, and scalped him. His wife heard his cries, and the report of two guns—ran out of the house, but was soon taken by the enemy, who carried her, with one of her own and two of her sister's children away with them, after setting the house on fire and otherwise destroying property.

A servant boy, who was at some distance, seeing this, ran to his neighbor, George Miess; though he had a bad leg, with his son, ran directly after the Indians, and raised a great noise, which so frightened the Indians, that they immediately took to their heels, and in their flight left a tub of butter, and a side of bacon, behind them. Mr. Miess then went to the house, which was in flames, and threw down the fences, in order to save the barn. The Indians had drunk all the brandy in the spring house, and took several gammons, a quantity of meal, some loaves of bread, and a great many other things with them.

Had Mr. Miess not been so courageous, they probably would have attacked another house. They shot one of the horses in the plough, and dropped a large French knife."*

Shortly after committing the above mentioned murder, the Indians killed a child of Lawrence Dippel's. The child was found cruelly murdered and scalped—a boy about four years old. Another lad about six years old was carried off.†

On the 26th of June, 1756, the Indians killed four persons, scalped them, and shot two horses. Two men, Franz Albert and Jacob Haendsche, and two lads, Frederick Weiser and John George Miess, were ploughing in the field of one Fischer, were surprised, murdered and scalped by the Indians, as appears from an extract taken from the *Schwatarer Kirchen Buch*:

In dem Wilden Krieg sind folgende vier Brueder, Franz Albert, Jacob Haendsche, zwei Maenner; Friedrich Wieser und John George Miess, zwei Knaben, die in der Hohl welche, da sie daselbst auf des alten Fischers Feld, um der Gefahr wegen gemein schaeftlich pfluegten Nachmittags, den 26 ten Juli, 1756, von den Wilden Indianern zugleich ploetzlich ueberfal-

* Pa Gaz , June 17, 1756
† Pa. Gaz , June 17, 1756

len, getoedet und gescalpt worden; und Sontags den 27 ten Juni, mit einer Starken Bedeckung von Sold aten und auderer Mannschaft aus der Hohl gefahren und mit einem Starken Gefolg von etwa zwei hundert Menschen, unter Bruder Friederich Schlegel's Liturgie, im Beysein des Bruder Samuel Herrs, der auch zu der Zeit hierwar, zugleich auf unser Gottes Acker, unter einem Gotlesfrieden beerdigt worden.

From the same book, it appears Franz Albert was born at Deux-Ponts, July 20, 1719—he was a shoemaker by profession, formerly a member of the Reformed Church. J. Haendsche was a mason by trade, also formerly a member of the Reformed Church. Weiser was born May 21, 1740, and Miess, September 28, 1739.

The Rev. Muhlenberg relates, in the Hallische Nachrichten, page 1029, an affecting case of a widow woman, who called at his house in the month of February, 1765. This lady had been a member of one of the Rev. Kurtz's congregations. She was a native of Reutlinge, Wirtemberg—she and her husband had emigrated to this country, and settled on the frontiers of this county. The Indians fell upon them, October the 16th, 1755—according to her statement, the Indians killed the old man, one of his sons, and carried off two small girls, while she and one of her sons had been absent. On her return home she found their dwelling reduced to ashes—she then fled to the interior settlements at Tulpehocken, and remained there.

The Rev. Todd, in his *Sabbath School Teacher*, alludes to the same affecting incident. In addressing his youthful readers he says:

You are aware, my dear pupils, that many of the early settlers of Pennsylvania came from Germany. Among the 'numerous emigrants, from that country, was a poor man with a large family. At that time "there were no schools here during the week, or on the Sabbath, and no churches. So the poor man used to keep his family at home on the Sabbath, and teach them from God's word—for he was a very good man. In the year 1754, a dreadful war broke out in Canada, between the French and English. The Indians joined the French, and used to go to Pennsylvania, burn houses, murder the people and carry off every thing they wanted. They found the dwelling of this poor German family. The man, and his eldest boy, and two little girls, named Barbara and Regina, were at home, while the wife, and one of the boys were gone to carry some grain to the mill, a few miles off. The Indians at once killed the man, and his son, and took the two little girls, one aged ten, and the other nine, and carried them away, along with a great many other weeping children whom they had taken after murdering their parents. It was never known what became of Barbara, the eldest girl; but Regina, with another little girl of two years old, whom Regina had never seen before, were given to an old Indian woman, who was very cruel. Her only son lived with her, and supported her; but he was sometimes gone for several weeks, and then the old woman used to send the little girls to gather roots and herbs in the woods, for the old woman to eat; and when they did not get enough, she used to beat them cruelly. Regina never forgot her good father and mother, and the little girl always kept close to her. She taught the little girl to kneel down under the trees and pray to the Lord Jesus, and to say over with her all the hymns which her parents had taught her. In this state of slavery these children lived for many long years, till Regina was about nineteen, and her little friend was about eleven years old. Their hearts all this time seemed to wish for that which is good. They used to repeat, not only the texts of Scripture which Regina could remember, but there was one favorite hymn which they often repeated over.

"In the year 1764, the kindness of God brought the English Colonel Bouquet to the place where they were. He conquered the Indians, and made them ask for peace. He granted it on condition that all the white prisoners should be given to him.— More than four hundred were brought to the Colonel; and among them, these two girls. They were all poor, wretched looking objects. The Colonel carried them to Carlisle, and had it printed in all the newspapers, that all parents who had lost children by the Indians, might come and see if they were among the four hundred poor captives." Parents and husbands went hundreds of miles in hopes of meeting lost wives or children. The collection amounted to several thousand, and the sight of beholding relatives, who had been cruelly sundered, again meet and rush into each others arms, filled the whole company with rejoicing. There was also mourning. Others who were disappointed in their expectations of finding relatives,. made much lamentation. Among them was "poor Regina's sorrowing mother. When she got to Carlisle she did not, and could not know Regina. She had grown up, and looked, and dressed, and spoke like the Indians. The mother went up and down among the captives weeping, but could not find her child. She stood gazing and weeping when Colonel Bouquet came up and said, 'do you recollect nothing by which your child might be discovered?' She said she recollected nothing but a hymn, which she used often to sing to her children, and which is as follows:

'Alone, yet not alone am I,
Though in this solitude so drear;
I feel my Saviour always nigh,
He comes the very hour to cheer;
I am with him, and he with me,
E'en here alone I cannot be!'

"The Colonel desired her to sing the hymn as she used to do. Scarcely had the mother sung two lines of it, when poor Regina rushed from the crowd, began to sing it also, and threw herself.into her mother's arms. They both wept for joy, and the Colonel gave the daughter up to her mother. But the other little girl had no parents. They had probably been murdered. She clung to Regina, and would not let her go, so she was taken home with Regina, though her mother was very poor. Regina began to ask after 'the book in which God speaks to us.' But her mother had no Bible—for the Indians burned her Bible when they burned her house, and killed her family. Her mother resolved to go to Philadelphia and buy a Bible, but her good minister gave her one, and it was found that Regina could read at once."—*Todd's Sabbath School Teacher*.

The following is from *Mr. Sarge*, in answer to a letter addressed him, on the subject of Indian incursions &c., he says:

"In 1834, an uncle of mine purchased a farm, three miles from Fort Smith, the house then (in 1834) on this farm, was evidently also a Fort—tradition has it so—there are, besides—

or were at least, when I saw the house in '34, marks of corroborating evidence, to conclusively show this to have been the case.   The *port-holes*, though plugged when I saw the house, and the scores of partial perforations made in the logs by bullets or balls, concur to sustain the truth of tradition. The house has, however, been since removed, and in its stead, another is erected.   The workmen, in sinking the cellar deeper, discovered a subterranean cave, which, it is surmised, served as a place of concealment and greater security for their wives and little ones, should the Fort be surprised by the Indians, in the absence of their men on their farms at work; for in those days the neighbors were, from want of necessity, compelled to aid each other on their farms, and at night all would resort to the Fort.

Mr. Mies, some years ago, informed my father that two of his brothers fell a victim to gratify the destructive propensity of the Indians.   The two brothers were ploughing, and thus were surprised by the indians.   One of them was shot dead on the spot; the other, for his life, made for the house; having nearly reached his goal, and while in the act of leaping a fence, a ruthless Indian, hard on his heels, sunk his tomahawk in the head of his victim—he expired instantly!

A man by the name of *Boeshore*,* while returning from his farm in the evening, with his family, espied some Indians near Fort Smith—he halted at that instant, an Indian levelled his deadly weapon at him, but fortunately, the bullet struck the cock of Boeshore's gun—for the gun was in that day a constant companion of the laboring man—his horses took fright and ran off in the direction of the Fort.   B. was, however, wounded in his left arm.   The Indians were fired upon; night advancing, and the Indians retreating, nothing more was done till next morning, when the settlers traced blood in the trail toward the Little mountain."

Bethel township has been materially changed since its first erection.   It is bounded on the north-east by Schuylkill and Berks counties, south-east by Jackson township, south by North Lebanon township, and west by Swatara.   Its greatest length is thirteen miles; breadth seven.   It contains about thirty thousand acres of land—the northern part of which is mountainous;

* Boeshore resided in Hanover township at the time.

the southern is level—and some of the best kind of soil, especially that portion which is limestone—though the greater proportion is slate and gravel; yet generally highly improved.
Many of the buildings are good; a few are still found covered
with tiles. There is considerable taste displayed—though somewhat grotesque—in the arrangements about their dwellings.

This township is well watered. The principal stream is the
Little Swatara creek, which rises at the base of the Kittatinny
—or Blue mountain—in Upper Tulpehocken township, Berks
county, and flows south-west, forming the boundary between
Bethel and Tulpehocken townships, in Berks; thence it crosses
Bethel and Swatara townships, Lebanon county, and falls into
the Great or Big Swatara creek, about one mile below Jonestown. It turns several mills. In its course, it receives, in
Bethel township, Elizabeth run and Deep run. In the forks of
the former lies Fredericksburg or Stumpstown. There are
several other smaller streams in the township.

In 1840, there were in this township, four stores, one furnace, one forge, three grist mills, one saw mill, two distilleries.

Fredericksburg—or Stumpstown—was laid out about the
year 1754 or 1755, by one Stump. Among its first inhabitants were Stump, Snevely, Meily, Mauerer, the first tavern
keeper in the place, Desch, Hauer and Siegfried. During the
Indian war, it was a place of retreat for the white settlers on
the frontiers.

In 1827, a great part of the town was destroyed by fire;
but has since been rebuilt. It is pleasantly situated, in a fertile, and well improved country. It contains between sixty
and seventy dwellings; nearly one hundred families; with a
population of about seven hundred and fifty. The village contains three stores, three taverns, and the usual number of handicrafts; also a Union church, in which Lutherans, German Reformed and Mennonites preach; also a church owned by the
Evangelical Association.

Population of Bethel township in 1830, 1,604; 1840, 1,662.
Average tax valuation for 1844, $538,011; county tax,
$807 01.

HANOVER TOWNSHIP.

Hanover township embraced originally, when first erected, what is now Hanover, in Dauphin county, Hanover, Union, and part of Swatara township, in Lebanon county. In 1729, when Lancaster was erected, and additional townships were laid off, Derry, Lebanon and Peshtank, (Paxton,) embraced nearly all Dauphin and Lebanon counties, till 1739, when Bethel was separated from Lebanon township.

Peshtank township, out of which Hanover was formed, was bounded in 1729, as follows:—"Beginning at the mouth of *Suataaro*, thence up the river to *Kehtotoning hill*, above Peter Allen's, thence eastward by the south side of said hill, to the meridian of Quetopohello, thence on a south course to the mouth of the same at *Suataaro*, and down *Suataaro* to the place of beginning."

Hanover township was erected, upon a petition of the inbahitants of Lancaster county, presented at the February session of 1736–7. "It was divided on the west from Peshtank, (Paxton,) by Beaver creek, from its mouth to the mountain—from Lebanon on the east, and Derry on the south, by Swatara creek, from Beaver to the forks, thence by the north branch to the mountain.

Prior to 1751, Hanover was divided into the *West End, and East End of Hanover;* the latter is now, principally, if not wholly, embraced within the bounds of Lebanon county. Many of the original settlers were Irish, who had emigrated principally from the north of Ireland. They were an enterprizing and daring race. Presbyterians by religious profession. Principally conspicuous as *militant* and *triumphant* members of community. They and their kindred of Paxton and Donegal, for many years bravely defended the frontiers against the Indians; and finally, when no other means answered, slaughtered "*friend and foe*" of the Indians. Allusion is had to "*Paxton affair*" in Lancaster.*

The taxables in the East End of Hanover, in 1750, were the following:—Jacob Musser, Peter Hettrich, Melchior Henry, Thomas Proner, Henry Bachman, Conrad

* See Appendix B, for a full statement of the "Paxton affair."

Clatt, Anthony Rosebaum, Jacob Mosher, Esau Ricker, William Clark, John Sibbins, John Schwar, James Young, John Gilleland, Peter Halman, Widow Work, Frederick Hoak, Jas. Sloan, Widow Gilleland, Jacob Sops, John Sops, Rudolph Hake, Joseph Hoof, Benj. Clark, Killion Mark, George Tittel, Isaac Williams, Adam Clannean John Casnet, James Williams, Anthony Tittel, Dennis Keril, Mathias Boor, John Sloan, Daniel Ankel, William Young, Abraham Williams, James Clark, Martin Lichty, Adam Roth, Ludwig Shits, John Stewart, John Foster, John Andrew, Walter McFarland, Joseph Brechtbill, William Robison, Philip Kolps, Onwal Jagle, Thomas Croil, Alexander Swan, Alexander Thomson, John Graham, Samuel Ainsworth, John Martin, Barnet M'Night, Widow Brown, John Humes, Andrew M'Keehan, Thomas Brewster, John Thomson, James Graham, John Cunningham, William Cunningham, Christopher Sies, John Meyers, Patrick Brown, John Andrews, John Strein, Antony M'Crath, George Shetley, Walter Bell, Leonard Long, Adam M'Neely, John M'Clure, John Henderson, William Woods, John Porterfield, Robert Haslet, John Crawford, William Watson, Henry Gantz, James Greenleaf, John Craig, Hugh M'Gowen, John Dickson, Joseph Willson, Adam Miller, Edward M'Murray, Jacob M'Cormick, John Ramsey, James Stewart, Humphrey Cunningham, Robert Kirkwood, James M'Coorey, William Thomson, Thomas Strain, Mathias Plank, Jacob Steiner, William Stoner, James Todd, John Young, James Dixon, Robert Bryson, William Bryson, Daniel Andrew, David Stevenson, William Cathcart, William Crosby, Benjamin Ainsworth, Patrick Bowen, Adam Harper, Lazarus Stewart.

These Irish Presbyterians—as they were called by some—defended their wives, children and country valiantly against the Indians. They were in good earnest.

Lazarus Stewart was the one who proposed to his neighbors, to go to Lancaster and storm the castle—alluding to what took place in December, 1763, of which a detailed account will be given in the appendix, or close of the book.

The inhabitants of Hanover, in common with the frontier settlers, were repeatedly alarmed, some murdered, others carried off by the Indians. We cannot fully appreciate the sufferings of the original settlers of this part of the county.—

They were not secure for one moment from being surprised or murdered by the savages lurking on the borders of these counties. From 1755 till 1763, Lebanon and Berks counties were scenes of murder, burning of houses, &c. They were exposed to the cruel incursions of barbarous Indians, whose delight was to shed human blood—who regarded neither age nor sex—all were, with them, alike objects of their cruelty.

The 16th of November, 1755, a party of Indians crossed the Susquehanna—commenced their bloody deeds, and murdered thirteen persons. In the autumn of 1756, a company of ten Indians, came to the house of Noah Frederick, while ploughing, killed and scalped him, and carried away three children that were with him—the eldest but nine years old.*

A large portion of the plantations had been abandoned in East and West Hanover townships. In West Hanover, the following persons had fled:—John Gordon, Richard Johnson, Alexander Barnet, James M'Caver, Robert Porterfield, Philip Robison, John Hill, Thomas Bell, Thomas Maguire, William M'Cord, Robert Huston, Benjamin Wallace, William Bennett, Bartholomew Harris, John Swan, James Bannon, William M'-Clure, Thomas M'Clure, John Henry, James Riddle, Widow Cooper, David Ferguson, Widow De Armand, James Wilson, Samuel Barnetts, James Brown, Widow M'Gowin, Samuel Brown, Thomas Hill, Jane Johnston, killed.†

In the East End of Hanover, the following had fled:—John Gilliland, John M'Culloch, Walter M'Farland, Robert Kirkwood, William Robison, Valentine Stoffelbein, Adam Cleaman, Rudolph Fry, Peter Walmer, John M'Culloch, jr., James Rafter, Moses Vance, John Brooner, Jacob Mosser, Philip Mauerer, Barnhart Beshore, Jacob Beshore, Mathias Beshore, William M'Cullough, Philip Culp, Casper Yost, Conrad Cleck, Christian Albert, Daniel Mosser, John M'Clure, Lazarus Stuart, Thomas Shirly, James Graham, Barnet M'Nett, Andrew Brown, William Brown, Andrew M'Mahon, Thomas Hume, Thomas Strean, Peter Wolf, Henry Kuntz, William Watson, John Hume, David Strean, John Stuart, John Porterfield, Anthony M'Crath, James M'Curry, Conrad Rice, Alexander Swan, John Gream. The following were killed—Andrew Ber-

* See page antea 64.
† See tax duplicate for 1756, at Lancaster, in which these are noted as having fled when the collector called.

ryhill, John Creigh, and his son taken captive; Samuel Ains-worth's son was also taken.*

A correspondence is mentioned in the Pennsylvania Gazette, of May, 1757, stating, that "in a letter from Hanover, Lancaster county, dated May 2, 1757, the house of Isaac Snevely was set on fire, and entirely consumed, with eighteen horses and cows—and that on the 17th of May, five men, and a woman, were killed and scalped by the Indians, about thirty miles from Lancaster, &c." The editor of that paper says, May 26, "We hear that more murders were committed—number uncertain, but it is thought there are about twenty destroyed, besides what may be carried off, and that the frontier inhabitants are in great distress, and moving from their plantations, &c.†

The inhabitants of this region of country were kept in continual alarm during the spring, summer and autumn of this year, on account of the murders committed by the Indians. One fails in the attempt to describe the perils of the frontier settlers at these times. The heart shrinks from portraying the scenes of horror—the barbarous murderers butchered the whites in the field—at their meals—in bed—at every unguarded hour.

Who would not sicken to view, in imagination, scalps clotted with gore, mangled limbs, women ripped open, the heart and bowels still palpitating with life, and smoking on the ground—see savages swilling, as it were, human blood, and imbibing a more courageous fury with the human draught—see the living, not captives, fleeing for life, while the Indians are in hot pursuit!

In a letter before us, dated Hanover, Lancaster county, August 11, 1757, it is stated, "That on Monday, the 8th, while George Mauerer was cutting oats in George Scheffer's field, he was killed and scalped. There is now," says the same writer, "such a severe sickness in these parts—the like has not been known—that many families can neither fight nor run away, which occasions great distress on the frontiers. Had it not been for forty men, which the province has in pay, in this township, little of the harvest could have been saved, and as the time for which they have been engaged, is nearly elapsed, the inhabitants hope the government will continue them in the service, else the consequences will be dreadful.

* See tax duplicate for 1756, at Lancaster, and page 66 antea.
† See page antea, 69–70.

The Pennsylvania Gazette of August, 1757, states,—"We learn from Lancaster that there was nothing but murdering and capturing, that on the 17th of August, one Beatty was killed in Paxton, that the next day James Mackay was murdered in Hanover, and William and Joseph Barnet wounded. That on the same day were taken prisoners, a son of James Mackey, a son of Joseph Barnet, Elizabeth Dickey and her child; and the wife of Samuel Young, and her child; and that ninety-four men, women and children, were seen flying from their places, in one body, and a great many more in small parties, so that it was feared the settlement would be entirely forsaken."

What rendered their condition still worse, nay hopeless, the fugitive and remaining inhabitants had no means to engage forces, rangers or scouters, to apprise them of the approach of Indians, and repel their incursions; and it was, it seems, in vain for them to appeal to a deaf government—their only appeal was to the sympathies of their fellow citizens for aid and means.* Patriotic individuals, who possessed means, would raise rangers at their own expense. *John Harris,* in an adjoining township, (Paxton) paid thirty men for their services as rangers, in watching and preventing the inroads of Indians. Harris did this on more than one occasion.

"On Monday, the 22d of May, Barnabas Tolon was killed and scalped in Hanover township. And we are," says the editor of the Pennsylvania Gazette, "well informed, that one hundred and twenty-three persons have been murdered and carried off from that part of Lancaster county, by the Indians, since the war commenced; and that lately three have been scalped and are yet living."

The Indians still continued to commit murders and depredations till December, 1763, when they were seen for the last time within the limits of Lebanon county.

East Hanover township is, at present, bounded on the north and west by Dauphin county; east by Union, and south by Anville and Londonderry townships. The surface of the country is diversified. In the southern portion, it presents gentle declivities; the northern part is mountainous, being crossed by the Blue mountain and the Second Mountain. There is quite a noted spring here, called the "Cold Spring," an agreeable watering place, and considerably frequented in the heat of summer.

* Page 75, antea.

There is also, a very large and commodious house of entertainment here; it was erected by an enterprizing, and public patronage deserving gentleman, *Samuel Winter, Esq.*

In the southern part of the township, is the well known
woollen factory on Indian creek, long owned by Gen. Harrison, but now in the possession of Mr. Lemberger.

The township is well supplied with streams affording abundant water power.   The Swatara creek, or river, is the principal one; it rises in Schuylkill county, on the south side of the
Broad mountain, and stealing its way through the Sharp and
Second mountains, enters Lebanon county on the north-east
angle, through which, in its sinuous course, it receives Quitopahilla, and other smaller tributaries; thence flows south-west
through Dauphin county, and empties into the Susquehanna
river below Middletown.   In its course, through this township,
it affords much water power.   The other streams are Indian
creek, Raccoon creek, and Reed's run.   In 1840, the township
contained four stores, one fulling mill, one woollen factory, already spoken of, five grist mills, six saw mills, one oil mill, one
paper mill, one tannery, one distillery.   Population in 1830,
2,498; 1840, 2,461.   Tax valuation for 1844, $452,674 00;
county tax, $679 01.

The following pensioners were still living in this township
in 1840—Thomas Koppenhaver, aged 80 years; John Hetrich,
77; Jacob Decker, 84; Philip Witmoyer, 90; John Gerberich,
81; James Stewart, 83 years.

It was in this township that the well known *Hollenback* was
born—to whom John Harris remarked, twenty or more years
before Harrisburg was laid out, that this place—*Harris's ferry*
—would become the centre of business in this section of the
country, and would be the seat of Government of Pennsylvania.—Strong and predictive faith, this.*

BIOGRAPHICAL NOTICE OF THE HON. MATHIAS HOLLENBACK.

The subject of this notice, was born of German parentage,
in Hanover township, upon the Swatara creek—then Lancaster—now Lebanon county.   Here he was inured to all the

* Napey's Harrisburg Directory for 1842, p. 9.

sufferings and privations incident to a frontier settlement at that early day. Possessed of a firm and vigorous constitution, and endued by nature with a strong, active and enterprising mind, at the age of seventeen he joined the first adventurous party, who came to make a permanent settlement, under the authority of Connecticut, in the valley of Wyoming. This was in the autumn of 1769. From this period, the history of his long and eventful life, is identified with the history of this part of the country.

In the controversy between Pennsylvania and Connecticut, he actively and firmly adhered to the latter, under whose auspices he had embarked his youthful fortunes, and whose claims he regarded as paramount to every other, until the right of soil and the right of jurisdiction to the country were decreed by a competent tribunal, to be in the former. From that moment, he yielded obedience to the constitution and laws of Pennsylvania, and contributed all in his power to quiet the turbulent, and to reconcile the disaffected to the legitimate authorities.

The dispute between Pennsylvania and Connecticut, had assumed all the characteristics of a civil war, and notwithstanding the conciliatory recommendations and remonstrances of the Continental Congress, it was continued during the revolutionary struggle. Whilst the poor and destitute settlers were suffering on the one side from the common enemies of the country, the British, the savage Indians, and the *worse than savage tories*, they were attacked on the other, and endured equal distress, by military parties under the authority of Pennsylvania.

Thus surrounded with difficulties and dangers, calculated to appal the stoutest heart, at a period too, when many good, but timid men, doubted, hesitated, and feared—young Hollenback, in want of every thing, but personal courage and patriotic feeling, was approached by one of those agents of the mother country, whose bland and fascinating manner, and duplicity of heart, marked him out as a fit emissary for "treason, stratagem and spoil." On the one hand, the effort making to free the country from British dominion, was represented as entirely hopeless, and that upon failure, poverty, shame and death, every where awaited the active partisan; on the other, by espousing the cause of the British King, money, office and honor would be immediately conferred, and a life of ease and independence secured. The youth stood firm—he was not to be allured

28*

from the path of duty. He had taken his resolution—staked his all upon the issue—and was willing to abide the result.

In 1776, and the following years, two companies were raised in Wyoming, in one of which young Hollenback was appointed Lieutenant. He was active and successful in filling up and preparing his company for active service—and, shortly after, joined the army under General Washington, in the State of N. Jersey. His merits were soon discovered and properly appreciated by the General, who frequently consulted him in relation to the frontier settlements, and the means of defending them against the incursions of the enemy. He participated in all the sufferings of our half fed, and half clothed troops, during the winter campaign, in the state of New Jersey—and was, on several occasions, employed by the General in the execution of confidential agencies.

Such was the patriotism of the Wyoming settlers, that, during the short period, when they were not immediately threatened with attacks from the enemy, almost every efficient man among them joined the army, and left their families without protection. This calm portended a storm. The defenceless state of the frontier invited aggression. The valley again began to suffer from the tomahawk, scalping knife, and fire brand— and early in 1778, it was discovered that a horde of British, Indians and tories, was collected upon the Susquehanna frontiers, and preparing to pour down upon the valley of Wyoming, and exterminate the defenceless settlers. The officers from Wyoming, urged the General to send a force for its protection, or to permit the two companies, drawn from this settlement, to return, for the purpose of defending their aged and helpless parents, wives and children. But such was the situation of the army, that no adequate force could be spared. An intense anxiety was felt among the officers—some obtained furloughs, and some resigned and returned to the valley. Every preparation was made in their power, to repel their invaders. About three hundred and fifty men marched out to meet the enemy. They were drawn into an ambuscade. The result is known— Wyoming was reduced to widowhood and orphanage. About fifty only escaped this disastrous battle, of whom the subject of this notice was one.

Articles of capitulation were made, in which security and protection of life and property had been stipulated, were no sooner made than they were violated, on the part of the faithless enemy. What property could not be carried away, was burned and destroyed, and the remnant of the settlers was driven naked and houseless to the surrounding mountains. Lieutenant Hollenback, whose property was all destroyed, still clung to the valley and participated in all its sufferings, until the conclusion of the war.

Upon the settlement of the controversy between Pennsylvania and Connecticut—and upon the promulgation of the laws of Pennsylvania in the disputed territory of 1786, Mr. Hollenback was chosen and appointed one of the justices of the courts of Luzern county; and upon the adoption of the Constitution, he was re-appointed an associate judge, which office he sustained with reputation, till the time of his decease. He was honored with the command of a regiment by his fellow citizens—a military officer being almost the only one in Pennsylvania, compatible with that of a judge.

In all the great political struggles which have agitated the country, Judge Hollenback was actively and firmly attached to the cause of the people. In a late conflict, although most of those around him, with whom he had been accustomed to act, entertained different views, and although he was exceedingly enfeebled by disease, he procured himself to be carried to the poll, and there, for the last time, exercised the right of suffrage in favor of a distinguished individual who succeeded to the presidency. He was firmly persuaded that the interests of the country demanded this preference, and he acted accordingly.

It is believed, that he was not a member of any Christian church, but it is known, that he reverenced the religion of the cross. Throughout his life, he contributed liberally to the support of that communion and its pastors, to which he was conscientiously attached, and it is feared, it will long feel the want of his supporting hand.

His life, was a life of temperance, industry, and attention to his business, the full fruits of which he enjoyed in almost uninterrupted health, until his last illness.

From the incidents of his life, the young may draw useful lessons for the regulations of their conduct, and from his death all may learn, that *man* is *mortal*. That neither riches, nor honors, nor virtue, nor age, can form any shield against the fell destroyer.— *Haz. Reg.*

LONDONDERRY TOWNSHIP.

Derry township organized in 1729, was then bounded as follows:—"The township of Derry, beginning at the mouth of Conewago, thence up Susquehannah to the mouth of Suataaro, thence up Suataaro to the mouth of Quetopohella, thence south to Conewago, and down the same to the place of beginning."

As then bounded, it embraced all within its limits, known as the "West End, and the East End of Derry;" or, as subsequently called, Derry and Londonderry. Derry was settled prior to 1720, and about the same time when the Semples, Pattersons, Mitchells, Galbraiths, Andersons, Scotts, Lowereys, Pedans, Porters, Whitehills and others settled in Donegal. They were principally Irish emigrants. As early as 1750, many of them moved to Cumberland county, among whom were the Works, Moores, Bells, Galbraiths, Whitehills, Hendersons, Sterrits, Mortons—all early settlers in the east end of Cumberland county.

In 1751, the following were taxables residing in the West End of Derry:—

James Semple, James M'Kee, Joseph Gandor, Thomas Hall, James Clark, John Allison, James Shaw, Robt. Ramsey, James Russel, Thomas Boman, James Chambers, James Long, David Campbell, James Inland, Patrick Down, John Vanlier, Robert Carothers, William Breedon, Charles Neely, Arthur Chambers, John Tice, John Laird, David Caldwell, Andrew Morrison, John Thompson, Alexander Felix, Alexander Robison, John Nicom, John Kerr, William Blackburn, Andrew Lockhart, David M'Nair, James Wiley, William Drennan, Christian Saddler, William Mitchel, Moses Willson, Michael Hour, Moses Patterson, James Russel, William Sterret, Robert Armstrong, Valentine Kloninger, Martin Brand, John Singer, Jacob Ionan, John Welsh, Hugh Laird, Wm. Irland, William Boor, James Harris, James Russel.

The taxables for 1751, of the East End of Derry, were the following:—

James Galbraith, James Wilson, James Campbell, James Walker, John Walker, Henry Walker, John M'Cord, David

M'Cord, William Robison, Archibald Walker, David Taylor, John Over, John Pinagel, William Wilson, James Miller, William Boyd, John M'Cosh, William Sawyers, George Espy, David Mitchel, Leonard Denie, John M'Culloch, Charles Connoy, David Shank, David Glenn, Michael Hoover, Hans Balmer, Henry Peters, Hans Kettering, Charles Clark, Thomas Macky, Andrew Moore, James Foster, Robert M'Clure, Felty Fillipo, Hugh Hall, Thomas Rutherford, William Rea, John M'Quinn, John Rea, Neal M'Callister, Christian Snider, Neal Dougherty, Thomas Logan, George Miller, John M'Callister, Joseph White, John M'Clelland, Robert Murdock, Moses Potts, David Johnson, Jacob Rife, Jacob Longenecker, Andw. Rowan, Hugh Hays, Patrick Hays, John Kerr, Duncan M'Donal, Thomas Willson, James Willson, John Campbell, John Hays, Widow M'Clan, Widow Sloan, John Maben, Patrick Kelly, James Duncan, John Duncan, William Hays, John Foster, Robert Foster, David Foster, Wilson Cooper, John Strean, John Cochran, Hans Adam Nai, Jacob Seiler, Hugh Miller, John Godfrey, Thomas Aiken, Anthony Hernsly, Christian Cochran, Albrecht Ziegler, Conrad Wisan, John M'Culloch, John Gingerich, William Miller, John Moore, John Hays, Thomas Freeman, William Huston.

Though the original settlers, in this township, were principally Irish, but few of their descendants are residing here; some as stated above, settled in the eastern part of Cumberland, others settled in the western portion, now Franklin county, called the Conococheague settlements, where are still to be found—the Campbells, McDowells, Smiths, Barrs, Welshs, McClellands, Finleys—the ancestors of Gov. W. Finley.

This township being more towards the interior, was not so much exposed, as the more northern townships, to the incursions of the Indians. Nevertheless, the barbarous savages penetrated into the more sparsely settled parts, and committed several murders and effected abductions. June 19, 1757, nineteen persons were killed in a mill on the Quitopahilla creek; and on the 9th of September, 1757, one boy and a girl were taken from Donegal township, a few miles south of Derry.*— About the same time, one Danner and his son, Christian Danner, a lad of twelve years, had gone out into the Conewago

* Loudon's Narrative, ii, p. 200—208.

bills to cut down some trees; after felling one, and while the father was cutting a log, he was shot and scalped by an Indian; and Christian, the son, was taken captive—carried off to Canada, where he was kept several years, till the close of the war—when he made his escape from them. Another young lad, named Steger, was, while cutting some whoop-poles, surprised by three Indians, and taken captive; but fortunately, after remaining some months with the Indians, made his escape.

Jacob and Henry Bowman, brothers, both young men, were taken by some Indians, who tied them in a secluded place, in the thickets, and proceeded, as was supposed, to the Conestoga Indians, with a view, when returning from thence, to take them to Canada; but in the interim, a Mr. Shally returned from Lancaster to Lebanon, and they perceiving him, called him, who immediately went to the place where they were tied, and unloosed them, and they returned to their parents, residing in the vicinity of the present Palmyra.

So much were the inhabitants constantly alarmed, that during the Indian troubles, the men attended church with loaded guns, and other defensive weapons. Their Pastor, the Rev. Elder, who ministered to their spiritual wants, and counselled them in those perilous times, had then charge of a congregation in Derry. It is said of him, he was doubly armed; first by faith in the certain protection of an all-ruling Providence: second in his gun, which he had often with him in the pulpit; for he was an unerring marksman.

It may be here added, " that the Rev. John Elder, a Scotchman, was the first clergyman settled west of the Conewago hills, towards Susquehanna—he preached fifty-six years in the Paxton church, about two miles from Harrisburg, and for many years in Derry.

" He wielded the sword of the flesh, though clothed with the helmet of salvation, as well as the sword of the spirit: for he held for several years a Colonel's commission in the provincial service; commanding the stockades and block-houses that extended from the Susquehanna to the Delaware, at Easton.

"It is said, as above intimated, that he often carried his rifle into the pulpit, and his congregation were prepared in the same way against the attacks from the Indians.

"About the year 1756, the church was surrounded by the

savages so closely, that, as was afterwards learned from an escaped prisoner, the rifles in the church were counted by the Indians, but as there appeared to be too many of them, the savages went off without molesting the congregation. In the year following, the congregation (at Paxton) was attacked after they had dispersed, and two or three were killed and others wounded."

The Rev. Elder died at the advanced age of 86, in the year 1792, on his farm, near Harrisburg, beloved in life, and much lamented by his survivors.

As late as 1763, in July, the reapers in this and other parts of Lancaster county, took their guns and ammunition with them into the harvest fields, to defend themselves against the Indians.

Londonderry township is bounded on the north by East Hanover township; north-east by Annville; east by Lebanon; south by Lancaster county, and west by Dauphin county. It contains nearly twenty-six thousand acres of land, some of the best, and some of the worst in the country. The middle portion of the township is level; limestone soil, and some gravel and slate. The northern part is undulating; the south and south-western, hilly and much of it covered with sienite bowlders, of huge size, and greywacke.

The Swatara creek runs along the northern boundary of this township, and receives Quitapohilla, a considerable stream, from the south-east. Klinger's run, a tributary of the latter, flows northwardly into it. The Conewago creek flows westwardly through the township, north of the Conewago hills, on which is Colebrook furnace, in operation for sixty years.— It is owned by Mr. Coleman. The Downingtown, Ephrata and Harrisburg turnpike passes through the township, on which is Campbellstown, a small village, containing a dozen or two of houses; and the Reading and Harrisburg turnpike, on which is Palmstown, or Palmyra, containing some twenty houses. There are several mills in this township. The improvements in this township, are generally good. In 1840, the following pensioners were still living in this township:—Jacob Lentz, aged 81; Jacob Keaner, 86; Andrew Robison, 81 years. Population in 1830, 1,874; 1840, 1,762. Average tax valuation for 1844, $794,285 00; county tax $1,191 43.

HEIDELBERG TOWNSHIP.

Heidelberg township originally embraced all that is now within the limits of Upper and Lower Heidelberg, in Berks county; and Heidelberg in Lebanon county, a part of Jackson. But when Berks was erected in 1752, the greater part *then* known as Heidelberg, was taken in with that county.

This township was originally settled by Germans; the first of whom had either directly emigrated from Germany, or from the State of New York, where many of them had arrived in 1710;* thence they emigrated to Pennsylvania, in 1723.

It was within the bounds of Heidelberg township, as first organized, that the German Baptists—commonly known by the name, Dunkards, had commenced a settlement as early as 1724. Many of these first emigrated from Germany and Holland, in 1709, and settled first at Germantown, and some years afterward established a church at Muelbach. One of their prominent members, Conrad Beissel, a native of Germany, arrived in America, in 1720, and took up his abode among them at Muelbach—he, and one Stuntz, built a house, and they were soon joined by Isaac Van Babern, George Steifel, and others.

Conrad Beissel being somewhat dissatisfied with some of the observances of his brethren, commenced promulgating his views, and eventually seceded from the Dunkard community, and formed a new sect, known as the German Seventh Day Baptist.

The following brief sketch of this society, taken from the History of Lancaster County, will afford the reader some idea of their rise and progress.

Conrad Beissel, wholly intent upon seeking out the true obligation of the word of God, and the proper observances of the rites and ceremonies it imposes, stripped of human authority, he conceived that there was an error among the Dunkers, in the observance of the day for the Sabbath; that the *seventh day* was the command of the Lord God, and that day being established and sanctified, by the Great Jehovah, forever! And no change, nor authority for change, ever having been announced to man, by any power sufficient to set aside the solemn decree of the Almighty; a decree which he declared that he had sanctified forever! He felt it to be his duty to contend for the

observance of that day.   About the year 1725, he published a
tract entering into a discussion of this point, which created some
excitement and disturbance in the society, at Mill creek; upon
which he retired from the settlement, and went secretly, to a
cell on the banks of the Cocalico, that had previously been occupied by one Elimelich, a hermit.   His place of retirement
was unknown for some time to the people he had left, and when
discovered, many of the society at Mill creek, who had become
convinced of the truth of his proposition for the observance of
the Sabbath, settled around him, in solitary cottages.   They
adopted the original Sabbath—the seventh day—for public
worship, in the year 1728; which has ever since been observed
by their descendants, even unto the present day.

In the year 1732, the solitary life was changed into a con-
venticle one, and a monastic society was established as soon as
the first buildings erected for that purpose were finished, May,
1733.   The habit of the Capuchins, or White Friars, was
adopted by both the brethren and sisters; which consisted of a
shirt, trowsers, and vest, with a long white gown or cowl, of
woolen web in winter, and linen in summer.   That of the sisters differed only in the substitution of petticoats for trowsers,
and some little peculiarity in the shape of the cowl.   Monastic
names were given to all who entered the cloister.   Onesimus
(Israel Eckerlin) was constituted Prior, who was succeeded by
Jaebez, (Peter Miller,) and the title of a Father—spiritual
father—was bestowed upon Beissel, whose monastic name
was Friedsam; to which the Brethren afterwards' added
Gottrecht; implying together, Peaceable, God-right.   In the
year 1740, there were thirty-six single brethren in the cloister,
and thirty-five sisters; and at one time, the society, including
the members living in the neighborhood, numbered nearly three
hundred.

The first buildings of the society of any consequence, were
Kedar and Zion; a meeting house and convent, which were
erected on the hill called Mount Zion.   They afterwards built
larger accommodations, in the meadow below, comprising a
sister's house, called Saron, to which is attached a large chapel
and "Saal," for the purpose of holding Agapas, or Love Feasts.
A brother's house called Bethania, with which is connected
the large meeting room, with galleries, in which the whole society assembled for public worship, in the days of their pros-
29

perity, and which are still standing, surrounded by smaller
buildings, that were occupied as a printing-office, bake-house,
school-house, almonry, and others, for different purposes; on
one of which, a one story house, the town clock is erected.

" The buildings are singular, and of very ancient architec-
ture; all the outwalls being covered with shingles, or clap-
boards. The two houses, for the brethren and sisters, are
very large, being three and four stories high; each has a chapel
for their night meetings, and the main buildings are divided
into small apartments, each containing between fifty and sixty;
so that six dormitories, which are barely large enough to contain a cot, (in early days a bench, and billet of wood for the
head,) a closet, and an hour glass, surrounded a common room,
in which each sub-division pursued their respective avocation.—
On entering these silent cells, and traversing the long narrow
passages, visiters can scarcely divest themselves of the feeling
of walking the tortuous windings of some old castle, and breath-
ing recesses of romance. The ceilings have an elevation of but
seven feet; the passages leading to the cells, or kammers, as
they are styled, and through the different parts of both con-
vents, are barely wide enough to admit one person, for when
meeting a second, he has always to retreat. The dens of the
kammers are but five feet high, and twenty inches wide, and
the window, for each has but one, is only eighteen by twenty-
four inches; the largest windows affording light to the meeting
rooms; the chapels, the saals, and even the kammers, or dormitories, are hung and nearly covered with large sheets of elegant penmanship, or ink paintings; many of which are texts
from the scriptures, executed in a very handsome manner, in
ornamented Gothic letters, called in German, *Fractur Schrif-
ten.* They are done on large sheets of paper, manufactured
for the purpose at their own mill, some of which are put into
frames, and which admonish the resident, as well as the casual
visiter, whichever way they may turn the head. There are
some very curious ones: two of which still remain in the chapel
attached to Saron.—One represents the narrow and crooked
way, done on a sheet of about three feet square, which it would
be difficult to describe; it is very curious and ingenious: the
whole of the road is filled up with texts of scripture, adverting
the disciples of their duties, and the obligations their profession
imposes upon them. Another represents the three Heavens: In

the first, Christ, the Shepherd, is represented gathering his flock together; in the second, which occupies one foot in height, and is three feet wide, three hundred figures in Capu-. chin dress, can be counted, with harps in their hands, and heads of an innumerable host; and in the third is seen the Throne, surrounded by two hundred Arch-Angels. Many of these Fractur-Schriften express their own enthusiastic sentiments on the subject of celibacy, and the virtue of a recluse life, whilst others are devotional pieces.

"A room was set apart for such purposes, called 'Das Schreib Zimmer,' the writing room, and several sisters devoted their whole attention to this labor, as well as to transcribing the writings of the founder of the society; thus multiplying copies for the wants of the community, before they had a printing press. Two sisters, named *Anastasia* and *Iphigenia*, were the principal ornamental writers. They left a large folio volume of *sample alphabets*, of various sizes and style, which are both elegant and curious, exhibiting the most patient application. The letters of the first alphabet are twelve inches long, sur-rounded by a deep border, in imitation of copper-plate engrav-ing; each one of which is different in the filling up. It was finished in the year 1750, and is still preserved in the hands of the trustees. There was another transcribing room appro-priated exclusively to copying music. Hundreds of volumes, each containing five or six hundred pieces, were transferred from book to book, with as much accuracy, and almost as much neatness, as if done with a graver.

"It was in contemplation, at one time, by the *Eckerlins*, three brothers, one of whom was a *prior*, and had the superin-tendence of the secular concerns, to make it a place of more importance than a mere religious refuge. They were from Germany, and had been brought up Catholics. They conceived a project of erecting extensive buildings, and connecting trades with it; and had some preparations under way; the timber all hewn, as all the buildings are of wood, even the chimneys, which remain in use at this day; and in readiness to erect a tower, and had sent to Europe, where they had extensive con-nexions, and got a chime of bells cast, unknown to the society, until they arrived at Philadelphia, and the bill for payment was forwarded to them. The society resolved not to receive them, but had them sold, and paid the loss.

"The commuity was a republic, in which all stood upon per-fect equality and freedom. No monastic *vows* were taken, neither had they any written covenants, as is common in the Baptist churches. The New Testament was their confession of faith, their code of law, and church discipline. The pro-perty which belonged to the society, by donation, and the labor of the single brethren and sisters, was common stock; but none was obliged to throw in his own property, or to give up any possessions. The society was supported by the income of the farm and grist mill, oil mill, fulling mill, and the labor of the brethren and sisters, in the cloister."

Many of the male members were men of education, and the school which they had established, attracted attention abroad; young men from Baltimore and of Philadelphia, were sent to this place to be educated. Ludwig Hacker, the teacher of the common school, projected the plan of holding a school in the afternoon of the Sabbath, or Saturday, and who, in connexion with some of the brethren, commenced it, to give instruction to the indigent children who were kept from regular school by em-ployments which their necessities obliged them to be engaged at during the week, as well as to give religious instruction to those in better circumstances. The precise time when this school was established is not known; it was after 1739.

The society, after an existence of fifty years, began to de-cline, from some cause, which we have not been able to learn. Some say that Beissel's successor, Peter Miller, wanted vigor of mind. This, says Doctor Fahnestock, is not, he believes, the case; for he assured us, in a conversation with him on this subject, in 1836, so far as he could learn, Peter Miller was a man of much greater powers of mind than Beissel, and that he had the management of the establishment during Beissel's time; and to whose energy and perseverance, is mainly attributable the great prosperity of the institution in its early days.

That Miller was a man of more than ordinary powers of mind, is evident from the testimony of the Rev. Jedediah An-drews, an alumnus of Havard College, of the class of 1695, Andrews speaking of Miller, in a letter, dated Philadelphia, 8th, 14th, 1730.

"There is lately come over a Palatine candidate of the min-istry, who having applied to us at the Synod (Scotch Synod) for ordination, 'tis left to three ministers, (these three were Ten-

ant, Andrews, and Boyd,) to do it.   He is an extraordinary
person for sense and learning.   We gave him a question to discuss about *Justification,* and he answered it, in a whole sheet
of paper, in a very notable manner.   His name is John Peter
Miller, and speaks Latin, as readily as we do our vernacular
tongue, and so does the other, Mr. Weiss."

At an early period, they established a German printing office,
which enabled them to distribute tracts and hymns, and afterwards to print several large works, in which the views of the
founder are fully explained.   Many of these books have been
lost and destroyed.   In the Revolutionary war, just before the
battle of Germantown, three wagon loads of books, in sheets,
were seized and taken away for cartridges.   They came to the
paper mill to get paper, and not finding any there, they *pressed*
the books in sheets.

"Music was much cultivated.   Beissel was a first rate musician and composer.   In composing sacred music, he took his
style from the music of Nature, and the whole comprising several large volumes, are founded on the Æolian harp; the singing is the Æolian harp harmonized; it is very peculiar in its
style and concords, and in its execution.   The tones issuing
from the choir imitate very soft instrumental music; conveying
a softness and devotion almost superhuman to the auditor.
Their music is set in four, six and eight parts.   All the parts,
save the bass, are led and sung exclusively by females—the
men being confined to the bass, which is set in two parts, the
high and the low bass—the latter resembling the deep tones of
the organ; and the first, in combination with one of the female
parts, is an excellent imitation of the concert horn.   The whole
is sung on the *falsetto* voice, the singers scarcely opening their
mouths, or moving their lips, which throws the voice up to the
ceiling—which is not high—and the tones, which seem to be
more than human—at least so far from common church singing
appears to be entering from above, and hovering over the heads
of the assembly."

The reader may form some idea of *their music* from the following extract of a letter, written by a tourist during the proprietary administration of Governor Penn: "The counter, tre-
ble, tenor and bass, were all sung by women, with sweet, shrill,
and small voices, but with a truth and exactness in time and
intonation, that was admirable.   It is impossible to describe to

your lordship, my feelings upon this occasion. The performers sat with their heads reclined, their countenances solemn and dejected, their faces pale and emaciated, from their manner of living, their clothing exceeding white, and quite picturesque, and their music such as thrilled to the very soul; I almost began to think myself in the world of spirits, and that the objects before me were ethereal. In short, the impression this scene made upon my mind, continued strong for many days, and I believe, will never be wholly obliterated."

This music is lost, entirely now, in Ephrata—not the music books, but the style of singing—they never attempt it any more. It is, however, still preserved and finely executed—though in a faint degree—at Snow hill, in Franklin county, where there is a branch of the society, and which is now the principal settlement of the Seventh Day Baptists.

This society attracted considerable attention. Men of various rank and standing visited the place.

George Thomas, formerly an Antigua planter, appointed in 1737, Governor of the province of Pennsylvania, visited Ephrata in 1741. He came, says Peter Miller, accompanied by a retinue of twenty horses, and a large number of distinguished gentlemen from Maryland and Virginia; they were all honorably received by the brethren. The Governor said he was much gratified to see such an institution. He spoke very favorably of their religious and economical arrangements. The motives of visit, it is believed, were sinister. Without doubt, he gained the object of his visit more easily by adulation than he would have otherwise. At this time, the talented and active Conrad Weiser, was a member of the association. It was the Governor's object, if possible, to secure once more the services of this man, in a capacity for which hs was felicitously suited, that of an Indian interpreter. He tendered him the appointment of justice of the peace, which he accepted. He was afterwards appointed provincial interpreter, in which capacity he rendered his country essential service for many years. Governor William Denny spent some time here, in 1756, and through an interpreter, had a long conversation with Beissel, touching the condition of the country.

Peter Miller was a native of Oberant Lautern—came to America in 1730; soon after his arrival, was ordained by a Scotch Synod, at Philadelphia—received as a member of the

Society at Ephrata, by being baptized in 1735, and remained sixty-one years, to the day of his death, September 25, 1796, a member thereof.—His remains rest in the grave-yard at that place.

He was well known in the religious and literary world. It is said he translated the Declaration of Independence into seven languages. His correspondence was extensive—he was visited by hundreds—General Lee, David Rittenhouse, Count Zinzendorf—and several noblemen of Europe—have been the guests of the establishment.

The following were taxables in Heidelberg township, a year after Berks county had been separated from Lancaster county:

Bastian Zimmerman, Abraham Stump, Godfried Loudermilch, Martin Kohl, Christian Smith, Yost Hoffman, Lorentz Bauman, Philip Kistaker, Jacob Kreider, George Trear, Henry Gring, John Dootweiler, John Lane, Nicholas Fellenberger, Jacob Durst, James Dutweiler, Henry Miser, Jacob Neaf, Nicholas Cress, John Stoler, Joseph Krotzer, John Wolfelsparger, Frederick Wolfelsparger, Peter Wolfelsparger, Adam Fritz, Barned Mous, Fridreck Miller, Hyronomus Troutman, Jacob Gishon, Peter Stone, Anthony Troser, John Shub, Christian Orendorf, Peter Edelman, George Conrad, Jacob Greeninger, Andrew Kreutzer, Philip Breidenbach, Christopher Noacker, Martin Noacker, Nicholas Miller, Valentine Herchelroth, Henry Bassler, Jacob Huy, John Ramler, Jacob Ramler, John Immel, Michael Spengler, Michael Coppenheffer, Christian Leaman, John Adam Mosser, Tobias Bickle, Jacob Brown, David Zeller, Henry Zeller, Geo. Micser, Lenhard Holstein, Michael Mieser, Andw. Ellig, Jacob Becker, David Lebenstein, Michael Brecht, Geo. Neff, Michael Neff, Ulrich Reasor, Joseph Pugh, Valentine Bowman, Christian Zwalle, Peter Borger, John Stock, Valentine Veeman, Ab'm Neff, Andw. Sholl, Stophel Stump, Widow Moore, Jno. Mire, John Knower, Henry Mire, Wendel Loudermilch, Casper Rebo, Andw. Reigand, Geo. Cogandoerfer, John Loudermilch, Lorentz Arnold, Michael Kapp, Peter Reem, Geo. Stoler, Jacob Neff, Mathias Albrecht, Henry Boyer, Lenhard Leidig, Conrad Heigberger, Daniel Clark, Ulrich Croll, Michael Schenck, John Grebill, Geo. Swingle, Martin Thomas, Thomas Durst, Alexander Sheffer, Valentine Urich, Peter Sum-

me, Ulrich Springer, Christian Miller, Peter Babler, Stofel Miller, Jacob Gensly, Peter Miller, Peter Schell, Hermanus Potorf, John Line, Thomas Copenhoefer, Christian Walborn, Martin Potorf, Wilhelm Hoster, Geo. Lash, Walter Newman, Nicholas Swingle, F. Newman, Andreas Strickler,· John Fague, Peter Zeller, Andreas Saltzgeber, John Null, Peter Brua, Michael Snider, Martin Eichholtz, Jacob Gass, Nicholas Bressler, Dietrict Marker, John Kuster, John Oxman.

The following resided in the south-east part of the township of Heidelberg, and on the borders of Warwick:
· Dillman Shite, David Taylor, Moses Irwin, Jacob Huber, Abraham Roland, Jacob Polinger, Ludwig Cole, Simon Tobias, Yost Blagher, Henry Stiegle, John Pofasberger, Nicholas Smith, Casper Simon, Martin Shoody, Stephen Beninger, Jacab Selzer, John Timothe, Tobias Hauk, Balser Shade, Michael Balmar, Henry Botts, Henry Hoyl, Han Nickle Entsminger, Han Nickle Entsminger, senr., Henry Wise, Stephen Yoacky, Jacob Gass, Christian Pence, Samuel Sellar, Mr. Shoufler, the tailor. Freemen—John Sheets, George Lidigh, George Hoyl, Peter Porgner, Yelia Swally, Jacob Stelly, Ulrich Bare, John Pile John Bale, George Ougansteen, John Switzer.

There is nothing special that occurred during the French and Indian war, not common to the townships of this county. The Indians committed several murders in the northern part of the township, (now Jackson.) They carried off several young children, one of them, named William Jackson, was returned, who had been held captive for some time, in 1762, at Lancaster. An extract of the proceedings of a conference with the Indians, held at Lancaster in 1762, is given.

LANCASTER, August, Friday 13, 1762.
James Hamilton, Esq., Lieut. Governor of Pennsylvania, recovered the following prisoners from the hands of King Beaver: Names of prisoners—Thomas Moore, taken from Potomack, Maryland. Philip Studebecker, taken from Conegocheague, Md. Ann Dougherty and Peter Condon, taken in Pennsylvania, Mary Stroudman, taken from Conegocheague, Pa., *William Jackson taken from Tulpehocken,* Pa., Elizabeth Adam, and John Lloyd, from Little Cove, Pa., Dorathy Shabrin, from

Big Cove, Eleanor Lancestoctes, from Pa., Hans Boyer, a boy, not known from whence taken. Richard Rogers, Esther Rogers, Jacob Rogers, Archibald Holtemon, and Rebecca, Walter, all from Virginia, about the South branch.

"Thursday, 19 Aug., 1762, the following were delivered: Elizabeth Williams, a young woman, delivered by Mussause, a Muncy Indian. Henry Williams, about eighteen years old, brother to Elizabeth Williams, delivered by Canyhocherato-quin, a Muncy. Peggy Dougherty, delivered by Eckgohson, a Muncy, Mary Tidd and her child, taken near Samuel Depuis, by Eckgohnson. Abigail Evan and her child, taken at Stony creek, in Virginia, by Cowachsora, a Seneca.

"A boy by Meightong, a Muncy. A little girl by Eckgoh-son, a Muncy. A little boy, Pessewanck, a Muncy. A boy of about fourteen years, by Eckgohson. A boy of twelve years, by Cowackslaira, a Seneca. A little boy of seven years, by Coracksaraa, a Seneca. These children's names unknown, as they cannot speak English, or give any account from whence they were taken."[*]

The neighborhood of Sheafferstown was, it is said, originally settled by German Jews. They were so numerous, at one time, as to have a synagogue, and a *rabbi* to read the scriptures and impart to them other instruction. As early as 1732 they had a grave-yard, around which was a substantial stone wall built, nearly the whole of which is still standing. The cement, or mortar used, must have been very adhesive, and must have been made of a larger proportion of lime than is generally taken; for it is, even now, quite as compact and solid as lime-stone itself. This grave-yard is about half a mile south of Sheafferstown—one hundred yards east from the Lancaster road, and a few hundred yards south of "Thurm-Berg," i. e., Tower-Hill—a hill on which William Henry Stiegel had erect-ed a tower, or castle, which will be noticed below. When this vicinity of Jewish settlement was pretty well populated, they left, and Germans of other denominations—Lutherans and Ger-man Reformed—settled here, among whom was Sheaffer, the proprietor of the present village.

Sheafferstown—laid out about the year 1745 or '46—is a pleasant village, south-east of Lebanon, and contains about one

[*] Provincial Rec. for 1762.

hundred houses, several stores and taverns—a Lutheran church built in 1765, and a German Reformed one—both built of stone. The inhabitants are Germans. It was here, as well as at Manheim, that the eccentric Baron Stiegel figured strangely. He was a man of singular fortune—his vicissitudes in life were varied. In Europe he was a Baron—in America an iron-master, glass manufacturer, a preacher, and a schoolmaster—now rich—then poor! In Sheafferstown, or hard by it, near the road to Lancaster, the spot on the hill, is still pointed out, where stood his tower, or castle—by those who saw the ruins of it—nothing is left to be seen of it now—which was built by the notorious German Baron.

Baron Stiegel was undoubtedly, with all his eccentricity, a man of much enterprise—of great skill in the arts, and of singular taste, as is still manifest from the house he erected in Manheim. The house is now occupied by Mr. John Arndt, of Manheim—and though Mr. Ardnt has, in having the house materially altered, so changed it, as to leave nothing of the Baron's pulpit, in a large upper saloon, where the Baron, as preacher, addressed *his hands*, he had employed at the glass factory, still much to excite admiration is to be seen. What remains of the internal, as decorations, has not its like in the United States. Its rich scenery painting, of falconry or hawking, on the side of the room walls—the tablets of China, curiously painted, the jambs, attract and excite the admiration of all who have the pleasure of spending a few moments with the affable owner of the house. Though he was proprietor of Manheim, and had a fine chateau there, he resided mainly in Philadelphia with his family, but was occasionally in the habit of inviting his friends into the country with him, to enjoy his baronial hospitality. He had two of these towers or castles erected, one at Sheafferstown, and another near Manheim—they were mounted with cannon, for the express purpose of firing a salute whenever he made his appearance in the country.

" This salute was the signal for his more intimate friends to repair to his castle, and enjoy with him the festivities of the occasion—and for all his workmen, at the furnaces and glass houses, to wash the dirt from their hands and faces, take up their musical instruments, and repair to the castle, to entertain their lord and his guests."

He lived beyond the competency of his means—he failed in business—was imprisoned for debt. A special act was passed for his relief, December 24, 1774, before the revolution of 1776 had cut "off his resources in Europe."* It is said he died as an obscure schoolmaster. *Sic transit gloria hominis!*

Newmanstown, which has been noticed, (page 195,) is on the borders of this township, on the road to Wommelsdorf.

Heidelberg township is bounded on the north by Jackson township, and by Berks county on the east; south by Lancaster county, and west by South Lebanon township. It contains thirty-six thousand acres of land, chiefly limestone, and generally well improved.

The township has several streams, affording water power to propel mills. Muelbach, or Mill creek, rises in the southern part of the township, and runs northward, and flows in Tulpehocken creek. In the south-west is Hammer creek, a branch of the Conestoga.

In 1840, this township contained six stores, one fulling mill, five grist mills, five saw mills, four tanneries and two distilleries. Population in 1830, 2,822; 1840, 2,827. Average tax valuation for 1844, $819,496 00; county tax $1,229 25.

SWATARA TOWNSHIP.

Swatara township was originally included in Bethel and Hanover townships; its boundaries have been changed since 1830, by erecting Union township. On the east it joins Bethel; Union on the west, and Lebanon on the south. The surface is diversified; the north and south are hilly; the centre level; soil, some of it limestone; the greater proportion gravel and slate, but generally well improved. It is well supplied with water, mills, &c.

This township possesses many advantages worthy the attention of capitalists, as will be seen from the subjoined communication, addressed to the writer.

* His. Col. of Pa., by Day, p. 421.

JONESTOWN, February 12, 1844;

Respected Friend:

When here, I promised to furnish you something touching our village, neighborhood, and surrounding country. This promise, it is my intention, to redeem, though a press of secular engagements, has hitherto prevented me to give the subject the attention it deserves.

I shall begin with the early history of our place. Williamsburg—this is the name of the town, now usually called Jonestown, was laid out into lots by William Jones, about the year 1761. The tract of land on which the town is built, was originally granted, by warrant, dated the 13th December, 1753, by the Honorable Proprietors, William Penn's sons, of Pennsylvania, to a Mr. Klein, who afterwards conveyed the same to William Jones.

Williamsburg or *Jonestown*, is situated near the forks of the Big and Little Swatara, seven miles north-west of the town of Lebanon, and on the main road leading from Harrisburg to Easton, on the Delaware river; it is 24 miles east of Harrisburg, and 77 from Easton; 32 from Lancaster; 31 from Reading, and 31 from both Pottsville and Orwigsburg, in Schuylkill county. The Big Swatara creek flows on the west of the town, and the Little Swatara on the south, at the base of Bunker Hill, and both unite within about one-fourth of a mile south west of the town—thence, with accessions from a number of tributaries, flow unitedly onward, and empty into the Susquehanna river, near Middletown, Dauphin county.

When this region was first settled, and about the time when Williamsburg was laid out, and for some years afterwards, the Swatara was considered one of the richest waters for fish, for its size, in the Province of Pennsylvania. This stream teemed with the finny race—the scaly salmon, the lubric eel and catfish, the coy shad, the slovenly mullet and *sui generis*—in short, "fish of all sorts," were abundant. Even within the last forty years—about 1804, 5, 6 and 7—five hundred shad were taken at a time, at the junction of the Swatara, with a common brush-net. These were days of no dry fun for us boys.

So plenty were fish—and some so large, as the old settlers will have it, that they were speared with a three, and four-tined dung fork. But those *sunny days* for piscators and lovers of fishy fun, are past, and it is feared, will never return so long as the fish are prevented from paying their visits by the interposition of, the to them, insurmountable barriers; for numerous mill, and other dams, have been erected in the Swatara, between *this* and Middletown; and as it is generally believed, not made "as the law directs," if they were, the salmon and shad would not disdain the waters here. Times have changed. But water still, naturally, runs down stream, unless forced up!

But to return to the town. It contains one hundred dwelling houses, with a population of five hundred and eleven human souls. The inhabitants, with exception of a few, are *Rank Germans*, of Pennsylvania birth. We have—we speak in common—several churches; one Lutheran, one German Reformed, one Union meeting house, for all orderly and well disposed persons, of every denomination, but, at present, principally used as a place of worship by the United Brethren, and the Evangelical Association, sometimes called "Albrechts Leute."

To accommodate the town and neighborhood—we can accommodate—we have six stores, four public houses, an apothecary, and of course a post office. Four school houses—*no* Academy yet—we expect one, if it should be raised on Bunker Hill!— Two of our school houses were built by individual subscriptions; and two by the public funds, collected by the Commonwealth, and paid over to us by the same authority. In these last, the common schools are taught under the law establishing that system. These two schools contain one hundred and sixty-five scholars, with two teachers, that is, one to each school. The crowd is so great that justice hides itself, and it is vain that parents look, that justice be done to all—we mean, to all the scholars and teachers.

For pleasantness of situation, a salubrious air, and consequently for health, our place cannot be surpassed; it has also other advantages. The town is situated on elevated ground— it commands a prominent eminence. The streets are wide, intersecting at right angles. It is not alone the eligible site that gave rise and progress to Williamsburg. What most contributed, was the navigation of the Swatara river, on which, from the time of the original settlements made here, and especially from the time the town was laid out, a vast quantity of lumber of all kinds, boards and other building materials were brought

30

to our place in rafts, floated down the Swatara in the spring, and in the fall freshets of the year. This raft navigation was carried on till in August, 1826, when the last rafts were landed. A stop was now put to it, in consequence of the Union Canal Company erecting a dam in the Swatara Gap, of immense altitude, for a dam: forty-five feet, is the height of it! This dam inundates about eight hundred acres of land; and the pond forms a complete artificial lake, and proves, occasionally, a death-place for some deer, which, to elude the chase of dogs, take to the deep and are there taken. There are still some deer in the mountains, not distant from the dam. The way hunters manage to take deer is, to set their dogs in pursuit of them, and during the chase, some of the party of the hunters do take stations near and along the pond or lake; when the deer are hotly pursued by the dogs, they make for the water, and thus are taken, in some cases alive, by the hunters.

The dam was constructed to serve as a reservoir, to feed the canal—it needs feeding, for it consumes much to keep all its functions moving—and also to answer as a slack water navigation, for the distance of six miles, towards Pine Grove, and the coal region. What changes! The tables have verily turned! Some years ago, lumber and building materials were floated *down* the Swatara to this place—now, similar materials are brought *up*, in boats, on the canal, from Middletown to our place, to Pine Grove, and intermediate places. The lumber brought down to Jonestown, formerly supplied all Tulpehocken, and the Muelbachers! These are reverses to many.

We shall leave the water and the glen awhile, to ascend "Bunker Hill"—we dont mean "the theatre of the first regular battle between the Provincial and British troop, in the war of the Revolution." We too have a *Bunker Hill*, and also still amongst us, *Revolutionary Soldiers*. But, to Bunker Hill. The prominent and rupic eminence, one half mile south of the town, is Bunker Hill. It is the highest point of the trap rock hills. The influence of these hills, says our friend Trego, Assistant State Geologist, has produced some curious and interesting modifications in the Geological features of the neighborhood.* Basalt and jasper are found here. In "Bunker, is a cave, or singular cavern, large enough to admit four or five persons—a small council for emergencies. There is something

* Geog. Pa. p. 274.

curious, as well as grotesque, in and about this rocky chamber. There is a stone two feet square and three feet high in the centre, which might have served as a table or altar, this is surrounded with seats of solid stone. In this cavern, tradition has it—internal evidence favors it—the Indians held councils.— The orderly arrangement of the massive furniture may have given rise to the tradition. It is well enough not to contradict so pleasing and so current a "Sage."

From the top of "Bunker," you have one of the most commanding prospects desirable. Place yourself on a rock—you have choice—look northward, you have a prospect, that presents a view of the coal regions through Swatara Gap, in the Kittitinny Hills—in this view lies spread before you, and between the mountain and Jonestown, a fine region of country, of sixty or more square miles. The eye tires not to view the variegated scenes—finely improved farms, interspersed with woods, and dotted with houses and barns. Contemplate on the past. See in imagination the savage Indians, thirsting for blood, crossing at Swatara Gap, in pursuit of marked victims. But, turn from so resiling a subject—wend your face south—there rises in view, for miles in extent, a lovely country; view that, while I tell you, that Bunker Hill also affords, to old and young, one of the most pleasant places of retreat and recreation in the summer season, and especially to the naturalist— here he can botanize and mineralize, while the carolling of the songsters of the wood heighten, by their varied notes, his pleasures in examining this part of our neighborhood, as to its plants, minerals, *et cetera*.

This, no doubt, had been a great place of resort for the Indians, on account of the commanding view afforded them of the country, on either side of the hill. Hundreds of arrow-heads are still found here, and go far to strengthen the hypothesis, that this was a common place of resort for the Indians, in all seasons of the year. Passing, it might be stated, that near the Little Swatara, variegated marble is found.

Other advantages, not generally considered, are to be met with here. There are some superior advantages for manufacturing purposes. I would venture the prediction, to say:— "This place will some day become a manufacturing town."— We possess water power in abundance for all such purposes.— Where need be more for propelling machinaries of all kinds?—

The facilities to transport, by canal, all raw materials to, and manufactured articles, from the place, are certainly not surpassed by any in Pennsylvania. Fuel, essentials to every one and at all times, is cheap and plenty, and can be readily supplied: the coal regions being not far distant. Capitalists and enterprising manufacturers, would do well to give this place a serious consideration. The investment would be more than "bank-sure."

Two miles above the Big Dam, in Swatara Gap, near the public road, is a beautiful cascade, which, it is confidently believed, is unsurpassed by any in the interior of the State. Four miles north of the cascade, on the summit of Sharp Mountain, is a prominent ledge of rupic projections, resembling very strikingly, at a distance, a group of houses; from the top of one of them, if you stand up there, you have a view of the Susquehanna Gap and Swatara Gap, where these streams, the former in its majesty rolls its way, and the latter sinuously steals through an opening in the Blue Mountain.

It is currently supposed—there is some ground for it—that the Indians were wont to build signal fires here: sort of telegraphs—for which Morse has a substitute—as they had a regular path from our neighborhood to Shamokin, which passed hard by this rupic town. These rocks are six miles north of Union Forge, where *Jacob Weidler* is always found, to hail and receive a friend. In the language of his favorite, Harrison,—"The latch string of his door is always hanging out."

Few only of our old settlers, are living. Among them are the following: Peter Rank, my aged father; George Heilman, Martin Meiley, John Seltzer, and John Bickel, Esq., the post master. He has held the office since it was first established in 1802. Comment is not necessary to show his fidelity as a public officer. Col. Valentine Schaufler is an old inhabitant, but has not resided here as long as some of the afore-mentioned.— He is an aged man—ninety-two years old. He was a soldier in the revolutionary army. I have heard the colonel often relate that, during the revolution of '76, he had been taken prisoner by the British, and afterwards deserted from them, and that he was obliged to swim several miles to effect his escape. This, said he, was near New York.

Five miles west from our town, Mr. Adam Harper settled himself, at an early period. His location was the most western in this county at that time. He was surrounded by Indians. They had a string of wigwams hard by his house. He kept the first public house in all this region of country. The place is still known as "Harper's tavern," on the Harrisburg road. Near this, in 1755 or 1756, th Indians killed five or six white persons, not half a mile from Harper's. A woman—a sister of Major Leidig—was scalped by the Indians, and incredible as it may appear to some, survived this barbarous act, and lived for years afterwards. This, however, agrees with what you stated, when here last winter.

In conclusion—once more to our own place. All tradition says, when this place was first settled, it was noted as a place for horse racing, gambling, &c., &c. But at present—and for a number of years past—it has been, and is a very moral place. Vice and immorality have turned their hideous faces t'other way. All we need now is a more general diffusion of knowledge, by means of Sabbath schools, schools of advanced standing, and preaching of the gospel in its purity and simplicity.

The thought has occurred to me that a well chosen site for an academy would be " Bunker Hill." Its advantages need no discussion. A trial would, undoubtedly, decide in its favor. I must close my epistle.

Believe me, I remain your friend,

WILLIAM RANK.

Swatara township contained a population in 1830 of 1,510; in 1840, 1,056—part of Union township having since been taken from it. Average tax valuation for 1844, $416,636,000; county tax, $624 96.

ANNVILLE TOWNSHIP.

Annville township was formed out of part of Londonderry and Lebanon. It is bounded on the north-east by East Hanover township; east by Lebanon; south and west by Londonderry. It contains nearly twenty-two thousand acres of land, principally level, and of the best limestone quality, and highly improved. Some portion of it is gravel. Some of the finest

30*

and best improved farms in the county, are to be met with in this township.   Many firm substantial farm houses and barns, principally of stone, indicative of wealth and taste, can be seen as one passes along the public roads.   Some old tile-covered houses are still to be seen.

This township is well supplied with streams of water, which afford abundance of water power for mills, &c.   The Swatara forms the boundary on the north; the Quitapohila flows through the township, and receives, in its course, Killinger's run.   There is a forge on the Quitopahila—Meadow run is the name of another small stream in this township.

In 1840 it contained one fulling mill, one woollen factory, eight grist mills, five saw mills, one oil mill, one distillery, and eleven stores.   Population in 1830, 2,736; 1840, 2,649: average tax valuation of 1844, $915,937 00; county tax $1,373 98.

The Harrisburg and Reading turnpike passes through this township.—Millerstown is on it.

Millerstown—this place was formerly called "Annville," and was laid out by Messrs. Riegel and Ulrich.   It is handsomely situated, and is a flourishing village on the Quitopahila.   It contains about one hundred and twenty houses, four or five stores, and the same number of taverns, and the usual handicrafts.   Several schools—one public school—and an academy, are in successful operation.   It contains several churches.

The names of the first settlers are given when speaking of Lebanon and Londonderry townships.

It was at this place—Rev. Dr. Dady—the noted impostor, first commenced, by aid of his fascinating eloquence, to gull the honest Germans.   To show what may be done among a people believing implicitly—"men untried,"—that place is given to the following.   A wholesome lesson may be deduced from it. When he failed, he tried another region, more genial to his purposes.

DOCTOR DADY.

~~~~~~~~~~~~~

The following account of that noted impostor, is taken nearly word for word from that written by the Hon. John Joseph Henry, and sent by him to Philadelphia with the convicted impostors. Judge Henry wrote the account from notes taken at the trial. It follows, in most things, the order of the testimony as given in by the witnesses.

Dr. Dady, who was a German by birth, came to this country with the Hessians during the American revolution. Possessing a fascinating eloquence in the German language, and being very fluent in the English, he was afterwards employed as a minister of the gospel by uninformed but honest Germans.

When the sacerdotal robe could no longer be subservient to his avaricious views, he laid it aside and assumed the character of a physician. As such he went to York county, and dwelt among the poor inhabitants of a mountainous part thereof, (now within the limits of Adams county,) where, in various artful ways, he preyed on the purses of the unwary.

Of all the numerous impositions with which his name is connected, and to which he lent his aid, we will mention but two. The scene of one of them is in what is now Adams county, where he dwelt; and of the other in the "barrens" of York county.

The following is an account of the Adams county imposition:—

Rice Willams, or rather Rainsford Rogers, a New Englander, and John Hall, a New Yorker, (both of whom had been plundering the inhabitants of the southern states by their wiles,) came to the house of Clayton Chamberlain, a neighbor of Dady, in July, 1797.

On the following morning, Dady went to Chamberlain's, and had a private conversation between Williams and Hall, before breakfast. After Dady had left them, Williams asked Chamberlain whether the place was not haunted. Being answered in the negative, he said that it was haunted—that he had been born with a veil over his face—could see spirits, and had been conducted thither, sixty miles, by a spirit. Hall assented to the truth of this. In the evening of the same day, they had another interview with Dady. Williams then told Chamberlain, that if he would permit him to tarry over night, he would show him a spirit. This being agreed to, they went into a field in the evening, and Williams drew a circle on the ground, around which he directed Hall and Chamberlain to walk in silence. A terrible screech was soon heard proceeding from a *black* ghost (!!!) in the woods, at a little distance from the parties, in a direction opposite to the place where Williams stood. In a few minutes a *white* ghost appeared, which Williams addressed in a language which those who heard him could not understand—the ghost replied in *the same language!* After his ghostship had gone away, Williams said that the spirit knew of a treasure which it was permitted to discover to *eleven* men —they must be honest, religious and sensible, and neither horse jockeys nor Irishmen.

The intercourse between Williams and Dady now ceased to be apparent; but it was continued in private. Chamberlain, convinced of the existence of a ghost and a treasure, was easily induced to form a company, which was soon affected.

Each candidate was initiated by the receipt of a small sealed paper, containing a little yellow sand, which was called "the power." This "power" the candidate was to bury under the earth to the depth of one inch, for three days and three nights —performing several absurd ceremonies, too obscene to be described here.

A circle, two inches in diameter, was formed in the field, in the centre of which there was a hole six inches wide and as many deep. A captain, a lieutenant and three committee men were elected. Hall had the honor of the captaincy. The exercise was to pace around the circle, &c. This, it was said, propitiated and strengthened the white ghost, who was opposed by an unfriendly black ghost who rejoiced in the appellation of Pompey. In the course of their nocturnal exercises they often saw the white ghost—they saw Mr. Pompey too, but he appeared to have "his back up," bellowed loudly, and threw stones at them.

On the night of the 18th of August, 1797, Williams undertook to get instructions from the white ghost. It was done in the following manner: He took a sheet of clean white paper, and folded it in the form of a letter, when each member breathed into it three times; this being repeated several times, and the paper laid over the hole in the centre of the circle, the instructions of the ghost were obtained. The following is a short extract from the epistle written by the ghost:

"Go on, and do right, and prosper, and the treasure shall be yours. I am permitted to write this in the same hand I wrote in the flesh for your direction—O————⌐⌐. Take care of your powers in the name and fear of God our protector—if not, leave the work. There is a great treasure, 4000 pounds a-piece for you. Don't trust the black one. Obey orders.— Break the enchantment, which you will not do until you get an ounce of mineral dulcimer eliximer; some German doctor has it. *It is near, and dear, and scarce.* Let the committee get it—but don't let the Doctor know what you are about—he is wicked."

' The above is but a small part of this precious communication. In consequence of these ghostly directions, a young man named Abraham Kephart waited, by order of the committee, on Dr. Dady. The Dr. preserved his *eliximer* in a bottle sealed with a large red seal, and buried in a heap of oats, and demanded fifteen dollars for an ounce of it. Young Kephart could not afford to give so much, but gave him thirty-six dollars and three bushels of oats for three ounces of it. Yost Liner, another of these wise committee men, gave the Doctor 121 dollars for eleven ounces of the stuff.

The company was soon increased to 30 persons, many of whom were wealthy. Among those who were most miserably duped may be mentioned Clayton Chamberlain, Yost Liner, Thomas Bigham, William Bigham, Samuel Togert, John M'-Kinney, James Agnew the elder, James M'Cleary, Robert Thompson, David Kissinger, George Sheckley, Peter Wikeart, and John Philips. All these and many other men were, in the words of the indictment, " cheated and defrauded by means of certain false tokens and pretences, to wit: by means of preten-

ded spirits, certain circles, certain brown powder, and certain
compositions called mineral dulcimer elixer, and Deterick's
mineral elixer."

But the wiles of these imposters were soon exerted in other
parts. The following is an account of their proceedings in and
about Shrewsbury township, in York county. Williams intimated that he had received a call from a ghost resident in those
parts, at the distance of forty miles from Dady's. Jacob Wister, one of the conspirators, was the agent of Williams on this
occasion. He instituted a company of twenty-one persons, all
of whom were, of course, most ignorant people. The same and
even more absurd ceremonies were performed by these people,
and the communications of the ghost were obtained in a still
more ridiculous manner than before. The communications mentioned Dr. Dady as the person from whom they should obtain
the dulcimer elixer, as likewise a kind of sand which the ghost
called the " Asiatic sand," and which was necessary in order
to give efficacy to the "powers." Ulrich Neaff, a committee
man of this company, paid to Dr. Dady ninety dollars for
seven and a half ounces of the elixer. The elixer was put
into vials, and each person who had one of them, held it in his
hand and shook it as he pranced round the circle; on certain
occasions he annointed his head with it, and afterwards, by
order of the spirit, the phial was buried in the ground.

Paul Baliter, another of the committee men, took with him
to Dr. Dady's, a hundred dollars to purchase "Asiatic sand,"
at three dollars per ounce. Dady being absent, Williams procured from the Doctor's shop as much sand as the money would
purchase. In this instance, Williams cheated the Doctor, for
he kept the spoil to himself, and thence arose an overthrow of
the good fraternity.

Each of them now set up for himself. Williams procured
directions from *his* ghost, that each of the companies should
despatch a committee to Lancaster to buy " Deterick's mineral
elixer," of a physician in that place. In the meantime Williams and his wife went to Lancaster, where they prepared the
elixer, which was nothing but a composition of copperas and
cayenne pepper. Mrs. Williams, as the wife of John Huber,
a German doctor, went to Dr. Rose, with a letter dated "13
miles from Newcastle, Delaware," which directed him how to
sell the article, &c. The enormity of the price aroused the

suspicion of Dr. Rose. In a few days the delegates from the committee arrived, and purchased elixer to the amount of $740 33. When the lady came for the money, she was arrested, and the secret became known. Her husband, Williams, escaped.

The Lancaster expedition naving led to a discovery of the tricks of the impostors, a few days after the disclosures made by Mrs. Williams, an indictment was presented in the criminal court of York county, against Dr. John Dady, Rice Williams, Jesse Miller, Jacob Wister, the elder, and Jacob Wister, the younger, for a conspiracy to cheat and defraud. The trial took place in June following, and resulted in the conviction of Wister, the elder, and Dr. Dady—the former of whom was fined ten dollars, and imprisoned one month in the county jail, the latter fined ninety dollars, and sentenced to two years confinement in the penitentiary at Philadelphia.

Dady had just been convicted of participating in the conspiracy in Shrewsbury, when he and Hall were found guilty of a like crime in Adams county—whereupon Hall was fined one hundred dollars and sent to the penitentiary for two years, and Dady was fined one hundred and sixty dollars, and sentenced to undergo an additional servitude of two years in the penitentiary, to commence in June, 1800, when his first term would expire.

Thus ended the history of Doctor Dady, who certainly was not devoid of talent, who possessed a most winning address, and was a thorough master in quick and correct discernment of character. He reigned, for a season, with undisputed sway, in what was then the western part of York county. His cunning, for a long time, lulled suspicion to sleep. The history of his exorcisms should teach the credulous that the ghosts which appear now-a-days are as material as our own flesh.— *His. York Co.*

MILLERSTOWN.

To return again to the vicinity of Millerstown. About one mile north-east from Millerstown, the first public house, in this region of country, was kept by the grand-father of Adam Ulrich, the present occupant. Mr. Ulrich also kept a small store, and traded with the Indians, many of whom staid weeks with him. Mr. Adam Ulrich's father, when a boy, frequently sported and played with the Indians, in the thickets. It appears there was a burying ground near Ulrich's house,

One evening, about the year 1756 or '57, Mr. Adam Ulrich's father, and grandfather, were feeding their cattle, when they were surprised by the Indians; but fortunately escaped and eluded the pursuit of them; whereupon, the Indians killed all the cattle, by cutting out their tongues. This happened on the farm now owned by Mr. Shenk.

During the late war of 1812, when a praiseworthy spirit pervaded community to resist British encroachments, and also to establish manufactories to manufacture goods for our own consumption, several wealthy gentlemen of Lancaster county, headed by the enterprizing Mr. Hentzelman, erected an extensive cotton and woollen factory, a few miles from Millerstown, at the enormous expense of $96,000—and for some time carried on business with success, but owing to the ruinous policy of *not protecting* American industry—opening our ports wide for foreign manufactures; they failed. Their goods were considered equal in quality to any manufactured in the country.

Free foreign importations—either of British goods, or British paupers—will eventually ruin the whole country. Our country should be protected against both, by wholesome restrictions. Our policy is too liberal. It is mis-directed charity, to open our ports for foreign goods, and foreign paupers, without salutary restrictions!!

JACKSON TOWNSHIP.

Jackson township—this township was originally embraced by Heidelberg and Bethel townships, to which the reader is referred for the names of some of the first settlers, a few of whom had come from Schoharie, in New York, others emigrated directly from Europe. This part of the county was embraced, in what is so well known, in the early history of Pennsylvania, as the "Tulpehocken settlement," or as the name is written in the Provincial Records, Turpyhocken.* It was through this region, that the Indians had their common course, in carrying their furs and skins from the west to the east, as may be learned from a proposal made by William Penn, in 1690, for a second settlement in the province of Pennsylvania. He says:—"It is now my purpose to make another settlement upon the river Susquehannagh, that runs into the Bay of Chesapeake, and lies about fifty miles west from the Delaware, as appears by the common maps of the English dominions in America. There I design to lay out a plan for the building of another city, in the most convenient place for communication with the former plantation on the east, which by land is as good as some already, a way being laid out between the two rivers very exactly and conveniently, at least three years ago, and what will not be hard to do by water, by the benefit of the river Scoulkill; for a branch of that river lies near a branch that runs into the Susquehannagh river, and is the common course of the Indians with their skins and furrs in our parts, and to the province of east and west New Jersey, and New York, from the west and north-east parts of the continent from which they bring them.†

The Honorable John Evans, Esq., Lieut. Governor of the Province of Pennsylvania, passed from the Susquehanna, through here on his way to Philadelphia, in July, 1707, as may be seen from the following extract from his journal.

"The Governor, with Messrs. John French, William Tonge, Mitchel Bezaillion, and one Grey, and four servants, set out from New Castle, the 27th of June, and the next morning arrived at Otteraroe, &c.‡

"On Tuesday, 1st July, we went to Conestogoe, and lay there that night, and the next morning proceeded on our journey, and arrived in the Evening within 3 miles of an Indian

---

* Min Prov Council ii, 196.
† Haz Reg., vol i, p 400
‡ Minutes of Prov Coun. ii, 404,—5.

Village, called Peixtan.   The Govr. had received Information
at Pequehan, that one Nicole, a ffrench Indian Trader, was at
that place, agst. whom great Complaints had been made to the
Govr. of which he acquainted the Chief Indian of Peixtan, as
also of his design to seize him; who willingly agreed to it, but
advised the Govr. to be very cautious in the manner: there
being only young People at home, who perhaps might make
some Resistance, if it were done without their first being told
of it; for this reason we lay short of the Village that night;
but Early in the morning we went within half a mile of the
Town, & leaving our horses, march'd a foot nearer the
same; from whence the Govr. sent Martine to the Village:
Ordering him to tell Nicole that he had brought 2 Caggs of
Rum with him, which he had left in the woods, for fear any
Christians were there; and withal to perswade Nicole to
go with him and taste the Rum.   Martine returned with
James Letort, & Joseph Jessop, 2 Indian Traders but could
not prevail with Nicole; upon this, Martine was sent back with
Orders to bring down some of the Indians, and Nicole with
them: then we drew nearer the Town, and laid ourselves in the
bushes, and Martine returned with 2 Indians, whom the Govr.
acquainted with his intent of taking Nicole, telling at the same
time, he had spoken with to the Uncle of one of them
upon that head, who ordered the Indians to submit to the
Govrs. Commands, with which they were contented, tho' we
perceived too well the contrary, by their inquiring how many
we were, and how armed; and by the Concern they seemed to
be in, when they found we were more men in number than they:
but still Nicole was wanting; it was therefore Resolved to
try once more if he could be got into the woods, accordingly Martine went again, and brought Nicole to the place where
we lay concealed, and asking him to Drink a dram, he seized
him; but Nicole started from him and run for it, when immediately we started out and took him, and presently carried him
to the Village, (thro' which we were obliged to pass,) and
there we found some Indians with Guns in their hands, who
lookt much displeased at what we had done, but we being in a
readiness against any surprize, they thought it not fit to attempt
any thing; here we stayed abot. half an hour, and then parted
for Turpyhocken; having mounted Nicole upon a horse, and
tied his legs under the Belly; we got within a mile of Turpy-

hocken about 2 of ye Clock, on fryday morning, and about 7 the Govr. went to the town, from thence we went to Mana- tawny that night, & the next day to Philadelphia."

During the French and Indian war, from 1755 to 1760, the inhabitants of this township, in common with many others, were repeatedly alarmed by the Indians. Several murders were committed by them within the borders of this township. On one occasion many of the inhabitants of this and adjacent town- ships, met at the house of Benjamin Spycker's, near the pre- sent site of Stouchstown. There, a company consisting of ris- ing of three hundred men, went in pursuit of the Indians, most of them well armed, though about twenty of them, had nothing but axes and pitchforks—all unanimously agreed to die toge- ther, and engage the enemy, wherever they should meet them. This happened in October 1755.*

In this, as well as other townships, there were several block houses, or forts, to which, in cases of emergency, the inhabit- ants would flee. There was one—we were informed by Mr. Breitenbach, on the farm now owned by him—a short distance east of Myerstown.

Philip Breitenbach, father of Mr. Breitenbach mentioned above, came from Germany—in 1754 he purchased the tract of land, on which a fort was afterwards erected, from Martin Noacker. Philip Breitenbach was wont, on many occasions of alarm, to take his drum and beat on an eminence near his house, to collect the neighbors from work, into the fort. On one oc- casion, the Indians pursued them close to the house, when one of the inmates took up a gun, and shot the Indian dead on the spot.

Jackson township is bounded on the north-east by Berks county—on the south by Heidelberg township, and on the west by South and North Lebanon, and Bethel townships; and con- tains nearly fifteen thousand acres of first rate land—limestone soil, and the surface is generally very level. The improvements are very firm. Buildings are—many of stone—large and com- modious.

This township is crossed by both the Reading and Harris- burg turnpike, and Union Canal. Tulpehocken creek, and the

* See Conrad Weiser's letter to Governor Morris, p 43—44 antea

Swatara, are the principal streams, affording water power for mills, &c. In 1840, this township contained three grist mills, one saw mill, two tanneries, two distilleries, four stores, and two lumber yards. Population in 1830, 2,120; 1840, 2,508. Average tax valuation for 1840, $1,031,326; county tax $2,546 99.

Myerstown, on the Reading and Harrisburg turnpike, seven miles east from the town of Lebanon, was laid out by Isaac Myers about seventy-five years ago. The locality is quite a pleasant one. The country around it is certainly not surpassed by any in the State, for fertility of soil.

The town has been much improved within the last twenty years. It contains several fine buildings; among others, the Lutheran church, built in 1812, which, in its way, makes a "modest" appearance. All the useful branches are taught here—with what success, it has not been stated to the writer. It is supplied with a School Library. This is a good feature in the general plan.

The Evangelical Association is erecting a house for public worship here. Sunday schools, and other schools are pretty well attended. The population exceeds 700 souls. Some three or four buildings are being put up at present.

UNION TOWNSHIP.

Union township has been erected within a few years, out of the contiguous townships. It has East Hanover on the west, and Swatara township on the east. The Big Swatara creek is its principal stream.

Fort Smith, it is believed, was in this part of the country, within the limits of Union township. Not a few seem to think, each of them has the honor of having it perpetuated, that Fort Smith was on his farm. Some with whom we have conversed, locate it at Union Forge. An intelligent gentleman, Jacob Weidler, Esq., in a communication of Feb. 13, 1844, says:—"The following facts I obtained from Mr. Daniel Musser, who is nearly seventy years old. He suggests that there may probably be an error to locate *Fort Smith,* where Union Forge is. Mr. Musser's maternal grandfather, Peter Heydrich, who emigrated from Germany and located, previous to 1738, about three-fourths of a mile due north from this place, it appears, owned the place on which Fort Smith was erected. My informant says, he knows that a fort had been erected on his grandfather's farm, to which, in great emergencies, the neighbors fled for safety.

The persons whom Mr. Musser remembers of having heard of that resided in this township, as old settlers, were Mr. Noacre or Noecker, who was shot dead in his field while ploughing, on the farm now owned by John Zehring. He says that one Philip Maurer was shot dead while cradling oats on the farm now occupied by John Gross. Martin Hess, who escaped unhurt, his house also had been a place of refuge—often half a dozen of families would resort to Hess's house, which was about one mile south-west from Peter Heydrich's, and a half a mile west from this place. Mathias Boeshore (your mother's relative) was also an old settler, who, on one occasion retreated from the enemy, the Indians, towards Hess's. Just as he had got inside the house, seized his gun, and turned upon his pursuers, levelling his deadly weapon at them, and while in the act of drawing the trigger, he received a shot from an Indian, which wounded him but slightly. The bullet of one savage's gun struck that part of Boeshore's rifle, to which the flint is attached; the ball glancing a little to one side, wounded him in the left side. Boeshore lived to be a very old man.

The land on which this fort was erected, is now owned by widow Elizabeth Shuey. The old people are unanimous in locating the fort on Mrs. Shuey's farm, at that time the property of Peter Heydrich. None of them seems to know that the house on Mr. Weidman's place here was ever used as a fort. May it not, like the house of Mr. Hess, have been only a kind of blockhouse; as the house of Hess, as well as the one here, has also some apertures, or port holes, which were evidently used to fire out upon the enemy?

Of Peter Heydrick, it is related, that on a certain occasion, the Indians appeared in great numbers—and nearly all the neighbors being in their own houses—Heydrich gave immediate notice to the people to resort to the fort, and in the meantime, (having both fife and drum in the fort, and could beat and fife well) took the drum and fife, marched *himself* into the woods or thickets, now beating the drum, then blowing the

31*

fife; then and again gave the word of command, *loud and distinct*, as if it had been given to a large force—though he was the only one to obey orders—by this *Guerre de ruse, slight of war*, he managed to keep the savages away, and collect his neighbors securely. *Noth bricht Eisen.*

The following letter from the pen of Adam Reed, Esq., dated in Hanover, Oct. 14, 1756, may cast some additional light on this point. The letter was addressed to Edward Shippen, Esq., and others.

" *Friends and Fellow Subjects*:
I send you in a few lines, the melancholy condition of the frontiers of this county. Last Tuesday, the 12th inst., ten Indians came on Noah Frederick, while ploughing, killed and scalped him, and carried away three of his children that were with him—the eldest but nine years old—and plundered his house and carried away every thing that suited their purpose; such as clothes, bread, butter, a saddle, and a good rifle gun, &c.—it being but two short miles from Captain Smith's fort, at Swatara gàp, and a little better than two miles from my house.

Last Saturday evening, an Indian came to the house of Philip Robeson, carrying a green bush before him—said Robeson's son being on the corner of his Fort, watching others that were dressing, flash by him—the Indian perceiving that he was observed, fled; the watchman fired, but missed him. This being about three-fourths of a mile from Manady Fort; and yesterday morning, two miles from Smith's Fort, at Swatara, in Bethel township, as Jacob Farnwal was going from the house of Jacob Meylin to his own, was fired upon by two Indians, and wounded, but escaped with his life; and a little after, in said township, as Frederick Henly and Peter Sample were carrying away their goods in wagons, were met by a parcel of Indians, and all killed, lying dead in one place, and one man at a little distance. But what more has been done, has not come to my ears—only that the Indians were continuing their murders!

The frontiers are employed in nothing but carrying off their effects; so that some miles are now waste! We are willing, but not able, without help—you are able, if you be willing, (that is including the lower parts of the county) to give such assistance as will enable us to recover our waste land. You may depend upon it, that without assistance, we, in a few days, will be on the *wrong side* of you; for I am now on the frontier, and I fear that by to-morrow night, I will be left two miles.

Gentlemen, *consider what you will do, and don't be long about it;* and let not the world say, that we died as fools died! Our hands are not tied, but let us exert ourselves, and do something for the honor of our country, and the preservation of our fellow subjects. I hope you will communicate our grievances to the lower parts of our country; for surely they will send us help, if they understood our grievances.

I would have gone down myself, but dare not, my family is in such danger. I expect an answer by the bearer, if possible.*

I am, gentlemen,
Your very humble servant,
ADAM REED.

P. S. Before sending this away, I would mention, I have just received information, that there are seven killed and five children scalped alive, but have not the account of their names.

A considerable portion of this township is hilly. The soil gravel and sienitic, some yellow shale and limestone, all of which is susceptible of high improvement. Average tax valuation, $178,890 00; county tax $288 34.

* Provincial Records, P , p. 69

CHAPTER II.

GENERAL STATISTICS OF LEBANON COUNTY.

PRODUCTS OF THE MINE.

Products of the mine are iron, manufactured into cast and bar iron. There were, according to the census of 1840, three furnaces in the county, and they produced three thousand and twenty tons of cast iron; three bloomeries and forges, which produced two hundred and ninety-seven tons of bar iron; the furnaces and forges consumed six thousand one hundred and eight tons of fuel—employed two hundred and thirty one men, including mining operations—capital invested, two hundred and thirty-three thousand dollars.

LIVE STOCK.

Live Stock.—Five thousand and fifty-six horses and mules; fourteen thousand seven hundred and eighty-one neat cattle; ten thousand nine hundred and seventy-seven head of sheep; thirteen thousand seven hundred and eighty swine; poultry of all kinds valued at seven thousand one hundred and thirty-five dollars.

CEREAL PRODUCTIONS.

Cereal productions.—Wheat, two hundred and fifteen thousand four hundred and twenty-eight bushels; two hundred and forty-five bushels of barley; oats, two hundred and thirty-two thousand six hundred and two bushels; rye, one hundred and forty-seven thousand two hundred and fifty-four bushels; eight hundred and thirty-five bushels of buckwheat; two hundred and thirty-nine thousand and thirty-one of Indian corn.

VARIOUS AGRICULTURAL PRODUCTS.

Various other agricultural products are: fourteen thousand nine hundred and forty-three pounds of wool raised; one hundred and one thousand six hundred and thirty-two bushels of potatoes; sixteen thousand five hundred and sixty tons of hay; one hundred pounds of silk cocoons; six thousand nine hundred and thirty-three cords of wood sold.

THE DAIRY.

Value of the products of the dairy, twenty-six thousand five hundred and twenty-two dollars. The value of the products of the orchard, six thousand one hundred and twenty-three dollars; fifty gallons of wine manufactured. Home made or family goods made, nine thousand seven hundred and twenty-two dollars.

COMMERCE.

There were fifty-eight groceries and stores, with an aggregate capital of two hundred and forty-one thousand nine hundred dollars; seven lumber yards, capital invested twenty-four thousand five hundred; employed one hundred and twenty eight men. Thirty-five persons were employed in internal transportation.

MACHINERY.

The value of machinery manufactured was estimated at six thousand dollars, and employed twenty-six men. Hardware and cutlery, two hundred dollars—employed three men. Bricks and lime, twenty-one thousand eight hundred and sixty dollars; two hundred and eleven men employed. Capital invested in the preceding manufactories, sixteen thousand nine hundred and ten dollars.

MANUFACTORIES.

The county is pretty well supplied with factories; four fulling mills, two woollen factories; value of manufactured goods
produced, four thousand one hundred and eighty dollars; thirty
persons employed; capital invested, one thousand four hundred
and eighty dollars.

Silk has received some attention, ninety pounds of reeled
silk were raised, valued three hundred and eighty dollars; employed six males and five females; capital invested limited, only
fifty-two dollars. The value of manufactured goods, eleven thousand and thirty-four dollars; persons employed, three hundred
and eighty-three; capital invested, five thousand four hundred
and fifty-one dollars. The raising of tobacco has received some
attention—the value of .the manufactured article amounted to
five thousand seven hundred and fifty dollars; employed twenty-six men; capital invested, three thousand and seventy-five
dollars

Value of hats and caps manufactured, eleven thousand nine
hundred dollars; nineteen persons employed; capital invested,
five thousand five hundred and fifty dollars.

TANNERIES, &C.

Tanneries, there were twenty two; tanned four thousand six
hundred and sixty-six sides of sole leather; two thousand eight
hundred and twenty-five sides of upper leather; fifty-two men
employed; capital invested, forty-six thousand eight hundred
dollars. There were twenty-nine saddleries; value of manufactured articles, estimated at thirty-four thousand four hundred and fifty; capital invested, fifteen thousand seven hundred
and sixty-four dollars.

SOAP AND CANDLES MANUFACTURED.

Soap, three thousand six hundred and eighteen pounds; tal-
low candles, seven thousand two hundred and twenty-five dollars—employed one hundred and thirty-seven—capital invested,
one thousand seven hundred and seventy dollars.

DISTILLED AND FERMENTED LIQUORS.

Twelve distilleries were in operation in 1840, which produced seventy-three thousand five hundred and twenty gallons;
two breweries made twelve thousand two hundred gallons of
beer—the distilleries and breweries employed twenty-four men;
capital invested, fourteen thousand three hundred and fifty gallons.

VALUE OF MEDICINES, DRUGS, &c. &c.

One thousand and fifty dollars. Five potteries produced in
value, one thousand eight hundred dollars—employed eight
men—capital, seven hundred and seventy-five dollars. One
sugar refinery—value of produce, one thousand two hundred
dollars. Confectionaries made to the value of twelve thousand
dollars—four men employed—capital, six thousand dollars.

PAPER MANUFACTURED, &c.

There was one paper manufactory—value of produce, six
thousand dollars—five men employed—capital, three hundred
dollars. Four printing offices—three weekly newspapers published and one periodical—thirteen men employed—capital, nine
thousand seven hundred and fifty dollars.

CARRIAGES AND WAGONS.

Were manufactured to the value of thirteen thousand and forty
dollars—employed fifty-eight men—capital invested, seven
hundred and fifteen dollars.

MILLS, &c.

The number of grist mills was thirty-seven, which manufactured two thousand six hundred and ninety barrels of flour.
Saw mills, twenty-four. Two oil mills. The value manufactured of saw and oil mills, was forty-three thousand two hundred and ninety-three dollars—employed seventy-eight hands—
capital invested, seventeen thousand nine hundred and sixty-five
dollars.

The number of brick and stone buildings built in 1840, was twelve, and twenty-two of wood—employed one hundred and nineteen men.

All other manufactures not enumerated above, amounted in value to one hundred and seventeen thousand two hundred and fifty-nine dollars—capital invested twenty-two thousand three hundred and seventy dollars. Total capital invested in all the manufactories, was one hundred and ninety thousand eighty-seven dollars.

———

POPULATION.

The Population of Lebanon county in 1840, was as follows:

Free white males under 5, one thousand eight hundred and seventy-seven; of 5 years and under 10, one thousand five hundred and thirteen; of 10 and under 15, one thousand four hundred and seven; of 15 and under 20, one thousand two hundred and ten; of 20 and under 30, one thousand seven hundred and eighteen; of 30 and under 40, one thousand one hundred and sixty-three; of 40 and under 50, nine hundred and five; of 50 and under 60, four hundred and ninety-nine; 60 and under 70, two hundred and eighty; of 70 and under 80, one hundred and twenty-six; of 80 and under 90, thirty-four; of 90 and under 100, one.

Free white females under 5 years, one thousand eight hundred and four; of 5 and under 10, one thousand five hundred and sixty two; of 10 and under 15, one thousand two hundred and seventy- six; of 15 and under 20, one thousand two hundred and ninety-seven; of 20 and under 30, one thousand nine hundred and nineteen; of 30 and under 40, one thousand one hundred and seventy; of 40 and under 50, eight hundred and eighty-six; of 50 and under 60, five hundred and seventy-nine; of 60 and under 70, three hundred and thirty-eight; of 70 and under eighty, one hundred and sixty; of 80 and under 90, forty; of 90 and 100, five.

Colored Persons.—Colored males under ten years, 17; of ten and under twenty-four 10; of twenty-four and under thirty-six, 9; of thirty six and under fifty-five, 10; of fifty-five and over one hundred, 4; colored females under ten, 19; of ten and under twenty-four, 11; of twenty-four and under thirty-six, 9; of thirty-six and under forty-five, 11; of fifty-five and under one hundred, 3. Total population of Lebanon county, 21,872; of these 27 are engaged in mining; 2,205 in agriculture; 122 in commerce; 4,324 in manufactures and trades; 2 in navigation on the ocean; 130 in the navigation on canals; 47 of the learned professions; 30 pensioners; of the borough of Lebanon, namely: George Hess, aged 79; Swatara, Peter Witmoyer, 80; Anna Barbara Yeagley, 78; Peter Sailor, 77; John Shalley, 79; Jacob Heim, 74; John Bickel, 88; Valentine Shoufler, 88; Martin Meily, 68; George Heilmen, 81; East Hanover, Thomas Kopenhaver, 80; John Hetrich, 77; Jacob Decker, 84; Philip Witmeyer, 80; John Garberich, 81; James Steward, 83 ; Londonderry, Jacob Lentz, 81; Adam Trist, 80; Jacob Keaner, Andrew Robeson, 81; Heidelberg, George Wolf, 79; Margaretta Leob, 79; Elizabeth Derr, 81; Lebanon, Andrew Hoover, 75; Dilman Doup, 81; Mary Weaver, 75; Bethel, Catharine Walborn, 85; Jackson, Mary Bainny, 75; Rebecca Bowers, 74; John Smith, 86.

Six deaf and dumb persons of 11 years and under 14; fourteen of 14 years and under 25; nineteen of upwards of 25 years; sixteen blind persons; twenty-six insane and idiots.

EDUCATION.

Four academies, one hundred and fifty-four scholars; thirty-six primary and common schools, one thousand three hundred and twenty-seven scholars; four hundred and twenty-four schooled at public expense. There are six hundred and eighty-nine white persons over twenty years of age, who cannot read and write.

32

CHAPTER III.

~~~~~~~~~~

GEOLOGY OF BERKS AND LEBANON COUNTIES.

In giving an account of the geology of a small district of a country, it requires, to enter minutely into it, a larger space than the design of this compilation will admit. Nothing original is presented. What is given, is from the pen of that distinguished and accomplished writer, the author of the *Geography of Pennsylvania,* a book that should be in every family in the State.*

BERKS COUNTY.

The geological character of this county is various in its different parts. On the southern border is the red shale of the middle secondary series; in the upper or northern portion of this red shale, the calcareous conglomerate rock, called Potomac marble, is abundant in several places, particularly near the Schuylkill below Reading. North of this are the hills of the South mountain range, which contain gneiss, sienite, and other primary rocks, together with the hard whitish sandstone which overlies the primary. Several of the little valleys interspersed between these hills, contain irregular belts of limestone.— Northward of this chain of hills is the great limestone formation of the Kittatiny valley, which extends along its south-eastern side from the Delaware river to the Maryland line; and adjoining it on the north, reaching to the Blue mountain, is the slate formation next in position above the limestone, which is equally extensive in its range. At several places in Berks county the

* The Geography of Pennsylvania by Charles B. Trego, Esq., Assistant State Geologist, published by E. C. Biddle, Philadelphia.

limestone contains belts of slate of considerable thickness, and in the neighborhood of Bernville and Womelsdorf, the limestone and slate formations appear to have no distinct line of division, but alternating strata of both are found. A dike of trap rock extends northward across the limestone, east of Sinking spring, crossing the Tulpehocken near the mouth of Cacoosing creek, and extending northward into the slate region.

Iron ore occurs in several parts of the county. At Mount Pleasant, in Colebrookdale township, the magnetic variety of ore has been mined to some extent, and is found in other places connected with the primary rocks. In Oley township, and near Boyerstown, are mines which were formerly worked for the supply of furnaces in that neighborhood. Brown argillaceous iron ore occurs near Kutztown, and at Moselem it is extensively mined, as also near the Lebanon turnpike, about eight miles west of Reading. A rock yielding hydraulic cement of good quality, is found near the Schuylkill, from which that article is manufactured in considerable quantity for use. Copper ore occurs at several places within the county, but generally in such small quantity and so mixed with iron as to render the expediency of working it very doubtful. Near Morgantown is a mine of this character, which is not at present in a productive state.

LEBANON COUNTY.

Being situated mostly within the Kittatiny valley, the physical features and geological character of this county, are similar to those of Berks and Dauphin, between which it lies.— Along the southern border are hills of sandstone and trap rock, and in the same region we find the middle secondary red shale, extending northward from Lancaster into the edge of Lebanon. North of this is a broad belt of the valley limestone extending to a line nearly parallel with, and a little north of the Reading, Lebanon, and Harrisburg turnpike, where it joins the slate formation. The next western part of Berks county, thin strata of limestone frequently occur, and belts of the slate are observed which are red, brown and yellow, thus differing from the general dark bluish colour of this formation. In the northern part of the slate region are some thick beds of coarse gray sandstone, occasionally containing imbedded pebbles.—

These may be observed in the hills on both sides of the Swatara creek, about three miles above Jonestown. Near Jonestown, on the south, are hills of trap rock, the influence of which has produced some curious and interesting modifications in the geological features of the neighborhood.

The northern part is mountainous. Proceeding northward from the Blue mountain, to the county line on the Fourth mountain, we pass, in succession, over the intermediate formations between the sandstones of the Blue mountain (IV,) and those of the Second mountain (X). In the valley of Stony creek is the red shale, (XI,) and above it, in the Third and Fourth mountains, the pebbly conglomerate, and sandstone (XII) next below the coal. In the narrow trough between these two mountains is the extended south-western point of the Pottsville coal basin.

Magnetic iron ore is found among the hills in the southern part of the county; it is mined at Cornwall, where specimens have been obtained yielding 70 per cent. of metallic iron. Indications of other varieties of iron ore occasionally appear, and in the limestone formation argillaceous and pipe ore has been dug in several places.

NOTES.

The Roman numericals IV, X, XI, and XII, refer to, and exhibit the order of stratification of the lower secondary formations of Pennsylvania, east of the Susquehanna.

For the information of those who have not the State Geologist's Reports, the following extracts are indispensable to understand the preceding article.

IV. This stratification consists of hard white and gray sandstones, and coarse massive conglomerates—contains impressions of several species of fucoides.

X. White and gray silicious sandstones, with dark bluish and olive colored slates, also coarse silicious conglomerates, alternating with gray, yellow and white sandstones, and bands of black carbonaceous slate; the latter is sometimes erroneously taken for coal slate.

XI. Red shales and soft argillaceous red sandstone, and occasional beds of compact silicious, red and gray sandstones; also a few thin calcareous bands.

XII. Coarse quartzose conglomerates, alternating with white and gray sandstones, and occasional thin beds of dark carbonaceous shale.—*Second Annual Report of the Geological exploration of the State of Pennsylvania, by Henry D. Rogers,* 1838.

CHAPTER IV.

~~~~~~~~

INTERNAL IMPROVEMENTS.

~~~~~~~~~~~

The internal improvements in, and passing through these two counties, were made by associated individuals, as incorporated companies, or by the Commonwealth. These shall be briefly noticed.

UNION CANAL.

In the year 1690, William Penn issued proposals for a second settlement or city in the Province, upon the Susquehanna river. In the proposals then made, he alludes to the practicability of connecting, by canal, a water communication between the city of Philadelphia, and the city to be, *in future*, erected on the banks of the Susquehanna. "It is now," says Penn, "my purpose to make another settlement, upon the river *Susquehanagh*, that runs into the bay of Chesapeake, and bears about fifty miles west from the Delaware, as appears by the common maps of the English dominion in America. There I design to lay out a *Plan* for building another city, in the most convenient place for the communication with the former plantations in the east: which by land, is as good as done already, a way being laid out between the two rivers, very exactly and conveniently, at least three years ago; and which will not be hard to do by water, by benefit of the river *Scoulkill*; for a

*Branch** of that river lies near a *Branch*† that runs in the *Susquehannagh* river, and is the common course of the Indians with their skins and furrs into our parts, and to the provinces east and west Jersey, and New York, from west and north-west parts of the continent from whence they bring them."

Turnpikes and Canals were not known in England at that time. It is acceded that Pennsylvania is entitled to the credit of having first directed public attention to canals and turnpikes in the United States. David Rittenhouse, the Astronomer, and William Smith, D. D., provost of the University of Pennsylvania, were the first movers in this matter.

Afterwards Robert Morris, the financier of the revolution, and still later Robert Fulton, the engineer, of whom Pennsylvania is justly proud, lent their powerful assistance. The writings of Turner Camac, William J. Duane, and Samuel Breck, Esqs.; and subsequently of Gerard Ralston, Richard Peters, Jr., Matthew Carey, Samuel Mifflin, William Lehman, John Sergeant, and Joseph McIlvaine, are too well known to require enumeration.

In the year 1792, David Rittenhouse, (and Dr, William Smith, we believe, at the same time,) surveyed and levelled a route for a canal to connect the waters of the Susquehanna and Schuylkill rivers, by means of Swatara and Tulpehocken creeks. The Union canal, which has since accomplished this object, passes over a portion of this route—the first, which was surveyed for a canal in the colonies.

The views of the projectors of this work were, if the difficulties of that period be considered, far more gigantic and surprising than have been entertained by their successors in any part of the Union. They contemplated nothing less than a junction of the eastern and western waters of Lake Erie and of the Ohio with the Delaware, on a route extending 582 miles. The Allegheny mountain was wisely deemed to offer an insuperable obstacle to a continuous navigation. A portage over this section was accordingly recommended: an expedient which we at the present day have been compelled to adopt.

Duly to appreciate the enterprise of that age, we ought to consider the great valley of the Ohio and Mississippi was al-

* The Tulpehocken creek, no doubt is alluded to.
† The Swatara creek, probably.

most one boundless forest; uninhabited, but by the beasts of the forest, or the Indians. Attainable moneyed capital was then almost unknown in the vocabulary of those days. No canal was then in existence in England. Sankey Brook and the Duke of Bridgewater's were yet unfinished. Public opinion even there, had yet to learn that canals were not visionary undertakings. The sneers of many were to be encountered; nevertheless, under all these discouragements, the earliest advocates for inland navigation commenced their efforts in Pennsylvania. In 1760 they induced the American Philosophical Society to order a survey for a canal to connect the Chesapeake bay with the Delaware. The provincial legislature about the same period, authorized a survey on a route, extending 582 miles, to Pittsburg and Erie. This survey was performed, and a report made strongly recommending the execution of the project. The adoption of the plan was postponed in consequence of the revolution. After the termination of that struggle, several works were commenced in North Carolina, Virginia, and Maryland. The canal through the Dismal Swamp, connecting the Chesapeake bay and Albemarle sound, with the works on the Potomac, James, and Rappahannock rivers, were commenced and partially finished, between the years 1786 and 1791.

The great project of Pennsylvania, was allowed to slumber until the 29th Sept. 1791, about a century after William Penn's first prophetic intimation, when the legislature incorporated a company to connect the Susquehanna and Schuylkill by a canal and slackwater navigation. Robert Morris, David Rittenhouse, William Smith, Tench Francis, and others, were named as commissioners. The intention of connecting the eastern and north-western parts of the state is distinctly expressed in this, and a subsequent act, of 10th April, 1792. By the terms of this last act, a company was incorporated to effect a junction of the Delaware with the Schuylkill river, by a canal extending from Norristown to Philadelphia, a distance of 17 miles. The Schuylkill river from the former city to Reading, was to be temporarily improved; and thus form, with the works of the Susquehanna and Schuylkill company, an uninterrupted water communication with the interior of the state; with the intention of extending the chain to Erie and the Ohio. Experience soon convinced the two companies that a greater length of canal was requisite, in consequence of the difficulties, of improving the channels of the rivers; hence the company last mentioned determined, (in compliance with the suggestion of, Mr. Weston, a British engineer, whom they had imported,) to extend *their* canal from river to river, a distance of 70 miles. In conjunction with the former company, they nearly completed 15 miles of the most difficult parts of the two works; comprising much rock excavation, heavy embankment, extensive deep cuttings, and several locks, which were constructed with bricks. In consequence of the commercial difficulties, (in which, it is known that some of the chief stockholders were shortly after involved,) both companies were compelled to suspend their operations, after the expenditure of $440,000. The suspension of these works, and some years after, of the Chesapeake and Delaware canal, had a most disastrous effect on every similar work which was projected for many years afterwards.

Frequent abortive attempts were made, from the year 1794, to resume operations; and notwithstanding the subscription of $300,000 stock, subsequently tendered by the state, these companies continued a mere languishing existence. In the year 1811, the two bodies were united, and reorganized as the Union Canal Co. They were specially authorized to extend their canal from Philadelphia to Lake Erie, with the privilege of making such further extension, in any other part of the state, as they might deem expedient. In 1819 and 1821, the state granted further aid, by a guarantee of interest, and a monopoly of the lottery'privilege. The additional subscriptions, obtained in consequence of this legislative encouragement, enabled the managers to resume operations in 1821. The line was re-located, the dimensions of the canal changed, and the whole work finished in about six years from this period; after 37 years had elapsed from the commencement of the work, and 65 from the date of the first survey. The Union canal is 89 miles in length, including the Swatara feeder, &c., from Middletown, on the Susquehanna, to a point on the Schuylkill, a short distance below Reading. It is calculated for boats of 25 to 30 tons burden. At Middletown, on the Susquehanna, it connects with the main line of Pennsylvania canals; at Reading, with the works of the Schuylkill Navigation Co. The descent from the summit to the Schuylkill is 311 feet; to the Susquehanna, 208.

The summit is 6 miles (between the Swatara and Tulpe-hocken) 78 chains in length; to which must be added the navigable feeder, which at present extends 6 3-4 miles. The summit passes over a limestone district: much deep excavation in rock was required. In consequence of the many fissures which abound in limestone rocks, the usual expedient of puddling did not succeed in retaining the water in the summit. After many experiments, it was found necessary to plank this section throughout. On the Schuylkill Navigation Co.'s canal, near Reading, which passes over the same limestone formation, a similar expedient was adopted. In both cases the plan was successful. On this section, the canal passes through a tunnel of 729 feet in length, excavated in solid rock. This summit is supplied by the water of the Swatara, conducted to it by the feeder already mentioned. As the summit is above the level of the feeder, two large water-wheels and pumps are resorted to for the purpose of raising the water to the requisite height. Two steam engines, one of 120, the second of 100 horse power, are provided for the purpose of supplying the feeder in case of accident to the water-works. [The feeder has since been continued to a point within four miles of the coal mines.]

A great error was committed in making the dimensions of this canal too small—an error which threatens to be fatal to its existence. It arose partly from the great scarcity of water, and partly from erroneous views entertained by engineers and others having charge of the work. The locks being adapted only for boats of 25 tons, while those of the state canals accommodate a boat of 40 or 50 tons, exclude the greater portion of the boats plying on the state works; added to which, the work has to contend with the competition of the railroad from Harrisburg and Columbia to Philadelphia. The latter competition discourages the Union Canal Co. from enlarging their locks.

In 1828, about $1,600,000 had been expended in the construction of the work, in addition to the proceeds of the lottery, and excluding the sums expended on the old work.

SCHUYLKILL NAVIGATION commences at Fairmount dam, near Philadelphia, and is continued up the Schuylkill by Norristown and Reading to Port Carbon in Schuylkill county; thus opening a communication between the city and the heart of the

Schuylkill coal region. It was commenced in 1815 and completed in 1826. This work, like the Lehigh navigation, is a series of pools formed by dams across the river, with intervening short lines of canal, sometimes on the east and sometimes on the west side of the river, which is crossed several times on the route. Near Reading it is intersected by the Union Canal, and thus has a communication with the Susquehanna, and with the State canals of the interior. Length of navigation from Philadelphia to Port Carbon 108 miles, of which 58 is canal and 50 slack water. The longest line of canal on the route is 22 miles, called the Girard, the upper end of which is 5 or 6 miles below Reading. Width of canal 36 feet at top, 22 at bottom, and 4 feet deep. Locks 80 by 17 feet: total ascent, 610 feet.

TURNPIKES.

Some interesting letters, it is said, are still extant of William Penn, Logan, and other early statesmen of Pennsylvania, which contain much interesting information relating to the improvement of roads, the structure of bridges, &c. In the preceding article, part of one of Penn's letters has been quoted, alluding to the practicability of effecting a communication by water, &c.

As to the actual construction of turnpike roads in Pennsylvania, nothing was done before 1792, when a company was incorporated to construct a turnpike from Lancaster to Philadelphia. This road was commenced 1792, and finished in 1794, at an expense of $465,000. The road is sixty-two miles long.

Since 1792, more than two hundred and twenty-five turnpike companies have been incorporated for the purpose of making roads.

The Berks and Dauphin county turnpike company was incorporated, and commenced the making of the turnpike in 1816, end finished it in 1817, at an average cost of $3,800 per mile. The original price of the shares was $50. Individual subscriptions amounted to $63,905. Subscriptions on the part of the state, $29,900.

The Perkiomen and Reading turnpike company was incorporated, and commenced a turnpike in 1811, and finished in
1815. The average cost of the road was $7,000 per mile.—
The individual subscription was $133,000; on the part of the
state $53,000. These two companies constructed the turn-
pike east and west of Reading, between Philadelphia and Harrisburg.

The Downington, Ephrata and Harrisburg turnpike company was incorporated, and began a turnpike in 1803, and finished
it in 1819. This turnpike passes through the western end of
Lebanon county. Besides these turnpikes, there is another in
Berks county, leading from Reading to Sunbury, through Alsace, Maiden creek, and other townships.

RAILROADS.

Philadelphia and Reading Railroad, connects with the Columbia Railroad, at the foot of the inclined plane, on the west
side of Schuylkill, near Philadelphia, and thence extends up
that river, by Reading, to Pottsville in Schuylkill county, thus
opening a line of communication between Philadelphia and the
Schuylkill coal region. Being connected with the railroads
which extend from the various mining districts to the river, it
will afford a means for the conveyance of coal to the city at all
seasons. The whole line, from Pottsville to Philadelphia, is
composed of levels and descending grades, which gives great
advantages to the descending transportation. A locomotive engine of 11 tons weight has conveyed from Reading to the Columbia Railroad near Philadelphia, at a single load, 101 cars,
with a gross burden of 423 tons, at an average speed of 10
miles to the hour. A part of this load consisted of 2002 barrels of flour, weighing 190 tons. There are three tunnels on
this road: one at Flat Rock, 8 miles from the city, 960 feet in
length; another near Phœnixville of 1832 feet; and the third
near Port Clinton, 1600 feet. Near the second tunnel, about
30 miles from Philadelphia, the road crosses to the east side of
the river, by a neat and well built viaduct, 228 feet in length,
and 24 feet above the water. Length from the Columbia Railroad to Reading 54 miles: from Reading to Pottsville 36 miles.

A branch, 5 miles in length, designed for the transportation of coal to the Delaware, leaves this road at the Falls of Schuylkill, and crosses eastward to the Delaware river at Richmond, about three miles above Philadelphia.

Public roads and bridges are numerous, convenient, and kept in good condition in various parts of these two counties.

33

CHAPTER V.

THE AMERICAN REVOLUTION.

As early as 1765, the British Parliament passed an act that all instruments of writing, such as promissary notes, bonds, indentures, &c., were to be null and void, unless written on paper or parchment stamped with specific duty. This measure was opposed in England and in this country; and being found unpopular, the act was repealed in 1766; but another act was passed by Parliament, declaring that the British Parliament had a right to make laws binding the colonies in all cases whatever; this act was soon followed by another, imposing, in the colonies, duties on glass, paper, painters' colors, and tea. These several acts kindled in every patriotic bosom, a strong opposition to the measures of the mother country, and one circumstance after another led to an open rupture between the colonies and the parent country, which happened about the year 1773, when the Bostonians *threw the tea overboard.* From that time on, a flame was kindled in every breast. Gen. Gage, from Britain, arrived at Boston in 1774, with more troops, some having arrived before, "to dragoon the Bostonians into compliance."—The Bostonians had to suffer much; but their sufferings excited the sympathy of others. Associations for their relief were formed in nearly all the colonies; even this county was not the *last nor least* to aid in relieving their suffering brethren, as will fully appear from the following:

Notices, headed "BOSTON PORT BILL," were posted up in Reading, calling meetings. The following are the proceedings of one of them:

At a meeting of a very respectable body of freeholders and others, inhabitants of the county of Berks, at Reading, the 2d of July, 1774, Edward Biddle, Esq., in the chair.

This assembly, taking into their very serious consideration, the present critical situation of American affairs, do unanimously resolve as follows, viz:

1. That the inhabitants of this county do owe, and will pay due allegiance to our rightful Sovereign, King George the Third.

2. That the powers claimed, and now attempted to be put into execution by the British Parliament, are fundamentally wrong, and cannot be admitted without the utter destruction of the liberties of America.

3. That the Boston Port Bill is unjust and tyrannical in the extreme. And that the measures pursued against Boston are intended to operate equally against the rights and liberties of the other colonies.

4. That this assembly doth concur in opinion with their respective brethren of Philadelphia, that there is an absolute necessity for an immediate congress of the deputies of the several advices, in order to deliberate upon and pursue such measures, as may radically heal our present unhappy disturbances, and settle with precision the rights and liberties of America.

5. That the inhabitants of this county, confiding in the prudence and ability of the deputies intended to be chosen for the general congress, will cheerfully submit to any measures which may be found by the said congress, best adapted for the restoration of harmony between the mother country and the colonies, and for the security and firm establishment of the rights of America.

6. That as the people of Boston are now suffering in the grand and common cause of American liberty, Resolved—

That it is the duty of all the inhabitants to contribute to the support of the said sufferers, and that the committee hereafter named, do open subscriptions for their relief. And further, that the said committee do lay out the amount of such subscriptions in purchasing flour and other provisions, to be sent by them to our said suffering brethren.

7. That Edward Biddle, James Reed, Daniel Brodhead, Henry Christ, Esqs., Christopher Schultz, Thomas Dundass, and Jonathan Potts, gentlemen, be, and they are hereby appointed a committee to meet and correspond with the committees from the other counties of the Province.

The thanks of the Assembly were unanimously voted to the chairman, for the patriotic and spirited manner in which he pointed out the dangerous situation by the unconstitutional measures lately pursued by the British Parliament, with respect to Boston; expressing, at the same time, the greatest loyalty to our Sovereign, and the most warm and tender regard for the liberties of America.

There never appeared to be greater unanimity of sentiment upon any occasion, than in the resolves made by the freemen of this county, all cordially agreeing to sacrifice every temporary advantage, for the purpose of securing liberty to themselves and their posterity.

Similar meetings had been held in Lancaster, in which citizens from that part of the county, now Lebanon, attended.—One of these meetings was held, at the court house in Lancaster, the 15th of June, 1774.

The following resolves were then adopted:—Agreed—that to preserve the Constitutional rights of the inhabitants of America, it is incumbent on every colony, to unite and use the most effectual means to procure a repeal of the late act of Parliament against the town of Boston.

That the act of Parliament for blocking up the port and harbor of Boston, is an invasion of the rights of the inhabitants of the said town, as subjects of the crown of Great Britain. That it is the opinion of the inhabitants at this meeting that the proper and effectual means to be used to obtain a repeal of the said act, will be to put an immediate stop to all imports, and exports, to and from Great Britain, until the same act be repealed.

That the traders and inhabitants of this town will join and concur with the patriotic merchants, manufacturers, tradesmen, and freeholders, of the city and county of Philadelphia, and other parts of this province, in an association or solemn agreement to this purpose, if the same shall be by them thought necessary.

December, 1774, the following persons of that. part of Lancaster, now Lebanon county, were chosen, with others of Lancaster county, as inspector at an election, to elect a committee to observe the conduct of all persons touching the general association of the general Congress; and as it was necessary that each township should elect a proper person to act as inspector, and receive the tickets of the electors, on the day of the election, &c., the following persons were chosen. From Hanover township, Timothy Green; from Londonderry, John Campbell; from Lebanon, Thomas Clark, Curtis Grubb, Henry Light; from Bethel, Ludwig Schuey, Casper Corr, John Bishon; from Lebanon Town, Henry Bealor.

The course pursued by the mother country, incensed the people of the several provinces and colonies—a continental congress was assembled at Philadelphia, September 4, 1774. Resolutions were passed, approving the course of Massachusetts, in opposition to Gen. Gage—the open and decided hostilities eventuated in bloodshed, at the battle of Lexington, April. 19, 1775, which was soon followed by another—the battle of Bunker Hill, June 17th. To meet the emergency, the provincialists and colonists held conventions, military and other meetings.

In this great conflict between the mother country and the colonists, the inhabitants of Berks and Lebanon, took in its incipient, progressive and consummating stage, an active part, in common with others of Pennsylvania, and the states generally.

Notice for a meeting of General Committee, on 2d of July, 1776.

In Standing Committee at Reading, Berks county, Thursday, June 27th, 1776.

NICHOLAS LUTZ, Chairman.

Resolved, That notice be immediately given to the members of the General Committee of this county, to meet at the Court House in Reading, on Tuesday next, the second day of July, on affairs of public importance, and very interesting at this critical time, especially to choose officers for six hundred and sixty-six men—and that the several members be desired to enquire what officers now in the Association are willing to go into immediate service on call.

33*

A public meeting was called at Lancaster, to which the military of Berks, as well as other counties, sent their ratio of men. The meeting consisted of the officers and privates of fifty-three battalions of the Association of Pennsylvania, to choose two Brigadier Generals, to command the battalions and forces in Pennsylvania. We give the names of those of Berks who attended the meeting. The meeting was held July 4, 1776.

The proceedings of that meeting, in the autograph of the Secretary, are still preserved by the Clymer family, of Reading. They are worthy a place here, as a reminiscence of '76— they cannot be too carefully preserved or too generally circulated.

Minutes of a meeting of the Officers and of the Private Associators of Pennsylvania, July 4, for the choice of two Brigadiers.

At a meeting of the Officers and Privates of fifty-three Battalions of the Associators of the Colony of Pennsylvania, at Lancaster, on the 4th day of July, 1776, on due notice to choose two Brigadier Generals, to command the Battalions and Forces in the said Colony.

Col. GEORGE ROSS, President.

Lieut. Col. Daniel Clymer, Secretary.

The Protest of the Board of Officers of the five Battalions, of the City and Liberties of Philadelphia, to the Assembly, was read.

No. 1. The Circular Letter, signed by the Chairman, Col. Roberdeau, was read.

No. 2. The Circular Letter from the Committee of Privates, of the City and Liberties of Philadelphia, signed by the Chairman, Mr. Sam'l Simpson, was read.

No. 3. The Protest of the Privates of the City and Liberties of Philadelphia, to the Assembly, signed by Mr. Samuel Simpson, was read.

By the returns of the City and Liberties of Philadelphia, and the several counties of the colony of Pennsylvania, the following persons were delegated to the Convention, to wit:

CITY AND LIBERTIES OF PHILADELPHIA.

First Battalion; Officers, Col. John Chevalier, Capt. Joseph Copperthwait. Privates: Mr. Thomas Nevil, Mr. George Nelson.

Second Battalion; Officers—Col. D. Roberdeau, Capt. Wm. Bradford. Privates: Mr. Thos. Montgomery, Mr. Wm. Pool.

Third Battalion; Officers—Major Robt. Knox, Capt. Sharp Dulaney. Privates: Mr. Paul Cox, Mr. Charles Prior.

Fourth Battalion; Officers—Capt. Jno. Kling, Capt. James Brewster. Privates: John Brower, Henry Keck.

First Rifle—Fifteenth Battalion; Officers—L. Col. Daniel Clymer, Capt. Lewis Bitting. Privates: Thos. Craig, Jacob Kitter.

Philadelphia County—First Battalion; Officers—Major Isaac Hews, Mr. Geo. Gray, standard bearer. Privates: Jesse Roberts, William Smith.

Second Battalion; Officers—Capt. Josiah Hart, Capt. Marshall Edwards. Privates: Robt. Whitten, John Simpson.

Fourth Battalion; Privates—James Hazelett, . William Hicks.

Bucks County—First Battalion; Officers—Capt. John Jarvis, Capt. John Folwell. Privates: Arthur Wats, Joseph Fenton.

Second Battalion; Officers—Capt. John Jameson, Adjutant Wm. Thompson. Privates: Ab'm Hollis, Wm. Harr.

Third Battalion; Officers—Col. And'w Kekline, L. Col. Josiah Bryan. Privates: John Patterson, Mich'l Stoneback.

Fourth Battalion; Officers—Col. Robt. Robinson. Privates: Tunis V'n Middleswart, Francis Titus.

Chester County—First Battalion; Officers—Major John Culbertson, Capt. Benj'n Wallace. Privates: Samuel Cunningham, And'w Boyd.

Second Battalion; Officers—Lt. Col. Wm. Gibbons. Privates: David Denny, Sam'l Culbertson.

Fourth Battalion; Officers—Col. Wm. Montgomery, Capt. Joseph Gardiner. Privates: John Mackey, John Fulton.

Sixth—Lancaster County—First Battalion; Officers—Col. Geo. Ross, Lt. Col. Adam Reigart. Privates: Christian Werts, Francis Baily.

Second Battalion; Officers—Col. Carlis Grubb, Major Philip Marstaler. Privates: James Sullivan, Ludwick Ziering.

Third Battalion; Officers—Lt. Col. Rob't Thompson, Major Thos. Smith. Privates: John Smiley, Isaac Erwin.

Fourth Battalion; Officers—Capt. Joseph Sherrer, Captain James Murray. Privates: Ab'm Darr, Wm. Leard.

Fifth Battalion; Officers—Col. James Crawford, Captain James Mirur. Privates: Henry Slaymaker, John Whitehill.

Sixth Battalion; Officers—Lt. Col. Lowry, Major James Cunningham. Privates: John Bealy, John Jameson.

Seventh Battalion; Officers—Col. M. Slough, Lieut. Col. Leon'd Rautfaung. Privates: Christian Bough, Simon Snider,

Eighth Battalion; Officers—Col. Peter Grubb, Capt. Henry Weaver. Privates: William Smith, George Wry.

Ninth Battalion; Officers—Lieut. Col. Chris'n Weyman, Major Michael Tire. Privates: Michael Diffebaugh, Anthony Debler.

Tenth Battalion—Rifle Battalion; Officers—Col. John Ferre, Lt. Col. And'w Little. Privates: George Line, Joseph Whitehill.

Eleventh—Rifle Battalion; Officers—Col. Timothy Green, Lieut. Col. Peter Heddricks. Privates: Wm. Barnet, George Little.

York County—First Battalion; Officers—Lieut. Col. Jos. Donaldson, *Capt.* Mich'l Smiser. Privates: Wm. Scott John Ewing.

Second Battalion; Officers—Major Hugh Donwiddie, *Capt.* Hugh Campble. Privates: Da. McConnaughy, Esq., Geo. W. Clinghan.

Third Battalion; Officers—Major Jos. Jeffereis, Major John Andrew. Privates: John Hamilton, Thos. Little.

Fourth Battalion; Col. Wm. Smith, Major Smith, Major John Finley. Privates: Jacob Shley, Josiah Scott.

Fifth Battalion; Officers—Col. Mathew Dill, Major Garrett Creft. Privates: James Nealor, Dan'l Messerty.

Cumberland—First Battalion; Officers—*Capt.* John Steel, Lieut. Wm. Blair. Privates: Jonathan Hogge, Eph'm Steel.

Second Battalion; Officers—Capt. John McClelland, Capt. Elias Davison. Privates: Jonathan Smith, Henry Pawling.

Third Battalion; Officers—L. Col. Wm. Clark, Capt. And, McFarland. Privates: James Brown, Wm. Sterrett.

Fourth Battalion; Officers—Lieut. Col. Fred'k Watts, Capt. Geo. Robinson.   Privates: John Hamilton, James Read.

Fifth Battalion; Officers—Col. Joseph Armstrong, Major James McCalmont.   Privates: James Finley, John Vance.

Berks County—First Battalion; Officers—Major Gabriel Heister, Lieut. Philip Cremer. · Privates: John Hartman, Peter Filbert.

Second Battalion; Officers—Col. Mark Bird, Major John Jones.   Privates: David Morgan, Benjamin Tolbut.

Third Battalion; Officers—Lieut. Col. Nich's Lutz, Capt. Geo. Keim.   Privates: Henry Spoon, Mathias Winrich.

Fourth Battalion; Officers—Major Mich'l Lindemut, *Capt.* George May.   Privates: Mich'l Moser.

Fifth Battalion; Officers—*Col.* John Patton, *Lieut. Col.* John Rice.   Privates: Jacob Selsir, Christ'n Winter.

Sixth Battalion; Officers—Major Conrad Leffler, Lieut. John Miller.   Privates: John Hill, Henry Larke.

Seventh Battalion; Officers—*Col.* Sebastian Swan, Adjutant Samuel Ebey.   Privates: Philip Wisters, Casper Smack.

Northampton—First Battalion; Officers—Major Ab'm Lebar, *Capt.* John Orndt.   Privates: Wm. McFarren, Jacob Upp.

Second Battalion; Officers—*Col.* Henry Geigar, *Capt.* Michael Snider.   Privates: Rich'd Barkhous, Peter Haas.

Third Battalion; Officers—Major John Sigfried, Captain Nich's Karn.   Privates: Robert Brown, Henry Best.

Fourth Battalion; Officers—Col. Jacob Stroud, Capt. Timothy Jayne.   Privates: John McDowel, jr., Derrick Von Fleik.

Northumberland—The Battalion under Col. Hunter—Officers—Capt. Ch's Gillespie, Lieut. Geo. Calhoun.   Privates: Fred'k Stone, Laughlan McCartney.

The Second battalion under Col. Plunkett—Officers—Maj. John Brady, Lieutenant Mordecai M'Kinzie.   Privates: Paul Gattes, Andrew Culbertson.

The Third Battalion under Col. Weiser—Officers—Col. Benjamin Weiser, Lieut. Col. Samuel M'Clay.   Privates: Seth Matlock, Jonas Yokan.   ·

The Fourth battalion under Colonel Potter; Officers—Lieut. Col. Robert Moodie, Capt. Wm. Gray.   Privates: James M'Clanahan, Benjamin Starret.

Westmoreland. First battalion; Officers—Capt. Vendle Orey,

Captain Alexander Thompson.   Privates: William Guthery, William Perry.

Second Battalion ; Officers—*Col.* Providence Mornly, Maj. James Smith.   Privates: John Carmichael, George Gray.

A question was put, whether the officers and privates shall vote by ballot, singly.

Resolved, unanimously, in the affirmative.

Resolved, That both *Brigadier Generals* be voted for at the same time, and the highest in votes to be the commanding officer.

Adjourned till 5 o'clock, *P. M.*

P. M., 5 o'clock, the officers and privates met, according to adjournment.

Resolved, that *Col. Mark Bird* and *Capt. Sharp Delancy,* with the *President,* be judges of the election for *Brigadiers General.*

The election came on the same day, and after casting at the poll, the votes stood thus for *Brigadier General:*

Daniel Roberdeau, 160; James Ewing, 85; Samuel Miles, 82; James Potter, 25; Curtis Grub, 9; George Ross, 9; Thomas M'Kean, 8; Mark Bird, 7.

The *President* immediately declared Dan'l Roberdeau 1st *Brigadier General,* and James Ewing 2d *Brigadier General.*

Resolved, That the *Brigadier Generals* shall have full power and authority to call out any number of the associates of this province into action, and that power to continue until superseded by the convention, or by any authority under the appointment.

Resolved, That the *President* of this board shall have full power and authority to grant *commissions* to the two *Brigadier Generals,* until *commissions* issue from the convention, or any authority they shall appoint to succeed them.

Resolved, That we will march under the direction and command of our *Brigadier Generals* to the assistance of all or any of the Free and Independent States of America.

Resolved, That the associators to be drafted out of each county, by the *Brigadier Generals,* shall be in the same proportion as that directed by the late *Provincial conference* in Philadelphia.

Resolved, That the thanks of this *Board* be presented to the *President* for his seasonable and correct speech this day in behalf of the Liberties of America, and of this *colony* in particular, and the cheerfulness, alacrity, and impartiality with which he conducted the business of the day, which the *colonel* reviewed, and politely thanked the *Board* for the honor done him in their address.

Resolved, That Col. Ross, Lieut. Col. Daniel Clymer, and Capt. Chas. Dulaney, be a committee to review and correct the number of the proceedings of this day, and they are hereby desired to publish them in the first newspaper of this Colony, and that they be signed by the President.

GEORGE ROSS, President.

D. Clymer, Secretary.

Lancaster, July, 4, 1776.

———

At a meeting of a board of Officers of the Five Battalions of the city and liberties of Philadelphia, and of the committee of Privates, at the College Hall, on Friday, the 14th of June, 1776.

Col. ROBERDEAU in the Chair.

A member of the committee of Privates, acquainted the Board, that the committee of Privates had prepared a Protest to the Assembly, against the appointment of Brigadier Generals, under a Resolve of Congress; Therefore

Resolved, by the Board of Officers, That an officer out of each *Battalion* be appointed to draw up a *Protest* against the Assembly's appointing Brigadier Generals under the Resolve of Congress.

Resolved, That Col. Matlack, Col. Dean, Major Bayard, Major Knox, and Captain Will, be appointed for that purpose.

The said gentlemen returned a *Protest,* which being read, paragraph by paragraph, was amended and unanimously agreed to.

Resolved, That the chairman sign the same, in behalf of this board of officers, and present it to the Assembly, which *Protest* is in the words following:

To the Honorable the House of Representatives of the Freemen of the province of Pennsylvania, in General Assembly met:

The Protest of the board of officers of the five battalions of the city and liberties of Philadelphia, respectfully sheweth:

That this board address you by the title heretofore used to the Honorable House of Assembly, in order to avoid the least appearance of disrespect to the Honorable members now sitting: '

That this board has received information, that the Honorable Congress of the United Colonies, has recommended to *this colony* to appoint two *Brigadier Generals* to command the Associators of this province: And we, apprehending that this House may be induced to take upon them to nominate and appoint the said *Brigadier Generals, without having authority of the Associators for that purpose:* And further apprehending, that any nomination made by this Honorable House will not give satisfaction to the Associators of the province, and, consequently, that they will not act under them: For these, and other important and weighty considerations, this board do hereby *Protest* against the Honorable House making, or attempting to making the said appointments.

Resolved, (*with one dissenting voice,*) That there is an immediate necessity of calling together a *Provincial Meeting of Associators,* for the purpose of appointing the said *Brigadier Generals.*

Resolved, That two officers and two privates, of each battalion in the province, be requested to attend in the borough of Lancaster, on Thursday, the fourth day of July next, for the purpose of appointing two *Brigadier Generals,* according to the recommendation of congress.

Resolved, That Colonel Matlack, Major Knox, Capt. Will, Capt. Wade, Capt. Loxley, and Capt. Humphreys, be a committee to draw up and send to the officers of the battalions, in this province, *a circular letter,* for the purpose of calling the said convention at the time and place aforesaid, and that the chairman sign the same.

Philadelphia, June 14, 1776.

Sir,—The above proceedings of the board of officers of the five battalions of this city and liberties, will inform you of their proceedings in a case which we conceive to be of the most important concern to the Associators of this province. The extreme dangers to which the province now stands exposed, we hope, justify us in requesting two officers and two privates of each battalion, to meet together at a time which we are very sensible, will be attended with great inconvenience to you. We flatter ourselves, that your zeal in the great cause of Liberty will induce you to a compliance with our recommendation, in appointing the delegation mentioned in our resolves, to attend in Lancaster, at the time mentioned therein. Various modes of appointing Brigadier Generals have been proposed and carefully considered; and we assure you that we have diligently attended to this very important altair, and are fully satisfied, that the mode we recommend is the *only one* which will effectually secure the rights and liberties of the associators of this province, and enable them to defend themselves against our inveterate and cruel enemies.

N. B. The Resolve of Congress is, That three Provincial Brigadier Generals be employed for the Flying Camp, two from Pennsylvania, and one from Maryland. That the said Brigadier Generals be appointed by the respective *Colonies* above mentioned.

D. ROBERDEAU, Pres't.

To the Privates of the several Battalions of Military Associators in the Province of Pennsylvania.

Gentlemen,—The Honorable Congress having resolved upon a flying camp of 10,000 men, for the protection of our Province and Maryland, viz: 6000 for this Province, 6000 for the lower counties, and 3400 for Maryland: and that Maryland should appoint one, and this Colony two Brigadier Generals; The Committee of Privates of the Associators of the city and liberties of Philadelphia, considering that an appointment made by any body of men, besides the Asssociators, would not be perfectly satisfactory, and being further convinced that it was their right to make the appointment, and that the security of their liberties depended greatly on the exercise of this right, and being desirous of having it enjoyed equally by all, have agreed with the Board of Officers, to call a Provincial meeting of As-

34

sociators, consisting of two Privates and two officers from each
Battalion, elected by said Battalions for the purpose of choosing said Generals, to meet in *Lancaster*, on *Thursday*, the 4th
of *July*. We attended particularly to the season of the year,
and the difficulty of your attending so near harvest; but yet, as
the matter was very important, and we were unwilling to do
any thing without consulting all, and giving them an equal opportunity with ourselves of exercising their right, we adopted
this measure: We therefore were persuaded, that freemen, associated for the defence of their rights, would overlook every
difficulty attending a perfect and free exercise of it.—Our Assembly, we mean such of its members as are not quite with us,
wished to have the appointment, but we prepared the following protest against it, as the whole of our success depends on
a *proper choice*. We trust you will see it in the same important light with us, and send the delegation above mentioned,
that every battalion in the Province may have a perfectly equal
representation—if said conference should unite in some test to
be taken by the Associators, that we might know who to depend on, it might be well. We wish to take nothing upon ourselves; but being the advance-guard, our duty requires that we
give the alarm.

We are, gentlemen, &c.
Signed by order of the Committee of Privates.
SAMUEL SIMPSON, President.

---

*To the Honorable the Representatives of the Freemen of the
Province of Pennsylvania.*

The Protest of the Committee of the Privates of the Military Association belonging to the city and liberties of Philadelphia, respectfully Sheweth:

That this Committee, understanding that the Honorable Congress has recommended to this Colony to appoint two Brigadier Generals to command the Associators of this Province, do
Protest against any Appointment of said Brigadier Generals to
be made by this House:

First. Because there is no regular Militia Law which obliges the Constituents of this House to become Associators, or to

find persons in their room, if they decline associating: And therefore the Association is not properly provincial, and of consequence this House is not properly constituted to be competent to the business, nor can the Appointment come before them as a Provincial Representation.

Second. Because many of the Associators have been excluded by this *very* House from voting for the Members now composing it, though this House was applied to on their behalf: And Therefore they are not represented in this House.

Third. Because the Counties which have the greatest number of Associators have not a proportional Representation, and therefore cannot be considered as having an equal voice in the nomination.

Fourth. Because the Association has been voluntary—and this House choosing, by their Resolutions respecting it, that it should remain so: Therefore cannot interfere, nor in any wise, consistent with decency, attempt to impose officers upon us not of our own choosing.

Fifth. Because many members of this House are the Representatives of persons in religious professions like themselves, totally averse to military defence: And therefore cannot be called the Representatives of Associators; nor do we wish to interfere so much with their religious sentiments as to reduce them to the necessity of quitting their seats, or joining in the nomination.

Sixth. Because it is well known that there are men in this House who have, ever since our first opposition to Great Britain, refused to concur in any measure necessary for defence; and we have reason to fear that some are disposed to break the Union of the Colonies, and submit to the Tyranny of Great Britain.

Seventh. Because this House is under no oaths of fidelity to their constituents, by which they would be bound to consult their interest; nor are they proper persons to make the oaths which are to bind themselves.

Eighth. Because, though the members of this House, who were under oaths of Allegiance to the Crown, consider themselves absolved therefrom, and have admitted the new-elected members to their seats without taking oaths, thereby dissolving the old Constitution, and finally abolishing the charter;—yet

effectual care is taken to head the several pages of their ic-
solves, as usual, with " *Votes of Assembly, John Penn, Esq.,*
Governor," without the assent of the people for this purpose.
These things wear such a face of design as renders the intentions of this House suspicious; and we think a House still con-
fessing the King's Representative their Governor, cannot safely be trusted with the appointment of Generals to command us,
lest it might give us such as would enable a certain party to
make up with the enemy, at the expense of our Lives and
Liberties.

Ninth. Because a House, which shewed itself so unfriendly
to the Association at a time when so much depended upon their
exertions, as after frequent and repeated applications for justice,
to impose no more than three shillings and six-pence fine on
non-Associators for every day of general muster, and that in so
lax a manner, that it is a question whether it will ever be collected, is not to be trusted with appointment of Generals to
command us, lest they should shew as little regard to our interest in the one case as in the other.

Tenth. Because, as this House was chosen by those only,
who were acknowledged the liege Subjects of George our enemy, and derived their sole right of electing this House from
that very circumstance. We conceive that the moment they
undertook to set aside this allegiance, they by that very act
destroyed the only principle on which they sat as Representatives; and therefore are not a House on the principles on which
they were elected, and having derived no new authority from
the people freed from such allegiance, they are a Representative body on no one principle whatever, and therefore can in no
manner undertake to do the business of Representatives farther
than the people indulge them, without usurping authority, and
acting arbitrarily.

Eleventh. Because the Associators have the right of appointing officers to command them, and mean ever to retain it.

We therefore protest against, and declare we will not submit to any appointment of General officers to command us,
which this House may think proper to go into.

Nevertheless, that the resolve of Congress may be fully complied with, we have taken the proper steps to have a number
of Associators, Representatives from every Battalion in the
province, collected together as soon as possible, to proceed to
the choice of said Brigadier Generals, under whom, we doubt

not, but the Associators will serve with cheerfulness, and they being the officers of their choice, will have the confidence of the Associators.

Signed by order of the committee of Privates.

SAMUEL SIMPSON, President.

———

List of persons in Middle Ward, in the City of Philadelphia, of the age of eighteen years and upwards, who are able and willing to bear arms, May 1, 1775.

Dan'l Clymer, Samuel Bush, Thomas Leonard, Ross Currie, Charles Lyon, jr., George Tudor, James Bryson, Will'm Huston, Wm. Falconer, Wm. M'Dougall, Nathaniel Parker, William Ritchard, Jno. Wigton, Thos. Tisdall, Wm. Oliphant, Jona'n Adams, Joseph Harper, Wm. Carson, Andrew Carson, Tobias Slidham, Ezek'l Getz, Gab'l Valois, Nathaniel Richards, John Sparhawk, Thomas Irwin, Wm. Sheaff, John Dupuy, William Stretch, Robert Smith, Daniel Craig, John Springer, A. Kuhn, Charles Simpson, Gust's Risberg, Robert Vallance, Joseph Warner, jr., Henry Strenbk, Alex'r Bartrum, James Huston, Thomas Palmer, Esmond Leonardnan, Richard Sweat, David McFee, Caspar Flesher, Thomas Logan, Jas. Burnside, Richard Hunt, Wm. Marshall, Adam Zantzinger, Sam'l Jervis, Wm. Thorne, Henry Salor, Tho. M'Kean, Thos. Montgome-ry, Joseph Vandegriff, James Suther, John Reynolds, Chris. Goffner, John Cobey, William Bombeger, Jacob Trosler, James Harris, William Rediger, Peter Gosner, John Book, Daniel Gosner, Elijah Coffing, Enoch Morrer, William Orr, Henry Taylor, Philip Warner, I. Sutter, Joseph Osborne, Jo-seph Hood, Pat'k Connelly, Chas. Torrence, Adam Clelan, Wm. Thompson, Archibald M'Lain, George Lufft, Wollore Ming, Rich'd Graham, John Wokel, John Warner, Nathan-Jones, Peter Wiltberger, John Handlyn, Sam'l Fletcher, Jo-Govell, John Halbarett, Patrick Doddey, William Reed, his mark X, Thos. Fisher, Jacob Shober, John Little, John Shea, — his mark X, Sachevol C. Wood, Bernard Harigan, his mark X, George Reinholt, Jeremiah Wilbaron, Benjamin Williamson, Andrew Graydon, John Withospoone, Michael Shoemaker, Jo-seph Burns, Jacob Frailey, John Koppold, Jacob Gubble, John Baker, John Park, William Marshall, Andrew Forrost, Wm. McCloster, James Porter, John Davison, Lawrence Seckel,

34*

John Bowman, Thomas Power, Franklin Rood, John Shop-
land,.—— McDonald, And'w Starrett, John Hanna.

———

To return to Berks—That the inhabitants of Berks and Lebanon as a body—*tories*, if any, excepted—were as ardently devoted to the cause of American freedom, and did as much as
any portion of the Union, is a matter of historical fact, and
needs not here to be repeated; nevertheless, a few extracts from
the *Minutes of the Committee of Safety*, and other documents,
letters, &c. are given, to show what was done, as it is believed.
will be read with interest, by those whose fathers took a part
in the ever memorable Revolution of '76, in favor of the
Whigs.

The extracts are given in detached order, without attempting to fill any hiatus.   It would occupy too much space to do
so.

An order was drawn, Sept. 2, 1776, on John S. Nesbitt,
Esq., Treasurer, and was directed to pay Mr. Isaac Levan,
£50, on account of the committee of Berks county, in supplying the families of poor Associators, who are now in actual
service, with necessaries to be charged to said committee.

The committee of Inspection and Observation, of Reading,
in Berks county, having respresented to the Board the necessity of keeping a guard in that town,

Resolved, That the committee of Reading be empowered to
appoint a small guard in that town, so long as the prisoners*
of war shall reside there, and the Board will take proper measures to defray the expenses attending it.

So determined were the patriotic soldiers of Berks, not to
suffer one transgressor or delinquent to escape condign punish-
ment or being publicly exposed; as will appear from the following communcation, addressed to the Committee of Berks
county:

Philadelphia, 21 Dec., 1776.
To the Honorable Committee of Berks, at Reading.
Gentlemen:
At our being properly quartered in Mr. Galloway's house in

* See pages 145, 146, antea.

the city, by the Quarter Master General, F——k R——p, one of our men, very imprudently and wickedly broke open a room, wherein were some valuable effects, which were the property, as is supposed, of said Galloway, and took off with him some loaf sugar, lawn, a diaper, table cloth, &c., and immediately deserted his company. These are, therefore, to request you'll take proper steps to secure said R——p, so that he may be brought to trial, for said offence, which is by no means countenanced by any of the officers—as we are likely to be greatly disgraced by such depredations or unwarrantable proceedings.

H——y M——r and B——r H——e, have also deserted— whom, we expect, may be secured and made a public example of, otherwise, we are determined never to serve longer in the cause. There is still remaining at home, numbers of others, belonging to the militia, well known to you all, enjoying their ease and pleasure, all of whom we request, you would, for the honor of Berks, order them to join us at the camp, to which place, we march to-morrow; otherwise, we will earnestly request, they may be published to the world, as enemies to their country—and we shall deem them as such.

We are, with great respect,

Gentlemen, your well wishers

and humble servants,

JOHN MEARS, Adj't.
GEORGE WILL,
JOHN DIEHL,
JOHN WITMAN,
DANIEL ROSE,
JOHN KIDD,
PHILIP KREMER.

Extract—Letter sent by Express.

CHESTER, 14th December, 1776.

James Read, Esq.—Dear Sir:

The Honorable Continental Congress having directed me to visit the Associators of the several counties of this State, and to endeavor, with the aid of several gentlemen of the Assembly, and of the freemen at large, to stimulate and encourage them to set forth, at this critical time, to the support of their country, I request the favor of you to convene the committee of your county, and to inform that we propose to meet the officers and Assooiators of the several battalions in your county, at the town of Reading, on Wednesday next, at 10 o'clock in the morning.

We depend much on the zeal and activity of yourself, and the other gentlemen of the committee, and trust that the appearance of your inhabitants on that day, will do honor to themselves and their country.

I have the honor to be your

Obedient Servant,

THOMAS MIFFLIN, Brig. Gen.

I am directed to pay the expense of Expresses, &c., which may be necessary to convene the inhabitants, which I will most cheerfully do.   T. M.

December 31, 1776; an order was drawn on Mr. John M. Nesbitt, for $2000, payable to John Biddle, jr., to be paid by him into the hands of Andrew Whitman, of Reading, to be subject to the drafts of the committee of said county, for to defray such expenses as they have incurred, by order of this Board.—*Minutes Com. Safety.*, iii, 3.

January 12, 1777; in council of safety, orders were given to Col. Morgan to have the second Battalion of militia in Berks county, which he is to command, to make all necessary preparations, and hold themselves in readiness to march on the shortest notice, and wait until further orders from the Board.—*Min. Com. Saf.*, iii, 29.

January 17, 1777; Captain Bickham was directed to pay Col. Henry Geiger, £89, 4s. 5d., for charges of apprehending and bringing to Reading jail the following persons, who are *suspected* of being tories, to whose account this sum is to be charged, viz: W——m T——s, P——p M——r, M——l O——d, C——r B——f, M——l B——k, H——y S——r, J——b O——t.—*Min. Com. Saf.*

January 18, 1777; Whereas this council is informed that many of the principal Associators of Col. Hunter's Battalion of Berks county, refused to march to join General Washington's army, at this important crisis, when so glorious an opportunity offers of crushing the enemy, and thereby have prevented and discouraged the rest, and proceeded even to dare them to enforce the Resolve of this council upon them.

Therefore, *resolved*, That Col. Hunter be directed forthwith to collect all the well affected in his Battalion, and to sieze upon the ringleaders, in this defection, and send them under guard to Philadelphia; and that he do execute the resolve of this council, of Dec. 7th, last, upon all who refuse to march, without favor or affection; and that they do collect blankets and other necessaries, for the use of those who are to march, paying a reasonable price for the same; and should any person refuse to deliver such necessaries as they can spare, the Col. is directed to take any pay for the same. Those that turn out to march the most direct road to head quarters.—*Min. Com. Saf.*, iii, 40.

The following notice was then served upon John Schuty and John Blattner, by John Fry.

READING, January 22d, 1777.

Sir—The committee at Reading, do order that you attend there on Saturday next, the twenty-fifth day of this instant, January, at ten o'clock in the forenoon, to give them information of such things as you know, relative to any person or persons discouraging the march of any part of the militia, hereof fail not.

By Order of the Committee.

JAMES READ, Chairman.

January 27, 1777, Captain Bickham was directed to pay to Captain Furry, £50, and to Captain Hederick, £62, 16, for subsistence money of their two companies, belonging to the

Third battalion of militia of Berks county—to be charged to Congress.

November 8th, 1777—In council of safety, ordered that the persons herinafter named, in the respective counties, be authorized and required to collect, without delay, from such of the inhabitants of the said respective counties, as have not taken the oath of allegiance or abjuration, or who have aided or assisted the enemy, by arms and accoutrements, blankets, woollen and linsey-woolsey, shoes and stockings, for the army— that they approve the same, when taken, according to the qua. lity, &c., &c.

The committee appointed, on this occasion, for Berks county, the following named gentlemen:

HENRY CHRIST,
HENRY HALLER,
THOMAS PARRY,
DANIEL UTREE,
PHILIP MILLAR,
NATHAN LEWIS,
JOHN LANER,
GODFRIED REAM,
JACOB SELTZER,
NICHOLAS SHAFFER,

Minutes of Committee of Safety, Vol. III.

CHAPTER VI.

EDUCATION

WILLIAM PENN, the founder of the colony of Pennsylvania, whom Montesquieu denominates the modern Lycurgus, seems to have well known that a sound education was indispensable among all classes to secure, enjoy, and perpetuate the blessings of civil and religious liberty.

A few extracts from his writings are here presented on this subject.

"Nothing weakens kingdoms like vice; it does not only displease Heaven, but disable them;"—"It is our interest to be good, and it is none of the least arguments for religion, that the piety and practice of it is the peace and prosperity of government; and consequently that vice, the enemy of religion, is, at the same time, the enemy of human society. What, then, should be more concerned for the preservation of virtue, than government? that, in its abstract, and true sense is not only founded upon virtue, but without the preservation of virtue, it is impossible to maintain the best constitution, that can be made. And, however some particular men may prosper that are wicked, and some private good men miscarry, in the things of this world, in which sense, things may be said to happen alike to all, to the righteous as to the wicked, yet I dare boldly affirm, and challenge any man to the truth thereof; that, in the many volumes of the history of all ages and kingdoms of the world, there is not one instance to be found, where the hand of God was against a righteous nation, or when the hand of God was not against an unrighteous nation, first or last; nor where a just government perished, nor an unjust government long prospered. Kingdoms are rarely so short lived as men; yet they also have a time to die; but as temperance giveth health to men, so virtue gives time to kingdoms; and as vice brings men betimes to their graves, so nations to their ruin.

Respecting modes of government, the memorable founder of that of Pennsylvania declares,—"There is hardly one frame of government in the world, so ill designed by its first founder, that, in good hands would not do well enough; and history tells us, the best, in ill ones, can do nothing, that is great or good; witness, the Jewish and the Roman states. Governments, like clocks, go from the motion, which men give them; and as governments are made and moved by men, so by them are they ruined too: wherefore governments rather depend upon men, than men upon governments. Let men be good and the government cannot be bad; if it be ill they will cure it: but if men be bad, let the government be never so good, they will endeavor to warp and spoil it to their turn."—"That, therefore, which makes a good constitution, must keep it, viz: men of wisdom and virtue; qualities, that, because they descend not with wordly inheritances, must be carefully propagated by a virtuous education of youth; for which after ages will owe more to the care and prudence of founders, and the successive magistracy, than to their parents, for their private patrimonies."

" I would think (says he in another place) that there are but few people so vicious, as to care to see their children so; and yet to me it seems a plain case, that, as we leave the government, they will find it : if some effectual course be not taken, what with neglect, and what with example, impiety and the miseries that follow it, will be entailed upon our children. Certainly it were better the world ended with us, than that we should transmit our vices, or sow those evil seeds, in our day, that will ripen to their ruin, and fill our country with miseries, after we are gone; thereby exposing it to the curse of God, and violence of our neighbors. But it is an infelicity we ought to bewail, that men are apt to prefer the base pleasures of their

present extravagances..to all.endeavors after a future benefit;
for, besides the. guilt, they draw, down. upon themselves, our
poor posterity must be.greatly.injured.thereby;. who. will: find
those debts and incumbrances harder to pay, than all the rest,
we can.leave them under."

"Upon the whole matter (continues he) I take- the freedom
to say, that, if we would preserve our government, we must
endear it to the people. To .do this, besides the necessity of
present, just and wise things, .we must secure the youth: this
is not to be done, but by the amendment of the way of their education; and that with all convenient speed and diligence. I
say, the government is highly obliged: it is a sort of trustee for
the youth of the kingdom; who, though now minors, yet will
have the government when we are gone. Therefore depress
vice, and cherish virtue: that through good education, they
may become good; which will truly render them happy in this
world, and a good way fitted for that which is to come. If
this be done, they will owe more to your memories for their
education, than for their estates."

Especially does the permanency of all Republics, depend
upon the enlightenment of the people. As education is therefore
encouraged or neglected, so will their foundations be sure and
stable, or loose and unsettled; and it is difficult to say, whether
in their moral relations or political privileges, this truth is most
self-evident. The certainty, stability and perpetuity of a republican government, with all its vast machinery of offices and
officers, such as the efficient administration of the government
by the Executive, the judicious and wholesome exercise of its
powers by the Legislature, the prompt and energetic administration of justice by faithful Judges, and above all, the just determination of the rights of parties by impartial Jurors, must
depend alone upon the people. There is no other foundation
upon which the structure can rest. This constitutes its chief
excellence, its greatest strength.

In a government then such as ours, based as it is upon acknowledged democratic principles, in the theory and practice
of which, it is admitted that the people are the source of all
power, making and unmaking at stated intervals all their func-
tionaries, from the chief magistrate of the nation, down to the
humblest officer created by a Borough charter, the necessity of
35

having that same people educated, will not for a moment be questioned. For, as they are enlightened or unenlightened so will their government be elevated in character, or depressed in a corresponding degree. Called upon as they are, to the frequent exercise of the elective franchise, and thus necessarily to judge of men and measures, their course of action must be determined, either by each man's own personal examination into the character of the one, and a careful investigation into the propriety or expediency of the other, or else it must be suggested, and fixed by the advice and opinions of others. And what a prolific source of abuse is this. It is seldom indeed that such advice is honest, for the most part, it is the gratuitous offering of interested men. How shall all those whose minds are obscured by the clouds of ignorance, be capable of discriminating between the correctness and incorrectness of questions of public policy? How shall they judge between the patriot and the ambitious, self-aggrandizing demagogue? Are they competent to arrive at a proper decision of the various complicated questions, necessarily arising for their determination, and by a reference to which, their choice, is to be regulated in the selection of officers and representatives? Let the people be educated, and thus each individual will be rightly impressed with the important truth, that his own interests are identified with those of the State. For no government is so free as that which is upheld by the affections of the people, and no community so happy as that in which the youth, by proper education, are disciplined to the exercise of all those moral virtues that ennoble human nature.

So thought and so acted, almost all of the early settlers of nearly every state in the Union. Although Colonists it is true, and perhaps entertaining not even the most remote idea of a separate existence, at any period of time, as a nation, they were in their Colonial government, if not essentially, at least partially democratic. Returning by a popular vote, their own Representatives, and—with the exception of their Governors—the greater part of all their prominent officers, they felt the necessity of so elightening this first great power, that at a very early day, schools and institutions of learning were established and founded by voluntary contributions among them. Such is the history of the Puritans of New England, the Roman Catholics of Maryland, the Quakers of Pennsylvania and the Huguenots of the Carolinas. True, their first efforts in this respect were feeble. The country was new, and surrounded as the inhabitants were by savage foes, the first elements of education which the children obtained, were communicated by the parents themselves, in the midst of dangers and unexampled hardships. By degrees, however, as the different settlements in· creased in number and strength, schools were established for the instruction of the children, in the ordinary branches of the education of the country from whence the parents had emigrated; and as in time, wealth began to flow in upon the Colonists, schools, academies and colleges came to be endowed, either by individual liberality or legislative munificence. Truly the good seed sown thus early by the settlers, has yielded abundantly, "some thirty, some sixty, and some an hundred fold."

In general terms and fewer words, we have thus described the progressive history of the education of almost every community in the United States. In some parts we admit, the advance has been accelerated more perhaps by the comparative extent of the information of the first emigrants and diminished number of obstacles encountered by them in subduing the country, than from any other cause. Under ordinary circumstances, this might therefore suffice for the object to which the present chapter is devoted; but as it is intended to present to the reader a detailed account of all matters of sufficient importance, and worthy of being embodied in a work of this kind, it is our duty as a faithful historian, to enter into details.

Schools were for many years, except a few among the Friends and Welsh settlers, exclusively under the control of German teachers. Many of the first German settlers in Berks and Lebanon, brought with them their school masters and ministers. The former in many instances, in the absence of the latter, officiated in a two-fold capacity, as school master and preacher.—. Of this number were J. C. Wirtz, at Sacany, and Casper Leutbecker, at Tulpehocken. Rev. Muhlenberg, speaking of him says, "Nach einiger Zeit kam ein Mann mit Namen, Casper Leutbecker, seiner Profession nach ein Schneider, nach. Tulpehocken (1745) setzte das Vorlesen in der Kirche fort, hielt Schule und Catichesirte."*

Common schools were very few in number in Berks and Le-

* Hall. Nach, 249.

banon, till 1750 or 1751. Some townships had none "In Oley," says Muhlenberg, "1748, sind Schulen sehr entfernt." No systematic efforts were made to improve the schools among the Germans, in Pennsylvania, till after 1751, when on the representation of the Rev. Michael Schlatter, who had been some time in Pennsylvania, to the churches of Holland. A scheme was started by a society of noblemen of Europe, for the instruction of Germans and their descendants, in Pennsylvania. These foreign gentlemen "were truly concerned to find that any of their fellow subjects, in part of the British dominions, were not fully provided with the means of knowledge and salvation. They considered it a matter of the greatest importance to the cause of Christianity in general, and the protestant interest in particular, not to neglect such a vast body of useful people, situated in a dark barren region, with almost none to instruct them, or their helpless children, who are coming forth in multitudes, and exposed an easy prey to the total ignorance of their savage neighbors on the one hand, and the corruption of their Jesuitical enemies, on whom they bordered, on the other hand; and of whom there were always, perhaps, too many mixed among them. Moved by these interesting considerations, these noblemen and others, did accordingly take the good design into their immediate protection, and formed themselves into a society for the effectual management of carrying out the scheme of instructing the Germans.*

Schools were subsequently organized at Reading, Tulpehocken, &c., under the direction of the Rev. Michael Schlatter, as Visitor or Supervisor General of the schools; but met with little or no success, at least not commensurate with the importance of the enterprize. The designing—these are always to be found—persuaded the more ignorant, that it was a scheme gotten up to enslave them! The scheme for, and its effects upon those whom it was intended to benefit, evanesced. The consequence was, that schools were still few till about the time when the Lutheran and German Reformed congregations were more permanently organized, through the efforts of the Rev'ds Muhlenberg, Schlatter, and their coadjutors.

At no part of this History better than the present, can it with greater propriety be observed, that almost co-existent with the establishment of the first Lutheran churches in Ger-

* See pages antea, 99, 109, where the scheme is given in detail.

many and of the Reformed churches in Switzerland and Holland, there sprang up a custom among their members, peculiar to themselves. Each congregation was regarded as a spiritual municipal corporation, and among other duties performed by those having its control or government, in order that "the word might not perish for lack of knowledge among the people," they employed a competent teacher, to instruct the youth of both sexes, without any regard whatever to the wealth or standing of the parents in society. Generally each church was supplied with an organ—indeed this instrument was regarded as indispensable to the proper worship of the Almighty, and the person employed to perform upon it during divine service, was required to unite with his skill and knowledge as a musician, the profession of a school teacher. He usually received a stated salary, and was furnished with accommodations for his school, himself and family, at the common cost of the congregation. In return for this, and in addition to his duty as an organist—as has been shown—he was required to teach the children of the congregation upon such terms as the vestry might from time to time determine. The sum thus fixed, was paid to him by the parents of such of the children, as were able to afford it, while the children of those who were in indigent circumstances, were taught the same branches without charge and in consideration of the salary paid by the congregation. This mode of educating their own poor, by a system as simple, was regarded as a religious duty. It was so taught from generation to generation, through successive years. And when the Lutheran and German Reformed churches were thoroughly organized and provided with settled pastors, they also had better qualified teachers, and schools regularly taught.

It was the unceasing effort of both the Revds. Muhlenberg, Schlatter, and their coadjutors, to establish schools in connection with churches. All great reformers appreciated, and will ever appreciate the importance of schools. Luther—the immortal Luther—when speaking of schools and schoolmasters, used the following emphatic language:—

Die Schulen sind kleine, doch sehr nuetzliche Concilien und die edelsten Kleinode der Kirche; und die Lehre derselben ein koestliches Amt und Werk. Ich wollte dass keiner zu einem Prediger erwaehlt wuerde, er haette sich denn Schon mit dem
35*

Unterricht der Kinder beschaeftiget. Wer dem Teufel in seinem Reiche einen Schaden zufuegen will, der ihn recht beisse, der mache sich an die Jugend und Kinder, und suche bey ihnen einen Grund zu legen, der fuer und fuer bleibe.

In the same light, schools should be ever regarded as the nurseries of virtue and piety. It is stated, however, with regret, that the citizens of Berks and Lebanon counties had, for some years, lost sight of these nuetzliche Concilien, in bestowing that fostering care upon them, so generally, as their importance demands; nevertheless, some attention was given to this subject at a comparatively early date, in the effort of establishing schools of advanced standing, in some sections of these counties. An academy was started at Reading, in 1778, but owing to a want of proper management and sufficient patronage, it was suspended till 1836—but subsequently revived, and sustains at present, a deservedly high character. The course of instruction is extensive, embracing the ancient and modern languages, mathematics, and the other branches usually taught in in academies and high schools.

A Female Seminary, located in Reading, was incorporated in the spring of 1838. This school, some private ones, and the public schools in the borough, sustain a very fair reputation.

At Wommelsdorf and Kutztown, are academies of advanced standing. These academies and seminaries, exert a wholesome influence upon a certain portion of community, and it is hoped their influence will be, before long, generally felt in the county, in liberalizing the views of those hitherto opposed to a general and advanced system of education. At present, but few of the districts of Berks county have accepted the provisions of the law in 1835. "In many instances," says Trego, "there has been much opposition in collecting the school taxes, building school houses, and making any improvements involving cost. The want of good teachers has been felt here, as in many other parts of the State; but it is believed that there is a general improvement in the schools as well as in the disposition of the public mind on this subject."

The state of education in Lebanon county, is nearly the same as that in Berks. There are three academies in this county, viz: at Lebanon, Myerstown, and Millerstown; all, except the last named, are in successful operation. Many gentlemen are to be found, in both counties, ardently devoted to the cause of education, exerting themselves in behalf of academies, seminaries, and common schools. These schools are the sure defences of our country. The patriot and the christian have reason to rejoice at the prospect of the ultimate, general adoption of the common school system—all should exert themselves with much anxiety, to aid in introducing the system, and supplying schools with well qualified teachers. Who even does not know that much depends upon teachers, to speed the labors of our legislators, magistrates, and the minister of the gospel. The teachers must be *virtuous* and *intelligent*, to make intelligent and useful scholars, or to aid the cause of intelligence; for without intelligence, on which the minister of the gospel, the legislator and magistrate, can act, and *principle*, cultivated in childhood, and matured in riper age, they will all act in vain. They may as well endeavor to remove mountains, as to attempt to accomplish much and prominent good without them. For, without these two—virtue and intelligence—it is truly said: "The Legislator, the Magistrate, and the Minister, will descend into the same gulf of ignorance and corruption."

Sabbath Schools—great auxiliaries in diffusing useful and indispensable knowledge among the junior portion of society—are fast gaining ground. Nearly all religious denominations foster them.

CHAPTER VII.

RELIGIOUS HISTORY.

Iu this chapter, brief sketches are presented, of the different religious denominations that existed, and are still found, in this part of Pennsylvania. It is not consistent with the limits of this compilation, to notice the doctrines of each, or to trace the origin of all. Those who wish more extensive information on the origin, rise, progress, doctrines and statistics of the religious denominations noticed here, and of all the sects in the United States, are referred to the writer's work, entitled " *He Pasa Ekklesia,* &c." published by Mr. James Y. Humphreys, Philadelphia, 1844.

If differences of opinion touching dogmas of religion and multiplicity of sects, serve as a standard of deep toned piety and Christian benevolence—charity in the true sense of the Gospel, then may the people of Berks and Lebanon lay some claim to a share of it—and it is undoubtedly true, they have claims of the kind—for the diversity of opinion, and sects or denominations, are not a few in Berks and Lebanon, as will be seen from the following brief and imperfect notices.

For the want of the *promised* materials, so kindly *proffered* by those on whom we called, or whom we addressed, the notices are brief and imperfect. They are made up of " *fragmentary rubbish,*" furnished, or gleaned *at a late hour.* Had these been furnished at an earlier date, though mere fragments, the writer could, if the reader will believe him, have rendered these *sketches* more worthy of his notice.

DIE NEUGEBOHRENE, OR THE NEW BORN.

A sect that assumed the appellation, *New Born*, existed about the year 1717 or 1719, in Oley, headed afterwards by one Bowman. Their peculiar tenets can only be gathered from detached fragments: a few of them are in the possession of the writer. From these it appears this sect existed for a period of some thirty or forty years.

The existence of this sect has been noticed in another part of this book—pages 233, 236.

John Peter Miller, contemporary with Bowman, speaking of this sect, says:—"Damals, Zwischen 1717—1721 entstand ein Volk in der Gegend Oly die man Neugebohrne nannte, und einer Matthies Bauman zum Anfaenger hatten. Ihr Vorgeben war, dass sie nicht mehr koenten suendigen, in einer in Deutschland gedruckten Schrift, genant, "Ruf an die Unwiedergebohrne Welt, klingt es _wunderlich, wan Bauman sagt, Pagina 13." Die Menschen sagen: Christus habe die Suende hinweg genommen, es ist war bey mir, wer sich also befindet, dass er also ist wie Adam vor dem Fall, als wie ich bin." Da, says Miller, setzt er sich neben Adam vor seinem Fall.

Und Pagina 17, machet er noch einen aergern Sprung, wann er sagt: "Wie Adam vor dem Fall war, sa bin ich gemacht, und noch fester." Was aber die Menschen am meisten aergert, war, was er Pagina 12 sagt: "Mit dem Leib kann Man nicht suendigen vor Gott, Sondern nur vor Menschen und andern Creaturen, und die kann der Richter schlichten." Daraus sie gefaehrliche Folgen zogen.

Sie ruehmten sich, zu seyn nur von Gott gesandt, um die Menschen irr zu machen, welches sie auch innerhalb zehn Jahren (1725—1734) fleissig getrieben; also dass man oft zu Mark-Zeit ihre Disputationen in Philadelphia mit Verwunderung hat koennen anhoeren, da auch Bauman sich einst erbotten, er wollte zum Beweiss, dass seine Lehre von Gott sey, durch den Delaware Strohm gehen.

* Col. Rec. 349—page antea, 233.

Bey ihrem Reissen durch Conestoga, allwo sie Eingang hin und wieder fanden, kamen sie endlich auch zum Vorsteher (Conrad Beissel zu Ephrata) und da brachte sich Bauman wegen der Wiedergeburt an. Der Vorsteher gab ihm kurtzen Bescheid, und sagte: Er sollte an seinem Unflat riechen, und betrachten ob dieses zur Wiedergeburt gehoere; darauf sie einen spitzigen Geist nannten und davon giengen. Man hat wargenommen, dass von derselben zeit an sie Kraft verlohren, ihre Verfuehrung weiter aus zu breiten: und ist mit den Urstaendern endlich abgestorben. Gedachter Bauman ist ums Jahr 1727, gestorben; er soll sonst ein redlicher Mann gewesen seyn, und die Welt nicht ueber die Gebuehr gesucht haben, aber Kuehlenwein,* Yotter, und andere senier Nachfolger waren in dem Weltlichen unersaetlich.

Dieser Mattheis Bauman war ein armer Tagloehner, aus der Stadt Lamsheim, in Churpfaltz. Im Jahr 1701 ist er mit einer harten Krankheit heimgesucht worden, da er in den Himmel verzuckt wurde, und Offenbahrungen an die Menschen empfieng. Als er wieder zu sich selbst kam rief er bey einer Stunde lang aus: "O! ihr Menschen!! bekehret euch!!! der juengste Tag kommt!!!!" Er fiel abermal in Verzuckung, und da wurde zu ihm gesagt: "Die Menschen meinen, sie leben bey Tage; sie sind aber alle verkehrt bey der Nacht!!"

Diese Verzuckungen haben vierzehn Tage angehalten, darunter die letzte vier und zwanzig Stunde gewaehrt, dass man auch meinte er waere gestorben, und Anstalt zu seinem Begraebniss machen liess. Als er wieder zu sich selbst kám, gieng er zum Prediger, und sagte ihm: "Gott habe ihn wieder in diese Welt gesandt, den Menschen zu sagen, dass sie sich sollten bekehren." Der Prediger aber, welcher meinte, er waere im Kopf verrueckt, suchte durch ein Weltbuch ihm die Grillen zu vertreiben.—*Chron. Ephra.* page 128—130.

They maintained they were impeccable, or that they had attained to a state of sinlessness. They were in their own estimation, *perfect!*

This is dogmatically asserted by one of them, a female in a. letter, dated Oley, May 14, 1718, to a friend of hers in Germany.

"I will apprise you of my present condition. I am in a bet-

* See page 233, 34, where the original is given.

ter state than I was while with you (in Germany).   Here God
has absolved me from all sin—I can sin no more; for which I
now praise, and shall ever laud his name."

"Teachers and hearers, none of them are christians, for they
are sinners; but Christ came to destroy sin.   He that is not
absolved from all sin, for him Christ has not appeared in this
world.   All teachers, in the whole world, not freed from sin,
and not in an impeccable state, are false teachers, be they pious
or impious.   In the kingdom of Christ, none but Christ prevails.
He that has not him is none of his; and where he is, there man
is set free from sin."

Under date of June 10, 1747, the Revd. Muhlenberg says
"I started from New Hanover, and eight miles from here, called
to see an aged person of the so *called New Born,* who had
married a widow woman some twenty years ago, with whom
he had five children, &c., &c.   The old gentleman says he was
new born in the Palatinate.   But the evidences of his being
new born, are simply these: According to his own oft repeated
declaration, that he has seceded from the Reformed Church,
and denounced the sacraments—and having refused to take the
oath of fealty to the then ruling elector, he, with others, was
brought before the consistory and imprisoned; and according to
his own notion, had suffered on account of Christ and the truth.
He will not listen to any rational counsel—rejecting all revealed truth—nor will he suffer himself to be taught, because he is
of a weak understanding—obstinately selfish, and a man of violent passions.

"After he had arrived in this country, he united with the so
called New Born.   They feign having received the new birth
through mediate inspiration, apparitions, dreams, and the like.
When one is thus regenerated, he fancies himself to be God and
Christ himself, and cannot, henceforth, sin no more.   Hence
they do not use the word of God as a means of salvation.   They
scoff at the holy sacraments.*

* Hallisch Nachrichten, p. 227

THE SWEDES.

The Swedes, who first settled within the limits of the province of Pennsylvania, as early as 1638, and within the bounds of Berks county, prior to 1700, had, undoubtedly, erected a church at Molatton, near Douglassville, about the year 1720 or 21. They were a "God-fearing and just people," and were the first to build sanctuaries, and by liberal donations, to establish permanent funds for the support of the ministry in other parts of the country. They had a church at Tinnecum Island prior to 1675, as is evident from the following:—

"At a special court, held at New Castle, in Delaware river, the 13th and 14th days of May, 1675, it was ordered that the church, or place of worship, be regulated by the court here, in as orderly and decent a manner as may. That the place for meeting at Craine Hoeck (opposite Wilmington) do continue as heretofore—that the church at Tinnecum Island do serve for Uppland, and parts adjacent.

"And whereas there is no church or place of worship higher up the river than the said Island, for the greater ease and convenience of the inhabitants there. It's ordered, that the magistrates of Uppland do cause a church or place of meeting to be built at Wickegkoo,* the which to be for the inhabitants of Passayunk, and so upwards. The said court being empowered to raise a tax for its building, and to agree for a competent fund for their minister: of all which they are to give an account to the next general court, and they to the governor for his approbation." Signed

E. ANDROSS."

The following extracts from the "Annals of the Swedes," by the Rev. J. C. Clay, go to show, that they were anxious to have the gospel preached in their new settlements, in the direction of Molatton.

"In 1705, the 'upper inhabitants'—meaning, I suppose, those at Upper Marion, or perhaps up the Delaware, towards Bristol—made application for occasional services in their neighborhood, in the winter season, because of their distance from

* Wickegkoo is Wiccacoe, above the Navy Yard, Philadelphia. Rev. Foot's Address, pa 17.

church. It was agreed that the rector should officiate twice during the winter season.

"About the year 1720, the Rev. Samuel Hesselius settled among the Swedes, in the lower part of Berks. This appears from the following, from the same author, Rev. Clay.

"1720—A meeting was held on the 27th of March, for the transaction of business, at which four clergymen were present: the Rev. Provost Andrew Hesselius, the Rev. Mr. Lidenius, of Racoon and Penn's Neck, and the Rev. Moses Lidman and Samuel Hesselius. The Provost proposed that the last named clergyman should take charge of those portions of the congregation residing at Kalkonhook and Neshamani. This was objected to by the lay members present, upon the ground that the Swedes living in those places might become weaned from the mother church at Wicaco.

"It being understood that one clergyman was competent to the duties at Wicaco, it was then proposed by Lidman, that as the people at Manatting—supposed to be Mollaton, four miles above Pottsgrove, on the Schuylkill—were a great distance from the church, they, perhaps, would be glad of his services there, and that he would cheerfully relinquish to him so much of the salary as was furnished by that part of the congregation. Marcus Hulings, and other respectable inhabitants of that part of the country, then present, earnestly seconded this proposition, promising to contribute to the extent of their means, towards his support. It was accordingly arranged that the Rev. Samuel Hesselius should settle at Manatting."

From all these it may be fairly inferred, that a congregation was organized at an early date, in the southern part of Berks county.

Molatton, for years afterward, and to this date, is an Episcopal church. The Rev. Muhlenberg, mentioned in the sequel, preached statedly here.

36

THE QUAKERS.

The Friends, or Quakers, were next to the Swedes in preaching the gospel within the borders of Berks. Two of them,
Anthony Lee and George Boone, settled in the interior of this
county, about the year 1716—1718, and were soon followed
by others, and without doubt, were visited by their ministers
or preachers. They had many self-denying men at that early
date, who not only visited their brethren, but preached the gospel to the tawny sons of the forest. Thomas Chalkley, who
came from England in 1701, was of that class; as early as 1705,
he visited the Indians living near Susquehannah, at Conestoga,
and preached the Gospel of Christ freely to them.

Some of their most eminent ministers in the county of Berks
were, Samuel Hugh, Ellis Hugh, Job Hugh, Enos Ellis, Abel
Thomas, Moses Embree, James Iddings, Amos Lee, Peter
Thomas, Judah Thomas. The Friends were very numerous between the year 1750 and 1780; their number, at the period alluded to, was rising of two thousand in the county; owing,
however, to the vast emigration to the western states, their
number does not, at present, exceed two hundred members.—
They have three or four meeting houses in the county; besides
the one in the borough of Reading, which was originally built
in 1751, and pulled down in 1766, and in its place the present
one story log house, built on Washington street.

The Friends, though not patrons of a classically educated
ministry, have always been the supporters of good schools.—
They have contributed much towards improving society.—
They are the friends of Peace and Universal Liberty, and of
unfettered tolerance. No where in the annals of history, can
the finger be pointed to this or the like sentence, as applicable
to the Quakers—"They persecuted others for opinion's sake."
This dark stain is not in their drab coats—it would show if it
were.

THE MENNONITES.

The *Mennonites* having settled about the year 1722 to '24, in the Southern part of Lebanon county, had meeting houses for public worship among their brethren, who were very numerous for many years.

In Europe, they had been sorely persecuted, and on the invitation of the liberal minded William Penn, they transported themselves and familes, into the province of Pennsylvania, as early as 1683. Those who came in that year, and in 1698, settled in and about Germantown. In 1709, other families of them arrived and commenced settlements in Lancaster county, in Pequea valley; these were the Herrs, Meylins, Kendigs, and others. They were soon followed by others in 1711, 1717, 1727—of these last, many settled in the more northern parts of Lancaster county, within the limits of Lebanon county.

Among their first preachers in America were, John Gorgas, John Conerads, Clas Rittinghausen, the grandfather of the celebrated David Rittenhouse, Jacob Gaedtschleck, Henry Kolb, Claes Jansen, Michael Zigler, Hans Burgholtzer, Hans Herr, Christian Herr, Benedict Hirschi, Martin Bear, Johannes Bowman, Velte Clemer, Daniel Langenecker, Jacob Beghtly Ulrich Breckbill, Hans Tschantz—all these were ministers prior to 1735.

They continued to increase till about the year 1790—'92, when a certain Martin Boehm, John Neidig, ministers, and many lay members, seceded from them, and afterwards connected themselves with the *United Brethren in Christ*, since when their number has diminished in Lebanon county. They still have a number of meeting houses in this county.

The Mennonites, in this county, as is well known, have been for the last forty years on the decline; but the indications at present seem rather more favorable to again resuscitate the doctrines, at least, among a portion of them,* which their ancestors so strenuously advocated.

The Mennonites never wasted money in rearing stately houses, in which to dispense the word of life, or in erecting massive college edifices, in which to impart useful knowleege, nor do they encourage theological seminaries. In this respect, like

* The Reformed Mennonites

the Friends, the Mennonites of this country have been content to walk in the ways of their fathers, and to hear the "word of life" expounded, by men of as simple taste and habits as themselves. Let none, however, reproach them with hostility to useful learning—learning for life, and not for school. Holding Peace principles, and taking little or no part in the affairs of government, they teach their young men, that the first great duty of life is, for each man *to mind his own business*. Practising upon this maxim, they encourage industry by their own examples, and discourage ambition by a representation of the evils necessarily following in its train. They spurn alike the honors and emoluments of office. Hence they deem an education, beyond the rudiments of a very common one, as superfluous, among all their members of society. They have, therefore, no ministers, to use a common phrase, classically educated. This is not, however, the case in Europe.

At Amsterdam, they have a college, in which all the useful branches are taught. Students of theology receive instruction in a room, containing the library, over the Mennonite chapel. The lectures are delivered in Latin; and each student before his entrance, must be acquainted with Latin and Greek. They attend at a literary institution for instruction in Hebrew, Ecclesiastical History, Physics, Natural and Moral Philosophy, &c. The college was established nearly a century ago, and was at first supported by the Amsterdam Mennonites alone; but lately, other Mennonite churches sent in their contributions.— Some of the students receive support from a public fund; they are all intended for the Christian ministry.[*]

THE BRETHREN, DIE TAEUFER, OR DUNKARDS.

This society, or members of it, emigrated from Germany and Holland, in 1719; some of them settled in Germantown, others in Oley, Conestoga, Muelbach, and elsewere. From a society organized at Muelbach, Conrad Beissel seceded and formed a new association, commonly called the *Sieben Taeger*, or German Seventh-day Baptists, of whom some account has been given in the preceding part of this book.

[*] Dr. Ypeij

The Brethren were numerous, from 1730 to 1745, in Oley; from that time on they seem to have declined; at least, their number in that neighborhood began, at that period, to decrease. In the year 1724, the Dunkards held a general meeting, or Grosse Versammlung, in Oley. Rev. Peter Miller, in his Chronicon Ephratensa, says:

"Sie, die Dunker, nahmen sich vor, einen allgemeinen Besuch zu machen—zu ihren Bruedern im ganzen Lande, und hierzu ward der 23ste October, 1724 ausgesetst, als an welchem der Besuch von Germanton absetzte, und zwar zuerst nach Schippack, Falkner Schwamm, hielten Brodbrechen da bei einem Bruder, Albertus genannt; von da reisten sie nach Oley, da sie eine Grosse Versammlung hielten und das Brodbrechen: dan nach ihren, Neugetauften Brueder an, der Schuylkill, wo sie Versammlung und Brodbrechen hielten, und zwei tauften, von da nach Conestogo."

This appears to have been a kind of Apostolischer Kreutzzug. Fourteen of the Brethren travelled in company, seven on foot and seven on horse.

Shortly after the arrival of Count Zinzendorf, there was another General meeting held in Oley, which was composed of Dunkards, German Seventh Day Baptists, Moravians, Mennonites, Separatists and others.

Im Jahr 1742, says Miller, ist noch eine Conferentz in Oley gehalten worden, da bey Vier Vaeter der Germeinde in Ephrata sind erschienen—Diese Versammlung wurde eigentlich von den Dunker gehalten—dann die Einsame Brueder hielten so verdaechtig von der Sach, dass sie sich nicht mehr wollten damit einlassen. Sie hatten eine Schrift von Ehestand aufgesetzt wie weit er an Gott reiche, und dass er nur seye eine loebliche Ordung der Natur, dieselbe uebergaben sie, worauf ein haeftiger Wortstreit erfolgte.

Der Ordinarius (Zinzendorf) sagte: Er waere keines weges mit dieser Schrift zufrieden, er haette seinen Ehestand nicht also angefangen, es stuende auch sein Ehestand hoeher als der Einsamen stand in Ephrata. Die Verordenten von Ephrata suchten die Sache wieder gut zumachen, und sagten, sie waeren keine Feinde des Ehestands, es waeren Familien in der Gemeinde, die alle Jahr ein Kind haetten. Darueber schlug er (Zinzendorf) die Haende zusammen, und sagte, Es wundere

36*

ihn, wie unter einem solchem wichtige Zeugniss, wie man vor-
gebe, die Menschen doch so fleischlich leben koenten.

Dorauf ist der Ordinarius in solchen Heftigkeiten ausgebro-
chen, dass er von seinem Amt, auf der Conferentz, ist ab-und
ein Schlottlaender, Statt seiner, eingesetzt worden, und also
lief endlich die Conferentz zur Aergerniss aller auseinander, zu
Ende.

Miller continues—Und weilen alle Gesinntheiten daȥu einge-
laden worden, wurde *ich* auch von meinem Vorsteher deputirt
dahin zugehen. Und als ich zum Conferentz kam, welche in
Oley gehalten worden, fand ich daselbst von unsern Taeufern,
Sieben-Taeger, Menonniten und Separatisten; der Graf aber
selbzt war Vorsitzer, daselbst hoerete ich wunderliche und
setlsame Sachen.

Als ich nun wieder heimkam, brachte ich mich bey meinem
Vorsteher an, und sagte, dass ich des Grafen Conferentz ansehe
als einen Fallstrick um einfaeltige, erwecktedente wider an die
Kindertaufe, und den Kirchengang, zu bringen, und das alte
Babel wieder aufzurichten. Wir hielten Rath, was zu thun
seye, und wurden einig, dieser Gefahr vorzukommen, weil schon
einige Taeufer sich an dieser nichtigen Lehre vergaft hatten,
jaehrlich eine Conferentz zu halten, oder wie wir es nannten
Eine Grosse Versammluug, und wurd zugleich Zeit und Ort
bestimmt. Diese ist der Anfang und das Fundament von den
Grossen Versammlungen der Taeufer—Chron. Eph. 128, 210.

The present number of Dunkards is comparatively small—
probably not exceeding two hundred in Berks and Lebanon
counties. Of their places of meeting, we have no estimate.

They, like the Mennonites, pay little or no attention to education. They are retrograding as to numbers in this part of
the country.

GERMAN SEVENTH-DAY BAPTIST.

Though these took their rise in this portion of Pennsylvania,
none are to be found, at present, residing in Berks and Lebanon.
Of their rise, we have spoken. The reader is referred to pages
336–343.

THE SCHWENKFELDERS.

A respectable number of these emigrated from Europe in 1734. Many of these arrived at Philadelphia the 22d Sept., others on the 5th October of the same year, and settled principally in Montgomery, Berks, Bucks, and Lehigh counties, where their grand children chiefly reside at present, on the branches of the Skippack and Perkiamen creeks, in the upper, middle and lower end of Montgomery county, and the lower or east part of Berks, and south corner of Lehigh.

The Rev. Wise was, it appears, one of their first ministers. He died in 1740. His successors were Rev'ds B. Hoffman, A. Wagner, G. Wagner, Christopher Schultz, sen., C. Kriebel, C. Hoffman, G. Kriebel, Messrs. Kriebel, Schultz, B. Schultz, A Schultz, and D. Schultz, assistants; I. Schultz, and last, the Rev. C. Schultz, who died March 1843. The Rev. C. Schultz, was the grandson of the Rev. Christopher Schultz, sen.—he was an eminent scholar, and distinguished writer; he was the author of their excellent Catechism, Compendium of Christian Doctrine of Faith; and of their Hymn Book. He was much esteemed as a sound Divine, and a man of undoubted piety, by all surrounding denominations. And on account of his devotedness and his eloquence, he was repeatedly called by the Reformed, Moravians, Mennonites, and others, to preach to them the gospel of everlasting salvation. His motto was:—"Soli Deo Gloria, et Veritas vincet."

The present young candidates in the Gospel Ministry of the upper district, in Berks county, are the Rev. Joshua Schultz, and William Schultz. In the middle and lower districts, the Rev. B. and A. Huebner, and Rev. David Kriebel.

They number about three hundred families; eight hundred members; have five churches and school houses.

By their strict church discipline, they keep their members orderly, and pure from the contaminating influence of corruption, so prevalent. They pay great attention to the education, the religious and moral training of their children. Many of them possess a respectable knowledge of the learned languages, Latin, &c. There is scarce a family among them that does not possess a well selected and neatly arranged library, among which are manuscript copies from their learned forefathers, which they held sacred on account of the purity of doctrine contained therein. They encourage Sabbath schools. They are practical temperance men. They exert a salutary influence upon the community, and it is hoped, their influence will soon be more widely felt.

MORAVIANS.

The Moravians took into consideration the conversion of the heathen as early as 1727, in North America. In 1735, the Rev. Augustus Gottlieb Spangenberger, late Theologus Adjunctus of the University of Hall, in Saxony, left his native country, and arrived that spring in Georgia, and remained there till 1737 when he came to Pennsylvania; and after spending some time here, he went to St. Thomas to hold a visitation there; from thence he returned again to Pennsylvania in 1739. Through him, it is said, the Brethren were made attentive to other Indian nations, having received notice of them from Conrad Weiser. Spangenberger returned to Europe in 1739, and there gave an account of the deplorable condition of the Indians; whereupon Christian Henry Rauch was sent to America, he arrived at New York in 1740, in July; in the month of August he went to Shekomeko, an Indian town, near the Stissik mountain, on the borders of Connecticut, where he labored among the Indians with success.

In 1740 Bishop David Nitschman, with a company of brethren and sisters, arrived from Europe, and settled, what is now called Bethlehem. Nazareth was soon afterwards settled.

In 1741 Count Zinzendorf came to Pennsylvania. as ordinary of the Brethren, with a view not only to see their establishments in general, but especially the fruits of their labor among the heathen. Shortly on his arrival, he proposed to hold a synod at Oley, which, as shown in a preceding page, was held the 11th of February, 1742, in the barn of Mr. Van Dirk, (De Turk,) on which occasion three Indians, from Shekomeko, were baptized.

In August, 1742, Count Zinzendorf visited the people at Tulpehocken. Shortly after this visit, a congregation was organized in Bethel township, (now within the limits of Swatara township, Lebanon county). The station was called Bethel. The Rev, Johannes Brandmueller officiated here about the years 1743 '44· Another congregation was organized at the Hebron station, near the present site of Lebanon, where they erected a church on the Quitopahilla, in which they held a synod in 1748. This building was of logs. In 1750 the "Oratoriam," now standing, was erected in 1750. Besides these two, there were two erected in Heidelberg and one in Oley, between 1742 and 1750.

Conrad Weiser co-operated with the Moravians for several years. In the month of September, 1742, he accompanied Count Zinzendorf to Shamokin, on the Susquehanna. While the Count was on a visit here, an incident fraught with interest occurred, which it is thought is deserving a notice here.

Zinzendorf and his little company, pitched their tents a little below Shamokin, on the banks of the Susquehanna. This. caused no small degree of alarm among the Indians; "a council of the chiefs was assembled, the declared purpose of Zinzendorf was deliberately considered. To these unlettered children of the wilderness it appeared altogether improbable that a stranger should brave the dangers of a boisterous ocean, three thousand miles broad, for the sole purpose of instructing them in the means of obtaining happiness *after death*, and that too without requiring any compensation for his trouble and expense; and as they had observed the anxiety of the white people to purchase lands of the Indians, they naturally concluded that the real object of Zinzendorf was either to procure them the lands at Wyoming for his own use, to search for hidden treasures, or to examine the country with a view to future conquest. It was accordingly resolved to assassinate him, and to do it privately, lest the knowledge of the transaction should produce war with the English, who were settling the country below the mountains.

"Zinzendorf was alone in his tent, seated upon a bundle of dry weeds, when the assassins approached to execute their bloody mission. It was night, and the cool air of September had rendered a small fire necessary to his comfort and convenience. A curtain formed of a blanket and hung upon pins, was the only guard to the entrance of his tent. The heat of his small fire had roused a rattlesnake which lay in the weeds not far from it; and the reptile, to enjoy it more effectually, crawled

slowly into the tent, and passed over one of his legs undisco-
vered. Without, all was still and quiet, except the gentle
murmur of the river at the rapids, a mile below. At this moment, the Indians softly approached the door of his tent, and
slightly removed the curtain, contemplated the venerable
man too deeply engaged in the subject of his thoughts, to
notice either their approach, or the snake which lay extended
before him. At a sight like this, even the heart of the savage
shrunk from committing so horrid an act, and quitting the spot,
they hastily returned to the town and informed their companions that the Great Spirit protected the white man, for they
had found him with no door but a blanket, and had seen a large
rattlesnake crawl over his legs without attempting to injure
him. This circumstance, together with the arrival, soon afterwards, of Conrad Weiser, procured Zinzendorf the friendship
and confidence of the Indians."* After spending twenty days
at Wyoming, he returned to Bethlehem.

THE LUTHERANS.

Though Lutherans had emigrated into America, between
1621 and 1650, and settled in New York, they had no ministers of their own denomination laboring among them before
1659. Their first minister, was Jacob Fabricius, who arrived
that year, and labored about eight years, when he left them, and
connected himself with the Swedish Lutheran church, at Wicaco, now Southwark, Philadelphia, where he preached fourteen
years; during nine of which he was blind. He died in 1792.

Who the immediate successors (in New York) of Fabricius
were, is not known; but from 1703 till 1747, their pastors
were the Rev. Falkner, Knoll, Rochemdaler, Wolf, Hartwick,
and others. All these labored in New York.

From 1682 and onwards, a number of Germans, among
whom were Lutherans, emigrated to Pennsylvania. "The tide
of emigration, however," says S. S. Schmucker, "fairly commenced in 1710, when about three thousand Germans, chiefly
Lutherans, oppressed by Romish intolerance, went from the
Palatinate to England, in 1709, and were sent by Queen Ann

* Chapman's His. of Wyoming

to New York, the succeding year. In 1713, one hundred and fifty families settled in Schoharie; and in 1717, we find in the Colonial Records of Pennsylvania, that the Governor of the province felt it his duty to call the attention of the Provincial Council to the fact, "that great numbers of foreigners from Germany, strangers to our language and constitution, had lately been imported into the province. The council enacted, that every master of a vessel should report the emigrants he brought over, and that they should repair to Philadelphia within one month, to take the oath of allegiance to the government,[*] that it might be seen whether they were "friends or enemies to his majesty's government."

In 1727, the year memorable alike for Francke's death, and the origin of the Moravians, a very large number of Germans came to Pennsylvania from the Palatinate, from Wirtemberg, Dormstadt, and other parts of Germany. This colony, (some of whom settled within the limits of Berks and Lebanon at an early period) was destitute of a regular ministry; there were, however, some school masters and others, some of whom were probably good men, who undertook to preach; and, as many emigrants brought with them the spirit of true piety from Germany, they brought also, many devotional books, and often read Arndt's True Christianity, and other similar works on mutual edification.

Among the first ministers who labored among the Germans, within the counties of Berks and Lebanon, was the Rev. Mr. Stoever, who had collected a congregation as early as 1732, near Lebanon, at the *Berg-Kirche*; and another congregation at Tulpehocken, or *Rieth's Kirche,* where a congregation was organized about the year 1730 or 1731.

Touching the *Berg-Kirche,* the Rev. Geo. Lochman, D. D., speaking of churches in Lebanon county, in 1812, says: Unter diesen ist die Bergkirch-Gemeine die aelteste. Schon im Jahr 1733 ist sie gesammlet worden, zu einer Zeit, da die Indianer noch haeufige Einfaelle in die Gegend machten und mordeten. Herr J. C. Stoever war zu der Zeit Prediger, und nahm sich der zerstreuten Schafen an. Man kam zusammen, nahm ein vacantes Stueck Land auf, und bauete eine hoelzerne Kirche. Anfangs begnuegte man sich damit, dieselbe unter Dach zu-

---

* Col. Rec. iii, p. 18.

bringen, und Blocke als sitze zugebrauchen, und erst nach manchen Jahren hat man sie ganz verfertigen koennen.

Der Hunger nach dem Wort Gottes, und der Eifer fuer den Gottesdienst, muesse zu der Zeit gross gewesen seyn, den die Zuhoerer kamen weit und breit zusammen, und liessen sich durch keine Gefahren abhalten. Man nahm oefters die Flinte mit zur Kirche, um sich unterwegs, nicht nur gegen die wilden Thiere, sondern auch gegen die noch weit wilderen Indianern zu vertheidigen; und wenn man Gottesdienst hielt, wurden oefters Maenner mit geladenen Gewehren auf die Wache gestellt. Die Kirche steht ohngefehr vier Meilen nordwestlich von Libanon.*

The Lutherans in the Tulpehocken settlement were destitute for some ten or fifteen, or more years, of a preacher of their own denomination; a certain John Peter Miller, a native of Oberant Lautern, of the electorate Palatinate, and a graduate of the University of Heidelberg, had arrived in Philadelphia, August 1730, and on application made to the Scotch Synod, was ordained, came to this place, and labored as a minister among the Germans here, several years—till 1734 or 1735.— In a letter to a friend, he states, alluding to his labors here, "In August 1730, I arrived in Philadelphia, and was there at the end of said year, upon order of the Scotch Synod, ordained in the old Presbyterian meeting house, by three eminent ministers, Tennant, Andrews, and Boyd. Having officiated among the Germans several years, I quitted the ministry and returned to a private life."

The Germans generally, Lutherans as well as others, were in a destitute condition, as to ministers, especially of their own denominations, till, and some time after, the arrival of the venerable patriarch of Lutheranism, the "Rev. Henry Melchior Muhlenberg, who came to this country in 1742, with qualifications of the highest order. His education was of the very first character. In addition to his knowledge of Greek and Hebrew, he spoke English, German, Hollandish, (Dutch,) French, Latin, and Swedish. But what was still more important, he was educated in the school of Franke, and had imbibed a large portion of his heavenly spirit. Like Paul, he had an ardent zeal for the salvation of his brethren, his kinsmen according to the flesh. He first landed in Georgia, and spent a week with the

* Evan. Mag. p. 20.

brethren, Bolzius and Gronau, to refresh his spirit and learn
the circumstances of his country; and then pursuing his course
by a dangerous coasting voyage, in a small and insecure sloop,
which had no accommodation for passengers, he arrived in
Philadelphia, November 25, 1742."

Shortly on his arrival, he entered upon the discharge of his
ministerial duties—visited, besides preaching statedly in Philadelphia, New Hanover, &c., other congregations, and dispersed
Lutherans in Montgomery, Berks, and Lancaster counties, and
organized a number of churches.

He was soon joined in his extensive field of labor, by other
highly respectable men, of excellent education, and of spirit
like his own; the greater part of whom were in like manner sent
from Germany, such as Brunnholtz and Lemke in 1745; Handschuh, Weygand, Kurz, and Schaum, 1748; Heinzelman and
Schultz, 1751; Gerock, Hausil, Wortman, Wagner, Schartlin,
Shrenk, and Rauss, 1753; Bager, 1758; Voigt and Krug, 1764;
Helmuth and Schmidt, 1769; Kunze, 1770. Some of these
labored in Berks and Lebanon.

"The greater part of these men were indefatigable" in their
labors. But none more so than Muhlenberg. Numerous and
arduous were the difficulties in his way. The population was
sparse, and in many instances unsettled. For the want of roads
in many directions, the difficulties of travelling were very great,
and in some instances, the tomahawk and scalping-knife of the
Indian impeded the way of the minister.

Muhlenberg, and his fellow ministers preached in season and
out of season, in churches, in dwellings, in barns, and in the
open air.

In the Hallische Nachrichten, page 584, Muhlenberg says,
under date of 1754. An sehr vielen Orten fehlet es nicht nur
an Haeusern, wo man das Wort in auesserlichen Ruhe vor dem
Bloecken der Schafe, Geschrei der Schweinen, Lermen der
Kuehe und Pferde, und dergleichen unvernuenftigen Creaturen,
in den an den Scheunen angebaueten Staellen predigen, und die
Sacramenten austheilen kann; sondern es fehlt uns noch manche
an einigen Gabaueden, worin man mit der armen Jugend die
Schul hatten.

Muhlenberg preached in many of the churches in Berks and
Lancaster counties. June 11, 1747, he preached in Alsace

township, in a church built in common by the Lutherans and German Reformed. The same month he preached at North-kill and Tulpehocken. Sometimes at Molattan, and also near Weaverstown. Speaking of these places, he says, 1753—"Ich hatte neben meinen weitlaüefigen Gemeine, ein Gemeinlein, aus Englische, Schwedische, und Deutschen Gliedern bestehende zu Molattan, ein paar Jahr mit grosser Beschwerlichkiet und Ruin meines Leibes-Kraeften bedient.

"Unsere Teutsche Lutheraner haben mit den Reformirten, drey Meilen von der Schwedischen Kirche (Molatton) ein gemein schaeftliches Schul—und Versammlung haus gebaut u. s. f."

He visited Reading, Heidelberg, Lancaster, &c., and preached the gospel in various parts of Berks, &c. A congregation, as already stated, was organized, at what is known as the *Riethen Kirche*, about the year 1729 or 1730. This congregation was visited by Moravian ministers, about the time Count Zinzendorf had visited this part of the country. They took possession of the first building, and as a consequence, some considerable dissensions arose, and a *militant* excitement prevailed for some time between the parties. The Moravians were triumphant for awhile; however, the church again fell into the hands of the Lutherans. While the contest was going on, a portion of them seceded from that congregation, and erected the church so well known as the *Die Tulpehocker Kirche*, in 1743. Three wealthy members of the church, whose farms joined, gave each five acres of land, gratuitously, for that purpose. Their names deserve to be perpetuated—they were Se- bastian Fisher, Christian Lauer, and George Unruh. Rev. To- bias Wagner was their first pastor. He labored two years and six months among them, when the Rev. J. Nicholaus Kurtz succeeded him. He ministered in spiritual things to the members of this and other congregations, for twenty-one years. Kurtz was succeeded by Rev. Christopher Schultz, who preached here for the space of thirty-eight years. In 1811, their present indefatigable pastor, the Rev. Daniel Ulrich, took charge of this, and other congregations of the neighborhood. This has always been one of the most prominent churches in Berks county, next to Reading, of which the following account is given:—

A HISTORICAL SKETCH OF THE EVANGELICAL LUTHERAN CONGREGATION OF TRINITY CHURCH OF READING.

"While there is probable reason to suppose the existence of this congregation prior to 1751, yet its history can only begin with any degree of precision and certainty, from March 20th, A. D., 1751, when we find Rev. Henry Melchior Muhlenberg, D. D., interesting himself in its welfare, while under the care of Tobias Wagner, (a self-constituted pastor, not connected with any clerical body,) who, living near the people of this congregation, held religious service with them in a private house.

" The congregation having increased, and their place of worship having been found too small, a congregational meeting was called, on January 6th, 1752, A. D., when, after the re-election of the officers of the previous year, viz: Peter Schneider, Christian Brentzer, William Marx, and Abraham Brosius—it was resolved to build a church for the use of the congregation. Peter Schneider and John Oehrlin were elected to superintend the building.

"At the same time, it was resolved to re-establish their organization, as an Evangelical Lutheran Congregation, upon the principles of the New Testament, as embodied in the 'unaltered Augsburg Confession,' and the symbolical books of the Evangelical Lutheran Church, an article was drawn up by subscription, to which the subscribers pledged themselves to the support of the congregation, on the principles above mentioned, and to the payment of the sums affixed to their names. This paper was subscribed by forty-nine names.

"It appears that the erection of the building was commenced at once, on a lot of ground designated by Conrad Weiser. This lot is located on the northern side of Washington street, near the jail, between 5th and 6th streets. The building was of wood, of simple structure, and of ordinary size—it had a steeple and a bell.

",The congregation, in this prosperous and growing state, desiring the· services of a regularly ordained pastor, frequently importuned the Rev. H. M. Muhlenberg, D. D., for the same, but as the ordained pastors of the Evangelical Lutheran church, were already stationed, the worthy Father (of the Evangelical Lutheran church) was unable to grant their request. Not discouraged by their unsuccessful efforts, the congregation appointed one of its members, a delegate to attend the synodical session, October, A. D., 1752, and to lay before this body a letter, signed by eighty-two members of the congregation, importunately asking, that a member of the reverend body might be appointed to deliver the first sermon in the newly erected church, as also ' to set things in good order' in the congregation.

"The appointment fell upon the Rev. H. M. Muhlenberg, D. D., who preached the first sermon in the church, in October 15th, 1752.

"The first pastor of this congregation was Rev. Schoertlin, of Magunshy, who administered for the first time in the new church, the holy supper of the Lord, on March 1st, 1753.

"But, as Pastor Schortlen could preach only every three weeks, and desirous of having the services of a pastor located among them, the congregation extended a call to Rev. Heinrich Gabriel Burchard Wordman, who accepted of the same, and entered upon his duties May 20th, 1753. During his pastorship, the church was consecrated to the service of the blessed Trinity, on Dominica Trinitates, (June 17th, A. D., 1753,) and named 'The Holy Trinity Church.' Rev. H. B. G. Wordman, leaving December 20th, 1753.

"The congregation passed successively into the hands of the

Revd. Schumacher, from March 1754, till March 1757.
"   Hausile, from November 1760, till Novem'r 1763.
"   Krug, from 1764 till 1771.
"   Henry Moeller, from 1775 till 1782.
"   Wildbahn, from March 1782 till March 1796.

During the pastorship of Rev. Carl Frederick Wildbahn, it was found necessary, on account of the decayed state of the church—in which the congregation worshipped—to erect a new house of worship, which was resolved upon and commenced in the year 1790, and finished in 1793.

This church is located upon the same lot of ground on which the old church stood. It is a brick church, strongly and substantially built—of the largest size, measuring 61 by 81 feet square—having large galleries, it will comfortably seat about 1500 persons. It has a steeple 201 feet high, in which hang three bells, the smallest of which is rung every week-day morning at 8 and 12 o'clock. The others are rung for all religious services.

After the removal of Rev. Wildbahn, the congregation came under the care, successively, of Rev'ds Mareard, Lehman, Scriba, and others, and in the year 1803, of the Hon. H. A. Muhlenberg, D. D., who continued his pastorship, among this people for 26 years, until 1729, when the present pastor, Rev. J. Miller, D. D., was called to the pastorship of the congregation.

Divine services had always been performed in the German language, until the pastorship of the Hon. H. A. Muhlenberg, D. D., who occasionally preached in the English language—which custom, for satisfactory reasons, was discontinued by him. Since that time the German continued to be the only language in which divine service were performed, until December 1842, when the congregation called Rev. F. A. M. Keller, as assistant pastor in the English language. At the present time, divine services are administered in the German language on the morning of every Lord's day, and in English on the evening of the same.

In connection with the congregation, is a Sunday school and week day school. The Sunday school has been in existence for many years. It has a morning and afternoon session on every Lord's day, in a house erected for the purpose, measuring 70 by 35 feet. The number of children enrolled as members of the school is 460. The average number in attendance about 400.

The week day school is held in the school house of the congregation, a very ancient building of stone, near the church. The instruction is given in the German language. In earlier years it was more numerously attended, than at present. The present tutor is Mr. J. C. Deininger.

The vacancies which occurred by the removal of the pastors above named, as well as those that follow, were temporarily supplied, as appears from the church records and Hallische Nachrichten. The names of those who filled these vacancies at the time are not noticed here.

This congregation is connected with three other country

congregations, viz:—Swartzwald, Spies, and Alsace, in all of which, Rev. J. Miller, D. D., officiates."

A few years ago, the Rev. James L. Schock, an alumni of the Seminary at Gettysburg, accepted of an invitation to preach exclusively in the English language, in Reading; after a short time, he succeeded in organizing a new congregation in the borough of Reading, and one or two in the country. Several churches are now building by the members of his charge.

In connection with the *Berg-Kirche*, already mentioned, the Rev. Stoever also preached to a congregation in Lebanon and other places. The congregation in Lebanon worshipped for some time in a private house; in 1766, they erected a church, under the care of Rev. Stoever—succeeded by Muhlenberg, Shultz, Kurz, and Geo. Lochman, who took charge of it in 1794. He preached here and at *Berg Kirche*, Ziegel Kirche, Millerstown, and Campbellstown, till 1815, when he was succeeded by the Rev. William G. Ernst, who has had charge of the congregation, and still preaches at Lebanon, Millerstown, Myerstown, Bindnagel's Kirche, and Campbellstown. The Rev. Rothrof has also charge of several congregations in Lebanon county. The congregation under his charge in Lebanon is now erecting a commodious church.

Besides these ministers, others labor in this county as Lutheran ministers—the Rev. Mr. Stein, at Jonestown, and one or two others.

To close this imperfect sketch of the Lutheran church, a brief memoir is added of one of their most eminent ministers.

REV. HENRY MELCHIOR MUHLENBERG, D. D.

Henry Melchior Muhlenberg, D. D., the father of the Lutheran church in America, was a native of Germany, born at Eimbeck, Hanover, September 6th, 1711; educated in the school of Franke, at Halle. His education was thorough, of the very first character. He was master of the Hebrew, Greek, Latin, French, Low-Dutch, Swedish, German and English.— He spoke the Latin fluently, in which he addressed his clerical brethren, more than once at their synodical meetings. He preached in the Swedish, Dutch, German, French, and English languages in America. "But what was still more important, he was not only educated in the school at Halle, but he imbibed a large portion of the heavenly spirit of Franke, the founder of the Orphan House at Halle."

"Like Paul, Muhlenberg, had an ardent zeal for the salvation of 'his brethren, according to the flesh.' He left his native country early in 1742; sailed for Georgia—on his arrival there, he spent a week with his brethren, Bolzius and Gronau, to refresh his spirit and learn the circumstance of the country; and then pursuing his course by a dangerous coasting voyage, in a small and insecure sloop, which had no accommodation for passengers, he arrived in Philadelphia, November 25, 1742.

"During this voyage, all on board endured many privations; and being delayed and tossed about by contrary winds, suffered much for want of water. So great was the destitution of water, that even the rats ate out the stoppers of the vinegar botties, and by inserting their tails, extracted the cooling liquid, and drew them through their mouths. And some of these animals had also been seen licking the perspiration from the foreheads of the sleeping mariners.*

"The Lutheran churches were in a deplorable condition when he arrived; for there were but five or six organized Lutheran churches in Pennsylvania, at the time—one at Philadelphia, one at Providence, (the Trappe,) one at New Hanover, a few miles above the Trappe, one in Lebanon, the Berg-Kirch, under the Rev. Stoever's care; Rieth's Kirche, in Tulpehocken, and one at York, whose first pastor was, Rev. Mr. Candler—all these he visited repeatedly. In passing back and forth in visiting the destitute Germans, he formed the acquaintance of Conrad Weiser, Esq., in 1743, and whose daughter Maria was given him in marriage, in 1745. Speaking on this subject, Muhlenberg says:—"Im Jahr 1743 ward Conrad Weiser mit mir bekannt—und gab mir seine Tochter† zur Ehegennossin." At this time he resided at Philadelphia.

The same year he married, he moved from the city, and settled at Providence, or *Trappe.* In 1761 he was, however,

---

* Hal. Nach , 9.

† Maria Weiser, born at Schoharie, June 27, 1727, was baptized by the Rev William Christopher Bockenmeyer, Lutheran minister—sponsors, Nicholas Feg and wife. Was married to the Rev H M. Muhlenberg, in Heidelberg township, Pa., 1743, in her 16th year. Priv. Jour. C. W

again recalled to Philadelphia, where he labored thirteen years. Leaving his son Henry, who had previously been appointed his colleague, in charge of the congregation in Philadelphia, he returned to Providence, or Trappe, in 1774, where he continued to reside till his death, October 7, 1787. His body rests in the burial ground at the Trappe church. His tombstone has this inscription:*

Hoc Monumentum
Sacrum esto memoriae beati ac venerabilis
Henrici Melchior Muhlenberg S. Theolog. Doctor
et Senioris ministerii, Lutheran Americani
Nati Sept. 6, 1711, *defuncti Oct.* 7, 1787.
Qualis et quantus fuerit non
ignorabunt sine lapide
futura Saecula.

He had labored for nearly half a century with indefatigable zeal, whilst Edwards was co-operating with the extraordinary outpourings of God's spirit in New England, and the Wesley's were laboring to revive vital godliness in England; whilst Whitefield was doing the same work in England and America; and the successors of Franke were laboring to evangelize Germany: Muhlenberg was striving with similar zeal and fidelity, to do the work of God among his German brethren in this western world.

Of him, as also of some of his early associates, it may be said, that " he was in journeyings often, in perils of waters, in perils of robbers, in perils by his own countrymen, in perils by the heathen, in perils in the city, in perils in the wilderness, in perils in the sea, in perils among false brethren, in weariness and painfulness, in watchings often, in hunger and thirst, in fastings often, and in cold and nakedness.

" He preached in season and out of season, in churches, in dwellings, in barns, and in the open air, until at last that divine Master, whom he so faithfully served, received him into the society of the apostles and prophets at his right hand, Oct. 7, 1787.†

* His Coll Pa , p 487
† He Pasa Ekklesia, 383, 384

THE GERMAN REFORMED.

It has already been stated, that from 1682, and at different intervening periods, Germans emigrated to North Carolina, New York, and the province of Pennsylvania. From 1708 to 1720 thousands of Germans, to flee from oppression, and to seek a place of security, emigrated from the Palatinate, and other parts of Germany, to England, thence sailed to New York, and afterwards settled at Schenectady, Schoharie, and other parts of New York. In one of these settlements, at a comparatively early period, the German Reformed had a church in *Weisers-dorff*. The Revd. Frederick Heger, a Reformed minister preached here in 1720, and the Rev. John Jacob Oehl, a German Reformed minister was, it appears, his successor. The Revds. John Bernhard von Duehren, and William Christian Bockenmeyer, Lutheran ministers, are mentioned by Conrad Weiser, in his *Private Tage Buch*, as having preached in that part of New York, between 1720 and 1724.

A large number of Germans arrived in Philadelphia, between 1715 and 1726, who, in the language of Father Muhlenberg : "Hatten zwar Prediger mit genommen, oder zufaelliger Weise bekommen." With these, they also brought some schoolmasters, of whose services they accepted as teachers for their children, and as readers of sermons for themselves—the two might, at present, be profitably united. Schoolmasters and sermon readers, should not be considered incompatible callings. Unfortunately for the German churches, those illy qualified schoolmasters, after reading sermons a short time, dreamed themselves qualified, assumed the sacred offices, to the non-edification of their hearers. Of this class was one J. C. Wirts, of Zurich.[*]

The early history of the German Reformed church, for the want of early records, is involved in obscurity. "It would seem," says Professor Nevin, " that the church at Goshenhoppen, in Montgomery county, is entitled to the highest antiquity among the early organizations. There is said to be documentary evidence of its having been in existence from the year 1717. The first pastor, it would seem, was the Rev. Henry

---

[*] Wirts, some years afterwards, made application to the Rev. Schlatter, to enable him to obtain, from the mother country, a regular ecclesiastical induction to the ministry.—Schlatter's Journal.

Goetschy, whose labors, however, in the end, included a wide field besides. He preached statedly to congregations at Skippack, Falconer Swamp, Saucon, Egypt, Maccungi, Moselem, Oley, Bern and Tulpehocken—his circuit comprising a district which is now covered by four counties—Montgomery, Chester, Berks and Lebanon."

In 1727, a large number of Palatines arrived, among whom was the Rev. George Michael Weis, V. D. M., a native of Stebback, in Neckerthal, Germany. He was a graduate of Heidelberg University—a profound scholar. "He spoke," says the Rev. Jedediah Andrews, "Latin, as readily as we do our vernacular tongue." After remaining here a few years, Weis, in company with an elder of the name of Reif, visited Holland, and other parts of Europe, about the year 1730, for the purpose of making collections in aid of the feeble congregations of Pennsylvania. Great interest was taken in their mission. Mr. Weis was received by the Synods of North and South Holland, as well as by smaller judicatories, with the greatest cordiality and regard."

In 1731, the Rev. Johannes Bartholomaeus Rieger, a native of Oberingelheim, Palatinate, and graduate of Basel and Heidelberg, arrived at Philadelphia. He took charge of a congregation at Seltenriech's, near New Holland, Lancaster county, and visited the dispersed German Reformed in other parts of the county.

Though the demand for German Reformed ministers was great, we find but the names of Goetschy, Weis, Rieger, Boehm and Dorstius, among them in Pennsylvania, till the year 1740. Still the church abroad, especially the church in Holland, carried the destitute churches here in her heart; an evidence of which appears in the fact, that not long before 1741, she had taken care to forward for their use, one hundred and thirty German Bibles, which were now waiting for distribution in the city of Philadelphia.

"No direct communication, however, was maintained with the distant spiritual plantation. But, in the year 1746, the Lord stirred up the heart of his faithful servant in Switzerland, to feel a more than usual solicitude in behalf of the German Reformed church in America. This was the Rev. Michael Schlatten, of St. Gall." Having learnt the destitute condition of the churches in this country, relinquished his pastoral charge, and with a commendable missionary zeal, set out for Amsterdam, with a view of being sent out regularly from that place. The Classis of Amsterdam was regarded as having proper jurisdiction over the German Reformed congregations in America, as well as over the Dutch. To this body, therefore, Mr. Schlatter applied for his commission to visit the destitute American churches. His application was accepted; and he received a formal appointment—embarked for America, June 1st, 1746, and on the 21st of July arrived at Boston. And on the 6th of September, he came to Philadelphia, where the elders of the Reformed Church received him with much tender affection and joy. '

"On the 7th Sept." says Schlatter, in his Journal, "I went to Witpen, 16 miles, to visit the oldest German preacher in this vicinity, the Rev. J. B. Boehm. The venerable man received me in the most friendly manner, and promised, after being made acquainted with my commission and instructions, to assist me heartily in counsel and in deed, which he also did to the extent of his power."

After visiting the Rev. P. H. Dorstius in Bucks county, and the Rev. G. M. Weis, at Goschenhoppen. Rev. Schlatter and Weis, "went in company over the mountain to Oly, and the following day to Lancaster, on Conestoga, to visit the Rev. Rieger and his church." Mr. Boehm, having in the mean time gone to Tulpehocken, to collect the two churches together, and preach a sermon preparatory to the communion; the Rev'ds Schlatter and Weis returned to Tulpehocken; where on the 25th Schlatter preached, as he expresses himself, with much divine assistance, and not without a blessing, to a congregation of more than six hundred persons assembled in a wooden building. The congregation listened to the publication of the word of God with much devout attention. The ardent desire for edification, and a regular organization, and the hope of obtaining a stated preacher might have been read in their countenances. They could not conceal the exceeding joy and surprise they felt in seeing three preachers together—a circumstance which had never been witnessed there before. The old and the young shed tears of joy. I can only say, that this was to me, and to my brethern, a day of much refreshment. I thought of the blessed Netherlands, where the company of heralds of the Gospel is numerous, while this extensive country is perishing for lack of teachers. This large church has never had a regular pastor. Mr. Boehm has administered the communion here annually, twice—travelling eighty miles from Philadelphia, for the purpose. After sermon, with the assistance of Mr. Boehm, I dispensed the holy communion to upwards of a hundred members.

"I afterwards informed them of my commission from the mother country, and made the same proposition to them, which I had made to the churches in Philadelphia and Germantown.— They obligated themselves to support a preacher in the two churches, situated five miles apart, consisting of about five hundred members; promising in money and produce about £50, as will appear by the *Call* forwarded on the 13th of October, to the Rev. Committees of the two Synods, and to the Classis of Amsterdam. I also chose Elders and Deacons, with the approbation of the church, and ordained them.*

The number of regularly ordained German Reformed ministers was small. There were but five, including Schlatter; namely, Mr. Dorstius, who was stationed in Bucks county; Mr. Rieger in the neighborhood of New Holland, Lancaster county; Mr. Weis in the region of Goshenhoppen; Mr. Boehm, now an old man, about 16 miles from Philadelphia. A Mr. Jacob Liscby, it is true, preached at York, but was formerly a leader and ordained teacher, or preacher of the Moravians. He accepted a call from the German Reformed congregation at York, in 1745.

'A few years after, Schlatter came, the Rev. Bartholomaeus, and two young men, students of theology, arrived—David Marinus and Jonathan Dubois. Messrs. Conrad Templeman, at Swatara, and J. C. Wirts, of Sacany, were on probation, as appears from the minutes of the Coetus, held at Lancaster, Oct. 20, 1749.

The Rev. Bartholomaeus took charge of the congregation at Tulpehocken, in 1748. His successors were the Revds. H. W. Stoy in 1752, William Otterbein in 1758, Johannes Waldschmidt in 1765, Johann Jacob Zufall in 1766, William Hendel, sen. in 1769, Andreas Horitz in 1785, Mr. Wagner in 1787, William Hendel, D. D. 1793. Thomas H. Leinbach, the present pastor, in 1826.

* Schlatter's Journal.

The Rev. William Otterbein, whose name is held in veneration by many in this country, was born in Nassau, Dillinberg, Germany, on the sixth day of November, 1726.

A friend, to whom we had applied, furnished the following brief memorial of Otterbein:—

" The time of Otterbein's arrival is unknown to me. From the records of the congregation at Lancaster, it appears that he became the pastor of that church in 1752. This is the first notice of him that I have found. It is probable that he had then but recently arrived in America; and this probability is strengthened, by the fact that the Rev. Mr. Schlatter returning from his visit to Holland, Germany and Switzerland, in behalf of the Reformed churches in this country, arrived at New York on the 27th of July, 1752, and brought with him six newly ordained ministers, who were destined for the churches of Pennsylvania. [Hallische Nachrichten, p. 502.] As Mr. Otterbein's name occurs frequently after this time, and not at all before, there is little doubt that he was one of these. In the autumn of 1758, meditating a visit to his native country, and undecided about returning to America, he resigned his charge at Lancaster; but the dangers of the approaching season, and of the war with France, which then prevailed, determined him to defer his voyage, in the hope of an early peace, until the ensuing spring; and to be usefully employed in the interval, he took the charge, temporarily, of two congregations in Tulpehocken. The war continuing, he remained in the same place, and in the fall of 1760, in pursuance of the wishes of the Coetus, he transferred his labors to Fredericktown, in Maryland, which is described as a large but very remote congregation, that could not be reached, like Tulpehocken, by supplies from neighboring churches. Before this time, he had been proposed as successor to Messrs. Rubel and Stoy, in the distracted congregation of Philadelphia, but declined. In 1761 the congregations of Reading and Oley, in Berks county, presented a call for him to the Coetus, which he also declined, on the ground that he could not relinquish a charge he had so recently assumed. Four years later, about the first of November, 1765, he removed to York, Pa., where he labored in the ministry until April, 1770. His long meditated voyage to Europe was now undertaken, and he left his flock to visit his home and his

38

friends in Germany, with the design, however, to return to his
labors here, if God permitted: and agreeably to this purpose
he did return, after an absence of about 17 months, and re-
sumed his ministry among the same people, in September, 1771.
In April, 1774, he took the pastoral care of the new church in
Baltimore. The Reformed congregation in that city, then under the care of the Rev. Christopher Faber,* had been rent by
a division in 1770; when a strong party, alleging that the pastor's ministry was cold and unedifying, seceded from the church
and built a new house of worship, having for their spiritual
guide a young man of piety and talents, of the name of Swope.
The Coetus wishing to re-unite the two parties, decreed that
both incumbents should withdraw, and their adherents be united
under another, who might be acceptable to all. Mr. Faber
retired and went to Taneytown, Md. Mr. Swope's party
would not suffer him to go. In consequence of this refusal,
their opponents called a Mr. Wallauer. Upon the removal
of Mr. Swope, the same party called Mr. Otterbein, who accepted their call. He was censured by the Coetus, though
informally; but he asserted his right to be governed, in such a
case, by his own convictions; and the Coetus ultimately sanc-
tioned the act, and recognized both congregations. The new
church seems to have consisted of the more pious portion of the
old congergation. Mr. Otterbein was more attentive to internal piety than to external forms, and pursued a course in his
ministry, which to many others appeared new and objectiona-
ble: and from this cause arose a coolness between his brethren
and him, which eventually alienated him, in a measure, from
the judicatories of the church. In his person, Mr. Otterbein
was portly and dignified; in his manner, urbane, affectionate,
and of child-like simplicity. He had been well educated, and,
to the close of his life, read Latin authors with as much ease
as those in his vernacular tongue. His piety was unfeigned
and glowing—his preaching solemn and impressive: but his
voice was weak, and his utterance, at least in his old age,
somewhat indistinct. The consistory of the church, in Philadelphia, in a letter to the Fathers in Holland, dated February,
1760, even where they indulge in an illiberal insinuation, bear
this testimony: ' He is a worthy man, and by reason of his
conduct in life, greatly beloved.' He went frequently on jour-

* A different person from the Rev. J. Theob. Faber, of Goshenhoppen.

neys to minister to remote and destitute congregations, and his ministrations left every where a grateful impression upon the hearts of his auditors. In the latter part of his life, his judgment failed, and left the goodness of his heart to be sometimes much abused by false pretenders. He died November 17, 1813, aged 88 years."

The early settlers of Alsace township were German Reformed, French Reformed, or Huguenots, Swedes and Germans. The two former classes held Calvinistic tenets; the latter were Lutherans. Tradition has it, that the Huguenots and German Reformed, held religious meetings within a mile or two of Reading, and in conformity with the good custom of their fathers in Europe, conducted their worship in the evening as well as in the day—they cultivated a spirit of genuine piety—they met after night in each other's houses, for social prayer. In this they imitated the example of primitive Christians. For the purpose of public worship they erected a church, more than one hundred and twenty years ago—it was a log building. After some of the Swedish and German Lutherans had settled in Alsace, they asked, and obtained privilege in the same old house—in which both congregations of the neighborhood worshipped, unitedly, till about the year 1751, when the Lutherans broke off, and erected a house of worship in Reading.

The German Reformed also, shortly afterwards, purchased a lot on Seventh street, erected a house on it, in which they worshipped till the old stone church was erected in 1761. The Rev. Michael Schlatter, and Johan Conrad Steyner, repeatedly visited this and other congregations.

They were, it seems, destitute for some time of a regularly settled pastor. At a Coetus, held at Lancaster, April, 1755, it appears from the Protocol, that Adam Coerper, an Elder, represented the interests of the congregation at Reading. At the same Coetus appeared Elders John Loescher and Casper Griefheimer, from Oley, and gave an account of the church of that neighborhood. The Elders united and petitioned for a minister, or supplies. The Revds. Weis, Schlatter, Leydick, Waldsmith and Steyner, were appointed as supplies for Reading and Oley.

The first stated pastor in Reading, was the Rev. John William Boos, who commenced his labors in 1771, who was succeeded by the Rev. Nebling, 1782; Bernhart Willy, 1784; John William Ingold, 1786; the Rev. Boosagain in 1789; he was then succeeded by the Rev. Philip Rhinehold Pauli, who preached here till 1814, when his son, William Pauli, took charge of this and other congregations connected with the Reading charge. Under his pastoral care, the present church edifice in Reading, was erected in 1832. The present pastor, the Rev. John Conrad Bucher, succeeded Mr. Pauli in 1842. Mr. Bucher was the first who introduced regular English preaching.

The present number of German Reformed churches, some of which are held jointly by them and Lutherans, is between thirty and forty in Berks county. The pastors residing, or preaching in this county, are, as far as we could learn, the following, the Revds. L. C. Herman, Philip Moyer, Mr. Hassinger, Mr. Bossler, A. L. Herman, Mr. Schultz, Charles G. Herman, J. Sasaman Herman, William Pauli, Augustus Pauli, J. C. Bucher, Isaac Miesse, and William Hendel, D. D., at Wommelsdorf, without a charge—all of whom preach German, and only one or two preach in English.

With this number of pastors—"if they will pursue the course which the Saviour took, and the apostles pursued, the course which the prophets went, in which the Reformers trod, and which the faithful minister of God in every age has pursued, ignorance, impiety, apathy in matters of religion, selfishness, and all the polluted offspring of the flesh, would soon be banished from the church, and she would, ere long, present that purity and loveliness which the Bride of Christ should exhibit." All who see the present condition of the German Reformed Zion, and pray, "Thy Kingdom Come," must devoutly wish for a more general reformation.

It appears that, besides at the Tulpehocken church, there was none ministering in spiritual things within the present limits of Lebanon county, prior to 1748, except Mr. Conrad Templeman, who, it seems, from the minutes of Coetus, held at Lancaster in October, 1749, had, though he was not regularly ordained, preached at Swatara.

The Rev. J. B. Rieger, as a supply, took charge of a congregation at Shaefferstown, as early as 1754 or 55; at the same time, the Rev. Johannes Waldsmith was stationed at Cocalico. Templeman preached at Lebanon and Swatara, till the year

1760, when through physical inability, he ceased officiating in the church. At a Coetus, held at Philadelphia, October 21 and 22, 1760, it is recorded, in relation to him. "*Templeman is stoek blynd, predikt maer zeer Zeldraum in zyn eygen huis,*" i. e., Templeman is stark blind, be preaches for some time in his own house.* It also appears that there was a vacancy at Tulpehocken, as well as at Swatara, about 1761. The Minutes of that date, state "Tulpehocken und Schwatara, warten mit Schmerzen fuer einen Prediger—gleichfals Reading und Oly."

Templeman was succeeded by the Revd. John Conrad Bucher, in 1768, who was succeeded by the Revd. Runkel in 1780, or 1781. Runkel's successors were the Revd. Loop, Hiester, Kroh, Henry Wagner, the present pastor of the churches at Lebanon, Jonestown, Anville, Millerstown, &c.

At present, there are but three German Reformed ministers stationed, and residing within the limits of Lebanon county. These are the Revd. Leinbach at Tulpehocken, Wagner at Lebanon, and John Gring at Stumptown—and in all, about fifteen congregations, numbering rising of two thousand members.

We shall close this imperfect sketch of the German Reformed church, with biographical notices of the Revds. P. R. Pauli, John Conrad Bucher, and Michael Schlatter.

* It is note-worthy here, that the greater part of the proceedings, reports, &c of the Coetes of the German Reformed Church were, until towards the close of the eighteenth century, conducted in Dutch or Latin. The extract above, from the Minutes, is Dutch—not German

BIOGRAPHICAL SKETCHES.

REV. PHILIP R. PAULI.

Philip Reinhold Pauli was born on the 22d of June, 1742, in the city of Magdeburg, in Prussia. His father, Ernest L. Pauli, was superintendent, consistorial counsellor, and court preacher, at the principality of Bernburg. He commenced his studies at the public school in Magdeburg, and afterwards was removed to the Soachim-Gynasium in Berlin: and finally completed his education at the Univeisities of Halle and Leipzig. He spent considerable time, according to the best information, after closing his studies, in tiavelling through Europe with a wealthy uncle. He arrived in this country in 1783, after an exceedingly distressing and dangerous voyage.

He began his useful labors in this country as a teacher of an Academy in Philadelphia, where he remained six years, and received the honorary degree of Master of Arts. He came to this country unmarried, and the 14th of February, 1784, was united to Elizabeth Musch, daughter of Mr. John Musch, of Easton, Pa. From the year 1789, he devoted himself to the work of the ministry, and for some years was pastor of the churches in Shippach and its vicinity. In 1793 he commenced his labors at Reading, as pastor of the G. R. Church, which he prosecuted with zeal and activity for 21 years and 9 months. In addition to his ministerial labors, he kept for several years a select Latin and French school. He seldom wrote his sermons, but collected materials for them during the week, and on Saturday arranged them into a regular disposition or skeleton. His sermons were generally simple and affecting; especially at funerals, where he seldom preached without weeping or causing others to shed tears. His church was generally well filled. His leisure hours were generally employed in reading. or visiting his members. As it respects the catechising of children, he generally devoted, during the summer season, the sabbath afternoon to this pleasing task, and previous to the confirmation of youth, he usually gave them instruction regularly for about two months. He was regular in attending synodical meetings, and always took an active part in the passing business. He was frequently invited to attend consecrations, and other public meetings, even at considerable distances. He was mild, cheerful, and generous in his disposition, and regular in his habits and course of life. He died on the 27th of January, 1815, and his departure was a sweet sleep, that transferred him to a better world. On the following sabbath his mortal remains were committed to the tomb. Notwithstanding the inclemency of weather, a large congregation assembled to offer the last testimony of regard to their aged pastor. The Rev. William Hendel delivered an appropriate funeral sermon on 2 Kings, ii, 12, in the large Lutheran church, after which the procession moved to the Reformed church, where a short but impressive address was delivered by the Rev. Mr. Dechant, Der Herr segne seine asche. W. P.

THE REV. MICHAEL SCHLATTER,

As already stated, was a native of St. Gall, in Switzerland; and, undoubtedly, a graduate of the Protestant college, which has, at present, fourteen professors.   When but quite a young man, he took a pastoral charge, but in consequence of information he had received of the destitute condition of the German Reformed churches in America, he relinquished his charge, and being a man of ardent temperament, and withal possessing much of the *romantique*, perhaps preponderating firmness and decision,—inspired with the zeal of a missionary, he at once set set out to visit his countrymen in the new world, and minister to them in things spiritual, " in the church and in the field."

He accordingly repaired to Amsterdam, to obtain from the Classis, there, such credentials as were requisite.   He obtained them from the Classis, and from the Synods of North Holland, in conjunction, a general commission to visit the churches, enquire into their condition, and organize, and as far as possible improve them.

He embarked on board of a ship at Amsterdam, June 1st, 1746, " and sailed for Boston, in North America, after having committed," says S. in his journal, "myself to the guidance and protection of God."   On the 11th we ran into the Orkney Islands on the North of Scotland, and remained till the 23d, during which time we only saw the sun on two days.   The inhabitants, who appear to be people of good disposition, assured us, that in those regions usually have nine months of winter, two of rough weather, and only about one month of good weather during the year.

After this we proceeded prosperously in our voyage until we reached Newfoundland.   On the 24th July we fell in, during an exceedingly dark night with Sable Island, a very dangerous place, at no great distance from Cape Breton, and I cannot recall to mind, without shuddering, and at the same time thanks to God, the imminent danger we were in of losing all, and perishing in the wild waves, had not God, who is mighty to redeem, rescued us contrary to all our expectations, and granted us, when we called upon him in trouble, deliverance from all our suffering, and brought us safely to Boston, our desired haven, in seven days, where we offered him our bounden tribute of thanksgiving.

In Boston—the largest and most populous city of the English Colonies in America, containing about 3000 well built houses—I was received with much affection and kindness by the honorable Mr. J. Wendel, a distinguished Holland Merchant, and a member of the Government. This reception allayed the anxieties I had felt on entering a land of strangers, and confirmed my hope, that God would make my way prosperous. After having sent on my baggage to Philadelphia and New York by water through the favor of my distinguished friend, I set out on the 4th of August on my journey by land, in the agreeable society of Dr. Bekman.

On the 7th, after travelling 70 English miles, we arrived at Newport, a considerable town on Rhode Island, which possesses a convenient and safe harbor, from which ships can run into the sea in the course of one hour. On the 11th, having travelled 230 more of these miles, we reached New York, or New Amsterdam, the capital of the province of New Netherlands, containing about 2000 houses. This city, as well as Long Island, and other places in the vicinity, and the shores of the North River to Albany, and the country beyond more than 250 miles, and even to Canada, is for the most part settled with well disposed native Low-Dutch inhabitants. During my stay in the city I received very special attention and kindness from the three Dutch preachers, but particularly from the venerable Father Du Bois, who is highly esteemed both by the English and the Dutch, and who has already labored in the ministry here for more than 50 years, and reached the age of 80. This is another proof that this climate is as healthy as that of Europe. Indeed, from my own experience, I can truly testify, that often, when seeing the towns, the level country, the climate, the prudent inhabitants, living in the same manner, and enjoying the same education, business and pursuits, and scarcely distinguishable in any thing from Europeans, I have hardly been able to persuade myself that I was, in reality, in a distant quarter of the world.

On the 6th September I came to Philadelphia, 95 miles from New York, where the Elders of the German Reformed church received me with much tender affection and joy, and provided lodgings for me with one of their number, in whose house I resided for eight months, though at my own expense.

On the 7th I went to Witpen, 16 miles, to visit the oldest German preacher in this vicinity, the Rev. J. B. Boehm, (whom the Lord has since released from his post.) The venerable man received me in the most friendly manner, and promised, after being made acquainted with my commission and instructions, to assist me heartily in counsel and in deed, which he also did to the extent of his power.

Sept. 8. I went out, 8 miles, to see Mr. J. Reif, and to require of him, according to the instruction of the Synods, an account of the monies collected in Holland, by him and Mr. G. M. Weis, sixteen years before (1731) for the benefit of the Pennsylvania churches. When he declared himself ready, I fixed the time of twelve days, and gave him the liberty to name the place of meeting for the purpose.

In order to lose no time, I returned immediately to Philadelphia, to make enquiry respecting the German bibles which had been sent thither some years before by the affectionate care of the Synods of Holland. I found them without much difficulty, in the careful hands of the honorable Benjamin Schumacher, who, when he saw my commission, and learned that the freight had been paid in Rotterdam to Mr. Z. Hoppe, cheerfully gave over to me one hundred and eighteen copies, all well preserved, without any charge for expenses. I sent, or carried one of these bibles to nearly every one of the churches in Pennsylvania for the use of the pulpit; fifty were placed at the disposal of the overseers of the churches, to be distributed according to their discretion for the benefit of the poor; others I lent to this and that poor man, to awaken and confirm their zeal for reading and examining the word of God. Six or eight of them I sold, in order to purchase catechisms for the school children, and about twenty-four copies still remain in my hands, to be disposed of as necessity may require.

On the 11th I administered the holy communion to about one hundred members in Philadelphia. Mr. Boehm assisted in this service. On the 13th I received a letter from Messrs. Weis and Reif, inviting me to the house of latter on the 21st to settle their accounts.

In the meantime I sought to restore order to the church of

Philadelphia, and unite it with Germantown in the support of a pastor, who may preach in both churches on every Lord's day.

The 16th I went into Bucks county, sixteen miles, to pay my respects to Mr. P. H. Dorstius, who, when made acquainted with my instructions, received me in a most friendly and fraternal manner, offered to render me his assistance, and promised to arrange his vestry at a convenient time, and give me information; after which, I returned to the city."

Schlatter had now entered his missionary field. He commenced to visit all the German Reformed ministers, and the destitute churches in Pennsylvania, Maryland and Virginia.

In the month of September, 1746, he visited the Rev. G. M. Weis at Goshenhoppen. Mr. Weis had recently fled from his church at Rhimebeck, near Albany, N. York, on account of the war. In the same month he visited the Rev. Rieger, in Lancaster county; the churches at Tulpehocken, where he organized several congregations. In the course of 1747, he organized six or seven congregations in Pennsylvania, besides visiting all the churches in Pennsylvania, and one or two at New Jersey. In 1748, he visited congregations in Maryland and Virginia. After spending several years in the faithful discharge of his officer, he returned to Holland, in 1751, where he laid a journal of his proceedings before the Synod.

Schlatter, faithful to his trust, and representing the true state of the German churches in Pennsylvania—stating that he found the harvest great—the laborers few, and thousands living here where the light of the Gospel reached them rarely, if ever; and that the greater portion was destitute of the means of the knowledge of salvation.

He made warm appeals to the Fathers of Holland—his appeals deeply affected them, and they accordingly devised a a plan and raised funds, to relieve and instruct the poor Germans and their descendants in Pennsylvania.*

A society of noblemen and gentlemen, for this purpose was organized, and the Rev. Schlatter was constituted Visitor, or Superintendant General of Schools opened by them in Pennsylvania; a duty which, on his return from Europe, he discharged with fidelity, though with much opposition from various quar

* See page 99, &c., antea.

ters!! This opposition, probably induced him to relinquish his Visitorial trust, and accept of a station "in the field."

In 1756, he was appointed General Chaplain to the British Army, by General Loudon of the fourth battalion of the Royal army of North America. He accepted the appointment. To other places besides, he also accompanied the army to Nova Scotia. In 1759, returned in good health, to Philadelphia.— The last notice we find of him, is in the *Hallische Nachrichten,* in which the Rev. Muhlenberg mentions that he staid with him all night, December 5th, 1762.

REVD. BUCHER.

THE REV. JOHN CONRAD BUCHER, a name associated with the Church and State of this country, whose genealogy has been preserved and recorded, consecutively, through twenty-nine different families, from January 21st, 1541, till it reaches the Hon. John C. Bucher, of Harrisburg, the grandson of the subject of this notice, was born the 13th of July, 1730, in Switzerland. He was the son of Jacob Bucher, Sheriff of Neunkirch. He was educated at the best schools in his native country. From all that is known of him, he pursued, with equal ardor, the various branches of study, gaining the highest honors in the schools which he attended. He was remarkable for having acquired a rich flow of language, and unprecedented copiousness and energy of thought, which rendered him useful, and attracted the attention of all who heard him.

At the age of twenty-five, he left Schaffhausen, in Switzerland; embarked, as is most probable, under the care of the English government, for America, seeking a place for future usefulness in life: he came to Pennsylvania, in 1755, and took up his abode at, or near Carlisle, Cumberland county, which was then a frontier settlement—where Fort Louther had just shortly before been erected.

Willing to wield carnal weapons of defence, in repelling the incursions of the savage Indians, who were instigated by the French to slaughter, indiscriminately, regarding neither age nor sex, Mr. Bucher was induced to accept the appointment as Lieutenant, of a company in the battalion of the Pennsylvania regiment of foot, as appears from a parchment commission—preserved in the Bucher family—signed by James Hamilton, Esq., Lieutenant-Governor and Commander-in-chief of the province of Pennsylvania, and counties of Newcastle, Kent and Sussex, on Delaware. The commission is endorsed by Richard Peters, Secretary, dated 19th April, 1760:—

To Conrad Bucher, Gentleman, Greeting, &c., appointing him Lieutenant, &c.

From documentary evidence, it further appears, he had been
39

in military service prior to his appointment to a Lieutenantcy. Previous to this appointment, he had married Mary M. Hoke, of York, whose parents had been among the first settlers of that place. They were married February 26, 1760.

He remained at Carlisle till 1762, when, as appears from the subjoined certificate, he was called to another station, or to itinerate as an officer at the command of his superiors.

" This is to show that the bearer hereof, Mary Bucher, has, for some years past lived in this congregation, and has behaved herself in a sober and decent manner, so far as it is to me known, and is now, at this time of her departure, here free from any church censure, or any thing to me known, exposing her thereto.

Carlisle, 4th day of November, 1762.

GEO. DUFFIELD, v. d. m.

Owing to his merits as an officer, in the faithful discharge of his duties, he was promoted to the captaincy of the Pennsylvania regiment of foot.

His commission is dated July 31, 1764.

Tranquility and peace having been restored about this time; for Col. Bouquet had conquered the Indians, and compelled them to sue for peace—Captain Bucher now exchanged the sword of the flesh for that of the spirit. The soldier became now a distinguished preacher of the gospel of Christ. A German Reformed congregation was organized at Carlisle about the year 1755, and it is probable he was the first German Reformed minister. It was about this time that he entered fully into the ministry. He became a preacher of singular power, and knew no other joy than to devote the energies of a vigorous constitution to the glory of his heavenly Father.

A vacancy presented itself at Lebanon, and having received a call from that congregation, he located at that place in 1768, and devoted all his time to the people of his charge, except what he spent in visiting destitute congregations, and discharging the duties of Chaplain in the Army in the commencement of the revolution, for some time.

He was one of the most devoted ministers of the gospel of his day—truly apostolic in his labors. He was a shining light, consuming itself, as it illuminated others by its splendor. In the language of Knapp—Er erlaubte sich keinen leeren Zwischenraum zwischen den verschiedenen Arten von Geschaeften die er zu verrichten hatte. An extract from his Pocket Almanac for 1768, shows that he was instant in season and out of season.

January, 1768. On the 1st, 2d, 4th and 5th, he preached at Carlisle—8th at Quitopahilla—9th at Lebanon—10th, the Lord's supper at Lebanon—11th at Heidelberg—12th at Weis Eichenland—17th at Carlisle—24th at Falling Springs—29th at Jonestown and Klopf's—30th at Camberlin's—31st at Lebanon, Quitopahilla, and at Carlisle.

In February, besides the places above mentioned, he preached at Rapho, Hummelstown, Middletown, Blaser's, Maytown, Sheafferstown.

In April, in Carlisle—at Doctor Schnebley's, Hagerstown, 14th—held catechising on the 16th, the 17th at Falling Springs.

In May the 8th, at Carlisle—12th at Falling Springs—15th Lord's Supper—21 and 22 at Quitopahilla and Lebanon—the 31st had nuptials at Lisburn.

In July he is again at Carlisle, Falling Springs, Conococheague, and Hagerstown.

In August, at the same places.

In September, at Reading, &c.

In October, 20th, at Carlisle—the 4th at Falling Springs—5th at Schnebley's—6th at Hagerstown—7th at Peter Spangs—8th at Sharpsburgh—9th at Fredericktown—16th at Hummelstown and Middletown; and almost every day then at some of his usual places.

November 6th at Bedford—13th at Redstone—20th at Redstone.

December—the whole month—at Carlisle.

In another Almanac, for 1771, he notices a number of night meetings he held. These were, no doubt, social prayer meetings.

He was unwearied in his Master's cause—faithfully discharging his pastoral duties, until in the Providence of God, he was called hence. He departed this life on the 15th of August, 1780. In the morning of that day, he had gone from Lebanon to Millerstown, a distance of five miles, to perform a marriage, and whilst among the nuptial party, he died suddenly.

As a testimonial of respect, high regard, and affection of the people for him, they carried his corpse on a sheet or bier, on their hands to Lebanon, where his earthly remains rest in the German Reformed grave yard—of which congregation he was pastor for twelve years.

He lived in the religion he professed; and wherever he was known, he was highly and universally esteemed. He died in the meridian of a life of usefulness; but in the triumph of his holy faith.

THE ROMAN CATHOLICS.

The protestants of every denomination, says Gordon, held the Roman Catholic communion in abhorrence; and the penal laws of England forbade the public exercise of that religion.*

Even the liberal minded William Penn was so much prejudiced against them, that it was with much reluctance he received any Roman Catholics into his province. They were considered enemies of the country, and often charged as French emissaries to spy out the condition of English subjects; that for the public safety, some were imprisoned.

As early as 1689, Governor Blackwell, Deputy Governor of Pennsylvania, convened a Council and laid before the members thereof *some rumors*.† He says:—"That ye reason of his calling them together at this time was to minde them that there had been formerly severall Rumors of danger from ye french & Indians, in conjunction with ye Papists, for ye Ruine of the Protestants in these parts, and of ye alarme formerly given, as if 9 thousand french & Indians were then neare approaching for yt purpose, upon wch ye Justices & Sheriff's of ye two Lower Countyes, with ye people thereof, had betaken themselves to armes for their defence; whereof he then gave ye Councill an account, from ye Letters he recd out of ye' sd Countyes: as also of a Letter he had recd from one Capt Le Tort, (a frenchman, living up in the Countrey,) agreeing therewith; which they did not see any reason to give heed unto:—And further, to acquaint them yt he had lately recd a letter from Mr. Joshua Barkstead, out of Maryland, advertising there was sufficient proof that ye Papists in Maryland had been tampering with ye french and Northern Indians, to assist them to cutt off ye Protestants, or at least to reduce them to ye See of Rome, &c."

* Gordon's Pa., 570.
† Min. Prov. Council, i., p. 257.

It afterwards appeared, that the danger apprehended was not great from the "Indians and papists." It was only to "skare the women and children."

Previous to 1730, not many Catholics resided in Pennsylva - nia. The few that had been in the province prior to 1730, were occasionally visited by missionaries from Maryland. So novel in this province, was the *mass*, that when it was first celebrated in *St. Joseph's* at Philadelphia, in 1733, it caused much agitation in the Provincial council, and Governor Gordon proposed to suppress it, as contrary to a statute of law 11 & 12, William III. The Catholics claimed protection under the provincial charter, and the council referring the subject to their superior at home, the Governor wisely resolved to suffer them to worship in Peace.*

Numerous German Catholics emigrated to this province, the principal part of them settled at Goshenhoppen and in the lower parts of Berks county. As early as 1755, they had a "very magnificent chapel at Goshenhoppen;" and shortly, on the defeat of General Braddock by the Freneh Catholics, they held "a large procession," which produced considerable excitement among the protestant population. They also had a priest at Reading, as early as 1755.

Their number, no doubt, would have been much greater prior to 1776, had it not been for the *oath of abjuration* they were compelled to take and subscribe to gain admittance. This oath, it is believed, was unfavorable to the increase of the Catholic church here—none would subscribe that oath, and still adhere to the church. An extract from it will best show the nature of it. The following is from a paper, subscribed by James Read, March 17, 1745.

"I, James Read, do swear that I do from my heart abhor, detest and abjure as impious and heretical, that damnable doctrine and position, that princes excommunicated or deprived by the Pope or any authority of the See of Rome, may be deposed or murdered by their subjects or any other whatsoever.

"I, James Read, do solemnly and sincerely, in the presence of God, profess, testify and declare, that I do believe that, in the sacrament of the Lord's supper, there is not any trans-substan-

* Gordon's Pa., 571.
† See p. 151 and 152. Provincial Records, Book N., 125.

tiation of the elements of bread and wine into the body and blood of Christ, at or before the consecration thereof by any person whatsoever, and that the invocation or adoration of the Virgin Mary or any other saint, and the sacrifice of the mass, as they are used in the church of Rome, are superstitious and idolatrous. And I do solemnly, in the presence of God, profess, testify and declare, that I do make this declaration and every part thereot in the plain and ordinary sense of the words now read to me as they are commonly understood by English Protestants, without any evasion, equivocation, or mental reservation whatsoever, and without any dispensation already granted me for this purpose by the Pope, or any person whatsoever, or without any hope of such dispensation, from any person or authority whatsoever, or without thinking that I am or may be acquitted before God or man, or any other person or persons or power whatsoever should dispense with or annul the same, and declare that it was null and void from the bebinning."

The Catholics have three chapels in Berks and one in Lebanon county. The present one in Reading was erected in 1791. The Revd. Steinbacher is officiating priest. He is a man highly esteemed by those among whom he ministers.

———

THE EPISCOPALIANS.

At an early period, in the province of Pennsylvania, the Episcopalians became numerous, and were increased by those who seceded from the Quakers under George Keith, in the year 1691.

George Keith had been an eminent preacher and writer among the Quakers for many years, and had published several well written treatises in defence of their religious principles; but afterwards seceded, and joined the Episcopal clergy in England, and served them for some time, as a vicar, ordained by the Bishop of London; he afterwards returned to America, when, as a clergyman, in orders, he officiated in this new function.   He drew many of the Quakers after him, and most cf them joined the Episcopal church.

As early as 1710, Christ Church in Philadelphia was founded, and in 1717, the Rev. Mr. Wayman, missionary to the Welsh settlements of Radner and Oxford, frequently visited Pequea, Conestoga and Indian settlements, within the bonds of Lancaster county.   He baptised many children of Quakers, and some who had been Quakers.

Episcopal churches were erected in several parts of the province prior to 1745; but neither their pastors nor their congregations were distinguished by zeal in making converts, and their churches were chiefly sustained by the accessions of members from England, and the progress of natural increase.

We cannot say with any definitiveness when the first Episcopal congregation was organized in Berks and Lebanon counties.   It is probable that immediately before, or shortly after the revolution, a church was organized at Molatton.

The congregation at Reading was organized within the last thirty years.   The present church was erected in 1826.   For the want of furnished statistics, so kindly promised us, neither the number of churches, nor ministers in the counties of Berks and Lebanon, can be stated—probably two or three of each. The Rev. R. U. Morgan officiates at present at Reading.

THE PRESBYTERIANS.

Previous to 1688 but few Presbyterians had become residents of the British provinces in America.   The Rev. Jedediah Andrews, from New England, settled in Philadelphia, about the year 1701.   He was the first Presbyterian minister in Pennsylvania.   In 1706, a primary ecclesiastical union of the American Presbyterians was formed.   It was the Presbytery of Philadelphia, and consisted of seven ministers—Samuel Davis, John Hampton, Francis McKemie, (the first Presbyterian minister on the continent,) and George McNish, all of Ireland, and residing in Maryland.   Nathaniel Taylor settled at Upper

Marlborough, and John Wilson officiating at Newcastle, both from Scotland, and Jedediah Andrews, of Philadelphia. To whom was added John Boyd, stationed at Freehold, the first candidate who was ordained by that presbytery, on October 29, 1706. From that time onward, they increased in numbers, respectability and influence. At present there is scarce a county in Pennsylvania where Presbyterian churches are not to be found. For many years they labored principally, if not wholly, among the Scotch, Irish and English; but within the last twenty-five years, they have succeeded to organized congregations in German communities, where their congregations are composed of English and Germans.

About the year 1736, 37. The Rev. John Elder, a Scotchman, settled west of the Conewago hills, towards the Susquehannah, and preached for fifty-six years. His labors extended into the settlements of the western part of Lebanon county.

It is very probable, that in 1745, when the Rev. David Brainerd visited the Indians on the Susquehanna, he may have visited the Rev. Elder, and his congregation.

Nearly twenty years ago, the Rev'ds Finney, Patterson, and others visited Berks county, whose efforts eventuated in the organization of a congregation in the Borough of Reading. In 1824, the present church in Reading, was erected—the congregation is in a prosperous condition. The Rev. William Sterling is the present pastor.

THE METHODIST EPISCOPAL CHURCH.

This denomination took its rise in England about one hundred years ago; and in the year 1766 the first Methodist Society was established in the city of New York. Their first preacher was Mr. Philip Embury, who was subsequently assisted by a Mr. Webb. He occasionally visited Philadelphia, preaching the gospel of Christ. From that time onward, this Society increased in numbers, respectability and usefulness, so that there is scarce a township, within the wide range of the inhabited parts of United States, where their influence is not seen—every where are men found of this denomination.

At what time minister were sent forth in this region of country, to itinerate and proclaim the glad tidings of the gospel, we cannot state with any degree of certainty, but it is probable, it was between the years 1780 and 1790; for as early as 1781, the Lancaster circuit, which embraced part of what is now Lebanon county, was formed.

The present church at Reading was erected in 1839, under the pastoral care of the Revd. Mr. Roach, then stationed here. The present pastor is the Revd. Mr. Koons.

They have also a church at Lebanon, and about one hundred members. The Revd. Greenbank has charge of this and several other congregations in this county. They have, probably, some six or eight houses of public worship in Berks and Lebanon county. They are on the increase.

THE UNITED BRETHREN IN CHRIST.

This denomination is, comparatively, of recent origin. Its first regular systematic organization was in 1789, when a conference, for that purpose, was held in the city of Baltimore, attended by the following preachers—Revds. William Otterbein, Martin Boehm, George A. Geeting, Christian Newcomer, Adam Lohman, John Ernst and Henry Weidner. For some years they were without a discipline. Shortly after the death of one of the most influential ministers who had met with them in 1789, a discipline containing the doctrines and rules for the government of the church, was presented at a conference held in 1815, at Mount Pleasant, Pennsylvania. It was adopted.

Having adopted the itinerant system of sending out ministers, and nearly all of them preaching German, they made considerable progress among the Germans in these two counties. They have a number of meeting houses, and some four or five ministers here. Of these are the Revds. John Lichty and Casper Lichty.

THE EVANGELICAL ASSOCIATION.

This denomination is sometimes called after its founder, Jacob Albrecht, "Albrecht's Leute." This sect was started about the year 1800, by the Rev. Jacob Albright, whose associates were the Reverends John Walker, George Miller, and others. Mr. Albright, not unlike the Methodists, commenced travelling and preaching the gospel, and soon made converts among the Germans, in various parts of Pennsylvania.

At present this denomination has some six or eight meeting places, besides some churches in Berks and Lebanon counties. The Revds. Danner and Sailor are ministers among them.

THE UNIVERSALISTS.

As a denomination, Universalists began their organization in England, about 1750, under the preaching of the Rev. John Kelly, who gathered the first church of believers in that sentiment, in the city of London.

The introduction into America, was by a Mr. John Murray, who had been converted from Methodism by the preaching of Mr. Kelly. Mr. Murray emigrated into this country in 1770, and soon after preached his peculiar views in various places in New Jersey, Pennsylvania, New York, Rhode Island and Massachusetts, and thus became the founder of the denomination.

Dr. George De Benneville, of Germantown, Pa., a learned and pious man, was a believer, and probably, says the Revd. A. B. Grosh, published the edition of *Siegvolk's Everlasting Gospel,* a universalist work, which appeared in 1763. Since that time, and Murray's preaching occasionally in Pennsylvania, the doctrine has spread generally through the United States.

The first society organized in Pa., was in 1787; the first meeting house built in 1808; first association held in 1829; convention in 1832. In Pennsylvania they have seventeen meeting houses and twenty-four preachers.

Universalist churches are not numerous in these two counties; there is but one in Berks. The Universalist church in
Reading was built in 1830. Their former pastor was the Rev.
John Parry. At present there is no stated pastor laboring
here. We have not had the means to ascertain what number
is actually connected with this church, in these counties, but
it is reported, there are many who avow universalist sentiments.
These are their sentiments, briefly stated:

I. "We believe that the Holy Scriptures of the Old and
New Testaments, contain a revelation of the character of God,
and of the duty, interest and final destination of mankind.

II. "We believe that there is one God, whose nature is love;
revealed in one Lord Jesus Christ, by one Holy Spirit of grace,
who will finally restore the whole world of mankind to holiness and happiness.

III. "We believe that holiness and true happiness are inse-
parably connected; and that believers ought to be careful to
maintain order and practice good works; for these things are
good and profitable unto man."

CHURCH OF GOD.

This denomination was formally organized in October, 1830,
at Harrisburg. A meeting was held, of which the Rev. John
Winebrenner was speaker, and the Rev. John Elliot, clerk,
of Lancaster. Since that time they have increased till they
number about fifty licensed preachers and six thousand church
members in Pennsylvania—a few of whom are found in Lebanon county—principally in and about Millerstown.

THE BAPTISTS.

This denomination has made, within the last ten or fifteen
years, efforts to organize congregations in Berks county. They

have succeeded to build several churches. Their first meeting house was in Reading, near the Schuylkill river; but as the location was considered rather unfavorable, they abandoned that, and erected another, in Chestnut street, in 1837. At that time tne Reverend E. M. Parker was pastor. Their pastors have been the Rev'ds Parker, Philips, and Davidson—at present they are building a church in the eastern part of Berks county. Their number is steadily increasing.

AFRICAN CHURCHES.

Of these there are three in the Borough of Reading:—The Union African church, the Presbyterian African church, and the Methodist African church. In the African churches, says Stahle, there are regular meetings on the Sabbath, accompanied with the usual religious exercises, and a pretty strict course of church discipline; with what results, may be partly gathered from the general good character, and industrious, steady habits of our colored population.

CHAPTER VIII.

HISTORY OF THE PRESS.

Four years after William Penn's first arrival in America, William Bradford, from Leicester, England, commenced printing, at Kensington, near Philadelphia. This was in 1686. Mr. Bradford removed from Philadelphia to New York in 1693.

The first newspaper published in Pennsylvania, was commenced by Andrew Bradford, in 1719, entitled "The American Weekly Mercury." Nine years afterwards, another paper was started by Mr. Keimer; the paper was called "The Universal Instructor in all arts and sciences, and Pennsylvania Gazette." This paper afterwards fell into the hands of Benjamin Franklin.

In 1739 Christian Sower commenced the publication of a paper, once a quarter. After some time it was printed monthly; but after 1744, it was printed every week, under the title of "the Germantown Gazette," by C. Sower, jr.

It is worthy of remark that C. Sower, sen., cast his own type, and made his own ink. Sower published *first* in the United States, a quarto bible, in German.

The first newspaper published in Reading, called the "Neue Unpartheyische Zeitung," was issued February 18th, 1789, by Messrs. Johnston, Barton and Yungman. The "Adler" was first issued by Jacob Snyder & Co., the 17th of January, 1797, and is still published, though much enlarged, by the Hon. John Ritter and Charles Kessler, Esq. This paper has an extensive circulation in Berks, and some of the adjacent counties. It is the political expositor of the Democratic party of Berks county.

"The Berks and Schuylkill" is the oldest English newspaper printed in Reading; the first number appeared June 17, 1816, and is now owned and published by John S. Richards, Esq. It is the organ of the Whigs.

"The Democratic Press," owned and conducted by Samuel Myers, Esq., and ".The Jefferson Democrat," by Joel Ritter, Esq., are both devoted to the cause of Democracy.

"The Reading Gazette," hitherto neutral, is owned by the Messrs. Getz and Boyer.

"The Liberale Beobachter," by A. Puwelle, Esq., and "Alt Berks," by William Schoener, Esq., are both German papers.

"The Hamburger Schnellpost und allgemeiner deutscher Anzeiger," published at Harrisburg, by Mahlon A. Sellers, Esq.

The oldest paper in the town of Lebanon, is "Der Wahre Demokrat und Volks-Advokat," by Joseph Hartman, Esq. This paper has reached its 29th Jahrgang.

"The Libanon Demokrat" is published by J. P. Sanderson, Esq.

"The Lebanon Courier," by George Frysinger, Esq.

There is also a small German sheet published at Myerstown.

SOCIETIES, CHARITABLE AND LITERARY—LIBRARIES.[*]

"It has been justly observed, that Reading is distinguished for the number of its societies, and the facility with which a society, for any purpose, may be started. An incredible number of associations have at one time or another had an existence, some of which were of an absurd· or ludicrous character. A large portion of them, however, were as readily abandoned as they were inconsiderately formed; insomuch that now, when a new association is announced, it is scarcely expected to sustain more than an ephemeral existence. This, however, is not the case with all; a part of those that were valuable, have survived

* Taken from the Stahle's description of Reading, in 1841,

for a number of years; and a few perhaps that are not of much value.

"In enumerating the societies of Reading, I shall follow the excellent classification of a writer in the Berks and Schuylkill Journal whom I have had already had occasion to quote:— "In Reading," he says, "we have now, or have had, the Masonic Fraternity and the Dorcas Society. The Red Men and the Soup Society. The Native Men and the Female Coterie. The Odd Fellows and the Sewing Society. The Masonic Fraternity and the Maternal Association. The Concert Club and the Tea Party jollifications. The Garrick Association and the Thespian Board. The Benevolent Society and the Free Trades' Union. The Franklin, Cordwainers, and Berks county Beneficial Societies. The Cabinet, Youth's Institute, Junior Association, Apprentices' Company, Mechanics' Institute, Mechanics' and Workingmen's Society, William Penn Institute, besides Bible, Education, Missionary, Sabbath School, Tract, Temperance, Colonization, Debating and other Societies.

" A large number of the above societies are long since defunct; and many more are in a very sickly condition. A few of them deserve a more particular notice."

" *Masonic Fraternity.*—The following account of this institution in Reading, was politely furnished by a gentleman who stands high in the Order. "The Masonic Order was established in Reading as early as 1794, under a warrant from the Right Worshipful Grand Lodge of Pennsylvania. The late William Bell, Esq., had the honor of being its first presiding officer.— Lodge No. 62, has ever embraced in its members some of the most respectable persons of Reading, and the county of Berks. There are now eighty-eight active members of the Lodge, besides a number of honorary members.—Chapter No. 152, holds its warrant from the Right Worshipful Grand Holy Royal Arch Chapter of Pennsylvania. This body is also in a very flourishing condition. The members of the Order contemplate erecting a Masonic Temple for their greater convenience, and the ornament of the Borough.'"

" *The Garrick Association of Reading.*—This Dramatic Association was formed several years ago, and has been continued in operation with a good share of prosperity to the present time. They have a hall in the old academy building, neatly fitted up and furnished for their performances. The society numbers about twenty members—all young men of the borough of Reading, of very respectable families and good standing in society."

" *The Cabinet.*—This association was formed about three years ago. Its design was to promote research and diffuse information upon scientific subjects, through the medium of lectures by the members. A small, but well chosen, chemical and other apparatus, and a collection of minerals were obtained; and the exertions of the association have been attended with interest and profit, to the members and others. Lectures are delivered regularly every Thursday evening during the fall and winter, and meetings for the transaction of business are held once a month during the remainder of the year. Several members have occasionally assisted in lecturing, but this duty has fallen principally upon Dr. J. P. Hiester, whose lectures and experiments upon chemistry have proved peculiarly interesting to the young, to whose interest and apprehension he has the happy faculty of explaining the most abtruse parts of the science."

" *William Penn Institute.*—This association has been in existence several years, under the name of the *Junior Association.* A short time since, the plan and constitution of the society were somewhat altered, and the present title adopted. It is composed principally of clerks in our stores, and young mechanics, and embraces a large number of young men, who are anxious for their own and each other's intellectual improvement. The debates of this society are held weekly in a convenient room, which they have elegantly furnished for their use, and which also serves them as a reading room. They have the present season got up a course of popular lectures, delivered by eminent men of this and other places, the avails of which are to be appropriated to increasing the library of the Institution."

" *Mechanics' Institute.*—This Society was formed between one and two years ago, and is composed chiefly of mechanics and apprentices. Feeling the importance of mental cultivation to them as men and members of society, and acknowledging

their deficiencies in this respect, they associated themselves
with the view of promoting their mutual improvement. They
are organized under an appropriate constitution and bye-laws,
to which strict obedience is rendered. Debates, Lectures, Essays and Recitations are among their weekly exercises, and are
conducted with a zeal and good feeling honorable to the members, and ensuring a high degree of success in the object for
which they are associated. The formation of a library is embraced in the plan of this society."

"*Library Companies.*—There are three libraries in Reading,
one German and two English.

The *German Library* contains a large number of well selected works, but is not at the present time open to the use of the
public. It is said that the Company is indebted to two or
three individuals, who have adopted the course of sequestering
the library for the security of their money. How long this
valuable collection of books will be suffered to remain in its
present precarious condition, or what disposition will finally be
made of it, it is difficult to conjecture."

"The *Reading Library,* is a large collection, containing
many valuable and standard works. There are, however, entirely too many novels; and a large portion of the other works
are rather ancient. These, however, are valuable, and if some
of the trashy novels and romances were cleared from the shelves,
and their places supplied with judiciously chosen modern works,
this would become a most excellent library."

"*Franklin Library.*—This library was formed to supply a
want that had been for many years seriously felt in Reading,
of some collection of useful books, which, by the low terms of
access, might be placed within the reach of all, especially of
the young who have a desire to read. The expense of membership is only fifty cents a year, which admits the individual
to the use of a choice selection of about two hundred volumes
—all useful and instructive works. This trifling sum may be
easily afforded by every person, and serves, through mere force
of the idea of possessing a share, to give the members a greater
interest in the library, and make them more likely to improve
its benefits, than if admission were gratuitous; and at the same

time, being carefully applied to the purchase of new books, it is sufficient to procure, in the course of a few years, an extensive and most valuable library. This institution has been in operation a little more than a year, and from the number of members and the extent to which the books are read, it seems to be well answering the purpose for which it was designed."

"Besides the above, there is a *Circulating Library*, kept by Mr. Harper. There are a good many excellent books in this collection, but a much larger share of novels and other light reading; and, unfortunately, this is the portion most read."

CHAPTER IX.

MISCELLANEOUS.

MAINTENANCE OF THE POOR.

Both counties have their Poor-Houses. An act was passed in 1824 for the maintenance of the poor of Berks county. The house is on a farm called "Angelica," formerly the property and residence of Governor Thomas Mifflin, of four hundred and eighty acres of superior land, three miles south-west of Reading. "The building was erected during 1824–5, the dimensions of which are as follows: The central building is 105 feet by 40, with a wing at each end by 42 and 27 feet; the whole building is two stories high.

"The first pauper was admitted on the 21st Oct. 1825, and on January 1st, 1826, the house contained one hundred and thirty inmates. Abram. Knabb was the first steward—served eight years. Henry Boyer was next appointed—served five years. Marshall B. Campbell served one year; and Daniel Kauffman, the present able steward, was appointed in 1839. The first Board of Directors elected, consisted of John Beiterman, one year; Daniel K. Hotterstein for two years, and Daniel

Bright for three years. The present Directors are Jacob W. Seitzinger, Abraham Kerper, and Daniel Baum.

" In 1837 an Hospital was put up 62 by 40 feet, two stories high. In 1843 another building was erected for the accommotion of the insane, 80 by 50 feet, two stories high. This building occupies the place or spot formerly taken up by the old Mansion, in which Gov. Mifflin, at one time, lived.

" Drs. Isaac Hiester and John B. Otto were appointed consulting Physicians. The present Consulting Board, are Drs. John B. Otto and William Gries. In 1825, Oct. 17, Doctors Banson and C. Baum, were appointed attending Physicians. The present ones are Drs. C. H. Hunter and P. F. Nagle. The number of inmates is 150—the number varies through the year from 150 to 180—the sick average about 25 through the year."

THE LEBANON POOR-HOUSE.

A farm was purchased pursuant to an act of the Legislature, passed the 16th of April, 1830, it contains one hundred and seventy acres of excellent limestone land, about a mile and a half east of the borough of Lebanon, on the south side of the Reading turnpike, and on the head of the Quitopahilla. There are fine buildings on the farm. The Poor-house is 114 feet long by 40 wide; there is, also, besides other suitable buldings, a large two-story one. The affairs are well managed.

THE COURTS OF BERKS AND LEBANON COUNTIES.

1. *The Court of Common Pleas.*—It is composed of a President and two Associate Judges. The Court can be held by the President alone, or by the two Associates.

2. *The Orphans' Court.*—It is held by *any two* of the judges of the Court of Common Pleas. Its jurisdiction extends to the appointment of guardians; the accounts of executors, administrators and guardians; the sale of decedents, real estate, &c.

3. *The Court of Oyer and Terminer and General Jail De-*

livery.—It is composed of the Judges of the Court of Common Pleas; or of *two* of them, the President being *one* of the *two.*

It has *exclusive* jurisdiction of cases of homicide, treason, sodomy, buggery, rape, robbery, arson, burglary, mayhem, concealing the death of an illegitimate child, in such a manner as to prevent its being known whether the child was born dead or alive; also of certain second, or any subsequent offences: and it has concurrent jurisdiction with the Quarter Sessions of *all other offences.*

4. *The Court of Quarter Sessions of the Peace.*—It is composed of *any two* of the Judges of the Court of Common Pleas. Its jurisdiction to all cases in the *county*, except those in which the court of Oyer and Terminer has *exclusive* jurisdiction.

The Register's Court.—It is composed of the Register and *any two* of the Judges of the Court of Common Pleas; and is convened in a case of a dispute on a will, or the right to administer.

The Judges at the present time for Berks county are,—the Honorable John Banks, President; Matthias S. Richards, and John Stouffer, Esqs., Associates.

The Judges for Lebanon are,—the Honorable Nathaniel B. Eldred, President; John Shindel and Samuel Goshert, Esqs., Associates.

The Court, and other officers for the county of Berks are,— Daniel Young, Prothonatory; John Green, Register; Henry Maurer, Recorder; William Scheuer, Clerk of the Orphans' Court; John L. Rightmyer, Clerk of Quarter Sessions, Oyer and Terminer; Henry Nagle, Treasurer; William Arnold, Adam Leise, John Shooman, County Commissioners; Joseph Ritter, Clerk to the County Commissioners.

MEMBERS OF THE BERKS COUNTY BAR.

John Biddle, Charles Evans, John S. Hiester, William Darling, Charles Davis, Henry W. Smith, Edward P. Pearson, William C. Leavensworth, Elijah Deckert, David F. Gordon,

Peter Filbert, James L. Dunn, Jacob Hoffman, Robert M. Barr, Joseph H. Spayd, Henry Rhoads, George M. Keim, William Strong, George G. Barclay, John Pringle Jones, John S. Richards, Dennis W. O'Brien, A. N. Sallade, George E. Ludwig, A. F. Miller, James Donegan, William Bets, Augustus F. Boas, Jeremiah Bitting, Samuel Sohl, Jeremiah Hageman, George W. Arms, John K. Longnecker, Charles Wireman, Henry Van Read, William M. Baird; Mathias Mingel, H. A. Muhlenberg, jr., Isaac Keim, Robert Fraser.*

LIST OF THE JUSTICES OF THE PEACE OF BERKS COUNTY.†

Albany township.	George Reagan	24 April, 1840.
"	John Miller	1 May, 1840.
Alsace.	John W. Burkhart	25 April, 1840.
".	Daniel Spengler	30 April, 1842,
Amity.	Charles Parks	23 April, 1840.
"	Solomon L. Custerd	1 May, 1840.
Bern.	Jacob Kline	6 May, 1843.
"	Geres Hain	7 May, 1844.
Bern Upper.	Henry Webber	11 May, 1840.
"	Wm. Sherrer	4 May, 1843.
Bethel.	Jacob Walborn	24 April, 1840.
"	Charles S. Cummens	27 April, 1840.
Brecknock.	Jacob M. Becker	27 April, 1840.
"	John M. Dewees	2 May, 1840.
Centre.	Jacob Miesse	27 April, 1840.
"	George K. Haag	1 May, 1840.
Cærnarvon.	David Finger	27 April, 1840.
"	‑ James E. Wells	30 April, 1840.
Colebrookdale.	Israel R. Laucks	27 April, 1840.

* As the names of the members of the Lebanon county Bar, have not been furnished as yet, they will be given in the list of subscribers in the Borough of Lebanon—to which the reader is referred.

† This list was kindly furnished by Chas. Kessler, Esq., Ed. of the "Adler."

Cumru township.	Charles H. Addams	14 April, 1840;
District;	Joseph Kemp	14 April, 1840·
Douglas.	Henry Feery	20 April, 1840.
"	Jacob Levengood	25 April, 1840.
Exeter.	John Guldin	27 April, 1840.
"	Jacob Gile	11 May, 1841.
Earl.	Daniel Clouser	25 April, 1840.
"	Abraham Hill	7 May, 1841.
Greenwich.	Peter Kline	28 April, 1840.
"	John Wagenhorst	28 April, 1840.
Hamburg Borough;	Israel Derr	27 April, 1840.
Heidelberg Lower.	Thos H. Jones	16 April, 1840.
"	David W. Eirich,	25 April, 1840.
Heidelberg Upper.	Jonathan L. Reber,	24 May, 1843.
"	George Schoch	19 June, 1843.
Hereford.	Adam Mensch	15 April, 1840.
"	George K. Rohrbach	6 May, 1840.
Kutztown Borough;	Jacob Graeff	28 April, 1840.
"	Charles Weirman	16 April, 1844.
Long-swamp.	Jonathan Haas	5 May, 1840.
"	William Trexler	25 May, 1843.
Maiden-creek;	Jacob Forney jr.	24 April, 1840.
"	John E. Addams	8 July, 1843.
Maxatawny.	John Kemp	4 May, 1843.
"	David K. Hottenstine	15 April, 1844.
Oley.	William Stapleton	16 April, 1840.
"	Henry H; Mowrer	16 April, 1840.
Pike.	Samuel Lobach	14 April, 1840;
"	Daniel Cleaver	27 April, 1840.
Penn.	Daniel Billman	8 July, 1842.
Reading, North ward	William Schoener	30 April, 1840.
"	William Betz	10 April, 1841.
Reading, South ward	David Medary	15 April, 1844.
Richmond.	William Lesher	27 July, 1840.
"	Reuben Shall	10 May, 1843;
Robeson.	Evan Evans	30 April, 1840.
"	Abraham Eargood	30 April, 1844.
Rockland.	Wm. Brentzighoff	30 April, 1840.
"	Lewis F. Kaufman	6 May, 1840.
Ruscombmanor.	Daniel Buskirk	10 July, 1841.
"	Solomon Hollenbush	13 July, 1841.

Tulpehocken twp.	Frederick Muth, jr.	30 May, 1840.
"	Adam Schoener	15 Aug. 1840.
Tulpehocken Upper.	John Potteiger	14 April, 1840.
"	John Riegel	30 May, 1840.
Union.	Jacob Rahn	1 May, 1830.
"	Caleb Harrison	27 June, 1840.
Windsor.	Samuel Hoffman	1 May, 1840.
"	James Anderson	15 May, 1840.
Washington.	Frederick Sigmund	22 April, 1840.
"	Daniel S. Schultz	29 April, 1842.
Womelsdorf Borough.	John Vanderslice	13 April, 1840.
"	Emanuel H. Hackman	13 May, 1844.

LIST OF SENATORS AND TIME OF ELECTION OF BERKS.

From 1790 to 1808, Berks and Dauphin counties constituted one senatorial district.

1790, Joseph Hiester and John Gloninger. Gloninger declined Dec. 4, 1792, and John A. Hanna, was elected and took his seat, Dec. 5, 1792.

1794, John Kean and Gabriel Hiester.

1796, Christian Lower.

1798, John Kean.

1800, Christian Lower.

1801, Henry Orth, in room of John Kean, who resigned.

1802, John Kean.

1804, Gabriel Heister.

1806, Melchior Rahn.

1808, Berks alone a district—after 1812, Berks and Schuylkill counties one district.

1808, Gabriel Hiester and John S. Hiester.

1812, Peter Fraily and Charles Shoemaker, jr.

1816, Peter Frally and Marks John Biddle.

1820, Conrad Fager and James B. Hubley.

1824, George Schall and William Audenried.

1828, David A. Bertolet and Jacob Krebs.

1832, Paul Geiger and Jacob Krebs.

41

1836, John Miller.
1840, Samuel Fegely.
1843, Samuel Fegely.

REPRESENTATIVES FROM BERKS COUNTY.

The time when members were elected is given. Sessions were usually fall and winter sessions. Elections, with few exceptions, for Representatives, were always held in October.

For 1752, Moses Starr; 1753, Moses Starr; 1754, Moses Starr; 1755, Francis Parvin; 1756, John Potts—June 27, returned in the room of Francis Parvin; 1756, Thomas Yorke; 1757, Thomas Yorke; 1758, James Boone; 1759; 1760, 1761, John Potts; 1762, 1763, 1764, John Ross; 1765, 1766, Adam Witman; 1767, 1768, 1769, 1770, Edward Biddle; 1771, 1772, 1773, 1774, 1775, Edward Biddle and Henry Christ; 1776, 1777, 1778, 1779, 1780, Henry Haller, John Lesher, Edward Biddle and Henry Christ.

1781, Baltzer Gehr, Gabriel Hiester, Daniel Hunter, Benjamin Weiser, Joseph Hiester and John Bishop.

1782, Daniel Clymer, Christian Lower, Abraham Lincoln, John Ludwig, John Patton and George Ege.

1783, Nicholas Lutz, Daniel Clymer, Christian Lower, Abraham Lincoln, John Rice and John Bishop.

1784, Nicholas Lutz, Abraham Lincoln, Christian Lower, Henry Spyker, David Davis and Martin Rhoads.

1785, Abraham Lincoln, Nicholas Lutz, Henry Spyker, Philip Kreemer, David Davis, Baltzer Gehr.

1786, Joseph Hiester, Philip Kreemer, Gabriel Hiester, David Davis, Daniel Clymer.

1787, Charles Biddle, Joseph Hiester, Gabriel Hiester, David Davis, Joseph Sands.

1788, Joseph Hiester, Gabriel Hiester, Joseph Sands, Daniel Brodhead, John Ludwig.

1789, John Ludwig, Joseph Hiester, Joseph Sands Nicholas Lutz, Daniel Leinbach.

1790, John Ludwig, Nicholas Lutz, James Collins, Gabriel Hiester, Daniel Clymer.

1791, Charles Shoemaker, Paul Groscop, John Ludwig, Nicholas Lutz, Baltzer Gehr.

1792, The whole of the members of 1791 re-elected, and also in 1793, except John Ludwig, in whose place Christian Lower was elected.

1794, Paul Groscop, Charles Shoemaker, John Christ, John Spayd, Baltzer Gehr.

1795, John Christ Paul Groscop, Charles Shoemaker, Baltzer Gehr, Christian Lower.

1796, Paul Groscop, Charles Shoemaker Peter Frailey, William Lewis, Baltzer Gehr.

1797, All the members of 1796, re-elected.

1798, Peter Fraily, Charles Shoemaker, Daniel Udree, Dan'l Rose, Baltzer, Gehr.

1799, All re-elected except Baltzer Gehr, in whose stead William Witman was elected.

1800, All of 1799, re-elected.

1801, Gabriel Hiester, William Witman, Daniel Rose, Dan'l Udree, Frederick Smith,

1802, All of 1801, re-elected.

1803, Jacob Roads, Isaac Adams, Gabriel Hiester, William Witman, Daniel Rose.

1804, Daniel Udree, William, Witman, Jacob Roads, Jacob Epler, Isaac Adams.

1805, Daniel Rose, Elias Radcay, Valentine Probst, Jacob Shaeffer, John Bishop.

1806, all re-elected except John Bishop, in whose place Daniel Ioder was elected.

1807, the same re-elected, except Elias Radcay—Bernard Kepner was elected in his stead.

1808, Jacob Snyder, David Kirby, Jacob Roads, James M'Larland, John M. Hyneman.

1809, Peter Fraily, John Spayde, David Kirby, Adam Ruth, Charles Shoemaker, jr.

1810, Conrad Feger, David Kirby, Daniel Rose, George Schall, Adam Ruth.

1811, Peter Fraily, Conrad Feger, David Rose, David Kirby, Charles Shoemaker.

1812, (from 1812 to 1829, Berks and Schuylkill formed one

Election District,) John Miller, Jacob Krebs, John Addams, Conrad Feger, Jacob Sassaman.

1813, Jacob Krebs, Conrad Feger, George Marx, John Addams, Jonathan Hudson.

1814, John Miller, David Kirby, Jacob Dreibelbis, Daniel Kerper. Daniel Rhoads, jr.

1815, Christian Haldeman, Jacob Epler, Daniel Rhoads, David Hottenstein.

1816, William Shoener, Godfried Roehrer, Daniel Rhoads, David Kirby, Michael Graeff.

1817, Joseph Good, Jacob Levan, Elisha Geiger, Jacob Greisemer, Michael Graeff.

1818, Jacob Levan, Joseph Good, John Neikerch, Michael Graeff, Jacob Greisemer.

1819, John Kohler, Godfried Roehrer, Abraham Mengel, John W. Roseberry, George Gernant.

1820, George Gernant, Samuel Jones, Joseph Good, Jacob Rahn, Jacob Schneider.

1821, Daniel Rhoads, David Hottenstein, William Addams, John Gehr, John Neikerk.

1822, William Addams, John Gehr, David Hottenstein, Godfried Roehrer, (William Audenried.)

1823, William Adams, David Hottenstein, Henry Boyer, James Everhart, (William Audenried.)

1824, James Everhart, George Rahn, Jacob Gehr, Henry Boyer, George U. Odenheimer.

1825, ames Everhart, Henry Boyer, Daniel A. Bertolet, Michael Graeff.

1826, Henry Boyer, Daniel A. Bertolet, David Hottenstein, Philip A. Good, George Rahn.

1827, Daniel A. Bertolet, George Rahn, Philip A. Good, Mordecai Lewis—[no election for the *fifth* member was effected.]

1828, John Stauffer, Thomas I. Rohrer, Geo. Kline, Paul Geiger, Philip A. Good.

1829, (Berks alone a district) Thomas J. Rohrer, John Stauffer, John Wanner.

1830, Paul Geiger, John Stauffer, John Wanner, John Potteiger.

1831, John Wanner, John Potteiger, William High, Henry Boyer.

1832, John Potteiger, Peter Kline, jr. Benjamin Tyson, Jacob U. Snyder.

1833, the same re-elected, except Benjamin Tyson, in whose stead Adam Schoener was elected.

1834, Lewis W. Richards, William Hottenstein, John Ulrich, John Jackson.

1835, John Ulrich, John Jackson, William Hottenstein, John Sheetz.

1836, Samuel Fegely, John Sheetz, John Jackson, Michael K. Boyer.

1837, Samuel Fegely, Jacob Walborn, Abraham Hill, James Geiger.

1838, Adam Schoener, Jacob Walborn, Abraham Hill, Samuel Fegely.

1839, Adam Schoener, Henry Flannery, Peter Filbert, Daniel B. Kutz.

1840, Daniel B. Kutz, Robert M. Barr, Samuel Moore, Henry Flannery.

1841, Samuel Moore, John Shenk, John Potteiger, John Bauchman.

1842, the same re-elected.

1843, John Potteiger, H. W. Smith, John C. Evans, Alfred J. Harman.

LIST OF SENATORS FROM LEBANON COUNTY.

From 1814, *Dauphin and Lebanon have been a District.*

1814, John Forster.

1818, John Sawyer.

1822, John Andrew Shulze. In 1823 Shulze was nominated for Governor, when he resigned, and John Harrison elected in his stead, who also declined, and Adam Ritscher was elected for the unexpired term.

1826, George Seltzer.

1830, Jacob Stoever.

1834, John Harper.

41*

1838, John Killinger. He resigned in 1841, when Levi Kline was elected for the rest of the term.

1842, Levi Kline.

LIST OF REPRESENTATIVES FROM LEBANON COUNTY.

Lebanon and Dauphin counties were one District in 1813 and 1814; afterwards Lebanon was a District.

1813, Amos Ellmaker, Peter Shindel, and David Ferguson.

1814, Peter Bucher, Peter Shindel, and Jacob Goodhart.

1815, '16, Jacob Goodhart and John Sawyer.

1817, John Harrison and John Uhler.

1818, George Seltzer and Adam Ritscher.

1819, Adam Ritscher and John Uhler.

1820, Joseph Barnett and John Uhler.

1821, John Harrison and John Andrew Shulze.

1822, George Seltzer and Adam Ritscher.

1823, George Orth and Gotlieb Seltzer.

1824, '25, James Bell and Charles Gleim.

1826, James Bell and Philip Wolfensberger.

1827, Philip Wolfensberger—Charles Gleim and Peter Shindel, each had 453 votes; neither of them elected.

1828, Peter Shindel and Philip Wolfensberger.

1829, Isaac Meyers.

1830, William Reily.

1831, '32, '33, David Mitchell.

1834, '35, John Krause.

1836, George Weidman.

1837, John Killinger.

1838, '39, Gotlieb Kintzel.

1840, '41, John Brunner.

1842, '43, Daniel Stine.

Delegates to the Provincial meeting of Deputies, chosen by the several counties &c., held at Philadelphia, July 15, 1774.

From Berks—Edward Biddle, Daniel Broadhead, Jonathan Potts, Thomas Dundas, Christopher Schultz.

———

Provincial Committee for Pennsylvania, held at Philadelphia, January 23, 1755.

Members from Berks—Edward Biddle, Christopher Schultz, Jonathan Potts, Mark Bird, John Patton, Baltzer Gehr and Sebastian Levan.

———

Provincial Conference for Pennsylvania, held at Carpenter's Hall, Philadelphia, June 25, 1776.

Delegates from Berks—Cols. Jacob Morgan, Henry Haller, and Mark Bird; Doctor Bodo Otto, Mr. Benjamin Spyker, Cols. Daniel Hunter, Valentine Eckert and Nicholas Lutz; Captain Joseph Hiester and Mr. Charles Shoemaker.

———

Convention held at Philadelphia, July 15, and continued by adjournment till the 28th of September, 1776.

From Berks—Jacob Morgan, Gabriel Hiester, John Lesher, Benjamin Spyker, Daniel Hunter, Valentine Eckert, Charles Shoemaker and Thomas Jones, jr.

———

Council of Censors convened at Philadelphia, November 10, 1783.

Members for Berks county.—James Read and Baltzer Gehr.

———

Convention to frame the Constitution of Pennsylvania, of 1790—commenced at Philadelphia, Nov. 24, 1789, closed Feb. 5, 1790.

Delegates from Berks—Joseph Hiester, Christian Lower, Abraham Lincoln, Paul Groscop and Baltzer, Gehr.

Members of the Convention to propose amendments to the Constitution, which assembled at Harrisburg, May 2, 1837.

From Berks county—John Ritter, George M. Keim, William High, and Mark Darrah.

From Lebanon county—Jacob B. Weidman and George Seltzer.

APPENDIX.

~~~~~~~~~~~~

B.

On page 223, the reader was referred to this place for a full statement of the *Paxton affair*.

The want of space, however, precludes a detailed account. The inhabitants of Lancaster and Berks counties being most exposed to the merciless Indians—these, having on numberless occasions, burnt dwellings, murdered with savage barbarity their helpless inmates, &c. The Paxtoxians and others, having, as they conceived, sufficient reason to believe that some of the Indians at Conestogue, or of Indian town, were exceedingly treacherous, and were accessory to murders committed upon the whites, had their feelings aroused—they resorted to Manor township, Lancaster county, and on "Wednesday, the 14th of December, 1763, at day-break a number of them, on horseback, attacked the Indian village, and barbarously massacred some women and children, and a few old men; amongst the latter, the chief—Shaheas—who had always been distinguished for his friendship toward the whites." The majority of the Indian villagers were abroad at the time of the attack. After slaying Shaheas, whose Indian name was Shea-e-hays, George or Wa-a-shen, Harry or Tee-kau-ly, Ess-ca-nesh a son of She-e-hays, Sally or Te-a-won-sha-i-ong, an old woman, and Ka-ne-un-qu-as, another woman—all who were at home, they set fire to huts, and most of them were burnt down.

"The magistrates of Lancaster sent out to collect the surviving ones, brought them into town, for their better security against any further attempt, and it is said condoled with them on the misfortune that had happened, took them by the hand,

and promised them protection. They were put into a recently erected workhouse, a strong building, as the place of greatest safety."

Here they were not safe; for on Tuesday, the 27th December, 1763, the Paxtonians and others assembled in great numbers in Lancaster, marched to the prison, forced the doors in, and, says Gordon, butchered all the miserable wretches they found within the walls. Unarmed and unprotected, the Indians prostrated themselves, with their children, before their murderers, protesting their innocence and their love to the English, and in this posture they all received the hatchet.

Those slain in the prison were Captain John, whose Indian name was Ky-un-que-a-go-ah, Betty or Ko-wee-na-see, his wife: Bill Soc or Ten-see-daa-qua, Molly or Ka-mi-an-guas, his wife; John Smith or Sa-qui-es-bat-tah, Peggy or Chee-na-wan, his wife; Qua-a-chon, Captain John's son; Jacob or Sha-ee-kah, a little boy; Ex-un-das, young Sheehay's boy; Christley or Ton-qu-as, a boy; Little Peter or Hy-ye-na-es, a boy; Molly or Ko-qua-e-un-quas, a little girl; Ka-ren-do-u-ah, a little girl; Peggy or Ca-nu-ki-e-sung, a little girl.

☞ "The names were taken from Peggy, wife of John Smith and Betty, wife of Capt. John—by John Hays, Sheriff. See. Provincial Records, Book S., p. 456.

ADDENDA.

The following we received from Dr. John Breitenbach, just as *this* form was going to press.

"Notes obtained from Mr. Peter Spangler, on the road leading from this village (Myerstown) to Shaefferstown. Mr. S. is eighty-three years old. He says, that about eighty years ago, a Mr. Guschweg lived on the farm now owned by Mr. Jacob Kapp. About seventy-five years ago, a Mr. Gring lived on Mr. Bleistein's place. About one hundred years ago, a Mr. Dreher owned the farm of my informant, Peter Spangler, grandson of Michael Spangler—about the same time Mr. Kissecker owned what is now John Eby's. A Mr. Duey lived on what is now William Haak's farm.

"Mr. Jacob Blecher, furnished me with the names of some of the early settlers of *"Haselteich,"* Hazel valley, so called from the abundance of hazels grown there. All the places spoken of above are in Jackson township.

"William Becher originally occupied Isaac Blecher's place; Jost Hoffman owned Mr. Hibschman's; George Smith, George Krum's; John Roth, Henry Haak's; Mr. Bollman, now Miller's at Muelbach district; Henry Strack, Jacob Wagner's.— These were all Germans from Wittenstein, Germany.

"The following I obtained from Christian Walborn, aged 84 or 85: He says, that one hundred years ago, the following were original settlers, as much as is known in the eastern part of Jackson township. Mr. Kitzmiller occupied what is now Hochstedder's farm—had the only mill in this part of the country. Christian Walborn originally owned John Tice's farm, below Myerstown; Batdorff, old John Walborn's; Hoster, Mi-

chael Keiser's; Lower or Lauer, the Rev. Daniel Ulrich's plantation near the Berks county line; Peter Diffenbach, what is
now known as Peter Diffenbach's; Etchberger, now Jacob
Stewart's near Berks; Weiser, known as Weiser's place. Some
sixty years ago a Mr. John Tice owned Mohler's place.

"Mr. Valentine Miller, residing in Myerstown, aged eighty
three, learned when a lad, from his father, that the vicinity of
Myerstown was first settled rising of one hundred years ago.—
The first settlers were Bassler, Herchelroth, Musser, Stamgast,
Ley, Immel, Bickel, Schell and others. The village itself was
originally settled by the following persons, residing in the central part of the town—Christian Maurer, a mason, near the
hill; Schnell, a weaver, both Moravians; Mr. Gasser, now
Diehl's tavern; Hoffman, at old Kintzle'e house; Henry Brill,
tailor, built and dwelt where Brehm now resides; Hussecker,
a Swiss; Schuhmacher—this man had one of his children carried off. The child was returned to him after two years absence. The house Mr. Schuhmacher erected by him is still
standing, having, however, been raised to two stories, and is
now occupied by a family of the name of Single; Nicholas Gast,
a mason, where Isaac Noecker now resides.

"The old German School house was also one of the first
buildings of the place. Here seven persons were massacred and
scalped—two women and five children; one woman made her
escape though scalped; another was hotly pursued by an Indian, but escaped being killed—while the Indian was in the act
of tomahawking her, a man not far off fired his pistol, at which
the Indian was alarmed and ran off, leaving his victim.

"A fort had been erected of palisades, hard by the road
leading across the Blue mountain, at Umbenhacker's tavern,
where usually a small body of Militia were stationed for the
protection of the settlers. On one occasion all the men except
five, had been absent, and the Indians being privy of the fact,
made an attack upon the fort; and before the entrance to the
fort could be secured, the savages entered, and murdered all
except one man—he fled, was pursued, having however concealed himself, and as an Indian in search of him neared him,
he shot the Indian. He soon made off further, and met some
of the militia, on their way to the fort, to whom he related what had transpired. To convince them that he had shot
an Indian, which they seemed first to doubt, they went to the

place, where they found the body of the Indian covered with brushes. The Indian who, it was supposed, had concealed the body of his fellow, was seen by one of the soldiers, at a short distance, among some tall grass—he immediately shot him. Now, believing all was well, (but sad to state,) he received a deadly shot from a concealed savage.

" Immediately below Myerstown, the first settlers were Herchelroth, (as stated above) Kuster, Noecker, Nicholas Miller, and Philip Breitenbach, my great grand father. He and Miller were direct from Germany—many of the other settlers were from Schoharie, in New York, though originally from Germany.

" There was, on my great-grandfather's farm, a block-house or fort, where, in time of danger, many took shelter.

" To conclude, I would add the names of some Revolutionary soldiers, &e. These were Martin Walborn, Leonard Batdorff, Tice, Koppenhaver, Schwengel, George Spangler, Capt. Leonard Immel, Captain Stoever of Swatara, Jacob Spangler, Sergeant Gloninger of Lebanon, Peter Lein, John Kreitzer, Peter Hoster."

MINERAL SPRINGS.

Rosenthal, or Rose-valley, (more commonly known as Kessler's spring, or run,) is a romantic and beautiful dell formed by the depression of neighboring mountains, which elevate their wood-crowned sides and summits to the height of several hundred feet above the level of the valley, excluding the oppressive rays of the summer's sun for many hours of the day, and rendering the place a delightful residence during the hot months. A limpid stream of the purest water meanders through the valley, adding greatly to its rural beauty, and affording agreeable promenades along its banks. The valley is well set with lofty trees, the remnants of the natural forest, affording a contiguity of shade and preserving an agreeable temperature during the hottest weather. The mineral spring affords chalybeate water, which is considered highly beneficial in several complaints, and is promotive of general health. The improvements have been greatly extended, by additions made recently, and are sufficient

42

to furnish accommodations to a large number of boarders. Plunging and Shower Baths are erected near the house, and the vicinity of the neighboring town will enable the proprietor to provide, at all times, whatever may be necessary to promote the health and comfort and gratify the tastes of his inmates. Reading, so well known for the beauty and salubrity of its situation, and the excellence of its society, is but three hours ride from Philadelphia, over the best railroad in the Union, traversing a country unsurpassed for its fertility and beauty.

"The waters," says Dr. Isaac Hiester, "I have found on examination with chemical re-agents, to contain iron, held in solution by carbonic acid gas, or fixed air; together with a small quantity of muriate of soda."

READING MUSEUM.

Since writing that portion which relates to *Reading*, Mr. C. S. Getz, proprietor of the Lancaster Museum, has also established one in the former place, which is highly spoken of; and, indeed, adds much to the place. A debt of gratitude, which should be well paid in money and kind offices, is due Mr. Getz, for his indefatigable efforts, both to instruct and amuse.

INDEX.

A.

B.

THE END.

SUBSCRIBERS' NAMES.

READING.

Hon. John Ritter & Co.,
James May Jones,
Jno. S. Richards, Esq.,
Boyer & Getz,
Hon. Henry A. Muhlenberg,
Matthias S. Richards, Esq.,
Morris M. Ancona, M. D.,
Rev. James L. Schock,
Jno. P. Hiester, M. D.,
Joel Ritter,
Isaac Hiester, M. D.,
Chas. Troxell, P. M.,
Saml. S. Young,
John L. Rightneyer,
Rev. J. O. Bucher,
Rev. Wm. Pauli,
Peter Nagle,
Rev. Pennell Coombe,
Rev. R. U. Morgan,
John S. Hiester, Esq.,
Hon. Jno. Banks,
Elijah Deckert, Esq.,
Charles Davis, Esq.,
Hiester H. Muhlenberg, M. D.,
S. Myers & Son,
Arnold Puwelle,
Wm. Gries, M. D.,
Jacob M. Long,
F. H. Behue, M. D.,
C. H. Hunter, M. D.
D. R. & W. H. Clymer,
A. H. Raiguel,

Samuel Bell,
D. M'Knight,
Wm. M. Seyfert,
Packer & Coleman,
Rev. William Sterling,
Rev. Samuel Davison,
Jno. Allgaier,
W. Darling, Esq.
J. Heitzmann,
J. L. Stichter,
Geo. G. Barckly, Esq.
Joseph Henry,
Geo. Boyer,
John Miller,
Zacharias H. Maurer,
John Green,
Rev. J'b Miller,
D. K. Shultz,
Boas Ketterer,
S. Warner,
Isaac Myers,
Chas. M. Pearson,
Jacob D. Barnet,
Henry Binckley,
Wm. Wunder,
Saml. S. Jackson,
Ger. G. Bisghoff,
William Betz, Esq.
Wm. B. Schœner,
Henry Brown,
And. M. Sallade, Esq.
M. B. Eckert, Esq.
J. Pringle Jones, Esq.

R. M. Barr, Esq.
John S. Schwear,
A. F. Miller, Esq.
John Goldsmith,
Fred. Louwen,
J. L. Dunn, Esq.
Gen. Geo. D. B. Keim,
Geo. W. Arms, Esq.
Beneville Keim,
Keim, Whitaker & Co.
Wm. Streeten,
James Fitzimmon,
John F. Moll,
Lewis Seider,
D. H. Dotterer,
Saml. Boone,
Adam Jones,
William Graeff, Jr.
David D. Maurer,
George Hantsch,
Daniel Boas,
Sol'n A. Stout,
Thomas S. Leaser,
Andrew Davis,
J. T. Jackson,
Levi S. Knerr,
Willm. R. Nicholls,
Thomas Barnett,
William Martin,
John E. Yager,
John E. Schaefer,
George Thorn,
Solomon G. Birch, M. D.
John Taxis,
Fredk. Lauer,
F. B. Shalter,
John Rapint,
John Miller,
S. Williams & H. Roch,
William Bingaman and Henry
　　Bindenger,
L. Mannerbach,

Philip Zieber,
A. Righteye,
G. D. Levan,
Sol. Brubaker,
Wm. Lotz,
Michael Riefsnyder,
J. & E. Eynicle,
Henry Van Reed, Esq.
Wm. Gensemer,
Charles Phillippi,
H. Rhoads, Esq.
Rev. F. A. M. Keller,
Rev. A. L. Herman,
A. F. Boas,
Gen. Geo. M. Keim,
Isaac Eckert,
Adam Johnston,
Robert Mills, Jr.
J. L. Dunn, Esq.
Albert G. Bradford,
Henry High,
John P. Miller,
Jas. V. Lambert,
George Garnant,
John S. Reifsnyder,
William A. Wells, Esq.
T. W. Hoffmand,
Herman Beard,
Richard I. Groff,
William Call,
Wm. Wanner,
John Kelly,
G. E. Ludwig,
Rev. William Sterling,
Rev. Samuel Davison,
Henry High,
John P. Miller,
James V. Lambert,
Sam. E. Griscom,
N. Soder.

CUMRU TOWNSHIP.
Adam W. Kauffman,

Elijah Ruth,
Bennerville Yoost,
Benjamin H. Wagner,
Solomon Reifsnyder,
Isaac M'Cardy,
Daniel Francis,
Wm. Lewis,
Jacob Dick, Esq.
D. B. Lorah,
Martin Fritz,
Hugh O'Neill,
David Rothman,
Geo. Freeman,
John Schwartz,
John Weidner,
Thos. J. Thomas,
Wm. Rohrbach,
Abel Thomas,
Jacob Shilling,
John Shoup, Jr.
Geo. Spohn,
Henry Mull,
A. H. Witman, M. D.
John Bush,
Hiram Miller,
Isaac Rollman,
M. Miller,
Benneville Miller,
Wm. Spohn,
Abr. Ruth, M. D.
Richard S. Ludwig,
Reuben Spohn,
Wm. Ruth,
George Ruth,
Elisha Beard,
Thos. Van Reed,
Daniel Ruth,
John B. Van Reed,
Rufus Addams,
David Marshall,
Peter Miller,
Jacob Winter,
Michael G. Moyer.

ALSACE TOWNSHIP.
F. A. N. Hiester,
Jonathan Derninger,
Thos. J, Webeer,
Daniel Baum,
Adam Phillips,
Jacob Madiera,
Daniel Spangler,
Simon Hoyer,
Jacob Klohs,
Lewis Miller,
A. Leize,
Jacob Gebert,
Wm. Hinnershitz,
Jacob Deisher,
John W. Burkhart,
Nicholas Mason,
Henry P. Birkinbine,
John Jackson,
Ezra High,
John Missimer.

ROBESON TOWNSHIP.
Henry A. Seyfert,
Samuel Kachel,
Wm. Wetley,
Nelson Dickinson,
Gains Dickinson,
Lewis M. Fawkes,
Daniel Serbe,
John Moore,
Geo. Moore,
Samuel Wolf,
Martin Glass,
Peter Schweitzer,
John Wetley,
John Stafferd,
Philip Witman,
Daniel Fry,
John Fry,
Levi B. Smith,
John E. Rigg,
Mathew Sample,
Evan Evans, Esq.

Geo. Sponagle,
Paul Geiger, Esq.
James Geiger,
John M'Nabb,
John Geiger,
Isaac Geiger,
Michael Walters,
Martley Potts,
Elisha Wells,
Cadwallader Morris,
Mahlon R. Parker,
John Kale,
J. S. Myers,
Isaac Templin,
Samuel Palsgrove,
Wm. Everhart,
Samuel Zink,
Peter Moore,
Jacob Fox,
Josiah Lewis,
Henry Homan,
Thos. Jacobs,
John Old,
John Miller,
G. S. Pierce,
Edw'd Brooke,
David J. Lincoln,
Abraham D. Hill,
Franklin M. Reazor,
John Saboldt,
S. E. Hirst,
Jacob H. Hill,
Joseph Mohr,
Daniel Hoffman,
Joseph F. Sarge,
Samuel B. Wetley,
W. Bell,
David Richard,
Wm. Welley,
Geo. Garman,
Peter Garman.

CÆRNARVON TOWNSHIP.
avid Morgan,

Daniel J. Bruner, M. D.
David Finger, Esq.
John Weidensaul,
Geo. Wert,
Wilson Hamilton
J. Pawling,
Wm. Pawling,
Milton Rutherford,
John Deihm,
John Morgan,
Davis Smith,
Menry Mengel,
Jacob Mast, sen.
Jacob Mast,
John D. Jones,
Wm. Vahgey,
H. B. Jacobs,
Daniel Fooman,
Abraham Heatrunft,
Geo. W. Johnson,
Evan Sheeler.

BRECKNOCK TOWNSHIP
Chr. Burckhart,
Christian Bowman
Peter Bowman,
Jacob Fritz,
Christian Huber,
John Becker, Esq.

UMIVU TOWNSHIP.
John Harrison,
Clement Brooke,
Isaac Wolf,
Jacob Giger,
George Wamsher,
Philip Fosnoch,
Jacob Hoffman,
Samuel Stamets,
Jacob Giger, jr.
Benjamin Grubb,
John M'Gowen, jr.
H. S. Rupp,
Wm. D. Munter,

George D. Putz.

DOUGLASS TOWNSHIP.
Jeremiah Van Reed,
Daniel Mauger.

AMITY TOWNSHIP.
H. M'Kenty,
William Jones, M. D.
David B. Mauger,
Washington Russell,
Doughten & Custer,
George Custer,
Peter Marquart, jr.
John Wagoner,
Henry Haus,
Abraham Babp,
William Yocom,
George Womsher,
Jacob Yocom,
Samuel Boone,
Jacob Kline,
Lot Rimby,
John Goodman,
Mahlon Aiman,
Amos Firing,
Hiram C. Baum,
Solomon Feather,
George Kline, jr.
Jacob S. Lachman,
Solomon Rhoads,
Ephraim Mauger,
George K. Lorah,
Jacob Strunck,
E. Lee,
Jeremiah Rhoads,
Lewis Beachtel,
Joseph Grisemer,
John Frances,
David K. Bortz,
Moses Stinbernger,
Samuel Rhoads.

COLEBROOKDALE TOWNSHIP.
John Staffer, Esq.

Rev. A. S. Basler,
Joel Bryan, M. D.
Jonathan B. Rhoads,
Henry B. Boyer,
Henry H. Gaubel,
Frederick Schawnhart,
David K. East,
Lewis Worman,
Jacob K. Boyer,
Frederick Witman,
Daniel Cressman,
Daniel Grau,
Daniel S. Sands,
David Fox,
Israel R. Lauchs, Esq.
Daniel Heller,
Benneville B. Rhoads,
Wm. Johnson,
Peter Kuser,
Wm. G. Fritz,
Wm. Ritter,
Solomon Rhoads,
Samuel Yost,
John S. Rhoads,

EXETER TOWNSHIP.
Jacob Hawk,
Jacob B. Brumbach,
A. Guldin,
Daniel Housum,
Avon Egolf,
Michael Koch,
G. Moyer,
Daniel Bishop,
John Esterly,
Henry Gilbert,
David Winters,
Jacob Esterly,
George Hartman,
Samuel Hechler,
Daniel Kehr,
Martin Goodhart,
Bartholomew Barto,
David B. Kline,

James Lee,
Isaac Crisman,

MAIDEN-CREEK TOWNSHIP.
John Keim,
John E. Addams, Esq.
James Darrah, M. D.
Samuel W. Althouse,
John Kehr,
John H. Gernant,
Adam Gernant,
T. S. Shoemaker,
John Smith,
Thos. Reber,
David E. Bosler,
Isaac Ely,
Thos. Evans,
Abraham K. Lesher,
Charles A. Yoch,
Peter Sell,
Charles Coleman,
John Housnet,
Solomon Kerby,
Jacob Hoffman,
G. W. Wily,
D. Neff,
Ely G. Fox,
Samuel Kerchhoff,
Joseph E. Peter,
Stinly Kerby,
Abraham Graeff,
John Dunkle,
Isaac Huy, jr.
Jacob Leightfoot,
Abraham Hughes,
Mordecai Lee,
Mary B. Lee,
William Willits,
Thos. Penrose,
Rees L. Davies,
Henry Moll,
Jacob Parvin,
Wm. Rahn,
David Huy,

Benneville Kline,
Henry A. Hottenstain,
Jacob Ulrich,
Jacob T. O'Brien,
Abraham Forney,
Jacob Graeff,
Augustus B. Hottenstain,
Jacob Dunkel,
Solomon Hovning.

LOWER HEIDELBERG TOWNSHI
Francis Sell,
Harrison Ruth,
Thos. B. Reber,
Samuel Hain,
William Fisher,
Adam L. Hain,
John Hoover,
Daniel B. Wenrich,
B. H. Guevlin,
John Saylor,
Adam Hain,
John B. Siegfried,
John A. Hain,
William Beidler,
Isaac Hain,
Henry Miller,
Hon. Wm. Addams,
Amos Miller,
Henry Z. Van Reed.

UPPER HEIDELBERG TOWNSHIP.
Samuel Fisher,
John Sohl, jr.
Jacob H. Boyer,
Daniel Ramsey,
Samuel Reed,
Andrew Taylor, jr.
John L. Fisher,
John Shitz,
G. B. Keiser,
Wm. M'Donell,
A G Morss, M D
E G Shulze,

John A C Stephen,
E P Smith,
John E Schwalem,
Wm Moore, M D
John Gregory,
Ezra Reed,
Col Jesse Renehold,
M Seltzer.

MARION TOWNSHIP.
Benjamin Hoffman,
John Lindsley,
J Kellar Burns,
Jno C Reed,
Rev Daniel Ulrich,
Samuel Shitz,
Peter Etschberger,
Jacob Tice, Esq
Edward Ellig, M D
Samuel Lindemuth,
Eli Klopp,
Jacob Jones,
Josiah Groh,
Sam'l L Stewart,
Edward H Becker,
Martin Brown,
Joseph Hollenbush.
Franklin Etchberger.

TULPEHOCKEN TOWNSHIP.
Philip Kline,
Francis A Harner,
Cyrus Geasey,
Valentine Brobst,
Henry W S Nipe,
Jacob Trion, M D
Peter Aulenbauch,
Henry Dewald,
Benjamin Klahr,
George Schaeffer,
Jacob Frantz,
Isaac Kurr,
Peter Lebo,
John Levengood,

Willougby H. Weiler,
John S Leisse,
Joseph Klahr,
Isaac Harner,
Samuel Miller,
Joseph Seyfert,
Samuel Heilig,

BETHEL TOWNSHIP.
Wm K Brobst,
Frederick Harner,
Charles J Commens, Esq
D L Batdorff,
Michael Slrmeltzer,
Daniel Walborn.

UPPER BERN TOWNSHIP.
Joseph Nunemaeher,
Wm. Sherrer,
Simon Riegel,
Wm Sauers,
Alber Sausser,
Geo. Reinzel,
Solomon Albright,
Daniel Seifert,
Franklin V Wagner.

WINDSOR TOWNSHIP.
Charles H Mohr,
Oliver Dyer,
Samuel L Becker,
William Reber,
Reuben Weidman,
Wm Mengel,
Joseph Seidle,
Jacob D Kline,
Wm Bowen,
Henry Billig,
Charles Keller,
Samuel Cox,
Charles Lawrie,
Anthony Richard,
John Stiner,
J Seiberling, M D

John Beitarmen,
Charles Stoud,
George Shollenberger,
Daniel Kern,
Peter Miller,
Wm E Shollenberger,
John Bailey,
Daniel Wolf,
J H Lewars,
Henry Lewars, Esq
Charles L Jaeger,
M A Sellers,
Thomas Smith,
Reuben Lintz,
Josiah Hearing,
John Sunday,
John S Boyer,
James G. Moyer,
Moses S Schock,
John Kirkpatrick,
Thomas Sieger,
Augustin Schulze, M D
—— Baum.

PENN TOWNSHIP.
Geo Beyerle
John Runkle
Wm Montgomery
Elias Staudt
Daniel Deppen M D
John Yeager
Henry Witman
John Reed
A A M'Donough M D
Edwin H Brockway
Levi S Stumm
Daniel Billman Esq
Gabriel O. Hiester
Joseph Greath.

RICHMOND TOWNSHIP.
John G. Kaufman
Nicholas W Hunter
Fred'k K Bechtel
Jacob Adam.

LOWER BERN TOWNSHIP.
Peter L Kershner
Daniel B Reber
Benneville B Reber
Joseph Reber
Samuel Albright
John R King
John Adam
John Epler
Peres Hain Esq
Jared Epler.

OLEY TOWNSHIP.
Daniel Bartolet sen
Daniel G Bartolet
Wm A Himelreich
Jacob de Kneuse
Gideon Hoch
Daniel Laucks
Jeremiah Y Bechtel
Isaac Bartolet
John A Bartolet
Abraham de Tirk
Frederick Glase
Samuel Spohn
Wellington B Griesemer
Isaac Van Sickle
Henry Tyson
John Maurer
Elmira H Sands
E B Gerben
Benneville Griesemer
John Y Antrim

CPSIA information can be obtained
at www.ICGtesting.com
Printed in the USA
LVOW10s1441190517

534965LV00011B/207/P